Revolt of the Admirals

Revolt
of the
Admirals

The Fight for
Naval Avaition 1945-1950

GOVERNMENT REPRINTS PRESS
Washington, D.C.

© Ross & Perry, Inc. 2001 All rights reserved.

No claim to U.S. government work contained throughout this book.

Protected under the Berne Convention. Published 2001

Printed in The United States of America
Ross & Perry, Inc. Publishers
717 Second St., N.E., Suite 200
Washington, D.C. 20002
Telephone (202) 675-8300
Facsimile (202) 675-8400
info@RossPerry.com

SAN 253-8555

Government Reprints Press Edition 2001

Government Reprints Press is an Imprint of Ross & Perry, Inc.

Library of Congress Control Number: 2001092329

http://www.GPOreprints.com

ISBN 1-931641-13-7

☉ The paper used in this publication meets the requirements for permanence established by the American Nation Standard for Information Sciences "Permanence of Paper for Printed Library Materials" (ANSI Z39.48-1984).

All rights reserved. No copyrighted part of this publication may be reproduced, stored in a retrieval system, or transmitted, in any form or by any means, electronic, photocopying, recording, or otherwise, without the prior written permission of the publisher.

Secretary of the Navy's Advisory Committee on Naval History

William D. Wilkinson, Chairman
CAPT Edward L. Beach, USN (Retired)
David R. Bender
John C. Dann
RADM Russell W. Gorman, USNR (Retired)
Richard L. Joutras
VADM William P. Lawrence, USN (Retired)
Vera D. Mann
Ambassador J. William Middendorf II
VADM Gerald E. Miller, USN (Retired)
Clark G. Reynolds
Daniel F. Stella
Betty M. Unterberger

The Author

Jeffrey G. Barlow has worked as a historian with the Contemporary History Branch of the Naval Historical Center since 1987. He is writing an official two-volume history on the U.S. Navy and national security affairs. During 1969–1970, while on active duty with the U.S. Army, he served as a staff member of the newly established U.S. Army Military History Research Collection at Carlisle Barracks, Pennsylvania. A Navy junior, Dr. Barlow graduated with a B.A. in history from Westminster College (Pa.) in 1972. At the University of South Carolina, where he was an H. B. Earhart Fellow, he studied under Dr. Richard L. Walker and received a doctorate degree in international studies in 1981. Dr. Barlow's contributions to published works include a biographical chapter on Admiral Richard L. Conolly in Stephen Howarth's *Men of War: Great Naval Leaders of World War Two* (New York: St. Martin's Press, 1993) and chapters on Allied and Axis naval strategies during the Second World War in Colin S. Gray and Roger W. Barnett's *Seapower and Strategy* (Annapolis: Naval Institute Press, 1989). His work has also appeared in *International Security* and *Air University Review*.

*To my father, Captain John F. Barlow, USN (Ret.),
and all of the other postwar naval aviators
who successfully brought carrier aviation into the Jet Age
and strengthened its capabilities during the
challenging years of the Cold War.*

Contents

	Page
Foreword	xv
Preface	xvii
Acknowledgments	xix
Introduction	1
Chapter 1. Air Power Doctrines	3
The Navy's Carrier Air Doctrine	3
The Air Force's Strategic Bombardment Doctrine	8
Doctrine at the Air Corps Tactical School	11
The Experience of War in Europe	13
The Air War in the Pacific	17
Conclusions	21
Chapter 2. Unification, Service Rivalries, and Public Relations	23
The Initial Fight Over Roles and Missions	32
The Air Force Public Relations Effort	44
Admiral Nimitz and the Continuing Controversy Over Unification	52
Louis Denfeld Becomes CNO	56
The Failure of Navy Public Relations	58
Conclusions	63
Chapter 3. Atomic Weapons and War Planning	65
The First Postwar Atomic Tests	68
Early Service Thinking on the Atomic Bomb	72
The AAF Position	74
The Navy Position	78
The Emerging Soviet Threat	81
War Planning	86
Some Air Force Planning Concerns	95
Forrestal's Concerns About the Strategic Air Offensive	99
Conclusions	103

Chapter 4. Navy Thinking on Atomic Weapons and the Strategic Air Offensive ... 105
    Carrier Delivery of Atomic Weapons ... 106
    Navy Doubts About the Strategic Air Offensive ... 108
    Navy Targeting Plans ... 115
    Air Force Opposition to a Navy Role ... 121
    Conclusions ... 130

Chapter 5. Super Carriers and B–36 Bombers ... 131
    The 6A Carrier ... 131
    The B–36 Bomber ... 145
    Conclusions ... 157

Chapter 6. A Time of Crisis and Change ... 159
    The Establishment of OP–23 ... 164
    James Forrestal Departs as Secretary of Defense ... 173
    Louis Johnson Takes Over ... 174
    Changes in the B–36 Program ... 177
    The Cancellation of *United States* ... 182
    John Sullivan Resigns ... 188
    Conclusions ... 191

Chapter 7. The Navy's Troubles Increase ... 193
    The New Vice Chief of Naval Operations ... 194
    The Air Force Again on the Offensive ... 197
    The Navy Gets a Brief Respite ... 201
    Francis Matthews Becomes Secretary of the Navy ... 205
    Drafting the Anonymous Document ... 206
    The Aborted B–36 Navy Fighter Tests ... 209
    Conclusions ... 212

Chapter 8. The Navy and the B–36 Hearings ... 215
    The Navy and the B–36 Hearings ... 216
    The Navy at Sixes and Sevens ... 222
    Burke and Radford Enter the Fray ... 224
    The B–36 Hearings Begin ... 226
    The Run-Up to October ... 233
    OP–23 Is Put Under Hack ... 237
    The Navy Gets Its Chance to Testify ... 243
    Conclusions ... 245

	Page
Chapter 9. The "Revolt of the Admirals"	247
Administration Reactions	254
Omar Bradley's Attack on Denfeld and the Navy	257
The Army Sides With the Air Force	263
The Hearings End	268
Conclusions	268
Chapter 10. Aftermath	269
Louis Denfeld Is Fired	270
The "Rebels" Are Put To Flight	277
The Results of the Unification and Strategy Hearings	283
Conclusions	289
Conclusions	291
Abbreviations	295
Notes	299
Bibliography	369
Index	401

Tables

1.	Principal Precision Target Systems in Europe, 1940–1945	16
2.	Operations for Carrier Task Force	116
3.	U.S. Atomic Weapons Stockpile, 1945–1950	128
4.	BUAER's New Categories of Bombing Aircraft	134
5.	Original Program—Project 6A Carrier	144
6.	Projected Capability of VHB Groups	147
7.	B–36 Selected Performance Data, 1941–1949	155
8.	Navy Operating Forces, Fiscal Years 1947–1949	161
9.	Defense Budgets for Fiscal Years 1948–1950	162
10.	The Decline of Carrier Aviation, Fiscal Years 1949–1951	224
11.	B–36 Performance as of Mid-1949	228

Charts

Navy Department Organization, May 1946	47
Office of the Chief of Naval Operations, January 1949	166
National Military Establishment, 30 September 1947	170
Department of Defense, August 1949	172

Illustrations

	Page
Wartime Navy leaders.	7
Essex-class carrier *Yorktown*	9
General Carl A. Spaatz briefs wing commanders	15
Formation of Boeing B–29s, June 1945.	18
Major General Curtis E. LeMay	20
Secretary of the Navy James V. Forrestal	26
Present and future Air Force leaders	31
Fleet Admiral Chester W. Nimitz	34
General Carl Spaatz, Commanding General, Army Air Forces	36
Navy leadership team in January 1946	37
Assistant Secretary of War for Air W. Stuart Symington	39
Navy admirals examine the XR 60–1 aircraft model	41
Major General Lauris Norstad	44
Stuart Symington and Steve Leo	51
Fleet Admiral Nimitz reads his "Valedictory"	55
Admiral Louis E. Denfeld's swearing in as CNO	57
Secretary of the Navy John L. Sullivan	60
Major General Curtis LeMay and Major General Earl E. Partridge	66
Able Test at Bikini	67
Ships damaged by atomic bomb test	69
Able Test damage to *Sakawa*	70
Damage to *Nevada* and *Pensacola* caused by the atomic blast	71
Damage to battleship *Arkansas*	72
Mushroom cloud of the Baker Test at Bikini	73
Vice Admiral William H. P. Blandy	78
Captain William S. Parsons	79
Formation of Eighth Air Force B–29s	96
Boeing B–50A	98
North American AJ–1 Savage	108
Three Service Secretaries, 18 September 1947	114
Chart showing carrier target coverage of the Soviet Union	118
Top military officials at Key West Conference	124
Lockheed P2V–3C Neptune	125
P2V–3C take-off from *Midway*	126
Joint Chiefs of Staff and Operations Deputies	129
Newport conferees at the Naval War College	130
Essex-class carrier *Shangri-la*	132
Midway in its original armored flight deck configuration	133

	Page
Midway in May 1947	135
Vice Admiral Arthur W. Radford	136
Chart showing sizes Navy aircraft carriers	138
Artist's conception of the large flush-deck carrier *United States*	140
United States model test at David Taylor Model Basin	142
United States model test with representative air group	143
United States model test at high speed	145
Secretary of the Air Force Stuart Symington and General Hoyt Vandenberg	151
Consolidated Vultee B–36A intercontinental bomber	153
Convair's conception of the jet pod-equipped B–36D	156
CNO Louis Denfeld with senior Navy officers	163
Air Force Secretary Symington at a press conference	164
Captain Arleigh A. Burke	168
Secretary of Defense James Forrestal's final meeting with the War Council	175
Joint Chiefs of Staff	178
Secretary of Defense Louis A. Johnson at press conference	181
Keel plate of *United States* being laid	185
Admiral Arthur Radford and Admiral Dewitt Ramsey	194
General Hoyt S. Vandenberg	198
Secretary of the Navy Francis P. Matthews	205
Take-off view of B–36D bomber, August 1950	229
Admiral Radford before the House Armed Services Committee	248
Admiral Radford during committee hearings	251
Admiral Louis E. Denfeld	252
Admiral Richard L. Conolly, CINCNELM	271
Admiral Forrest P. Sherman	276
Rear Admiral Robert L. Dennison	281
Sherman conferring with Radford	283
Attack carrier *Forrestal* during sea trials	284
Forrestal underway at flight quarters, March 1956	286
A–3D all jet-powered heavy attack aircraft	287

Foreword

This study examines the debate that took place during the years immediately following World War II over the role of naval aviation in the national security of the United States. Jeffrey G. Barlow's comprehensive study assesses the full complexity of this issue. He includes extensive coverage of the background, nature, and development of the highly publicized dispute over service roles and missions that was at the core of the debate, and shows how major changes in the organization of the nation's Armed Forces affected the issue. Dr. Barlow also demonstrates the influence of the large-scale demobilization of the United States after World War II and the impact of the emerging Cold War that imposed additional responsibilities on the American military.

In the 1990s the Navy is once again engaged in defining the role of its aviation arm as a component of the nation's defense structure. Although there are always some fundamental differences between the past and the present, the Navy's historians hope that today's naval and defense professionals, as well as students of modern military history, will benefit from Dr. Barlow's study of a famous debate on aviation roles and missions that took place more than four decades ago.

Several key individuals within the Naval Historical Center made major contributions to the direction and publication of this history. They include Dr. Edward J. Marolda, Head of the Contemporary History Branch; Sandra J. Doyle, the Center's Senior Editor; and Dr. William S. Dudley, our Senior Historian. I also give particular thanks to three scholars from outside the Naval Historical Center who generously provided comments and advice on earlier drafts of this manuscript. They are Captain Edward L. Beach, USN (Ret.), a prominent author and a member of the Secretary of the Navy's Advisory Committee on Naval History; Dr. Alfred Goldberg, the Historian for the Office of the Secretary of Defense; and Herman Wolk, Senior Historian with the Center for Air Force History. It should be understood, however, that the views expressed in this study are solely those of the author and do not reflect the opinions of the Departments of the Navy and Defense.

Dean C. Allard
Director of Naval History

Preface

Forty-five years have passed since the events occurred that have been labeled the "revolt of the admirals," the culmination of a period of intense rivalry between the Navy and the Air Force over the fate of air power in the post-World War II period. This competition still exists, even in an era of putative military "jointness": witness recent claims from some quarters that air power almost single-handedly won the war in the Persian Gulf. Such rivalry is to be expected. For as long as there are differing strategic perspectives and doctrines, there will be service competition over roles and missions.

Our view of the events of 1948–1949 has become distorted for a variety of reasons. It is not surprising that such distortions occur. After all, writing contemporary history is a very difficult process. Inasmuch as society depends on the written accounts of observers for knowledge of the past, it is to such accounts that we must look for the sources of inaccuracies that plague us in the present. Historical errors arise almost inevitably when historians draw conclusions based on incomplete information. In the case of the "revolt of the admirals," such problems were magnified by the security classification of most of the relevant documents and by the reticence of many of the key individuals involved, particularly naval officers, to discuss the roles they played in events that generated heated disagreements between the armed services.

The passage of time, however, has a way of freeing historians from some of these problems. In the past fifteen years many of the classified records relating to these occurrences have been declassified and are now available for scholarly research.

This study, therefore, is an attempt to provide a new, more balanced perspective of the "revolt of the admirals"—one that more closely mirrors the complexities of the time—using the large amount of official documentation that is now available from Navy, Air Force, and other records, together with selected interviews with participants.

It has had a long gestation. I was first introduced to the strong emotions generated by the "revolt of the admirals" while serving at the U.S. Army Military History Research Collection, Carlisle Barracks, Pennsylvania in 1969–1970. One of the many interesting things I worked on in those years was the papers of General of the Army Omar N. Bradley. Scattered among that collection were numerous contemporaneous newspaper accounts of the "revolt" and of General Bradley's role in the congressional hearings.

I next returned to the story during 1974–1975 while working on my master's thesis on the services' unification fights during Harry S. Truman's presidency. My research during these years allowed me to examine at great length the voluminous congressional hearings for the period. Yet it was in 1977, while conducting my first lengthy interview with Admiral Arleigh A. Burke, in connection with my doctoral dissertation on the role of the Joint Chiefs of Staff during the Kennedy administration, that I got my initial first-hand account of the "revolt."

My primary purpose for the interview was to question the admiral about his experiences as Chief of Naval Operations under Presidents Dwight D. Eisenhower and John F. Kennedy. I began, however, by asking Admiral Burke about some of the formative experiences of his naval career. He quickly and not unexpectedly got to his service as head of OP–23 during the tumultuous months of 1949. In the years since my initial interviews with Admiral Burke I have had the opportunity to discuss the "revolt" with him on many other occasions.

Another part of the story fell into place in the early and mid-1980s when I was fortunate enough to be able to examine the papers of Admiral Arthur W. Radford at the Naval Historical Center's Operational Archives. As one of the members of Navy Secretary James V. Forrestal's brain trust on unification matters and later Vice Chief of Naval Operations, Radford had accumulated an invaluable collection of materials on the Navy's roles and missions disputes with the Air Force and Army. These and numerous other documents relating to his role in the events of the "revolt" were later organized into a separate section within his personal-official papers devoted exclusively to unification issues.

The final spark leading to this study was the research I conducted for a paper on the "revolt of the admirals" given at the U.S. Naval Academy's Naval History Symposium in 1987, shortly after I joined the staff of the Naval Historical Center. The chance to reexamine Arleigh Burke's and Arthur Radford's papers at length and to interview officers closely involved in the events of 1949 convinced me that there was sufficient material available for a full-length reevaluation of the "revolt." With the support of the then Director of Naval History, Dr. Ronald H. Spector, and the Center's Senior Historian, Dr. Dean C. Allard, and the concurrence of my immediate superior, Dr. Edward J. Marolda, I was allowed to put aside other projects and undertake the present study. After the passage of more than forty years, it is certainly time to correct the record.

Acknowledgments

Inevitably in a project of this size an author incurs many debts for the help he has received. I first wish to thank the men who allowed me to interview or correspond with them about their experiences: Captain Charles S. Arthur, USN (Ret.), Vice Admiral Frederick L. Ashworth, USN (Ret.), Stuart B. Barber, Captain Edward L. Beach, USN (Ret.), Admiral Arleigh A. Burke, USN (Ret.), the late Admiral Robert B. Carney, USN (Ret.), the late Rear Admiral Thomas D. Davies, USN (Ret.), the late Admiral Robert L. Dennison, USN (Ret.), the late Rear Admiral Emerson E. Fawkes, USN (Ret.), Admiral Charles D. Griffin, USN (Ret.), Rear Admiral Joseph L. Howard (SC), USN (Ret.), the late Vice Admiral Fitzhugh Lee, USN (Ret.), Captain Frank A. Manson, USN (Ret.), Rear Admiral Alfred B. Metsger, USN (Ret.), the late Rear Admiral Harold B. Miller, USN (Ret.), Captain Robert A. Rowe, USN (Ret.), and the late Brigadier General Samuel R. Shaw, USMC (Ret.).

During the course of my research I have been helped by a number of historians, archivists, and librarians in various parts of the country; some at my request had records reviewed for declassification, while others provided access to materials in their collections or suggested possible new avenues of research. I particularly wish to thank Dennis Bilger of the Harry S. Truman Library, James Leyerzapf of the Dwight D. Eisenhower Library; James Hutson and the rest of the staff of the Manuscript Division, Library of Congress; John Taylor, Richard von Doehnhoff, Barry Zerbe, Wilbert Mahoney, Richard Boylan, Dr. Cary Conn, Dr. Timothy Nenninger, and Richard Myers of the National Archives; Velecia Chance and Michael Waesche of the Reference Service Branch, Washington National Records Center; Herman Wolk, Chief of the General Histories Branch, and his colleagues of the Center for Air Force History, Dr. George Watson, Dr. Walton Moody, and Sheldon Goldberg; Timothy Cronen of the National Air and Space Museum; Dr. Ronald Grele of the Oral History Research Office, Columbia University; and Nancy Bressler of the Seeley Mudd Library, Princeton University.

Throughout the lengthy process of researching and writing this study Edward Marolda provided guidance and strong support for my efforts. The Center's Senior Editor, Sandra J. Doyle, and Editorial Assistant, Wendy Karppi, proved similarly skillful in guiding the manuscript through the editing and publishing process. Detailed editing of the manuscript was efficiently carried out by Shirley Sirota Rosenberg and the staff of SSR, Incorporated.

Over the years portions of my manuscript were read by and discussed with a number of present and former colleagues in the Contemporary History Branch, including Robert J. Cressman, Dr. Lynne K. Dunn, Dr. Mark H. Jacobsen, Dr. Theresa L. Kraus, Dr. Michael A. Palmer, Dr. Gary E. Weir, and Dr. Clarence E. Wunderlin, Jr. Their comments were always stimulating and their criticisms frequently proved helpful.

I am also grateful to those colleagues in the Naval Historical Center who provided expert archival, bibliographic and photographic assistance. I particularly wish to acknowledge the help of Bernard F. Cavalcante, Head of the Center's Operational Archives, and that of past and present reference archivists on his staff, including George W. Pryce III, Kathleen K. Lloyd, Regina T. Akers, and Richard M. Walker. The library services provided by John E. Vadja, Head of the Navy Department Library, and his staff were extremely important to my research efforts. The photographic assistance provided by Charles R. Haberlein, Head of the Curator Branch's Photographic Section, and Edwin C. Finney, Jr., was vital to the manuscript's completion. I would also like to thank Ella W. Nargele, the Center's Information Security Specialist, for helping to clear the completed manuscript quickly through the required security and policy review process.

I also wish to thank those individuals who read and commented on the manuscript as members of review panels. These include Dr. Allard, Director of Naval History; Dr. William S. Dudley, Senior Historian; Dr. Marolda; Dr. Jacobsen; Captain Steven U. Ramsdell, USN, and Lieutenant Commander Richard R. Burgess, USN, of the Center's Naval Aviation History and Publication Division; Captain Edward Beach; Herman Wolk; and Dr. Alfred Goldberg, OSD Historian.

In addition I want to acknowledge the moral support provided to me by those people with whom I informally discussed this writing project over the years. These individuals deserve special thanks for allowing an author to talk at excessive length about a subject that probably wasn't of equal interest to them, all the while providing encouragement and advice. These include my father, Captain John F. Barlow, USN (Ret.), Admiral Burke, George W. S. Kuhn, Dr. David Alan Rosenberg, Dr. Thomas C. Hone, Vice Admiral Gerald E. Miller, USN (Ret.), Vice Admiral William P. Lawrence, USN (Ret.), Admiral Thomas H. Moorer, USN (Ret.), Captain Frank Manson, Captain Paul F. Stevens, Jr., USN (Ret.), the late Captain Paul R. Schratz, USN (Ret.), Captain William C. Chapman, USN (Ret.), Captain T. K. Woods, Jr., USN (Ret.), Patricia S. Kotzen, Harold (Hal) Andrews, Captain Peter M. Swartz, USN (Ret.), Captain Kenneth L.

Coskey, USN (Ret.), Norman Polmar, Dr. Robert W. Love, Jr., Richard A. Russell, Dr. Robert J. Schneller, and Dale Sharrick.

Finally, I must express my deep appreciation to my wife, Martha, and my sons, Robert and Andrew, for the support they gave me during these years of effort. Invariably, a project of this size consumes a portion of one's attention at home as well as at work. But when I was with them, they did their best to keep me focused on things other than naval aviation.

The aforementioned help notwithstanding, any errors of fact or interpretation found in this study are mine alone.

Introduction

The incidents commonly linked to the "revolt of the admirals" took place from late March through November 1949. On 28 March 1949, James V. Forrestal, the first Secretary of Defense and a former Secretary of the Navy, had left office. He was succeeded by Louis A. Johnson, a lawyer who had served as Assistant Secretary of War in the late 1930s. In the months leading up to World War II Johnson had been actively involved in strengthening the Army's Air Corps.[1] He thus came into his new office with the reputation of being a partisan for the Air Force. Less than a month after becoming Defense Secretary, Johnson halted construction of the newly laid flush-deck aircraft carrier *United States*, a postwar-designed ship capable of operating the larger and heavier aircraft that were entering the fleet. Moreover, he did this at a time when Secretary of the Navy John L. Sullivan was out of town, thus failing to give Sullivan a chance to present his views on the carrier's importance to the Navy. To protest the Defense Secretary's action, John Sullivan resigned.

To replace Sullivan, Johnson selected Francis P. Matthews, a Midwest lawyer and businessman who possessed neither military nor government experience. Matthews quickly saw himself as a representative of the Secretary of Defense.

In early May 1949 an anonymous document was delivered to several members of Congress. It alleged that serious improprieties had occurred in the Air Force's procurement of the B–36 bomber and implied that Air Force Secretary W. Stuart Symington and Defense Secretary Johnson had benefited financially from the procurement. The author of this document was subsequently revealed to be Cedric R. Worth, the special assistant to Under Secretary of the Navy Dan A. Kimball. Although the charges leveled against Symington and Johnson were later found to be totally baseless, they inspired two sets of hearings by the House Armed Services Committee: the first on the B–36 bomber program, and the second on matters of defense unification and strategy. During the latter set of hearings the Navy presented its views on issues concerning overall national strategy, cancellation of the flush-deck carrier, and the value of Air Force procurement of additional B–36 bombers.

In the course of these hearings senior naval officers, led by Admiral Arthur W. Radford, contended that naval aviation was being denuded of its resources by a Secretary of Defense enthralled by the supposed war-deterring and war-fighting capabilities of strategic bombing. The press labeled the Navy's stand the "admirals' revolt."

In the immediate aftermath of this second set of hearings Secretary of the Navy Matthews fired the Chief of Naval Operations, Admiral Louis E. Denfeld, for supporting his fellow naval officers. Several other naval officers, including Captain Arleigh A. Burke, were also punished by a Navy Secretary intent on forcing the service into line behind Louis Johnson's policies.

Following the hearings, the Secretary of Defense continued budgetary policies that cut deeply into the Navy's existing aviation assets. Thus the overall outcome of the "revolt" was seen by almost everyone as a Navy defeat. In fact, the serious depletion of naval aviation strength was not reversed until the start of the Korean War necessitated a drastic upturn in defense spending.

The "revolt" received a great deal of attention in the press. It contained many of the elements of human passion that make a good story: secret (and perhaps sinister) dealings by individuals and organizations; anonymous charges of malfeasance and financial corruption in connection with an important defense contract; and an openly aired rivalry between two powerful military services, the Navy and the Air Force. Some of the dozens of newspaper and magazine articles were thoughtful and many were interesting, but none accurately represented the larger reality behind the hearings.[2]

Unfortunately, because much of the material related to the Navy–Air Force fight was classified, historians writing about these events during the quarter century that followed were forced to rely too much on this contemporaneous reporting for their facts. But this author's own evaluation of the events of 1949 and earlier leads him to reject the accepted view that the outcome of the Navy's presentation before the House Armed Services Committee was a defeat for that service. It is argued in this study that the strength of the Navy's presentation and the vehemence with which it was delivered by many of the service's most senior officers served to convince the committee that naval aviation had a vital role to play in the nation's defense strategy. This realization by important congressional leaders such as Carl Vinson set the stage for a revitalization of carrier aviation that would probably not have occurred in the absence of the "admirals' revolt."

Chapter 1

Air Power Doctrines

To understand the imperatives that drove Navy and Air Force actions during the pivotal months of early May to late November in 1949, it is necessary to grasp the strong differences between the two services in matters of doctrine. By the end of World War II the Navy considered its carrier aviation to be a part of a larger, balanced fighting force, albeit its most powerful offensive component. The Army Air Forces (AAF) saw its strategic bombing force as the preeminent weapon of attack, a concept that occupied a dominant position in Western military thinking in the immediate postwar years.

Navy Carrier Air Doctrine

The Navy's carrier air doctrine evolved gradually during the interwar years from the individual concepts contributed by a number of naval officers—both aviators and enthusiastic Blackshoes (regular line officers). Because in carrier aviation the aircraft was inseparably linked with its operating base—the aircraft carrier—refinements in air doctrine and tactics were usually worked out during exercises at sea, not in the classroom. This fact undoubtedly lent a realism to the development of carrier aviation doctrine during these years.

Although some in the Navy were slow to recognize aviation as an indispensable element of naval power, in June 1919 the General Board—composed of senior officers tasked with advising the Secretary of the Navy on major issues—was farsighted enough to call for the most complete utilization of fleet aviation. In its report on "Future Policy Governing Development of Air Service for the United States Navy," the board stated, "To ensure air supremacy, to enable the United States Navy to meet on at least equal terms any possible enemy, and to put the United States in its proper place as a Naval power, fleet aviation must be developed to the fullest extent. Aircraft have become an essential arm of the fleet."[1]

The Navy Department was slow to heed the General Board's strongly worded appeal. Naval aviation had gained a certain bureaucratic prominence within the Office of the Chief of Naval Operations (OPNAV) during the final months of World War I when it was made a division of the Material Branch under a director of aviation, but the first months of peacetime saw it reduced in status. Once postwar demobilization had taken hold, the Chief of Naval Operations (CNO), Admiral William S. Benson, saw no reason to continue aviation's enhanced wartime position. The new director of aviation, Captain Thomas T. Craven, was reduced to a section head in the Plans Division of the CNO's office, and his personnel were scattered throughout the various other divisions of the office.[2]

It took Benson's retirement in 1919 and the pressure of outside events to effect a change. In 1919 and again early the following year, pro-naval aviation members of Congress had proposed establishing a bureau of aeronautics within the Navy Department. In both cases the department's senior leaders repudiated the idea.[3] But their opposition quickly turned to support. The principal reason for this change of heart was Brigadier General William (Billy) Mitchell's public campaign for an independent air force.

Mitchell, who had commanded the air units of the U.S. First Army in France during the war, appeared before a House Appropriations subcommittee on 3 February 1920 to call for support for a strong air force that could assume the Navy's traditional role as the country's first line of defense: protecting the United States against an enemy invasion fleet through attacks by pursuit (fighter), bomber, and torpedo aircraft. The U.S. Army Air Service officer said that air officers were convinced that surface fleets could not stand up under attack from the air and that, in the face of such attacks, "it was only a question of a very short time before a navy will get under the water and stay there."[4]

Following Mitchell's impassioned testimony, which was well received in Congress and the press, Rear Admiral David W. Taylor, Chief of the Bureau of Construction and Repair, convinced Admiral Robert E. Coontz, Benson's successor as CNO, and Navy Secretary Josephus Daniels that the Navy might lose its air arm if it failed to counter Billy Mitchell's efforts.[5] Taylor proposed that the department draft a bill establishing both a bureau of aeronautics and a separate naval flying corps. Following the concurrence of the Secretary of the Navy's council, Secretary Daniels called a conference to draft such a bill. The final version sent to Congress provided for both a bureau of aeronautics and a flying corps made up of some 500 officers and 5,000 men.[6] The latter provision was of particular concern to some senior naval officers who felt that the new organization might be influenced by officers with no sea experience and no direct connection with or interest in the ongoing activities of the fleet.

The Navy's reversal on the issue of a bureau of aeronautics was heartening to Representative Frederick C. Hicks (R–N.Y.), a member of the House Naval Affairs Committee and sponsor of the earlier bills in Congress to create a bureau of aeronautics. Hicks drafted his own version of the Navy's bill, leaving out the provision for a separate flying corps. The bill did not pass during that session of Congress.[7] The following year, shortly after the Harding administration took over, Hicks reintroduced the bill. With strong support from the new Secretary of the Navy, Edwin Denby, and CNO Admiral Coontz and the endorsement of President Warren G. Harding, the bill was incorporated into the annual Naval Appropriations Act for 1922 and passed on 12 July 1921. The new bureau was formally established by the Navy Department a month later.[8] Captain William A. Moffett, who had succeeded Thomas Craven as director of aviation in March 1921, was appointed bureau chief. Moffett's energetic and highly effective direction of the bureau quickly made itself felt.

The primary duties of the Bureau of Aeronautics (BUAER) included the development of naval aircraft and their engines and accessories, and the procurement of adequate numbers and types of aircraft for the naval aviation units. In addition the bureau was responsible for aircraft installations on fleet vessels, the development of aircraft carriers, the training of aviation personnel, and the maintenance of naval stations ashore.[9] For some years thereafter other bureaus, including Construction and Repair, Ordnance, Engineering, Navigation, and Yards and Docks, continued to retain responsibility for certain aviation-related functions that might have been transferred to the Bureau of Aeronautics.[10] Nonetheless, with the establishment of BUAER, naval aviation—and carrier aviation in particular—gained a departmental sponsor that was to serve it well during the succeeding years.

The decision not to create a separate naval flying corps was fortuitous for the Navy as a whole. By not having a group of specialist officers set apart from their fellow line officers, the Navy ensured that naval aviators thought of themselves as naval officers first and aviators second. Despite their special skills the officers were required to undertake the traditional "responsibilities of command" of the naval service.[11] Moreover, by remaining integrated, aviators and Blackshoes were able to appreciate each other's viewpoints and concerns to a much greater extent than would otherwise have been possible.

The integration of naval aviation squadrons with the fleet, afloat and ashore, during the interwar years brought about an understanding that the interdependence of surface, subsurface, and air operations was vital for the successful prosecution of a naval campaign. The wide variety of technical specialists both in the fleet and at installations ashore often collaborated with their generalist compatriots to solve problems of mutual concern and generate doctrines applicable to forces employed for war at sea. Furthermore, because seaborne aviation ultimately had to be tested in its operating element, the practicability of particular naval air operational techniques and doctrines was most often readily validated or disproved in fleet exercises.

The advent in 1922 of the first Navy aircraft carrier, *Langley* (CV 1), a converted collier, provided a test bed for fleet aviation. In 1925 *Langley* and its aircraft first participated in a fleet exercise, albeit in a minor way. But two years later the carrier participated more fully in Fleet Problem VII. *Langley* was assigned to the BLUE Fleet, which was tasked with escorting a large, slow overseas convoy and then establishing a base in the face of BLACK Fleet opposition. From this base further operations were to be conducted against BLACK. During the exercise, *Langley* suffered delays in launching and landing aircraft because of the need to conform to the maneuvers of the fleet.[12] *Langley*'s experience demonstrated the need for carrier mobility and resulted in the recommendation that Commander Aircraft Squadrons be given "complete freedom of action in employing carrier aircraft."[13]

In the late 1920s naval leaders had categorized fleet aviation into four principal tasks—scouting, gunfire spotting, screening, and delivering offensive attacks on the enemy, with scouting considered the most important.[14] As Navy Captain Frederick J. Horne explained in a 1928 lecture to the students of the Army's Air Corps Tactical School, "Superior information regarding actual conditions is of tremendous value to a Naval Commander, for it assures the effectiveness of his strategic and tactical dispositions, prevents surprise by the enemy, and aids definitely toward success."[15]

Offensive attacks by fleet aircraft were seen largely as augmenting the main attacks conducted by the surface warships. Neither side was expected to attempt to launch air attacks in strength before the surface forces were at least in tactical contact. Similarly, gaining local control of the air was seen as necessary for victory but not in itself a guarantee of it. Surface forces of near equality with the enemy were required since, as Frederick Horne explained to his audience, aviation alone could not "win a sea battle."[16]

Another problem facing the Navy at that time were the weight penalties imposed on Navy fighter aircraft throughout the 1920s and 1930s (when aircraft were generally underpowered) by the need for tailhooks and stronger undercarriages to enable them to make repeated arrested landings on aircraft carriers. The extra weight meant that carrier aircraft were slower and less maneuverable than their land-based counterparts. This weight penalty led many aviators, particularly those in the Army Air Corps, to believe that carrier aircraft could not effectively stand up against first-line, land-based fighters; if they did engage in air combat with a major land-based air force, the carrier planes would suffer prohibitive losses.

Wartime Navy leaders at a planning conference in San Francisco in 1944. Left to right: Admiral Raymond A. Spruance, Commander Fifth Fleet; Admiral Ernest J. King, COMINCH/CNO; Rear Admiral Charles M. Cooke, Jr., COMINCH Deputy Chief of Staff; Secretary of the Navy James V. Forrestal; Vice Admiral Randall Jacobs, Chief of Naval Personnel; Admiral Chester W. Nimitz, CINCPAC/CINCPOA; and Vice Admiral Aubrey W. Fitch, DCNO (Air).

Naval aviators believed that Fleet Problem IX in 1929 demonstrated the importance of carrier mobility for magnifying the enemy's defensive worries. In this problem the attacking carrier, *Saratoga* (CV 3), was able to launch successful strikes on the Panama Canal even though the defending forces had an accurate fix on the carrier's position.[17] The lesson was that the only effective defense against such carrier strikes was attacking the carriers before they reached their launching positions.[18] Captain Horne commented, "The only positive method of defense is a counter-attack at the source. In other words, the defending forces must prevent the launching of the enemy aircraft by seeking out and attacking the floating base before the carrier can arrive within striking distance of the objective on shore."[19]

During the late 1920s and early 1930s squadrons operating on board the new aircraft carriers *Lexington* (CV 2) and *Saratoga*, both commissioned in late 1927, worked to perfect basic operating techniques and develop combat skills.[20] In his annual report for 1930–1931, Admiral J. V. Chase, Commander in Chief, U.S. Fleet, commented:

> Progress has been made in all phases of carrier operations, particularly in the landing operations where the landing interval has been reduced considerably. The scouting squadrons were qualified in night carrier landings. Advanced aircraft practice was conducted by the carriers for the first time, involving the actual arming and re-arming of the airplanes.[21]

The following year, Chase's successor, Admiral Frank H. Schofield, stressed that the Navy's greatest aircraft-related need was more carrier decks, particularly those of battle-line aircraft carriers like *Lexington* and *Saratoga*.[22]

By the mid-1930s the general assessment of the offensive capabilities of carrier aviation had been upgraded significantly. In the intervening years greater attention had been devoted to increasing the striking power of carrier-based aircraft in attacks against surface craft. In the words of Commander P. N. L. Bellinger, carrier aviation, already considered the "eyes of the fleet," was now being looked upon as one of the "fists of the fleet."[23] Although air strikes were not expected to actually sink battleships, they were expected to inflict sufficient damage to reduce the battleships' effectiveness materially, as well as to sink all other types of warships.[24] Similarly, in a number of fleet exercises that occurred during the 1930s, carrier aviation demonstrated a significant potential for striking and damaging specific land targets such as the Panama Canal.

When war came to the United States in 1941, naval aviators had to use all of their training just to stave off the advancing Imperial Japanese Navy in the first terrible months of the Pacific war. Nonetheless, during the final years of the war, the carriers of the Fast Carrier Task Force piled up an enviable record of successes against Japanese land-based air power as its aircraft hammered away at enemy shore targets, including those in the Japanese Home Islands. From 1 September 1944 to 15 August 1945 alone U.S. Navy F6F and F4U fighters destroyed 2,948 Japanese fighters (1,882 of them first-line Zeke [Zero] or other advanced model aircraft) in combat at a cost of only 191 American planes.[25] Such achievements by U.S. naval aviators dispelled the prewar belief that carrier aviation could not go up against, much less defeat, land-based aircraft.[26]

The Air Force's Strategic Bombardment Doctrine

Unlike the Navy, whose carrier air doctrine grew primarily out of experiences at sea, the Army Air Corps developed a strategic bombing doctrine

Air Power Doctrin

National Archives 80-G-417154

The *Essex*-class aircraft carrier *Yorktown* (CV 10) operates in waters off Japan in July 1945.

that can be traced back to a few pivotal aviation figures in the closing years of the First World War and the early years of the peace. These men included Major General Sir Hugh M. Trenchard of Great Britain, Lieutenant Colonel Edgar S. Gorrell and Brigadier General Billy Mitchell of the United States, and General Giulio Douhet of Italy.[27] Although the views of Trenchard and Gorrell contributed to the ideas underpinning U.S. strategic bombardment doctrine, Mitchell and Douhet were more influential.[28]

Billy Mitchell's writings, although in large measure designed to popularize his drive for an independent air arm, demonstrated a pragmatic approach to important air power issues. Mitchell's pragmatism no doubt reflected his wartime experiences as an operational commander. In contrast Douhet's writings were more reflective and theoretical, arguing that an independent air force was a necessity for an industrialized country hoping to prevail in future wars, with strategic bombardment the preeminent role for such a force.

Despite the polemical nature of many of Mitchell's writings, they reveal the thinking of a man who, in the immediate postwar years, was far from doctrinaire on the subject of air power. During the early 1920s

Mitchell continued to view air power as a mixture of essential components: pursuit, bombardment, and attack (i.e., ground support) aviation.

In 1921, in his first book, *Our Air Force—Keystone of National Defense*, Mitchell contended that the proportion of financial, material, and operational effort devoted to the various air power components should include 60 percent for pursuit aviation and 20 percent for bombardment aviation.[29] These projected allocations were in line with his belief that mastery of the air—attainable only through the air battle of pursuit aviation—was a precondition for successful bombing.[30]

At this time Mitchell viewed the role of bombardment aviation as striking at the enemy country's military forces rather than at its concentrations of industrial sites or civilian population.[31] Before 1924 Mitchell asserted that civilian objectives would be attacked only "as an act of reprisal."[32] In later years he began according greater importance to strategic bombardment, with an explicit emphasis on targeting vital industrial centers.[33] According to Alfred Hurley, Mitchell's biographer, "Mitchell's broader conception of aviation distinguished his approach from that of Douhet's apparent single minded concern with strategic bombardment."[34]

Giulio Douhet, convinced of the tremendous promise of military aviation as early as 1909, began his major public writing following retirement from government service in 1921.[35] His first and most influential book, *The Command of the Air*, published by the Italian war ministry that same year, came as a revelation to enthusiasts of military aviation. In a reasoned and logical manner it set forth the theoretical bases for creation of independent air forces.

Douhet contrasted the situation prior to military aviation with that in the present and, more important, in the future. One of the principal differences was the status of the civilian populations. In the past civilian populations of warring nations had been spared the worst of combat because they remained largely beyond the reach of the opposing armies.[36] The advent of the airplane had changed the distinction between combatants and noncombatants irrevocably, since air power now made it possible to range far behind the enemy's lines without first breaking through enemy defenses.

He asserted that in future wars armies and navies would no longer be capable of guaranteeing the security of national borders. The battlefield would be limited "only by the boundaries of the nations at war, and all of their citizens will become combatants, since all of them will be exposed to the aerial offensives of the enemy."[37] Douhet argued that the only effective way for a country to protect its territory and population from an enemy's air attacks was to use its own air force to seize command of the air.[38] He saw aerial bombardment as the most effective means of achieving such a command, preferably by destroying the enemy's "airports, supply bases, and centers of production."[39]

Once command of the air was attained, the independent air force would deliver mortal blows to the heart of the enemy, in a short span of time and without the high costs in lives and treasure imposed by a slow-moving war of attrition.[40] The overwhelming power of the bombing attacks, when coupled with the rapidity with which they could be delivered, would be sufficient to collapse the enemy's war effort and crush its morale.

General Douhet believed that breaking the will of the enemy nation should be the primary objective. Aerial offensives could be directed "not only against objectives of least physical resistance, but those of least moral resistance [i.e., mental and emotional hardiness for war] as well."[41] The country's citizens, demoralized by the death and destruction inflicted upon their cities and deprived of essential needs by the breakdown of governmental structures, would then rise up and demand that their leaders sue for peace.[42]

The centerpiece of Giulio Douhet's concept of the independent air force was the bomber. According to Douhet, a fully activated air force was potentially capable of destroying as many such targets as it had "bombing units" (four- to twelve-plane groups of bombers).[43] He stated that the guiding principle of bombing actions should be the complete destruction of each bombing target in a single attack, making further attacks on that target unnecessary.[44]

Douhet stressed that the independent air force should always operate en masse to inflict the "greatest damage in the shortest possible time," and thus always be able to penetrate enemy defenses.[45] Any enemy pursuit aircraft encountered during its operations would be driven away by escorting "combat" (fighter) units, whose sole responsibility was facilitating the bombers' arrival over the targets.[46]

Doctrine at the Air Corps Tactical School

As Douhet's work was becoming known to the world at large, his ideas played a substantial role in shaping the air power doctrine that developed in the United States during these years.[47] In 1920 the U.S. Army Air Service was establishing a school for the study of air tactics and doctrine, the Air Service Field Officers School at Langley Field, Virginia. In 1922, as the renamed Air Service Tactical School, its course and enrollment were changed to provide intensive training in air tactics and techniques for both junior and senior officers. Its name underwent another change in 1926—to the Air Corps Tactical School (ACTS)—when the U.S. Army Air

Service became the Army Air Corps. Five years later the school was moved to Maxwell Field, Alabama.[48] During the 1920s and 1930s ACTS emphasized air tactics, a subject that encompassed not only tactics but also doctrine and strategy as applied to pursuit, bombardment, attack, and observation aviation.[49]

In 1926 the school issued *Employment of Combined Air Force.* Unlike the school's earlier textbooks, this volume forcefully stressed the potential of aerial bombardment. Echoing Douhet, it argued that the true objective in war was to crush the enemy's will to resist and that this will could be reduced at the beginning of the war by attacks on its bases of power.[50]

However, the text emphasized the need for precision attacks on particular targets, whose destruction would greatly hinder the enemy war effort, rather than the more generalized attacks on industrial and population targets. This preference for precision attacks was a carryover from earlier thinking. The textbook indicated that attacks should be made against such significant targets (or subtargets) within a target system as the "vital parts of the enemy's sources of supply," "sensitive points" of the enemy's rail system, and (as part of the fight for command of the air) aircraft assembly plants.[51] It was the first ACTS text to stress the importance of winning command of the air.

While strategic bombardment doctrine was gaining primacy at the school, pursuit doctrine was rapidly losing ground. By 1930 the faculty had accepted the premise (first put forth by Douhet) that a defensive bomber formation could provide sufficient self-defense to overcome attacks by enemy pursuit formations without the aid of escorting pursuit aircraft. The view adopted at the school was that "a well planned and well conducted bombardment attack, once launched, cannot be stopped."

By the early 1930s strategic bombardment had become the dominant doctrine at the Air Corps Tactical School. Among the fundamental premises taken from Douhet's writings were the views that strategic bombardment constituted the preeminent weapon of an air force; independent strategic air attacks against the vital centers of a hostile industrial country could break the enemy's will to resist; and a properly led, unescorted bomber formation could fight its way through to any target with acceptable losses. Billy Mitchell also influenced the school's doctrinal developments, but the impact of his writings was clearly overshadowed by the example he set for his fellow Army aviators by sacrificing his career in his quest for an independent air force.

During the mid-1930s the school's faculty continued to refine its thinking on strategic target selection. For example, petroleum and electric power systems were added to the list of important economic targets first identified in 1926.[52] An even more significant development was the concept of targeting key points in a nation's industrial fabric in an effort to rend or unravel the fabric.[53] The culmination of the school's thinking on strategic target selection during this period was the development of the concept of the national economic structure. A major conclusion was that target selection required a complete analysis of a nation's industry, "a study for the economist, statistician or technical expert, rather than the soldier."[54]

In June 1941, when the newly created U.S. Army Air Forces (AAF) began planning the buildup of American military air power, the school's basic tenets of strategic bombardment served as the foundation for the effort. Under the tutelage of Colonel Harold L. George, former head of the Air Tactics and Strategy Department at the Air Corps Tactical School, the AAF's Air War Plans Division produced a basic plan (AWPD-1) centered around the expected capabilities of strategic bombardment.

The Experience of War in Europe

The U.S. Army Air Forces entered combat in Europe in August 1942 without fully understanding the operational lessons learned at great cost by the British and Germans during the first years of that war. During 1939 and early 1940 Britain's Royal Air Force (RAF) had attempted daylight precision bombing attacks by heavy bombers operating in close, self-protective formations. Severe losses to German antiaircraft fire and, more important, to fighter attacks pressed home against the bomber formations, soon persuaded the RAF that unescorted daylight bombing attacks were too costly. After March 1941 continuing high losses forced the RAF to shift from night precision bombing to night area bombing of German targets.[55]

Even after U.S. airmen were warned of the difficulties of engaging in unescorted daylight precision bombing over Germany, they continued to insist that the well-armed, American B-17 bombers and superior American tactics could overcome the difficulties. General Henry H. (Hap) Arnold jotted down in a note early in the war, "Either I'm an optimist or just plain dumb, but I think the British still have much to learn about bombing."[56]

The AAF believed that the Royal Air Force's problem lay not so much with the concept of precision bombing in the face of enemy defenses but with a general British dislike of precision bombing and a lack of élan.[57] Major General Carl A. Spaatz, the first commander of the U.S. Eighth Air Force, wrote to Hap Arnold in the first flush of enthusiasm following his command's initial bombing missions:

> The operations of the past week, limited as they have been, have convinced me of the following:

a. That daylight precision bombing with extreme accuracy can be carried out at high altitudes by our B–17 airplanes.
b. That such operations can be extended, as soon as the necessary-size force has been built up, into the heart of Germany without fighter-protection over the whole range of operation.[58]

In this same letter Spaatz went so far as to assert that combat experience in Europe and the Far East up to that time had shown that bombing accuracy did not diminish under enemy fire but actually increased.[59]

In large part because of optimistic assessments of the correctness of their strategic bombing doctrine, American airmen began combat operations with unrealistic expectations of success. Unfortunately the limited nature of American bombing operations during the AAF's first months of combat in Europe failed to reveal just how unrealistic these expectations were. The first American bombing strikes in Europe were small-scale operations carried out against targets in occupied France and the Low Countries close to the English Channel coast. In addition, during these missions the bomber formations were heavily protected by RAF fighter escorts. Consequently U.S. bomber losses were not large.

The strong influence of these circumstances apparently was not grasped by the American commanders. Major General Ira C. Eaker, the new commander of the Eighth Air Force, was convinced that by employing 300-bomber missions, the Eighth Air Force could attack any target in Germany "with less than 4% losses."[60]

A few months later the vulnerability of the American bomber formations to German fighters became readily evident. In May 1943 German fighters began employing air-to-air rockets against the bomber formations. These weapons not only outranged the bombers' 50-caliber machine guns but also proved highly effective against tight formations.[61] As American bombers flew ever-deeper missions into Germany, losses mounted. By mid-October 1943 the situation forced the AAF to acknowledge that its doctrine on unescorted bomber formations was flawed. In four unescorted, deep-penetration raids in Germany during October, the Eighth Air Force lost 148 heavy bombers to attacks by German fighters—some 12.6 percent of the attacking forces.[62] According to one analyst these losses represented about 30 percent of the current fully operational B–17s and B–24s in the Eighth Air Force's tactical units and 35 percent of the combat-effective heavy bomber crews.[63]

In the weeks that followed Black Thursday (the name applied to the Schweinfurt raid by one of the surviving bomber crews), the staggering losses forced the Army Air Forces to admit that it could no longer afford to launch deep bomber raids into Germany without fighter cover. Commented one AAF source a year later, "Beyond fighter cover the Germans

Air Power Doctrines 15

General Carl A. Spaatz, Commanding General U.S. Strategic Air Forces in Europe, briefs wing commanders of the Eighth Air Force in 1944. Pictured to Spaatz's left are Lieutenant General James H. Doolittle, Commanding General Eighth Air Force, and Major General William E. Kepner, Commander VIII Fighter Command.

now appeared to have the better of unescorted bombers. It must be soberly admitted that a few more battles beyond fighter cover might have condemned daylight strategic bombardment for all time."[64]

Deep penetration strikes into Germany were curtailed for the rest of 1943 pending the arrival of long-range fighters in numbers sufficient to protect the bombers on such missions. The arrival of the long-range P–51 Mustang escort fighter, together with shorter-legged P–47 and P–38 fighters, enabled the Eighth Air Force to resume its daylight bombing of Germany in 1944 and eventually to seize control of the air from the Luftwaffe.

In the final sixteen months of the war the heavy bombers pounded away at German target systems—including aircraft factories, Luftwaffe air bases, oil production facilities, the ball-bearing industry, and the motor transport industry—with ever greater freedom of action. Nevertheless the sudden collapse of German resistance did not occur. The war in Europe ended in the traditional way, with Allied armies overrunning German territory and seizing the German capital of Berlin to compel a Nazi surrender.

Contrary to the expectations of its proponents, strategic bombing in Europe proved to be an ambiguous success. The actual results failed to measure up to the promises of the doctrine. None of the attacks on the principal target systems, for example, had succeeded in destroying or completely disrupting these systems. And achieving the desired bombing results required hitting the target systems again and again.[65]

After the war the United States Strategic Bombing Survey (USSBS) found that German oil production was the target system attacked with the most decisive results. Bombing strikes on this system caused a drastic decline in production beginning in mid-1944, but they still failed to bring the German war machine to a halt.[66] Similarly attacks on the German aircraft industry, designed to nullify the threat from the Luftwaffe, proved only partially successful.[67] And bombing strikes on the German ball-bearing industry, which can be viewed as an adjunct to the attacks on the aircraft industry, were found by the USSBS to have been wholly unsuccessful in affecting the output of finished munitions of any type.[68]

TABLE 1. *Principal Precision Target Systems in Europe, 1940–1945*

1940–1942	Submarine pens and yards, transportation
1943	Submarine pens and yards, aircraft production, rubber and rubber products, antifriction bearings industry, transportation
1944	Aircraft production, antifriction bearings industry, transportation, oil production and storage, airfields
1945	Oil production and storage, selected armaments factories, transportation, aircraft production, airfields

SOURCE: USSBS, *The Effects of Strategic Bombing on the German War Economy* (Washington: Overall Economic Effects Division, USSBS, 1945), Tables 1–4, 2–5.

The Eighth Air Force devoted a significant part of its bombing effort to German submarine pens and yards in an effort to reduce U-boat production, particularly during the first half of 1943. Nonetheless this massive effort had a negligible influence on German output. As the USSBS commented, "There were 138 major attacks against yards, U-boat bases, ports, shipbuilding and naval installations, aggregating about 100,000 tons or about 4 percent of the total bomb tonnage on *all* targets during the war.... The attacks had little effect on production of submarines until 1945."[69] The most effective attacks on these targets were made not by mass formations of heavy bombers; they were made by small numbers of RAF Mosquito bombers dropping 4,000-pound bombs with high accuracy.[70]

Because the nature of the German transportation system, with its numerous targets of varying types, proved daunting to air planners, the Eighth Air Force scheduled strikes against transportation targets in the early part of the war only when weather or other factors had ruled out attacks on primary targets.[71] Attacks on transportation facilities, railroad-equipment manufacturing companies, and marshaling yards (which had a strong potential for decisive results if pursued with sufficient effort) therefore were not conducted in a systematic manner until far too late in the European war.[72] When heavy strikes did begin in earnest following the Allied landings in Normandy in June 1944, Allied bomber commands alternated between attacks designed to serve tactical and strategic ends. This situation delayed the ultimate impact of the transportation attacks.[73]

Another aspect of the AAF's strategic bombardment doctrine suffering from the test of reality was the belief in high-altitude precision bombing. The bombing accuracy of the heavy bomber formations was much worse than had been expected before the war. One 1946 official report commented, "One of the first impressions conveyed by Intelligence reports is the exaggeration implicit in the loose term 'pinpoint' bombing, which is used promiscuously to characterize bombing employing the Norden [bomb] sight. Neither visual nor radar bombing ever achieved pin-point bombing."[74]

Radar bombing was introduced into the Eighth Air Force in September 1943 and used increasingly whenever the cloud cover (generally on days where clouds were covering 40 to 50 percent of the sky) precluded satisfactory visual bombing. However, the H2X radar bombing never achieved the accuracy of visual bombing.[75] Weather degraded bombing accuracy far more than enemy defenses did. Given the frequency of poor visibility in northern Europe (30–50 percent or more cloud cover), it is easy to understand why a USSBS study noted, "In many cases bombs dropped by instruments in 'precision' raids directed against specific targets fell over a wide area comparable to that covered normally in an 'area' raid."[76]

The Air War in the Pacific

The Army Air Forces had much less time to test the validity of its strategic bombardment doctrine in the Pacific, but the results proved similar to those in Europe. It was not until April–May 1944 that the first B–29 VHB (very heavy bomb) units moved into the China-Burma-India Theater to begin operations against Japan. From the beginning these XX Bomber Command missions were undertaken at great operational and logistic cost.[77]

Because of the distances involved the most important strategic objectives in Japan—those in the Tokyo-Nagoya-Osaka area—were beyond the reach of these VHB units. Only western Honshu, Kyushu, and Manchuria

Formation of three Boeing B–29s over Laredo Army Air Forces Base, Texas, 22 June 1945.

were within the 1,600 nautical-mile combat radius of the B–29s staged from Chengtu, China. The targets included portions of Japan's steel industry, oil storage and refineries, aircraft plants, and naval dockyards located in smaller urban and industrial centers. The total weight of the bombing effort was small, and the bombing attacks were at best only moderately successful.[78] Because of range limitations, Chengtu-staged B–29s could carry bomb loads of only 3,000 to 4,000 pounds to targets in the Japanese Home Islands.[79] With such limitations the XX Bomber Command dropped only 2,880 tons of bombs on all targets during its first five months of operations (June–October 1944).[80]

On balance the cost of this effort far outweighed the military benefits.[81] Only about 14 percent of XX Bomber Command's combat capability could be employed against the Japanese. The rest was absorbed in using the command's B–29s as tankers to ferry fuel from India to China for the few operational missions.[82]

In November 1944 B–29 units were finally operating from the Mariana Islands, located less than 1,300 miles south-southeast of Tokyo. From here the B–29s were able to begin attacks in force against the Japanese

Home Islands. From late November 1944 until early March 1945 the XXI Bomber Command was occupied largely with adjusting to the B-29 and learning to make best use of its capabilities. During this period the AAF remained committed to its doctrine of high-altitude, daylight, precision bombing, which was quickly shown to be militarily ineffective. According to the USSBS report on VHB operations against Japan:

> Weather constituted the most serious obstacle confronting our combat units.... Intervening clouds often obscured a clear view of the aiming point thereby resulting in an unsuccessful bombing approach, or necessitating a radar drop on the secondary target. Bombing accuracy, as a result of these conditions, was not satisfactory during the first phase of operations.
>
> Urban areas, readily identifiable on the radar scope were usually designated as secondary targets since accuracy limitations of the APQ-13 radar *prevented successful radar bombing of pinpoint industrial targets from high altitudes.*[83]

Other factors contributing to the unsatisfactory bombing effectiveness of the B-29s included the planes' relatively small bomb loads, the high rate of failure in bombing primary targets, and the serious effect of concentrated Japanese fighter attacks on the unescorted bomber formations.[84]

The unsuccessful nature of B-29 operations during this phase of the campaign led to a change in bombardment tactics. In early March 1945 Major General Curtis E. LeMay, commander of the XXI Bomber Command, ordered the B-29s to undertake maximum-strength, low-level incendiary strikes on Japanese urban areas. This change in tactics was influenced by three considerations—the cost of unescorted daylight missions, the predicted vulnerability of Japanese cities to incendiary attacks, and the continuing ineffectiveness of precision bombing with high-explosive bombs.[85]

The change in tactics enabled the bombers to mount a remarkably successful campaign against the built-up areas of Japanese cities. In a series of strikes during a ten-day period, the bombers of the XXI Bomber Command burned 32 square miles of the urban-industrial centers of Japan's four principal cities—Tokyo, Nagoya, Osaka and Kobe.[86]

Originally aimed at destroying Japan's war production, these fire raids soon were seen by some AAF leaders as a method by which strategic bombing could single-handedly crush Japan's will to resist.[87] As General LeMay wrote to Brigadier General Lauris Norstad on 25 April, "I am influenced by the conviction that the present stage of the development of the air war against Japan presents the AAF for the first time with the opportunity of proving the power of the strategic air arm. . . . I feel that the destruction of Japan's ability to wage war lies within the capability of this command."[88]

The conversion from precision to area bombing in the war against Japan marked a significant departure from AAF bombardment doctrine.

Major General Curtis E. LeMay, Commanding General XXI Bomber Command, 1945.

Author's Collection

For the rest of the war, area fire bombings of Japanese cities constituted the AAF's primary effort, although a number of medium-altitude precision attacks were carried out against specific Japanese industrial targets.[89] The area bombings, however, promised decisive results and thus garnered primary AAF attention. So thoroughly was the XXI Bomber Command burning out Japan's urban-industrial areas that in mid-June General LeMay boasted at a press conference, "In a few months we will be out of targets. We will be fresh out of Japan, too."[90]

In the end, however, strategic bombardment's promise also went unfulfilled in the Pacific. By early August 1945 the newly operational Twentieth Air Force was almost out of targets, having burned out 51.57 percent of the urban areas of Japan's cities in incendiary attacks, including 50.8 percent of Tokyo's built-up industrialized area. And yet, the Japanese government would not surrender.[91] It took a final series of cataclysmic circumstances, including dropping atomic bombs on Hiroshima and Nagasaki and the Soviet Union's entry into the war, to compel Japan's leaders to sue for peace.

Conclusions

By the end of World War II the Army Air Forces and naval aviation had fully tested their major air doctrines. The AAF's strategic bombardment doctrine was found wanting in significant areas, yet few of its senior leaders saw it as flawed. Men such as Arnold and Spaatz were aware of certain limitations in strategic bombing as demonstrated by aerial combat in Europe and the Pacific. However, they blamed strategic bombing's failure on the AAF's inadequate resources and the high proportion of its effort foolishly diverted to assist land and naval campaigns, rather than on the doctrine itself. Moreover, the awesome power unleashed by the atomic bombs at Hiroshima and Nagasaki appeared to AAF leaders to promise a future decisiveness for strategic bombing that could overcome the limitations that had diminished its effectiveness during the war just ended.

By and large Navy carrier air doctrine proved successful in combat. Much of this success came about because the doctrine evolved significantly during the course of the Pacific war.

Naval aviators took serious losses in carriers and aircraft in the first months of the fighting, learned from their mistakes, and went on to devise new and highly effective ways to reduce such losses in the final two years of the war. At one point in late 1942, following the sinking of *Hornet* (CV 8), the U.S. Navy was down to a single operational fleet carrier in the Pacific. With the arrival of sizable numbers of new *Essex*-class CVs and *Independence*-class light carriers (CVLs) in 1943 and 1944, the mid-1943 introduction of outstanding fighters, such as the F6F Hellcat and improved F4U Corsair, and the establishment of the Fast Carrier Task Force under the experienced leadership of Vice Admiral Marc A. Mitscher, U.S. carrier aviation came into its own. The availability of large numbers of fast carriers enabled Mitscher to utilize several multicarrier task groups of three or four carriers each as the offensive striking components of his force. Improvements in radar-assisted fighter direction of the Fast Carrier Task Force's combat air patrols and better ship damage control enabled U.S. fast carriers to operate effectively within range of Japan's land-based air power in the last years of the war without the loss of a single *Essex*-class ship.

By war's end the Navy's carrier air doctrine rested on a number of fundamental beliefs. One of the strongest was the belief that, for the Navy to maintain control of the seas, its carriers would have to be capable of launching limited offensive strikes against selected land targets in the initial stages of a war. In this way they could eliminate enemy submarines in their pens (before they could pose a vastly dispersed threat at sea) and destroy enemy land-based aviation positioned to threaten the task forces.

Chapter 2

Unification, Service Rivalries, and Public Relations

In many respects disagreements and rivalries between the Navy and Air Force in the postwar period reflected animosities between Navy and Army airmen that had first arisen during the fight for an independent air force in the years immediately following the First World War. The campaign by Brigadier General Billy Mitchell and his supporters to amalgamate Army and Navy aviation into a unified air service earned these airpower advocates the enmity of Navy leaders. As the campaign progressed into the mid-1920s, Billy Mitchell combined his call for air autonomy with the concept of an overall Department of National Defense under which a separate air arm would be one of three main components. Mitchell's proposal had congressional adherents, but it solidified the Navy's opposition to major changes in the existing organizational structures.[1]

During the 1920s and 1930s the War Department sided with the Navy Department in opposing unification of the armed services. Indeed in 1932 when the House of Representatives came within a few votes of approving service unification as an economy measure, Army Chief of Staff General Douglas MacArthur was one of the strongest opponents of such a change. As he stressed in a letter, "No other measure proposed in recent years seems to me to be fraught with such potential possibilities of disaster for the United States as this one.... Each [service] must be free to perform its mission unhindered by any centralized and ponderous bureaucratic control."[2] The continuing opposition of both military departments to unification during this period proved an adequate deterrent to congressional enthusiasm for radical change.

The onset of the war in Europe in 1939 and the U.S. entry into the conflict two years later aroused renewed interest in service unification, but this time the Navy found itself without its Army ally. The Army's new thinking on the issue of unification was revealed in late 1943 when Army Chief of Staff General George C. Marshall submitted a paper to the Joint Chiefs of Staff (JCS) on "A Single Department of War in the Post-War Period." In this paper drafted by the Army's Special Planning Division, Marshall acknowledged that he was in general agreement with the basic idea of a single department of war, and he proposed that the Joint Chiefs approve the idea for planning purposes and settle the details later.

The paper stated that a unified military department would provide unity of command and eliminate duplication and overlapping by centralizing numerous functions then under the separate services, thus effecting significant economies in funds, personnel, and facilities. The department would be headed by a Secretary and organized into three major groups—ground forces, air forces, and naval forces—plus a general supply department. In addition, the paper called for the appointment of a chief of staff to the President, who would serve him in the exercise of his duties as commander in chief of the armed forces and would head a U.S. (joint) general staff composed of the chiefs of staff of the three armed services and a chief of staff for supply.[3]

The Navy Department's uniformed leaders had good reason to oppose a unified department of war. The Army paper advocated this "radical reorganization" of the armed forces to facilitate postwar planning at a time when the U.S. war experience was far from complete. Moreover Navy leaders were convinced that an "efficient mechanism" already existed for handling wartime operations and planning postwar demobilization in the form of the Joint Chiefs of Staff.[4]

There was an even more powerful reason to oppose such unification—the realistic concern of many senior naval officers that under such a department of war, the new air component would either absorb naval aviation entirely or deprive it of most of its funding.

Retired Admiral Harry E. Yarnell put this concern most forcefully in a memorandum to the Chief of Naval Operations. Yarnell told the CNO that, once the war ended, the Army Air Forces would undoubtedly make every effort to secure independence. If this happened, one of two situations would pertain—either the "Independent Air Force" would include all military and naval aviation (as in Great Britain after the First World War), or the Army and Navy would be left with only their tactical aviation components while the independent air force would handle "strategic" operations. In the second case Yarnell noted, there would be three separate and distinct air forces, each requiring large sums of money for maintenance and encroaching on the spheres of interest of the others. In such an event he stressed, "The natural result will be in peace time when considerations of economy prevail over those of military efficiency, for Congress to concentrate air activities under the most powerful branch—the 'Strategic' Air Force, and to starve or abolish the others."[5]

Deprived of Navy support, the Army proposal languished in the JCS for some months. During this time, however, Congress began to examine the issue anew. On 9 March 1944, James W. Wadsworth (R–N.Y.), a member of Congress with a long-standing allegiance to the Army, introduced a resolution in the House creating the Select Committee on Post-War Military Policy to investigate all matters of U.S. postwar military requirements.[6] Following House approval in late March, the new committee, under its chairman, Representative Clifton A. Woodrum (D–Va.), began preparations for hearings.

The Woodrum Committee hearings opened on 24 April 1944 with witnesses from the War Department. Among the first was Secretary of War Henry L. Stimson. At the beginning of the war he had opposed a proposal for a joint general staff because it "would involve such radical changes and meet with such bitter opposition that it would probably be impossible even if it were advisable."[7] In this instance, however, he came out strongly for a single department, in substantial part because he knew that Navy Secretary Frank Knox also favored unification.[8] Stimson told the committee, "The creation of a single Department of the Armed Forces... is essential if our Nation is adequately and most effectively to carry on its wars under modern conditions, which have revealed that even our great Nation has limitations in manpower and resources."[9]

Overall the Army witnesses stressed two reasons for adopting this major defense reorganization. The first was that a single department of war would provide large economies by eliminating duplications in administration, procurement of personnel and material, and services and supply. The second reason was that unified command was needed at the highest military level. Army witnesses argued that the cooperation achieved in the Joint Chiefs of Staff during the war was largely a matter of personalities and could not be counted on to continue in the future.[10]

From the Navy's perspective the most contentious aspect of the single-department plan was the role of the air component. The most candid War Department witness, Assistant Secretary of War for Air Robert A. Lovett, acknowledged that the Army Air Forces leaders expected that, under this scheme, a separate air force would take over all land-based aircraft in operation, including those planes owned and operated by the Navy for long-range reconnaissance and antisubmarine warfare (ASW). He also told the committee that, to effect "economies," the air force should serve as the department's research and procurement agency for aircraft and all aviation-related items and as its sole elementary, primary, and basic flight-training establishment.[11]

An issue of particular concern to the Navy Department's Marine Corps component was the fate of the Corps under an Army-inspired unification plan. Marine senior officers were well aware that the Corps' wartime expansion to a peak combat strength of six Marine divisions was considered by Army leaders to be far in excess of the needs of the naval service. These officers were fearful that the capability of the Marine Corps to perform its missions would be severely hampered by a drastic reduction in its fighting strength.

James Vincent Forrestal, Secretary of the Navy from 19 May 1944 to 17 September 1947.

When the first Navy witnesses appeared before the Woodrum Committee on 28 April, they were led by Navy Under Secretary James Forrestal. Ironically Secretary Knox had been hospitalized following a heart attack just before the committee began its hearings. Forrestal, unlike Knox, was vehemently opposed to unification. It was fortunate for the Navy Department that the committee decided to hear Army witnesses first, allowing the Navy witnesses to formulate their thoughts after hearing the other side's case.[12]

James Forrestal told committee members that his department believed the unification issue needed an objective and thorough study. Without such an examination the Navy was unwilling to assume, even in principle, that a single department of war would be a beneficial organizational change.[13] The other Navy Department witnesses followed Forrestal's lead in calling for further study of the issue. In addition they questioned various aspects of the Army plan that they deemed problematic, without directly opposing the plan. In particular, a number of the Navy witnesses denied there was unnecessary "waste and duplication" in the War and Navy Departments and expressed strong doubts that unification would produce substantial economies—an issue that seemed especially to have captured the committee's attention.[14]

With the Navy Department's opposition to any immediate change fully evident, the Woodrum Committee concluded its hearings the day after the final Navy witnesses testified. On 15 June 1944 the committee issued its report on the hearings. In a conclusion that represented a Navy victory, the report stated, "The committee does not believe that the time is opportune to consider detailed legislation which would undertake to write the pattern of any proposed consolidation, if indeed such consolidation is ultimately decided to be a wise course of action."[15]

Despite his department's success in delaying congressional action, James Forrestal, who had "fleeted up" to Navy Secretary following Frank Knox's death on 28 April, was convinced that the hearings had generated substantial congressional and public support for unification. Several months later he wrote to a friend, "I have been telling King, Nimitz and Company it is my judgment that as of today the Navy has lost its case, and that either in Congress or in a public poll the Army's point of view would prevail."[16]

In early May 1945 the Navy's top leadership began to examine how the Navy could best fight for its position in the face of a renewed War Department or congressional push for unification. On 3 May Assistant Secretary of the Navy for Air Artemus L. (Di) Gates wrote to Admiral Ernest J. King:

> It has always been my conviction that to take an effective stand against a Single Department of Defense and to defend the organization which we have, we, the Navy, must be sure that our own house is in order.... I still don't think our own house is in order, i.e. the relationship of Naval Aviation to the Navy. Therefore, any arguments we present are weakened because of defects in our own system.[17]

To correct these defects, Gates proposed strengthening the position of naval aviation within the office of the Commander in Chief, U.S. Fleet (COMINCH), by giving the Deputy Chief of Naval Operations (DCNO) for Air additional duties as Deputy Commander in Chief, U.S. Fleet (Air). King and his staff would then look to him for everything pertaining to aviation. Gates also advised adding another naval officer (possibly an aviator, to balance the Army Air Forces' influence) to the Joint Chiefs of Staff.[18] King did not accept these suggestions.

A few days later, Di Gates briefed Navy leaders on his views of the unification fight.

Having gone before the Woodrum Committee last year and been a party to their postponing consideration at that time, I feel that we have got to be very positive this time in some kind of plan which is a Navy plan. I don't think we can be negative any further as far as Congress is concerned.[19]

Navy Assistant Secretary H. Struve Hensel then suggested that the Navy set up an organization to study the problem and present the Navy's views to the public.[20] This step would put the Navy Department on a much better footing than it had during the Woodrum Committee hearings the previous year. Gates remarked to the group about the earlier experience, "The Woodrum Committee got off to a bad start. It allowed the Army to put forward a proposal, which put us on the defense because instead of being objective, we had to see what was wrong with the Army's proposal."[21]

Coincidentally, a week later, Secretary Forrestal received confirmation of these ideas in a letter from Senator David I. Walsh (D–Mass.), Chairman of the Naval Affairs Committee. Walsh wrote that he doubted if any useful purpose would be served by merely objecting to plans to consolidate the War and Navy Departments. Instead, Walsh noted, those who believed that such a consolidation would not be effective should attempt to formulate a more effective plan to accomplish the reformers' objectives. The senator suggested that the Navy Department undertake a thorough study of the subject to see if a proposed council on national defense should be set up as an alternative to departmental consolidation.[22]

In his answer to Senator Walsh, Forrestal agreed that the Navy Department must come up with a "positive and constructive recommendation."[23] In early May 1945 James Forrestal contacted Ferdinand Eberstadt, an old friend and former business associate, whose wartime assignments had included serving as chairman of the Army and Navy Munitions Board and then as vice chairman of the War Production Board.[24] Eberstadt agreed to head an investigation of a national security organization. In an initial meeting at the Navy Department on 9 June, Eberstadt and his newly selected executive secretary, E. F. Willett, met with the Secretary's advisory group to work out many of the arrangements.[25] Ten days later, Forrestal sent Eberstadt a formal request to study and report on unification and other defense organization matters.[26]

Ferdinand Eberstadt and his small, primarily Navy Department staff worked tirelessly throughout the summer of 1945 to complete the work. In the course of the study Eberstadt, who had come to the project with an open mind on the question of unification, gradually became convinced that the Navy's position on defense organization better reflected existing realities than the Army's.[27] Eberstadt later wrote James Forrestal, "As you know I started the study somewhat predisposed toward unification, but as

I went into the matter further, I became convinced that it not only would not produce its heralded benefits but that it would raise an entirely new, and in some respects serious, set of problems."[28]

On 27 September Eberstadt delivered his 250-page report to Secretary Forrestal.[29] The Eberstadt Report rejected unification but did recommend the creation of two new coordinating bodies—the National Security Council and the National Security Resources Board—designed to overcome deficiencies in coordination that had been revealed during the war in relations between the State Department and the War and Navy Departments and between the JCS and the U.S. industrial mobilization agencies.[30] The new bodies were meant to strengthen the diplomatic and economic aspects of U.S. security. In addition the report recommended the creation of an air department equivalent to the existing War and Navy Departments. It was a recommendation that Forrestal could not yet bring himself to accept. He wrote to Eberstadt on 6 October 1945:

> I am entirely confident that we would have... [the War Department's] complete support on the thesis of a department for Air, but I must say that I haven't quite yet reached that conclusion.... If I were sure that we could confine a separate air arm to strategic operations I would be for it, but with our own arm, the tactical arm of the Army, and the Marines' tactical units, I am afraid it will be an easily salable idea to the public that all should be rolled together, and while I am no expert on war I have seen enough of this to know that as far as the Navy arrangement is concerned that would be fatal.[31]

While the Navy was busy developing its platform on defense reorganization, the Army was further refining its earlier unification proposals. By this time the Army was supporting a single department of national defense for a mixture of theoretical and practical reasons. For example, its support for a powerful, single chief of staff who would have a controlling influence over the budget of the new department derived from the service's traditional organizational theory. As political scientist Demetrios Caraley explained, "Implicit in the testimony of the Army leaders was the belief that in any decision-making situation, there was an optimum solution with respect to maximizing military effectiveness that was in the 'real interest' of all the services."[32]

Such a solution, however, could not come through a committee such as the Joint Chiefs of Staff but only through a single military decision maker, standing above the parochial interests of any particular military service and thus able to weigh the issues dispassionately. As General George Marshall remarked, "Committees at best are cumbersome agencies, especially when the membership owes loyalty and advancement to chiefs installed in completely separate governmental departments. Local service enthusiasms become a source of weakness instead of a source of strength."[33]

This viewpoint contrasted sharply with the Navy's concept of collective decision making at the highest military levels. Navy leaders believed that strategic decisions, in the words of Demetrios Caraley, "were not susceptible to optimal determination."[34] They believed that a JCS committee system would provide the most realistic solution. In such a system, decisions of how best to allocate military forces to accomplish national goals would be made through compromise, following a thorough airing of competing service viewpoints.[35]

The Army's practical reason for supporting a single defense department was that their ground forces might well lose out in the postwar competition for funds to the more glamorous Air Force and Navy, if a single department were not present to allocate the monies Congress provided in a rational manner.[36] Forrestal recalled a conversation that he had with General Marshall in the spring of 1945:

[Marshall] said that [after the First World War] the Army faced the fact that the country wanted to disarm; the further fact that the Secretary of War didn't take a very aggressive interest in the affairs of the Army, and he stopped General Pershing's attempt to create a General Staff, and in fact forbade Pershing to see the President of the United States without his permission.... Marshall said that the result of that was that all of the experience that the Army had gathered out of the First World War was practically to all intents and purposes lost.... They weren't able, of course to get much money to do anything with, and he said—he was very frank about it, saying that the Navy was a popular service because it gave people to believe that it would keep war away from this country, and it always had more visible appeal than the Army had. There wasn't much sex appeal to promenading over an Army post and watching soldiers spade up the garden.[37]

In a single department of national defense—one, moreover, in which a powerful chief of staff, who would, by definition, be above narrow service interests, would have the controlling influence on budget matters—the Army would be less likely to suffer in the competition for funds.

The Army Air Forces' position on unification was straightforward. It saw support for a single department as the means to its separation from the Army and its acquisition of a coequal position with the Army and the Navy.[38] The senior airmen were convinced that the role the AAF combat forces had played in World War II demonstrated the need for an independent air force in the postwar period. They did not believe, however, that a separate status, analogous to the Army and the Navy, was inevitable.[39] They had only to look back to the 1920s and 1930s, when opposition from the War and Navy Departments thwarted AAF attempts at

Present and future Air Force leaders at an awards ceremony in Luxembourg, April 1945. Left to right: General of the Army Henry H. Arnold, Commanding General Army Air Forces; General Carl A. Spaatz, Commanding General U.S. Strategic Air Forces in Europe; and Lieutenant General Hoyt S. Vandenberg, Commanding General Ninth Air Force.

achieving independence. They recalled how congressional support for change had weakened in the face of strong service opposition. And they believed that, if support for their position was not at least strengthened by the war's end, the Army Air Forces could revert to its prewar, subordinate position within the Army's organization.

AAF Commanding General Hap Arnold was convinced that, to perform its postwar mission effectively, the Air Forces had to become coequal with the Army and Navy. Separate service status would provide the AAF with the same access to Congress possessed by the other two services and give it an equal chance to present its views at the top levels of government.[40] More important, perhaps, separate service status would enable the Air Forces to fight for funding on the same footing as the other services. Arnold was concerned that, if the AAF remained part of the War Department, it inevitably would receive a budget share far below that needed to carry out its missions in the postwar world. In a memorandum to General Marshall in June 1945 he commented, "Acceptance of the assumption that the third major force—sea power—will continue to receive its traditional proportion of approximately half the budget for the Armed Forces ultimately may result in the absorption by the Navy of missions which logically should be assigned to the Army Air Forces."[41]

Despite the AAF's vital interest in unification the real impetus behind the campaign for a single department continued to come from General Marshall and planners in the War Department's Special Planning Division. Yet, many of the naval officers analyzing the issue for the Secretary mistakenly linked the War Department's 1945 call for unification with the Air Corps' interwar efforts to achieve an independent status. They therefore believed that the Army Air Force leaders were behind the "renewed agitation."[42] This misapprehension, understandable in light of the earlier history, strengthened the resolve of many senior Navy leaders, and particularly the aviators, to fight the War Department proposals.

This is how matters stood on 17 October 1945 when the Senate Military Affairs Committee began hearings to examine two unification bills introduced by several members of the committee. During two months of hearings, War Department and Navy Department witnesses fought to a near standstill. Although the committee came out in favor of unification, neither of the proposed bills was passed by Congress. This situation created a policy vacuum into which President Harry S. Truman moved. Just two days after the conclusion of the Senate committee hearings, the President sent a unification message to the House of Representatives. Truman was convinced that some form of unification would emerge once the Army-Navy stalemate had been overcome. Throughout 1946 he continued to exert his personal influence on Forrestal and Secretary of War Robert P. Patterson to reach an accommodation.

The Initial Fight Over Roles and Missions

In early 1946, even as Congress was drawing up new unification legislation, the Joint Chiefs of Staff took steps that aroused concern on both sides about the issue of service roles and missions.[43] On 20 February 1946 the Joint Strategic Survey Committee (JSSC) issued a report to the JCS on missions of the land, sea, and air forces. The report noted that the primary missions could be assigned to the Army, Air Forces, and Navy "principally" by the element in which they normally operated. The JSSC report, however, was split between its Army and Navy members on a number of major issues, including the responsibility for land-based aviation, the operation of air transport, and the role of the Marine Corps.[44]

The Army version of the report noted that the AAF was capable of providing the land-based air component used in conducting antisubmarine warfare and also capable of performing reconnaissance for the Navy. Although both of these functions would be performed under the Navy's operational control, the Army version stated explicitly that the land-based planes necessary for these functions should be "designed, manned, operated and commanded" by the Army Air Forces.

The Navy version called instead for the continuation of the service's existing responsibilities in these fields, commenting with some acerbity, "Anti-submarine warfare and naval reconnaissance are not part-time jobs that can be assimilated in part-time training and accomplished in part-time operations.... Temporary loan of Air Force units... will produce inadequately trained and insufficiently capable personnel for these vital naval purposes."[45]

The JSSC report set off a prolonged debate among the Joint Chiefs over roles and missions (detailed in the JCS 1478 series memoranda) that did much to cloud Army-Navy relations throughout the rest of 1946 and well into the following year. The debate began quietly enough when Fleet Admiral Chester W. Nimitz, the new Chief of Naval Operations, submitted a paper to the JCS calling for revision of the JSSC report to reaffirm the wartime Army-Navy agreement on land-based air responsibilities.[46]

This paper elicited a blunt reply from Army Air Forces Commanding General Carl Spaatz. His March 1946 paper on roles and missions was a departure from the noncommittal position that his predecessor, Hap Arnold, had taken just a few months before. Arnold, concerned that discord over the land-based air issue would impede a final Army-Navy agreement on unification, had wisely decided to leave the decision to the new Secretary of National Defense, once the War and Navy Departments had been unified.[47]

Spaatz, however, believed in meeting the issue head on. This direct approach was in line with his willingness, in the immediate aftermath of the war, to examine all of the contentious air issues anew. In the early weeks of the peace he had even been willing to look at the issue of the Air Forces' control of carrier aviation. For example, on 19 October 1945, in a conversation with Major General Lauris Norstad, Assistant Chief of Air Staff for Plans, General Spaatz had remarked, "Whether or not under a single department the air units utilized on carriers should be a part of the Navy or part of the Air Forces is one question which should be given very careful study. *I personally believe that a well-trained air unit can*

34 *Revolt of the Admirals*

Fleet Admiral Chester W. Nimitz, Chief of Naval Operations from 15 December 1945 to 15 December 1947.

be rapidly trained to operate aboard a carrier."[48] Spaatz had gone on to say that whether or not carrier air remained in the Navy, he believed that naval aviators should receive their primary and basic training in Air Forces schools.[49]

In his March 1946 JCS Paper, Spaatz stated "The concept of the three services—land, sea and air—is derived from the ideal principle that the land forces should operate all forces on the land, the Navy all forces on the sea and the Air Forces all forces in the air."[50] Although the AAF commanding general allowed that certain exceptions to this principle appeared necessary to meet the needs of the Navy, the operation of land-based aircraft was not one of these. He declared, "The Army Air Forces can perform all the functions of the armed forces requiring the use of land-based aircraft and I recommend that they be charged with this responsibility in its entirety, thus insuring maximum use of the inherent flexibility of air power."[51]

General Spaatz's paper was followed immediately by an equally blunt one from General of the Army Dwight D. Eisenhower, Marshall's successor as Army Chief of Staff. Although Eisenhower seconded Spaatz's comments on land-based air, his primary intention was to recommend severe restraints on the size and capability of the Marine Corps.[52]

Navy leaders were completely taken aback by the severity of these assaults on the Navy's position on roles and missions. Vice Admiral Forrest P. Sherman, Deputy Chief of Naval Operations for Operations and one of Chester Nimitz's closest advisers, stressed to the admiral:

> Both papers attempt to reject all previous agreements and all previous legislation. General Eisenhower further expresses the belief that further exchange of papers on the subject would serve no useful purpose and recommends that resolution of the matters at issue be effected by conversation among the JCS or, failing agreement, taken to a higher level—presumably the President.[53]

Linking the AAF and Army positions with the impending congressional actions on unification, Sherman advised Nimitz that the best policy for the Navy was "deliberate delay" on the issue. He remarked, "Certainly when the Army presses for immediate action it is to our interest to delay, particularly as this question would seem part of an accelerated campaign directed at influencing Congressional action on the basic problem."[54] The Spaatz and Eisenhower papers were handed over to Vice Admiral Arthur W. Radford, DCNO (Air), and General Alexander A. Vandegrift, Commandant of the Marine Corps, for their detailed comments.[55] Thereafter JCS debates over the various roles and missions papers continued without resolution until 7 June 1946, when the Joint Chiefs finally agreed

General Carl A. Spaatz, Commanding General, Army Air Forces, 1946.

Unification, Service Rivalries, and Public Relations 37

NHC, Radford Papers

The new Navy leadership team, January 1946. Left to right, *front*: Admiral Dewitt C. Ramsey, VCNO; Fleet Admiral Chester Nimitz, CNO; Secretary Forrestal; John L. Sullivan, Assistant Secretary of the Navy for Air; and Admiral Charles P. Snyder, Naval Inspector General. Left to right, *rear*: Rear Admiral Edmund W. Burrough, head of OPNAV's Joint Plans Division; Vice Admiral Forrest P. Sherman, DCNO (Operations); Vice Admiral William H. P. Blandy, DCNO (Special Weapons); Vice Admiral Louis E. Denfeld, Chief of Personnel and DCNO (Personnel); Vice Admiral William S. Farber, DCNO (Logistics); Vice Admiral Richard L. Conolly, DCNO (Administration); and Vice Admiral Arthur W. Radford, DCNO (Air).

to suspend further consideration of the 1478 series memoranda until such time as presidential or legislative action required it.[56]

The impasse in the JCS, however, did not end the Army Air Forces' attempts to settle the issue in its favor. The Navy feared that President Truman would side with the Army-AAF view that the Navy should be denied land-based aircraft for reconnaissance and antisubmarine warfare. Its concerns proved justified. On 15 June 1946 the President issued a public letter to the Secretaries of War and Navy in which he stated, "Land-based planes for Naval reconnaissance, anti-submarine warfare and protection of shipping can and should be manned by Air Force personnel."[57]

The announcement deeply concerned Arthur Radford and most of the other senior naval aviators.[58] On 19 June Secretary Forrestal met with the President to express the depth of the naval aviators' misgivings. He told Truman that "the Navy felt so strongly as to be fanatic about it, that they *must* have the means with which to carry out their mission."[59] He apparently persuaded the President that the language of Truman's letter had not been intended to deny the Navy "sufficient land-based planes for reconnaissance and 'search and strike' purposes."[60] On 24 June Forrestal reaffirmed the substance of this discussion in a letter to the President. This Navy Department letter so clouded the issue that the administration was precluded from taking overt action to strip the Navy of its land-based aircraft.[61]

Not to be dissuaded from taking at least some steps towards its goal of controlling Navy land-based air, the Army Air Forces began campaigning to deny the Navy any appropriations for purchase of additional land-based aircraft. AAF views on the issue found a favorable reception at the Bureau of the Budget. On 21 and 22 October the Navy's Bureau of Aeronautics briefed the Bureau of the Budget on the fiscal year 1948 naval aviation requirements. Within a few days it was apparent that the funding for land-based aircraft was a particular bureau target.[62] Admiral Radford urged Forrestal to persuade the Bureau of the Budget that the President had modified the view expressed in his original letter and, therefore, that the Navy could continue to procure land-based antisubmarine warfare and reconnaissance aircraft. However, Forrestal was reluctant to do anything, remarking to Radford that soon things would be changing for the better.[63] The Secretary apparently was referring to the stories he had heard that Assistant Secretary of War for Air W. Stuart Symington and the AAF were becoming unhappy with the lack of progress on the unification issue and with Secretary of War Patterson's unwillingness to negotiate with the Navy.[64]

In an attempt to exploit the AAF's apparent interest in talking, Forrestal arranged a luncheon meeting at his house with Symington and Lieutenant General Lauris Norstad for 7 November. By prearrangement Radford and Vice Admiral Forrest Sherman joined the group after the luncheon for a discussion on unification. During the session Symington expressed the AAF's fear that the Navy might set up a strategic air force of its own and thus threaten AAF's existence. Radford and Sherman explained that the Navy had no such intention, but that it feared the loss of its land-based patrol aircraft. After some further discussion Symington and Norstad expressed their support for "the continuance of Naval patrol landplane squadrons for anti-submarine warfare."[65]

The Army Air Forces' apparent agreement to the continuation of Navy land-based air had no effect on changes already in train, however. In mid-November the Bureau of the Budget requested the Navy's written views on why it believed it was necessary to maintain a land-based avia-

Assistant Secretary of War for Air W. Stuart Symington in early 1947.

tion program for naval reconnaissance, ASW, and the protection of shipping.[66] On 6 December 1946 General Spaatz sent a letter to Budget Director James E. Webb. Ignoring the assurances that Symington and Norstad had given Navy leaders just a month earlier, Carl Spaatz told Webb that the Navy's request for long-range, land-based aircraft was for "strategic bombers similar in character to the long range bomber which is the backbone of our Strategic Air Force." He characterized the naval officers seeking such planes as "advocates of the theory that the Navy should now be permitted to build up a Strategic Air Force."[67] The AAF commanding general explained to Webb that the Army Air Forces was fully capable of performing long-range naval reconnaissance and anti-submarine tasks; thus, there was no need for the Navy to duplicate the AAF's capabilities in these areas. In fact he stressed, "The resources and economy of the country could scarcely afford in war time, and certainly cannot sustain in peace time, a duplicate Strategic Air Force."[68]

It was about this time that the budget director killed the Navy procurement request for land-based air, citing the President's 15 June letter as authority.[69] This proved the final straw for most of the Navy's senior aviators, already upset over a series of internal Navy Department actions indicating to them that naval aviation was being downgraded. The aviators were not just imagining a loss of influence within the Navy Department. Some of the senior surface officers in the Office of the Chief of Naval Operations were expecting a diminution of naval aviation's influence within the service either as a result of unification or because of a general reduction in carrier aviation capabilities caused by newly developing technologies.

One example of this new viewpoint was a 25 November eyes-only memorandum from Vice Admiral Robert B. Carney, Deputy Chief of Naval Operations for Logistics, to the CNO (via the Vice Chief) on the Navy's new position on unification. In this memorandum Carney, a surface officer, provided a gloomy prediction of naval aviation's future:

> An inference from these trends [of larger and heavier aircraft] is that the carrier may be at the crossroads; such aircraft as can be operated from the carriers in the future may be so inferior to similar land-based aircraft as to seriously restrict both offensive and defensive capabilities of such aircraft.[70]

Carney considered this development to be a death knell for carrier aviation. He argued that the Navy Department could not afford to reverse its newly emerging position in favor of a separate air force in deference to the concerns of naval aviators, who might be forced by technological circumstances to leave the Navy and join the air force anyway.[71]

The chief departmental action that convinced the aviators of their loss of status, however, was the revelation, made in a briefing to the Flag Selection Board on 21 November, that the Secretary of the Navy had decided to commit the Department to the establishment of a separate air force despite the continued strong resistance of the naval aviation community.[72] The Secretary got a sudden indication of the depth of the aviators' feelings on 4 December when, at a luncheon meeting, Arthur Radford told him that the naval aviators feared that granting the AAF departmental status was only a first step in the Army Air Forces' more ambitious plans for taking over "the whole business of national defense."[73]

James Forrestal's reasons for giving up his long-standing objections to a separate air force included his belief (not shared by many senior naval aviators) that AAF leaders had given up any intentions they may have had of stripping naval aviation of its primary missions. By late 1946 a belief in the inevitability of AAF independence was also a strong component of Forrestal's thinking. Some months later he wrote to a naval aviator:

> While I have the same reservations as you about the separate department for air, the fact is that the Army Air people have already pretty well established autonomy, will not be happy unless a legislative seal is put upon it,

NHC, Radford Papers

Rear Admiral Leslie C. Stevens, Assistant Chief of BUAER for Research, Development, and Engineering; Vice Admiral Arthur Radford, DCNO (Air); and Rear Admiral Harold B. Sallada, Chief of BUAER, examine a model of the XR 60–1 Constitution—the largest airplane built to that time for the Navy—at a press conference in August 1946.

and if they don't get it, will have a sense of frustration which will lead to continued friction.[74]

The issue came to a head on Saturday, 11 January 1947, when Secretary Forrestal held a conference in his office with the Navy's senior aviators to discuss their differing views on unification. Those at the conference who supported a separate air force included Forrestal, Under Secretary John L. Sullivan, Fleet Admiral Nimitz, and two aviators—Admiral DeWitt C. (Duke) Ramsey, the Vice Chief of Naval Operations (VCNO), and Vice Admiral Forrest Sherman, the Navy's principal negotiator of the unification compromise with the War Department. The aviators opposed to such a plan represented a veritable cross-section of naval aviation[75] and included Admiral Marc A. Mitscher, Commander in Chief, Atlantic Fleet; Vice Admiral Radford; Rear Admiral Harold B. Sallada, Chief of the Bureau of Aeronautics; and the three naval air training chiefs.[76]

The conference became a no-holds-barred debate between the two groups. Forrestal viewed the proposed unification legislation as the best the Navy could expect to obtain under the circumstances. As he commented a few weeks later, "If I were writing a bill solely for the Navy, I might have some different bill, but this bill has been written, number one, for the USA, and then second, for the Navy, and it represents, in my opinion, the best combination of those two objectives that we could get."[77]

The naval aviators were not persuaded by the Secretary's reasoning. They argued that establishing the Army Air Forces on a par with the Army and Navy would be "just the initial step in a continuing campaign by the Army Air Force people to absorb all Naval aviation."[78] One evidence of the strong emotions that day was the accusation during the meeting by VCNO Duke Ramsey that the aviators were being disloyal to the Secretary by maintaining their strong uncompromising stand. The session broke up with the aviators still convinced that the Secretary and the CNO were mistaken in agreeing to unification. Moreover the vehemence with which the opposing views had been expressed undoubtedly left bad feelings on both sides.[79]

The views of the aviators were put into perspective in a confidential personal letter that Rear Admiral Felix B. Stump, Chief of Naval Air Technical Training, wrote to Admiral Nimitz a few days after the conference. Stump began by stressing that every one of the attending officers was wholeheartedly convinced that having "a well-balanced Navy, air, surface and sub-surface" was essential to the national defense. He noted that the two groups differed only in the methods they believed necessary to accomplish that purpose. Admiral Stump went on to say, "I do feel that the development of Naval Aviation and all other forms of sea power must be sparked and controlled by Naval officers, air and surface."[80] He explained to Nimitz his concern that the aviators had been castigated as being troublemakers by the Vice Chief for expressing their strong opposition to a separate air force. Stump recounted:

> I expressed the thought and conviction that we could do more with the Navy and for the Navy by guiding the development of the air force from within than by standing up against them from without. This is what "Duke" Ramsey, whom all of us [who] know [him] both love and respect, mentioned as "heresy".[81]

The CNO responded to Stump's thoughtful letter by reaffirming his belief in the importance of naval aviation to the service.[82]

With the Navy Department's opposition to a separate department of air overturned, the final major impediment to service unification disappeared. In mid-January 1947 Forrestal and Secretary of War Robert Patterson signed a joint letter to the President informing him that they had reached agreement on all aspects of unification.

The impending arrival of unification, however, did nothing to alleviate the Navy's immediate concerns over its land-based aircraft program. James Forrestal sent a letter to President Truman on 13 January in an effort to overturn the Bureau of the Budget's veto of funds for procurement of Navy land-based aircraft.[83] On 24 January, after receiving the advice of his budget director, President Truman responded. He informed Forrestal that the matter could now be worked out in accordance with the principles laid down in the recent Patterson-Forrestal agreement on unification.[84] That compromise had allocated the responsibility for naval reconnaissance, ASW, and protection of shipping to the Navy, subject to the proviso that the air aspects of these functions were to be coordinated with the Air Force.[85] This letter officially ended the Navy's concerns over its continued possession and employment of land-based air. Nevertheless its struggle with the AAF over the issue was not yet finished.

The Army Air Forces, relying on the wording of the draft Executive Order concerning coordination of the air program, continued to frustrate Navy efforts to obtain funding for new aircraft. On 29 January Admiral Radford submitted a memorandum to the Aeronautical Board requesting support for continued production of the P2V and P4M aircraft.[86] Two days later Radford received a letter from General Spaatz that stated:

> The Air Force 1948 budget provides no funds for the provision of a type of aircraft especially adapted to the mission of sea search and anti-submarine warfare. The Budget Bureau was told that the Strategic Air Force would be trained to the performance of this task as one of its missions if and when it were called upon for that purpose.[87]

Spaatz went on to say that, in light of the new agreement assigning sea search and antisubmarine missions to the Navy and the President's statement that the missions were to be accomplished within the present allotment of funds, the Navy might take a number of AAF B–29s to determine their adaptability for its needs.[88]

Radford wrote Spaatz on 4 February and again on 8 February, requesting Spaatz's concurrence on the funding for the Navy P2V and P4M program.[89] Two days later General Spaatz finally replied:

> I must tell you that on our side of the house there is complete agreement that we will not make representations to the Congress which might result in exceeding the budget for our service for 1948.... As you know, we had a considerable number of airplanes which we considered very essential... which had to be eliminated for economy.[90]

Major General Lauris Norstad, Assistant Chief of Air Staff for Plans, January 1946.

Accordingly Spaatz informed Radford that he "could not be a party" to testifying for the Navy in an effort to have its budget enlarged. He remarked further that in the interest of economy, "We should give the B–29 a thorough tryout" before building a special type of aircraft for the ASW mission.[91]

The matter was not concluded to the Navy's satisfaction until mid-March 1947, when Spaatz grudgingly accepted the Navy view.[92] By then he had been convinced by General Norstad that his continued intransigence on this issue could affect the unification agreement worked out with the Navy.[93] After some fourteen months of wrangling, the fight over the Navy's right to operate land-based aircraft in support of maritime missions was at an end.

The Air Force Public Relations Effort

In the closing months of the war the Army Air Forces had begun gearing up for a major public relations (PR) effort designed to garner public and, more important, congressional support for the postwar establishment of an autonomous air force. In September 1944 a significant study on AAF public relations was prepared for General Arnold by the AAF's public relations staff. The study redefined the PR mission in light of the approaching end of the war in Europe and the coming shift of the AAF effort to the Pacific theater. It was explicit about the primary goal of the AAF effort: to maintain high public confidence in the Army Air Forces during both the remaining months of the war and the postwar period. As the study defined the current situation:

> Today, the Army Air Forces has completed one major phase of World War II, by building and manning the world's greatest air force, and has almost completed a second major phase, *by knocking out Germany* in history's first major employment of air power in warfare....
>
> Today, the picture of war has changed. The AAF has already won a tremendous victory and, paradoxically, it now faces a potentially serious public relations situation....
>
> The American public has a historic tendency — to build up idols, and to knock them down. The AAF has been and is the idol of the American public. The public's acceptance and support must be carefully planned and jealously guarded.[94]

The Army Air Forces' counter to the powerful public relations position the Navy had attained in the Pacific would have to be a strong publicity campaign on the Twentieth Air Force's long-range bombing of Japan. The report stressed:

> The Twentieth Air Force has the mission of applying V.L.R.B. [Very Long Range Bombardment] and it also, from the AAF viewpoint, has the mission of serving as an implement for selling the AAF as the proper hand to wield air power and to advance the AAF goal of independent operations under a joint department of war.[95]

General Arnold took this advice seriously. Just three days after receiving the public relations staff's report, he sent strong letters to his three top-level AAF commanders—Carl Spaatz, Ira Eaker, and George C. Kenney. His letter to Spaatz read in part:

> I realize fully the difficulties incident to a proper presentation of the part the air has played in the success of the campaigns conducted by various Theatre Commanders. However, you must apply pressure in Europe while I apply it here, to the end that our press releases more nearly picture in proper balance the relative contribution of ground, sea and air forces in our approach toward complete victory over our enemies....

I consider the whole subject of realistic reorientation of the public's concept of the effect of air power upon the outcome of the war so important that I will scour the country to provide you with the men most capable of putting into words the achievements of the Army Air Forces.[96]

By October 1945 the AAF had taken an official position that its independent status could best be assured under the War Department's concept of a single department, wherein it would have coordinate and coequal status with the Army and the Navy.[97] In the event that a single department was not created, its fall-back position was establishment of the Air Force as a separate, completely unified department.[98]

By this time AAF thinking also had coalesced around most of the major themes that would be stressed in its postwar PR effort to achieve independent status. The first theme was that air power had become the nation's dominant military force. General Spaatz asserted in October 1945, "The aeronautical advance of the past few years has ushered in the 'Air Age.' Its primary force is Air Power. As sea-power was the dominant factor in the destiny of nations in the nineteenth century, so today the dictate is Air Power."[99] Where before, the Navy had served to protect U.S. shores from enemy invasion, in the air age only air power could defend the United States from the devastation wrought by an enemy air force.[100]

The air power referred to, however, was AAF air power, not the combined aviation of the Army and Navy.[101] The Army Air Forces, echoing Giulio Douhet, saw air power as an indivisible entity operating under the control of the air commander.[102] The AAF had expressed this theme in 1943: "The inherent flexibility of air power is its greatest asset.... Control of available air power must be centralized and command must be exercised through the air force commander if its inherent flexibility and ability to deliver a decisive blow are to be fully exploited."[103] AAF leaders saw separate service air forces as manifestly weak air forces—each unable to function as effectively in combat as could a single integrated air force.

A second theme, linked directly to the first, was that the Army Air Forces, as the only true exponent of air power, had become the first line of defense for the United States. Armed with the atomic bomb, the AAF stood ready to defend the United States against air attack and to launch an early counteroffensive employing its devastating weapon.[104]

A third theme was that strategic bombardment remained the most important function of an air force. To the leaders of the Army Air Forces, strategic bombardment had proven its decisiveness in war, even without the atomic bomb.[105] As General Spaatz wrote to Lieutenant General Barney M. Giles, AAF Deputy Commanding General, in March 1945, "There has been no lack of evidence that the strategic bombing of Germany has been a major, *if not the major*, factor in its impending defeat."[106] Showing

Navy Department Organization, May 1946

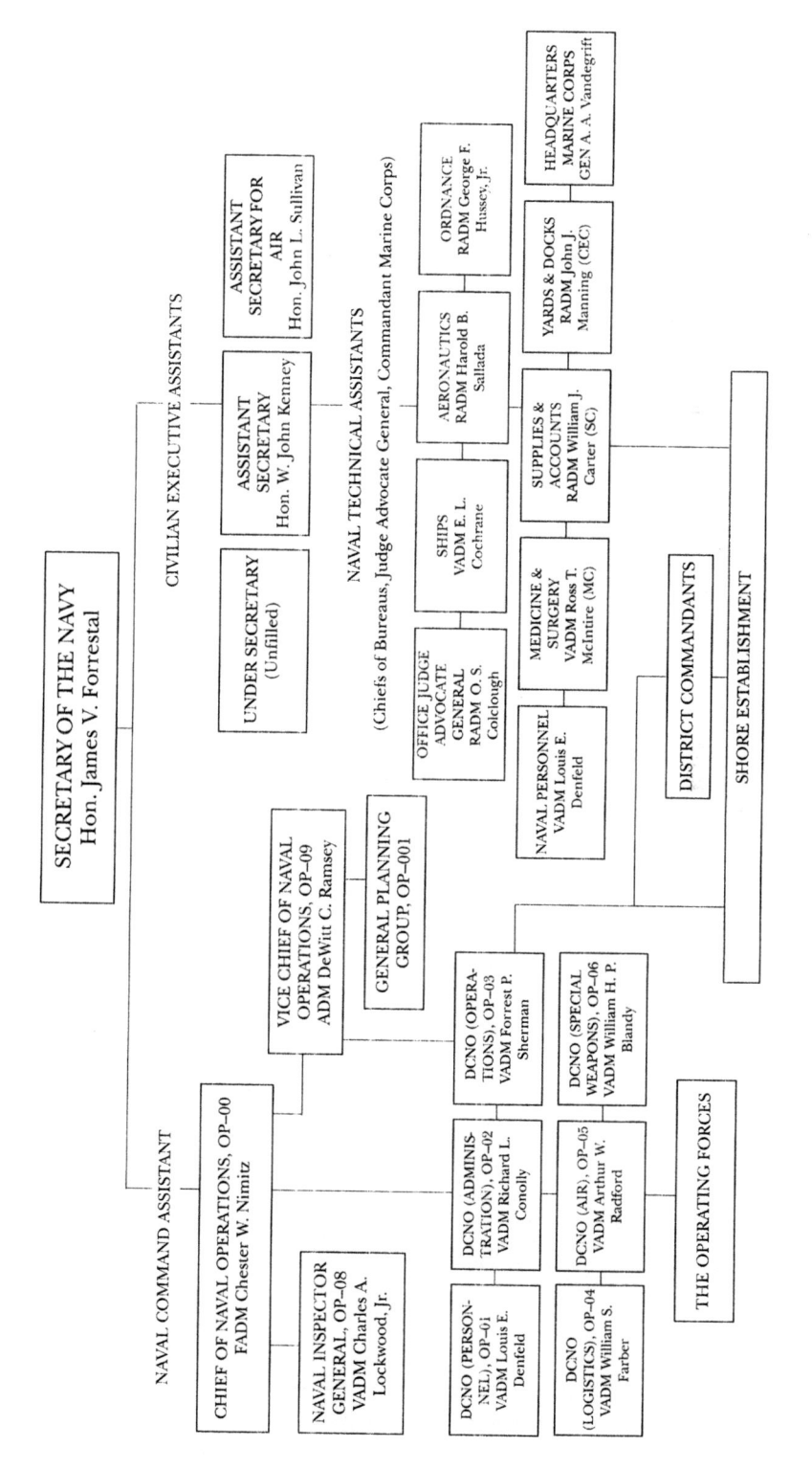

SECRETARY OF THE NAVY
Hon. James V. Forrestal

CIVILIAN EXECUTIVE ASSISTANTS

- **UNDER SECRETARY** (Unfilled)
- **ASSISTANT SECRETARY** Hon. W. John Kenney
- **ASSISTANT SECRETARY FOR AIR** Hon. John L. Sullivan

NAVAL TECHNICAL ASSISTANTS
(Chiefs of Bureaus, Judge Advocate General, Commandant Marine Corps)

- **OFFICE JUDGE ADVOCATE GENERAL** RADM O. S. Colclough
- **NAVAL PERSONNEL** VADM Louis E. Denfeld
- **SHIPS** VADM E. L. Cochrane
- **MEDICINE & SURGERY** VADM Ross T. McIntire (MC)
- **AERONAUTICS** RADM Harold B. Sallada
- **SUPPLIES & ACCOUNTS** RADM William J. Carter (SC)
- **ORDNANCE** RADM George F. Hussey, Jr.
- **YARDS & DOCKS** RADM John J. Manning (CEC)
- **HEADQUARTERS MARINE CORPS** GEN A. A. Vandegrift

NAVAL COMMAND ASSISTANT

- **CHIEF OF NAVAL OPERATIONS, OP-00** FADM Chester W. Nimitz
  - **NAVAL INSPECTOR GENERAL, OP-08** VADM Charles A. Lockwood, Jr.
  - **VICE CHIEF OF NAVAL OPERATIONS, OP-09** ADM DeWitt C. Ramsey
    - **GENERAL PLANNING GROUP, OP-001**
    - **DCNO (OPERATIONS), OP-03** VADM Forrest P. Sherman
    - **DCNO (SPECIAL WEAPONS), OP-06** VADM William H. P. Blandy
    - **DCNO (ADMINISTRATION), OP-02** VADM Richard L. Conolly
    - **DCNO (AIR), OP-05** VADM Arthur W. Radford
    - **DCNO (PERSONNEL), OP-01** VADM Louis E. Denfeld
    - **DCNO (LOGISTICS), OP-04** VADM William S. Farber

- **THE OPERATING FORCES**
- **DISTRICT COMMANDANTS**
- **SHORE ESTABLISHMENT**

SOURCES: *Manual of Organization Charts: Bureaus and Offices of the Navy Department*, NAVEXOS P-63 (Washington: Navy Department, 20 Jan 1947) for chart diagram; "Office of Chief of Naval Operations OP-Sheet," 15 May 1946, Navy Department Library, NHC, for personnel list.

an even greater confidence in the ability of AAF air power to end the war, General George Kenney, Commander Allied Air Forces Southwest Pacific Area, wrote to Hap Arnold early that same year, "I believe that the Nip [Japan] is tottering so badly that an overwhelming and continuous air assault may very easily gain the final decision."[107]

In the early weeks of the peace, the full weight of the AAF public relations effort was directed toward the campaign for service unification. An important part of this effort was the attack on the Navy's antiunification position and wartime accomplishments, which helped to legitimize unification in the public's mind. These attacks had to be made in such a way that the public would remain unaware of the AAF's direct role, because such adverse publicity would reflect badly on the Air Forces. The attacks on the Navy therefore had to be done indirectly.[108]

The most important example of this technique was the AAF's secret support of the writings of William Bradford Huie. A professional writer who had served briefly in the Navy during the war while working on articles about the Seabees, Huie was a strong proponent of air power. In 1942 he had written *The Fight for Air Power*—a book castigating the War and Navy Departments for their stands against an independent air force.[109] With the war over, Huie decided to write a book that would provide strong support for unification of the services by attacking the Navy, the most powerful opponent of unification.

In late September 1945 Huie met with Major General Hugh J. Knerr, Commander Air Materiel Command, to seek his and the AAF's assistance in the attack on the Navy.[110] Knerr, a graduate of the Naval Academy class of 1908, had transferred to the Army in 1912 and become a Signal Corps pilot five years later.[111] A formidable crusader and sometime polemicist for strategic air power, he had a personal antipathy toward the Navy dating back to his days of naval service, when he was denied a chance at flying duty.[112] Knerr, moreover, was an old comrade-in-arms of Huie's.[113]

General Knerr, who had returned to active duty during the war, was planning to retire for a second time in September 1945. It was this circumstance that apparently provided the final motivation for William Bradford Huie to contact Knerr for his help in writing the new book. Huie followed up a luncheon meeting with Knerr on 27 September—a meeting at which Knerr presumably agreed to help with the effort—with a letter in which he detailed the assistance that the Army Air Forces had agreed to secretly provide him.[114]

> I have had several long conferences with General [Frank F.] Everest and the Air Force people. They are using me as a civilian adviser in planning the campaign for unification.... They are anxious for me to write the

book as planned, and I am going ahead with it. They are undertaking to do a lot of research for me.[115]

Huie described the thinking of General Everest and his AAF personnel on how to fight the Navy's position.

> They have little hope that Arnold will really put his shoulder to the wheel, so they want to make James H. (Jimmy) Doolittle *and you* their chief inactive duty spokesmen. But since Doolittle has political aspirations, they want to keep him on a "high plane." ... Several of them want to blossom out as "writers" to support the Cause. Spaatz is willing to write a series of articles, and even Arnold has expressed such a willingness.[116]

In the closing paragraphs, Huie said that he was hoping that the book, "tentatively entitled THE CASE AGAINST THE ADMIRALS," could be co-authored by Knerr and Doolittle (or Knerr and Arnold).[117]

He was soon disappointed in this hope of publicly acknowledged expert help. Knerr decided not to retire and apparently felt it unwise, under the circumstances, to become publicly linked to the book. Huie went ahead with the project anyway.[118]

Its publication in mid-March 1946 generated some initial publicity, in part because the Navy Department had obtained galley proofs and made it clear to the press that it found the book to be error-prone and propagandistic.[119] The Navy's strong reaction to Huie's book was no surprise, since the author had made his purpose clear at the outset, stating that he meant "to attack the cabal of admirals which is obstructing consolidation of our armed services."[120] The Navy was so concerned over the negative impact of Huie's book that it took the issue up directly with the Army before the book was published. Secretary Forrestal talked with Secretary Patterson about it. Similarly, in a letter to his Army colleague, Dwight Eisenhower, Chester Nimitz stressed, "The net result of publication will be harmful to both services and particularly unfortunate at this time when further evidence of disunity between the services can be used to our national disadvantage."[121]

The new Army Chief of Staff was completely unaware that elements of the AAF's leadership had aided and abetted Huie's effort. In a 9 March memorandum to Generals John E. Hull and J. Lawton Collins, Eisenhower commented, "All our personnel should be aware that ... [the] W.D. [War Department] does not approve of methods intended to discredit another service; we must be objective, logical and *public* minded.... The job of the officer is not that of a political conniver!"[122]

Despite the initial spate of publicity *The Case Against the Admirals* lost much of its public visibility after a few weeks.[123] Huie's book thus did not have the major impact on public opinion on unification that he and the AAF had hoped. Nonetheless it served to reinforce the concern of many senior officers in the Navy, and particularly the naval aviators, that the proponents of unification would go to great lengths to achieve their goal.

With hopes for a rapid passage of the unification legislation and, as a result, early independence from the War Department fading by early 1946, the Army Air Forces began according greater attention to its postwar organization for public relations. Because Congress would have the major role in the ultimate outcome of unification, it soon became the chief target of this PR effort. A September 1946 memorandum to then Assistant Secretary of War for Air Stuart Symington stressed, "*Our campaign for unification should be aimed with a rifle at the 531 senators and congressmen who are actually going to vote on unification rather than with a shotgun at the 140,000,000 citizens who are not.*"[124]

With strong support from the highest levels of AAF, the Office of Public Relations was placed on a solid organizational footing during the latter half of 1946. The effectiveness of Air Force public relations was improved even more, however, during 1947 and 1948. The most important improvement was the appointment of Stephen F. Leo—in Symington's words, "the best young newspaper man I know"—as Director of Public Relations for the new Service.[125] Steve Leo was a superb choice to head up the Air Force's PR effort. He stood head and shoulders above other service public relations people of the day. As Navy Captain Frank A. Manson recalled, "He was *absolutely* a superior PR manager for those days. He understood how to do it."[126]

With the direct support of Air Force Secretary Symington, Leo had the authority to oversee the public relations aspects of all Air Force activities. In addition to being Director of Public Relations, a job that included oversight responsibility for the Service's legislative and liaison activities, Steve Leo also served as Special Assistant to the Secretary—a position that allowed him access to matters that weren't covered under his public relations function.[127] Leo was convinced that having the PR effort headed by a civilian was the major factor in its success:

> There were many things that the military person in the PR function could not properly do.... If you were dissatisfied with a civilian you could always replace him, and if you were satisfied with him he would have a freedom of operation that was not available to a uniformed officer within the then existing proprieties.[128]

The team of Steve Leo and Stuart Symington was formidable. Symington had a true politician's flair for dispensing rewards and punishments to gain desired ends. Symington and Leo's principal object was to have the Air Force considered "essential" to U.S. security. To do that, they had to overcome the "slanted" stories put forth to the press by anti-Air Force groups.[129]

The Air Force's top flight public relations team: Stuart Symington and Steve Leo in early 1947.

In regard to PR, Symington was a firm believer in the adage "don't get mad, get even." In practicing this philosophy, Symington and Leo were always the first to officially protest any anti–Air Force newspaper or magazine article that seemed to be inspired by another service. At the same time they turned a blind eye to Air Force–inspired pieces that attacked Navy or Army positions. A memorandum for Navy Secretary John Sullivan summed up the situation in early 1948: "The Air Force apparently contends that it is perfectly alright to disseminate their ideas widely in the public magazines. [Yet] it objects to the Navy issuing material setting forth the Navy's position."[130]

One indication of the success that the Air Force public relations effort appeared to be having with Congress was disclosed in a survey that Captain Lyman A. (Red) Thackrey had done for the Secretary of the Navy in March 1948. Thackrey then headed the staff of the Secretary's Committee on Research on Reorganization (SCOROR)—the departmental group set up after the war by James Forrestal to work on unification issues. The SCOROR staff reviewed the *Congressional Record* from January through March 1948, tabulating the articles, speeches, and editorials dealing with the Navy and the Air Force that had been inserted by members of Congress. The survey found eleven pro-Navy and eleven anti-Navy pieces in the January–March period. Twenty-eight pro-Air Force and no anti-Air Force pieces had been inserted in the *Congressional Record* during the same period.[131] This situation was seen as a clear indication that the Air Force had been doing a better job than the Navy of getting its viewpoint across to Congress. As Captain Thackrey informed the Secretary of the Navy, "It is apparent... that there is either considerably more natural interest in the Air Force by members of Congress, or that the Air Force itself is more assiduous in discharging its responsibility with regard to enlightening public understanding. The latter is believed to be the case."[132]

The Navy received another, more emphatic, indication when several prominent senators announced that they supported the Air Force's 70-group program (the service's planning figure comprising 70 groups and 22 separate squadrons for the minimum necessary peacetime strength needed to carry out its national defense responsibilities), even if it had to come at the expense of the Army and Navy.[133] In April 1948 Admiral Louis E. Denfeld wrote his friend Dudley White, President of Sandusky Newspapers, "I am a little disturbed because Bob Taft, Joe Martin, and Styles Bridges have come out for the '70 Group Air Force' and Bob has said that they should have it at the expense of the Army and Navy. I am sure that they are being fed the regular Air Force propaganda."[134]

Admiral Nimitz and the Continuing Controversy Over Unification

On 26 July 1947 the National Security Act of 1947 was signed into law by President Truman. Among its provisions was the creation of a National Military Establishment, composed of three services—the Army, the Navy and the Air Force—to be coordinated by a secretary of defense.

To Admiral Nimitz, then in his final months as Chief of Naval Operations, passage of the National Security Act was proof that men of good will who held differing views could sit down together and work out their differences.[135] He continued to hold this view throughout 1947–1950. Nimitz's optimism was reflected in a December 1948 letter, written to his friend Ted Dealey, president of the *Dallas Morning News*, a year after he had retired as CNO. Nimitz commented that he was a "great booster of the National Security Act of 1947" and suggested that Dealey have one of his reporters interview Secretaries Sullivan and Forrestal to get the real story on how much progress had been made on unification under the new act.[136] Dealey took Nimitz up on his suggestion.

The result was not what Nimitz expected. The correspondent, David Botter, observed to the managing editor of the newspaper:

Forrestal's staff is very frank in saying that unification is not working and they are putting the blame on the Air Force, which has great ambitions. The administrative setup is absolutely impossible because any of the departmental secretaries can bypass Forrestal to go either to the White House or Congress.[137]

Botter concluded, "I am afraid Admiral Nimitz is going to be disappointed."[138]

No sooner was the National Security Act passed than the Navy's conflicts with the Army and Air Force began anew. A prime example was the War Department's 11 August 1947 publication and subsequent circulation of a classified study, *Final Report: War Department Policies and Program Review Board*. The study's purpose was to review War Department policies and programs concerning the regular Army and draw up recommendations that could be coordinated at the appropriate time with the Navy Department. Unfortunately the report contained language that clearly struck at the Navy's view of its missions and capabilities. In the section on the Navy the report listed five requirements for naval forces: control of sea areas (with emphasis on antisubmarine warfare), amphibious lift, naval support and protection of amphibious forces and convoys, outlying bases, and mobilization.[139] The list omitted any requirement for Navy offensive capabilities. In apparent connection with this omission the report asserted:

> For the foreseeable future there will be no naval threat to the United States in any portion of the world except by the submarine.... In the absence of such naval threat, the determination of the relative proportion between naval and land-based aviation in U.S. air power as a whole should be based on the most careful consideration of roles and missions, and strict evaluation of characteristics and capabilities.[140]

The War Department study, which the Navy received late in 1947, had an immediate, negative impact on Navy-Air Force relations. It provided the impetus for drafting two Navy documents that had a pronounced effect on service interactions during 1948 and 1949. The first was the so-called Nimitz Valedictory. The second was the "Gallery memorandum," written in December 1947 but leaked by persons unknown to newspaper columnist Drew Pearson a few months later.

Two individuals in SCOROR were primarily responsible for the Nimitz Valedictory. A few days before Admiral Nimitz was detached as Chief of Naval Operations on 15 December, Rear Admiral Thomas H. Robbins came to the CNO with a proposal. Robbins was upset that the War Department's report had indicated that the Navy was useful only as a transportation, service, and escort force for the other two services. He wanted

Nimitz to refute this view. He explained in a letter shortly thereafter, "I was so upset about this paper that I recommended that Admiral Nimitz write a JCS paper to counter it. I was told to go ahead."[141]

After receiving the CNO's permission, Robbins huddled with Red Thackrey, his assistant in SCOROR, to work out a response. Thackrey drafted the paper and gave it to Admiral Forrest Sherman to take in to Nimitz. According to Tommy Robbins, the CNO then decided how it would be presented.

> Admiral Nimitz himself dreamed up the idea that it should not be submitted to the JCS, because of the fact that the JCS would then take note of it, file it, and it would never see the light of day. Instead, he said, it was to be given the widest possible publicity.[142]

In the weeks following the admiral's retirement the valedictory was painstakingly cleared through Navy, civilian, and military channels and then printed as a small pamphlet. To avoid having it ground into "pulp" by the PIO "mill," the procedure was handled outside the Navy's normal public information channels. It then was distributed in large numbers within the Navy Department and to the press.[143]

Entitled *The Future Employment of Naval Forces*, the Nimitz Valedictory set forth in historical context the requirement for strong Navy offensive forces in the event of future conflicts:

> *Offensively*, it is the function of the Navy to carry the war to the enemy.... It is improbable that bomber fleets will be capable, for several years to come of making two-way trips between continents... with heavy loads of bombs.... In the event of war within this period [then], if we are to project our power against vital areas of an enemy across the ocean before beachheads on enemy territory are captured, it must be by air-sea power....[144]

This view of naval offensive capabilities echoed the strategic thinking of Navy planners in such then classified studies as the Strategic Plans Division's NSPS 3, entitled "Study of Carrier Attack Force Offensive Capabilities."[145]

The valedictory created quite a stir in the press, and senior naval officers considered the response highly favorable.[146] Nimitz was pleased with the results of his paper. A month after his retirement he wrote to his friend and protégé Forrest Sherman, who was in the process of leaving OPNAV and preparing to take over as Commander U.S. Naval Forces, Mediterranean:

Fleet Admiral Nimitz, retiring as CNO, reads his "Valedictory," 15 December 1947.

NH 62367

You probably did not hear of the storm of criticism that came from the Air Force on the publication of the report I submitted to The Secretary on future employment of naval forces....

That ... immediately got me in hot water with the authorities in Washington.... Even if I have been privately spanked, *I believe I have done a public service in speaking as I did.*[147]

Sherman, too, was pleased with the reception that the valedictory had gotten. He later wrote Admiral Nimitz, "I think that there is little doubt that your final paper did more for the Navy than any other single effort in recent times."[148]

The Nimitz Valedictory proved to be only a transitory victory for the Navy in its ongoing public relations battle with the Air Force. Air Force leaders seized on it as proof that the Navy was out to overturn the National Security Act of 1947 and usurp the Air Force's responsibility for strategic air warfare.

On 7 January 1948 General Spaatz sent a memorandum to Air Force Secretary Symington in which he quoted the almost spur-of-the-moment comments he had made to the Air Board upon hearing of the Nimitz Valedictory. Spaatz had told the assembled senior officers of the Air Force, "Although we have a separate Air Department, we haven't established firmly in the minds of some people, particularly the Navy, that there is only going to be *one Air Force.*"[149] Spaatz had also noted, "If the Navy is trying to spend hundreds of millions of dollars building aircraft carriers of a hundred thousand tons to move 36 bombers somewhere close to the hostile shores to deliver devastating attacks, it shows an utter lack of realization of what the hell strategic air and what air power is."[150] He had ended his remarks to the Air Board by stating that, if the Air Board could come up with suggestions as to "how to carry this *battle* through to its logical conclusion," it would be doing the best job it had ever done.[151]

General Spaatz's reaction, though extreme, was representative of the Air Force's increased militancy in the months following passage of the National Security Act. With Chester Nimitz gone from OPNAV, a new Chief of Naval Operations was left to figure out how to respond to these circumstances.

Louis Denfeld Becomes CNO

Nimitz's successor as Chief of Naval Operations was Admiral Louis Denfeld. Denfeld, Commander in Chief, Pacific and Pacific Fleet at the time of his selection, came to the job possessing a broad range of professional experience. Nonetheless he had not seen extensive combat service in World War II nor had he held a major wartime command as his predecessor had.[152] Denfeld was picked in large part because his background as the first postwar chief of the Bureau of Personnel (BUPERS) and DCNO (Personnel) had provided him with excellent ties to Capitol Hill.[153] In this regard his appointment echoed a return to the prewar CNO selection process that favored men with backgrounds as former Chiefs of the Bureau of Navigation (BUPERS' predecessor); among the most notable was Fleet Admiral William D. Leahy.

Louis Denfeld was selected over two other front-running candidates for the job, Duke Ramsey and William H. P. (Spike) Blandy, through effective lobbying efforts by Admiral Leahy and Sidney Souers in the White House, Senator Styles Bridges (R–N.H.) and Representative John McCormick (D–Mass.), among others from the Hill, and the naval aviation community in general. This last group saw the fine hand of unification-supporter Forrest Sherman behind Duke Ramsey's candidacy and were equally upset by Spike Blandy's too-obvious promise to name Sherman as his Vice Chief.[154]

The choice of Denfeld was logical, given concerns for the Navy's fate in the appropriations process under the new National Military Establishment,[155] but it was not universally applauded in OPNAV. Admiral Robert Carney, DCNO (Logistics) at the time, recalled, "It should have been

Navy Secretary John Sullivan congratulates Admiral Louis Denfeld on his swearing in as Chief of Naval Operations, 15 December 1947.

National Archives 80-G-704743

Blandy [as CNO]. Blandy had technical knowledge. He had the operating service, particularly in the Palaus."[156] And Admiral Charles D. (Don) Griffin, who had worked for Admiral Denfeld as a captain, remarked years later, "People liked him ... [but] I think that most people did feel that ... it was questionable whether he was strong enough."[157]

Louis Denfeld chose Vice Admiral Arthur Radford to be his Vice Chief of Naval Operations. He had singled Radford out from the beginning.[158] Denfeld had been convinced for some time that it was important to choose a strong naval aviator for the number two spot. As he wrote to Rear Admiral T. L. Sprague, Chief of Naval Personnel, in October 1947, "In a Vice CNO I would want an aviator who had the complete confidence of Naval Aviators, both young and old, one who had a good war record and one who would be completely loyal in working out the unification legislation as it affects the Navy."[159]

Radford was an excellent choice for the assignment. As DCNO (Air) during the critical months prior to the enactment of the National Security Act of 1947, he was looked on by most of the senior naval aviators as their leader. Furthermore, Radford understood that keeping naval aviation strong in the face of ongoing unification quarrels would require an active effort. He wrote to Denfeld in August 1947, "In my estimation the most serious mistake that we can make in the Navy at this time is to assume that everything insofar as naval aviation is concerned is alright.... It will take bold and aggressive leadership after careful advance planning to combat the Air Force arguments and drive when it comes."[160]

The Denfeld-Radford team was a good one for OPNAV at the time.[161] Though not a strong CNO, Denfeld had solid administrative skills and maintained excellent personal contacts on the Hill. Radford possessed sharp intelligence, strength of character, and a dedication to the maintenance of the Navy's role in the national defense.[162] He was prepared, given Denfeld's blessing, to fight it out with the Army and the Air Force in order to preserve the Navy's position. The situation was shaping up as a difficult time for the Navy, and the two men realized that they would need to rely on each other's strengths to succeed.

The Failure of Navy Public Relations

From 1945 through 1949 the Navy had to cope with the highly effective Air Force public relations effort when their own public relations organization was amateurish by comparison.[163] For the most part this situation was the Navy's own fault. Professional naval officers possessed little understanding of what a good public relations job entailed. Because publicity was anathema to them they wanted no part in PR activities themselves; neither did they sufficently respect the competence of those department reservists or civilians who did the necessary PR work for the Navy. Rear Admiral Harold B. (Min) Miller, director of the Navy's Office of Public Information, told Secretary Forrestal in October 1945, "The major problem we are faced with in post-war public information is that of educating the naval officer. He still doesn't realize and appreciate what can be done by letting the people know what is going on."[164] Forrestal, who agreed with this assessment, remarked, "There are two jobs: to do the work you have got to do and at the same time make an exposition to the public, and I confess it's quite a job."[165]

Ironically Louis Denfeld possessed an advantage over his predecessor as CNO; he recognized the seriousness of the continuing struggle with the Air Force and understood the importance of a strong public relations effort for maintaining public support for the Navy. Frank Manson noted, "Admiral Nimitz... simply was not aware... during his entire tenure as CNO, of the seriousness of the struggle. That's my impression. Now, Denfeld was very much aware of it when he came in.... And that's how come we were assigned to his staff—Captain [Walter] Karig and myself."[166]

Although Denfeld believed in the need for an enhanced Navy PR effort, the new Secretary of the Navy, John Sullivan, was not convinced that such was necessary. The Navy's Office of Public Information—and thus its main public relations effort—was under the control of the Secretary, not the CNO.

When Forrestal left the Navy Department in September 1947 to take over as the first Secretary of Defense, Under Secretary Sullivan was appointed Secretary. Sullivan, who had been Assistant Secretary of the Treasury in the Roosevelt administration, apparently had hoped to return to that department as Secretary following his stint at the Navy Department.[167] A likeable man, Sullivan was not considered a particularly aggressive Navy Secretary by some Pentagon officials.[168] However, in his continuing loyalty to Secretary of Defense James Forrestal, Sullivan went to great lengths to make the National Security Act work, even when it meant that the Navy Department was forced to remain passive in the event of attacks by its critics. Vice Admiral J. W. Reeves commented on this point to Admiral Radford in September 1949:

> When Mr. Sullivan was Secretary, it appeared to me that he refused to take any stand himself and would not let anybody else take one. Probably this was the result of a sincere desire to conform with what the Secretary of Defense expected. In any case, it was ruinous for us when those whose avowed policy was to eliminate us did not play under those rules.[169]

Captain Frank Manson agreed with this view. He recalled, "Sullivan simply *would not* fight. And in this kind of a situation with Symington—Symington was a fighter."[170] Under the Secretary's control the Navy's Office of Public Relations was precluded from taking an effective stance against the anti-Navy and pro-Air Force pieces that were appearing with great frequency in the press from 1947 through 1949, even if it had been capable of doing so.

Admiral Denfeld's most important decision on public relations was establishing the position of special adviser for public relations (OP–004) within his immediate office. In early March 1948 Captain Walter Karig, the head of the writing section of SCOROR, was assigned to Denfeld's office as the new OP–004. Frank Manson came with him as his assistant.[171]

In the following months Karig did his utmost to educate OPNAV on the need for effective PR. In a June 1948 memorandum to Denfeld, Karig stressed the urgency of solving the public relations problem. He told the CNO, "Vice Admiral Radford said at [the] DCNO meeting Friday that the fate of the Navy will be determined in the next two years. I think the time is shorter than that, in a public relations sense."[172] This memorandum and

John L. Sullivan, Secretary of the Navy from 18 September 1947 through 24 May 1949.

National Archives 80-G-K-9358

several subsequent ones by Karig on the state of Navy public relations were copied and sent to Secretary Sullivan by Admiral Denfeld in early July 1948, but such efforts failed to change the Secretary's thinking on the issue.[173] The Air Force continued to press ahead on the public relations front; the Navy Department stood by and watched.

Under such circumstances it is not surprising that some in the Navy Department began taking it upon themselves to counter Air Force publicity. Two of the busiest were Navy Department civilian employees Hugh L. Hanson and Stuart B. Barber.

Hugh Hanson was an aeronautical engineer working at BUAER. He had served in the Navy during the war and had retained his Reserve commission. Hanson started writing to the AAF's Office of Public Relations in his spare time in 1946, questioning aircraft performance figures in AAF publicity releases and press stories. In 1947 he also began sending letters to the editors of newspapers, such as the *Washington Post*, questioning the accuracy of stories on the performance of Air Force aircraft. In early 1948 Hanson began writing to members of Congress.

These activities quickly came to the attention of Stuart Symington.[174] At first, the Air Force attempted to convince Hanson to drop his letter-writing. When this failed, Symington took the matter up with John Sullivan.[175] Then Symington began complaining about Hanson directly to Secretary of Defense Forrestal. In late March 1948, after several months of complaints from Symington, Forrestal directed Sullivan to fire Hugh

Hanson—an action that was averted only when Forrestal was informed that Hanson might not go quietly.[176] When this ploy failed, Steve Leo made several unsuccessful attempts to hire Hanson to work in the Air Force public relations shop.[177] Finally, after further Air Force pressure on Forrestal and Sullivan, Hugh Hanson was transferred to California.

Stuart Barber was a statistical expert in the joint DCNO (Air)–BUAER office set up to monitor work under the integrated aeronautic program. As a Navy air intelligence officer during the war, Barber had been in charge of the Commander Air Force Pacific Fleet (COMAIRPAC) office that compiled combat aviation statistics and distributed classified analyses of Pacific air operations to all Air Pac units.[178] He was a strong believer in the importance of naval aviation to the Navy and the country. Barber began his own letter-writing efforts as a way of calling attention to a naval aviation viewpoint that he believed was being ignored by the Navy public relations shop. In July 1947 he wrote to Navy Secretary Forrestal:

> The principal heat in the unification controversy has been generated by the divergence between the exclusive or monopolist theory of air power advanced by the expansionist Air Forces, and the parallel-development ... theory of the Navy. ...
>
> The main area of conflict is thus not unification per se, but whether one theory of warfare shall dominate or whether two shall live side by side, complementing each other.[179]

Barber was particularly upset by instances where the Navy had had the chance to stress the wartime importance of naval aviation but had failed to do so.[180] One such instance had occurred in 1946, when the Navy had suppressed a classified Office of Naval Intelligence publication entitled *Naval Aviation Combat Statistics: World War II*, because of SCOROR's concern that some of the statistics might be used by the AAF against the Navy.[181]

Barber then began writing letters to the editor of the *Washington Post* on subjects such as the "AAF's Vulnerable Bomber," and "Naval Air Power."[182] As Stuart Barber recalled, Air Force attention was not long in coming.

> After two or three things were printed on various subjects, I got some *adverse attention*. ... While this had nothing to do with my job, and I was very careful not ever to say that I was working for the Navy, ... the Air Force found out pretty quick that I was with the Navy. So they started beating on the Navy.[183]

He was first called into the office of the DCNO (Air) and told by Vice Admiral Donald B. (Wu) Duncan to "lay off." When this stance didn't work, Barber remembered, "I was called in by the Assistant Secretary [for Air], John Nicholas Brown [and told] to desist *or else.*"[184] At this stage Barber told Bob Esterbrook, who was running the letters-to-the-editor column at the *Post,* about the matter. Esterbrook, upset that the Air Force was attempting to suppress Barber's pro-Navy views, offered to print Barber's letters under a pseudonym. From that point on, Barber's letters to the *Post* and other Washington papers such as the *Evening Star* and the *Times Herald* began appearing under pseudonyms such as Diogenes, Isaiah, Progressive, Veritas, and Neptunus.[185]

The crowning achievement of Barber's career as an anti-Air Force publicist, however, was his article on U.S. naval aviation in the Pacific published by the *Buffalo Evening News* in May 1948. The Navy was planning to celebrate the thirty-seventh birthday of naval aviation in the spring of that year. Barber proposed the article to friends in Navy public relations (including Captain Leroy Simpler).[186] With their encouragement Barber compiled a group of tables giving naval aviation combat statistics and drafted an explanatory text to go with it.

The article was approved in Navy public relations, but getting it through the National Military Establishment's review process proved another matter entirely. Even though the Navy piece dealt solely with naval aviation's record against Japanese air power, Steve Leo, Air Force Director of Public Relations, refused to concur in its publication. He argued that although the release *appeared* to be dealing with subjects completely internal to the Navy, it actually was an evaluation of land-based versus carrier-based aviation.[187] As the result of the Air Force's objection the Navy Department decided to release only the statistical tables without Barber's interpretative text.[188]

This decision angered Stuart Barber so much that he contacted a recent acquaintance, A. H. Kirchhofer, managing editor of the *Buffalo Evening News*, asking if his paper would be interested in printing his interpretation of the bare statistics that the Navy would be releasing in May.[189] Kirchhofer agreed and also promised to ensure that no one would trace the article back to Barber.[190] On 9 May the Navy issued its press release containing the statistical tables on naval aviation's record in the Pacific War.[191] The following day the *Buffalo Evening News* published an article by "Richard Essex" providing an interpretative commentary on the statistics. The article began:

> U.S. naval aviation is air power—as fully as is the U.S. Air Force—but the Navy can't say so....
>
> The Air Force has for three years conducted a vigorous propaganda campaign to identify itself as the exclusive proprietor of American air power. In this way the Air Force planned that it alone would cash in on the popularity of air power.[192]

Kirchhofer followed up the publication of this article by sending copies, together with his editorial supporting it, to every member of Congress. For days the Richard Essex article was a major topic of conversation around Washington. Publication of the piece was a publicity boon for the Navy. Naturally, the Air Force's leadership was highly displeased by the attention the article received. Although it did its best to lay the article at the Navy's doorstep, the Navy Department replied truthfully that it had had nothing to do with it.[193] Indeed no one in the Navy Department's senior leadership apparently knew, then or later, who the real author was.[194]

Conclusions

The private letter-writing campaigns of Hugh Hanson and Stuart Barber demonstrated the strong feelings supporters of naval aviation had regarding the Air Force's PR effort, as well as the lengths to which these individuals would go in the face of Navy Department passivity. A year later the efforts of others to fight the enfeeblement of naval aviation would prove far more explosive for both services.

By 1948 the Navy Department was well aware that its position on naval aviation in the postwar era was under attack by the Air Force. It had its own doubts about the vaunted strategic air power of its sister service, doubts expressed in meetings within the National Military Establishment. Nonetheless the department chose to do nothing on the public relations front because the Secretary of the Navy saw a public fight with the Air Force as harmful to the spirit of unification that Secretary of Defense James Forrestal continued to encourage. As the result of its public passivity, the Navy gradually lost much of the public and congressional support it had held throughout the war years and in the first years of the peace. Therefore the Navy was poorly prepared to handle the crucial shocks it received in the early months of 1949.

Chapter 3

Atomic Weapons and War Planning

In the immediate aftermath of the atomic bombing of Hiroshima and Nagasaki, planning elements of the Joint Chiefs of Staff began developing a postwar military policy and strategic plan. The JCS took these measures in light of foreseeable developments in new weapons and possible countermeasures to such weapons.[1] Similarly, in a paper on the atomic bomb submitted to the JCS on 18 August 1945, Army Chief of Staff George Marshall stated, "It is desirable that a concerted viewpoint of the military on the overall effect of this new weapon on warfare and military organization be developed as soon as possible."[2] At Marshall's recommendation the JCS instructed the Joint Strategic Survey Committee (JSSC) to undertake this analysis.[3]

The JSSC tendered its report to the Joint Chiefs on 30 October. One of the report's important conclusions was that possession of the atomic bomb by other nations would greatly hinder U.S. security. In such an event the Atlantic and Pacific Oceans would no longer serve as defensive bulwarks for the continental United States.

The report specifically contrasted U.S. vulnerability with that of the Soviet Union, the only country seen as having comparable military strength. "In contrast to our concentrations of industry and population and our exposure to attack by bombs launched from the sea, Russia is inaccessible from the sea and its industry and population are widely dispersed over vast areas."[4] The only active defenses available against the atomic bomb would be to take effective action against its source before it was launched or to destroy its carrier in flight. To accomplish the first type of defense, the United States would need not only an effective intelligence system to warn of an impending attack and an adequate stockpile of atomic bombs and systems to carry the bombs, but also a willingness to strike first.[5]

With regard to the atomic bomb's effect on the composition of U.S. military forces, the report noted that the new weapon did not justify elimination of conventional armaments or major modification of the armed forces. Because of the difficulty in manufacturing the bomb, only a limited number were likely to be available in the early postwar period. The atomic bomb was seen therefore as a strategic rather than a tactical weapon:

Using a scale model, Major General Curtis LeMay, Deputy Chief of Air Staff for Research and Development, points out the proposed ground zero for the upcoming atomic tests at Bikini Atoll to Brigadier General William F. McKee and Major General Earle E. Partridge.

The atomic bomb, in the foreseeable future, will be primarily a strategic weapon of destruction against concentrated industrial areas vital to the war effort of an enemy nation....

On the other hand, the atomic bomb is not in general a tactical weapon suitable for employment against ground forces or naval forces at sea, because they normally offer targets too widely dispersed to justify the use of a weapon of such limited availability and great cost.[6]

This initial report was subsequently modified by the JCS. The revised statement called for the United States to maintain a variety of active and passive measures for defense against atomic attack. These measures included an effective worldwide intelligence service, forward bases from which to intercept enemy attacks and to launch counterattacks, and balanced military forces capable of undertaking immediate retaliation.[7]

Atomic Weapons and War Planning 67

Author's Collection

The Able Test at Bikini, 1 July 1946. The air-dropped Mk III atomic bomb exploded some 550 feet above the array of ships.

The First Postwar Atomic Tests

The accuracy of these early views on the influence of the atomic bomb on warfare was validated by weapons testing that took place nine months later. The idea of new atomic tests was first broached in a speech by Senator Brian McMahon (D–Conn.) on 25 August 1945: "In order to test the destructive power of the atomic bomb against naval vessels, I would like to see these Japanese naval ships taken to sea and an atomic bomb dropped on them."[8] On 18 September General Hap Arnold, acting on suggestions from senior AAF officers, proposed to the Joint Chiefs of Staff that the Chiefs determine military requirements for Japanese naval vessels "suitable for future experimentation with conventional bombs, atomic bombs, guided missiles and other possible new weapons" that could be made available to the Army Air Forces.[9]

This suggestion was in line with advice the Chief of Naval Operations was receiving from officers in his own department. Accordingly, on 16 October 1945, Admiral Ernest King proposed to the JCS that Arnold's proposal be broadened to include the use of U.S. surplus warships but that the tests be conducted under JCS control, so that "all services and other interested agencies of the Government could make the determinations they consider essential."[10] He suggested that two atomic tests be conducted on the target array—an air burst of an atomic bomb and a shallow underwater burst—at a location in or near the Caroline Islands in the Pacific.[11]

Following JCS approval the proposal was submitted to the Joint Staff Planners (JPS) for drafting an outline plan on atomic testing. The JPS, in turn, gave the job to an ad hoc subcommittee chaired by Major General Curtis LeMay. Despite vigorous debate on specific issues the subcommittee managed to accomplish its task in six weeks. Its plan, which called for three tests (a deep underwater burst was added), was approved on 28 December 1945 by the JCS and on 10 January 1946 by President Truman. The Joint Chiefs of Staff chose Vice Admiral W. H. P. Blandy to head the tests and designated him Commander Joint Task Force One. It was Blandy who proposed the test site of Bikini Atoll in the Marshall Islands. After JCS agreement with his detailed plan on 24 January 1946, the operation was designated CROSSROADS.[12]

The Able Test—the air drop of an atomic bomb by an AAF B–29—took place on the morning of 1 July 1946 (the afternoon of 30 June in the United States).[13] The bomb exploded some 550 feet above the array of eighty-eight ships and small craft located in the waters of Bikini Atoll and sank five ships that were within 650 yards of ground zero: two U.S destroyers, two U.S. transports (APAs) and the Japanese cruiser *Sakawa* (which sank twenty-five hours and forty minutes after the explosion). Six other ships, including the U.S. battleships *Nevada* and *Arkansas* and the

Atomic Weapons and War Planning   69

Able Test. Aerial view of the center of the target array, showing the ships receiving major damage.

National Archives, RG 341

Able Test. Close-up view of the topside damage on the Japanese cruiser Sakawa.

light carrier *Independence*, were temporarily immobilized by ruptures of their uptakes and boiler casings. Minor fires were started on an additional twenty-three ships.[14]

There was much less damage from the atomic explosion than many people (particularly in the Army Air Forces) had expected.[15] Other than the five ships sunk by the blast, none of the target ships suffered any appreciable underwater damage or flooding. Also, except for *Independence* no ship suffered appreciable loss of military efficiency from the fires alone.[16] The limited extent of the damage to the key target ships (positioned in the center of the array) was due in part to the inaccuracy of the bomb drop. Although *Nevada* had been the intended bull's-eye, the actual point of burst was some two thousand feet from that ship because of the effects of wind on the fall of the bomb.[17]

The Baker Test—the shallow underwater detonation of an atomic bomb—took place at Bikini on 25 July 1946. The bomb was suspended in the lagoon 90 feet below a Navy landing ship (LSM), with the seventy-four target ships and small craft arrayed at varying distances from the center. Twenty ships were within half a mile of the Zero point, and another twenty were within a mile. The explosion sank or capsized nine

National Archives, RG 341

Able Test. Damage to the battleship *Nevada* seen from the starboard quarter. The cruiser *Pensacola* is in the background.

ships, including the battleship *Arkansas* and the fleet carrier *Saratoga*, the closest targets to the point of detonation, and the Japanese battleship *Nagato*, which didn't sink until almost five days later.[18]

The damage produced by the Baker Test was caused largely by the underwater shock wave. The most impressive result of the test, though, was the extensive radioactive contamination of the target ships caused by the tons of irradiated water from the underwater explosion plunging down on them. Over 90 percent of the target array was affected by this radioactivity.[19]

The deep underwater test was never conducted. At the urging of Major General Leslie R. Groves, head of the Manhattan Engineer District (MED), who feared a further disruption of the U.S. atomic weapons research and development activities at Los Alamos, the JCS agreed to suspend further testing at Bikini Atoll.[20]

The final report of the Joint Chiefs of Staff Evaluation Board for Operation CROSSROADS was delivered almost a year later, on 30 June 1947. It stated that the wartime atomic explosions over Hiroshima and Nagasaki and the Bikini tests showed that the atomic bomb was "pre-eminently" a weapon for use against people and activities "in large urban and industrial areas." With regard to naval vessels, it noted, "The Bikini tests would

Able Test. View of damage to the battleship *Arkansas*, taken from the bridge structure and looking aft.

strongly suggest that ships under way will rarely constitute suitable targets for atomic bomb attack."[21]

Early Service Thinking on the Atomic Bomb

As the Joint Strategic Survey Committee was undertaking its analyses of postwar military forces and the effects of the atomic bomb on warfare, the military services were beginning their own examination of these issues. In the fall of 1945 the Army Air Forces was determining its proper postwar structure. The uniformed Navy, in turn, was in the process of consolidating top-level offices, which had been operating since 1942 under two sepa-

Atomic Weapons and War Planning   73

Baker Test at Bikini, 25 July 1946. The Mk III bomb was exploded while suspended some ninety feet below the surface of the lagoon. Note the huge amount of water carried up into the mushroom cloud by the explosion.

Author's Collection

rate chains of command—CNO and COMINCH—back into a single one under the Chief of Naval Operations. The question was what effect U.S. possession of the atomic bomb was likely to have on this organization.

The AAF Position

Initial AAF interest in the issue had appeared just days after the end of the war. Lieutenant General Hoyt S. Vandenberg, Assistant Chief of Air Staff for Operations, Commitments, and Requirements (AC/AS-3), directed his Requirements Division to study the effects of the latest scientific developments and trends, particularly the atomic bomb, on future AAF programs.[22] That effort was only a few days old when, on 30 August 1945, Major General LeMay, Chief of Staff for the U.S. Army Strategic Air Forces in the Pacific, in a message to AAF Deputy Commanding General Ira Eaker, recommended that the AAF's program for delivering atomic weapons be accorded top priority. The 509th Bomb Group, which had dropped the atomic bombs on Hiroshima and Nagasaki, would form its nucleus.[23]

On 14 September Eaker designated Generals Carl Spaatz, Hoyt Vandenberg, and Lauris Norstad to be members of a board charged with determining the effect of the atomic bomb on the size, organization, composition, and employment of the postwar AAF.[24] After meeting in continuous session from 18 September to 23 October, the Spaatz Board submitted its final report to General Arnold. Reflecting early AAF thinking on the atomic weapon, it concluded that, because the atomic bomb was tremendously expensive in terms of critical materials and industrial effort, its availability would be limited, and that "the atomic bomb in its present form is primarily an offensive weapon for use against large urban and industrial targets."[25]

The Spaatz Board noted that the atomic bomb did not warrant a material change in the employment or composition of the postwar AAF. The board also concluded that "the atomic bomb has not altered our basic concept of the strategic air offensive but has given us an additional weapon." Indeed the report stressed the continuing need for forces armed with conventional bombs for use against targets that could not be effectively or economically attacked with atomic bombs.[26]

The board's reluctance to see the atomic bomb as a military panacea reflected its conservative viewpoint on changes to existing AAF doctrine and organization. Its members apparently believed it was too early to stake the future of the AAF on a single weapon, regardless of its revolutionary potential. Nonetheless the members recognized that to maintain the most capable offensive and defensive capabilities in the future, the AAF needed to mount a large-scale, scientific research and development program for the development of new air weapons. They advocated the appointment of a senior officer responsible for overseeing this program.[27]

General Arnold directed immediate implementation of the report's recommendations,[28] emphasizing "that the national interest demands relentless efforts, operationally and technically, in research and development, especially as they relate to future air weapons."[29] As an indication of the importance he placed on this matter, he appointed General LeMay as the new Deputy Chief of Air Staff for Research and Development.[30] LeMay's responsibilities included overseeing all of the AAF's research and development (R&D) activities and acting as AAF liaison with the Manhattan Engineer District for all atomic energy matters.[31] His stature within the Air Staff was assured by his additional role not only as the Commanding General's adviser on all AAF research and development matters but also by his position as the Chief of Air Staff's right-hand man on R&D policies.[32]

Shortly thereafter the air staff began planning the composition of an Atomic Bomb Striking Force. This name was soon dropped at the suggestion of General Eaker, who feared that if a portion of the AAF's long-range bombers was designated as its atomic striking force, this force would become in the eyes of the War Department and Congress "the only strategic air force we will require."[33]

In a major AAF reorganization in March 1946 General Spaatz, the AAF's new Commanding General, ordered the demise of the Continental Air Forces, which was responsible for training and continental air defense. In its place he ordered creation of three major combat air commands; one was the Strategic Air Command (SAC).[34] SAC's mission was to "be prepared to conduct long range offensive operations in any part of the world," using the "latest and most advanced weapons."[35]

SAC was assigned two air forces, the Eighth and the Fifteenth. Only a few dozen of the aircraft assigned to SAC were then capable of carrying atomic weapons. Just one of SAC's nine very heavy bomb groups[36]—the 509th—was equipped with B–29 bombers modified to carry atomic weapons (designated SILVERPLATE aircraft) and trained for the atomic striking mission.[37] Over the following months the Strategic Air Command quietly began converting its entire bombing force into an atomic striking force. But because of funding delays and conversion difficulties, the 509th's three dozen B–29s remained SAC's only atomic-capable striking force for the next two years.[38]

The AAF's biggest problem in the first eighteen months in readying its forces for the atomic-bombing mission was its lack of detailed technical knowledge on atomic weapons. Development of the atomic bomb had been conducted by the Manhattan Engineer District under the highest secrecy and without direct participation of AAF personnel.[39] As a 1949 Air Force study recounted, "From the beginning of [the] Manhattan Project both the Army (Corps of Engineers) and the Navy provided personnel to occupy key policy and administrative assignments.... During this period, the U.S. Air Force did not concern itself greatly with the technical aspects of atomic weapons nor with their evaluation as weapons of war."[40] Although the AAF's 509th Bomb Group had provided the aircraft and the crews that dropped the atomic bombs on Japan, the fully assembled weapons had been turned over to the crews just before takeoff and the Navy had supplied the weaponeers (air crew atomic-bomb technicians) who armed the bombs and monitored their condition during the flights.

This situation remained basically unchanged well into the early postwar period. The Manhattan Engineer District continued to function under its wartime leader, Major General Groves, until January 1947. Security restrictions on disseminating atomic energy data allowed only a handful of Army Air Forces personnel to become acquainted with the technical aspects of the atomic bomb.

The question of AAF access to atomic energy information first was raised by Major General E. M. Powers, Assistant Chief of Air Staff for Materiel (AC/AS-4), in mid-September 1945. In a memorandum to the Chief of Air Staff, Powers stated, "It is recommended that formal channels be established whereby A.A.F. engineering activities will be given access to sufficient technical data on atomic energy to permit research and development leading to possible applications to present and future weapons and equipment."[41] No immediate action was taken on Powers's request, but two months later General Spaatz, responding to the recommendation in his capacity as recent chairman of the board of senior officers that had examined the effect of the atomic bomb on Air Forces' size and composition, recommended to Brigadier General Reuben C. Hood, Jr., Deputy Chief of the Air Staff, that no further action on Powers's memorandum be taken. He noted, "The War Department has named Major General LeMay to the advisory board serving Major General Groves.... It is thus within the realm of General LeMay's prerogatives to inform General Groves of the need of the Air Force for specific information and the extent to which it should be disseminated."[42]

Despite LeMay's position and his access to Groves the process of clearing AAF personnel for atomic energy information was glacially slow, even for those Army Air Forces personnel who met MED requirements.[43] In March 1946 General Eaker informed Major General F. L. Anderson, Assistant Chief of Air Staff for Personnel (AC/AS-1), "General LeMay spoke to me about the urgent necessity for having Air Force personnel made sufficiently familiar with the Manhattan Project so that we will have the trained know-how to carry out operations with the atomic bomb if and when needed." Eaker urged Anderson to work very closely with LeMay in selecting the necessary personnel.[44]

The circumstance that finally forced the issue was the AAF's coming participation in the first postwar atomic tests at Bikini Atoll.[45] To enable the Air Forces to supply the weaponeer for the Able Test weapon, the Manhattan Engineer District trained the first few AAF officers in the technical aspects of the atomic bomb.[46] This effort was only a stop-gap improvement.

In late July 1946, a few days after the second Bikini test, Major General St. Clair Streett, SAC's Deputy Commanding General, wrote to General Spaatz, "To what extent will Air Force personnel in the atomic striking force be responsible for the handling of the atomic munition? In the past, Air Force personnel had little to do with the bomb until its delivery to and loading on the airplane.... What special training will be provided by the Manhattan District?"[47]

The Manhattan Engineer District had by this time trained just ten AAF weaponeers in the handling of atomic weapons. Five were senior officers scheduled for assignment to AAF Headquarters, SAC, and Air Materiel Command, plus two lower-echelon SAC commands. The other five were junior officers designated to form a cadre for training personnel within the Strategic Air Command. Another four junior officers had been selected for future MED training.[48]

In response to Streett's memorandum, General Hood informed the Commanding General, Strategic Air Command, that specially selected air ordnance personnel from SAC's atomic striking force would indeed be responsible for storing and preparing atomic weapons and that General Groves had also indicated a willingness "to consider the AAF proposals for increased responsibilities pertaining to the atomic bomb." However, an acceptable definition of these responsibilities had not yet been worked out by Groves and the AAF, so Air Forces Headquarters was unable to tell SAC what its atomic weapons responsibilities would be.[49] This situation lasted through 1946. No wonder that Major General David M. Schlatter, Assistant Deputy Chief of Staff, Operations for Atomic Energy (AFOAT), later commented on this early period:

> In 1946, the Air Force found itself with a revolutionary weapon they were not prepared to employ. True, there were a few B-29 airplanes modified to carry the then existent atomic bomb, [and] there were six trained Air Force weaponeers. But, on the other hand, the Air Force plans did not include realistic consideration of the potential of the atomic bomb; programs then were not directed to exploit the bomb as we have it today, nor were there than any airplanes in research and development which would take full advantage of new atomic weapons then known (by scientists) to be possible....[50]

Vice Admiral William H. P. Blandy, Deputy Chief of Naval Operations (Special Weapons), in 1946.

The Navy Position

Although the Navy had its own problems with regard to atomic weapons, a lack of technical knowledge about the atomic bomb was not one of them, since a number of naval officers had been heavily involved in the bomb's development from the Manhattan Project's early days. The Navy's problems concerned how (and even whether) this new weapon would be integrated into the fleet, particularly since the existing types of atomic bombs (the Mk I "Little Boy" gun-type weapon dropped on Hiroshima and the Mk III "Fat Man" implosion bomb used on Nagasaki) were too bulky and heavy to be carried by Navy carrier-based aircraft.[51]

The Navy initially dealt with the issue by establishing a division within the Office of the Chief of Naval Operations to handle atomic energy and related matters. On 13 November 1945, following approval by Navy Secretary James Forrestal, Chief of Naval Operations Fleet Admiral Ernest King established the Special Weapons Division of the Office of the Chief of Naval Operations (OP–06).[52] Its responsibilities were to coordinate all matters relating to the research and development of atomic

Captain William S. Parsons, senior technical member of the Manhattan Engineer District and weaponeer on the atomic bomb mission over Hiroshima, in his temporary office on Tinian, July 1945.

energy, guided missiles, and related technologies for the Navy Department; and to represent the department in joint organizations dealing with these technologies.[53]

Vice Admiral Spike Blandy was picked to head OP–06 as Deputy Chief of Naval Operations for Special Weapons. His Assistant Chief (ACNO) was Commodore William S. Parsons, the Navy's senior expert on atomic energy. During the war Parsons had served in a senior position in the Manhattan Engineer District and had been the weaponeer on the atomic bombing mission to Hiroshima. OP–06 coordinated atomic energy and guided missile matters for the next twelve months. During much of this time, though, it was occupied almost completely with arrangements for the first postwar atomic tests at Bikini Atoll.[54]

In early November 1946, just three months after the second Bikini test, OPNAV disestablished the office of the Deputy Chief of Naval Operations for Special Weapons because of continuing friction between OP–06 and other Navy organizations over assigned responsibilities.[55] OP–06's atomic energy and atomic weapons development responsibilities were assigned to the new Atomic Defense Division (OP–36) headed by now Rear Admiral William Parsons. The division operated under the Deputy Chief of Naval Operations for Operations (OP–03). OP–06's guided missiles responsibilities were turned over to a Guided Missiles Division (OP–57) established in the office of the DCNO (Air).[56]

By late 1946 senior naval officers such as Fleet Admiral Chester Nimitz and Vice Admiral Forrest Sherman, DCNO (Operations), believed that, for at least the next decade, atomic weapons would not necessitate major changes in naval forces.[57] They dismissed the view that because no potential enemy of the United States possessed a major navy, the current naval establishment was excessive in size. As they saw it, such a view misrepresented both the character of a potential naval threat to the United States and the functions required of the fleet in a war against a major power, whether or not this power possessed a large navy. Furthermore they noted the Soviet Union's considerable submarine fleet that could pose tremendous hazards to U.S. shipping in the event of a war.[58] Navy leaders saw the need during the near term for three general types of naval forces—aircraft carrier groups, amphibious forces, and general escort forces, including antisubmarine warfare ships. Aircraft carriers constituted "the only truly mobile tactical air forces—in which the air bases as well as the aircraft themselves are highly mobile and enjoy all the advantages of mobility such as ability to concentrate and to achieve surprise."[59]

These leaders envisioned two methods of delivering atomic weapons to a target—via large bombing aircraft such as the B-29 and via long-range rockets such as those evolving from the German V–2 rocket of World War II. They did not expect an operational capability for rockets with a range of thousands of miles for at least twenty-five years.[60] Furthermore they doubted the ability of large bombers to deliver atomic bombs against a "strong and well-alerted enemy," given the technological trend "decidedly in favor" of defense over offense in ordinary strategic bombing. This trend stemmed from improvements in aircraft detection and interception, the introduction of proximity-fuzed guided or homing antiaircraft missiles, and jet propulsion for fighter aircraft. In such an environment Navy leaders saw the need for short-range but very high-speed jet bombers or supersonic missiles capable of delivering atomic weapons. However, such weapon systems would require the use of outlying bases located close to the territories of potential enemies.[61]

In the wake of the Bikini atomic tests Navy leaders recognized a need for a somewhat greater tactical dispersion of naval vessels at sea and at anchor. Such dispersion would reduce the damage of an atomic explosion to a deployed fleet. Still these leaders were not excessively worried about the effects of an atomic attack on naval forces.[62]

The Emerging Soviet Threat

By the early months of 1945 JCS committees had begun an unwelcome reappraisal of the intentions of the Soviet Union.[63] In light of the Soviet Union's stiffening attitude toward its British and American allies and its unilateral attempts at achieving territorial and other advantages, U.S. military and State Department officials began wondering just what the Soviet postwar aims were. Their questions were succinctly expressed in early June 1945 by the naval advisor to the U.S. Delegation to the European Advisory Commission. His memorandum to Admiral Harold R. Stark, Commander U.S. Naval Forces, Europe (COMNAVEU) asked:

> Will the Soviets go their own way, unilaterally pursuing a path of aggression which is not only not that of her Allies, but may result in increasing difficulties and even direct conflict with them, with the future control of Germany as the stakes—or—will the Soviets, overcoming suspicion, painful memories, and presently existing conflicts of interest, determine that their greatest security lies in cooperation with the Allies?[64]

That same month the Soviet Union revealed its interest in expanding into the Northern Tier countries of the Near East. In a meeting with Selim Sarper, Turkey's ambassador to Moscow, Soviet Foreign Minister Vyacheslav Molotov informed him that the price of a treaty between the Soviet Union and Turkey would include the return of the Turkish areas of Kars and Ardahan (originally ceded to Turkey in 1921), agreement to Soviet bases in the Dardanelles, and USSR-Turkish agreement to a revision of the 1936 Montreux Convention on the Straits.[65] The Turkish government rejected these proposals.

In mid-July 1945 the Joint Chiefs of Staff informed the State Department (through the State-War-Navy Coordinating Committee) of the JCS's strong opposition to any concessions to the Soviets in regard to Turkey.[66] A few days later, during the Potsdam Conference, Molotov (and later Joseph Stalin) brought up the issues of abrogating the Montreux Convention and securing Soviet base rights in the Dardanelles. But President Harry Truman and British Prime Minister Winston S. Churchill were able to put off a final decision on the matter.[67] Thereafter the USSR began a war of nerves, utilizing (among other tactics) press and radio attacks on Turkey and troop movements close to Turkey's borders in an attempt to soften the Turkish government's intransigent attitude.

The Soviet Union was exerting similar pressures on Iran, Turkey's neighbor to the east, at about the same time.[68] At the end of August 1945 the Democratic Party of Azerbaijan was formed and subsequently strengthened with substantial Soviet help. In November 1945 large-scale uprisings broke out in Iran's province of Azerbaijan, which was under the control of the Soviet army. When Iran tried to put down the uprisings, Soviet forces prevented its troops from entering Azerbaijan. U.S. and British protests over Soviet actions were almost summarily dismissed by the Soviet Union. By 12 December, the Democratic Party of Azerbaijan had formed a National Assembly and proclaimed its province the autonomous Republic of Azerbaijan. Three days later, Kurdish separatist leaders, accompanied by several armed Soviet officers, announced the creation of the Kurdish Republic of Mahabad in northwestern Iran, sandwiched between Turkey's eastern border and the new republic of Azerbaijan.

These Soviet actions confirmed U.S. military fears about increasing Soviet hostility toward the Western Allies. Historian Bruce Kuniholm remarked, "In 1945, Allied negotiations demonstrated that high-minded principles and diplomatic conferences were ineffective in deterring the Soviets' ambitions to secure their southern flank and acquire a springboard to the Eastern Mediterranean and the Middle East."[69]

On 9 October 1945 the Joint Strategic Survey Committee submitted a report, undertaken on its own initiative, that reviewed the military position of the United States in light of recent Soviet policies. The JSSC report noted that six months before, the United States had been "the greatest military power in the history of the world." This position had changed completely with the increasingly swift demobilization of its military machine, urged on by the American public's interest in "liquidating" U.S. military forces to some vaguely defined minimum size. The report contrasted this situation with that in the Soviet Union, where, if one accepted Russian statements about its demobilization, there would still be 5.5 million men under arms after 1 January 1946.

The JSSC study also discussed the Soviet Union's successes in controlling Eastern Europe and its unfulfilled demands in Turkey and elsewhere: "As an extreme toward which Russian policy may conceivably be heading, that nation may be pushing toward a domination of Europe, comparable with that which inspired the Germans, and toward the control of the eastern Mediterranean, the Persian Gulf, Manchuria, Northern China, and Korea."[70] The JSSC report therefore recommended that the Joint Staff Planners examine present and prospective U.S. military capabilities on a priority basis and determine the areas of the world where these American capabilities could successfully resist an attempted Soviet aggression.

By mid-December 1945 JCS planning organizations were drawing up preliminary Soviet threat assessments for use in war planning.[71] The Soviet Union's ground forces were seen as its most formidable offensive weapon, capable of quickly overrunning Western Europe, the Near East, the Persian Gulf, and major portions of East Asia.[72] These assessments reflected the views of the individual service intelligence offices.[73] Although the size and fighting ability of the Red Army continued to receive major attention in subsequent assessments, as 1946 progressed service intelligence studies accorded increasing importance to a future offensive capability of the USSR's air force.[74]

In the early postwar period the Soviet air force, *Voyenno-vozdushnyye sily* (VVS), was essentially still a tactical air force. During the war Soviet airmen had not adopted the concept of strategic bombing as the AAF and Britain's Bomber Command understood it, in part because of a shortage of aircraft and a lack of training. In the VVS's heaviest wartime attacks on cities such as Warsaw and Berlin, the strength of Soviet long-range bomber forces employed had been less than two hundred aircraft, and average raids had numbered only seventy-five to a hundred aircraft.[75]

In early 1946 the most capable aircraft in Soviet long-range aviation, *Dal'naya aviatsiya* (DA), was the twin-engined ER–4 medium bomber, which had a combat radius of about a thousand miles and carried a bomb load of forty-four hundred pounds.[76] Although adequate for bombing enemy rear areas in support of Soviet Front (Army Group) operations, it (and its less-capable counterpart, the TU–2) clearly posed no serious threat to the continental United States (CONUS).[77]

During the same period, however, the Soviet air force's offensive ability in areas contiguous to Soviet-controlled territory was accorded great respect. For example, in April 1946, the Pacific Air Command, U.S. Army (PACUSA) estimated that, in the event of a war in Korea, one to two hundred Soviet medium bombers could subject U.S. air bases and installations in the Japanese Home Islands to night attacks upon the opening of hostilities. In addition, once the Soviet Union's occupation of southern Korea had been completed (estimated to take from six to ten days), Soviet air forces could subject most of the U.S. bases in Japan to daylight attacks by fighter-escorted bombers and strafers, and could also deliver night bombing raids on U.S. installations in the Ryukyus.[78]

By late 1946 the perception of a limited Soviet threat to the continental United States began to change, driven in part by the Soviet Union's development of the TU–4 heavy bomber. During 1944 two AAF B–29s had landed "wheels down" in the Vladivostok area (one on 29 July and the other on 11 November) and were "interned" by the Soviets.[79] In the following months Soviet aircraft designers, working under Lieutenant General A. N. Tupolev, copied these aircraft down to the minutest detail. An unmarked B–29 was first seen flying over Moscow by two members of the U.S. Military Attache's office in early April 1946, and another was spotted by U.S. military attaches on the ground at Bykovo Military Airfield in mid-October. Although AAF intelligence analysts could not be certain that these weren't the original American aircraft, they had good reason to believe they were Russian copies of the B–29. Aircraft experts from Wright Field, Dayton, Ohio, estimated that, by using the American B–29s as a starting point, the Soviets could have come up with a production model in twenty months. If they had begun the process in August 1944, the first production aircraft could have been ready in April 1946—a date that accorded with the first U.S. sighting. Using this date as a reference point, U.S. analysts estimated that the Soviets could have 150 B–29–type heavy bombers by 1 January 1947, 1,000 by 1 January 1948, and 2,550 by 1 January 1949.[80] With a range comparable to that of the U.S. B–29, 4,600 statute miles, the new Soviet bomber could attack a number of targets in CONUS on one-way flights.

In late December 1946 Army Air Forces intelligence confirmed the Soviet production of B–29–type aircraft when it got the word that the Russians had requested maintenance parts and manuals for the B–29 and had also tried unsuccessfully to place an order with Goodyear Tire and Rubber Company for twenty-five sets of B–29–type tires, wheels, and brake assemblies.[81] The new aircraft eventually was given the U.S. designation TU–4 Bull.

Although there was no doubt that Soviet ground and air forces had impressive capabilities for military action in Western Europe or the Near East, the greater concern of U.S. policymakers in this period was over Soviet intentions. Did the Soviet Union intend to use these forces to expand its territorial control by overt military action? On this question there was more reason for optimism. Despite the threatening nature of Soviet ideological attacks and diplomatic pressure during 1946 over issues such as the Dardanelles, there were valid reasons for believing that these actions represented a war of nerves rather than preparations for a military assault on the West. The Director of Central Intelligence, Lieutenant General Hoyt Vandenberg, informed President Truman in August 1946, "There appears to be no reason, from the purely economic point of view, to alter our previous estimate that because of the ravages of war, the Soviets have vital need for a long period of peace before embarking upon a major war."[82]

Major General Lauris Norstad expressed this same view in October 1946 in a briefing prepared for President Truman on the War Department's thinking regarding the postwar military establishment:

> There are ... several factors which would tend to indicate that resort to force of arms by the Soviets is not imminent. Among these are: a depleted war potential; an incomplete assimilation of the satellite nations; lack of a strategic Air Force or an effective defense against such a force; and our possession of the atomic bomb.[83]

Norstad did not see the Soviet Union initiating a major war for at least five years (and possibly even ten).[84]

The USSR's lack of atomic weapons was seen as a key factor in deterring near-term Soviet military action. U.S. military analysts believed that the Soviet Union would be unlikely to use conventional military forces while only the United States possessed the atomic bomb.[85] Thus the state of the Soviet Union's atomic energy program became an issue of overriding importance. In October 1946 the United States was still in the dark about the pace of Soviet atomic developments.[86] Intelligence personnel were aware of reports that the USSR was intensely pursuing atomic energy research in the Ural Mountains and the Kazakh area, but they did not know how far the Soviets had progressed.[87] This uncertainty led to differing assessments within the U.S. intelligence community as to the earliest date when the Soviet Union would have the bomb.

From late 1946 through 1947 AAF Intelligence believed that the Soviets could possess atomic bombs on an operational basis as early as 1949. They placed the start of a serious Soviet atomic program in 1942 and argued that the release of the Smyth report[88] in 1945 allowed the Soviets to eliminate the thermal diffusion and gaseous diffusion processes and concentrate instead on development of plutonium pile reactions. The Assistant Chief of Air Staff for Intelligence believed therefore that the Soviet Union would have the atomic bomb at least by 1949.[89]

The other service intelligence offices were more conservative. Both the Director of Intelligence on the War Department General Staff and the Chief of Naval Intelligence believed that, although it was possible that the USSR would successfully develop its first atomic weapons in 1950, the most probable date was 1952.[90] This assessment was in line with the initial thinking of intelligence analysts of the Central Intelligence Group, the predecessor to the Central Intelligence Agency.[91] In March 1948 the scientific representatives of all three service intelligence offices arrived at an agreed position on estimated Russian atom bomb production, approved informally by the Joint Intelligence Committee:

1. It is believed that the Soviet Union does not have atomic bombs now.
2. It is estimated that:
    a. The earliest date by which the Soviets may have exploded their first test bomb is mid-1950.
    b. The probable date by which the Soviets will have exploded their first test bomb is mid-1953.
    c. Based on a mid-1950 test explosion, the greatest possible number of bombs in the Soviet stockpile in mid-1955 is about 50.

d. Based on a mid-1953 test explosion, the probable number of bombs in the Soviet stockpile in mid-1955 is about 20.[92]

The combination of long-range TU-4 bombers and atomic bombs would provide the Soviet Union with a force capable of posing a substantial threat to the continental United States even though the aircraft would have to be expended on one-way missions.[93] This forecast was of particular concern to military leaders since U.S. air defenses in the 1946–1950 period had a negligible capability against incoming bomber aircraft and would have to be drastically improved to cope with even limited attacks by atomic-armed, long-range bombers.[94]

War Planning

On 19 September 1945 the Joint Staff Planners submitted a report, concurred in by the JSSC, on a strategic concept and plan for the employment of U.S. military forces, together with a statement on U.S. military policy.[95] This report stated that destruction of Germany and Japan had removed the most immediate military threat to the Soviet Union and the major opposition to Russian expansion on the Eurasian landmass.[96] Noting that a stable peace required amicable relations between the United States, the Soviet Union, and the British Empire, the JPS study acknowledged that if relations between the powers broke down, the USSR would present the most difficult problems from a military point of view. The report stressed that the most likely cause of war with the Soviet Union "would be her demonstration of intent to overrun western Europe or China."[97]

Keeping the prospective enemy at the greatest possible distance from the continental United States was essential to defending vital U.S. installations in an era when new weapons of great destructive capacity were available. The JPS report urged the development and garrisoning of an "integrated system of strategically located bases" situated along an outer perimeter. These bases would allow wide-ranging reconnaissance and surveillance, interception of enemy forces and missiles, protection of vital air and sea lines of communication, and effective offensive operations against U.S. enemies. These operations would utilize special weapons, including atomic bombs, and the mobility of U.S. air and sea-based striking forces to destroy or disrupt the enemy's offensive capability and war-making capacity.[98] After slight revision the JPS report was approved by the Joint Chiefs of Staff on 9 October and subsequently was concurred in by the Secretary of War and Secretary of the Navy.[99]

In December 1945 the Joint War Plans Committee (JWPC) began developing a detailed concept of operations upon which a joint outline war plan for war against the Soviet Union could be based.[100] In the first draft presented to the Joint Staff Planners in March 1946, the committee stressed that although it did not believe the Soviet Union sought a war with the United States, war might occur as the result of the Soviet policy of territorial expansion. The Near and Middle East, where the USSR was even then putting pressure on the Turkish and Iranian governments, was the most likely source of potential military conflict.

Since it was deemed fruitless to attempt to match the Soviet Union's strong ground forces in the event of a war, the report called for securing and defending forward bases and lines of communication in the general areas of the British Isles, Egypt, India, and possibly Italy and western China. From these bases long-range bomber forces, armed with atomic weapons, would be launched immediately to attack the USSR's war-making capacity. In addition U.S. naval forces would destroy the Soviet Union's navy and merchant marine and blockade its coasts.[101]

On 27 April 1946 JWPC submitted a Joint Outline War Plan to the Joint Staff Planners, based on the recently developed concept of operations. Designated PINCHER, it provided the basis for preparing a joint basic war plan and the supporting service war plans covering U.S. military action against the Soviet Union in the next three years. After amendment, the JPS approved PINCHER as the "basis for further planning" in mid-June. In a subsequent decision, the JPS directed the Joint War Plans Committee to keep the plan's concept of operations up to date and to prepare a series of geographically oriented strategic studies based on it.[102] A sizable number of such studies were drafted during the next year, including ones dealing with operations in the Pacific area; an intelligence estimate of specific areas in Southern Europe, the Middle and Near East, and Northern Africa; and the Soviet threat to the Iberian Peninsula.[103]

In July 1946, while the initial PINCHER studies were being drafted, Clark Clifford, Special Counsel to the President, directed Admiral William Leahy to have the JCS furnish the President with certain information Truman needed prior to participation in the Paris Peace Conference. The requested information included U.S.–Soviet wartime military agreements, estimates of present and future Soviet military policies, and the recommended military policy toward the USSR.[104] Answering the President on 26 July, the Joint Chiefs of Staff noted, "In a war with the USSR we must envisage complete and total hostilities unrestricted in any way on the Soviet part.... Preparations envisaged on our part and our plans [also] must be on this basis. They must envisage that gas, bacteriological warfare, and atomic weapons will be used."[105]

The employment of atomic weapons, however, remained in dispute within the JCS during 1946 and much of 1947. In June 1946 Admiral Nimitz wrote to General Dwight Eisenhower suggesting that the joint planners avoid affirming in their plans that atomic bombs would be used, since such weapons might be outlawed by international agreement or the United States might choose not to employ them.[106] A few days later in a related action, VCNO Duke Ramsey recommended to the JCS that a sentence stating that atomic weapons would be used if the United States became involved in a major war be removed from a list of general assumptions scheduled to be issued for joint planning purposes.[107] Eventually the JCS accepted a compromise proposal offered by General Spaatz; it modified the wording to read, "Until such time as atomic weapons are limited by international agreement, such weapons may be used by either side in a major war."[108] Nonetheless, the compromise did not settle the overall issue.

The Navy's objections to the inclusion of statements in joint planning papers about U.S. employment of atomic weapons were in line with President Truman's developing policy calling for international control of atomic energy.[109] However, Army Air Forces planners viewed such actions by Navy leaders as an attempt to frustrate the AAF's attempts to plan for a strategic air offensive.[110]

In the absence of authoritative word from the White House the Joint Chiefs of Staff were unable to resolve the contending viewpoints during 1946. As a result, war planning during this period was predicated on U.S. employment of a strategic air offensive using only conventional high-explosive bombs. This outline war plan (JCS 1725/1) prepared in February 1947 by the Joint Staff Planners to provide strategic guidance for a joint industrial mobilization plan for the 1947–1949 period did not include U.S. use of atomic weapons. The JPS document stated:

> The outline plan has been prepared on the conservative assumption that weapons of mass destruction, such as the atomic bomb, will not be used by the United States and its allies, even though it appears almost certain that these could be made available in considerable quantities initially and an additional number produced over the three year period covered by this guidance.[111]

This troublesome situation was finally rectified by the JCS several months later. In commenting on this JPS outline war plan, Army Chief of Staff Dwight Eisenhower stressed, "There is considerable probability, if not a certainty, that atomic weapons would be used in any such war as envisaged in J.C.S. 1725/1."[112] He recommended that the Joint Staff Planners, as a matter of priority, draft a study similar to JCS 1725/1, but one that assumed the use of atomic weapons. On 30 April 1947 the Joint Chiefs of Staff approved this recommendation, and JPS was instructed to develop such a study.[113]

Three and a half months later the Joint Chiefs of Staff came to a further decision on atomic planning. The decision concerned the link between the continuing hopes of the United States for international control of atomic energy (under the Baruch Plan) and the question of whether the United States might employ atomic weapons in a general war with the Soviet Union. On 14 July 1947 the JSSC issued a report on the military aspects of U.S. policy to be adopted if international control of atomic energy remained at an impasse. It concluded that the Soviet Union was bent on developing its own atomic weapons and had no intention of accepting international control of atomic energy on American terms. The JSSC stressed that, under these circumstances, it was essential to accelerate production and stockpiling of atomic weapons to the "maximum practicable rate" and to establish a system of strategically located overseas bases from which "*all . . . offensive weapons*" could be employed.[114] On 13 August the JCS approved a slightly amended version of this report and directed that its conclusions be sent to the Secretaries of War and Navy.[115]

Even as the initial PINCHER studies were being drafted in 1946 by the joint planning bodies, the individual services were preparing their own plans designed to parallel the emerging joint plans. In the late spring of 1946 the office of the Assistant Chief of Air Staff for Plans (AC/AS-5) developed a rough outline setting out how the available Army Air Forces units would be used in the event of an emergency. Later that year the Air Staff recognized that the Air Forces should have on hand a "top drawer" emergency plan showing in detail how its ready forces would be committed during the initial months of hostilities. The effort was assigned to AC/AS-5's Strategy Branch and code-named MAKEFAST.[116]

MAKEFAST was essentially a scaled-down version of the U.S. strategic bomber offensive against Germany during World War II, refined by wartime lessons and directed against the Soviet Union.[117] Focusing on bombing with conventional high-explosive weapons, the plan placed its principal targeting effort on the Soviet petroleum industry, which was seen as the most critical target system that would be vulnerable to a conventional bombing attack on the scale allowed by the size of the available postwar U.S. forces. In consonance with the U.S. bombing doctrine followed in the wartime European Theater, MAKEFAST did not specifically target enemy population centers. Attacks were to be directed instead at the USSR's petroleum refineries—a target system of known importance for immobilizing Soviet air and ground forces in a short period of time. Moreover, the refineries could be knocked out using a much lower conventional bomb tonnage than necessary for other important target systems such as the Soviet Union's rail network or its electric power industry.[118]

Although MAKEFAST, which was completed in late October 1946, was worked out in greater detail than the earlier plan had been, it did little more than earmark the units that might be available for use and designate their deployment locations. In connection with this plan General LeMay, Deputy Chief of Air Staff for Research and Development, was separately tasked with developing a special weapons (i.e., atomic weapons) annex giving a rough outline of how the AAF would conduct atomic bombing operations.[119]

When General Spaatz was briefed on MAKEFAST, he directed that AAF short-range emergency planning be a continuous process and that a new version of MAKEFAST, based on Army Air Forces capabilities as of February 1947, be drafted. This new version, EARSHOT, was completed in February 1947. Although it featured a special weapons annex, EARSHOT still lacked detailed logistical considerations.[120] Nonetheless, using EARSHOT and a summertime revision, EARSHOT JUNIOR, the Strategic Air Command drew up its first detailed plan for conducting strategic air operations: SAC Operation Plan (OPLAN) 14-47.[121]

The Joint War Plans Committee concluded in mid-July 1947 that PINCHER planning had progressed sufficiently to enable the planners to prepare a joint war plan for the initial stages of a war with the Soviet Union within the next three years. Following concurrence by the Joint Staff Planners, on 29 August 1947 JWPC was directed to prepare such a plan, designated BROILER. The planners were instructed to assume that the United States would use atomic weapons.[122]

While work on BROILER was going on, the Joint Strategic Survey Committee completed an estimate of atomic weapons requirements for the JCS. Initial thinking on this issue had begun in earnest in February 1947. This followed a request from General Eisenhower that the JSSC furnish the Joint Chiefs of Staff with a long-range estimate of total military requirements for fissionable material in connection with the recommendations of the Atomic Energy Commission (AEC) to the President on production in calendar year 1947.[123] The JSSC's initial report proved of little value, since it noted only that the existing supply of atomic weapons was inadequate to meet U.S. security requirements and that application of the entire supply of fissionable material available during 1947 would fall "far short" of the total military requirement.[124]

In July 1947 Lieutenant General Lewis Brereton, the AAF's representative on the Military Liaison Committee to the AEC, wrote to General Spaatz:

The present strategic planning regarding [atomic weapons] stock piling has progressed no further to date than a position to the effect that all that can be produced is not enough. It seems to me, therefore, that it is highly important that the strategic planners produce specific requirements even if they must be reviewed frequently.[125]

General Hoyt Vandenberg, Spaatz's deputy, replied that this idea was even then under study, both in the Air Staff and in the JSSC and the Joint War Plans Committee.[126]

In September 1947 the JSSC was tasked by the Joint Chiefs of Staff with preparing, in collaboration with the Joint Staff Planners, long-range estimates of the total U.S. military requirement for fissionable material.[127] In late October the Joint Staff Planners submitted to the JSSC their study on the long-range requirements for atomic weapons and fissionable material. It was based principally on a targeting study prepared by the Air Staff and envisioned sufficient bombs to provide for attacks on approximately one hundred different urban targets.[128] The JPS subsequently informed the Joint Chiefs of Staff that, for war purposes, a military requirement existed for approximately four hundred atomic bombs of destructive power equivalent to the Nagasaki-type implosion bomb.[129] According to the subsequent JSSC report to the JCS several weeks later, this number of bombs could probably be attained by 1 January 1953 if two modifications to the implosion bomb's design, scheduled for testing in the spring of 1948, proved successful. If the modifications did not prove out, the required stockpile probably could be attained by 1956.[130]

The JCS passed this information to the Atomic Energy Commission in mid-December 1947. The Chiefs noted that this number of bombs would probably be satisfactory until the time any possible enemy possessed atomic weapons in quantity and an air force capable of launching a massive attack on the United States. In such an event the atomic bomb objective would have to be raised, perhaps radically.[131]

The Joint Strategic Plans Group (JSPG), the successor to the Joint War Plans Committee,[132] completed Joint Outline War Plan BROILER in early November 1947. BROILER envisioned the Soviet Union's overrunning of Western Europe and parts of the Far East. Tasks for the United States and its allies would then include securing the Western Hemisphere, the United Kingdom, and the Cairo-Suez area and undertaking a strategic air offensive against "vital elements of Soviet war-making capacity." The targets for U.S. conventional and atomic bombs—selected "to achieve the maximum systematic destruction of elements of vital importance to the Soviet war effort and [the] maximum psychological effect of the atomic bomb"—would be Soviet industrial, political, and control centers. Although BROILER did not specify the number of atomic weapons to be used, the scale of effort suggested by a target study earlier in 1947 was delivery of thirty-four atomic bombs on twenty-four Soviet cities.[133]

In November 1947, work also began in the JSPG on a Joint Outline Long Range War Plan, designated CHARIOTEER, in the event of a war with the USSR during 1955.[134] As initially completed, it served principally as an exercise in mobilization planning.

BROILER was submitted by the JSPG to the Joint Strategic Plans Committee (the former Joint Staff Planners) in February 1948 and was approved for planning purposes by the JCS in March. A few days later a slightly revised version, FROLIC, was presented to the JCS for submission to Secretary of Defense Forrestal.[135] It envisioned the initiation of an air offensive using atomic and conventional weapons launched from England, Okinawa, and Karachi, India, rather than the Cairo-Suez area, against the vital elements of Soviet warmaking capacity, starting at D-Day plus 15 days (D+15).[136]

During April 1948 planners from Great Britain, Canada, and the United States met in Washington to discuss common strategic problems and interests. They approved an abbreviated version of BROILER, designated HALFMOON, as the basis for development of "unilateral but accordant" plans in each country. HALFMOON provided for a strategic air offensive initiated by D+15 by Strategic Air Command bomb groups operating from the United Kingdom, Cairo-Suez, and Okinawa.[137] In conjunction with HALFMOON (and the earlier FROLIC) the Air Staff of the U.S. Air Force prepared an emergency war plan designated HARROW.[138] This plan contained an atomic annex that called for the delivery of fifty atomic bombs on target systems in twenty Soviet cities. Air Force planners believed that this attack would cause an "immediate paralysis of at least 50 percent of Soviet industry."[139]

Fleet Admiral Leahy briefed President Truman on emergency war plan HALFMOON on 5 May 1948. Truman was particularly concerned that the plan was "completely dependent upon full use of atomic bombs for success."[140] The next day the President directed Admiral Leahy to inform the JCS that an alternate war plan must be developed that employed only conventional forces because atomic bombs might be outlawed by international convention before war came; in any case the American people would not tolerate the bomb's use for "aggressive purposes."[141]

Although the JCS approved HALFMOON for planning purposes on 19 May, they did instruct the joint planners to begin work on a conventional alternative to the plan. Work on the new plan, ERASER, was aborted before completion by the U.S. response to international events.[142]

The most serious concern to the Truman administration centered on Berlin, deep in the Soviet occupation zone, where after 24 June 1948 Soviet Forces cut off the former German capital from all surface traffic from the West.[143] The United States and Britain were now providing the minimum requirements of food, coal, and other supplies to their forces in Berlin and the German population in the city's western sectors through a combined airlift from their zones in Germany. In light of the dramatically increased tension over Berlin, certain American leaders started pondering what the United States would do if war was forced upon it and how such a war could be fought successfully in the face of the Soviet Union's overwhelming superiority in ground forces.

On 19 May 1948 Army Secretary Kenneth C. Royall sent a memorandum to the National Security Council (NSC) concerning U.S. policy on atomic warfare. Arguing that there was doubt in some government quarters that atomic weapons would be used in a war, Royall recommended that the NSC consider "the position of the United States with respect to the initiation of atomic warfare in the event of war, including a consideration of the time and circumstances of employment and the type and character of targets against which it would be employed."[144] Although the subject had been raised by the Secretary of the Army, opinion within the National Military Establishment was divided on how to proceed with this question for some weeks, given President Truman's evident feelings and the possibility of a negative NSC ruling.[145] Defense Secretary Forrestal met with the President on 15 July. In the course of conversation, the subject of atomic weapons was raised. Forrestal told Truman that he did not propose to ask him for a decision on their use because he felt confident that Truman's decision would be the correct one "whenever the circumstances developed that required a decision." Truman remarked that he proposed to keep the decision to use atomic weapons in his own hands, since he did not propose "to have some dashing Lieutenant-Colonel decide when would be the proper time to drop one."[146] Forrestal apparently came away from the meeting convinced that Truman would not rule out the use of atomic weapons altogether.

On 28 July 1948 Secretary Forrestal met with Secretary of State George Marshall, Army Secretary Royall, and Army Chief of Staff Omar N. Bradley. Forrestal said that, in view of the European situation, he found it difficult to carry out his responsibilities as Secretary of Defense "without resolution of the question [of] whether or not we are to use the A-Bomb in war." Bradley remarked that although the JCS was considering a war plan centered around the use of atomic weapons, Admiral Leahy had expressed a wish for a conventional war plan at the present time. Later that afternoon Forrestal, on his own responsibility, directed the Joint Chiefs of Staff to give top priority to a war plan employing atomic weapons and give low priority to a conventional one.[147]

By early September 1948 talks on the Berlin issue had broken down between the Western powers and the Soviet Union. The Truman administration became alarmed that the United States and the USSR were on the verge of a final showdown. Reacting to the same situation, the National Security Council finally resolved the question of general U.S. policy on atomic warfare later that month. Using an earlier Air Force paper as a basis, the council agreed in NSC 30 that the National Military Establishment must be ready to "utilize promptly and effectively" all appropriate military means available, including atomic weapons, but that the decision to use them would be made by the President.[148] Truman approved the conclusions of this paper on 16 September.

In a related decision two months later, the National Security Council declared in NSC 20/4 that U.S. general objectives with respect to Russia should be to reduce Soviet power and influence to limits that no longer constituted a threat to the peace and stability of the nations of the world and to bring about a change in the Soviet Union's conduct of international relations. In the event of war, the United States would endeavor to eliminate the following: Soviet domination in areas outside the existing borders of the Russian state, the Soviet Union's (or a successor's) military-industrial power to wage "aggressive war," and the ability of any remaining Communist regime to fight and defeat other regimes that might exist on traditional Russian territory after the war.[149]

In December 1948 joint planners completed an atomic weapons annex for a new short-range Joint Emergency War Plan designed to replace FLEETWOOD (the renamed HALFMOON). The new plan, TROJAN, was approved by the Joint Chiefs of Staff on 28 January 1949. It called for atomic attacks on a broad range of urban-industrial target systems located in seventy Soviet cities. The primary target systems were urban-industrial concentrations and governmental control centers. Secondary target systems, to be hit by conventional bombing once the primary ones had been destroyed, were the petroleum industry (much of it already destroyed because of its location in the targeted urban-industrial areas), inland transportation, and the electric power industry. In all, 133 atomic bombs were to be delivered to Soviet targets. Fifteen were to be dropped in an initial strike on Moscow and Leningrad, cities with large populations and high concentrations of the USSR's war industry. The atomic bombing and follow-on conventional bombing were to be carried out by B–29 and B–50 medium bombers flying from airfields in the United Kingdom, Cairo-Suez, and Okinawa, and by B–36 heavy bombers flying from Alaska.[150]

In November 1949 TROJAN was superseded by OFFTACKLE. It was approved by the JCS a month later. Like its predecessor, OFFTACKLE called for a strategic offensive in Europe and a strategic defensive in the Far East. The strategic air offensive was to be aimed at the vital elements of Soviet war-making capacity and at retarding Soviet advances in western Eurasia. Specific target systems included twenty-six war-supporting industries located in 104 Soviet urban centers and known elements of the petroleum industry, the transportation network, and military and political control and communication "mechanisms." OFFTACKLE posited the use of 292 atomic bombs (220 plus a re-attack reserve of 72) and 17,610 tons of conventional high-explosive bombs against these targets systems during the first three months.[151]

From 1949 until well into the 1950s U.S. plans for war against the Soviet Union were increasingly oriented around U.S. ability to deliver ever-greater numbers of atomic weapons on (for the most part) increasing numbers of Soviet urban-industrial targets. In follow-on plans such as REAPER and SHAKEDOWN, the Strategic Air Command's responsibilities were increased even more dramatically, even as its forces and capabilities were enlarged and improved in an effort to keep pace.[152]

Some Air Force Planning Concerns

From its first assumption of responsibility for the strategic air offensive in the early postwar period, the Army Air Forces found itself beset by problems. Some of the problems were imposed by external factors, such as demobilization, overzealous atomic secrecy, and straitened defense budgets. But others were of its own making. These problems, for better or worse, shaped AAF's response to the security challenges of the early Cold War years.

From an operational standpoint the military readiness of the Strategic Air Command was the major issue. For a variety of reasons, between 1946 and 1948 SAC was, in the words of historian and Air Force officer Harry Borowski, a "hollow threat"—a command that was poorly trained and ill-prepared for its mission.[153] However, in this period the Army Air Forces as a whole was in poor shape. In mid-1947, for example, the AAF had only two groups in the continental United States capable of action within fifteen days in the event of an emergency: SAC's 43d and 509th Very Heavy Bomb Groups.[154] Of these two only the 509th was equipped with the SILVERPLATE aircraft capable of delivering atomic weapons.

There were other problems of equal concern from the Air Staff planners' perspective. One was the sheer size of the Soviet Union. Although some major Soviet urban-industrial centers such as Moscow, Gorki, and Leningrad were within manageable flying range from the Soviet Union's borders, many others had been built up during World War II in the central fastness of the country (Siberia and the area east of the Ural Mountains) so as to escape the invading German armies, and thus were difficult to reach. An Air Intelligence briefing given to the Air Policy Board in September 1947 noted, "You can see quite readily how deep in her interior Russia's vitals are. . . . They have developed their industrial sinews

A formation of Eighth Air Force B–29s of 509th Composite Group participates in Operation BIG TOWN, May 1947.

roughly along the median line of the earth's broadest land mass."[155] Moreover, little intelligence on these remote targets was available.[156]

Between 1946 and 1948 the U.S. Air Force (USAF) had two aircraft capable of long-range bombing—the B–29 and the B–50; the latter an upgraded B–29, featuring design improvements, more defensive firepower, greater fuel capacity, and larger reciprocating engines. The B–29's operational radius while carrying a 10,000-pound bomb was 1,800 statute miles, and the B–50's radius was approximately 2,100 statute miles.[157] This limitation meant that SAC's bombers were incapable of attacking many significant Soviet urban-industrial targets on round-trip missions. During 1947 and early 1948, therefore, a number of senior AAF people were giving serious thought to using the bombers on one-way missions (expending the planes and crews in the attempt at hitting targets deep in the Soviet Union's interior). As Major General Earl E. (Pat) Partridge, Assistant Chief of Air Staff for Operations and Training (AC/AS-3), explained to the members of the USAF Aircraft and Weapons Board at its first meeting in August 1947:

We should plan to do the job with the airplanes which we have available, which we now call a "work-horse," a B–29 or a B–50, on a one-way basis.... We can afford, in the economy of the country, to build, in my opinion again, eight bombers for every [atomic] bomb there is. Easy. It will be the cheapest thing we ever did. Expend the crew, expend the bomb, expend the airplane all at once. Kiss them goodbye and let them go. This is a pretty cold-blooded point of view, but I believe that it is economically best for the country.[158]

Air Force Secretary Stuart Symington agreed. He told the Combat Aviation Subcommittee of the Congressional Aviation Policy Board in January 1948, "In my opinion...we would do quite a considerable amount of what might be called 'suicide' bombing.... Maybe the boys could get out. You might say that is a 'one-shot' operation of retaliation."[159]

These views were not universally shared within the Air Force hierarchy, and following serious objections that such plans might preclude the SAC crews from following through on their bombing missions, Air Force leaders began searching for ways to accomplish the necessary targeting without sacrificing the planes and crews.[160] Therefore increased support was generated within the Air Staff for the limping B–36 intercontinental-range bomber program and for development of aerial refueling for the existing bomber types.[161]

Another concern had to do with the nature of AAF's atomic targeting. The Spaatz Board's initial survey suggested that, because of its cost and limited availability, the new weapon be used primarily against large urban and industrial targets.[162] In a study written at about the same time for General Leslie Groves, the AAF's Plans Directorate had posited that the rapid destruction of "enemy centers of industry, transportation, and *population*" would so damage the enemy state's infrastructure that it would make a prolonged war unimaginable.[163]

By mid-1946, however, analysts within the Requirements Division of AC/AS–3 were unconvinced that this adaptation of the AAF's World War II concept of strategic bombing was valid, particularly since the targets for atomic attack had not been defined with any clarity. None of the possible targets for atomic attack—industrial systems, cities, enemy military power, ports and harbors, and atomic bomb, gas, and secret weapon manufacturing sites—appeared to offer an early defeat of an enemy country. The analysts noted that even "immediate and total destruction" of vulnerable industrial systems would not affect the enemy's war potential for at least a year. With regard to attacks on the enemy's cities, they commented:

Destruction would not affect the enemy military machine, with the possible exception of communication services, for an indefinite period of time. It is

The Boeing B–50A, the postwar version of the wartime B–29 Superfortress, possessing larger engines, greater fuel capacity, and increased defensive firepower.

assumed that if *sufficient* force were applied in a *short* enough period of time against the major cities of a modern nation, a morale collapse would end the war. This force has never been calculated and there is grave doubt that we could counter-attack on such a target system on a decisive scale even assuming we were not seriously crippled by the first blows of the enemy. Also, a dictator nation might calculate that the United States could still be beaten even if we did destroy its cities.[164]

They called instead for the evolution of a new AAF concept of strategic bombing, both for atomic and conventional weapons.

The Air Staff's MAKEFAST plan for a strategic air offensive utilizing conventional weapons, completed in the fall of 1946, stressed avoiding attacks against enemy population centers and instead targeting specific systems vital to the enemy's war-making capacity. By early 1947, however, AAF's Air War Plans Division again began to emphasize atomic attacks against "large industrial centers" and targets such as enemy governmental control centers, communications, and population.[165]

During the following months target studies by the Directorate of Intelligence focused on the issue of target co-location. Many of the most vital

Soviet industrial target systems, such as steel, tin, machine tools, heavy and light electrical equipment, and aircraft-engine manufacturing facilities, were found to be located within the seventy most important Soviet urban areas. Knowing this, some Air Force planners quickly suggested that atomic attacks might be better directed against Soviet cities rather than against specific industrial target systems. After all, they argued, many Russian urban-industrial areas were easier to recognize on a radar scope than were discrete industrial facilities. If bomb-aiming points could be located between two or more important targets within an urban-industrial area, and if atomic weapons of sufficiently large yield were used, a single bomb's destructive effects could be maximized. From this thinking arose the concept of "bonus damage"—the idea that, in an attack against an urban-industrial area, a properly aimed atomic bomb would not only destroy the intended industrial targets but also kill or incapacitate large numbers of the population working or residing in the target area. One member of the Directorate of Intelligence recalled, "It was a sort of a shock to a lot of people when a few [planners] began to talk about bonus effects... and particularly when some began to ask what was a city besides a collection of industry."[166]

The concept was seen to have particular merit while the existing U.S. atomic stockpile remained extremely small. The Strategic Air Command under its new commander, Lieutenant General Curtis LeMay, was particularly intrigued by the idea of bonus damage, in part because it minimized the influence of bomb-aiming errors. Accordingly, SAC's first emergency war plan (SAC EWP 1–49) selected aim points "with the primary objective of the annihilation of [the urban-industrial] population, with industrial targets incidental."[167] By late 1948, therefore, population targeting had become an accepted, indeed vital, part of Air Force war plans.

Forrestal's Concerns About the Strategic Air Offensive

Secretary of Defense James Forrestal first began to have doubts about the likely effectiveness of the strategic air offensive in early October 1948, after rancorous budget sessions with the Joint Chiefs of Staff over the fiscal year 1950 budget. On 4 October Admiral Louis Denfeld voiced his concerns about the effectiveness of a "one-shot" war and the Air Force's ability to deliver the atomic offensive as planned.[168] Some ten days later, in another budget meeting, Forrestal heard Army Chief of Staff Omar Bradley express concern that cutting Army and Navy forces to the bone so that additional funding could be provided for the strategic air offensive would amount to putting "all your eggs in one basket." At this same session Air Force Vice Chief of Staff Muir S. Fairchild admitted to having doubts about the U.S. ability to launch a successful air offensive from Great Britain. As Fairchild told the Defense Secretary, "Whether we can or cannot mount an offensive from Britain is the question in my mind. I think it would be wrong to count for certainty on the ability to mount a full scale [strategic air] offensive from Britain." [169]

With the success of the country's war plans riding on the outcome of the strategic air offensive, James Forrestal needed reassurance that the offensive could be carried out as planned and that it would have the intended effects. On 23 October 1948 he sent a memorandum to the Joint Chiefs of Staff directing that they evaluate the chances of successfully delivering "a powerful strategic air offensive against vital elements of Soviet war-making capacity." In this study the JCS were to assume that war would occur before 1 April 1949 and that atomic bombs would be used by the United States. Two days later Forrestal sent the Joint Chiefs a second memorandum directing that they evaluate the effect of this air offensive on "the war effort of the USSR." This study was to include an appraisal of the psychological effects of atomic bombing on the Soviet Union's will to wage war.[170]

Forrestal's first memorandum was referred to the Air Force Chief of Staff on 25 October for a proposed reply to the JCS. After some delay General Vandenberg finally submitted his reply to the JCS on 21 December 1948, stating that the strategic air offensive could be delivered as planned. He argued as well that although certain risks did exist, they were not unreasonable and could be managed without "unduly jeopardizing" the successful execution of the air offensive.[171]

During the next several months, Vandenberg's memorandum was the object of intense debate in the JCS. Initially Admiral Denfeld, and later the Joint Intelligence Committee, questioned some of its assumptions such as the location and identifiability of Soviet industrial targets and the relative effectiveness of Soviet antiaircraft defenses.[172] Eventually, in late April 1949, the issue was handed over to the recently created Weapons Systems Evaluation Group for joint evaluation.[173]

Secretary Forrestal's second memorandum was referred to the Joint Strategic Plans Committee (JSPC), in collaboration with the Joint Intelligence Committee, for comment and recommendation. The JSPC returned a report to the Joint Chiefs of Staff on 6 December 1948 recommending that a series of additional studies be prepared before attempting an overall evaluation of the strategic air offensive.[174] Three days later the JSPC agreed to note and file the report and to recommend the creation of an ad hoc committee, consisting of two officers from each service, that would prepare the necessary evaluation. Agreeing with this recommendation, the JCS designated such a committee on 12 January

1949, with Lieutenant General Hubert R. Harmon, USAF, as the senior member.[175] The Harmon Committee began meeting later that month.

Meanwhile Secretary Forrestal chose to resolve his doubts in a more direct manner. He called in various senior officers for personal discussions on the subject. One such discussion took place in early November 1948 during a dinner attended only by Forrestal, Stuart Symington, General LeMay, John Sullivan, and Rear Admiral William S. Parsons.

LeMay had been in his new job as SAC's commanding general for only a little over two weeks, having replaced George Kenney on 19 October. He had been brought in to straighten out SAC's terrible combat readiness after more than two years of inadequate attention, skewed priorities, and outright command mismanagement by Kenney and his deputy commander, Major General Clements McMullen. The Strategic Air Command that LeMay found when he reported in was limping along with serious staff, supply, and administrative problems. Many of its aircraft were nonoperational because of uncorrected mechanical defects. Its crews were only marginally trained for their combat missions, and the command's bombing accuracy was abysmal.[176] LeMay commented years later, "We didn't have one crew, not one crew, in the entire command who could do a professional job. Not one of the outfits was up to strength—neither in airplanes nor in people nor anything else."[177]

At the dinner, however, when Forrestal began questioning the General about SAC's ability "to drive home attacks on targets in Russia," LeMay decided that for the sake of the Command and that of the Air Force, he could not tell the Defense Secretary what he really thought. Admiral Parsons recorded the discussion several days later:

> General LeMay, in his replies, several times emphasized that he was basing his statements on the *present* situation.... It was LeMay's opinion that *if* the United States could strike immediately (in a matter of several days) on the opening of hostilities, with about 80 percent of the atomic stockpile, these attacks would find the defenses so uncoordinated that we might come off unscathed, and certainly should not suffer heavy losses.[178]

Parsons, who had served as the weaponeer on the Hiroshima mission, was dumfounded that LeMay was so optimistic. Moreover, as Deputy Chief of the Armed Forces Special Weapons Project, Admiral Parsons was well aware of the general state of atomic training in the United States, and he couldn't believe that SAC's existing peacetime organization was in such good shape. Nonetheless he refrained from casting doubt on LeMay's credibility. As he later noted:

102 *Revolt of the Admirals*

> In view of LeMay's World War II experience in Europe and the Pacific, his reputation, and the fact that he now has the Strategic Air Command, I did not feel that it was appropriate for me to take issue with him in statements which would immediately raise a question as to the efficiency of his command.

Parsons did raise the point that attacks under the conditions outlined by General LeMay required "letter-perfect" navigation under wartime conditions by crews which had either no combat training or combat experience that was several years old. LeMay answered that the present crews were "*better* than the ones who hit Japan from the Marianas."[179] Parsons, unable to respond in detail, said that this might be true on average but the wartime lead crews and the ones he had flown with "had successfully completed twenty to fifty missions over Europe and the Pacific."[180]

Forrestal remained unaware of how badly General LeMay had deceived him. In a memorandum he drafted a month later, the Defense Secretary noted:

> Throughout my recent trip in Europe I was increasingly impressed by the fact that the only balance that we have against the overwhelming manpower of the Russians, and therefore the chief deterrent to war, is the threat of immediate retaliation with the atomic bomb. . . .
>
> The central question, of course, is whether or not our bombers can get in to deliver this attack. A year ago I had substantial misgivings, and while nobody can say anything with certainty about war, *I now believe the Air Force can get in with enough to deliver a powerful blow at the Russian capacity to make war.*[181]

Despite his overconfident words to Secretary Forrestal, General LeMay knew that only a priority effort at the Headquarters USAF level to provide SAC's needs would allow him to build up his command's capabilities sufficiently to carry out its awesome responsibilities under the joint war plans. He pushed his case at Exercise DUALISM, held at the Air University in December 1948. There he informed the assembled senior officers of the Air Force that as Commanding General of SAC, he intended "to develop the *capability* to deliver in one mission all of the [atomic] stockpile made available to us."[182] To accomplish this task, SAC equipment and budgetary requirements needed top priority in the Air Force. The assembled group agreed to his proposal.[183]

Much had to be done to make SAC combat ready. Just how much was demonstrated in January 1949 when SAC carried out a practice mass-bombing mission against Dayton, Ohio. The crews were provided with an outdated intelligence photograph of the city, similar to what was expected to be available for many of their Soviet targets. They were told to "bomb" their intended targets using radar at a combat bombing altitude of 30,000 feet rather than at the 15,000 to 20,000 feet they were used to in practice.[184] The results were unbelievably poor. The circular error probable (CEP) for the mission averaged 10,100 feet (i.e., half of the "bombs" fell within a circle 3.8 miles in diameter centered on the aiming point; the other half fell outside it).[185] General LeMay later remarked in disgust, "You might call that just about the darkest night in American aviation history. Not one airplane finished that mission as briefed."[186]

From this low point the Strategic Air Command began a gradual climb toward true combat readiness under Curtis LeMay's forceful leadership. It took several years of dogged effort, but by the early 1950s SAC had finally become the preeminent atomic deterrent force that LeMay and the Air Force had envisioned.

Conclusions

Developing realistic joint war plans against the Soviet Union proved a slow and halting process in the early postwar years. Even slower was the recognition at the highest levels of the U.S. government that such plans would have to give serious attention to the employment of atomic weapons, both as a deterrent to Soviet military action in Europe and as a way of compensating for the Soviet Union's superiority in ground and tactical air forces in the event of war.

By late 1948 U.S. strategic planners knew that a strong strategic air offensive was vital to U.S. security. But the forces to make such an offensive a reality did not yet exist. Unfortunately neither Secretary of Defense James Forrestal nor President Truman was fully aware of this stark and unsettling fact.

Chapter 4

Navy Thinking on Atomic Weapons and the Strategic Air Offensive

The Navy and Air Force disagreements over strategic warfare, exhibited in testimony during the House Armed Services Committee's B–36 and Unification and Strategy hearings in the summer and fall of 1949, were not sudden and unexpected. They had been building gradually since the end of the Second World War. In certain aspects they were symptomatic of service animosities dating back to the Air Service's fight in the 1920s for a single department encompassing all military and naval aviation. For the most part these disagreements represented fundamental differences in postwar thinking on the pivotal issues of how best to deter and, if necessary, wage war against the Soviet Union, using atomic and conventional weapons.

Air Force leaders were convinced that the only hope of deterring or effectively responding to Soviet military action in Western Europe was the rapid employment of a powerful strategic air offensive that would lay waste to Russian urban-industrial targets vital to the Soviet Union's war-making capacity. They believed that the atomic and conventional attacks by the Strategic Air Command's heavy and medium bombers would disrupt Soviet industry, undermine the will of the Soviet government and people to continue the war, and eventually disarm the Soviet armed forces. They saw no other way of defeating a Soviet offensive in Western Europe, believing that the United States could not afford the high costs of recruiting and maintaining the large conventional ground forces needed to fight the Red Army successfully and that U.S. naval forces would have little utility in a war against a major continental power lacking a significant navy and merchant marine.

Navy leaders had a far different perspective. Although they believed in the necessity of mounting an early strategic air offensive, they were far less sanguine about its chances of bringing the war to a successful conclusion. Navy leaders also believed in the importance of using ground forces to hold Western Europe west of the Rhine River against Soviet attack and in the necessity of holding a Mediterranean line of communications and securing the Middle East oil-producing areas. They were convinced that these objectives—none of which could be obtained through air attacks on the Soviet heartland—required the maintenance of significant naval forces to establish and hold the essential sea and air lines of communication to Europe and Africa.[1] Navy leaders envisioned using carrier task forces, operating in forward areas such as the Mediterranean and the Norwegian Sea, as power projection forces. The carriers would employ their air assets, not only to strike Soviet naval and air targets that threatened control of waters adjacent to Western Europe and Asia, but also to provide air support for the ground campaign.

Carrier Delivery of Atomic Weapons

From the beginning the Navy's interest in atomic weapons was linked to a belief that the service had a right—indeed an obligation—to make use of new or emerging military technologies that appeared capable of improving the effectiveness of the fleet. One Navy study expressed this viewpoint in the following manner: "We must foster and perform scientific research and development, particularly in the field of atomic energy and other new forces, with a view to maintaining a naval establishment built around the newest techniques."[2] The establishment of the Special Weapons Division (OP–06) in the office of the Chief of Naval Operations in November 1945 was a concrete expression of the Navy's determination to pursue the military applications of atomic energy, including both the adaptation of atomic weapons for naval use and the employment of atomic energy for powering ships.[3]

In early 1946 the chief stumbling block to the Navy effort to develop a capability for delivering atomic weapons was its belief that it lacked the authority to employ the atomic bomb in warfare. On 15 August 1945 President Harry Truman had issued a memorandum on atomic energy to the Secretaries of State, War, and Navy; the Joint Chiefs of Staff; and the Director of the Office of Scientific Research and Development, directing the appropriate departments of the government and the JCS to take steps to prevent the release of information on the development, design, or production of the atomic bomb, "or in regard to its employment in military or naval warfare, except with the specific approval of the President."[4] OPNAV inaccurately interpreted the directive to mean that the Navy had to seek presidential approval to develop ships and aircraft designed specifically to deliver the atomic bomb. Navy leaders were at first unsure whether it was best to approach Truman on the matter through the Joint Chiefs of Staff or have the Secretary of the Navy go directly to the President. After a period of vacillating they decided on the latter course. Accordingly on 22 July 1946 OP–06 drafted a letter for John L. Sullivan, the acting Secretary of the Navy,[5] to send to the President. It was finalized and sent to Truman two days later. This letter read in part:

> In order to enable Carrier Task Forces to deliver atomic bombs, it will be essential to modify carrier aircraft and alter aircraft carriers to provide servicing facilities. This will require advance peacetime preparations....
>
> I strongly urge that you authorize the Navy to make preparations for possible delivery of atomic bombs in an emergency in order that the capabilities of the Carrier Task Forces may be utilized to the maximum advantage for national defense.[6]

Three days later, in a letter to Sullivan, President Truman replied that, inasmuch as he had already discussed the subject with Secretary James Forrestal in a Cabinet meeting, he believed that a memorandum from him was unnecessary.[7] When Forrestal returned from the Bikini tests, he confirmed that the President had authorized the Navy to proceed with such preparations. With this implicit clearance from the President the Navy began planning to equip its ships and aircraft for atomic operations.

Some initial steps had already hastened the Navy's acquisition of an atomic capability. The 52,000-pound XAJ–1 heavy attack aircraft, later modified to carry the 10,300-pound Mk III atomic bomb, was already under development, and the flush-deck aircraft carrier, designed to operate a much larger, long-range attack aircraft, was undergoing design study. However, the President's authorization sanctioned an emphasis on the atomic delivery aspects of these development projects and allowed the Navy to modify its existing ships for atomic delivery. On 19 November 1946 the Chief of Naval Operations directed Vice Admiral Robert Carney, DCNO (Logistics), to modify the three *Midway*-class carriers (CVBs 41, 42, and 43) to permit the operation of AJ aircraft with atomic bomb loads. Modifications to these carriers were to include strengthening the flight decks, adding larger bomb elevators, and furnishing atomic bomb stowage, handling, and loading facilities.[8]

Having initiated a program to provide the fleet with a limited atomic delivery capability, Navy leaders gradually sought Army and Air Force acceptance of this capability for purposes of strategic planning. The Navy's leadership, however, encountered immediate and sustained opposition from the Air Force. Executive Order 9877, "Functions of the Armed Forces," issued by President Truman in July 1947 as part of the agreement with the services on the National Security Act, stated that the Air Force had the specific function of organizing, training, and equipping air forces for the "strategic air force."[9] Air Force leaders viewed Navy efforts to ready its forces for delivering limited, long-range atomic attacks as an unwarranted infringement on their service's responsibility. This issue was a source of increasing friction between the two services during 1948 and 1949.

108 *Revolt of the Admirals*

NHC USN 419521

A North American AJ-1 Savage heavy attack aircraft with markings of the Naval Air Test Center, Patuxent River, Maryland, flying over Philadelphia in 1949 or 1950.

Navy Doubts About the Strategic Air Offensive

Although the Navy had neither the interest in nor the intention of usurping the Air Force's responsibility for strategic air warfare, its establishment of a limited, long-range atomic attack capability was influenced to some degree by its generally negative assessment of the likely effectiveness of a strategic air offensive in the 1946–1950 period. The Air Force concept of a strategic air offensive in the mid- and late 1940s was essentially unchanged from the one developed and refined by the Air Corps Tactical School during the interwar period. It relied upon the destruction of vital enemy urban-industrial targets to bring a war to a successful conclusion.

In the early postwar period, though, the emphasis on *precision attack* of individual industrial targets, which had been a cornerstone of the Eighth and Fifteenth Air Forces' targeting efforts during the air war in Europe, began to shift to *area attack* of more readily identifiable, large-scale urban-industrial complexes. This shift was due to higher bombing altitudes and a greater reliance upon radar bombing, increasing the difficulty in identifying and striking precision targets.

In this period Army Air Forces personnel, nonetheless, were convinced that strategic bombing had had a decisive effect in ending World War II and, given the use of atomic weapons, would be likely to have a far more decisive, possibly war-winning, effect in future conflicts.[10] But Navy personnel were far less certain. As the months progressed and advances were made in militarily applicable technologies, such as jet-powered aircraft and radar, that promised improved air defenses, these doubts increased.

Naval aviators were in the forefront of those in the service who questioned the ability of the Air Force to mount a successful strategic air offensive against an enemy as formidable as the Soviet Union. One early question concerned the appropriateness of counting on the United Kingdom as a geographic base from which to launch retaliatory attacks on Soviet territory and forces. Throughout the 1947–1949 period, in joint outline emergency war plans such as Frolic, Halfmoon, and Offtackle, the United Kingdom was included as a base for operating a substantial portion of SAC's air offensive forces.[11] In February 1947, however, almost a year before Frolic was drafted, Captain Herbert D. Riley, head of the Air Liaison subsection of the Navy's Strategic Plans Division, sent a memorandum to the Director of Strategic Plans questioning the common planning assumption that the United Kingdom would remain available as a geographic base some time into a war with the Soviet Union:

> Our present plans and studies occasionally mention possible loss of the UK, but so far as I can ascertain, no great amount of study has been devoted to our strategy in the event that this blow materializes. . . .
>
> To me, it is inconceivable that the strategists of the USSR will not realize the importance of putting the UK out of the war as their initial step, thereby eliminating one of their two major enemies from further consideration and, at the same time, denying the other of the use of this most important forward base.[12]

Riley went on to state that, in his view, upon deciding to go to war, the Soviet Union would launch a "devastating, annihilating attack" on the United Kingdom with atomic and biological weapons. The expected targets for this attack would be Britain's urban centers. He argued that their destruction would isolate the United Kingdom from the rest of the world as effectively as if it were a separate planet.[13] It was several years, though, before senior Air Force officers acknowledged the vulnerability of the United Kingdom as a base for SAC medium-bomb groups.[14]

Naval officers had two principal concerns about the strategic air offensive: the likely decisiveness of a strategic bombing campaign directed against specific, vital target systems, rather than the massive destruction of Russian urban-industrial areas apparently emphasized in Air Force target planning, and the ability of the Air Force's relatively slow, medium and heavy bombers to penetrate Soviet air space and reach their intended targets.[15] Navy planners objected to the massive destruction of an enemy's urban-industrial centers for a mixture of practical and moral reasons. They saw this strategy as extremely costly in terms of the resources expended to accomplish it and also unnecessary because these resources could be better applied against specific target systems of military importance in the USSR and its Satellites.

On a moral basis Navy planners were opposed to infliction of massive casualties on an enemy's civilian population, whether such casualties resulted from the intentional targeting of the enemy's urban population for psychological or retaliatory reasons or from the collateral damage arising from *excessive* urban-industrial targeting. In the Navy's thinking only collateral civilian casualties incurred in carrying out the minimum targeting necessary to accomplish the mission were justified.

As Rear Admiral W. F. Boone, Assistant Chief of Naval Operations for Strategic Plans, explained to the students at the Air War College, Maxwell Air Force Base, Alabama, in the spring of 1949:

> We hold that engaging in wholesale bombing for the purpose of destroying large industrial areas and population centers is the most expensive type of warfare, not to mention the moral principle involved....
>
> Indiscriminate strategic bombing of urban areas and populations could at best, from a psychological viewpoint, create among the people a numbed, resentful, and frustrated state of mind from which only some time advantage might be gained. The roots of Communism will not have been destroyed; on the contrary, they will be watered by starvation, suffering, and confusion.[16]

Boone also urged the students to remember that such bombing was not consistent with certain U.S. national objectives set forth by the National Security Council, including creating conditions conducive to a mutually beneficial relationship between the Russian and American people and developing an effective world organization based on the purpose and principles of the United Nations.[17]

Because of their concerns about the decisiveness of an unaided strategic air offensive against the Soviet Union, Navy planners saw the value of employing Air Force and Navy offensive air assets in tandem, in precision attacks against those vital enemy target complexes best suited to their capabilities. A draft briefing prepared in 1948 expressed the issue:

> [National air power] must consist of a land-air force and a sea-air force (carrier task forces), each developing the weapons and tactics for the *precision*, instead of mass, destruction essential to the successful prosecution of

atomic warfare.... Through the maximum exploitation of faster, lighter, fully escorted and more evasive bombers trained for the precision placement of atomic explosives a decisive effectiveness never realized by mass bomber tactics can thus be achieved.[18]

The aviators' and strategic planners' concerns about the decisiveness of strategic bombing were spurred by their analyses of the reports of the United States Strategic Bombing Survey. They interpreted the reports as showing that strategic bombing had failed to be decisive in the war against Germany and Japan.[19] One of the most articulate proponents of this view was Rear Admiral Ralph A. Ofstie. As the senior naval member of the United States Strategic Bombing Survey, Ofstie had headed the Naval and Naval Air Branch of the USSBS Military Studies Division during its investigations following the end of the war in the Pacific.[20] From November 1946 to July 1950, although he was assigned outside OPNAV (as Naval Member of the Military Liaison Committee to the Atomic Energy Commission), Admiral Ofstie maintained a significant influence on Navy thinking on issues of air power and strategic bombing through an active correspondence with officers in OPNAV and through lectures to the Service war colleges.

In 1947 Ralph Ofstie drafted a paper setting forth his thoughts on the effects of the bombing of Japan on the outcome of the Pacific war. Ofstie noted that before the Army Air Forces could be employed in direct attacks on the Japanese homeland, it had been necessary to capture bases close enough to permit attacks, to defeat or heavily weaken the Japanese air force, and to laboriously build up the air power in sufficient strength. Because of the many months required to accomplish these prerequisites, the heavy AAF and Navy carrier air attacks on the Japanese economic structure did not begin until the spring of 1945. By this time, he noted, the lack of raw materials in the Home Islands (because of the effectiveness of the U.S. submarine campaign against Japanese merchant shipping) had resulted in a large and rapidly increasing amount of unused capacity in Japanese manufacturing plants. Admiral Ofstie argued that the net consequence of this situation was the failure of both the area bombing of Japan and the precision attacks against its economic target systems to bring on the collapse of the Japanese war effort.[21]

In Ofstie's view the one target system that should have been pursued with greater vigor earlier in the bombing campaign was the attack against Japan's communications network (railroads and internal shipping). He believed that such targeting would have complemented the effort against another portion of Japan's communications—the Twentieth Air Force's highly successful mining campaign directed at Japanese shipping in the Inland Sea. Among the lessons which Admiral Ofstie drew from his study of the bombing campaign against Japan was "that great destruction of an enemy's wealth as represented by his urban and industrial areas is not necessarily a gauge of the effectiveness of the attack on him."[22]

In July 1947 Admiral Ofstie was the Navy's official representative at a British exercise—THUNDERBOLT—the purpose of which was to reexamine the strategy and conduct of the Combined Bomber Offensive from January 1943 to the end of the war in Europe and to deduce lessons that could be applied to future strategy.[23] The exercise was conducted in August 1947 at the Royal Air Force (RAF) Station, Old Sarum, England, with a majority of the most senior officers of the RAF in attendance. The lectures and discussions proved to be frank in pointing out the deficiencies of the bombing campaign against Germany.

Upon his return to the United States, Admiral Ofstie reported to the CNO the most important conclusions reached during the exercise:

> a. The strategic bombing attack of urban and industrial areas was a failure.
>
> b. The target *system* attack as opposed to the *area* attack is the only correct form of bomb employment. This requires much greater precision than has heretofore been attained.
>
> c. There is need for vastly improved economic intelligence of the enemy to serve as a basis for correct target selection which is the essence of useful air bombing.
>
> d. Deep mass penetration by bombers is not possible in daylight until the Air War is won.[24]

By early 1948 Admiral Ofstie's views were shared by many, if not most, of the Navy's strategic planners. They were convinced that the Air Force plan for the strategic air offensive suffered from significant deficiencies. Rear Admiral C. W. Styer, Acting DCNO (Operations), pointed out some of the serious operational problems in a memorandum to the CNO in April 1948:

> The Air Force plan is based upon long range flights made by slow speed bombers operating unescorted deep into enemy territory. These planes cannot protect themselves and they will be an easy prey to Russian jet interceptors.... While it may be argued that it only takes one A-bomb to demolish a city, large operational losses will be suffered if a single plane is to get through."[25]

The personnel in the DCNO (Air)'s shop had almost identical views. Commenting on Styer's memorandum to the CNO, Rear Admiral E. A. Cruise, Chief, Air Readiness Division, stated that in his opinion the B–29 and the B–50 had neither the speed nor the bombing ceiling "to hope for any measure of success deep in hostile territory even against present-day defenses."[26] He argued that the Air Force and Navy should work together on a development program for long-range bombers capable of high altitude (above 40,000 feet) bombing at *supersonic* speeds.[27]

By the spring of 1948 concerns about the effectiveness of the proposed strategic air offensive were so strong within OPNAV that they were raised in meetings of the Joint Chiefs of Staff. For example, in a memorandum to the JCS on medium-range war planning, CNO Admiral Louis Denfeld commented:

> The concept in FROLIC places entire reliance for the defeat of Russia upon the success of long-range air operations against the interior of Russia.... In view of the great difficulty of these operations at the start, which must be carried out at long ranges against heavy opposition, I do not consider sole reliance should be placed on this type of warfare because:
>
> (1) If the operation does not succeed, we shall have lost so much territory, so many allies, strategic positions, and vital resources, and so much *time* as seriously to jeopardize the possibilities for ultimate victory. At best, we shall find ourselves committed to a long war and one ruinous to ourselves and to our allies, even if we are eventually to win it.[28]

Of course such official challenges to the Air Force view on the strategic air offensive did nothing to increase the Air Force's support for Navy positions within the JCS.

The height of official Navy-Air Force discord over the strategic air offensive, however, was reached in early October 1948 during the debates over the fiscal year 1950 budget. At a meeting attended by Secretary of Defense Forrestal, the Service Secretaries, the Service Chiefs, and some of their senior deputies, Admiral Denfeld attempted to convince those assembled that the budget must include money for conventional forces necessary to hold the Mediterranean and aid in the defense of Western Europe. At one point Denfeld commented on the strategic concept behind the McNarney plan[29] for allocating money to the services:

> The McNarney plan as it developed places sole reliance on a single initial offensive measure—the atomic offensive....
>
> It is a concept of a "one-shot" war, and makes no provision for possible failure of the atomic offensive to terminate the war in a matter of months....
>
> The unpleasant fact remains that the Navy has honest and sincere misgivings as to the ability of the Air Force successfully to deliver the weapons by means of unescorted missions flown by present-day bombers, deep into enemy territory in the face of strong Soviet air defenses, and to drop it on targets whose locations are not accurately known.[30]

The three Service Secretaries at their swearing in, 18 September 1947. Left to right: Secretary of the Air Force W. Stuart Symington, Chief Justice of the Supreme Court Fred M. Vinson, Secretary of the Navy John L. Sullivan, and Secretary of the Army Kenneth C. Royall.

The reaction in the meeting from representatives of the other two services was immediate and highly negative. Air Force Secretary Stuart Symington, taking exception to another portion of Admiral Denfeld's statement—that the armed forces might not be given approval to use the atomic bomb—responded, "It seems to me... the [Navy's] idea is to substitute a larger Navy for the atomic bomb."[31] And Army Secretary Kenneth Royall remarked, "I don't want to comment on this now... but I don't want my silence to leave the inference that I think Admiral Denfeld's statement is either factually correct or sound or that I do not fail to recognize its purpose."[32]

The Army and Air Force bitterness against the Navy viewpoint that came out during the morning's debate on the budget was evident to Navy attendees Sullivan, Denfeld, and Carney. They left the meeting fully aware that, in the future, the Navy could expect little support for its programs from the other two services.[33]

Navy Targeting Plans

The Navy's choice of targets for atomic attack and its views regarding its own level of participation in the strategic air offensive were influenced to a greater or lesser degree by the concerns it had about the effectiveness of the strategic air offensive. From the outset Navy atomic (and conventional) targets were predominantly strategic and tactical targets of naval interest (enemy submarine pens, naval bases, ports, shipyards); targets designated in later war plans as retardation targets, picked to slow down Soviet armies and tactical air forces advancing into Western Europe and Turkey (petroleum-oil-lubricants [POL] facilities, advanced air bases, railheads, and major road junctions); and fixed enemy airfields that posed a threat to carrier operations.[34] These targets, which were of primary importance to the Navy, were likely to be struck late or not at all by a strategic air offensive oriented toward attacks on major Soviet urban-industrial areas.[35]

By mid-1946 Navy strategic planners had decided that to cope with the expected menace of large numbers of fast Soviet submarines (based on captured German Type XXI U-boats),[36] the Navy would have to resort to offensive mining and bombing of Soviet submarine pens and building yards—"attack at the source," in the planners' parlance.[37] As Captain George W. Anderson, Jr., commented in a memorandum:

> I have long held the view that the most effective type of anti-submarine warfare is that which prevents the enemy from putting submarines to sea. This involves destroying submarines in port, preventing any egress from port by blocks or mines, destroying base facilities and by an effective strategic attack upon the industries essential to submarine production and operation.[38]

Other targets of interest to the Navy were similarly picked because their destruction would facilitate wartime fleet operations in waters contiguous to Eurasia or would retard Soviet advances in Western Europe or the Mediterranean area.

In March 1947 the Strategic Plans Division issued planning study NSPS 3, which postulated aircraft carrier offensive capabilities in a war with a major land power. In addition to discussing the targeting of Soviet air power and selected shore objectives for naval purposes, this study suggested that limited and temporary targeting of inland objectives could be undertaken by aircraft carriers, if necessary, while awaiting the arrival of shore-based strategic air at overseas bases. The clear preference in such targeting, however, was for transportation targets (also called LOC [lines of communication] targets), to retard Soviet ground advances.[39] For example, an accompanying appendix to NSPS 3, which discussed carrier air support to oppose Soviet moves to overrun Turkey,

116 *Revolt of the Admirals*

Iran, and the Levant, specifically listed a variety of transportation targets (railheads, bridges, and POL refineries) in the USSR and Soviet-controlled territory as objectives for the carrier attacks.[40]

TABLE 2. *Operations for Carrier Task Force*

- Support the withdrawal of our own and Allied forces
- Destroy enemy naval forces, naval bases, and installations [1]
- Conduct and provide necessary air cover for mining operations
- Destroy enemy aircraft and facilities at bases which threaten our control of sea areas and locations [2]
- Hinder enemy advancement of air bases and stockpiling of material in his forward areas [2]
- Support and participate in the strategic air offensive, as ordered [3]
- Support allied (British and Turkish) and our own ground forces
- Interdict enemy LOCs[4]
- Provide supplementary air defense when necessary
- Participate in the air battle

[1] The task force would operate from the Barents Sea, Norwegian Sea, North Sea, and Mediterranean Sea. Russian-controlled naval bases exist at Split and Kotor Bay in Yugoslavia, and at Durazzo and Valona in Albania.

[2] These two operations not only retard the enemy advance but contribute to successful air protection for our LOCs and forces in the Mediterranean by cutting down enemy air capabilities.

[3] Objectives will be the precision bombing of smaller elements of the selected target systems—elements which are not suitable for high-altitude bombing but which must be destroyed to make the overall effort effective.

[4] By the destruction of key transportation facilities, rolling stock, coastal shipping, and airborne support transport.

SOURCE: "Navy Budgetary Presentations Before the JCS (or Representatives) Fiscal Year 1951: Review of Plans, Phase II Part I," vol. 1, 16 Jun 1949, 30 (chart), 31-33, box 30, T/S Control Office Files, OA.

Other targeting in NSPS 3 was specifically designed to help the Air Force carry out the strategic air offensive. It could include targets designated for attack under the strategic air plan that required "immediate neutralization by tactical bombing"; targets necessary for operational success which could not be hit by land-based air because of unforseen circumstances; and air power targets whose destruction would reduce Soviet fighter strength around the periphery of the Soviet Union, facilitating penetration of Soviet airspace by the Air Force's heavy bombers.[41] The study clearly saw such targeting as an *augmentation* of Air Force capabilities for accomplishment of the strategic air offensive, not as a *replacement* for land-based strategic bombing.

This limited concept of targeting remained the official Navy thinking on the issue throughout the 1947–1949 period and beyond.[42] On several occasions in 1948 and 1949, however, offices outside the OP–03 and OP–05 planning shops drafted papers or statements that failed to adhere to this limited concept of Navy atomic targeting. In these cases the rhetoric outpaced accepted policy. Despite such lapses the Navy's strategic planners did not attempt to expand their concept of targeting beyond the relatively limited areas sketched out in NSPS 3.[43] They continued to view naval participation in the strategic air offensive as an adjunct to SAC's air offensive, designed to increase the effectiveness of the overall effort by applying offensive strength to certain areas where the Air Force's effort might be weak.[44] As Navy planners explained to their joint colleagues in a March 1949 briefing on Navy forces for Joint Outline Emergency War Plan OFFTACKLE:

> [The carrier task force will be called upon to] . . . support and participate in the strategic air offensive, as ordered—specializing in the precision bombing of smaller elements of the selected target systems—elements not suitable for high altitude bombing but which must be cleared up to make the effort effective.[45]

Nevertheless, this limited Navy concept for its targeting may not have been as apparent to the Air Force as it should have been. It is unlikely that senior naval officers fully understood the strong concerns that the Air Force leadership had about possible infringements on their service's responsibility for the conduct of strategic air warfare. Undoubtedly, a specific reason for possible Air Force confusion on the Navy's ultimate aims in this regard was the publicity attendant to the so-called "Gallery memorandum." In December 1947, Rear Admiral Daniel V. Gallery, ACNO (Guided Missiles), wrote a memorandum to the DCNO (Air), Vice Admiral Wu Duncan, commenting on the Final Report of the War Department Policies and Programs Review Board, which had been circulated within OPNAV on 4 December.

In this memorandum Gallery expanded upon certain ideas he had been formulating for some weeks.[46] He argued that the Navy should use the opportunity afforded by the publication of the War Department report to present its case as the branch of the armed forces best suited to deliver the atomic bomb. He stated, "If the Navy makes delivery of the atom bomb its major mission, and if we develop the proper ships, planes, and tactics, the Navy can become *the principal offensive branch of the National Defense system, the branch that actually delivers the knock-out blows.*"[47] In such a situation, the Navy should have the primary mission of delivering

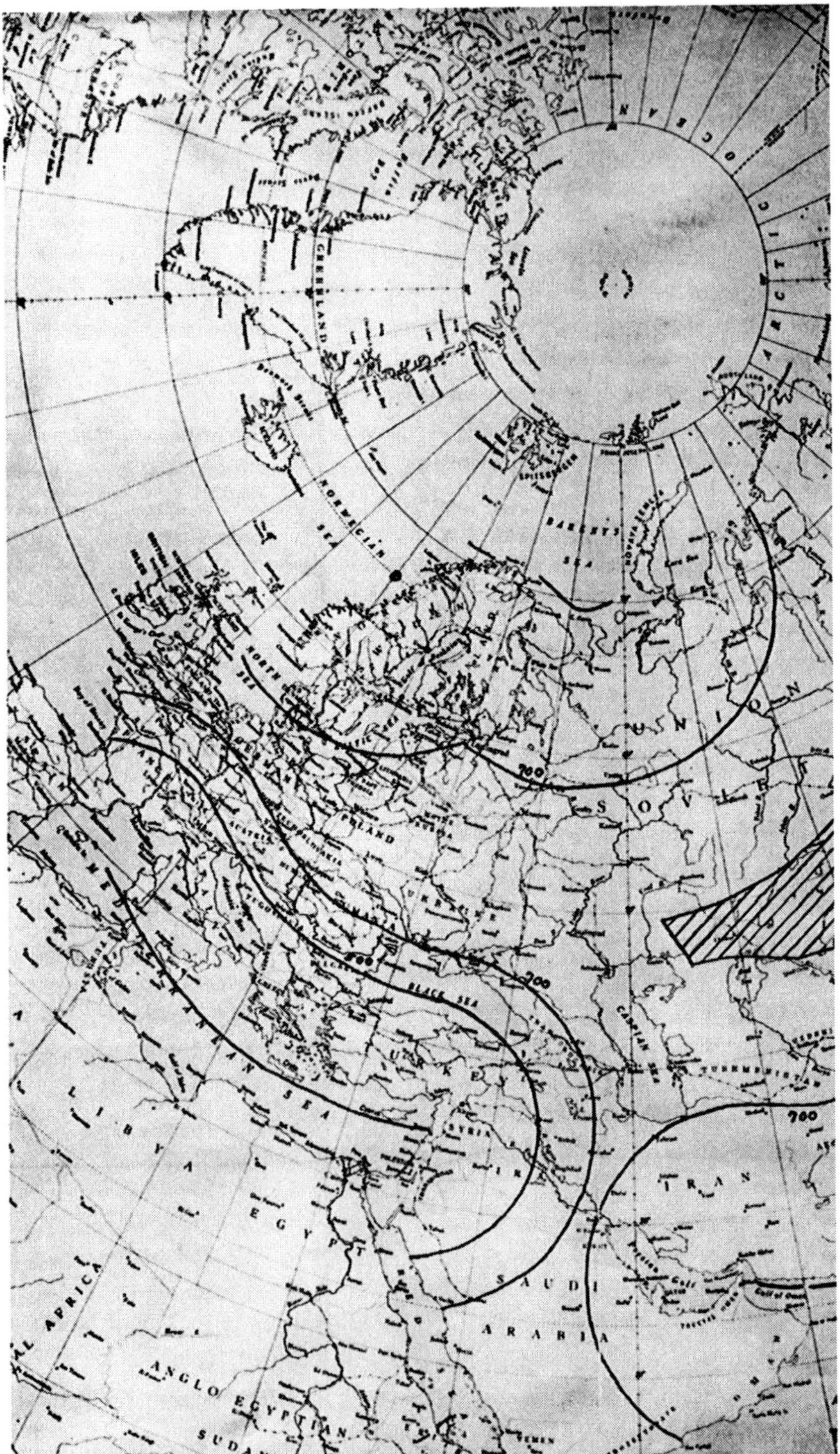
GREENLAND
NORWEGIAN SEA
BARENTS SEA
NORTH SEA
POLAND
BLACK SEA
S O V I E T
U N I O N
I R A N
SAUDI
ARABIA
E G Y P T
L I B Y A
ANGLO EGYPTIAN
SUDAN
700

This late-1947 chart shows the target coverage of the Soviet Union provided by projected attack aircraft of various ranges operating from attack carriers located in the Norwegian Sea, the Mediterranean Sea, the Arabian Sea, the Bay of Bengal, and the Yellow Sea. The hatched area is the portion of the Soviet Union that could not be reached by carrier aircraft with a combat radius of 1,200 miles or less.

NHC, Strategic Plans

atomic attacks on the capital and industrial centers of the enemy, while the Air Force should have the primary mission of defending the United States against air attack, with only a secondary mission of delivering atomic attacks from overseas bases.[48]

Gallery's provocative idea of having the Navy take over the strategic offensive mission, though considered by senior officers in OPNAV to be conceptually interesting, was not accepted as a guide for action. It was seen as neither logical nor operationally feasible to make the Navy responsible for all atomic bombing.[49] Vice Admiral Forrest Sherman, DCNO (Operations), commented on the memorandum, "I think this is a fine paper up to the point where it follows the Air Force error of wanting *exclusive* responsibility for bombing strategic targets."[50] Similarly, Admiral Duncan noted, "I do not think we can claim exclusive rights to the Navy for the delivery of A bombs."[51]

If this had been the end of matter, nothing would have happened to stir up Air Force resentment. But Admiral Gallery had distributed a sizeable number of copies of his memorandum within OPNAV. Some weeks later an Air Force sympathizer happened to see a copy of this memorandum and surreptitiously made a copy of it, which was quickly passed to Air Force Secretary Stuart Symington.[52] Incensed at Gallery's suggestions, Symington sent two memoranda to Navy Secretary Sullivan, on 15 and 16 March 1948, protesting this apparent intrusion upon the strategic bombing mission of the Air Force.[53]

A few days later word of the Gallery memorandum mysteriously found its way to Representative Albert J. Engel (R–Mich.), Chairman of the House Appropriations Committee's Army Subcommittee. He contacted the Secretary of the Navy and requested a copy of the Gallery memorandum. It was sent to the congressman on 22 May, together with a joint letter from Navy Secretary Sullivan and Admiral Denfeld stressing that the ideas expressed in Admiral Gallery's memorandum were not the official views of the Navy Department on strategic air warfare.[54]

In early April Denfeld sent a memorandum to Sullivan suggesting that the matter be closed by giving Admiral Gallery a private reprimand for making "an extensive and somewhat uncontrolled distribution of a classified document."[55] At about the same time, however, the Gallery memorandum was leaked to columnist Drew Pearson by an unknown individual.[56] Publication of the contents of the classified memorandum in Pearson's columns in the *Philadelphia Inquirer* and *Philadelphia Bulletin* on 10 April 1948 forced the Navy Secretary to release a copy of the Navy's letter to Engel and make Gallery's censure public that same day.[57] In a statement released to the press at the same time, the Navy acknowledged that its position was that strategic bombing was a job "primarily for the Air Force."

Coming only a few months after the publicity surrounding the Nimitz Valedictory, release of the Gallery memorandum beyond the confines of OPNAV convinced some senior leaders in the Air Force that the Navy intended to take over the strategic bombing mission. Such was not the case, but this perception obviously placed added burdens on the Navy's effort to maintain support in the National Military Establishment for carrier aviation. The Navy's failure to adequately allay Air Force fears on this matter at the time would prove difficult to overcome in the coming months.

Air Force Opposition to a Navy Role

Air Force opposition to the Navy's use of atomic weapons and, in particular, to a Navy role in strategic bombing, gathered force in early 1948. Air Force Chief of Staff Carl Spaatz told the Air Board in January 1948, "I have heard it said by the Navy that they do not even consider the Executive Order of the President [on roles and missions] binding. Well, that starts off the fight again."[58] The renewed Air Force attack was directed against the most powerful portion of naval aviation: carrier air. To Air Force leaders it was the continued development of carrier aviation that threatened the preeminent position of the Air Force as the embodiment of U.S. "air power."[59] Air Force concern over carrier air power was a mixture of worry that such aviation would absorb monies that were needed for an expanding Air Force and belief that, in the postwar period, aircraft carriers were obsolescent and highly vulnerable platforms. The Air Force's belief that carriers would have little utility in a war against a major land power such as the Soviet Union sprang from postwar AAF and Air Force analyses of carrier operations during World War II which concluded:

1) aircraft carriers are highly vulnerable to a variety of attacks by an enemy's air force and submarines;
2) carriers would be unable to operate in waters within range of a first-rate land-based air force;
3) carrier aircraft are inherently inferior to land-based aircraft in range, speed, and combat capability;
4) carrier aircraft lack the requisite range to hit significant targets in the interior of a large land power;
5) the weight of a bombing effort that a carrier task force could employ against land targets is relatively insignificant.[60]

As the result of such analyses, senior Air Force officers dismissed aircraft carriers as effective weapon systems. They were particularly harsh in their judgments on the value of carriers in the Mediterranean, an area which was of special interest to the Navy strategic planners in this period. Major General George McDonald, the AAF's Assistant Chief of Air Staff for Intelligence, wrote General Spaatz in October 1946, "A Navy in the Mediterranean cannot *reach*, even through its carrier aircraft, any significant portion of Russia's national strength.... The real military worth of the carriers may come in trading carriers sunk for time, measured in weeks, while land based air power can arrive on station."[61]

The Air Force began analyzing aircraft carrier capabilities for atomic warfare in 1948. Their interest was aroused by press attention to the subject following the Nimitz Valedictory. A 1948 Air War College study on the employment of carrier forces for strategic atomic attacks, which was summarized for Air Force Chief of Staff General Hoyt Vandenberg, reached certain negative conclusions about the carrier's capability for such attacks.

   a. Because of vulnerability to submarines and to aircraft, the ability of carriers to reach appropriate launching areas is questioned.
   b. The ability to penetrate enemy defenses to reach the target is seriously in question as a result of a disparaging comparison of carrier and land based [aircraft] types in terms of speed, range, etc.
   c. Assuming 1,000 nautical miles radius of action and assuming launching areas close to the continent, limited percentages of Russian industry are in range.
   d. The weight of attack required for decisive effect leads to a prohibitive expenditure.[62]

By early 1948, Air Force opposition to allotting aircraft carriers even a subsidiary role in atomic bombing was being openly displayed. On 23 January Admiral Arthur Radford spoke with former Representative Melvin J. Maas, who was working with the Congressional Aviation Policy Board. The board, which was studying the country's military and civilian aircraft requirements, was hearing testimony from a variety of witnesses; one was Air Force Secretary Symington. Maas told Radford, "'Stu' [Symington] said if the Navy keeps this up to get in on strategic bombing the Army and Air Force were going to turn to and finish up with a single Air Force."[63] In late January 1948, General Spaatz discussed the issue of strategic bombing in a meeting with Defense Secretary Forrestal and Admiral Radford. When Radford said that he did not want any arbitrary restrictions being placed on the development of Navy airplanes, either in their carrying capacity or range, Spaatz argued that the matter would hinge on funding. He stated that the amount of funding made available to each of the services must be based on the war plan existing at the time. Spaatz commented further, "Super-carriers might be very expensive."[64] The implied threat to the flush-deck carrier was not lost on Radford or Forrestal. In the latter part of

February 1948 a dismayed James Forrestal wrote to Admiral Sherman, now in the Mediterranean, that the Air Force was opposing any new aircraft carriers for the Navy. Sherman wrote back, "I am sorry that the Air Force has chosen to oppose our building new carriers because they thereby vastly increase the difficulty of establishing the 'live and let live' attitude which is so badly needed in our interservice relationships."[65]

The continuing service controversy over roles and missions caused Secretary Forrestal to convene a meeting of the Service Chiefs and their Operations Deputies at Key West, Florida, on 11 March 1948. During several days of tough bargaining sessions the participants worked out a revision of the Executive Order on roles and missions signed by President Truman the previous July.[66] The Key West agreement assigned the primary function of strategic air warfare to the Air Force.[67] The Navy, however, was assigned the collateral function to be prepared to participate in the overall air effort as directed by the Joint Chiefs of Staff.[68]

The key issues at stake, though, were how the term *strategic* was to be interpreted and whether the Navy could bomb inland targets in connection with the naval campaign. Secretary Forrestal had gone into the Key West meetings determined that although the Navy must be allowed to have the air assets necessary for its mission, it could not create a strategic air force.[69] During the course of the meetings, the Navy representatives reiterated that their service had no intention of setting up a strategic air force. Accordingly, the group as a whole (including the Air Force representatives) finally agreed that the Navy could attack inland targets and could employ atomic weapons in carrying out its tasks. Forrestal recorded in his diary:

> Air Force recognizes right of Navy to proceed with the development of weapons the Navy considers essential to its function but with the proviso that the Navy will not function as a separate strategic air force.... However, the Navy in the carrying out of its function is to have the right to attack inland targets — for example, to reduce and neutralize airfields from which enemy aircraft may be sortying [sic] to attack the fleet.[70]

In his briefing to President Truman on the results of the Key West meeting, Forrestal stressed that it had been decided that the Navy was "not to be denied use of [the] A-bomb."[71]

An immediate problem arose, however, from the fact that no secretarial record of the Key West meetings had been taken. Each service had its own interpretations of what had been agreed to, which could neither be proven nor falsified by reference to a written transcript of the proceedings. Accordingly, the issue of just what rights to participate in strategic air warfare and atomic bombing the Navy had been granted at Key West remained in contention during the next few months.

124   *Revolt of the Admirals*

NHC USN 705090

Top officials of the National Military Establishment attend a conference on roles and missions at Key West, March 1948. Left to right, *front*: Admiral Louis E. Denfeld, Chief of Naval Operations; Fleet Admiral William D. Leahy, Chief of Staff to the Commander in Chief; Secretary of Defense James V. Forrestal; General Carl A. Spaatz, Air Force Chief of Staff; General Omar N. Bradley, Army Chief of Staff. Left to right, *rear*: Vice Admiral Arthur W. Radford, Vice Chief of Naval Operations; Major General Alfred M. Gruenther, Director of the Joint Staff; Wilfred J. McNeil, Special Assistant to the Secretary of Defense; Lieutenant General Lauris Norstad, Air Force Deputy Chief of Staff for Operations; and Lieutenant General Albert C. Wedemeyer, Director of Plans and Operations, Army General Staff.

On 1 July 1948 Secretary Forrestal finally issued a memorandum approving, with slight changes, the JCS Memorandum for the Record on the Key West agreements. The Memorandum for the Record had attempted to clarify the extent of the Navy's participation in the overall (strategic) air effort,[72] but it was ambiguous on the matter of whether the Navy had the right to attack selected targets with atomic bombs. Captain Fitzhugh Lee, Aide to the Secretary of the Navy, explained to John Sullivan, "'Strategic Bombing' means many things to many people. The basic issue as to whether or not carriers can be utilized for atomic bombing on selected targets remains unresolved."[73] A few days later, Lee sent the Secretary a further memorandum on the subject, noting, "The question is—'May the

A Lockheed P2V–3C Neptune heavy attack aircraft takes off from *Midway* (CVB 41) with JATO assistance, 7 April 1949.

Navy plan to drop an atomic bomb on an inland target, and if so how far inland?'"[74] After commenting that the Air Force wanted the Navy to have no part in atomic bombing, Lee then quoted from answers on the issue which had been given by Secretary Forrestal in a recent press conference. He concluded that Forrestal's responses on the subject were not clear-cut and that until the Defense Secretary did make some clear-cut answers "the majority of the important planning will be considerably handicapped."[75]

It was in this context that Sullivan took up the issue directly with Air Force Secretary Symington. During the conference at which the subject was first raised, Symington told Sullivan that the Air Force should have the exclusive wartime use of the atomic bomb. When Sullivan later requested that the Air Force Secretary put his answer in writing, Symington sent him a somewhat evasive response.[76]

On 19 July Secretary Forrestal had dinner with the three Service Secretaries. During the dinner the issue of which service should have use of the atomic bomb was raised. Sullivan remarked that the Navy conceded that the responsibility for strategic warfare belonged to the Air Force.

The P2V-3C completes its take-off from *Midway*, 7 April 1949. This shot was captured from the deck of the accompanying *Kearsarge* (CV 33). Note the extensive smoke left on *Midway*'s flight deck by the use of JATO.

He noted, however, that the Navy was not willing to be denied "the use of the atomic bomb on particular targets." Army Secretary Kenneth Royall replied that the Navy should accept practical control of the atomic bomb by the Air Force and that any use the Navy made of the weapon should be "subservient to the Air Force."[77]

Following this meeting, at which Sullivan again asked for a clarification of Symington's earlier response, the Air Force Secretary sent Sullivan a memorandum forthrightly explaining his service's views.[78] As to whether the Navy should be authorized to drop the atomic bomb in the event of war, Symington stated, "If the Naval organization and equipment required to perform *the normal Naval missions* can be used to deliver an atomic bomb against a target or targets, the destruction of which is necessary to carry out the strategic plan, *and which target cannot be destroyed by the Air Force,* Naval equipment should be used to conduct atomic bomb operations." The memorandum noted, however, that there was no justification for the development by the Navy of special equipment or organization for dropping the atomic bomb unless there were enough resources to provide not only for the normal missions of all three services but also for "consideration of additional military tasks" for each service, and unless it would result in equal or greater economy in the use of fissionable material.[79] The latter qualification was a backhanded swipe at the Navy's plan to use P2Vs carrying Mk I Little Boy (gun-type) atomic bombs as an interim carrier atomic capability.[80] This was because the gun-type weapon was less efficient in the use of fissionable material than the Mk III implosion bomb carried by Air Force bombers.[81]

John Sullivan responded by sending Stuart Symington a paper outlining the Navy's position. In his cover memorandum, Sullivan told Symington in no uncertain terms, "A unilateral development program directed toward achieving atomic weapon delivery systems restricted to one Service would be unsound and fraught with gravest consequences."[82]

Tied in with the Air Force's desire to maintain its primacy in strategic air warfare by keeping the Navy out of the atomic-weapons delivery business was the whole issue of atomic-weapons scarcity between 1945 and 1948. Throughout this period the Air Force was concerned that its initial strategic air offensive against Soviet targets would require all of the atomic weapons likely to be available in the stockpile for years to come. The original implosion design for the Mk III weapon being stockpiled relied upon an all-plutonium core. But by early 1947 U.S. production of plutonium at its Hanford, Washington, reactors had fallen to a fraction of wartime levels. And although uranium-235 (ORalloy) production at its Oak Ridge, Tennessee, gaseous diffusion, separation, and enrichment facilities was significantly higher, ORalloy could only be used in the Mk I gun-type weapon, which was not then being stockpiled.[83] As a result of this shortage of fissionable material, there were still few atomic weapons in the stockpile by mid-1947.

Early postwar advances in core design, including the so-called "levitated" core, and the development of composite (plutonium/uranium-235) cores were tested successfully in three full-scale weapons tests during Operation SANDSTONE in April and May 1948. The three tested designs released energy yields equivalent to 40.8 kilotons (kt) of TNT, 43 kt, and 18 kt, respectively; two of the three yields being almost double the 22 kilotons available from the Mk III, or Fat Man (FM), design then in the stockpile.[84] These tests demonstrated that the new designs could use the available stock of fissile material far more efficiently. As Chuck Hansen noted in his definitive history of U.S. nuclear weapons, "The most immediate military effect of these tests was to make possible within the near future a 63% increase in the total number of bombs in the stockpile and a 75% increase in the total yield of these bombs."[85] With the adoption of the SANDSTONE-proven core designs, the introduction of new mechanical assemblies (particularly the Mk IV bomb assembly), and improvements in U.S. fissile materials production, the United States' long-term atomic weapons scarcity was alleviated by 1951.[86]

TABLE 3. *U.S. Atomic Weapons Stockpile, 1945–1950*

	Nuclear Components		Mechanical Assemblies	
Date	Implosion	Gun-type	Implosion	Gun-type
June 30, 1945[1]	2	0	2	0
June 30, 1946	9	0	9	0
June 30, 1947	13	0	29	0
June 30, 1948	50	0	53	2
June 30, 1949[2]	?	?	228	12
June 30, 1950[2]	[at least 292][3]		660	28

[1] These numbers may apply to December 31, 1945.
[2] There were more mechanical assemblies than nuclear cores to match them in 1949 and 1950.
[3] The figure in brackets was supplied by David A. Rosenberg on the basis of non-Department of Energy information.

SOURCE: Taken from Table 1 in David A. Rosenberg, "Nuclear stockpile, 1945–1950," *The Bulletin of Atomic Scientists* 39 (May 1982): 26. The 1945–1948 official figures, supplied by the Department of Energy and first published in Rosenberg's article, were separately confirmed in Steven Rearden's OSD history. See Table 8 in Rearden, *The Formative Years*, 439.

It was also during 1948 that the question of control over the Armed Forces Special Weapons Project (AFSWP)—the interservice training and support organization responsible for the handling and assembling of atomic weapons released to military custody by the Atomic Energy Committee—was being fought out in the JCS.[87] Air Force Chief of Staff Hoyt Vandenberg wanted to assume control over AFSWP as the Joint Chiefs of Staff's requisite executive agent for atomic warfare matters.[88] The Navy was against giving this control to the Air Force because it feared that such control would effectively deny the Navy staff support for its own emerging atomic weapons capability.

The Navy had good reasons for its concern, since the Air Force continued to object in National Military Establishment meetings, not only to the Navy's employment of atomic weapons but also to its procurement of the flush-deck aircraft carrier, which would enable it to undertake limited long-range bombing. On 28 July 1948, when Forrestal talked with General Vandenberg about the issue of assigning control of atomic weapons to the Air Force, Vandenberg said that "the nation could not afford to continue spending money for two duplicating programs, particularly when one *involved the use of obsolescing weapons* [i.e., aircraft carriers]."[89]

The continued Air Force-Navy squabbling over atomic weapons and strategic air warfare induced Secretary Forrestal to elicit the views of two retired elder statesmen—General Carl Spaatz and Admiral John H. Towers—on 9 August 1948. The specific questions that they were asked to look at included whether the aircraft carrier had any useful role in

Radford Papers, OA USN 705984

The Joint Chiefs of Staff and their Operations Deputies meet with Secretary of Defense Forrestal to resolve roles and missions disputes, Newport, August 1948. Left to right: Major General Alfred Gruenther, Director of the Joint Staff; General Hoyt Vandenberg, Air Force Chief of Staff; Admiral Louis Denfeld, Chief of Naval Operations; General Omar Bradley, Army Chief of Staff; Secretary of Defense James Forrestal; Lieutenant General Albert Wedemeyer, Director of Plans and Operations, Army General Staff; Vice Admiral Arthur Radford, Vice Chief of Naval Operations; and Lieutenant General Lauris Norstad, Air Force Deputy Chief of Staff for Operations.

strategic air operations; whether the Air Force should be given operational control over atomic weapons as a matter of dominant interest; and whether the Navy's use of atomic weapons should be limited either to sorties upon strategic targets under the Air Force's operational control, or to sorties upon targets of purely naval interest.[90] Although the two men did reach agreement that carriers could have a useful role in strategic air operations, they were unable to agree on specific aspects of service control over atomic weapons.[91]

With this matter at an impasse, Forrestal eventually decided to bring the Chiefs together for a second series of meetings on roles and missions. Accordingly, from 20 to 22 August 1948 Forrestal met in seclusion with the Joint Chiefs of Staff and their Operations Deputies at the Naval War College in Newport, Rhode Island.[92] After lengthy and sometimes heated debate, those present agreed that although the Air Force would be desig-

The Newport conferees outside on the grounds of the Naval War College, August 1948.

nated the interim executive agent for AFSWP, the Navy would be allowed to participate in atomic bombing, both for tactical purposes and, in assisting in the overall air offensive, for strategic purposes as well.[93]

Conclusions

The Newport meetings marked a major concession on the part of the Air Force in acknowledging that the Navy had a right to the use of atomic weapons and a role to play in assisting the Air Force in the conduct of the strategic air offensive.[94] For many months the Air Force had done everything it could to keep the Navy out of atomic warfare. Its concession was a grudging one, made under pressure from a Secretary of Defense who actively sought service compromise and who, moreover, was sympathetic to the Navy viewpoint. To the Navy's dismay it proved to be a concession that did not remain firm but had to be reviewed over and over again during day-to-day planning decisions reached during the course of the continuing deliberations of the JCS. Throughout the rest of 1948 and during all of 1949, the Navy had to fight to maintain the role in atomic warfare planning and operations that it had been granted at the Newport conference.

Chapter 5

Super Carriers and B–36 Bombers

From 1946 to 1950 the differing Navy and Air Force perspectives on roles and missions and the nature of future warfare were represented by two offensive weapon systems that the services were developing. The Navy's was the large, flush-deck aircraft carrier, designed to operate the larger and heavier aircraft entering the Navy's inventory, including attack (bombing) planes capable of flying long-range missions. The Air Force weapon system was the B–36 bomber, designed during the war and capable of carrying a huge bomb load over intercontinental distances.

In 1946 both weapon systems had been accorded a relatively modest priority, reflecting the stage of development each had then reached. By the end of 1948, however, they had become the principal repositories of their services' hopes for effective offensive capabilities in the near future. As each weapon system increased in importance to its respective service, it became a more prominent target for attack by those in other services who held differing viewpoints on the appropriate national military strategy and the forces necessary to support it.

The 6A Carrier

The Navy began thinking about the design of a successor class to the *Midway* (CVB 41) class aircraft carriers during the final months of World War II.[1] In late April 1945 an Informal Advisory Board was appointed to restudy the Navy's aircraft carrier requirements and submit its recommendations to the Deputy Chief of Naval Operations for Air.[2] On 10 May in a related action, Secretary James Forrestal proposed building new ships that would incorporate "changes dictated by war experience" and improvements derived from research and development and up-to-date operating methods.[3] One was to be a new fleet carrier with aviation facilities equal to those of *Franklin D. Roosevelt* (CVB 42)—the second *Midway*-class carrier.[4]

In the summer of 1945 the Bureau of Ships (BUSHIPS) began studying aircraft carrier designs with standard displacements in the range of 35,000

The *Essex*-class aircraft carrier *Shangri-la* (CV 38) underway in the Pacific with the crew at quarters, August 1946.

to 50,000 tons.[5] However, concerns about the labor and material costs of a new fleet carrier soon oriented BUSHIPS' thinking toward an intermediate-sized carrier with a displacement in the lower end of that range—one that would be larger than the CV 9 (*Essex*) class but smaller than the CVB 41 class.[6] The design study (C–1) eventually settled on for this CV of "improved standard type . . . capable of handling any present or proposed standard carrier aircraft" was for a carrier of 39,600 tons standard displacement.[7] This proposed carrier was improved in speed and endurance over the *Midway* class. It had an additional catapult but smaller flight and hangar decks. Thus it could neither accommodate as large an air group nor handle large aircraft as efficiently as the *Midway*-class carrier.[8]

In a parallel but separate action, naval aviators in the Bureau of Aeronautics initiated a call for large, carrier-based bombers and a large aircraft carrier to operate them. BUAER planning for an aircraft capable of carrying an 8,000- to 12,000-pound bomb load started in the late spring of 1945, at the same time evaluations were begun on the U.S. Strategic Bombing Survey's analyses of U.S. bomb damage to Germany.[9] The idea was not officially advanced outside the bureau, however, until 11 Decem-

Midway (CVB 41), the first of the Navy's wartime-designed aircraft carriers with armored flight decks, in its original configuration, October 1945.

ber 1945, when BUAER Chief Rear Admiral Harold Sallada sent a memorandum to the CNO on the development of large bombers for carrier operations, stating:

> The largest bomb regularly carried by carrier-based aircraft in World War II was the 2000 lb. G.P. [general purpose] bomb, and the maximum striking radius of carrier-based aviation was about 400 nautical miles. Analysis of bombing results in Germany has revealed that lethal damage to many targets required 4000 lb. bombs, and lethal damage to some targets required 12,000 lb. bombs.[10]

The document noted that BUAER had conducted a series of preliminary studies to determine the increases in range and bomb size that would be possible in carrier-based aircraft in the foreseeable future through technological advances. These studies revealed that the development of propeller-turbine engines would enable three categories of bombing aircraft to be developed. Category A would be able to operate fully from present CVB-class aircraft carriers. Category B would be able to operate from the same carriers in a restricted manner.[11] Category C would require the development of a new class of aircraft carriers with larger, stronger, or increased-capacity arresting gear, catapults, elevators, and so forth.[12] The weight and capabilities of each of these aircraft categories are shown below.

TABLE 4. BUAER's New Categories of Bombing Aircraft

	A	B	C
Gross weight, fully loaded (lbs.)	30,000	45,000	100,000
Gross weight, landing (lbs.)	20,000	30,000	65,000
Bomb size (lbs.)	8,000[1]	8,000[1]	8,000[1]
Vmax/alt. (mph/ft)	362/S.L.	500/35,000	500/35,000
Combat radius (naut. mi.)	300	1,000	2,000

[1] 12,000-lb. bomb can be carried with sacrifice of fuel and range.
S.L. = sea level.
SOURCE: Memo, Sallada to CNO, 11 Dec 1945, encl. A to memo, DCNO (Air) to CNO, 8 Jan 1946, "A19/2 Key West Conferences (Briefing Pamphlet) S&C" folder, Series II, OP–23 Records, OA.

Sallada's memorandum recommended initiating a program to extend the ranges and bomb capacity of carrier-based aviation. It specifically called for the rapid development of an aircraft of the category B type, with a fully loaded gross weight of 41,000 pounds and a landing weight of 28,000 pounds and employing a combination of reciprocating engines and turbo jets to attain a combat radius of 300 nautical miles (345 statute miles).[13] This proposed aircraft became the AJ–1 Savage. It had not originally been designed to carry an atomic weapon,[14] but in late 1946, on the initiative of Captain Frederick L. Ashworth of OP–36 and Captain Joseph N. Murphy of BUAER, the AJ's bomb bay was reconfigured to provide the plane with the capability of carrying atomic weapons.[15] It thus became the Navy's first aircraft designed for the heavy attack (long-range atomic bombing) mission, capable of carrying the 10,300-pound, Mk III Fat Man atomic bomb (then the principal atomic weapon in the U.S. stockpile) to a combat radius of some 750 nautical miles (864 statute miles).[16]

Admiral Sallada's memorandum did not call for an immediate start on the design and development of a category C aircraft and the aircraft carrier to operate it, even though these were a primary BUAER concern.[17] In keeping with the BUAER plan to get the category B aircraft program off the ground without engendering major OPNAV opposition, the memo listed the design of the 100,000-pound bomber and the large aircraft carrier as the third part of its suggested four-part program, after the early development of the category B reciprocating-engine/turbo-jet aircraft and the development of a category B turbine-propelled aircraft.[18]

Midway's flight deck is packed with Curtiss SB2C Helldiver bombers, off Norfolk, Virginia, May 1947.

On 28 December 1945 the Chief of Naval Operations approved the development of the first, second, and fourth parts of the BUAER program. He deferred action on the development of aircraft requiring a new class of carriers pending further consideration. He noted in conclusion, though, that the program proposed by Admiral Sallada should "form the basis of post-war effort in the carrier aviation field."[19]

Strong support from DCNO (Air) Vice Admiral Marc Mitscher led to an early decision within OPNAV to develop the new larger carrier. In 1944 Mitscher had been Commander Task Force 58 during the battles in Philippine waters. His carriers were forced to operate in the Bight of Luzon, close to the enemy shoreline, in order to attack Japanese air bases that posed a threat to the fleet. This sacrifice of carrier mobility, occasioned by the relatively short combat radius of Navy aircraft, subjected the carriers to continuous air attack by the Japanese. This situation emphasized to Mitscher and other carrier admirals the need for longer range (thus larger and heavier) fighter and attack aircraft and the larger carriers to operate them.[20] Mitscher was also convinced that the larger carriers should be flush-deck ships because he believed this design would

National Archives 80-G-705757

Vice Admiral Arthur W. Radford served as Vice Chief of Naval Operations from 3 January 1948 to 16 May 1949.

facilitate the Navy's required transition to all-weather carrier operations.[21] Admiral Arthur Radford succeeded Admiral Mitscher as DCNO (Air) in mid-January 1946 and therefore had a primary role in supporting construction of the new carrier during the next two years. Radford believed the flush-deck carrier would be valuable for operating large reconnaissance aircraft in addition to large attack planes and fighters.[22]

The concept of the flush-deck carrier appealed to naval aviators in general because a flight deck completely free of vertical obstructions allowed much larger aircraft to be operated from the ship. As an aircraft's overall size and weight increased, so too did its wing span, and in the days of straight-deck aircraft carriers, the presence of an island imposed serious restraints on the size of aircraft that could be safely launched and recovered.

In early January 1946 Admiral Mitscher wrote a memorandum to the Chief of Naval Operations recommending that the CNO initiate a design study of a new carrier class and approve the development of 100,000-pound bombers.[23] Admiral Chester Nimitz instead referred the matter to Assistant Secretary of the Navy for Air John Sullivan. In a memorandum submitting the BUAER–DCNO (Air) recommendations to Sullivan, his aide, Captain William V. Saunders, pointed out that "we risk a brush with the Air Force in any such project." Nevertheless Saunders supported the authorization of design studies of the aircraft and carrier, since he believed the Navy would be remiss in its planning if it did not conduct studies "looking towards the exhausting of all the possibilities of carrier aviation."[24] Sullivan was concerned about the costs associated with the new carrier and aircraft, but, on being assured that no expenditure of funds was contemplated at present, on 23 January he approved the studies pending a six-month progress report.[25] Two weeks later the CNO directed the DCNO (Air) to proceed with a detailed design study of the 100,000-pound bomber and directed the DCNO (Logistics) to conduct a preliminary design study of the new carrier class.[26]

The Ship Characteristics Board (SCB) began studying the carrier problem using the 90,000-pound (100,000-pound fully loaded) ADR–42 BUAER design-study aircraft as a basis. Meanwhile BUSHIPS began its sketch designs for the ship, designated CVB–X.[27] So it could have some concrete aircraft characteristics to work from in January 1946, BUSHIPS's Preliminary Design Section based its estimates on the Navy's largest land-based bomber, the P2V patrol aircraft, which weighed 60,000 pounds and possessed a wing span of 100 feet. BUSHIPS completed its initial design study for the new carrier on 20 May 1946. According to this study, the CVB–X would have a standard displacement of 69,200 tons and a trial displacement of 82,000 tons. It would have an overall length of 1,190 feet and a beam of 130 feet. The maximum width of the flight deck would be 132 feet, enabling the carrier to operate twenty-four ADR–42 aircraft.[28] Since the study did not provide for a hangar deck, these aircraft would have to remain on the flight deck for maintenance and storage.

At this point CVB–X was intended to be a single-purpose, special-type carrier, designed solely for conducting atomic strikes with 100,000-pound, long-range attack aircraft.[29] As noted earlier, these Navy atomic strikes were to be directed against enemy targets of naval interest, air power targets on the periphery of the Soviet and Satellite territories, and retardation targets designed to slow Soviet advances into Western Europe and the Middle East. They were not intended to be directed against the Soviet urban-industrial complexes that were the primary objects of the Air Force's strategic air offensive. Because the CVB–X was to be a single-purpose ship, OP–03 had not specified the need for a hangar to store additional aircraft such as fighters. Fighter protection for the carrier was to be provided by the other, multipurpose CVs in the task force. In June 1946 Vice Admiral Forrest Sherman commented on this point:

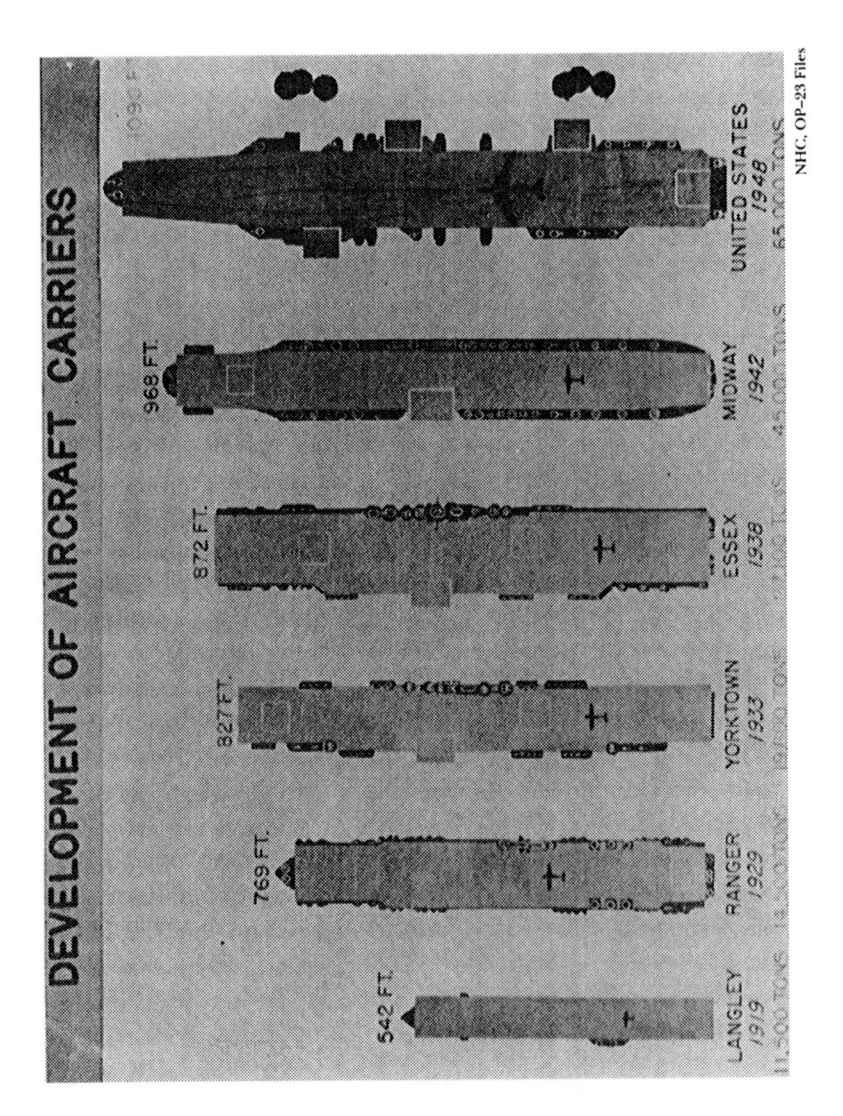

This chart shows a size comparison of various classes of Navy aircraft carriers from *Langley* to *United States*. It was an enclosure to the Navy memo submitted in April 1949 to Defense Secretary Louis Johnson in support of the flush-deck carrier program.

The Operations Division does not consider that any employment of this strictly offensive type will be warranted without far heavier fighter support and CAP [combat air patrol] than could be provided by fighters carried aboard. This ship would always be accompanied by at least two CV's. Accordingly, no sacrifice of primary characteristics is considered to be warranted in order to get fighters on the same bottom.[30]

This initial design was not for a true flush-deck carrier. BUSHIPS designers were concerned that a flush-deck design would create serious problems, both in handling stack gases from the ship's power plant and in ship control. Therefore the CVB–X design featured a small island with navigation, flag, and communication bridges and uptakes for the stack gases. The inclusion of an island proved a stumbling block to the aviators. They were concerned that an island of any size would reduce the effective width of the flight deck and thus place a restriction on the size of future aircraft.[31] They were reluctant to foreclose their options on such aircraft.[32]

In addition to the problem with the ship's island, the design of the ADR–42 aircraft had not progressed sufficiently to provide enough data for planning the details of ship construction, such as the strength of the flight deck.[33] On 18 July 1946, the DCNO (Air) recommended to the Vice Chief of Naval Operations that the redesignated 6A carrier[34] not be included in the fiscal year 1948 shipbuilding program but be funded as a design study instead.[35] This recommendation was followed.

The Bureau of Aeronautics design conceptualization of the ADR–42 was also progressing. By late 1946 the ADR–42 was envisioned as a swept-wing aircraft some 87 feet in length and 32 feet in height (28 feet with the tail folded), with a wing span of 110 feet.[36] The wings would be folded for stowage of the aircraft. It was to be powered by four De Laval turbine engines hung in nacelles (or "pods") under the wings. The ADR–42 was projected as having a top speed (Vmax) in excess of 440 knots (506 mph) at 40,000 feet, a cruising speed in excess of 350 knots (403 mph), and a combat radius of 2,000 nautical miles.[37]

By early 1947 the design for a flush-deck carrier was making good progress. On 13 February the SCB produced the first tentative set of proposed characteristics for the 6A carrier. The carrier was to have a hangar of sufficient clearance to accept the largest aircraft in its air group. For planning purposes the air group for this carrier was to consist of either twelve to eighteen ADR–45A attack aircraft—a smaller, 57,000-pound, 750-nautical-mile-radius plane—and fifty-four XF2D–1 fighters or twelve ADR–42 attack aircraft and fifty-four XF2D–1s.[38]

On 20 June 1947 the SCB submitted a recommended Shipbuilding and Conversion Program for fiscal year 1949 to the CNO. It accorded priority 2 to the Project 6A carrier. Five days later the CNO forwarded the SCB's rec-

National Archives 80-G-706108

Artist's conception of *United States* by Bruno Figallo, October 1948. The aircraft are not drawn to scale. For example, the fighter aircraft shown taking off and those taxiing to the forward starboard catapult, which vaguely resemble McDonnell FH-1 Phantoms, are depicted as if they were almost as large as North American AJ-1 Savage heavy attack aircraft.

ommendation to the General Board, which held a hearing on 23 July. During this hearing Admiral Robert Carney told the General Board that the question of the Navy's aircraft carriers was considered by the Ship Characteristics Board to be "one of the most vital factors in the maintenance of seapower." Also, in light of aircraft development trends, the continued effectiveness of the carrier weapon depended on modernizing the *Essex*-class carriers and initiating a replacement carrier program. Carney noted that the SCB was in favor of including the 6A carrier in the fiscal year 1949 program, so long as BUAER believed that its thinking on the limiting size and weight of future aircraft characteristics had crystallized sufficiently.[39] The General Board submitted its recommendations on the fiscal year 1949 program on 1 August, with the Project 6A carrier listed as priority 4.[40]

On 22 August Admiral Carney, as senior member of the SCB, submitted the board's proposed characteristics for the flush-deck carrier to the CNO, with the recommendation that they be approved (subject to revision) for the purpose of preparing preliminary plans by BUSHIPS. The 6A carrier was to have an estimated length (on the waterline) of 1,000 feet and a beam of 125 feet with a standard displacement of 60,000 tons.[41] The size of the carrier's air group was increased over the air group specified earlier, to a total of eighteen ADR-42 attack aircraft and eighty XF2D-1 fighters, with the option of substituting twenty-seven ADR-45A attack aircraft for the eighteen ADR-42s.[42]

The carrier characteristics were approved by the CNO on 2 September 1947. He submitted the fiscal year 1949 Shipbuilding and Conversion Program to the Secretary of the Navy that same day, with Project 6A assigned priority 2.[43] The program was approved by Acting Secretary W. John Kenney the following day.

The Ship Characteristics Board presented the fiscal year 1949 program to the Bureau of the Budget's Review Board on 24 October 1947. Although the Budget Review Board approved the program, it requested a written statement that the 6A carrier had been approved by the Joint Chiefs of Staff. However, after consultation between the interested parties in the department, Secretary of the Navy Sullivan decided that clearance with other defense agencies was not necessary and he so informed Budget Director James Webb.[44]

In hearings before the Bureau of the Budget on 16 December 1947, Webb informed the Navy that he was not in favor of the new 1949 Shipbuilding and Conversion Program because of the enormous cost already required for completion of the Navy's wartime shipbuilding program under Public Law 291 (1946).[45] After consultation with the CNO and the Secretary of Defense, Secretary Sullivan offered to stop work on certain vessels then under construction in order to assure sufficient funds to build the 6A carrier. Webb agreed to this arrangement. On 19 December he informed Sullivan by letter that President Truman had approved the modified 1949 shipbuilding program[46] with the understanding that work would be stopped on the battleship *Kentucky* (BB 66) and the large cruiser *Hawaii* (CB 3) and that the Navy would sponsor legislation to permit the work stoppage.[47]

When the Joint Chiefs of Staff met with Defense Secretary Forrestal at Key West to work out disagreements on roles and missions in March 1948, the flush-deck carrier was used in illustrating collateral service functions. The JCS agreed that while the Navy might not be able to establish a requirement for the carrier solely on the basis of its naval function, combining that with its contribution to strategic air warfare "might be enough to warrant its construction."[48] On 15 March Forrestal reported to President Truman on the results of the Key West meeting. He told Truman that agreement had been reached on allowing the Navy "to proceed with development of 80,000 ton carrier and development of HA [heavy attack] aircraft to carry heavy missiles [*sic*] therefrom."[49]

142   *Revolt of the Admirals*

NHC, OP-23 Files

Seakeeping model of an early design of *United States* under testing in the wave tank at the David Taylor Model Basin, Carderock, Maryland.

In May 1948 the Navy testified before Congress in support of its fiscal year 1949 program. In hearings before the House Navy Appropriations Subcommittee and the House Armed Services Committee, Secretary Sullivan and CNO Denfeld stated that the 6A carrier had received the approval of the JCS as well as that of the Secretary of Defense and the President.[50] When he was informed of this, newly retired Air Force Chief of Staff Carl Spaatz objected. He argued that the carrier project had not been referred to him or to the Joint Chiefs of Staff for decision.[51] Secretary Forrestal therefore requested that the JCS formally consider the flush-deck carrier. Vice Admiral John Dale Price, DCNO (Air), made the presentation on the 6A carrier to the JCS on 26 May 1948. Following consideration of the matter, three of the four members of the JCS—Admiral William D. Leahy, Chief of Staff to the Commander in Chief; General Omar N. Bradley, Army Chief of Staff; and Admiral Denfeld—approved the project. General Hoyt Vandenberg, the new Air Force Chief of Staff, refused to approve it. He argued that since the budgets of the three armed services had been prepared on a unilateral basis, he could neither ap-

Super Carriers and B–36 Bombers 143

NHC, OP-23 Files

The *United States* model under testing at David Taylor. The representative air group appears to be composed of Vought F7U Cutlass fighters and large attack aircraft vaguely resembling Douglas A3D Skywarriors without their underwing engine nacelles.

prove nor disapprove one part of a single service's budget without a thorough consideration of the budgets of all three services.[52]

Whatever the Air Force's viewpoint may have been, President Truman believed that the issue of the flush-deck carrier had been settled. When Captain William G. Lalor, Secretary of the JCS, took the memorandum on the 6A carrier to Leahy, the admiral told him:

> I mentioned to the President this morning something of the discussions we had yesterday afternoon about the 6A carrier. The President said that he was under the impression that the Joint Chiefs of Staff in commenting to him on the 1949 budgets had approved the construction of the 6A carrier. Further, the President stated that he had recently called in those fellows on this business of presenting a united front to these questions and that *he expected that that would be done.*[53]

OPNAV had originally planned to build four 6A carriers, beginning one in each of four successive fiscal years (1949 through 1952). OPNAV expected that all four would be operational by fiscal year 1955 and would

TABLE 5. *Original Program—Project 6A Carrier*

	Building	Operational
Fiscal year 1949	1	—
Fiscal year 1950	2	—
Fiscal year 1951	3	—
Fiscal year 1952	3	1
Fiscal year 1953	—	2
Fiscal year 1954	—	3
Fiscal year 1955	—	4

SOURCE: Taken from memo, RADM W. F. Boone, ACNO (Strategic Plans), to OP–34, OP–30 X ser 098P30, 19 Jul 1948, box 244, Strategic Plans, OA.

provide the long-range offensive backbone for four carrier task groups.[54] Indeed in April 1948 the Ship Characteristics Board had drawn up a proposed Shipbuilding and Conversion Program for fiscal year 1950 that included the second 6A carrier.[55] However, in the course of testimony before the subcommittee of the Senate Appropriations Committee, Secretary Sullivan told the senators that the fiscal year 1949 6A carrier was to be a prototype: "I think it would be a very great mistake for us to build any more of these big carriers until this one that we now propose be completed and operated."[56] This statement, which apparently had not been coordinated with OPNAV, effectively killed the 6A carrier being planned for the fiscal year 1950 shipbuilding program.

Sullivan was likely reflecting the view held by Forrestal—that the Navy could expect to retain support for the flush-deck carrier only by selling it as a prototype design that would be thoroughly tested before any others were requested.[57] In OPNAV, perplexed planners from OP–03 and OP–05 started casting about for a way to maintain the momentum of the Navy's overall carrier program. At the beginning of August 1948 the Chief of Naval Operations sent a memorandum to the Secretary of the Navy stating that the Project 6A carrier program should be resumed at the "earliest possible time" in order to provide a total of four ships of this class.[58]

Congress authorized construction of the 6A carrier as part of the fiscal year 1949 program and appropriated the initial money for its construction in Public Law 753 on 24 June 1948.[59] On 22 July the Secretary of the Navy approved a new naval vessel classification for the Project 6A aircraft carrier—CVA (Heavy Aircraft Carrier)—and assigned the first 6A carrier the classification CVA 58.[60] The following day President Truman authorized construction of several ships, including CVA 58.[61]

After many months of effort by the Navy Department, it looked as though it was going to get the large aircraft carrier that would enable car-

OP-23 Files, OA

The *United States* model under testing at David Taylor. Three large 90,000-pound attack aircraft are shown on the flight deck—one spotted on the centerline catapult, one taxiing from the aft starboard elevator, and one parked on the fantail. Note the water breaking over the ship's bow, an indication of a high-speed test run.

rier aviation to keep pace with the increased size and weight of aircraft in the jet age. The Navy had approached the flush-deck carrier program in a slow, deliberate manner, and its cautious, step-by-step approach appeared to have worked. In July 1948 the Navy's leaders were not unaware that powerful forces continued to be arrayed against the construction of the 6A carrier, but they thought that proper handling of the issue would continue to hold these forces at bay. Time was to prove this assumption wrong.

The B–36 Bomber

Air Corps planning for the intercontinental bomber that eventually became the B–36 first began in the spring of 1941, some eight months before the Japanese attack on Pearl Harbor.[62] At that time the Air Corps was concerned that a defeat of Great Britain by Nazi Germany would leave the United States to face the Axis Powers alone, without European allies and with no bases outside the Western Hemisphere from which to project its military power across the Atlantic. Foreseeing a significant requirement for a bomber capable of carrying a heavy bomb load from the continental United States to Europe, the Air Corps initiated a design competition for an intercontinental bomber on 11 April 1941.[63] Consolidated Aircraft and Boeing were invited to submit preliminary design studies for such a plane.

In the wake of Germany's June 1941 invasion of the Soviet Union the interest by the Army Air Forces in an intercontinental bomber was heightened. At a 19 August meeting Robert Lovett, Assistant Secretary of War for Air; Major General George H. Brett, Chief of the Air Corps; and senior members of the Air Staff agreed to push the intercontinental bomber project. The revised preliminary military characteristics called for an aircraft possessing a 10,000-mile range (providing an effective combat radius of 4,000 miles with a 10,000-pound bomb load), a 40,000-foot ceiling, and a cruising speed of 240 to 300 miles per hour.[64] On 3 October 1941 Consolidated's design was chosen from among the preliminary designs submitted. Two weeks later Major General Hap Arnold, Army Air Forces Chief, approved the procurement of two experimental models of Consolidated Aircraft's intercontinental bomber, designated the B–36.

By mid summer of 1942 Consolidated had progressed far enough on the aircraft's development to suggest that the AAF place a contract for production aircraft.[65] Because an operational capability for the aircraft remained far in the future, at that point the AAF did not follow through on Consolidated's suggestion. A year later, however, in response to concerns about the lack of bases from which to launch a sustained bombing campaign against Japan, the AAF reevaluated the proposal of the renamed Consolidated Vultee Aircraft Corporation (Convair).[66] On 19 June 1943 General Arnold directed the procurement of 100 production B–36s, without waiting for the outcome of service tests on the experimental models under contract. Arnold decided that an early procurement decision would speed up the first deliveries of the production aircraft. Nevertheless he placed the order with the understanding that the contract would be cut back or canceled if excessive production difficulties were encountered with the aircraft. The first experimental model (XB–36) was scheduled for delivery in May 1944. The other 101 aircraft (including YB–36, the second experimental model) were to be delivered by the end of October 1946.[67]

During the next two years the B–36 program suffered from design problems and shifting AAF production priorities. The June 1943 specifications for the B–36 called for an aircraft with a 10,000-mile range and a 265,512-pound gross weight, carrying eleven crewmen, twenty 500-pound bombs and 18,881 gallons of fuel. Its estimated performance at this weight was a top speed of 369 mph at 30,000 feet, and an average

TABLE 6. *Projected Capability of VHB Groups*

Radius of Action (stat. mi.)	Tons of Bombs Per Group Per Month	
	B–36	B–29
3,000	2,496	—
2,000	4,320	—
1,500	5,616	3,744
1,000	—	912

SOURCE: Taken from AAF Office of Statistical Control, "Capabilities of VHB, HB, and M&LB Groups," SC–SS–1463, 1 Oct 1945, encl. to memo, COL Charles B. Thornton, Chief Office of Statistical Control, to GEN Spaatz, 4 Oct 1945, box 24, Spaatz Papers, MD–LC.

speed of 288 mph, with a service ceiling of 40,000 feet.[68] Increases in the aircraft's design weight and changes in engine design soon degraded the B–36's estimated performance, however. In July 1944 the AAF directed Consolidated to speed up its B–32 program at the expense of engineering effort on the B–36. Work continued on the B–36 but at a lower priority.[69] The projected production schedule slipped accordingly, and May 1944 passed with the XB–36 still months away from completion.

The war's end in August 1945 ironically provided impetus to an intercontinental bomber program that, by now, was four years old. The need for an intercontinental bomber was reaffirmed to AAF planners by the costs which had been paid for capturing the advanced Pacific bases needed for B–29 operations against Japan. Further, the planners realized that, in a future war, delivery of atomic bombs could not wait upon the seizure of advanced bases for operating shorter-ranged bombers.[70] On 9 August 1945 Lieutenant General Hoyt Vandenberg, Assistant Chief of Air Staff for Operations, Commitments and Requirements, recommended the formation of four B–36 Very Heavy Bomb groups to constitute an "effective, mobile task force" for the postwar AAF.[71] Earlier studies of bomber operating costs had led the Air Staff to recommend continuing Convair's 100-airplane B–36 contract on the grounds that the B–36 was the most efficient bomber for long-range missions.[72] Subsequent bomber capability studies also projected a superior performance by the B–36.

During the last half of 1945 and the first months of 1946, completion of the XB–36 continued to suffer from engineering and materiel delays. In July 1945 AAF inspectors found evidence of faulty workmanship and the use of substandard materials in the XB–36.[73] These deficiencies were gradually corrected by the contractor. In late March 1946, because of the continuing troubles with the B–36 program, the AAF Assistant Chief of Staff for Materiel (AC/AS-4), Major General Edward M. Powers, directed Lieutenant General Nathan F. Twining, Commanding General of the Air Materiel Command at Wright Field, to review the project. Twining was to furnish AC/AS-4 with an up-to-date summary of the project that could be presented to General Ira Eaker and General Spaatz. Among the items that Powers wanted explained were the thirty-mile-per-hour decrease in the airplane's high-speed requirement and a 20,000-pound increase in its weight from the initial estimates.[74] In a memorandum sent a week later, General Powers questioned Twining on changes made to the aircraft's radar bombing system that required reducing the plane's defensive armament. Powers stressed, "Since this airplane is relatively unmaneuverable and slow, it must incorporate *the maximum of defensive fire power*, as well as the best radar bombing equipment, if its primary mission is to be accomplished."[75]

The airplane finally rolled out of the plant on 1 June 1946. Engine run-up tests, in preparation for the XB-36's first flight, began on 12 June. The first flight of the XB-36 finally took place on 8 August 1946, more than two years after the aircraft had originally been scheduled for delivery to the AAF.

Despite the disturbing delays in the B-36 program, AAF leaders were determined to use the aircraft as part of the public relations effort to boost the American public's perception of Air Forces' strategic bombing capability. In late August 1946 after returning from a globe-circling tour of air installations, Assistant Secretary of War for Air Stuart Symington gave an interview to a reporter from the *St. Louis Globe-Democrat*. According to Symington, "Our new 10,000 mile bombers can fly easily across the North Pole and the Arctic Region. From bases in the continental U.S. or from our outlying bases, they can reach any of the capitals of industrial centers of Europe."[76] On 7 November 1946 the AAF Press Section of the War Department's Public Relations Division issued a press release extolling the new bomber, "The six-engine Consolidated-Vultee B-36 heavy bomber could carry an atomic bomb to any inhabited region in the world and return home without refueling in the event of an enemy attack."[77]

These boasts about the B-36's capabilities were not missed by interested people in the Navy Department. Undoubtedly both Hugh Hanson and Stuart Barber were intrigued to find that the AAF was pressing a claim for a bomber that was not in its operational inventory and that was, moreover, suffering serious development problems. The coming months found both men writing letters to the editors of local Washington papers, questioning the accuracy of these claims for the B-36.

Despite the public relations efforts, by late 1946 the outlook for the B-36 remained sufficiently discouraging that General George Kenney,

Commanding General of the Strategic Air Command, wrote to General Spaatz about the B–36's capabilities. Relying on SAC projections that the B–36's usable range would be only 6,500 miles, Kenney told Spaatz:

> A 3,000 mile radius operation with a 10,000 pound bomb load is not sufficient to permit the B–36 to reach and return from profitable targets in Europe and Asia from bases in the United States and Alaska. Further, the airplane is relatively slow and only moderately armed, making it a vulnerable target for fighters.[78]

Noting that the B–36 production airplane would be inferior in all respects except range to the B–50 (an upgraded B–29), Kenney suggested to Spaatz that the present B–36 contract might be curtailed to provide only a service-test quantity of B–36s. The savings from such a curtailment could then be spent on procuring a more modern bomber with greater range and speed potential.[79]

Air Materiel Command (AMC) was asked to comment on Kenney's proposal. General Twining acknowledged the plane's shortcomings, stating that many of them were "inherent in any design directed toward the fulfillment of extreme long range bombing." Nevertheless he noted that a number of highly successful aircraft, including the B–17, the P–47 and the B–29, would have been lost to the AAF if it had canceled these aircraft projects merely because marked design improvements could be made if new projects were initiated. Twining called for exerting every possible influence to ensure the continuation of the B–36 program; stressing that, while the B–36 was not the best solution that could be envisioned, it was "a workable solution, which is a solution in fact, not in vision."[80] Spaatz agreed strongly with Twining's views and wrote to Kenney that the B–36 contract would be continued in full.

AMC's principal concern regarding the B–36's design during 1947 was the attempt to increase its range and speed by upgrading its engines. In December 1946 AC/AS–4 had concurred in AMC's request to substitute Pratt & Whitney R–4360–41 3,500-horsepower (hp) engines for its R–4360–25 3,000-hp engines, starting with the twenty-third B–36A production aircraft. Under this decision, the last seventy-eight aircraft built under the 100-plane contract would be the modified B–36B aircraft. The more powerful water-injection engines in the B–36B would enable the bomber's gross weight to be increased to its structural limit of 328,000 pounds (from the present 278,000 pounds), thereby allowing it to carry the additional fuel necessary to approach its 10,000-mile range requirement. Furthermore, the new engines would increase the B–36's top speed by 13 mph (to 330.5 mph) and its cruising speed by 10 mph.[81]

In March 1947 Convair proposed that a more powerful version of the 4360 engine, fitted with a variable discharge turbine (VDT) already in development, be adapted for the B-36. The contractor estimated that the VDT engine would provide the bomber with a high speed of 410 mph, a cruising speed of 336 mph, a service ceiling of 45,000 feet, and a 10,000-mile range with a 10,000-pound bomb load.[82] The proposal was presented by Air Materiel Command officers at a staff conference in Washington on 25 March. Attending AAF officers turned down the proposal on the grounds that Research and Development funds were too limited to be spent on modernizing existing weapons.[83]

On 30 August the first production model B-36A was flown from Convair's Fort Worth, Texas, plant to Wright Field for delivery to AMC as a static test article.[84] Five days later Consolidated Vultee approached the Air Force with a proposal to install VDT engines in the last thirty-four B-36s at the cost of a five-plane reduction in the original contract and a six-month delay in the delivery of the final aircraft.[85] The modified aircraft was to be known as the B-36C. This proposal received immediate and serious consideration by the Air Staff.[86] Because the principal Air Force concern about the B-36 was the need to increase its speed, Convair's offer to install a much more powerful engine in the aircraft at little additional cost proved very tempting. So, despite some concerns expressed about Convair's optimistic schedule for delivery of the VDT-equipped aircraft, the Air Force approved the proposed change. In early December 1947 Vice Chief of Staff Hoyt Vandenberg directed Air Materiel Command to implement the proposal.[87]

During late 1947 and early 1948, however, SAC's Commanding General continued to be unenthusiastic about the capabilities of the B-36. On 3 November 1947 George Kenney informed Carl Spaatz that he was against the proposal for equipping the B-36 with the VDT engine because he believed the Convair claims were too optimistic. He thought the aircraft would be incapable of successfully performing its combat mission:

> There is no doubt in my mind that the B-50 would have a far greater chance in arriving at a fighter defended war-time target and returning to its base than the more vulnerable B-36c. In view of the limited numbers available of certain types of bombs [i.e., atomic weapons], it might be questionable whether or not it would be advisable to send them out on a combat mission in a bomber *whose chances of even getting to the target were small.*[88]

In late January 1948 Kenney wrote to General Spaatz, "At this weight [278,000 pounds—the B-36A aircraft's maximum weight] the maximum range with 10000 pounds of bombs is 8000 miles or 3000 miles operating radius. When loaded to a gross take-off weight of 328,000 pounds

Super Carriers and B–36 Bombers 151

National Air and Space Museum, Smithsonian Institution, 34735

Secretary of the Air Force Stuart Symington and General Hoyt Vandenberg, Air Force Chief of Staff, September 1948.

the maximum range [of the B–36B] is only increased to 9300 miles as by that time they are burning gasoline to carry gasoline."[89] Kenney's negative opinion of the aircraft was further strengthened when the B–36 VDT-engine program proved to be unexpectedly short in duration.

In mid-April 1948, following an engineering conference at Fort Worth attended by representatives from Air Material Command, Convair, and the other contractors, Consolidated Vultee submitted new data on engine-cooling requirements to AMC. Based on recomputation of these requirements Convair's estimates of aircraft performance with the VDT engine were reduced significantly. The B–36C's cruising speed was lowered by 60 mph from the earlier estimate and its maximum range was decreased by more than 1,800 miles.[90] These reductions made the projected B–36C inferior to the B–36B. On 21 April 1948 General Joseph T. McNarney, Air Materiel Command's new chief, recommended cancellation of the VDT modification and reevaluation of the B–36 program. McNarney provided the Air Force Chief of Staff with four alternatives for the program: 1) revert to the original program by reinstating B–36Bs for the final thirty-four aircraft; 2) cancel the last thirty-four aircraft; 3) terminate the contract at the forty-first B–36 airplane (leaving the Air Force with eighteen operational B–36Bs and twenty-two operational B–36As); or 4) cancel the entire program except for the twenty-two aircraft that were essentially shop-completed.[91]

In response to General McNarney's letter, Lieutenant General Lauris Norstad, Deputy Chief of Staff, Operations, sent a memorandum on 24 April to Lieutenant General H. A. Craig, Deputy Chief of Staff, Materiel, that called for terminating B–36 construction at sixty-one aircraft (McNarney's second alternative). According to Norstad, this would provide the Air Force with one Heavy Bomber Group equipped with B–36Bs. The B–36As would be used for transition and training, with possible later conversion to tanker aircraft.[92] General Craig concurred with General Norstad's recommendation.

On 21 May 1948 senior Air Force officers met with Secretary Symington to decide the fate of the B–36 program. The new Air Force Chief of Staff, Hoyt Vandenberg, General McNarney, and Major General K. B. Wolfe, AMC's Director of Procurement and Industrial Planning, came into the meeting favoring cancellation of the program after the sixty-first airplane. Arthur S. Barrows, Air Force Under Secretary, and Lieutenant General Muir Fairchild, Vice Chief of Staff, favored continuation of the full program. After discussion, the conferees agreed to cancel the VDT engine for the B–36 and to accept at least sixty-one of the ninety-five aircraft under contract. However, the group decided to defer a decision on the fate of the final thirty-four aircraft for two weeks, giving Secretary Symington time to visit Convair's Fort Worth plant to see the B–36 for himself.[93]

Stuart Symington's 26 May visit to Fort Worth marked the turning point for the B–36 program. Symington watched the B–36 perform a short take off and landing and was shown performance figures for the untested B–36B model aircraft that convinced him it was a good airplane. He was particularly impressed by the as-yet-unconfirmed information that the B–36 would be capable of operating at 40,000 feet.[94] Following his inspection he immediately dictated a memorandum to Secretary Forrestal, expressing his support for the B–36 and deriding recent criticisms of the airplane that had appeared in the press.[95] Symington followed up this first memorandum to Forrestal with another, hand-delivered on 5 June, in which he remarked,

> I personally investigated the operation incident to the production of this ship at Fort Worth and was much impressed with what I saw, including the fact that unless there are further engineering changes, the ... [B–36's performance] *will be within the original estimate, this despite all the changes that have been made to date.*[96]

Super Carriers and B–36 Bombers 153

The Consolidated Vultee B–36A intercontinental bomber, March 1948. Powered by six pusher-type, 28-cylinder, 18,000-hp Pratt & Whitney Wasp Major engines, the huge aircraft had a wingspan of 230 feet, a length of 163 feet, and a gross weight of 278,000 pounds.

By this time Symington had apparently decided the full B–36 program should go forward. He was certain that much, if not most, of the public criticism of the aircraft was coming from sources connected in one way or another to the Navy, and he was determined to defend the program from such attacks.[97] In an undated memorandum dictated in June 1949, Symington recalled, "I remember that some [of the anti-B–36 letters to the editor] were signed by 'Diogenes' [one of Stuart Barber's pen names] and others by a man named Hanson, whom I subsequently was informed was an employee of the Navy."[98]

While Secretary Symington appeared to be satisfied with the heavy bomber, many of the Air Force's senior officers still needed to be convinced of the B–36's operational suitability. On 15 June 1948 the Secretary met with his top military and civilian advisers to make a final decision on the future of the program. The group reviewed envelope curves (graphs showing aircraft performance under different conditions), which had been prepared by Convair, comparing the B–36B with the B–50 and the B–54 (a modernized B–50 equipped with the VDT engine).[99] The comparison showed the B–36 to be superior to the B–50 in cruising speed at long range and capable of far greater combat range than either the B–50 or the B–54. Although the B–54 possessed a higher maximum speed over the target than the B–36, overall the comparison showed the B–36 to be "well qualified" for its designed mission.[100] At a follow-up meeting on 24 June, Symington, Norstad, Kenney, and several others reviewed the program a final time. Air Materiel Command had affirmed the performance data. Following discussion of economic concerns related to the B–36 contract, and with recent Soviet actions over Berlin as an unavoidable backdrop to the decision, the group unanimously agreed to continue the B–36 contract through the full ninety-five aircraft.[101]

Two days after the final decision on the B–36 contract was made, the Strategic Air Command received its first five B–36A aircraft, which were to be used for training and crew conversion.[102] With more B–36s available in the second half of 1948, the Air Force was finally getting a chance to evaluate aircraft performance based on accumulated operational flight data.[103] Following the B–36A's third maximum range flight on 18–19 July 1948—designed to test its performance while flying a B–29/B–50-type bombing mission—Major General Powers found it necessary to restrain Secretary Symington's enthusiasm for the B–36 as the answer to most of the service's bombing needs. Responding to Symington's question of whether the B–36 was better than the B–50 or B–29, Powers noted:

> The B–36 accomplished the B–50—B–29 5,000 nautical mile type mission at better speed and altitude than those planes, *however, it is an extravagant way of doing the job*. Over twice the fuel, five or six more crew members, greater logistical support, etc. are needed. We need B–50's for the 5,000 mile job and the B–36's for the 7,000.[104]

The B–36 was proving more successful than had been expected just a few months before, but by no means had it turned into a "wonder weapon." Even though the aircraft's high-altitude capability was being demonstrated in flight tests and its long-range performance was deemed acceptable, if not yet up to contract requirements, the Air Force continued to be concerned about its speed over the target. The B–36B's maximum speed of 376 mph might have been acceptable in the World War II days of reciprocating-engine fighters, but it was another thing entirely in the postwar era of jet fighters with maximum speeds of over 600 mph.

One fix for this problem—the VDT engine—had already been tried and failed. In October 1948 Consolidated Vultee proposed another solution—mounting two paired General Electric turbojet engines under each wing of the B–36 aircraft. The self-contained installations, with each pair of GE J–47 engines enclosed in a separate nacelle, would provide jet assist to boost the aircraft's maximum speed over the target from 376 mph to 435 mph.[105] This was of particular interest to the Air Force, because even a moderate boost in speed over target would help to reduce the bomber's vulnerability to the new Russian jet fighters and interceptors.

Table 7. *B–36 Selected Performance Data, 1941–1949*

	Contract Spec.	Convair Claim AMC Est.	(B–36B) B–36B	B–36A AMC Est.
Range (stat. mi.) [1]	10,000	10,000	9,700 [2]	10,000 [3]
Combat radius (stat. mi.) [1]	4,000	4,600	3,881 [4]	4,272 [5]
Combat ceiling (ft)	40,000 [6]	40,000	35,800	37,500
Average cruising speed (mph)	240–300	—	218	222
Maximum speed at optimum altitude (mph)	369	382	345	376

[1] With 10,000-pound bomb load.
[2] Combat range—7,277 stat. mi.
[3] Combat range—7,998 stat. mi.
[4] Combat radius based on *combat* range (7,277 stat. mi. x .40)—2,910 stat. mi.
[5] Combat radius based on *combat* range (7,998 stat. mi. x .4272)—3,417 stat. mi.
[6] Service Ceiling

SOURCES: The data used for the contract specifications are from the discussion of the 19 August 1941 "Revised Military Characteristics" in Marcelle S. Knaack, *Encyclopedia of U.S. Aircraft and Missile Systems*, vol. 2, *Post–World War II Bombers, 1945–1973* (Washington: Office of Air Force History, USAF, 1988), 6; and Meyers K. Jacobsen and Ray Wagner, *B–36 in Action* (Carrollton, TX: Squadron/Signal Publications, 1980), 5. The data dealing with Convair's claimed performance of the B–36B are from a typescript Air Force briefing (with charts) titled "The Intercontinental Bomber—the B–36," n.d. [early 1949], 10, box 157, Cabinet File, President's Secretary's File, Truman Library. The data used for the portion of the table dealing with AMC's estimates of B–36A and B–36B performance are taken from B–36 performance data sheets attached to memo, MAJ G. S. Curtis, Jr., Office of the Director, Research and Development, AMC, to COL Garman, HQ USAF, S–57609–A, 29 Jun 1949, box 27, Strategic Air Group, RG 341, NA. The figures for range in statute miles and speed in miles per hour were derived by recomputation from the figures for nautical miles and knots given in the original document.

NOTE: The maximum speed (at sea level) of the Soviet MiG–15 fighter that became operational in late 1948 exceeded 660 mph, and its service ceiling was 50,000 feet.[106]

At this juncture the Air Force staged a major press demonstration of the B–36B, apparently to sell the airplane to the public. At the presentation, in which senior Air Force representatives participated, the aircraft's capabilities were significantly overstated. For example, the totally unfounded assertion was made that the B–36B bombers were "capable of delivering atomic bombs over a 12,000 mile range."[107]

Because the J–47 engine had already been developed for use in the B–47 bomber program, Convair expected that the prototype installation could be accomplished within four months. The chief drawback of the proposal was that the jet engines would have to be installed after com-

Convair's February 1949 conception of the jet pod-equipped B–36D. Note that the engine nacelles have been painted on a retouched photograph of a B–36B by a company artist.

pletion of the airplane, since production of the remaining B–36 aircraft was too advanced to incorporate the change on the assembly line.

After examining additional information from the contractor, AMC decided that the proposal was promising and subsequently recommended a prompt decision on procurement of a prototype.[108] However, while the matter was under study, events conspired to delay a decision. A board of officers that convened in November to review the service's requirements for reconnaissance aircraft recommended the modification of a number of B–36Bs into reconnaissance aircraft.[109] This recommendation took precedence over the proposal to mount jet engines on the bombers.

The following month administration budgetary restrictions forecast for fiscal year 1950 necessitated the revision of the Air Force's entire aircraft procurement program.[110] It was not until mid-January 1949 that a decision was made to procure thirty-two B–36B aircraft equipped with jet pods and the K–1 bombing system.[111] And another nineteen months would pass before the service could accept the first of these improved bombers, designated B–36Ds.[112]

Thus although the B–36's future was improving, by 1949 a great deal still remained to be done to enable the bomber to meet important aspects of its original contract specifications and the increased demands of the jet era. Consolidated Vultee's bomber was an aging, wartime-design airplane with a number of serious weaknesses, but in the years since 1946 its development had become extremely important to the Air Force. It was now the only intercontinental bomber available to the service in the near term. And SAC was increasingly concerned over the potential vulnerability to Soviet air attack of the overseas bases required for launching strikes with the shorter-ranged B–29 and B–50 bombers. Air Force leaders were aware that new bomber designs, such as the intercontinental-range XB–52, promised to far surpass the B–36 in capability, but such designs took time to mature. And they believed that it was vital to keep the B–36 program on track during the interim if SAC was to carry out its responsibilities under the existing war plans.

Conclusions

By the end of 1948 the Navy and the Air Force had each staked a significant portion of its plans for increased near-term offensive capabilities on a single expensive and technically complex weapon system. Each program had endured the vagaries of initial design troubles. Each had surmounted the problem of maintaining support during stages in the development process when there was little concrete data to reassure decision makers of the program's success. Nonetheless, neither program escaped these trials unscathed.

In large part because the 6A carrier and the B–36 bomber were highly visible examples of their services' differing strategic perspectives, they became increasingly important targets for attack by the other services. Yet as 1949 began, few could foresee the tremendous battering that both programs would undergo in the coming months.

Chapter 6

A Time of Crisis and Change

The fall of 1948 and the winter of 1948–1949 were for the Truman administration times of continuing crises in the international arena. Western access to Berlin continued to be the most serious concern. From the peak of tension reached in September 1948, however, the Berlin crisis gradually began easing. At the end of January 1949 Joseph Stalin indicated that the Soviet Union would be willing to resume direct negotiations on the issue, and secret talks eventually led to the May 1949 ending of the blockade.

Yet even as the U.S.-Soviet conflict over Berlin appeared to be diminishing after January 1949, events in China were looming ever larger for the U.S. government. The American-supported Nationalist armies of Chiang Kai-shek's Kuomintang government had long since lost the military initiative to Mao Tse-tung's Communist forces. By the end of 1948 Chiang's troops in northern China had been destroyed and the Communists had seized the major cities north of the Yangtze River. In April 1949 the Communist armies began their long-anticipated invasion of southern China by crossing the Yangtze and quickly capturing the Kuomintang capital of Nanking. With the Nationalists' capital in their hands and Chiang's armies reeling southward in defeat, the Chinese Communists' final victory in China appeared to be only a few months away.[1]

While these events were occurring overseas, the U.S. military services were engaged in a continuing battle of their own—the fight over the fiscal year 1950 defense budget. This battle was only the latest manifestation of military frustrations over an increasingly downward-moving defense-budgeting roller coaster that the armed services had been on since the end of the war. The Navy's funding in particular had suffered at the hands of both the Truman administration and Congress for several years.

For fiscal year 1947 the Navy had originally proposed a budget of $6.325 billion.[2] This was to have provided a Navy of 500,000 personnel, with 319 major combatant ships and 12,000 aircraft.[3] The Bureau of the Budget and the President cut this figure to $4.225 billion.[4] This amount provided for only 437,000 personnel with 291 major combatants and

8,851 aircraft.⁵ Congress in turn voted to scale the figure back by some $125 million, to $4.1 billion.⁶

The Navy's fiscal year 1948 budget told an even more woeful tale. The department submitted a budget of $5.790 billion to the Bureau of the Budget. It was to provide for 515,000 personnel, with 279 major combatants and 6,130 operating aircraft. After extensive hearings in the fall of 1946 the Bureau notified the Navy that its fiscal year 1948 budget was to be $3.952 billion (including $170 million in contract authority for aircraft and $127.8 million in new money and contract authority for Public Works slated for later submission as a 1948 supplemental appropriation). As submitted to Congress in early 1947 (without the monies for aircraft procurement and Public Works), the Navy budget stood at only $3.654 billion.⁷

The House Naval Appropriations Subcommittee proved unsympathetic to even this reduced funding request, in large part because its pro-Navy chairman, Representative Harry R. Sheppard (D–Calif.), had been succeeded by Charles A. Plumley (R–Vt.), a man who saw economy and efficiency as the watchwords for postwar spending. Under Plumley's leadership the House cut almost $400 million from the Navy's request. Following Senate action that increased the funding slightly, the final sum appropriated by Congress for the Navy for fiscal year 1948 was $3.3 billion.⁸

For its fiscal year 1949 budget the Navy Department originally estimated that it would need $5.393 billion to meet its requirements. However, it was operating under a Truman-imposed policy that the ceiling for fiscal year 1949 could not exceed the level provided by Congress for fiscal year 1948. Accordingly, the Navy submitted a request for $3.667 billion to the Secretary of Defense.⁹ The figure for Navy Department appropriations that was eventually transmitted to Congress was $3.511 billion.¹⁰

From mid-February to early March 1948, while Navy witnesses were testifying on their fiscal year 1949 budget, events in Europe changed the defense budget picture. On 25 February the Communists seized power in Czechoslovakia. Just a week later, on 5 March, General Lucius D. Clay, U.S. Military Governor in Germany, sent a "war warning" message to Washington, stating that war with the Soviet Union might come "with dramatic suddenness."¹¹ Under guidance from Defense Secretary James Forrestal, the services began drawing up plans for a supplemental budget request within a few days. Harry Truman finally allowed the National Military Establishment to submit a Supplemental Estimate of Appropriation to Congress totaling just under $3.1 billion.¹² The Navy's portion was to be approximately $710 million of this amount.¹³

Table 8. *Navy Operating Forces, Fiscal Years 1947–1949*

	Maximum Wartime	FY 1947	FY 1948	FY 1949
Major combatants	1,307	291	288	293
Attack carriers	20	15	11	11
Light and escort carriers	78	11	9	10
Battleships	24	6	4	1[1]
Cruisers	96	39	30	31
Destroyers	445	182	154	160
Submarines	259	80	80	80
CV/CVB groups	53	15	13	24
Patrol squadrons	113	42	34	34
Marine squadrons	132	28	23	31
Operating aircraft [2]	24,000	6,130	5,793	8,035
Personnel (Navy & Marine Corps)				
Officers	375,359	62,000	49,019	57,540
Enlisted	3,611,022	600,000	475,000	494,460
Total military personnel [3]	3,986,381	662,000	524,019	552,000

[1] Reduced complement.
[2] Excludes Naval Air Reserve and Civilian Component aircraft.
[3] Excludes one-year Navy and Marine Corps enlistees, Continuous Active Duty USN and USMC Reserve personnel, and Aviation Cadets.

SOURCES: OP–31 R, "Location of US Naval Aircraft," No. 15 45, 7 Apr 1945, 14–18, 38–41, and No. 16 45, 14 Apr 1945, 14–18, 39–42; OP–03 4R, "Location of US Naval Aircraft," No. 32 45, 4 Aug 1945, 1–8, and "Location of US Aircraft," No. 37 45, 7 Sep 1945, 1–8, all in box 192, WW II Command File, OA; Office of Budget & Reports, Navy Department, "1949 Budget Review," 22 Aug 1947, box 7, Top Policy Correspondence, RG 80, NA; Table B in "Information with reference to Fiscal Year 1948 Navy Budget Estimates," n.d. [early Feb 1947], encl. to ltr, SECNAV Forrestal to Senator Charles Gurney, OP–001B Ser 012P001, 7 Feb 1947, box 7, Top Policy Correspondence, RG 80, NA; "U.S. Navy Summary of Programs," 1949, box 3, Denfeld Double Zero Files, OA; "Brief of Operating Forces," n.d. [mid-1951], box 7, Sherman Papers, OA; Robert Sherrod, *History of Marine Corps Aviation in World War II* (Washington, 1952), 434.

NOTE: Numbers from different sources do not always agree.

Despite the worsened international situation the Navy's fiscal year 1949 budget again suffered at the hands of both Plumley's subcommittee and the House of Representatives. Even after some of the House budget cuts were restored by Senate action in the House-Senate conference committee, the Navy's appropriations stood at only $3.75 billion.[14] Moreover, five weeks before the Navy Department appropriations bill was passed, President Truman informed Forrestal, the service secretaries, and the service chiefs that during fiscal year 1949 the services could not increase their

TABLE 9. *Defense Budgets, for Fiscal Years 1948–1950*
(*in billions of dollars*)

	1948	1949	1950
OSD	—	.007	.011
ARMY	4.562	4.217	4.420
NAVY	3.935	4.924	4.183
AIR FORCE	1.260	4.793	4.433
Total	9.757	13.941	13.923

SOURCE: Kenneth W. Condit, *History of the Office of the Joint Chiefs of Staff*, Vol. 2, *1947–1949* (Washington, 1978), Appendix II, 555.

NOTE: New Obligational Authority for Military Purposes.

personnel or build their force structures in a manner that would require more than $15 billion to maintain during fiscal year 1950.[15] Thus, the military buildup was capped before it had even started.

Skirmishing over the fiscal year 1950 budget began in July 1948 when President Truman imposed a limit of $14.4 billion on the new defense budget—a figure far below the amount the military services considered necessary to maintain the forces required to carry out their responsibilities in the event of war with the Soviet Union. Each of the services based its budget request on what it believed was necessary for the country's security. But, to a greater or lesser extent, each service had a different strategic outlook that influenced its views on the types and combination of forces required. In the ensuing attempts by Secretary Forrestal and the Joint Chiefs of Staff to bring the National Military Establishment's budget figure into line with the President's, each service's programs thus came under question by the other services.[16] During this process the size of the Navy's force of aircraft carriers came under particular attack by the Air Force and the Army.[17] By November and December 1948 it was evident to the Navy's leadership that the service's fights with the Air Force (and to a lesser extent with the Army) over differing perspectives on strategy, procurement programs, and defense funding were likely to be even more intense in 1949. An additional factor that some senior naval officers found unsettling was a subtle change in James Forrestal's attitude toward the Navy. Even as SECNAV, he had most valued those officers who supported his own opinions. As Defense Secretary he had struggled unceasingly during 1947 and 1948 to get the service chiefs behind a unified defense budget, but to little avail. As General Dwight Eisenhower noted, Forrestal held a "terrific, almost tragic, disappointment in the failures of professional [military] men to 'get together.'"[18]

The Chief of Naval Operations in conference with senior Navy officers, June 1948. Left to right: Admiral Richard L. Conolly, CINCNELM; Admiral Dewitt C. Ramsey, CINCPAC/CINCPACFLT; Vice Admiral Arthur W. Radford, VCNO; Admiral Louis E. Denfeld, CNO; and Captain Howard A. Yeager, Executive Assistant and Aide to the CNO.

As the defense budget outlook worsened during 1948, the Joint Chiefs of Staff were forced to place ever greater reliance in their war planning on the strategic air offensive, at the expense of conventional forces. Navy leaders were invariably the least inclined to go along on this strategy without a fight. The resulting impression that the Navy's uniformed leadership was thwarting SECDEF's attempts at unifying the National Military Establishment's budgetary and planning processes was strengthened by the steady barrage of anti-Navy complaints and accusations directed to Forrestal in Eyes Only memoranda from Air Force Secretary Stuart Symington.[19] The outcome was an inevitable decrease in Forrestal's personal confidence in and regard for the Navy's senior officers. To a beleaguered James Forrestal it was as if he was being deserted by his own people. After talks with the Secretary in February 1949, Eisenhower confided in his diary:

Air Force Secretary Stuart Symington at a press conference, November 1947. The man to Symington's right is Steve Leo.

At one time he accepted unequivocally and supported vigorously the navy "party line," given him by the admirals. Only today he said to me, "In the army there are many that I trust—Bradley, Collins, Gruenther, Wedemeyer, and Lemnitzer and Lutes, to name only a few. In the navy I think of only Sherman and Blandy among the higher ones. Possibly Conolly, also."[20]

In addition to the budget wrangling, the costly compromises on roles and missions, reached during 1948 at Key West and Newport, were subject to all the stresses of continuing service antagonisms in a time of straitened defense spending. John Sullivan and Louis Denfeld were convinced that a way needed to be found to unite the Navy in an effort to maintain its fundamental beliefs and purposes against unwarranted assaults by the other services.

The Establishment of OP–23

In mid-December 1948 the Secretary's Committee on Unification (UNICOM) was dissolved by the Secretary of the Navy following an unfortunate incident in which a letter prepared for the signature of a senior official in the department was leaked to the press.[21] UNICOM, which had replaced the unofficial organization SCOROR, had functioned since June 1948 as the Navy Department's central agency for coordinating departmental action on "unification problems relative to Navy basic concepts, doctrines and policies."[22]

With UNICOM dissolved, the Secretary of the Navy and the Chief of Naval Operations saw a need for an organization to carry on the coordination of unification matters and, at the same time, bring a renewed sense of purpose to the Navy's efforts in this area. Marine Brigadier General Samuel R. Shaw recalled how he first became involved in this process:

> I got a call one afternoon from Headquarters [Marine Corps] and [was] told to come up and see the Commandant.... So I went up there [from Quantico] and sat in on this conference, and [General Clifton B.] Cates did all the talking. He said he'd spent several conferences with the Secretary of the Navy and Denfeld.... And they were determined that something had to be done to get the Navy back into believing in itself.[23]

Cates told Shaw that Sullivan and Denfeld had rejected the idea that the new organization be simply another SCOROR under the control of the Secretary of the Navy. Instead they decided the new, strengthened organization should be put under the CNO. They further decided that the head of this new organization would have to be a naval officer who could garner the support of the service.

Sullivan and Denfeld eventually settled on Captain Arleigh A. Burke as their choice for the job.[24] Burke, a highly decorated combat veteran of World War II, was a noted destroyerman who had served during the final two years of the Pacific war as Chief of Staff to Admiral Marc Mitscher, the preeminent commander of the Fast Carrier Task Force. He was known to have the admiration and respect of both the surface officers and the naval aviators. His work in the postwar period, particularly while serving on the General Board, had demonstrated his ability to analyze problems, formulate solutions, and write clearly on major issues of importance to the Navy.[25] To Sullivan and Denfeld, Burke was just the man for the job.

Captain Burke, the commanding officer of the light cruiser *Huntington* (CL 107), was on board his ship in the Philadelphia Navy Yard a day or so before Christmas when he received a telephone call from Rear Admiral Charles Wellborn, Jr., DCNO (Administration). Admiral Burke recalled, "Without any preliminary conversation except to say he was glad I was back in the States again, he said it was necessary that I report in Washington just as soon as possible."[26] To his dismay Burke found out

Office of the Chief of Naval Operations, January 1949

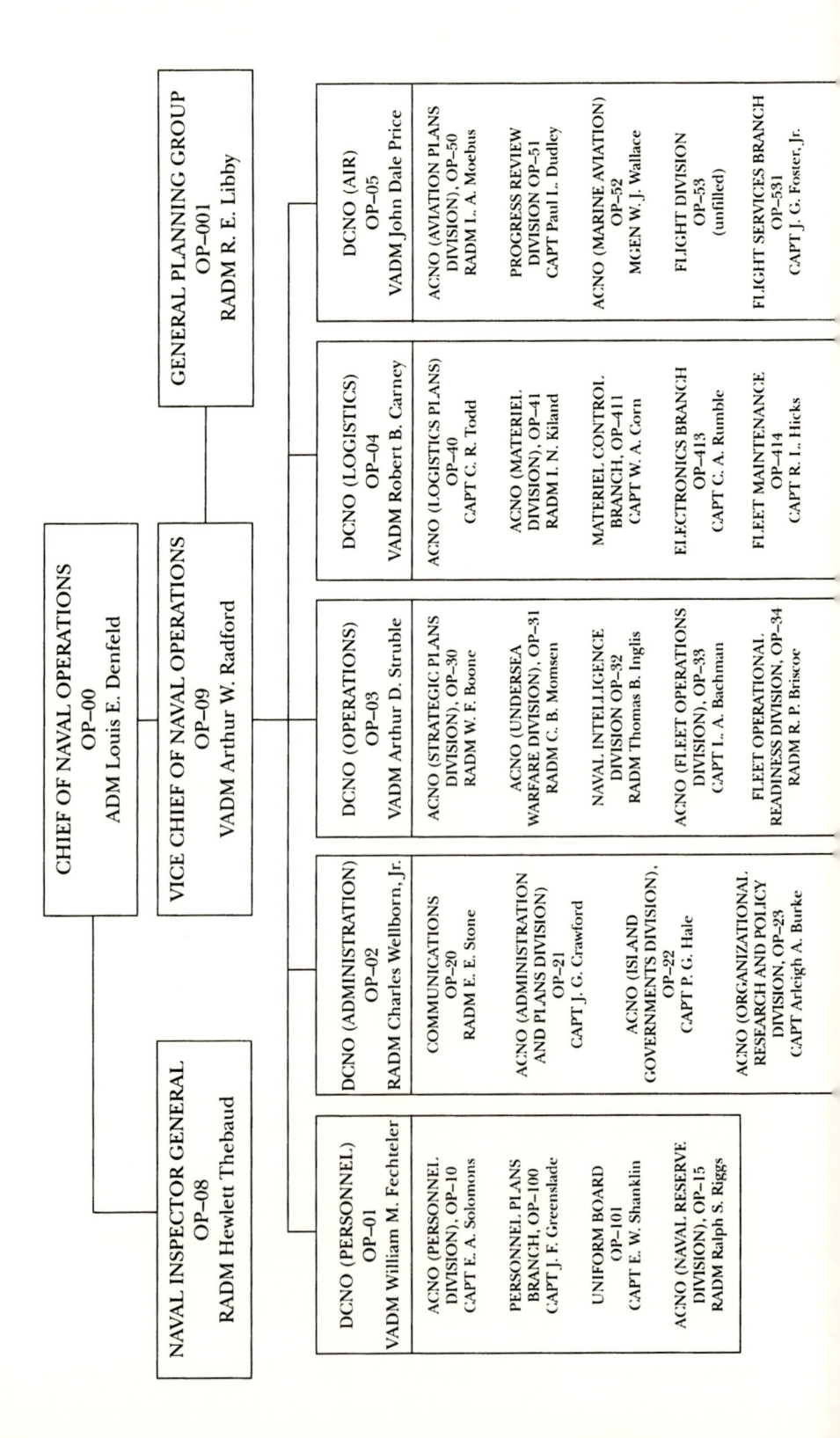

CHIEF OF NAVAL OPERATIONS
OP-00
ADM Louis E. Denfeld

VICE CHIEF OF NAVAL OPERATIONS
OP-09
VADM Arthur W. Radford

NAVAL INSPECTOR GENERAL
OP-08
RADM Hewlett Thebaud

GENERAL PLANNING GROUP
OP-001
RADM R. E. Libby

DCNO (PERSONNEL) OP-01
VADM William M. Fechteler

- ACNO (PERSONNEL DIVISION), OP-10
  CAPT E. A. Solomons
- PERSONNEL PLANS BRANCH, OP-100
  CAPT J. F. Greenslade
- UNIFORM BOARD OP-101
  CAPT E. W. Shanklin
- ACNO (NAVAL RESERVE DIVISION), OP-15
  RADM Ralph S. Riggs

DCNO (ADMINISTRATION) OP-02
RADM Charles Wellborn, Jr.

- COMMUNICATIONS OP-20
  RADM E. E. Stone
- ACNO (ADMINISTRATION AND PLANS DIVISION) OP-21
  CAPT J. G. Crawford
- ACNO (ISLAND GOVERNMENTS DIVISION), OP-22
  CAPT P. G. Hale
- ACNO (ORGANIZATIONAL RESEARCH AND POLICY DIVISION, OP-23
  CAPT Arleigh A. Burke

DCNO (OPERATIONS) OP-03
VADM Arthur D. Struble

- ACNO (STRATEGIC PLANS DIVISION), OP-30
  RADM W. F. Boone
- ACNO (UNDERSEA WARFARE DIVISION), OP-31
  RADM C. B. Momsen
- NAVAL INTELLIGENCE DIVISION OP-32
  RADM Thomas B. Inglis
- ACNO (FLEET OPERATIONS DIVISION), OP-33
  CAPT L. A. Bachman
- FLEET OPERATIONAL READINESS DIVISION, OP-34
  RADM R. P. Briscoe

DCNO (LOGISTICS) OP-04
VADM Robert B. Carney

- ACNO (LOGISTICS PLANS DIVISION), OP-40
  CAPT C. R. Todd
- ACNO (MATERIEL DIVISION), OP-41
  RADM I. N. Kiland
- MATERIEL CONTROL BRANCH, OP-411
  CAPT W. A. Corn
- ELECTRONICS BRANCH OP-413
  CAPT C. A. Rumble
- FLEET MAINTENANCE OP-414
  CAPT R. L. Hicks

DCNO (AIR) OP-05
VADM John Dale Price

- ACNO (AVIATION PLANS DIVISION), OP-50
  RADM L. A. Moebus
- PROGRESS REVIEW DIVISION OP-51
  CAPT Paul L. Dudley
- ACNO (MARINE AVIATION) OP-52
  MGEN W. J. Wallace
- FLIGHT DIVISION OP-53
  (unfilled)
- FLIGHT SERVICES BRANCH OP-531
  CAPT J. G. Foster, Jr.

NAVAL DISTRICT AFFAIRS DIVISION AND ACTIVITIES CONTROL, OP-24 CDR B. McCandless	ACNO (INTERNATIONAL AFFAIRS DIVISION), OP-35 RADM E. T. Wooldridge	BASE MAINTENANCE OP-415 RADM J. E. Maher	CIVIL AVIATION BRANCH OP-532 CAPT E. Grant
HYDROGRAPHIC OFFICE OP-25 CAPT A. Hobbs	ATOMIC ENERGY DIVISION OP-36 RADM William S. Parsons	ACNO (TRANSPORTATION DIVISION), OP-42 RADM A. J. Wellings	AIR TRANSPORTATION BRANCH, OP-533 CDR W. H. Newton
NAVAL OBSERVATORY OP-26 CAPT G. W. Clark		NAVAL TRANSPORTATION SERVICE, OP-421K CDR D. R. McMullen	AVIATION PERSONNEL DIVISION, OP-54 RADM F. W. McMahon
PAN AMERICAN AFFAIRS AND U.S. NAVAL MISSIONS DIVISION, OP-27 RADM O. B. Hardison		PETROLEUM AND TANKERS BRANCH, OP-422 CAPT J. M. Boyd	AVIATION TRAINING BRANCH, OP-542 CAPT J. B. Moss
CNO CIVIL ADMINISTRATIVE DIVISION, OP-28 Mr. J. N. Stonesifer		BOARD OF INSPECTION AND SURVEY, OP-45 RADM F. A. Braisted	ANALYSIS SECTION OP-542D CAPT R. W. Denbo
NAVAL RECORDS & LIBRARY AND CURATOR OP-29 CAPT J. B. Hefferman (Ret.)			AIR WARFARE DIVISION OP-55 RADM E. A. Cruise
			MILITARY REQUIREMENTS AND DEVELOPMENTS BRANCH, OP-551 CAPT W. K. Godney
			TACTICS AND COMBAT TRAINING BRANCH, OP-552 CAPT F. B. Schaede
			PHOTOGRAPHY BRANCH OP-553 CAPT R. S. Quackenbush, Jr.
			ACNO (AIR LOGISTICS DIVISION), OP-56 CAPT Paul E. Pihl
			ACNO (GUIDED MISSILES DIVISION), OP-57 RADM Daniel V. Gallery

SOURCE: "Office of the Chief of Naval Operations OP-Sheet," 1 Jan 1949, Navy Department Library, NHC. Note the location of Arleigh Burke's OP-23 under the office of the DCNO (Administration).

Captain Arleigh A. Burke, Assistant Chief of Naval Operations for Organizational Research and Policy from 28 December 1948 to 3 November 1949. His division—OP–23—was under cognizance of the DCNO for Administration.

immediately that the new assignment was to be permanent. He was to relieve Captain Red Thackrey in OPNAV.[27]

Captain Burke reported to Admiral Wellborn on 28 December 1948. Wellborn told Burke that he was to be an Assistant Chief of Naval Operations in OP–020. He was to head the newly formed Organizational Research and Policy Division (OP–23). The next day Burke met with CNO Denfeld and asked about the offices responsibilities. Admiral Burke recalled:

> [Denfeld] replied ... by saying the charter included the best guidance he could give me: OP-23 was to familiarize itself on all matters pertaining to unification; advise him and keep him and other senior officers informed on all unification matters ... and be the clearing house within the navy for unification matters.[28]

The CNO couldn't give Captain Burke any detailed instructions on what the job would entail, since he simply didn't know.[29] Clearly though, one of the OP–23's most important tasks would be keeping senior naval leaders aware of how unification issues could impinge on service missions and responsibilities.

Although the division's daily work would likely involve its personnel in difficult and contentious matters, it was work that was entirely above board, not sinister or duplicitous—a vital point to recognize, since during and after the "revolt of the admirals," OP–23 was negatively characterized in the press. Indeed, Paul Y. Hammond wrote "Op. 23 was treated by the Navy from the beginning like a dirty business; and the press had soon drawn the same conclusion."[30] Arleigh Burke realized within the first hours of reporting in that he had been ordered in to OPNAV to do a job that nobody else wanted—to fight the continuing Army and Air Force efforts to strip the Navy of much of its service independence.[31]

One of the first people in OPNAV that Burke went to see in his new assignment was the CNO's public relations adviser, Captain Walter Karig. Lieutenant Commander Frank Manson, who was present when Arleigh Burke walked in, asked the captain what he was doing in OPNAV and was told that Burke was taking over OP–23. He remembers thinking to himself, "Oh, my God. What a *terrible* thing this is to do to a nice, future Admiral."[32] Manson believed that Burke was being placed in an almost untenable position, because the job could entail fighting a dirty, political battle with the Air Force.[33] Captain Burke was aware of the dangers of his new undertaking, but he was most concerned with how the Navy as a whole would respond to OP–23's efforts. He wrote to his old friend and classmate Captain W. E. (Goat) Mendenhall, "Certainly somebody must lay down definite policies for the Navy to follow. The danger comes in that we cannot (probably) develop any policy which will receive the strong support of all the various components of the Navy."[34]

During frequent discussions with his officers in the first weeks, Captain Burke compiled a list of rules to ensure OP–23 would be effective and, at the same time, would continue to be allowed to operate. Burke knew that as soon as its efforts were made known outside the Navy, OP–23 was likely to become a target for those who opposed the Navy's stands. Accordingly, he believed that the organization could not afford to engage in any practices that might redound to its (or the Navy's) discredit.[35]

Among the rules Burke promulgated within OP–23 were:

1) OP–23 had to know and reflect the views of most naval officers;
2) it had to have the trust and confidence of the Navy's senior officers;
3) OP–23 could not engage in secret operations or anything the rest of the service could not know about;
4) it had to be absolutely ethical in its activities, even if others were not operating in that way;

National Military Establishment, 30 September 1947

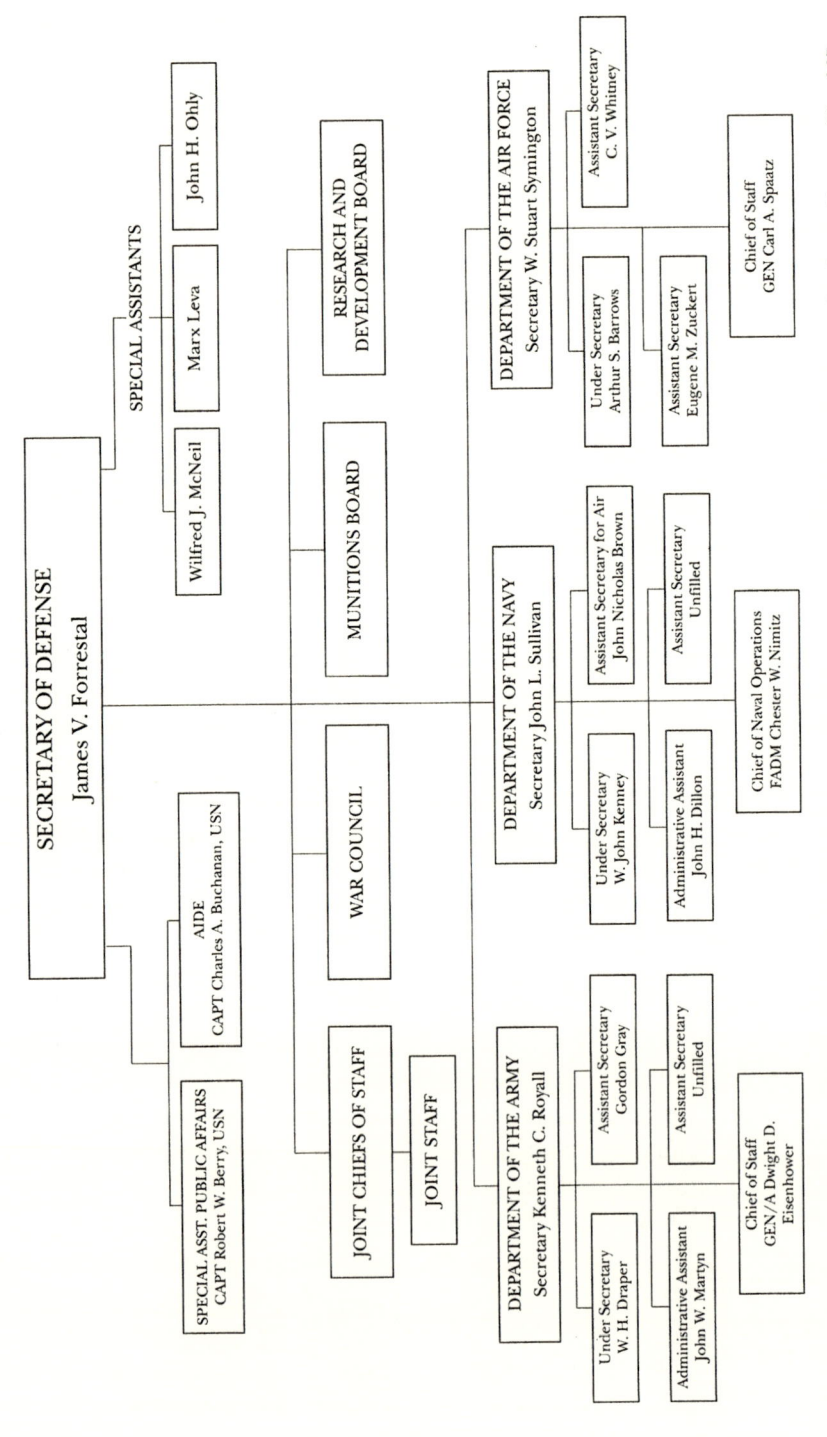

SECRETARY OF DEFENSE
James V. Forrestal

- AIDE: CAPT Charles A. Buchanan, USN
- SPECIAL ASST. PUBLIC AFFAIRS: CAPT Robert W. Berry, USN

SPECIAL ASSISTANTS
- Wilfred J. McNeil
- Marx Leva
- John H. Ohly

JOINT CHIEFS OF STAFF
- JOINT STAFF

WAR COUNCIL

MUNITIONS BOARD

RESEARCH AND DEVELOPMENT BOARD

DEPARTMENT OF THE ARMY
Secretary Kenneth C. Royall

- Under Secretary W. H. Draper
- Administrative Assistant John W. Martyn
- Assistant Secretary Gordon Gray
- Assistant Secretary Unfilled
- Chief of Staff GEN/A Dwight D. Eisenhower

DEPARTMENT OF THE NAVY
Secretary John L. Sullivan

- Under Secretary W. John Kenney
- Administrative Assistant John H. Dillon
- Assistant Secretary for Air John Nicholas Brown
- Assistant Secretary Unfilled
- Chief of Naval Operations FADM Chester W. Nimitz

DEPARTMENT OF THE AIR FORCE
Secretary W. Stuart Symington

- Under Secretary Arthur S. Barrows
- Assistant Secretary Eugene M. Zuckert
- Assistant Secretary C. V. Whitney
- Chief of Staff GEN Carl A. Spaatz

SOURCE: Adapted from Steven L. Rearden, *History of the Office of the Secretary of Defense*, vol. 1, *The Formative Years, 1947–1950* (Washington, 1984), chart inserted between 26 and 27.

5) OP–23 had to distribute its efforts through regular Navy channels to all sections that could use them; and

6) since it did not have responsibility for public relations or legislative liaison, and since the nature of its work might trigger outside requests for information, all material furnished would be done through regular channels.[36]

The importance of obeying these rules was carefully impressed on all OP–23 personnel.

In addition to its self-generated responsibilities, the new organization was soon tasked with drafting letters and speeches on a variety of naval and unification subjects for senior officials and officers in the department.[37] From Arleigh Burke's perspective the most important assignment in its first weeks was OP–23's drafting of a statement of fundamental principles to guide naval thinking in the Navy Department.[38]

Another issue of importance to the Navy at this time was pending legislation—the Tydings Bill (S. 1269)—to change the National Security Act of 1947. From February 1949 through the summer of that year, OP–23 was busily engaged in analyzing the potential effects of these changes on the department's status.

The National Military Establishment had become involved in the revisions to the act in the months following May 1948. Ferdinand Eberstadt, Forrestal's old friend and the newly appointed chairman of the Committee on the National Security Organization of the Commission on Organization of the Executive Branch of the Government, announced that his committee would take testimony on defense organization and functions from various officials of the National Military Establishment.[39] The Eberstadt Committee held hearings from June through October 1948, interviewing most of the top civilian defense officials and senior military officers, including Defense Secretary Forrestal and the three service secretaries.[40]

In early August 1948 Forrestal sent a memorandum to the services, requesting that they submit recommendations concerning revisions in the National Military Establishment.[41] In response Air Force Secretary Stuart Symington sent Forrestal a list of changes that, in addition to strengthening the position of the Secretary of Defense, called for setting up a single chief of staff who, under the Secretary, would have "adequate authority and power of decision over purely military matters." To assist him in discharging his responsibilities, Symington proposed that the chief of staff be provided with a military staff "adequate in size and composition."[42] Army Secretary Kenneth Royall had expressed a similar sentiment to Forrestal the month before.[43]

The proposal for a chief of staff with the power to decide military matters and assisted by a military staff raised the specter of a general staff system along German lines. This possibility was anathema to Navy leaders,

Department of Defense Organization, August 1949

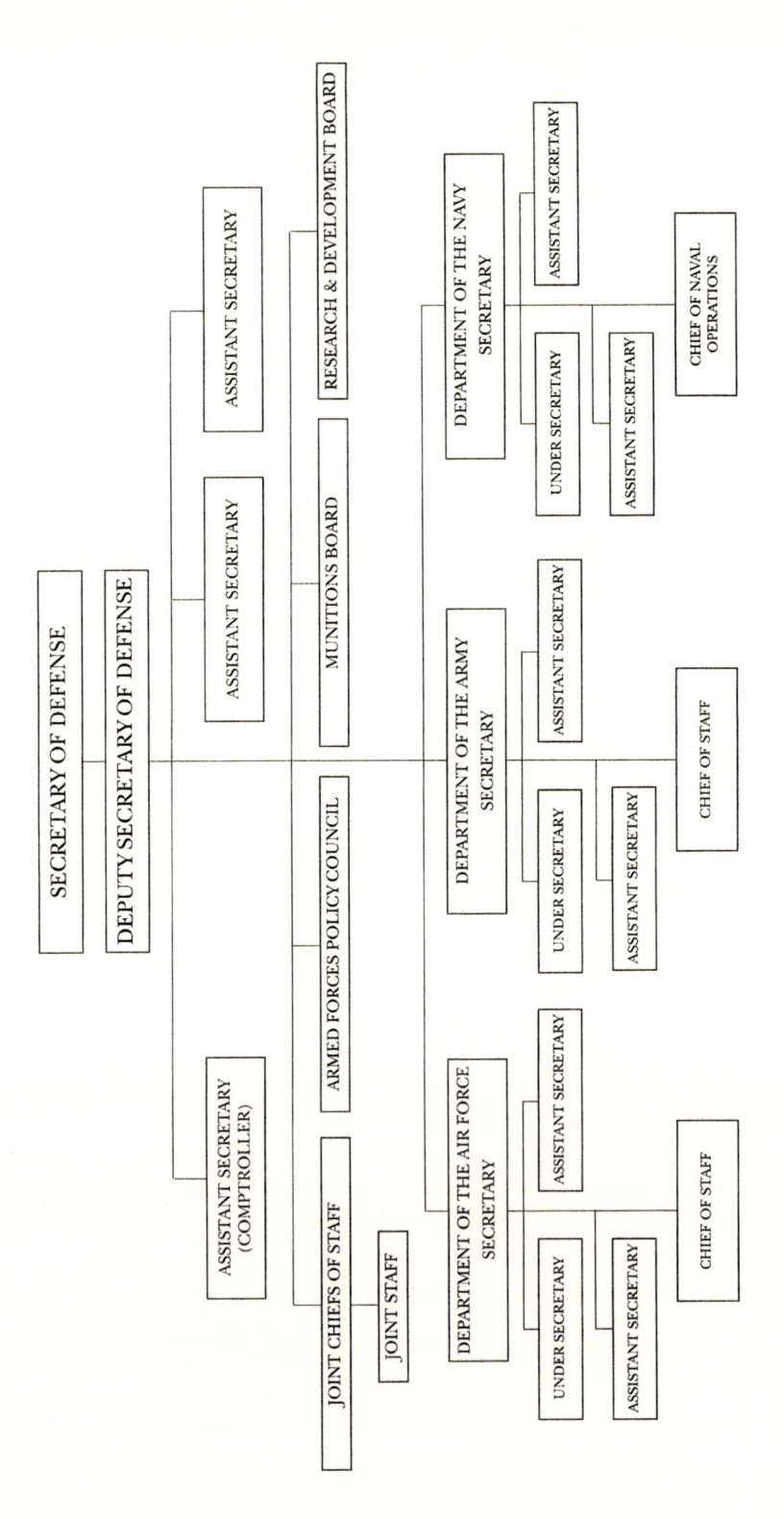

- SECRETARY OF DEFENSE
- DEPUTY SECRETARY OF DEFENSE

- ASSISTANT SECRETARY (COMPTROLLER)
- ARMED FORCES POLICY COUNCIL
- ASSISTANT SECRETARY
- ASSISTANT SECRETARY
- MUNITIONS BOARD
- RESEARCH & DEVELOPMENT BOARD

- JOINT CHIEFS OF STAFF
  - JOINT STAFF

DEPARTMENT OF THE AIR FORCE SECRETARY
- UNDER SECRETARY
- ASSISTANT SECRETARY
- ASSISTANT SECRETARY
- CHIEF OF STAFF

DEPARTMENT OF THE ARMY SECRETARY
- UNDER SECRETARY
- ASSISTANT SECRETARY
- ASSISTANT SECRETARY
- CHIEF OF STAFF

DEPARTMENT OF THE NAVY SECRETARY
- UNDER SECRETARY
- ASSISTANT SECRETARY
- ASSISTANT SECRETARY
- CHIEF OF NAVAL OPERATIONS

SOURCE: Adapted from Steven L. Rearden, *History of the Office of the Secretary of Defense*, vol. 1, *The Formative Years, 1947–1950* (Washington, 1984), chart inserted between 55 and 57.

who had successfully fought earlier Army attempts at imposing this system on the military services in the name of unification. Thus, from early December 1948 when Secretary Forrestal submitted his initial draft of National Security Act revisions to the White House until 10 August 1949 when the National Security Act Amendments of 1949 were signed into law, the Navy went to great effort to make certain that SECDEF's proposal for a Chairman of the Joint Chiefs of Staff did not become the single Chief of Staff desired by the Army and the Air Force.

During the spring and summer of 1949, therefore, the personnel of OP–23 kept a careful watch on the progress of the Tydings Bill. Several factors helped ensure that the Tydings Bill was sufficiently modified to preclude the establishment of a general staff system within the new department. They included the organization's painstaking efforts to keep the Navy's top leadership and its congressional allies apprised of the emerging situation; the opposition of witnesses such as Ferdinand Eberstadt, former President Herbert Hoover, and members of the Joint Chiefs of Staff, to a strong JCS Chairman with military authority over the chiefs; and the active efforts of members of Congress (particularly Carl Vinson) opposed to a highly centralized Defense Department.[44]

Their work was mentally taxing and the hours were long, but the personnel in OP–23 were dedicated to keeping the Navy abreast of the ongoing unification developments in the National Military Establishment. Arleigh Burke, a believer in hard work since his days as a midshipman, took the demanding schedule in stride. He found time in early February 1949 to joke to his predecessor, Red Thackrey, "This is a hell of a job you left me. I see no movies, I drink no liquor, I do nothing but work and very little of that."[45]

James Forrestal Departs as Secretary of Defense

By the final months of 1948, it had become evident to a number of senior people in the administration that Defense Secretary Forrestal was under increasing mental and physical strain that was beginning to affect his performance. Those who worked closest to Forrestal in the final months noticed little more about his condition than his increasing tiredness brought about by excessively long workdays.[46] But people who did not see him on a daily basis noticed a deterioration in his decision-making ability.[47]

One of these people was President Truman. Admiral Robert L. Dennison, the President's Naval Aide, recalled a conversation he had with Truman. The President asked Dennison if he knew who the Secretary of Defense was. Dennison, playing along, remarked, "Yes, sir, Jim Forrestal." To this Truman replied, "You're wrong. *I'm* the Secretary of Defense.... Jim calls me up several times a day asking me to make a decision on matters that are completely within his competence, but he passes them on to me."[48]

President Truman finally decided in January 1949 to replace Forrestal. His reasons were never specifically stated. They probably included not only Truman's feeling that Forrestal's control of the job was slipping, but also the increasing divergence he saw between his own views on foreign policy and defense budgeting matters and those of his Defense Secretary.[49] On 28 January Forrestal was called to the White House for an off-the-record meeting with the President. He was told by Truman that Louis A. Johnson would be replacing him as Defense Secretary on 1 May 1949.[50] Events proceeded ever faster thereafter. Forrestal's command of his job continued to slip, and on 1 March the President told him to submit his letter of resignation at once. He did so the following day. In his letter Forrestal asked that he be relieved of his duties on 31 March 1949.[51] This date was subsequently moved up a few days, and Forrestal turned over the job of Secretary of Defense to his successor on 28 March.

Louis Johnson Takes Over

The new Secretary was a self-assured and forceful man. Historian Forrest C. Pogue described the Louis Johnson of a decade earlier as a ruthless, energetic, and ambitious man.[52] Other people, especially some who worked directly with Johnson in later years, were less charitable. General Harry H. Vaughn, Truman's Military Aide and confidant, characterized Louis Johnson as "the only bull I know who carries his own china shop around with him."[53]

Johnson, though a practicing lawyer, was also an energetic politician. Following his First World War Army service he had helped to found the American Legion veterans organization. Realizing its potential influence on the national political scene, he maintained strong ties with the Legion. In 1932 he was named National Commander of the American Legion. That same year he served as head of the veterans division of the Democratic Party during its national presidential campaign.[54]

His national political ambitions apparently dated from the time of his appointment as Assistant Secretary of War in 1937. He took the position expecting that he would shortly succeed Secretary Harry H. Woodring.[55] As the months passed and Woodring continued to occupy his office, Louis Johnson began undercutting his superior in the Roosevelt administration and planting attacks on him in the newspapers.[56] The power struggle in the War Department eventually became an open fight, one only resolved by President Franklin D. Roosevelt's decision in 1940 to bring in prominent Republican statesman Henry Stimson to head the War Department.

National Air and Space Museum, Smithsonian Institution, 35619

Secretary of Defense James Forrestal's final meeting with the War Council, 25 March 1949. Left to right: Under Secretary of the Navy W. John Kenney (acting in the absence of Secretary Sullivan), Secretary of the Air Force Stuart Symington, Secretary of the Army Kenneth Royall, Secretary Forrestal, Army Chief of Staff General Omar Bradley, Chief of Naval Operations Admiral Louis Denfeld, and Air Force Chief of Staff General Hoyt Vandenberg.

Although Johnson left the War Department following Stimson's arrival, he kept his contacts with the Roosevelt administration, undertaking a number of tasks at presidential request during the war years. His close association with the Air Corps, which had begun during his time at the War Department, was further cemented by his 1942 appointment as a director of the Consolidated Aircraft Corporation—a company that specialized in producing bombers for the Army Air Forces.[57]

Louis Johnson owed his appointment as Secretary of Defense to a number of circumstances. The most important was his yeoman service during Harry Truman's 1948 presidential campaign. In the summer of 1948 Truman desperately needed help in his catch-up race against Republican challenger Thomas E. Dewey. At the time, pollsters and columnists around the country were predicting a Truman defeat. Even the national Democratic Party was concentrating its major efforts on the congressional races in order to avoid being dragged down by a losing presidential candidate.

At this juncture Johnson accepted the position as chairman of the Democratic finance committee. It is reported that he even donated a large amount of his own money to the Truman campaign.[58] When Truman was elected by a narrow margin, Johnson was in an excellent position to ask for a major appointment in the Truman administration. One rumor then making the rounds in Washington was that he could choose any Cabinet post he wished.

Louis Johnson did not wait long.[59] On 13 January 1949, a week before Truman's inauguration, he went to see the President. Columnist Drew Pearson, a friend of Johnson's, recorded Johnson's account of this meeting in his diary:

> Louis Johnson . . . took the bit in his teeth and went to see Truman regarding Secretary of Defense Forrestal. . . .
>
> As Louis was about to leave, Truman said, "Now about this job of Secretary of Defense. . . . " Louis says he held up his hand and said: "Mr. President. I don't want to talk about that or anything else. You don't owe me anything. *I just want to tell you some time how Forrestal tried to cut your throat during the campaign.*"[60]

Within three months of this meeting, Forrestal had relinquished his position and Johnson had become the new Defense Secretary.

Interestingly, Admiral Denfeld's initial impression of Louis Johnson was a positive one. He first talked to Johnson in early March 1949 at a luncheon with Dean Acheson and John E. Peurifoy.[61] That afternoon he wrote Admiral Dennison:

> I was very much impressed with Louis Johnson, and I think we will be able to get along all right with him. *He assured me in front of the other guests present that he was not going to let anything happen to the Navy as long as he was Secretary of Defense* and he wanted to say it before witnesses so that I could hold him to it.[62]

Others who met Johnson were less sure of his support for the Navy. Captain Edward C. Holden, Jr., USNR, Commander of the American Legion's Merchant Marine Industries' Post, reported to Admiral Denfeld that bringing Louis Johnson around to a pro-Navy stance was going to be a difficult task.

> I am authoritatively informed that the party in question [Johnson] is for the Navy "least of all." This information comes from close confidantes. . . .
> I am told that L.A.J. will not be persuaded one bit by anything except "political pressure" for the Navy—that his mind only functions from a "politi-

cal viewpoint"— and that he will lend a willing ear to one who has any sizable "bloc" of potential votes.[63]

Although many naval officers felt that Louis Johnson was entirely anti-Navy in his outlook from the beginning of his tenure as Defense Secretary, his actual view was somewhat more complex. He understood that the country needed a Navy but, to his way of thinking, it should be a Navy that concentrated on its basic defensive tasks in light of its potential adversary, not one that used its varied capabilities for a whole range of offensive and defensive tasks. As Dwight Eisenhower remarked in a letter to his friend Edward E. (Swede) Hazlett:

> You say that . . . [Johnson] has an "anti-Navy" slant, but I doubt such a generalization is completely accurate. I know that he came into his present job with the feeling that our present Navy could scarcely be justified on the basis of the naval strength of any potential enemy particularly when it is clear that any other navy worthy of the name belongs to a traditional ally. On the other hand he, like everybody else, had and has a healthy respect for hostile submarines and he was very anxious that the Navy consolidate all resources and brains in the field of anti-submarine warfare.[64]

Changes in the B–36 Program

In January 1949 the Air Force finally made its decision to allow Convair to mount jet pods under each wing of the B–36 to boost its maximum speed. To free up the additional money for this expensive conversion program, the Air Force decided to cancel the funding for a number of other aircraft already in its budget.[65] On 17 January Major General E. M. Powers, Acting Deputy Chief of Staff for Materiel, directed the Commanding General of the Air Materiel Command to begin negotiations with Convair to procure thirty-two B–36B aircraft with jet pods and K-1 bombing systems, and seven RB–36B aircraft with jet pods and the required reconnaissance equipment.[66]

Eleven days later Air Force Secretary Stuart Symington sent a memorandum to Defense Secretary Forrestal requesting the deletion of certain aircraft from the supplemental fiscal year 1948 program and asking for certification of a portion of the released funds for new B–36 procurement. Symington's reasons for the changes were that the Air Force needed a reduction from fifty-nine active groups in fiscal year 1949 to forty-eight groups in fiscal year 1950, an increase from two to four Heavy

The Joint Chiefs of Staff. Left to right: General Hoyt Vandenberg, Air Force Chief of Staff; Admiral Louis Denfeld, Chief of Naval Operations; and General Omar Bradley, Army Chief of Staff.

Strategic (B–36) Bomb Groups, and a reevaluation of the other aircraft types in light of technological developments.[67]

The Fairchild Board, appointed by Symington in late December 1948 to review the composition of the service's forty-eight group program, had recommended that the Air Force double the number of B–36 bomb groups and decrease the number of B–29 and B–50 bomb groups by two. The board's decision was based on its finding that the primary mission of the Air Force must be the launching of "a powerful air offensive designed to exploit the destructive and psychological power of atomic weapons against the vital elements of the Soviet war-making capacity" and an austere air defense of the United States and selected essential base areas.[68]

A total of 240 aircraft were to be deleted for a reduction of $269,761,000. From this amount, Symington requested that $172,949,000 be certified by the Secretary of Defense for procurement of the jet pod-equipped B–36 and RB–36 aircraft.[69] At the conclusion of his memorandum the Air Force Secretary noted that funds for a further B–36 modification program would be requested by separate correspondence.

On 3 February 1949 Secretary Forrestal sent a memorandum to the Joint Chiefs of Staff enclosing a copy of Symington's communication. Forrestal informed the Chiefs that he proposed to act on the matter by 9 February.[70] The JCS was being given the Symington memorandum merely for its information. The matter required no action unless one of the service chiefs desired to do something about it on his own initiative.[71]

The second Air Force memorandum requesting funding for B–36 modifications was sent to the Secretary of Defense on 4 February. It requested that $182,600,000 (the rest of the amount freed by the Air Force's deletion of the aircraft from the supplemental fiscal year 1948 program) be certified and released to provide for modifications to B–36, B–50, and B–54 bombers. Specific changes to the B–36 program included converting twenty-one B–36As to B–36Bs with jet pods and modifying seventy-three B–36Bs to include jet pods and K–1 bombing systems (the modified aircraft eventually being designated the B–36D).[72] According to an annex appended to the basic memorandum, the increased speed and improved bombing accuracy provided by these modifications would materially improve the Air Force's ability to undertake the strategic air offensive.[73]

James Forrestal also sent this Air Force memorandum to the Joint Chiefs of Staff, again for purposes of information only. Therefore the JCS took no action on it. A few days later, however, Forrestal decided that he needed the Joint Chiefs' formal advice and comment on the Air Force requests. He sent a memorandum to the JCS on 12 February requesting their views as a matter of "high priority."[74] The JCS reply, signed by Admiral Denfeld for the Chiefs, was sent to Secretary Forrestal on 21 February. It stated that the JCS had discussed the matter with the Air Force Chief of Staff, who assured the group that "the release of the funds requested will involve no change in the strategic concept or basic composition of the forces concerned." The JCS, therefore, had no objection to Forrestal's approval of the request.[75]

Despite this clear indication of support for the Air Force requests, the Defense Secretary continued to delay his final action on the matter. He was concerned about a staff study he had received from the Research and Development Board's Committee on Aeronautics, expressing doubt about the advisability of equipping all B–36 aircraft with jet pods until a prototype jet pod-equipped aircraft had been tested.[76] However, after receiving reassurances on the matter from General Dwight Eisenhower, who was serving as an adviser and as temporary presiding officer of the JCS, the Defense Secretary transmitted the Air Force requests to President Truman in early March 1949, recommending approval of the release of funds for the purposes stated.[77]

The final action on B–36 procurement occurred just three days after Louis Johnson had taken over as Defense Secretary.[78] On 31 March 1949 the Air Force requested that its procurement of forty-three B–54 bombers—which, just a month before at the Air Force's request, had been approved for an additional $13,307,000 to equip them with K–1 bombing systems[79]—be canceled and the funds, totaling $179,000,000, be used to procure thirty-six additional B–36 bombers.[80] The new Defense Secretary quickly approved the request.

Because of Johnson's previous service as a director of Convair, his motives in this decision later became a source of speculation, but at this point the whole issue was largely pro forma.[81] In fact, Johnson had asked Forrestal to make all of the decisions regarding the B–36 before leaving office. But Forrestal's early departure prevented him from settling this last issue.[82]

By this time, there had been a 79 percent increase in the number of B–36 aircraft procured at an additional cost of $354.5 million over the original B–36 procurement program. In hindsight it appears that the Air Force requested the increases in an incremental manner in order to obtain the Secretary of Defense's approval without raising fears that the service was making a basic change in its strategic concept or the composition of its forces.

Although this tactic proved successful in gaining the Secretary of Defense's concurrences with a minimum of trouble, the Air Force's third request was sufficiently obvious to elicit a negative reaction from the Bureau of the Budget. On 1 April Frank Pace, Jr., Director of the Bureau of the Budget, sent a memorandum to General Eisenhower, presiding officer of the JCS. Pace noted that the Joint Chiefs of Staff had approved the earlier Air Force requests (totaling $269.7 million) with the understanding that these would involve no changes in the present strategic concept or basic composition of the forces concerned. Pace said, however, that he believed the elimination of the B–54 and other aircraft did constitute a change in the strategic concept. He informed Eisenhower that he would withhold approval for the expenditure of these funds until this part of the Air Force program was approved by the JCS.[83]

Pace's memorandum arrived at the Pentagon when Eisenhower was out of Washington. It was therefore referred to Secretary Johnson, who quickly notified Stuart Symington that General Hoyt Vandenberg needed to obtain the Chiefs' concurrence in the B–54 cancellation. Vandenberg discussed the matter informally with General Bradley and Admiral Denfeld that same day and obtained their unofficial concurrences.[84] To make this action a matter of formal record, however, he decided to send a paper to the JCS for decision.[85] On 2 April Johnson

The confident new Secretary of Defense, Louis A. Johnson, at his first press conference, 29 March 1949. Left to right: Secretary of the Air Force Stuart Symington, Secretary of the Army Kenneth Royall, Secretary Johnson, and Secretary of the Navy John Sullivan.

sent Frank Pace a memorandum stating that he had spoken with Eisenhower on the matter and that the general concurred "most heartily" with the Air Force request.[86]

Air Force leaders nevertheless decided that the matter couldn't risk a delayed JCS response. So on 5 April the issue was brought up at the conclusion of a meeting of the War Council—the group composed of the service secretaries and the service chiefs that met with the Defense Secretary to advise him on matters of broad military policy. As a Navy brief recounted:

> On 4/5/49, in a meeting of the War Council with SecDef Johnson, Mr. Symington (or General Vandenberg) attributed great urgency to the ... reallocation of funds and, noting that all the Chiefs were present at the meeting, suggested ... that the JCS act on 1979/4 at that moment. Accordingly, the JCS approved General Vandenberg's request that they *note* the proposed adjustment.[87]

Admiral Denfeld brought this news back to his understandably perturbed office staff, who were in the process of preparing the Navy's position on this request.[88] Denfeld attempted to mollify his people by stating that the JCS had *noted* the intended action by the Air Force, not *approved* it.[89] At 11:30 that same morning, the Air Force issued a press release stating that the JCS had approved the cancellation of B–54 procurement and the reallocation of funds for purchase of additional B–36s.[90] Over the next several days OPNAV went about its (by now academic) task of drawing up a formal Navy position on the Air Force paper.

In due course the Navy formally agreed to a JCS decision to note the proposed adjustment in the Air Force procurement program. On 9 April 1949 the Chiefs informed the Secretary of Defense of its decision.[91] By this time, however, the Air Force's third request had already cleared Pace's office in the Bureau of the Budget, and the first portion of the requested funds for B–36 procurement had been certified by President Truman.

After months of patient effort the Air Force finally obtained the much stronger B–36 procurement program that it believed was necessary to increase the effectiveness of Strategic Air Command's planned strategic air offensive. Moreover, it accomplished this change through direct application to the Secretary of Defense, thereby avoiding the possibility of an objection from the Joint Chiefs of Staff. The Navy was not as lucky in its efforts to maintain support for the flush-deck carrier.

Cancellation of *United States*

In December 1948, a few weeks before he started to work as military consultant to the Defense Secretary, General Eisenhower wrote Forrestal a memorandum detailing his thinking on current defense issues. These views were the result of several days of consultation with various senior members of the armed forces. Eisenhower expressed his support for the flush-deck carrier.[92] However, after spending some days in the Pentagon listening to the disagreements between Air Force and Navy proponents, Eisenhower became aware of just how deep the gulf between Air Force and Navy thinking was on issues such as the strategic air offensive. He remarked in his diary, "The bitterness of the fight between Air and Navy is so noticeable that it is never absent from any discussion."[93]

In early February OPNAV spent several days briefing Eisenhower, at his request, on its strategic planning and its thinking on such matters as the Navy's role in national defense and the importance of the aircraft carriers and carrier aviation to its missions.[94] These briefings convinced Eisenhower that the Navy now viewed its main mission as "projection of American Air power against [the] enemy."[95] Although this impression was not a completely accurate representation of Navy thinking, it was one shared by senior Air Force leaders.[96]

The belief that the Navy intended to undertake a major role in the strategic air offensive undoubtedly reinforced Air Force opposition not only to the flush-deck carrier but also to the Navy's existing fleet carriers (CVs and CVBs).[97] The Air Force's active opposition to the flush-deck carrier had been held in check during 1948 and early 1949 by the continuing presence of a Secretary of Defense who favored its completion. However, the arrival of Louis Johnson at the end of March 1949 as the new Defense Secretary introduced a new factor into the equation.

There is little direct proof that senior Air Force leaders approached Johnson privately with the idea of canceling the flush-deck carrier, but the evidence that does exist suggests this to be the case. By February 1949 construction of the carrier was an all-but-foregone conclusion. Congress had appropriated the money for its construction the previous June, and President Truman had authorized its construction a month later. Nonetheless in early February 1949—just days after word had been received that Secretary Forrestal was being replaced by Louis Johnson—the Air Force began positioning itself for a reversal of the carrier decision. Air Force consultant W. Barton Leach prepared a memorandum for General Vandenberg to send to Forrestal, setting straight the Air Force position on the "Super-Carrier."

> a. Probable military usefulness of an aircraft carrier larger than existing types has not been established. . . .
>
> d. The project for a super-carrier should be given careful, detailed and objective study by bodies [i.e., the Weapons Systems Evaluation Group] upon which the three services are represented.[98]

The primary purpose of the memo was, in Leach's words, "to prevent Congress from committing itself still further in approving the CVA–58."[99] To this purpose, the memorandum urged that the Air Force information be called to the attention of the Congressional Armed Services and Appropriations Committees.[100]

General Vandenberg personally handed the memorandum to Secretary Forrestal on 5 March 1949. Forrestal, however, took issue with one of the statements in the enclosed paper on the Air Force's position and returned the memo to Vandenberg's office that same day. Thereafter the senior Air Force leaders decided to hold the paper in abeyance, awaiting changed circumstances. Secretary Symington in particular, believed that "no paper should go forward to the Secretary of Defense or JCS on this matter *at the moment.*"[101] Ten days later Leach talked with Lieutenant General John E. Hull, the Director of the Weapons Systems Evaluation Group, to persuade him that the Air Force was being above-board in voicing new criticisms of the flush-deck carrier and to find out how his organization would respond to a call for it to evaluate the carrier program.[102]

On 15 April 1949, only eighteen days after taking over as Defense Secretary, Louis Johnson sent a letter to General Eisenhower, who was in Augusta, Georgia, recuperating from an illness. The Secretary noted that he would like to have the judgment of the Joint Chiefs of Staff on the proposed new aircraft carrier "tentatively designated USS UNITED STATES."[103] He stated that he had not gone deeply into the matter and did not intend to until he had "received the views of the Chiefs."[104] Johnson ended the letter by reiterating that he had "no preconceived notions with respect to the advisability or inadvisability of continuing to go forward with the construction of the carrier."[105] These words were belied, however, by the way in which the matter was reopened. On the Defense Secretary's order copies of the letter to Eisenhower were distributed to each member of the Joint Chiefs of Staff to ensure that staff work on the matter could begin prior to Eisenhower's return to Washington.[106]

Louis Johnson's letter came as a disturbing surprise to the Navy Department.[107] The day after its arrival, Captain C. W. Wilkins, Admiral Denfeld's Administrative Aide, wrote a hasty note to Vice Admiral John Dale Price, who had just relieved Admiral Arthur Radford as Vice Chief of Naval Operations.[108] The note attached to Denfeld's copy of the Secretary of Defense's letter, stated, "Adm Denfeld wishes you to prepare a 'very comprehensive' paper on this subject."[109]

On 18 April Navy Secretary John Sullivan met with Louis Johnson to discuss a variety of subjects. The matter of the flush-deck carrier was raised by the Defense Secretary. Sullivan recalled, "He asked me if I were to start all over again would I bother to build the ship, and I replied that I most definitely would, that it had been approved by the Congress twice and by the President twice, and I saw no reason not to go ahead."[110] Sullivan then spoke about the issue of aircraft carrier vulnerability. But before he had talked "more than a minute," Johnson cut the conversation off, pleading that his schedule was too busy for further discussion at that time.[111] Sullivan remembered that, before he left the office, he said to Johnson, " 'Now I'm leaving for Corpus Christi on Friday. I'm addressing a Reserve Officers' convention down there on Saturday, and do I have your word that nothing will be done about this until I have a further opportunity to talk with you?' He said, 'You have my word.' "[112] That same afternoon, the keel of the flush-deck carrier—newly designated the *United States*—was laid officially in a brief ceremony at Newport News shipyard.[113]

On 19 April the form of the JCS reply to the Secretary of Defense was discussed at the Chiefs' Tuesday afternoon meeting. They were unable

The keel plate of *United States* being laid at the Newport News Shipbuilding and Dry Dock Company, 18 April 1949. Five days later construction was canceled and the keel plate was broken up.

to agree on a single reply and therefore agreed to submit separate views to the Secretary.[114]

The following day Barton Leach sent an Eyes Only letter to Stuart Symington, expressing his hopes for the outcome. He commented, "Taking the optimistic view that Bradley, Eisenhower, the Secretary, and the President will oppose the big carrier, the problem then arises of getting Congress to backtrack." Leach suggested that Symington could avoid problems from House Armed Services Committee Chairman Carl Vinson by placing in his hands "the material which will permit him gracefully to change his position"—the Air Force's "proof" that the Navy had misled the committee on the certain aspects of the carrier program. Finally Leach informed Symington that if the carrier was indeed "thrown in the ash can," the Navy was likely to ask for the released funds to be used for other Navy shipbuilding projects. He asked the Air Force Secretary to consider warning Louis Johnson that this could occur, noting that if the scrapping of the flush-deck carrier was to produce a real saving, the Office of the Secretary of Defense would have to "watch the whole Navy program like a hawk."[115]

During the week of 17–23 April, OPNAV made several efforts to draw up a Navy response to the letter. The initial attempt was made in the office of the DCNO (Air). Working with the assistance of OP–03, OP–05 completed the draft and submitted it to Admiral Denfeld on 21 April.[116] OP–05's draft stressed the status of *United States* as a prototype and its continuity with earlier aircraft carrier designs.[117] The draft concluded:

> I am informed that there may be a rather unusual challenge to the need for this new ship on the grounds that no carrier plane can carry the newest A-Bomb. This is categorically incorrect—we have such planes; they have been service tested with loads tailored to the weight of the heaviest A-Bomb now in prospect.[118]

Although OP–05 may not have realized it, this was not the kind of argument designed to sell the new carrier to Secretary Johnson. This draft was rejected by the CNO. On 21 April Captain George Anderson was brought in to write a new draft based on materials from files in the Vice Chief of Naval Operations' office.[119]

Toward the end of that week the Joint Chiefs of Staff were hurriedly informed that their views would have to be given to the Secretary of Defense by Friday afternoon, 22 April, and that the Secretary would be making his decision the following morning.[120] The final version of the Navy's memorandum was finished on 22 April and sent over to the office of the Secretary of the JCS late that afternoon.[121] The Navy memorandum signed by Admiral Denfeld stressed, "It is axiomatic that failure to progress is to accept unwarranted deterioration of our strength. I consider that the construction of the *United States* is necessary for the progressive improvement of naval capabilities and is fully warranted as insurance to cover the unpredictable exigencies of the future."[122]

The Army and the Air Force memoranda on the construction of the *United States* presented views much different from the Navy's. The Army memorandum, signed by General Bradley, reached the JCS Secretary's office at about four o'clock that afternoon.[123] In this memorandum, Bradley did a complete turnabout from the previous year when he had been in favor of the flush-deck carrier.[124] Denying that the carrier was needed, Bradley stated:

> If the existing carriers are adequate for . . . [the Navy's] primary tasks then the construction of a super carrier cannot be justified. The fundamental purpose for which the super aircraft carrier is designed, namely to facilitate the employment of heavy, long-range, bombing aircraft, is included within a primary function of the Air Force, which already has adequate means and capabilities to perform this function.[125]

The Air Force memorandum, signed by Major General Frank Everest for the Air Force Chief of Staff, was the last to arrive in the JCS Secretary's office, not coming in until 6:30 or 7:00 p.m.[126] The judgments on the flush-deck carrier contained in this memorandum were harsh and direct:

> The relative military value of the large carrier, when compared to other weapons systems procurable with the same resources, is of a low order. This carrier is designed for bombardment purposes. The resources required to make it an operational weapon could produce in land-based aviation capabilities considerably greater than the capability of the carrier.[127]

Because the separate service memoranda were received late on Friday, the JCS Secretary and his staff were not able to assemble them in proper form until the following morning. It was not until almost 10:30 a.m. on 23 April that the three memoranda, together with the forwarding memorandum from Admiral Denfeld, were sent over to Louis Johnson's office.[128] Slightly more than half an hour later, Admiral Denfeld received a copy of a mimeographed press release that the Secretary of Defense's office was handing out to reporters announcing that the carrier's construction had been discontinued.[129] The press release, obviously prepared some hours earlier, included a memorandum from the Defense Secretary to the Secretary of the Navy, which read in part:

> With further reference to the proposed aircraft carrier USS UNITED STATES, I have now received the views of the Chiefs of Staff and, *after careful consideration* and discussion of the matter with the President, I have reached the conclusion that appropriate orders should be issued discontinuing the construction of the vessel.[130]

Louis Johnson's peremptory cancellation of the carrier's construction was a clear indication that he had decided upon this course of action well before he read the considered opinions of the Joint Chiefs of Staff.[131] He later testified that he had been able to act so quickly because he had already discussed the matter with the individual Chiefs and with General Eisenhower and had read their memoranda in preliminary, draft form. But this was largely a prevarication.[132] He certainly did not see any Navy draft memoranda, since OPNAV did not even have an acceptable draft until 22 April. And Johnson's sole contact with senior people in the Navy Department during that week was his brief meeting with Secretary Sullivan on the 18th. Sullivan recalled, "Immediately after I had finished my speech [in Corpus Christi] I got on the phone to talk with . . . Denfeld and I said, 'Louis, the Secretary of Defense must have given you a hard time this week.' He said, 'I haven't even seen him.' "[133]

It is evident, too, that Johnson had not received General Eisenhower's substantive views before canceling the carrier, since the two did not discuss the matter at all.[134] Moreover, even after the carrier had been canceled, Dwight Eisenhower remained uncertain of where he stood on the matter.[135]

Although Johnson never provided an explicit reason for his cancellation of *United States*, many at the time saw it as an economy measure on the Defense Secretary's part.[136] Indeed, from his first days on the job, Johnson had proclaimed the need for drastic economizing in the National Military Establishment. It was therefore natural for historians to associate the decision with the Secretary's desire for economy in defense spending.[137]

Johnson's real reason for the decision, though, had much less to do with budgetary savings than it did with his belief that the Navy should not be allowed to participate in strategic air warfare. He saw the flush-deck carrier as a weapon system that would allow naval aviation to participate in long-range atomic bombing in a significant manner, and this he refused to countenance. Johnson revealed his thinking on the 6A carrier in an interview given to independent newsman Davis Merwin a few weeks after the cancellation.[138] As Merwin wrote to a friend:

> Johnson told me himself that the Navy was promoting the new [carrier] design as a means of competing with the Air Force, that *while he was SecDef the Navy would have no part in long range or strategic bombing*, and that he was going to permit an extension of carrier aircraft combat radius from what he said was a present 530 miles to 750 miles, in which we are giving them an additional 200 miles, which is all they are going to get.[139]

Because of Secretary Johnson's strong pro-Air Force sentiments, the Navy Department's many months of patient effort were overturned with the stroke of a single pen.

John Sullivan Resigns

Secretary of the Navy Sullivan returned to Washington from his speaking engagement in Texas in a very angry mood. He had been told of the cancellation in a long-distance telephone call from the Navy Department, just as he entered the Reserve Officers' convention in Corpus Christi. By the time he flew back to Washington the next day, he had decided to resign in protest if he could not get the decision reversed. As he later told Navy Under Secretary John Kenney:

> Without consulting either Louis [Denfeld] or me or anybody in the Navy... [Johnson] announced on Saturday while I was down in Texas—he sent an order to me to discontinue ... [the carrier]. So, if I am not even going to be consulted about the things in my Department there is no need of staying.[140]

When he returned to Washington that afternoon, Sullivan sent President Truman a written request for an appointment to discuss the matter.[141] Although the President agreed to see him, the Secretary was informed that Truman supported Louis Johnson's action.

Now determined on his course, Sullivan assembled a group of people to assist him in drafting his letter of resignation. One of the people he called upon was Robert Dennison, the President's Naval Aide. Admiral Dennison recalled,

> He... was absolutely infuriated. He called me at the White House and asked me to come down to his office. As I recall, it was about 6 o'clock or so in the evening. Several other people were in his office.... He had been waiting to dictate to Kate Foley, and the minute I came in and sat down he started. Well, this was a letter of resignation addressed to the President, and it was a pretty strong letter.[142]

Dennison was concerned both because the President was not responsible for the action and because Sullivan was a loyal Democrat still in the administration's good graces. Therefore, Dennison left Sullivan's office and telephoned Charles Ross, the White House Press Secretary, from the Navy Secretary's outer office and informed him of the situation. Ross hurriedly called Sullivan and tried to persuade the Navy Secretary that he couldn't send this letter to the President.[143] Ross suggested instead that Sullivan send it to Louis Johnson. Sullivan remained unpersuaded, arguing with Ross that it was the President, not Johnson, who had appointed him.[144] The letter was eventually sent over to the White House as written.[145]

When Sullivan, accompanied by Admiral Denfeld and Vice Admiral Price, saw the President in an off-the-record meeting shortly before noon the following day,[146] the discussion between the two men was cordial but unproductive. The Navy Secretary, as he had expected, was unable to persuade President Truman to reverse the decision of his recently appointed Secretary of Defense. Truman, in turn, attempted to get Sullivan to stay on as Secretary of the Navy but without success. Sullivan stood firm in his commitment to resign if the cancellation remained in force.[147] During the next twenty-four hours Charlie Ross continued to urge Sullivan to change his mind on sending his strongly worded resignation letter to the President. Finally, on Tuesday, 26 April, Ross came to

Sullivan's office and, after ascertaining that he was still determined to resign, persuaded him to take back his original letter. Sullivan agreed to write a new letter of resignation to the President and to send his strongly worded letter instead to the Secretary of Defense.[148] This was quickly accomplished.

John Sullivan's letter to Louis Johnson castigated the Defense Secretary for his drastic and arbitrary action in discontinuing the construction of the *United States* without consulting the CNO or the Secretary of the Navy.[149] The letter also noted Sullivan's belief that this action represented "the first attempt ever made in this country to prevent the development of a powerful weapon" and his fear that it would result in a renewed effort "to transfer all Naval and Marine Aviation elsewhere."[150] When Sullivan's letters to Johnson and Truman were publicly released at 2:30 p.m. the same day, they added to the flurry of stories in the press about the cancellation of the *United States*.[151] For the most part, however, Sullivan's letter to Johnson had little effect on the press's sentiments, which were largely favorable to Johnson's action.[152]

Nonetheless, the fact that Sullivan's well-argued criticisms of the Secretary of Defense's actions had become public knowledge bruised Johnson's ego and earned Sullivan the Secretary's permanent enmity. Just how angry Johnson was with Sullivan was revealed two months later during a conversation he had with Davis Merwin. Merwin recounted:

> At three points . . . I mentioned Sullivan, whose name literally threw Johnson into apoplexy. He rattled on at some length, and with obvious bitterness, in an attempt to discredit Sullivan completely as a man of utter incompetence who not only knew nothing about his job but was possessed of characteristics appreciated only by his mother.[153]

It was at this point in the conversation that Johnson first voiced a slander that he would later repeat and embellish during the Unification and Strategy hearings. Johnson stated that Sullivan had actually resigned in March because of his inability to go along with unification but had used the carrier incident in April as an excuse to leave gracefully.[154]

John Sullivan left office as Secretary of the Navy on 24 May 1949, almost a month after submitting his resignation. Under Secretary John Kenney left with him, having resigned as a gesture of solidarity with Sullivan.[155] The Navy gave Sullivan an excellent send-off in a brief ceremony on the Mall side of the Pentagon.

Interestingly Louis Johnson decided to attend the ceremony. As Johnson's confidant, Louis H. Renfrow, recalled:

The day he was to leave, that morning, Johnson came into my office and he said, "Come on, go with me."

I said, "Where are you going?"

He said, "I'm going over to tell John goodbye."

I said, "Mr. Secretary, you can't do that. Even Al Capone, when he kills them in Chicago, he sends them flowers but he doesn't go to their funeral."

He said, "John and I are good friends. He understands."[156]

Johnson did not stay long at the departure ceremony, however. John Sullivan had prepared a page of remarks that he delivered to the assembled crowd of supporters. The second sentence stated, "I have been privileged to serve with you men and women of the greatest Navy the world has ever known—a Navy that has never been defeated by a *foreign foe*."[157] When Sullivan read this passage, Johnson hurriedly left the gathering.[158]

Conclusions

Louis Johnson's 1949 return to government as Secretary of Defense initiated a series of events that appeared to predestine the devastation of naval aviation. Johnson's pro-Air Force sympathies were all too quickly borne out in his peremptory decision to cancel the construction of the Navy's flush-deck aircraft carrier. The resulting resignation of Navy Secretary John Sullivan unfortunately opened the way for even greater attacks by Johnson on the position of the Navy within the National Military Establishment, and on naval aviation in particular. None of the Navy's leaders were prepared for what was to follow.

Chapter 7

The Navy's Troubles Increase

By early May 1949 the Chief of Naval Operations was in an unenviable situation in the department. Never a particularly forceful CNO, Louis Denfeld found himself suddenly bereft of the strong, organizationally astute assistance he had been receiving from his Vice Chief, Arthur Radford. Just before *United States* was canceled, Radford had left Washington headed out to Oahu as the new Commander in Chief, Pacific (CINCPAC) and Commander in Chief, Pacific Fleet, as the relief for the retiring Duke Ramsey.

Admiral Radford was very pleased with the new assignment and was happy to be leaving Washington. Some speculated at the time that Louis Johnson had had a hand in Radford's departure as Vice Chief of Naval Operations, but this was not the case.[1] Admiral Ramsey, the outgoing CINCPAC, had written Admiral Denfeld in mid-March 1949 of his decision to seek retirement in order to move back to Washington and accept an attractive civilian job with the Aircraft Industries Association.[2] Following discussions between Denfeld and Radford about Ramsey's plans, the CNO informed his Vice Chief that he was recommending him as Duke Ramsey's relief.[3]

In May 1949 Radford wrote to his friend Rear Admiral A. K. (Artie) Doyle, about the move:

> I can assure you ... that I had my choice as to whether I stayed or came out here. It seemed to me that it was best for the Navy that I move. Principally because I felt that Mr. Symington had succeeded in convincing Mr. Forrestal (and subsequently Mr. Johnson) that I, personally, was the stumbling block to unification. That being the case, my usefulness was distinctly circumscribed for the time being.[4]

Arthur Radford's assignment as a major unified commander was good for him personally, providing him with new challenges and the perquisites of four-star rank. However, it left the top echelons of the Navy Department bereft of strong, committed leadership at a time when the service's fortunes were about to take a turn for the worse. Had Radford known that his strength and commitment to the Navy's cause were still needed in Washington, he probably would have refused the new assignment. But neither

NHC, Radford Papers

In conjunction with his appointment as CINCPAC, Admiral Arthur Radford is sworn in as High Commissioner of the Trust Territory of the Pacific Islands by his predecessor, Admiral Dewitt Ramsay, May 1949.

he nor anyone else in OPNAV knew then that Louis Johnson was about to launch a major assault on the viability of naval aviation.

The New Vice Chief of Naval Operations

Radford's hand-picked replacement as Vice Chief, Vice Admiral John Dale Price, was a highly respected naval aviator—most recently the Deputy Chief of Naval Operations (Air)—and an excellent officer. Radford had supported Price as his relief knowing that Price was fully conversant with the Navy's aviation concerns. Price also had long-standing friendships with many senior Air Force officers—friendships that Radford believed might make it easier to reduce the tensions between the two services.[5] For all his virtues, though, Price lacked Radford's incisive mind, his well-honed skills for competing in interservice infighting over roles and missions, and his speed in getting work accomplished. Frank Manson, who as the assistant to Captain Walter Karig regularly attended the Vice Chief's morning meetings with the Deputy Chiefs, remembered Price's largely passive style of leadership on Navy-Air Force issues:

> I used to attend his meetings every morning at eight o'clock.... The best way I could describe it, ... in the log book on a destroyer ... we'd start the first line [each day] ... "steaming as before." Well, with a meeting with John Dale, it was "steaming as before."... If you needed to get him *behind* you on a project you were working on and you asked him for his support, he'd give it to you. But he was not an initiator.[6]

Because Admiral Price was less equipped by background and temperament than Radford to handle the ongoing fight with the Air Force, he proved unable to provide the day-to-day policy support in Joint Chiefs of Staff matters to which Denfeld had become accustomed. The resulting vacuum in OPNAV was filled instead by Vice Admiral Arthur D. (Rip) Struble, DCNO (Operations). Struble was an extremely competent naval officer with an amphibious warfare background, but he lacked a full appreciation of the importance of carrier aviation to the Navy. Furthermore, by temperament he disliked disagreements over issues arising in the Joint Chiefs of Staff. Manson, who worked closely with him during this period, recalled, "His tendency [was] to try and keep peace in the valley. And if he could work out a compromise [with the other services] that would be suitable and ... not rock the boat too much, that was his tendency."[7] For this reason, during his tour as VCNO Admiral Radford had sought to insulate Struble as much as possible from high-level Navy participation in JCS matters, preferring to handle the complexities of interservice bargaining himself.

The concern held by a significant number of senior officers in OPNAV about Rip Struble's views on unification had been demonstrated in February 1949. On the morning of 1 February a group of officers assembled in Admiral Denfeld's office to brief General Dwight Eisenhower on undersea warfare, carrier operations, and the need for the 6A carrier. The group included Vice Admirals Radford, Struble, and Price; Rear Admiral L. A. (Fish) Moebus, Assistant Chief of Naval Operations for Air; and two officers from Admiral Struble's Operations shop—Rear Admiral C. B. Momsen, ACNO (Undersea Warfare), and Rear Admiral W. F. Boone, ACNO (Strategic Plans).[8] Admiral Denfeld was on a trip to Key West and Guantanamo at the time.[9]

The group briefed General Eisenhower from 10:00 a.m. to about 12:25 p.m.[10] After the departure of Eisenhower and Struble the rest of the assembled officers joined in a free-wheeling discussion. Lieutenant Robert A. Rowe of OP–23, the most junior officer present, was in the back of the room and had the unexpected privilege of being privy to the admirals' private discussion. Years later Rowe recalled:

> The gossip session was over... the high-level officers of the Navy that supported this [pro-]unification view and those that didn't. And one of them was Struble.... Well, the consensus of the opinion of the room was that they had to get rid of Struble. [But the admirals noted] "We['ve] gotta find a three star job [for him] equal to or better than this [one]." They kicked around all kinds of jobs. So they came up with the conclusion that in the ... summer of 1949 ... they'd [get the CNO to] relieve Struble and send him ... [as] Commander Seventh Fleet. "He can't do us any harm there."[11]

Despite the import of this informal discussion Admiral Struble stayed on as DCNO (Operations).[12] In fact, when Admiral Radford left for Hawaii to take over as CINCPAC, Struble assumed much of the former's influence over decision making within OPNAV. As the Navy's Deputy for Operations, Struble was also one of the Operations Deputies (Little Chiefs), a group composed of the Deputies for Operations for each of the services and the Director of the Joint Staff. They met regularly to resolve service differences on joint matters before they reached the Joint Chiefs of Staff's level.

The effect of Arthur Struble's increased influence in the JCS system was quickly evidenced by the more frequent Navy compromises favoring Air Force and Army positions at the Little Chiefs' level. Internal OPNAV decisions were also having a disproportionately negative impact on naval aviation. These distressing trends were so apparent by the summer of 1949 that aviation admirals in billets outside Washington began openly remarking on Struble's harmful influence. On 8 August 1949 for example, Vice Admiral J. W. Reeves, Jr., Chief of Naval Air Training, wrote to Admiral Radford:

> You know only too well the adverse situation resulting from decisions made by the little JCS, which have frequently been against both the Navy's, and particularly Naval Aviation's, interest. This means two strikes when the proposition gets to the big JCS....
>
> Naval Aviation had a representative in OP–03. If it isn't entitled to one now, then it ought to fight for it.... There is a lot of talk about Air being the backbone of the modern Navy but, when the chips are down, Air takes 50% of the proposed cuts, while the rest of the people maybe take 25%. What's left is not a backbone—it isn't even a rib.[13]

Reeves suggested to Radford that situation could improve if Struble were given the three-star amphibious job and an aviator such as Donald B. (Wu) Duncan or Felix B. Stump was brought in as OP–03.[14] Several weeks later

Reeves again wrote Radford, noting that putting Wu Duncan in as OP–03 was a "must" and that it was important for the naval aviators to form a common front with other threatened minorities in the department, such as the Marines, the amphibious community and the submariners.[15]

On 30 August Admiral Radford answered Admiral Reeves's earlier letters. Radford agreed completely with Reeves's viewpoint on Admiral Struble:

> Struble has done more harm to the Navy in the time that he has been there [as OP–03] than anyone else could have possibly done. I discussed this with Louis [Denfeld] before I left in April, and at that time Louis assured me that he would appoint a separate JCS Assistant. . . . If Struble were relieved of his contacts with the JCS he could not do so much damage—although I would favor getting him completely out of the operations picture.[16]

Nevertheless Struble remained as OP–03 for the rest of that year and well into the next one.

The Air Force Again on the Offensive

In the days immediately following the aircraft carrier *United States*'s cancellation, senior naval officers saw how isolated the Navy's position really was under a Louis Johnson-controlled National Military Establishment. Yet the Navy's problems lay not just within the Pentagon but with Congress and the public as well. Years of effective Air Force public relations had clearly reduced political support in Washington for a strong Navy.

For the Air Force's leadership the happy turn of events in the spring of 1949 marked a time not for resting on its laurels, but for attacking with renewed vigor until the Air Force truly became the dominant service. In March 1949 Air Force Chief of Staff Hoyt Vandenberg set forth the service's "policy line" designed to assist in achieving this result.

In a memorandum to Major General William F. McKee, the Assistant Vice Chief of Staff, General Vandenberg made it clear that the Air Force could not afford to give the impression in its public statements that it accepted a *balanced* military establishment, as reflected in the fiscal year 1950 defense budget. He stated, "The attitude that we are a member of a joint team of land-sea-air power is an excellent one to support and applaud WHEN a truly balanced force has been established. A military force is *properly balanced* when it is shaped to meet the task set for it."[17]

The Air Force Chief of Staff then came to the heart of the matter, as he stressed to McKee:

National Air and Space Museum, Smithsonian Institution, 146338 AC

General Hoyt S. Vandenberg, Chief of Staff of the Air Force, in his Pentagon office, May 1948.

I believe that the sound policy line for public statements which the Air Force should pursue is: First, the Air Force advocates shaping the Military Establishment so as to provide the maximum deterrent effect upon potential aggressors by virtue of overwhelming and apparent capability to deliver a retaliatory blow immediately. Second, that the Military Establishment be shaped so as to provide the maximum capability of engaging the enemy decisively as soon as possible after war begins.[18]

Vandenberg informed the Assistant Vice Chief that while the United States needed a military establishment composed of Army, Air Force, and Navy forces, the major portion of that military establishment must be Air Force.[19]

The harshness of the Air Force's public relations attack on the Navy in the winter and spring of 1949 was epitomized by a series of articles which appeared in *Reader's Digest* from December 1948 through April 1949. They were written by the Navy's old antagonist, William Bradford Huie.

The genesis of these articles shows how the Air Force PR viewpoint was effectively marketed to a mass audience. In the fall of 1948 Major General Hugh Knerr, the Air Force's Inspector General, talked with Defense Secretary James Forrestal to determine the Secretary's personal attitude on whether active duty and retired military personnel should be allowed (or even encouraged) to make public statements on issues affecting the National Military Establishment.[20] Earlier that year Forrestal had issued a directive that no article on a controversial subject could be published without the Defense Secretary's prior approval.

In the course of their conversation Knerr got Forrestal to admit that he would have no part in an attempt at "thought control." The Secretary did reiterate, however, that he "would not tolerate" the public castigation of the motives of military personnel.[21] Knerr interpreted this conversation as a license to sponsor anti-Navy articles. As he noted, "The upshot of this interview was that I proceeded to foster the series of articles published this spring in the *Reader's Digest*."[22]

The *Reader's Digest* was undoubtedly chosen as the vehicle for disseminating the Air Force PR viewpoint because of its stature as the American magazine with the largest circulation[23] and because its stable of editors believed that the Air Force should be the dominant armed service. As the magazine's senior editor, Paul Palmer, wrote to retired General Carl Spaatz, following a meeting in which they had discussed how the magazine could best campaign for a strong Air Force, "We [*Reader's Digest*] are going to pursue vigorously our campaign urging the supreme strategic Air Force for our country."[24]

The first article in Huie's series castigated the Navy for maintaining a large and duplicative air force:

> We are now buying and maintaining two separate, vast, and expensive air forces. One of these air forces can deliver the nuclear weapons to Moscow and is, therefore, an influence for peace. The other of these air forces is short-ranged, useful only on the seas, and is therefore comparatively worthless since our enemy has no reason to fear it. Against Russia what role is there for a carrier-based air force?[25]

Captain Walter Karig was so incensed by what he took to be blatant Air Force propaganda in Huie's article that he wrote in protest to Alfred Dashiell, the magazine's managing editor.[26] Several weeks later Karig and Commander William Lederer, an officer from the Navy's public relations magazine section, traveled to New York to interview the editors of the *Digest*, whom they knew personally. They were told in no uncertain terms that their efforts to have *Reader's Digest* present both sides of the issue were wasted. Karig noted in a subsequent memorandum on the meeting sent to the Under Secretary of the Navy, "We were told that the *Digest* is dedicating itself 'as a great public service' to depriving the Navy of its air arm, and concentrating all military aviation in a more powerful Air Force."[27] By April 1949 when the fourth and last article in Huie's series had appeared, the American public had received a large dose of pro-Air Force and anti-Navy views.[28]

It was only in the aftermath of the *United States'* cancellation that the Navy's leaders finally realized the extent to which the Air Force's public relations campaign had convinced key members of Congress that strategic air power had become all important to America's defense posture. Of these key members, Representative Carl Vinson was perhaps the most influential, both because of his position as chairman of the House Armed Services Committee and because of the way he used the power of his position. Vinson was considered the father of the modern Navy because of his pivotal role in strengthening the service while chairman of the House Naval Affairs Committee during the 1930s. Nonetheless, since passage of the National Security Act of 1947, he had also taken an increasing interest in strengthening the Air Force. Navy leaders hoped that this newfound enthusiasm for the Air Force would not supplant Vinson's longstanding appreciation for the Navy, but they were uncertain how his two interests would coexist. The question in the minds of Louis Denfeld and other politically attuned officers was which side Carl Vinson would take on defense issues that affected both the Navy and the Air Force.

Unfortunately for the Navy, by early 1948 the Air Force's effective selling job had helped to convince Carl Vinson that the Strategic Air Command was the only effective military means for deterring the Soviet Union from expanding into Western Europe or punishing her if deterrence failed. Vinson's feelings on this issue were fully revealed in a conversation he had with columnist Stewart Alsop in January 1949. Alsop recounted the conversation in a letter to Martin Sommers, an editor for *The Saturday Evening Post*:

> I talked with Carl Vinson the other day. His long love affair with the Navy is now definitely at an end—if he talks to the Admirals the way he talked to me they must be muttering about the sharpness of serpents' teeth. His line is—and it seems to me a sensible line—that our only potential enemy is Russia, that we can't touch Russia with a navy, that we can't hope to equal Russia in ground forces, and that the only way we can really and immediately bring our superiority to bear is by air. And he's convinced that the Congress will go along with him.[29]

Admiral Denfeld did not become aware of Carl Vinson's current beliefs on the Navy until mid-1949, in the days following the cancellation of *United States*.

The Navy Gets a Brief Respite

The Navy's fiscal year 1950 Shipbuilding and Conversion Program had been severely curtailed by the Bureau of the Budget, in part because of the funding needed for *United States*[30] to progress at the required building rate.[31] Following the cancellation of the flush-deck carrier, the office of the DCNO (Logistics) proposed a supplemental building program for fiscal year 1950 to cover certain priority ship conversions and new construction: two *Essex*-class carrier conversions (to the 27A configuration),[32] five destroyer escort conversions, one antisubmarine submarine (SSK) conversion, and the procurement of two mine countermeasures devices. The cost of this supplementary program was estimated to be $129,780,000.[33]

On 3 May 1949 Admiral Denfeld sent a memorandum to Dan A. Kimball, the Acting Secretary of the Navy, urging him to approve this supplemental building program and submit it to the Secretary of Defense. The CNO argued that, in the wake of the stoppage of work on *United States*, radical curtailment of the fiscal year 1950 shipbuilding program was no longer necessary. He noted that the proposed supplemental program would partially remedy the deficiencies caused by the cancellation of *United States*.[34] Kimball approved the proposed program and the following day sent a letter to Secretary Johnson requesting its consideration. His letter pointed out that the cost of the program was considerably less than the probable savings accruing from the *United States*'s cancellation.[35]

After holding Kimball's letter for several weeks, Secretary Johnson referred it to the Joint Chiefs of Staff on 16 May with the request that the JCS provide recommendations on submission of the Navy's program to the President and Congress. Johnson asked the JCS to submit its recommendations as early as possible, in view of the likelihood that Senate Appropriations Committee would hold early hearings on the fiscal year 1950 appropriation bill.[36] It was accordingly placed on the agenda for the Chiefs' 18 May meeting.[37] The JCS, however, took no immediate action.

The Air Force's reaction to this plan to modernize two additional *Essex*-class carriers was completely negative. In fact within a few days of Secretary Johnson's cancellation of the flush-deck carrier, the Air Force had embarked on a campaign to strip the Navy of all its existing large (CV and CVB) aircraft carriers. On 26 April 1949 General Vandenberg had sent a memorandum to the Secretary of Defense setting forth his views on these carriers:

> I have agreed to the full number of carriers, CVE/CVL's, proposed by the Navy as necessary for anti-submarine operations and the protection of shipping; but *I have not agreed to any large carriers, CV/CVB's, designed primarily for attack or bombardment operations* which, certainly on a minimum adequate basis, can be performed by the Air Force.[38]

After weeks of waiting, concern began mounting in OPNAV over the fate of its supplemental shipbuilding request. It was clear to Navy leaders that the proposal to modernize two additional *Essex*-class carriers was the likely cause of the delay. To the senior aviators in OPNAV, the modernization was imperative in the wake of the flush-deck carrier's cancellation. In their professional judgment modernization of additional World War II-vintage aircraft carriers was desperately needed to enable the Navy's carrier task forces to operate the longer-legged attack aircraft necessary to strike the targets that needed to be hit, while the carriers remained far enough at sea to reduce their vulnerability to enemy air attack.[39] The senior aviators also recognized that the Navy could not meet its mobilization requirements under existing plans if the schedule of *Essex* conversions was not increased to compensate for the absence of the 6A carrier.

Others in OPNAV, particularly senior surface officers in OP–03 and OP–04, were not as strong in their support for the carrier conversions. Indeed some of them seemed willing to give up the request entirely to save the rest of the supplemental shipbuilding program. Captain William H. Hollingsworth, the Vice Chief's Administrative Aide, recorded the contending views on the issue at the upper levels of OPNAV:

> 03 [Admiral Struble] says we will not get approval of the 2 Essex class conversions... [and] suggests that we drop the request for the CV conversions and attempt to put through the remainder of the program. He says we can take up the CV conversion issue later. OP–05 [Admiral Durgin], OP–02 [Admiral Wellborn] and Admiral Gardner [ACNO (Operations)] says [sic] this would be a mistake and that if we drop this item now we will never get it reinstated. They say we should submit a split [JCS] paper and get an official turndown. OP–04 (Admiral Kiland [ACNO (Logistics)]) and OP–01 [Admiral Fechteler] feels [sic] we should face the situation and drop our request for Item 1 (CVs) in order to gain Items 2, 3 and 4.[40]

On 31 May at the Vice Chief's morning conference with the DCNOs, Admiral Robert Carney, DCNO (Logistics), suggested again that to save the rest of the supplemental program, OPNAV drop its support for the *Essex* conversions until after the "resolution of forces" for the coming year.[41] Instead the group made a tentative decision to stand behind the original Navy submission in follow-up memoranda on the issue to the Secretary of Defense and the Joint Chiefs of Staff, but doing so in language that suggested a certain willingness to give up the carrier conversions, if this was necessary to save the rest of the shipbuilding program.[42]

On 1 June 1949 Admiral Struble sent the other service Operations Deputies a proposed compromise recommendation for the Secretary of

Defense.[43] The next day at their regular meeting the Operations Deputies agreed to send the compromise paper to the Defense Secretary.[44] It was amended in the JCS the same day and signed for the Chiefs by General Omar Bradley in the absence of Admiral Denfeld, the senior member of the JCS. It was then sent to Louis Johnson.

Struble's compromise paper had not been coordinated with the Vice Chief, John Dale Price. Thus when Admiral Price later obtained a copy of the JCS memorandum, he spoke with considerable agitation about it to Denfeld and Under Secretary Kimball. All three men strongly disagreed with the conclusions that had been expressed in the document by the Army and Air Force chiefs of Staff. This sudden meeting resulted in an afternoon conference on 6 June with Secretary Johnson, attended by the new Secretary of the Navy, Francis P. Matthews,[45] Under Secretary Kimball, Admiral Denfeld, and Admiral Carney.[46] Kimball and Admiral Denfeld presented the Navy's case for the *Essex* conversions to Secretary Johnson, stressing

> The Essex conversions are definitely required to accommodate those types of modern carrier-based aircraft which will be necessary to accomplish approved roles and missions of the Navy.... For example, modernization of Essex-class carriers is an immediate necessity if fighter aircraft in production and in the fleet *today* are to be carrier operated.[47]

Johnson told the group that he was in favor of building up naval aviation but did not "favor the Navy developing huge 1,700 mile radius bombers."[48] He also commented that the JCS memorandum lacked sufficient information from the Navy on which he could make a decision and that the Army-Air Force views presented therein "stink."[49] He said that he was returning the memorandum to the Chiefs for rewriting.

A revised JCS memorandum incorporating the rewritten service views on the *Essex* conversions was sent to Secretary Johnson on 10 June.[50] Three days later Johnson informed the service secretaries and the Joint Chiefs of Staff that, before making his final decision, he wished to hear a discussion of the subject.[51] A special 17 June meeting of the War Council was scheduled for this purpose.

Unbeknownst to the services Johnson had already made up his mind to allow the *Essex* conversions. On 17 June, prior to the 11:15 a.m. special meeting of the War Council, the VCNO's Administrative Aide received a draft copy of a speech that Secretary Johnson was planning to deliver to the National War College on 21 June. Drafted for the Secretary by Lieutenant Colonel Chester B. Hansen (General Bradley's assistant), the speech specifically announced Johnson's support for the carrier conversions. When he read the draft that morning, Captain Hollingsworth commented, "If this paper is correct[,] SecDef has already made up his mind to approve our request despite Army and Air Force objections. Politics is a wonderful thing!"[52]

At the meeting of the War Council Secretary Johnson allowed both sides to vent their feelings on the issue. General Vandenberg took the lead in attacking the Navy proposal, while Admiral Carney headed up the Navy's defense.[53] After a number of heated exchanges the meeting ended without Johnson announcing his decision. Admiral Carney recalled that when he got up to leave, he was indignant about "the whole damn thing" and refused to speak to Secretary Johnson. The others in the group had already left the room. As Carney walked by, Johnson grabbed him by the arm and said, "Hold on there. You're gonna get your carrier[s]. You're gonna get your carrier[s]."[54] It was then that Admiral Carney realized that the whole meeting had been a sham.[55]

On 21 June Louis Johnson sent a memorandum to the service secretaries and the Joint Chiefs of Staff announcing his decision in favor of the *Essex*-class carrier conversions. That same day he delivered a speech to the graduating class of the National War College, using the occasion to dismiss recent criticisms of his actions by Navy supporters and to affirm his belief in the continuing need for naval aviation. Johnson interrupted his prepared remarks to announce his approval of the Navy request for $80 million to modernize two *Essex*-class carriers, in order to give them the capability of launching heavier, longer-range aircraft.[56]

Although it remained unstated, Johnson clearly saw his support for the *Essex* conversions to be part of a quid pro quo—the carrier conversions for an end to the Navy's complaints about anti-Navy actions in the National Military Establishment. One man in the Navy Department who was eager to accept the proffered bargain was Dan Kimball, the new Under Secretary of the Navy.[57] Kimball had been a World War I Army Signal Corps aviator and had gone through flight training with Jimmy Doolittle. He believed that the existing tensions within the National Military Establishment were not necessarily harmful and could be reduced through friendly and patient effort.[58]

On the day that Johnson announced his support of the *Essex* conversions, Kimball wrote a letter to Frank Hecht, the president of the Navy League. Kimball enclosed a copy of Johnson's speech, which, he said, answered "practically all the questions that have been bothering the Navy League" and some parts of the Navy, for the past several years. He added, "I personally feel from my contacts with Mr. Johnson and Mr. Early that they fully realize the part the Navy plays in the team, and will support it wholeheartedly."[59] The Navy Under Secretary urged Hecht to give Johnson's speech the publicity it deserved with members of the

Francis P. Matthews, Secretary of the Navy from 25 May 1949 to 31 July 1951.

Navy League. He then he sent a copy of this letter to Deputy Secretary of Defense Stephen T. Early, together with a brief note that read, "Dear Steve: *I'm trying to call the dogs off.*"[60]

Francis Matthews Becomes Secretary of the Navy

Following the announcement of John Sullivan's resignation Louis Johnson immediately began looking for a replacement for the Navy Secretary. Because Johnson took a largely political approach to his job as Secretary of Defense,[61] he decided to replace Sullivan, one of the most prominent Catholics in the Truman administration, with man who had a background as a noted Catholic layman.[62] John Sullivan later recalled being told that "Secretary Johnson phoned around to his old American Legion friends and specifically requested that they recommend a prominent Catholic to take my place."[63]

Although a number of people were considered, the post was eventually offered to Francis Matthews, an Omaha, Nebraska, lawyer-businessman with no previous administrative experience in the federal government or military service. From Johnson's perspective Matthews's professional credentials were less important than his standing as a prominent Midwestern Catholic.[64]

When offered the appointment as Navy Secretary by President Truman, Matthews was somewhat nonplussed, since prior to this time he had only expressed his willingness to serve as the Ambassador to Ireland.[65] At the urging of friends, especially the Right Reverend Maurice S. Sheehy, a faculty member of the Catholic University of America and a strong Navy supporter, Matthews accepted the job. He was sworn in as Secretary of the Navy on 25 May 1949.

Few realized how detrimental Johnson's choice was to be for the Navy. Father Sheehy saw Matthews's appointment as beneficial to the service and expressed this view to Admiral Radford:

> I have known him for fifteen years. He is a forthright, honest man, the exact antithesis of John Sullivan. However Johnson pushed his name through and he will have to play along with Johnson. This can be done at present without too much damage to the Navy because, after the reaction to the carrier cancellation, Johnson is not inclined to give the Navy any trouble immediately.[66]

But Father Sheehy underestimated Matthews's need to frame his views in terms of what his boss Louis Johnson expected of him.

In fact Matthews's almost complete subservience to Johnson, his unfamiliarity with the Navy, and his lack of experience proved to be overwhelming handicaps in his administration of the Navy Department. Within a few weeks of taking over, naval officers in the department were derisively referring to him as "Rowboat" Matthews.[67] It was a reference to an early, unguarded comment he had made to the press that his only familiarity with his new responsibilities as Navy Secretary came from having owned a rowboat in Minnesota.[68] During his succeeding months in office Francis Matthews's lack of knowledge and his continuing debt to Louis Johnson for his appointment only strengthened his reliance upon the Defense Secretary, to the overall detriment of the service he represented.

Drafting the Anonymous Document

In 1947 and 1948 the Air Force's campaign in the press to sell strategic bombing as the ultimate component of national defense had, for the most part, gone unanswered by the Navy. This situation had induced individuals in the Navy Department, such as Hugh Hanson and Stuart Barber, to fight back by conducting their own campaign through letters and articles in the press critical of the Air Force positions and favoring naval aviation. In April 1949 the declining fortunes of naval aviation in the National Military Establishment (as evidenced by Louis Johnson's cancellation of the Navy's new flush-deck aircraft carrier) engendered a similar but far more serious reaction by other individuals. The Anonymous Document (as it came to be known) was the brainchild of two men who were apparently convinced that something drastic had to be done to bring the dramatically worsening plight of naval aviation to the attention of Congress.[69] The first of these men was Cedric R. Worth, Special Assistant to the Under Secretary of the Navy.

Worth, a journalist by training, had served as a Naval Reserve officer during the Second World War. From January 1945 until he left active duty in July 1946 then Commander Worth had served as the public relations officer for the Chief of Naval Operations.[70] In November 1946, when John Nicholas Brown took office as Assistant Secretary of the Navy for Air, he needed someone familiar with Navy Department organization and practice to advise him on matters requiring research and study. Cedric Worth was recommended for the job and was appointed as Brown's special assistant that same month.[71]

When Brown resigned as Assistant Secretary for Air in March 1949, Worth stayed on as special assistant for his successor, Dan Kimball. And, when Kimball fleeted up as Under Secretary of the Navy in May 1949, Cedric Worth went with him. Worth's duties as Special Assistant to the Under Secretary of the Navy included conducting research; advising the Under Secretary on issues such as personnel, administration and organization, budget, legislation, and public relations; preparing speeches; and facilitating the day-to-day flow of business in the Under Secretary's office.[72]

The other individual who had a principal role in the drafting of the Anonymous Document was Commander Thomas D. Davies.[73] Davies was a distinguished naval aviator who had set the world's nonstop, long-distance flying record of 11,236 statute miles in a P2V aircraft, nicknamed "The Truculent Turtle," in 1946. He had served as the P2V project officer and the assistant head of the VP (patrol plane) Design Branch in the Bureau of Aeronautics. In the spring of 1949 Tom Davies was serving as a special assistant to the Assistant Secretary of the Navy for Air, reporting through Cedric Worth to the Assistant Secretary.[74] He was also assigned in an additional-duty capacity to OP–23, Captain Arleigh Burke's Organizational Research and Policy shop.[75] In this duty he served as one of the officers performing writing assignments, particularly those having to do with naval aviation matters.[76]

From the outset Worth and Davies' ultimate goal was to somehow interest Congress in the plight of naval aviation. Captain Frank Manson recalled, "Tom Davies used to come over to my office, and I . . . [can] see him now, standing with his . . . foot up on the window [sill] there and his . . . hand on his chin, . . . talk[ing] about this situation, you know. And he was trying . . . [to determine how to get Congressional interest in the situation, wondering] 'How can we get a Congressional hearing?' "[77]

Although it is difficult to determine when Worth and Davies first decided to draft the Anonymous Document, it is evident that they began accumulating material for it some weeks before Louis Johnson canceled the construction of United States.[78] Worth and Davies were finally spurred to complete the paper that became the Anonymous Document by a meeting the two men had with Glenn L. Martin, chairman of the board of the Glenn Martin Aircraft Company, and Harold G. Mosier, a Martin Company representative. At the end of this cordial meeting Worth commented to Martin and Mosier that an account of the B–36's procurement problems would make an interesting story. As Mosier recalled, "Mr. Worth said that there were a lot of very interesting clippings, excerpts of magazines and so forth that, if put together, would make a very interesting story. . . . Mr. Martin said that he—if it was done—would like to read it. And Mr. Worth said, 'Well, I'll see that you get a copy.' "[79]

With this inducement Cedric Worth and Tom Davies proceeded to draft a paper that would fulfill Worth's promise to Martin. The initial version was apparently finished within a week after the 13 April meeting.[80] The completed document was a nine-page paper containing fifty-five numbered sections (most a single paragraph in length), each detailing a particular fact or rumor relating to the B–36 procurement program.[81] Paul Hammond later summarized the document:

> The gist of . . . [the] charges was that the B–36 was a "billion dollar blunder" by the Air Force which remained uncorrected because the Secretary of Defense and the Secretary of the Air Force had a personal financial interest in its continued production; and because political and personal favors were owed to Floyd Odlum, whose company was the manufacturer.[82]

Cobbled together from aeronautical industry gossip and wild suppositions, and casting highly negative aspersions on the reputations of senior officials in the National Military Establishment, the Worth-Davies document was not one its authors could be proud of writing. Although it served its purpose, it did so in a manner that eventually redounded to the discredit of its purveyors. It remains unclear how much of this information the authors themselves believed at the time, but even years later, Tom Davies could not bring himself to admit his major role in its drafting.[83]

Sometime during the week of 17–23 April Worth telephoned Glenn Martin and told him that the paper was finished. Martin came to Washington and picked up his copy of the Anonymous Document the same day he received the call.[84] During the next few days Glenn Martin had two additional copies of the document made; one to be sent to Senator Millard E. Tydings (D–Md.).[85]

After a few days of inaction following his delivery of the paper to Glenn Martin, Worth decided to send additional copies of the Anonymous Document to a few members of Congress in hopes of generating some anti–Air Force attention. One of those congressmen was James E. Van Zandt (R–Pa.), a member of the House Armed Services Committee and a long-time proponent of Navy interests. Van Zandt had recently delivered a statement on the floor of the House decrying the anti-Navy articles by William Bradford Huie in *Reader's Digest*.

The Worth plan slowly began to bear fruit. A short time after he received a copy of the Anonymous Document, Representative Charles B. Deane (D–N.C.) called Worth and asked if he might show the document to the Speaker of the House, Representative Sam Rayburn (D–Tex.). Worth gave his permission. A week later Deane called again to ask if he might give a copy to Chairman Carl Vinson of the House Armed Services Committee.

With the Anonymous Document in the hands of several influential members of Congress, Cedric Worth and Tom Davies sat back to see what would develop. They had every reason to expect that their document was explosive enough to produce the reaction they sought—a congressional investigation of the B–36 program and an eventual examination of the need to strengthen naval aviation.

The Abortive B–36 Navy Fighter Tests

At about the same time that the Anonymous Document was beginning to circulate on Capitol Hill, another B–36-related matter came under scrutiny. It had been initiated unintentionally several months before by a flurry of pro-B–36 publicity issued by Convair and the Air Force.[86] It started with an article in the 14 March 1949 issue of the industry magazine *Aviation Week* on the new jet-pod–equipped B–36D that the Air Force had ordered. The article extolled the heavy bomber as "the sledgehammer" of the service's intercontinental bombing force for at least the next six years. It went on to assert its relative invulnerability to fighter interception:

A series of test interceptions pitting the Lockheed F–80C, Republic F–84 and the North American F–86A against the B–36B has indicated that the jet fighters are unable to make [a] significant percentage of successful attacks on the bomber and never have been able to make an interception until after the bomber reached its target and dropped its bomb load.[87]

The article stated that early warning radar provided a less-than-thirty-minute warning of a B–36's approach; yet it took Air Force fighters twenty-six minutes to reach the bomber's operating altitude of 40,000 feet.[88]

On 15 March an article in the *Washington Daily News* presented the view of naval aviators that the B–36 *could* be intercepted successfully by present-day fighters, even at 40,000 feet.[89] After a short period of attention the issue then simmered—appeared occasionally in newspaper and aviation industry editorials—until after Louis Johnson's cancellation of the carrier *United States* on 23 April.

Four days after the cancellation Congressman Van Zandt wrote identical letters to Air Force Secretary Stuart Symington and Navy Secretary John Sullivan asking whether their services had fighters capable of successfully intercepting and shooting down the B–36.[90] Symington did not want to answer the letter, knowing that whatever answer he gave might be used against the Air Force by anti-Air Force stalwarts. Furthermore he was aware that Van Zandt was himself a strong supporter of Navy programs. He took the letter to Carl Vinson and asked him if he should answer it, since a reply would give away "military secrets with respect to the security of the United States." Vinson told Symington that under the circumstances he should not answer the letter and should so inform Van Zandt.[91] Symington's office was still drafting a reply to Van Zandt when, a few weeks later, the matter was overtaken by events.

In the Navy Department the letter was turned over to Dan Kimball, the Assistant Secretary for Air. Because of the nature of Van Zandt's letter the Bureau of Aeronautics's Technical Section drafted the reply.[92] Kimball signed the letter and sent it to the congressman's office on 2 May. The letter stated that the Navy's McDonnell F2H–1 Banshee fighter, then being delivered to the Fleet, would be "able to accomplish interception and successful attack against the B–36B throughout the latter's range of possible performance, as that performance is known to or estimated by the Navy based upon information which has been obtained from Air Force sources." It also noted that, based on this same information, the Grumman F8F–2 Bearcat, the Chance-Vought F4U–5 Corsair, and the Grumman F9F–2 Panther (in order of increasing ability) should all be able to cope with the B–36B at the speeds and altitudes employed on its long-range flights.[93]

The issue was brought to the attention of the press again on 8 May, during a familiarization cruise on board the carrier *Franklin D. Roosevelt* for a civilian party that included newsmen. The Navy demonstrated the ability of its new F2H Banshee fighters to launch from the carrier and climb to 40,000 feet in just seven minutes. Admiral Spike Blandy, Commander Atlantic Fleet, pointed out the demonstration's lesson by noting, "If actual war games were held with the Air Force and the Banshees proved themselves, it would weaken the Air Force's claim that its B–36 super bombers are almost impossible targets for interceptors above 40,000 feet."[94]

During the next several days columnists and editorial writers from a number of major newspapers commented on the story. On 17 May 1949, even as people in the Pentagon were telling reporters that the military was thinking about holding tests pitting the B–36 against Navy jet fighters, Scripps-Howard staff writer Jim Lucas broke the story of Dan Kimball's letter to Congressman Van Zandt.[95]

This press attention resulted in the House Armed Services Committee unanimously adopting a resolution on 18 May 1949 that the Pentagon conduct impartial tests between the B–36 bomber and U.S. Navy and Air Force fighters, to determine the vulnerability of the B–36 to fighter attack.[96] The committee's resolution was sent the following day to Defense Secretary Johnson together with a letter from Chairman Vinson. The Secretary of Defense turned the matter over to the Joint Chiefs of Staff for their recommendation.[97] Johnson was not at all pleased with the prospect of holding interception tests with the B–36. He hoped that the Joint Chiefs would get the National Military Establishment "off the hook" by providing written confirmation that such tests would be prejudicial to U.S. national security.[98] To maintain confidentiality for the deliberations Johnson issued an order that no one in the National Military Establishment could disclose information on the subject to the press.

When the letter from Johnson was received in OPNAV, the naval aviators on the staff were overjoyed at the prospect of tests between their fighters and the B–36 bomber.[99] They were well aware of where the Air Force stood in its testing of high-altitude intercepts and were convinced from their own testing that the Navy's lower-wing-loading fighters would be able to "wax" the B–36 in any face-off.[100] Admiral Radford, who was watching from his vantage point as CINCPAC, expressed the feelings of many of these naval aviators when he wrote to an acquaintance:

> Truth will out in time but I only hope that the result of the tests against the B–36 will be conducted in such a way that the Air Force position will be exposed. In spite of the fact that they are supposed to be enthusiastic, I know perfectly well that they don't want any impartial tests made.[101]

Unfortunately for the naval aviators' position Secretary Johnson's pressure on the JCS to reject specific testing of B–36-fighter interceptions was sufficiently strong to dissuade Admiral Struble and Admiral Denfeld from taking an independent Navy stance on the issue. On 27 May 1949 the Joint Chiefs submitted their answer to Johnson. The JCS memorandum, signed for the Chiefs by Admiral Denfeld as the senior member, advised against holding B–36 interception tests.[102] On 31 May Johnson wrote Vinson and enclosed a copy of the Joint Chiefs' recommendation against conducting the tests. Vinson immediately decided to drop the matter "for security reasons."

That same day the Chiefs' memorandum was declassified at Johnson's request and given out to the press.[103] This action was a master stroke apparently designed to split the Defense Secretary's Navy opposition by convincing many naval officers that the CNO had sided against them and in favor of their Air Force and Army opponents. A number of major newspapers specifically pointed to the fact that Admiral Denfeld had gone against his own service on the issue. Jim Lucas summed it up in this way, "The Denfeld signature on the Joint Chiefs memorandum was masterful strategy on someone's part, Navy fliers conceded. It left some admirals wondering where their chief stood."[104]

The cancellation of the interception tests proved a further blow to the morale of the naval aviation community. The aviators had been anticipating that the tests would demonstrate the hollowness of the Air Force's reliance on the B–36 bomber. Vice Chief of Naval Operations John Dale Price wrote to Admiral Radford about it:

> We were all set, having completed interception problems with Banshees representing B–36's—all successfully.... Over 100 flights have been made above 40 thousand feet and several above 45 thousand including shooting the 20MM guns. McDonnell is installing tail burners [afterburners] in the Banshees which will push them up to 40 thousand feet within 3 minutes from a standing start.[105]

Yet, even as the decision on the tests was being announced, events were in train that were to overshadow this aspect of the Navy–Air Force rivalry.

Conclusions

In May 1949 the Navy found itself under continuing attack from those in the National Military Establishment who denied there was a need for a significant carrier aviation capability. Bereft of his strong, bureaucratically astute Vice Chief, Arthur Radford, and saddled with a Navy Secretary who was obliged to Louis Johnson for his position, Admiral Denfeld was at a loss as to how to cope with an ever more unfavorable situation for his service.

Johnson's approval of the *Essex*-class carrier conversions, although heralded by some in the Navy as a sign of an improving situation, was quickly shown to be only an exception to an increasingly bleak picture for the future of naval aviation. This situation was the one looming before the Navy's leaders as the summer of 1949 began.

Chapter 8

The Navy and the B–36 Hearings

As the first part of May 1949 passed without any sign on Capitol Hill that the charges contained in the Anonymous Document were going to be investigated, Cedric Worth began to wonder if the document should be given a wider audience. There were several reasons for the apparent inaction of the members of Congress who had received it. Although Senator Millard Tydings, Chairman of the Senate Armed Services Committee, was a friend of Glenn Martin and thus had a reason to support an investigation of the Anonymous Document's charges, he was wary of the paper's absence of documented facts.

Carl Vinson, Chairman of the House Armed Services Committee, had reasons of his own for ignoring the Anonymous Document. He was particularly concerned that continuing service public relations campaigns for specific weapon systems and the attendant sniping by Air Force and Navy partisans at these service programs might damage public and congressional support for defense appropriations.[1] His concern had been sparked by a spate of Air Force-inspired publicity for the B–36 in March 1949, which coincided with that service's request for an additional number of these bombers. The highlight of this campaign was the revelation to United Press reporter Charles Corddry of the highly classified information that joint planners had selected seventy Russian cities as targets of strategic bombing attack in the event of a war with the Soviet Union.[2]

Corddry's story, which appeared in a number of major newspapers under various headlines (the *Washington Daily News* headline "B–36 Can Blast 70 Red Bases, AF Says" being the most colorful) stated:

> Conclusions from recent tests [have shown] that the mammoth [B–36] aircraft is virtually immune from interception and has the range to attack any Russian target from North American bases....
>
> Military planners have marked off some 70 strategic targets in Russia as possible objectives in the event of a war. The Air Force has given assurances that they are within the range of bases in Alaska or Labrador.[3]

Vinson found out about this leak of classified information before it was published. On 12 March he wrote to Air Force Secretary Stuart Symington demanding an investigation and explanation of this potentially serious security violation.[4] Symington eventually informed Vinson that an investigation showed that the Air Force was not responsible for the leak.[5]

Whatever the source of such information Carl Vinson wanted these damaging PR efforts to stop. At his request the House Armed Services Committee unanimously approved a statement on 5 April:

> If persons in the armed services or in their employ continue to pass statements to the press which are calculated to deprecate the activities of a sister service and which, at the same time, jeopardize the national security, the committee will step in with a full-scale investigation.[6]

Given his feelings regarding this issue, it is little wonder that Vinson avoided doing anything about the Anonymous Document.

Van Zandt's Role in Initiating the B–36 Hearings

Aware that his committee chairman was doing nothing to respond to the charges in the Anonymous Document, Congressman James Van Zandt decided to act on his own account.[7] Sometime during the week of 15–21 May he called on Frank McNaughton, a friend who was a correspondent for *Time* magazine, and asked McNaughton to write a speech for him based on the Anonymous Document's charges.[8] Working from Van Zandt's copy of the Worth document, McNaughton drafted a firebreathing speech for the congressman over the weekend. Frank Manson, a close friend of McNaughton's, recalled:

> I don't know how in the world Frank ever got the job to write Van Zandt's speech. But he was working on it [on Sunday afternoon], and every thirty minutes or so, he'd call me and say... "Chief, how am I doin' on this?"... And man, he would unload another [zinger].... He [would say]... "How'd that sound to you?"... Do you think it'll turn them on their ear?"[9]

On 25 May 1949 Van Zandt introduced a resolution in the House to establish a select committee of five members to investigate the matter of aircraft contract awards and cancellations since 8 May 1949.[10] The following day Van Zandt supported his resolution by delivering the McNaughton speech on the House floor. He began, "Ugly, disturbing reports are beginning to circulate through the Congress and through Washington.... I say that the seriousness of their nature, the insistence with which they are going the rounds... imperatively demands that this Congress set up an unbiased House Committee to make a full and complete investigation."[11] He then proceeded to recount many of the Worth document's most damaging rumors concerning Convair's B–36 contracts and the putative roles of Louis Johnson and Stuart Symington but without mentioning the document as the source of these rumors.[12] He concluded by calling on Congress to support a full investigation into these matters.

The Van Zandt resolution and speech and the attendant flurry of press attention alarmed Carl Vinson. Under House procedure it was customary to give the author of such a resolution the chairmanship of the investigating committee. Vinson apparently saw this situation as a challenge to his stature as chairman of the House Armed Services Committee and a threat to the committee's power. Having ignored the Anonymous Document's rumors for weeks, he did a sudden about-face and, on 1 June 1949, submitted a resolution to the House requesting that the Armed Services Committee be authorized to conduct "thorough studies and investigations relating to matters involving the B–36 bomber."[13] Vinson knew that the House would recognize his committee's jurisdiction over an investigation of B–36 procurement and that House adoption of his resolution would obviate the requirement for a special committee.

The Vinson resolution was considered by the House on 8 June and agreed to, as amended, the same day. The following day the House Armed Services Committee adopted an eight-item agenda for its B–36 investigation:

1. Establish the truth or falsity of all charges made by Mr. Van Zandt and by all others the Committee may find or develop in the investigation.

2. Locate and identify the sources from which the charges, rumors and innuendoes have come.

3. Examine the performance characteristics of the B–36 bomber to determine whether it is a satisfactory weapon.

4. Examine the roles and missions of the Air Force and the Navy (especially Naval aviation and Marine aviation) to determine whether or not the decision to cancel the construction of the aircraft carrier *United States* was sound.

5. Establish whether or not the Air Force is concentrating upon strategic bombing to such an extent as to be injurious to tactical aviation and the development of adequate fighter aircraft and fighter aircraft techniques.

6. Consider the procedures followed by the Joint Chiefs of Staff on the development of weapons to be used by the respective Services to determine whether or not it is proposed that two of the three Services will be permitted to pass on the weapons of the third.

7. Study the effectiveness of strategic bombing to determine whether the nation is sound in following this concept to its present extent.

8. Consider all other matters pertinent to the above that may be developed during the course of the investigation.[14]

The scope of the investigation was far broader than the issue of B–36 procurement. It ranged over such major issues as national military strategy, service roles and missions, and the effects of unification on service weapon programs. What Carl Vinson hoped to accomplish with such a wide-ranging investigative agenda remains a mystery, but it clearly offered all three services an opportunity to express their viewpoints on national military policy and strategy.

On 9 June Vinson sent copies of the committee's agenda to each of the service secretaries, with a letter informing them that they would be given advance notice as to when the committee would expect their appearance.[15] The Air Force, the service principally affected by the announced investigation, had already begun to act. On 2 June Symington had appointed W. Barton Leach the "Director-Coordinator" for the Air Force's portion of the investigation.[16] Leach, a professor at Harvard Law School, had served in the Army Air Forces during World War II as Chief of the Operations Analysis Division, Army Air Forces Headquarters. In mid-1949, in addition to holding a reserve commission as an Air Force colonel, he was serving as a paid special consultant to the Secretary of the Air Force.[17]

Barton Leach immediately set to work on an Air Force defense against the anonymous charges. In a memorandum to Symington on 2 June Leach stated that the Air Force would do well to set out the following objectives with regard to the House Armed Services Committee's investigation: "(1) We do not want to have to defend strategic bombing as a method of warfare; (2) we should have only to defend B–36's as intercontinental strategic bombers."[18]

Given his legal background, Barton Leach sought to organize the Air Force defense as he would a major litigation. Thorough preparation for the case would require an analysis of hostile statements and distillation of the charges in these statements; preparation of answers to the charges; detailed memoranda on such matters as JCS action on the B–36, the nature of the aircraft industry, and Secretary Symington's policies regarding that industry; and a chronological compilation and comparison of all Air Force statements on the B–36, together with the preparation of explanations for any discrepancies found in them.[19]

Since Symington had directed that Leach's requests for assistance should be given top priority within the Department of the Air Force, from the outset Leach was able to call upon top level assistance of all kinds. Air Force General Counsel Brackley Shaw was to prepare a Bill of Particulars—a compilation and analysis of statements hostile to the Air Force—and the answers to these allegations. To assist in this task a special projects office, headed by a colonel, was set up in the Office of the Secretary. General Lauris Norstad, Deputy Chief of Staff for Operations, was to compile all pertinent JCS actions on the B–36. Under Secretary Arthur Barrows and Major General Kenneth Wolfe, Commanding General, Air Materiel Command, were assigned the task of "establishing the effect of the Air Force on a 'healthy aircraft industry.'" General Wolfe was also responsible for obtaining and analyzing aircraft industry rumors on the B–36. Brackley Shaw and Major General Frederick H. Smith, Jr., Assistant for Programming in the office of Deputy Chief of Staff for Operations, were to collect statements on the heavy bomber program and prepare a chronological history of B–36 procurement. Other senior officers, including Air Force Chief of Staff Hoyt Vandenberg, were to detail their recollections of events with regard to the Air Force's policy on the B–36 or to review Air Force correspondence on the matter.[20]

The Navy's top-level response to the matter was far slower than the Air Force's. On 9 June 1949 Rear Admiral J. H. Cassady, Assistant Chief of Naval Operations (Air), wrote a rough draft of a personal memorandum concerning the upcoming congressional B–36 investigation that he wished to submit to Vice Chief of Naval Operations John Dale Price. He sent the draft to several officers, including Rear Admiral Ralph Ofstie and Captain Arleigh Burke, seeking their comments before sending the paper to Admiral Price. In this paper Cassady called for the Navy to immediately organize a task force to prepare for the investigation—one similar to the task force formed for the Eberstadt Committee hearings the year before. Cassady set out a series of themes that a Navy presentation could cover, and suggested individuals who could staff the task force, including Rear Admirals Ofstie, Robert P. Briscoe, R. E. Libby, and W. F. Boone, and Captains Burke and George Anderson.[21]

Cassady's memorandum was enthusiastically greeted by its initial recipients as the first sign of an OPNAV action on the congressional investigation. Ofstie noted in his response to Cassady's memorandum that the congressional investigation was an opportunity to present the fact that U.S. air power was composed of two elements—the Air Force and naval aviation—and that "both of these must be directly aimed to the support of the overall concept of war." But, as Ofstie commented, the most important thing was to get interested senior people in the department together as soon as possible to discuss the initial course of action.[22]

With this encouragement John Cassady discussed his memorandum with Admiral Price on 13 June. Later that day Vice Admiral Arthur Struble informed interested DCNOs that OP–03 and OP–05 had been directed to jointly prepare the paper setting forth the Navy's views on the House Armed Services Committee's agenda. That same afternoon Rear Admiral Charles R. (Cat) Brown, Chief of Staff to the President of the Naval War College, arrived from Newport to assist in the effort.[23]

On 14 June 1949 Carl Vinson sent letters to Secretary Francis Matthews and Admiral Louis Denfeld asking them to provide their detailed views on each item of the committee's investigative agenda by 1 July.[24] This action forced Matthews to act officially in a matter he would have preferred to avoid.[25] During the next few days Cassady and Price discussed the Navy's response to the House investigation with Denfeld and Under Secretary Dan Kimball. Yet to the interested people in OPNAV little appeared to be happening.[26] On 17 June Arleigh Burke sent a detailed eight-page memorandum to Admiral Struble on the points that should be considered for the Navy's testimony before Vinson's committee.[27] He sent copies of this paper to a sizable number of interested flag officers in OPNAV. The reactions to this memorandum proved sufficient to prevent further delay.[28]

On 20 June Dan Kimball issued a memorandum to the Chief of Naval Operations, establishing a task force to prepare for the congressional investigation. Composed of four rear admirals (Ofstie, Briscoe, Brown, and Libby) and four captains (Burke, Paul E. Pihl, Alexander S. McDill, and Charles D. Griffin) with Cat Brown as the steering member, this group was to report to Under Secretary Kimball. The group began its work with alacrity. During its first session the following day members reviewed the correspondence between Congressman Vinson and Secretary Matthews, discussed the nature of the Secretary's reply to Vinson, and parceled out assignments. Individual members were assigned responsibility for drafting a response to each item listed in the House Armed Services Committee's investigative agenda.[29]

During the rest of June and the early part of July the Under Secretary's Task Force labored to finish the drafts of the Navy's position on the Vinson committee agenda items. On 5 July 1949 Cat Brown sent copies of his paper, "Study of the Nature of a Future War," to offices in OPNAV. At this point task force support began to disintegrate. Brown's paper, which departed in several places from approved JCS strategic thinking (as reflected in joint war plans), was not well received. Rear Admiral Boone, ACNO (Strategic Plans), first commended the paper as "an excellent general strategic treatise," but went on to criticize it on a number of specific points. He questioned its value as a basis for the testimony of Navy witnesses before the Vinson committee, remarking, "Since CNO has approved [Joint Emergency War Plan] TROJAN, he cannot in good conscience now put forth a Navy concept substantially different from that of TROJAN."[30]

The reaction of Rear Admiral M. B. (Matt) Gardner, ACNO (Operations), was even harsher. Gardner reiterated his opinion expressed in an earlier meeting "that in attempting to tie the question of the B–36 investigation to matters of global strategy, we are getting far afield and on dangerous ground." He therefore strongly recommended that the paper be withdrawn from circulation and that the task force discontinue further effort in this direction because it served "no useful purpose."[31] Not surprisingly Vice Admiral Struble, DCNO (Operations), agreed with Matt Gardner that the study should be withdrawn from further circulation.[32]

On 7 July Cat Brown submitted a seven-page preliminary draft of the Navy positions to the CNO, the VCNO, and the Deputy Chiefs.[33] Brown's draft, based on the task force's supporting papers, took a strong anti-Air Force position on each of the agenda items. This paper, too, received a negative reaction from a number of the recipients. Vice Admiral Robert Carney, DCNO (Logistics), criticized the discussions of all but one of the agenda items, noting in conclusion, "*I again wish to view with alarm the dissemination of any writings which could vitiate the gains which the Navy appears to have made on many fronts recently.*"[34] VCNO John Dale Price was similarly concerned that a strong paper would be inopportune. He noted that the JCS had already taken a position on Item 7, and he did not see how the Secretary of the Navy could properly take a view on it that was not in accord with the JCS position "unless it is desired to precipitate another fiery controversy."[35] Things continued to go downhill for Admiral Brown thereafter.

When Under Secretary Kimball first read the draft task force statement of the Navy's views, he commented that "if the remarks which were contained in this Report were true... something drastic had to be done by the Navy."[36] The next morning he met with Admirals Denfeld and Price to discuss the draft. The three men agreed to recall the paper and place the task force under the strategic direction of OP–03.[37]

During the next few days the draft was watered down under OP–03's guidance to reflect a much weaker reply on the issues under investigation.[38] In this form it received Kimball's approval and was typed up as a letter for the Secretary's signature. After a delay of several days Francis Matthews reluctantly signed this letter, and it was sent to Vinson.[39]

With the departmental replies to Vinson out of the way, Cat Brown and the task force continued putting finishing touches on the supporting studies for each agenda item. These were completed by 21 July and combined into the task force report.[40] The following day in a private conference, Brown presented the report to Kimball. The supporting studies that constituted the report offered hard-hitting critiques of the Air Force position on the B–36 and strategic bombing and strongly supported the Navy's position on the issue of roles and missions and on the need for the carrier *United States*. Indeed the studies reflected even more strongly the views that Kimball had wanted toned down in the Secretary's reply to Carl Vinson a few days before.

Dan Kimball was furious. He attacked the task force report as too extreme and not representative of the Navy Department's viewpoint. Admiral Brown gamely fought back, defending the validity of the task force findings.[41]

The result was inevitable—Kimball relieved Cat Brown on the spot and directed him to return to his duties at Newport. In a letter written to Admiral Arthur Radford that day, Arleigh Burke wrote laconically, "Admiral Brown has been detached as of today to report to Newport. It may be possible that he will be ordered back. I don't think so."[42] That same afternoon Kimball met with the remaining task force members. He informed the group that Rear Admiral Briscoe, Director of Operational Readiness, would take charge of the task force.[43] Several weeks later, from his vantage point at Newport, Cat Brown wrote to Burke:

> I have been rather pleased with the reactions of the various Deputies. Apparently that very mealy-mouthed letter of ours was necessary—much as it went against the grain. Now, even if nothing comes of it immediately, there will be authoritative statements available against future events.
>
> I am afraid you are right in your estimate as to what is going to happen to the investigation. I wonder what would have been the result if a MAN had been there to back up our first short answer instead of opposing it?[44]

The Navy At Sixes and Sevens

July and August 1949 were difficult months for a Navy leadership already reeling from a rapid decline in support within the National Military Establishment. OPNAV was principally occupied with deliberations over the fiscal year 1951 defense budget. By mid-June 1949 several schemes for solving service budget wrangling had been tried without success. The Navy was laboring to derive fiscal year 1951 budget costs under the latest proposals suggested by General Dwight Eisenhower (labeled IKE I and IKE II) based on keeping operational six CV and four CVB attack carriers, respectively. At this juncture Admiral Struble suggested that the Navy voluntarily "lower its 'standards'" for naval aviation by cutting aircraft procurement, reducing flying hours, and extending the operating life of its planes. This step, he believed, would reduce the Navy's fiscal year 1951 budget projection by an additional $300 million, thereby possibly preventing a further loss in ships from the active fleet. The Vice Chief heatedly objected to this idea.[45] To the naval aviators in OPNAV, Struble's proposal was only the latest example of an anti-naval air viewpoint that had manifested itself in the top levels of the Office of the Chief of Naval Operations in the weeks since Admiral Radford had departed.

On 27 June Vice Admiral C. T. (Cal) Durgin, DCNO (Air), sent a memorandum to Vice Admiral Carney, the Navy's Budgetary Assistant, expressing OP–05's strongly held concerns about the likely impact of the IKE I and II programs. The DCNO (Air) noted that the direct and indirect savings proposed in the IKE II program, which involved cutting eight carrier air groups, four attack carriers, and eleven Marine fighter squadrons from the active forces, would amount to some $400 million.

> For this amount, out of a total Navy budget exceeding $4 billion and an NME budget of $14-$15 billion, the United States would lose its possibility of holding the vitally strategic area of the Mediterranean and its environs, of providing direct military assistance and encouragement to Allies and potential Allies (Spain and Turkey), and of inflicting severe damage on the advancing military forces of the Soviets.[46]

He urged Carney to accept a general plan for scaling down the Navy that did not cut the Navy's attack carriers below the eight already provided for in fiscal year 1950.

This was not to be. A few days later President Truman announced that, because of national economic conditions, the fiscal year 1951 defense budget would have to be reduced to $13 billion—$2 billion below the level the services had been using as the basis for planning.[47] On 5 July Secretary Louis Johnson sent a memorandum to the service secretaries and the JCS, laying out forces and ceilings for fiscal year 1951 for the three services. Under this new plan the Navy was tentatively allowed only four attack carriers.[48]

The budget looked bleak for the Navy. Out of the $13 billion allocated for defense, the Navy's share was $3.8 billion—$300 million less than that being given to the Army and $700 million less than that going to the Air Force.[49] In a briefing on the National Military Establishment budget prepared for the Chief of Naval Operations, Admiral Carney laid out the sobering facts. Since fiscal year 1949 the National Military Establishment had taken a $1.5 billion cut in funding. Of this amount, the Navy had absorbed $1 billion—two-thirds of the total. Carney then compared each service's ability to carry out its D-Day tasks under existing war plans. Since fiscal year 1949 the Air Force's ability to carry out these tasks had increased slightly, and the Army's ability had remained relatively constant. The Navy's ability, on the other hand, had declined by 30 percent.[50]

On 8 July 1949 Arleigh Burke wrote to Radford about the bleak situation: "The outlook a month ago was very rosy. The outlook now is extremely black.... I think that naval aviation will take a drastic beating and that a lot of us on the side lines are going to suffer therefrom."[51] Four days later the Joint Chiefs of Staff met at White Sulphur Springs,

TABLE 10.   *The Decline of Carrier Aviation, Fiscal Years 1949–1951*

	1949 Planned	1949 Approp.	1950 Approp.	1951 Planned[1]	1951 1/50	1951 6/50
Carriers (CV/CVB)	12	11	8	4	6	7[2]
Carrier air groups	24	24	14	6	9	9
Carrier aircraft	2,366	2,366[3]	1,554	690	1,035[4]	1,035[4]

[1] In response to OSD guidelines, July 1949.
[2] On 15 February 1950, SECDEF approved CNO's recommendation to retain a seventh carrier in commission
[3] Based upon "FY 49 Planned" figure.
[4] Calculated on basis of 115 a/c per carrier air group (used for "FY 51 Planned" figure).

SOURCES: Untitled chart marked "This data worked up at request of OP–00 for use at White Sulphur Springs," n.d. [early Jul 1949], box 25, Radford Papers, OA; encl. 1 to memo, ACNO (Strategic Plans) to DCNO (Operations), OP–301F1 ser 08P30, 11 Jan 1950, 1, and encl. 1 to memo, Director, Strategic Plans to DCNO (Operations), OP–301C5 ser 0001031P30, 1 Dec 1950, 1, both in box 257, Strategic Plans, OA; and DOD Office of Public Information Press Release No. 226–50, 15 Feb 1950, Sherman bio folder, box 573, Officer Bios Collection, OA.

West Virginia, to discuss the budget and other matters.[52] In the following days the Navy Department began working on a brief Basic Naval Establishment Plan based around four attack carriers and reduced numbers of escort carriers, cruisers, destroyers, and submarines.[53]

As the department sought to keep its fiscal year 1951 budget proposal in line with Secretary Johnson's new figures, evidence mounted that naval aviation would absorb an ever bigger share of the internal cuts, not only in aviation ships and aircraft but also in personnel. Although the Navy was reducing its total personnel strength by 5.5 percent, its aviation personnel (less aviation cadets) were being reduced by 8.2 percent, and pilot output was being reduced by 10 percent.[54] The concern in DCNO (Air) over disproportionate cuts in aviation personnel reached such a peak that at one point OP–05 drafted a memorandum for the CNO (which wasn't submitted) baldly stating, "If it is the desire of the Chief of Naval Operations to reduce naval aviation to a lesser role within the Navy, it is believed that such a policy should be promulgated as an aid to planning."[55]

Burke and Radford Enter the Fray

Following Admiral Cat Brown's sudden departure for Newport, the Navy's preparation for the House Armed Services Committee investigation had virtually come to a halt. Although Rear Admiral Briscoe and Vice Admiral Durgin were designated to go ahead with the service's preparations for the B–36 hearings, neither Matthews nor Admiral Denfeld issued directives outlining their desires on the matter.[56] With the Under Secretary's task force essentially rudderless there was little forward movement in OPNAV during the final weeks of July. This inactivity might have lasted for a considerable period were it not for events that drew Admiral Radford back into the Washington arena.

On 19 July 1949 Commander A. B. Metsger, an aviator on the staff of Commander Air Force, Pacific Fleet, who had served as an assistant to the task force, wrote to Radford at the suggestion of his boss, Vice Admiral Harold Sallada. He acquainted Radford with the seriousness of naval aviation's situation and said that, if the admiral felt it worthwhile, he would fly out to Pearl Harbor to brief him.[57] As Metsger expected, Admiral Radford did ask him to come to Hawaii.[58]

On 26 July Metsger privately briefed Radford on events in OPNAV as he saw them, stressing the following:

Crisis. Air Force and other offices have us on the ropes....

Surface Navy abandoning us, salvaging all possible.

Top policy [in OpNav] has abandoned air as a primary naval weapon, is emphasizing ASW. No continuing defense of Naval Air visible....

Naval Aviation at present rate will be finally licked with the '51 budget.[59]

Metsger strongly encouraged Radford to take on the job of presenting the aviators' case to Congress.[60]

Arthur Radford was deeply concerned by what he had heard. Metsger's briefing confirmed the seriousness of naval aviation's situation and the need for Radford to become personally involved in the fight. Arleigh Burke had already informed the admiral that it was likely he would be called upon to testify before the House Armed Services Committee. Following Metsger's visit, Radford detailed Fitzhugh Lee to assist him in drafting the statement he would make to the committee and in assembling the supporting material he would need for background.[61] On 30 July Radford wrote to Burke that he would be ready to come back "any time I'm called.... For my money the whole Navy had better realize that this B–36 investigation is no pink tea, and will probably mean all or nothing in the long run."[62]

At the beginning of August 1949 OPNAV was still uncertain whether the B–36 hearings would actually take place and, if they did, what tack they would take. On 2 August Burke wrote to Fitzhugh Lee, expressing his surprise that the hearings, previously rumored to be delayed, were apparently going to start within a few days. He suggested to Lee that, although it was not likely Admiral Radford would be recalled to testify in the near future, it would do no harm to be ready.[63] Events a few days later proved the value of Burke's suggestion.

On 4 August Chairman Carl Vinson pledged that the Armed Services Committee would begin its investigation of the matter shortly and continue straight through if it had "to run until Christmas."[64] In a conversation the following day with Captain McDill of the Navy's Congressional Liaison office, Vinson recalled that Radford had told him the United States was not getting the proper aircraft for its money. The congressman told McDill that he was going to send a dispatch to Radford asking his current opinion. McDill suggested that Vinson send this request to Radford through the Secretary of the Navy.[65] Accordingly on 6 August Vinson wrote to Secretary Matthews that matters relating to the committee's investigation of the B–36 made it desirable for Vinson to confer with Admiral Radford. He requested that Radford be ordered back to Washington to meet with him on 10 August.[66] Two days later Matthews informed Vinson that Radford would arrive in Washington to confer with him.[67]

The B–36 Hearings Begin

The House Armed Services Committee held its first session on the B–36 investigation on 9 August 1949. That day the committee questioned Robert Lovett, who as Assistant Secretary of War for Air during World War II had been involved in awarding the contract for the B–36 to Consolidated Aircraft Corporation. Lovett made it clear to the committee members that there had been no ulterior motives in awarding the B–36 contract to Consolidated.[68] Major General Frederick Smith, the Air Force's Assistant for Programming, followed Lovett to the witness table. Smith began to read to the committee a detailed program history for the B–36 that had been compiled for use in the hearings.[69]

The next morning before the hearings reopened Admiral Radford and two assistants—Arleigh Burke and Commander Tom Davies—met with Carl Vinson in the congressman's office. Vinson said that he wanted Radford to sit in on all of the Air Force testimony and assist the counsel in evaluating the testimony.

In the hearings that morning General Smith completed reading the B–36 program history. From the extensive material provided by Smith it was apparent that although the B–36 program had suffered a number of serious design problems over the years, there was no indication that the Secretary of the Air Force and the Secretary of Defense had made contract decisions influenced by their own personal financial considerations.

On 11 August Radford, Burke, and Davies entered the hearing room for the first time and took their places at the counsel's table. That afternoon they listened to testimony on the virtues of the B–36 bomber from General George Kenney, former Commanding General of the Strategic Air Command, and Lieutenant General Curtis LeMay, his successor. General Kenney acknowledged that for much of the B–36's development history he had held serious reservations about its usefulness as a strategic bomber. Nonetheless he told the committee that in the months just before he was relieved as commander of SAC, noticeable improvements in the B–36's characteristics had led him to reevaluate his earlier reservations and to come out in favor of the aircraft.[70] However, he still did not believe the B–36 could operate effectively over enemy territory in daylight. As he had written Stuart Symington some weeks earlier:

> Under conditions of blue sky day operations I would expect the modern day fighter [one at least equivalent to the USAF's F-86 in performance], who merely has to look for the vapor trails in order to locate the high altitude bomber, to give the B–36 a lot of trouble.[71]

Kenney believed, though, that the plane was perfectly safe from interception at night or in bad weather. He explained to the committee members, "Particularly as a night bomber at 40,000 feet, it would be almost perfectly safe to fly the thing anywhere in any time of war against any country, because no one has a night fighter that can go up there and do anything at night."[72]

General LeMay, the current SAC commander, was far more supportive of the B–36 in his testimony. Asked by the committee's General Counsel whether he agreed with General Kenney on the advisability of bombing at night with the B–36, LeMay responded, "We have the capability and we intend to continue developing the capability of bombing in daylight or in darkness, in good weather or in bad weather, by individual airplane or by formations."[73] He further stated that it would be difficult for a day fighter to shoot down the B–36 at an altitude of 40,000 feet.[74]

The SAC commander made it evident to the committee that he utterly dismissed the Soviet Union's capability of detecting, intercepting, and shooting down the B–36 in the near term. Under questioning, he remarked at one point, "I believe we could run the B–36 in over a target at the present time, and not only get it over—I doubt if they would ever know it was there until the bombs hit."[75] LeMay also told the people present that if an airplane could go high enough, it could get over the present radar equipment without being picked up, and he noted that the B–36 was such a plane.

On Friday, 12 August, Radford and the others were again in the hearing room for the testimony of Air Force Chief of Staff Hoyt Vandenberg

TABLE 11. *B–36 Performance as of Mid-1949*

	B–36B	B–36D (jet pods)
Combat radius [1]	4,272 stat. mi. at avg. speed of 222 mph	3,708 stat. mi. at avg. speed of 228 mph
Combat range [1]	7,998 stat. mi. at avg. speed of 213 mph	7,600 stat. mi. at avg. speed of 214 mph
Combat speed	362 mph	414 mph
Maximum speed	376 mph [2]	435 mph [2]
Ceiling	37,500 ft. [3]	40,500 ft. [3]

[1] With 10,000 pound bomb load.
[2] Attainable at 35,000 feet.
[3] Altitude where feet per minute = 500 at maximum power and combat weight.

SOURCE: B–36 performance data sheets attached to memo, MAJ G. S. Curtis, Jr., Office of the Director, Research and Development, Air Materiel Command, to COL Garman, HQ USAF, S–57609–A, 29 Jun 1949, box 27, Strategic Air Group, RG 341, NA. The figures for range in statute miles and speed in miles per hour were derived by recomputing from the figures for nautical miles and knots given in the original document. The original data was extracted by Air Materiel Command from standard current "Characteristics Summary Sheets" and compiled according to RAND Rules.

and Air Force Secretary Stuart Symington. General Vandenberg ably defended the Air Force's concept of strategic bombing and the procurement decisions made in connection with the B–36. However, when he was questioned about the B–36's military capabilities, he threw aside his heretofore cautious answers. One committee member asked him how effective the B–36's bombing would be on a specific target from 40,000 or 45,000 feet, using an atomic bomb. Vandenberg replied, "I questioned General LeMay about that a week ago.... He assured me that the accuracy was just as good and in some places and in some cases better with trained crews than it was [during World War II] with the B–17s." When pressed to give his own answer to this question, the Air Force Chief of Staff stated that he believed a B–36 at that altitude could accurately deliver an atomic bomb.[76] Vandenberg also agreed with LeMay that the B–36 could not be detected on radar at 40,000 feet.[77]

In his testimony Secretary Symington provided the committee with a point-by-point refutation of the charges from the Anonymous Document that Congressman Van Zandt had read in the House on 26 May 1949. He also seconded Vandenberg's support for the B–36 as a bomber, stating that, judged by the standard performance criteria for military airplanes (range, speed, altitude, and fire power), the B–36 was a good choice for its mission.[78] Symington seemed particularly proud of the B–36's defensive armament, consisting of sixteen 20 mm cannons directed by a new fire-control system, which the Secretary termed "by far the heaviest known [aircraft armament] in the world."[79]

National Air and Space Museum, Smithsonian Institution, 23561

First take-off view of the production model B–36D bomber, August 1950. The aircraft was equipped with four J–47 jet engines in underwing nacelles and six 3,500-hp piston engines.

This was one bit of hyperbole that Symington might better have left out. Although the B–36's defensive armament was theoretically top notch, the Air Force had been unable to get it working properly. For months the Secretary had been receiving biweekly reports on the technical difficulties causing delays in delivery of operational B–36 aircraft to Strategic Air Command units. The 7 July 1949 report had indicated that the 20mm guns installed in the B–36's turrets were not functioning satisfactorily, both because of trouble with the electrically primed ammunition and gun jamming caused by ammunition extraction problems. In light of the number of technical difficulties involved, the report noted that production fixes for the 20mm gun would not be ready until 1 September 1949.[80]

The problems were brought up again in a report issued two weeks later. A final report, given to Secretary Symington on 4 August, just eight days before he testified, revealed the 20mm gun problems to be even more serious than anticipated. The report specifically moved the date for successful production fixes from 1 September 1949 to 1 January 1950 and noted that the Armor Institute, the Ordnance Department, and Air Materiel Command were working on a high-priority, overtime basis to solve this difficulty.[81] It undoubtedly was fortunate for all concerned that no hint of these problems was ever picked up by Vinson's committee.

Although Stuart Symington did not have the opportunity to testify about it before the committee, a later leak to the press revealed that the Air Force Secretary knew that the Navy was responsible for the Anonymous Document's slandering of his and Johnson's reputations. *Time* magazine intoned in its 22 August issue:

> What, then, was the basis for the charges of political skulduggery?
>
> Air Force Secretary W. Stuart Symington thought he knew for sure. The charges had been embodied in a rambling anonymous document, prepared by a group of Navy regulars and reservists and furtively delivered to Congressman Van Zandt, himself a Naval Reserve Captain and one-time national commander of the Veterans of Foreign Wars.[82]

The completion of Vandenberg's and Symington's testimonies provided a useful stopping place. At the end of the day's session Chairman Vinson announced that the committee would recess until 22 August.[83]

After attending two days of the B–36 hearings, Radford, Burke, and Davies were aware that the Air Force witnesses had presented a strong defense against the principal charge of the Anonymous Document, namely, that Secretaries Symington and Johnson had made decisions on the B–36 contract for financial gain. But they were also aware that, in defending the aircraft itself, a number of these witnesses had failed to answer certain questions about the bomber or had seriously misstated facts about the B–36's bombing capability and its vulnerability to attack by enemy fighters.[84] An OP–23 review of Air Force testimony noted:

> Certain questions have not been answered. For instance when General Kenney was asked about guided missile interception, he replied with remarks about night fighters. Similarly, when General Vandenberg was asked about the correctness of LeMay's statement that sufficient altitude conceals planes from ground radar, he did not give a definite answer.
>
> The Air Force in their statements regarding the vulnerability of the B–36 against detection by present day radar and by fighters presently available have completely ignored reports of their own proving ground at Eglin Field which as early as July 1948 reported successful detection and intercept of B–36's at altitudes of 40,000 feet.[85]

While attending the committee hearings, Arleigh Burke had thought about the Navy's participation in the hearings, particularly questioning what he and the other Navy representatives were doing there, and what would be the likely nature of the Navy's future participation. Burke wondered if Carl Vinson had had the Navy representatives attend the hearings to demonstrate to the Navy the seriousness of the situation.[86] On 15 August Burke sent a lengthy memorandum to Rear Admiral Briscoe:

> I think that we are not organized or prepared, nor are we moving fast enough to defend ourselves against the attacks which will probably be made against us. This thing is no longer an investigation of the B-36. It may turn, at any time, into an investigation of the Navy and if we are not prepared with our testimony, well coordinated and with witnesses who are prepared to testify, the Navy will be in a very sad position.[87]

Burke urged that a high-ranking officer be appointed, with a rear admiral as an assistant, to coordinate the Navy's activities for the hearings. He also suggested that the technical issues should be handled by specifically assigned teams for aviation, radar, and budget matters.[88]

Although copies of this memo were sent to a large number of senior officers in OPNAV, including the CNO and VCNO, no decision for an expanded Navy effort was made. Admiral Briscoe's position as head of the task force was merely advisory, and the ones in a position to decide—Matthews, Kimball, and Denfeld—did not want to make a decision.[89] However, because Burke was still in daily contact with Admirals Briscoe and Durgin concerning the Navy's preparation for the hearings, OP-23 gradually assumed a de facto role as the shop tasked with coordinating OPNAV's response to the House Armed Services Committee hearings.

The committee resumed the B-36 hearings on 22 August. Admiral Radford was back in Washington that week but did not attend the sessions, preferring to work on his draft statement in the time he had available.[90] On 24 August Radford submitted to the committee a list of the prospective Navy witnesses and the order of their presentations. This list had been prepared some days earlier by OP-23 at the request of the Assistant Counsel to the committee's General Counsel.[91] Under this proposal Admiral Radford was to lead off the Navy's testimony by setting forth the major points. He was to be followed by the technical team—captains and commanders who would provide specialized briefings on issues such as the general intercept problem, radar, jet fighter performance, and bombing accuracies. Then senior active duty and retired flag officers would discuss naval strategy and warfare. The final presentation would be given by the Chief of Naval Operations.[92]

The same day Radford submitted the list of Navy witnesses, Cedric Worth was called to testify before the House Armed Services Committee. His startling revelation that he was the author of the Anonymous Document brought the hearings to a sudden close.[93] *Newsweek* magazine reported, "The B–36 'scandal' blew up last week.... Nobody was hurt except the men who had made and repeated the charges; they were left red-faced and penitent."[94]

Stuart Symington, in particular, was relieved that Worth had admitted his authorship. As he wrote to Barton Leach some months later:

> Do you know the day I was really frightened? In Vinson's office when you said, "It is going to be rough so do your best." I tried hard to whistle in the dark and hope I deceived you and went in with a bucket of false assurances and could have embraced Worth when he pulled me out despite Keenan—what a story and what a world.[95]

The Worth revelation was a major blow to the Navy's credibility, since many in the press looked upon Worth's action as part of an orchestrated effort by the Navy hierarchy. The headline in the *Washington Daily News* on 25 August, following Carl Vinson's questioning of Under Secretary Dan Kimball on the matter, read "Navy Fathered Memo on B–36, Vinson Says."[96] And the issue of *Time* magazine for that week intoned:

> Would Worth ... admit to the committee that the whole scheme had done the Navy no good? Worth would go further than that: "I will state to anybody that I've done the Navy no good."
>
> ...
>
> Most committee members believed that Bureaucrat Worth could not have done it without a lot of help from Navy officers.[97]

Those preparing for the Navy's part in the hearings didn't have to be told of the seriousness of Worth's admission. Arleigh Burke wrote to a friend, "We didn't realize the seriousness... [of the situation] until the last several days when it was found that our Mr. Worth had written the anonymous document. This makes it very difficult for the Navy to present any other side of the story."[98]

After a final day of hearings on 25 August Chairman Vinson declared that "not one scintilla of evidence" offered in the hearings supported charges that corruption or influence had played any part in the procurement of the B–36 bomber. He then recessed the committee until 5 October 1949.[99]

The conclusion of the B–36 hearings was a major public relations victory for the Air Force. The Department of Defense's review of press and radio accounts of the final week of hearings noted:

> *SecDef Johnson and SecAir Symington* considered completely vindicated before Worth testimony. Allegations in anonymous document generally conceded to be unfounded....
>
> *Consensus is that AF made out good case* for itself and for the B–36 by all of its witnesses.[100]

It was now up to the Navy to try to recover the ground that had been lost with Congress and the public by Cedric Worths' revelations.

The Run-Up to October

Only a few days after the B–36 hearings were concluded, an event occurred that was to have a major effect on U.S. strategic planning in the months and years to come. It was the Soviet Union's first test of an atomic weapon. On 3 September 1949 an Air Force weather reconnaissance aircraft on patrol from Japan to Alaska received indications of higher than normal radioactivity in the atmosphere. These indications were quickly confirmed by other sampling aircraft, and within four days laboratory analysis revealed that the radioactivity was the result of nuclear fission.[101] President Truman was given the momentous news on 19 September and, at the strong urging of his defense advisers, issued a statement to the press on 23 September.

This event was a major concern to military planners since it revealed that the Soviet Union had tested an atomic device almost a year earlier than the most pessimistic recent American intelligence estimate had predicted. Several months later it was determined that instead of the Soviet Union having a likely stockpile of twenty atomic weapons by mid-1955 (according to the probable mid-1953 date of a first Soviet atomic test), it would have ten to twenty bombs by mid-1950.[102] This dramatically increased Soviet offensive capability in turn required drastic revisions in U.S. planning for continental defense.

In a matter of more immediate consequence to the Navy Department at this time, certain naval officers who were aware of how slowly their service was preparing for the upcoming congressional hearings wondered why their senior leaders were not being more responsive. One of these officers was Fitzhugh Lee. At the end of August, Lee wrote to Arleigh Burke:

I am more than ever convinced that more people in the Navy (particularly the non-aviators) must know what is happening and how important it is that the navy be permitted to tell its story in public in October. It is apparent that many sincere high-ranking officers think *now* that the navy would do better to slink away and stay quiet until Louis Johnson leaves office. Yet those same officers would be in there pitching if they knew the full story as it is known to you and a few others.[103]

These weeks were busy ones for the Navy. On 29 August 1949 a Naval Court of Inquiry convened to examine the circumstances surrounding the preparation of the Anonymous Document.[104] Secretary Matthews was particularly determined to get to the bottom of the matter.[105] Over the following three weeks the Court of Inquiry met another seven times before adjourning to await additional evidence. In its deliberations the court was clearly hampered by the lack of Air Force cooperation. It was denied access to the report on the Anonymous Document prepared by the Air Force's Office of Special Investigations, which had been turned over to Carl Vinson.[106] Moreover, Stuart Symington, who had been requested to appear before the Court of Inquiry to give testimony, later declined to appear, commenting that any testimony he might give would have the appearance of entering into an interservice controversy.[107]

Although several Navy witnesses—Tom Davies, in particular—were closely questioned by the court regarding assistance given to Cedric Worth, none were charged with having knowingly participated in writing or distributing the Anonymous Document.[108] The absence of direct evidence linking others to Worth's writing effort proved too difficult a hurdle for the court to overcome.

At the end of August Secretary Matthews left Washington for a visit to CINCPAC. He arrived on Oahu on 2 September and during the next five days had several opportunities to talk at some length with Admiral Radford.[109] One of the things Radford attempted to do in these personal meetings—his first with the new Secretary of the Navy—was to acquaint Matthews with the problem the Navy was facing in the Johnson Defense Department. As Admiral Radford recalled:

> I... explained to him at considerable length the fact that the Navy was facing a show-down in the Department of Defense Organization because of an accumulation of circumstances dating back almost to the end of the war and brought to a head largely by the policies adopted by Mr. Forrestal... [who] had urged Navy to keep quiet and to help him... adjust differences of opinion gradually.[110]

Radford urged Matthews to read the volumes of the 1947 hearings on the National Security Act in order to learn the history of unification. This the Secretary agreed to do.

Despite Francis Matthews's promise, Admiral Radford retained a vague feeling of uneasiness about the new Navy Secretary's bluff sense of self-assurance. Matthews appeared to believe that his judgment "was best at all times and in every detail." Radford remarked:

> In my conversations with Mr. Matthews...I came to the conclusion that Mr. Matthews, like a great many civilians who have had no military service, had the feeling that in a military service a senior officer simply spoke and others did as they were told. During the war, I came in contact with many civilians who were surprised to find out that in a military service, particularly the Navy, senior officers listened to arguments from their juniors.[111]

Upon his return to Washington Matthews hastened to assure Radford that their talks had been helpful.[112] However, the Secretary's views about the nature of the Navy's presentation to the House Armed Services Committee were guided by a subsequent telephone call he received from committee General Counsel Joseph Keenan. On 14 September, Keenan told the Secretary that the Navy should present its views to the committee but its presentation should avoid criticizing the actions of the Defense Department or the Air Force. He said, "Now off the record I have had a little chat with Steve Early about it...[and] I think Steve rather has the feeling that if...[the Navy presentation] isn't done that there will be a good deal of criticism if this is a one-sided affair, nevertheless...it ought to be on a high level."[113]

The Secretary quickly passed these newly adopted views on to Admiral Denfeld. Radford's concerns about Matthews were not eased when the CNO wrote him of a talk with the Secretary following the latter's return from Hawaii. Denfeld remarked, "He of course is very much disturbed about this B–36 investigation and hopes that we will make objective presentations. He feels that we should tell them what we can do and not discuss the B–36 or the Air Force unless we have to do it in answering questions."[114]

In early September rumors were rife on Capitol Hill that the House Armed Services Committee would not resume its hearings to examine the other items on its agenda. Both the Air Force and the Truman administration were said to be arguing against a resumption. Admiral Radford was convinced that additional hearings *would* take place because he had received assurances from Representative Dewey Short (R–Mo.), the ranking Republican on the committee.[115] However, others in the Navy, particularly those on the fringes of the fight, were doubtful that the hearings would resume. One such skeptic was naval aviator Captain John G. Crommelin.

Crommelin, then serving on the Joint Staff, had been bothered by what he saw as a lack of appreciation in the Pentagon for the capabilities of naval aviation. Indeed for several months John Crommelin had been going occasionally to OP–23 to discuss his feelings with his classmate Arleigh Burke.[116] OP–23 staffer Joe Howard had been present at one of these meetings, and he recalled, "In capsule form, Crommelin's view was that we should (as he had been doing) leak anything we deemed appropriate to the press to make the Navy's points, make a big public 'splash' . . . and 'martyr' ourselves if necessary to get our message to the world."[117] Burke instead counseled patience, arguing that Secretary Matthews and Admiral Denfeld would support naval aviation when they were made aware of the true situation.[118]

Expecting to be called as a witness before the House Armed Services Committee, Captain Crommelin had prepared a strong statement of his views on unification. But when the hearing recessed on 25 August without his being called, he became convinced that committee members were unwilling to hear the Navy's views. Crommelin decided to act on his own. On the morning of 10 September he assembled a group of reporters from the wire services at his home and gave a press conference.[119] His formal statement released at the time declared that the real cause of the B–36 controversy and the cancellation of the carrier *United States* was the domination of the Pentagon by the officers and civilians imbued with the "General Staff concept" of complete and autocratic military control.[120] Although Crommelin's statement was almost irrelevant to the agenda of the B–36 investigation, it received a good deal of attention in the press. Many commentators saw the statement as an effort by the Navy to ensure the reopening of the hearings.[121]

Soon a number of other naval officers, including Fleet Admiral William F. Halsey, publicly announced their support for Crommelin's position. However, the officers closely involved with preparations for the hearings were concerned that Crommelin's press conference might have hurt the Navy's case. On 14 September Arleigh Burke passed along to Crommelin a caution from Admiral Radford, "Please don't go off on tangents. . . . Be circumspect."[122]

The public support by other naval officers for Crommelin's stand angered Secretary Matthews. He viewed these acts as indicative of a general anti-unification viewpoint among naval aviators. On 14 September he issued a message to all major commands that officers who wished to express views on the matter should transmit them to him through the appropriate channels.[123]

One officer who responded to the Secretary's request was Vice Admiral Gerald F. (Jerry) Bogan, Commander First Task Fleet. In a Confidential memorandum sent up the chain of command, Admiral Bogan commented, "The morale of the Navy is lower today than at any time since I entered the commissioned ranks in 1916.... In my opinion this descent, almost to despondency, stems from complete confusion as to the future role of the Navy and its advantages or disadvantages as a permanent career."[124] In his endorsement on the memorandum Commander in Chief, Pacific Fleet Arthur Radford seconded Bogan's view noting, "Right or wrong the majority of officers in the Pacific Fleet concur with Captain Crommelin and with the ideas of Vice Admiral Bogan."[125] Admiral Denfeld's endorsement also echoed Radford's concern.[126]

OP-23 Is Put Under Hack

The final days of September 1949 were incredibly busy ones for OP-23 as it hastened to research and edit the statements of Navy witnesses, arrange for mimeographing the presentations, and coordinate the Navy's appearance before the House Armed Services Committee.[127] Just keeping up with a flurry of last-minute changes in the Navy's presentation required a major, all-hands effort by the personnel in Arleigh Burke's shop.

On the afternoon of 27 September the B-36 investigation's assistant general counsel, James M. Gillin, and its attorney, Solis Horowitz, called on Secretary Matthews in an attempt to persuade him to support their proposal for ending the hearings.[128] Vice Chief of Naval Operations John Dale Price and Assistant Judge Advocate General Captain Edwin E. Woods were also present at this meeting.[129]

Gillin talked to Matthews and the others for about thirty minutes on the quesion of continuing the B-36 investigation. As a memorandum on the substance of the meeting recorded:

> [Gillin] stated that the counsel felt that the whole purpose of the [House] resolution had now been heard because they had thoroughly covered Items 1 and 2 [of the committee's agenda]. They had determined that there were no irregularities in the purchase of the B-36, and they had also determined the author of the charges. They were therefore constrained to recommend to the policy [sub-]committee of the House Armed Services Committee that *the rest of the agenda* was not pertinent to the resolution, and they therefore expected to recommend to the policy sub-committee that no further hearings should be held. Mr. Gilliam [*sic*] further stated that they were in Mr. Matthews' office in order *to explore Navy help*.[130]

To this, Admiral Price commented that, as far as the public was concerned, the "baby" was now in the Navy's lap. He noted that the impression conveyed in the hearings to date—that the B–36 program was completely satisfactory—left the Navy in an unfavorable public relations position.[131] Price argued that the Navy should have an opportunity to present its case.

In rebuttal, Gillin replied that although he was sympathetic to the Navy's position, if the Navy was allowed to testify on other items of the committee agenda and get into matters that the Air Force had not discussed, it would cause "consternation in the Air Force as well as in the Navy." And if this were to happen, and the Air Force was given the opportunity to rebut the Navy's testimony, it would result in hearings that lasted "perhaps a year or more." James Gillin argued further that the strategic concept of war and the technical details of U.S. weapons would be subjected to public discussion, perhaps causing much harm to national security.[132]

At this point, Francis Matthews spoke up and agreed with Gillin that the remaining agenda items were not necessary to carry out the committee's mandate. However, he also commented with an air of apparent puzzlement, "[W]hat was the Navy to do now—shut up?" After rambling along in this vein for a few minutes, Matthews finally let the discussion drop.[133]

In the face of Admiral Price's continuing reluctance to give up the Navy's right to be heard by the committee, the participants finally agreed that the Navy could attempt to rewrite a single agenda item for the hearings that could be used by the Navy to relate its "scheme of things."[134] Gillin and Horowitz, however, made it clear to Matthews and the others that they, at least, believed the agenda item selected should be one acceptable to the Air Force.[135]

Following this meeting, Admiral Price instructed Captain Woods to give Arleigh Burke a thorough accounting of what had taken place. Price knew that Burke would acquaint Fitzhugh Lee and Arthur Radford out in Hawaii with what had occurred in the meeting. The VCNO specifically directed Burke to inform Admiral Briscoe of events of the meeting. Price further ordered Burke to have his shop prepare a draft of a single agenda item for the Navy that would cover the earlier agenda items three through seven.[136]

At ten o'clock the following morning, in a Top Policy Group meeting, Secretary Matthews met with his senior service advisers to discuss the Navy's participation in the B–36 hearings.[137] Those present included Admiral Denfeld, Admiral Price, Marine Corps Commandant Clifton Cates, and Rear Admiral George L. Russell, the Navy's Judge Advocate General. Matthews quickly laid down the law to Denfeld, telling the CNO, "The President doesn't want this. It's got to stop. We're not going to have the Navy go up there and ... make a display of all this disunity."[138]

Admiral Denfeld protested somewhat weakly that the Navy had to testify because Congressman Vinson had requested it.[139] Matthews then changed tack and told the group that if the Navy testified it would have to stick to its own issues and not attack the Air Force's position on the B–36.[140] By the end of the meeting, though, the question of whether the Navy Department would request the chance to deliver testimony at the hearings still remained up in the air.

After the group had left his office, Matthews continued the discussion with Admiral Denfeld. He told the CNO that "the proper order of presentation which is now tentative should be, Radford, Blandy, Conolly, Denfeld, *period.*"[141] It was left that the Navy personnel then scheduled to testify in supporting roles should remain ready to testify, even though a decision to allow them to do so had not been made.

Admiral Price sent for Arleigh Burke after the meeting to inform him that he needed several additional drafts of the single agenda item by that afternoon. The VCNO stressed to Burke that there could be no mention of the B–36 or the implications of the bomber in the draft. He did indicate though that the issue of strategic bombing could be mentioned.[142] As Burke was leaving Price's office, the CNO sent for him. Admiral Denfeld asked Burke if he had a copy of Radford's proposed statement for the hearings. Burke told the CNO that he didn't have the current version and suggested that Admiral Denfeld wait until the evening of 30 September when Radford would be in Washington and could give it to him personally. The CNO then requested that Burke make up a folder containing copies of the proposed statements for Matthews, Denfeld, Conolly, and Blandy, for his and the Secretary's use.[143]

Arleigh Burke placed a transpacific telephone call from OP–23's new Pentagon offices to Fitzhugh Lee in Hawaii that afternoon.[144] With Admiral Radford listening in on the line, Burke read to Lee a carefully worded account of the events of the past two days. At the conclusion of the call, Lee asked if Burke felt that he and Radford should continue with their plans to come back to Washington. When Burke said that he certainly did, Lee commented, "We will continue to do that unless I hear otherwise."[145]

That night John Dale Price invited his friend Jack Norris, a *Washington Post* reporter, over for a drink and proceeded to give him an account of Matthews's recent meetings in some detail, neglecting, however, to say that this information was "off the record."[146] The next morning, 29 September, the *Post* played up the story in full under the headline "Navy Cramps Admirals in B–36 Inquiry."[147] Norris's story provided a fairly detailed version of the decisions made by Secretary Matthews:

> Navy Secretary Francis Matthews . . . has ordered naval officer witnesses to make no mention of the B–36 bomber in testifying before the House Armed Services Committee when that group resumes its probe next Wednesday. . . .

These same congressional sources also said that Matthews contemplates limiting the Navy's witnesses to four top admirals and may hold them to a defense of the place of the Navy under current and future world conditions.[148]

There was a special Top Policy Group meeting at 9:14 that morning to further discuss what the Navy should do about testifying. In addition to the regular attendees, James Gillin and Solis Horowitz of the House Armed Services Committee's staff were there.[149] It was in this meeting that Matthews attempted to pressure Admiral Denfeld and the others into informing the committee that the Navy believed the hearings should not be resumed until sometime in the new year. As it was later recounted to newsman Davis Merwin, "Matthews stated that Denfeld, the two admirals Hill [Harry W. Hill, Chairman of the General Board, and Tom B. Hill, Director of OP–36—the Atomic Energy Division] and Admiral Russell, I believe, and one or two others, had all agreed and voted with him to write a recommendation to the Committee that the recessed hearing not be resumed until after the first of the year."[150]

It was at this point that John Dale Price spoke up and said that the group should await the next day's arrival of Admiral Radford from the Pacific before reaching a decision on this matter. When Admiral Price's sudden suggestion received support from Admiral Denfeld and the other officers, an inwardly seething Francis Matthews grudgingly went along.[151]

When Matthews had first read the *Post*'s story that morning he was furious. Norris's account had pictured him (correctly) as attempting to muzzle the Navy's testimony before Congress, and he didn't like being depicted in this manner. As he told columnist C. B. Allen the following morning:

> I don't mind being criticized for mistakes that I have made but I don't like to be accused of unworthy purposes or unworthy motives. I think this, and I think you'll agree with me. In an organization, a Military organization, you have to have discipline, you have to have order, and there are certain things that have to be respected and observed. . . . [152]

He was determined to find out who had leaked the story to the press, so that severe punishment could be meted out.[153] With his morning business out of the way he set about doing just that.

Shortly after noon, Secretary Matthews summoned Admiral Denfeld and Rear Admiral Allan R. McCann, the recently appointed Naval Inspector General, into his office.[154] In the CNO's presence, he gave McCann verbal orders to investigate the leak. At 1:20, Captain Eddie Woods, Assistant Judge Advocate General, paid a call on SECNAV.[155] A concerned Woods told the Secretary that he had information that might be related to the leaking incident. He said that he had been instructed "by a certain unnamed admiral" to prepare the minutes of the 27 September meeting and turn them over to OP-23.[156] Although Captain Woods did not tell the Secretary that he thought OP-23 had leaked this material to Jack Norris, Matthews immediately drew the inference that this was the case.[157] Following some additional meetings that afternoon, Matthews called in Admiral McCann shortly before 4:00 and told him he suspected Arleigh Burke's shop was responsible for the leak.[158] McCann now had a solid lead on where to direct his investigation.[159]

OP-23 staffer Commander Snowden Arthur was in the habit of "cruising by" the CNO's office once in a while, to chat with a certain Reserve lieutenant who was a fund of flamboyant stories. It just so happened that he ran into the lieutenant that afternoon shortly after the IG had decided to target OP-23. The man told him, "They're gonna raid you. The IG's... headed toward you."[160] Commander Arthur hurried back to OP-23 to warn Arleigh Burke. Burke had no way of knowing what was really going on, but he decided to take no chances. With Arthur's help, he rapidly began pulling some of his most sensitive papers out of the files and filling up a briefcase with them.

Admiral McCann reached the OP-23 offices between 4:30 and 5:00 p.m.[161] Sam Shaw recalled, "He came in and... you looked at that man and you knew something was afoot.... And he says, 'Arleigh, I want to talk to you for a moment out in the hall.' So they went out in the hall and closed the door."[162] OP-23's spaces were divided with two doors opening onto the passageway. Commander Arthur happened to be in the other half of the office holding the briefcase of documents when Admiral McCann announced himself: "I heard the Inspector General come in and say, 'Arleigh, it's a raid!' And 'poom,' I took off like a catapult."[163] Arthur didn't stop until he met a friend in OP-30 who agreed to put the briefcase in his safe for the time being. Thereafter, Arthur walked the passageways in the Pentagon for some time before finally deciding to go home.[164]

Back in the OP-23 offices, Sam Shaw and Joe Howard were quickly adjusting to the situation. Admiral Howard remembered, "Sam Shaw seemed to sense, right away, what... [Admiral McCann's visit] was all about. I didn't but Sam Shaw did. And he and I—just the two of us—began frantically to adjust our files and make damn sure that if they were gonna go through the files that there would be some things that they wouldn't be able to find."[165] The things that they were trying to protect were items that provided the names of people in the Air Force and Army who agreed with the Navy's positions.[166] Shaw and Howard had no particular reason to expect that the IG's people would release such information to offices outside the Navy, but, then again, they had no faith in the judgment of Secretary Matthews and no way of knowing what he might do, so they took no chances.[167]

Following the arrival of additional IG personnel a few minutes later Arleigh Burke was directed to order all his people to remain in their offices. Sam Shaw remembered, "Burke came back in by himself, and he was so furious he was white. That man was *just about* to burst. The first thing he said was, 'Sam, how many people have left to go home?'... I told him. [He said,] 'Get 'em all back.' You know, just like that."[168] Joe Howard was also aware of just how upset Burke was when he reentered the office: "Burke was pissed off as hell. And you could tell that. But at the same time, I think that he was aggravated because, for some reason or another, his officers were now also involved, whereas he felt as though whatever responsibility there is, [if] you're gonna hold me here— namely Burke—why okay, but let my officers go home."[169]

Those OP-23 personnel who had already left for the day and who could be reached were hurriedly recalled to the Pentagon. For the next nine or ten hours Burke and his people were held incommunicado while the IG team searched OP-23's files. While Marines guarded the doors into the offices, McCann's officers handled the telephones, telling callers only that OP-23 personnel could not be reached. If Burke's people had to use the bathroom, they were escorted. They could not leave the rooms to get dinner; sandwiches were brought in.[170]

Sometime between 6:00 and 7:00 p.m., IG interviews of OP-23's personnel began.[171] Each of those questioned was taken individually to an office somewhere in the bowels of the Pentagon, as Sam Shaw remembered it, and sharply interrogated by Admiral McCann and his assistants. A still angry Arleigh Burke was the first to be interviewed, and his questioning took a considerable period of time. Allan McCann and his people proved cool and correct in their manner of interrogation but went strictly by the book, making no attempt to put their subjects at ease. Naturally enough, for Burke's people, the atmosphere in the interview room was tense. Sam Shaw likened the experience to being under questioning in a police stationhouse.[172] Admiral Howard commented, "Well, I didn't get the impression myself of there being... the strobe light down on top of you and being beaten... by hoses and whatnot.... But there was certainly a kind of... Star Chamber type of a thing."[173]

The questions centered around the daily work of the office and OP-23's contacts with reporters. McCann gave no indication why OP-23 was being investigated or what he was attempting to determine. Joe Howard later remarked, "I couldn't fathom what it was... that they were going after."[174] Nonetheless, at least a few of the people had deduced that the Norris article was probably the cause.[175] The interrogations went on into the early hours of 30 September without obtaining any confirmation that OP-23 had leaked the story to Jack Norris. Allan McCann was thus forced to admit defeat, but not before the IG team's severe questioning had reduced some of the women staffers to tears and everyone to a state of mental exhaustion.[176] It was 2:00 or 3:00 a.m. when Admiral McCann finally told Arleigh Burke that he and his people were released from the investigation and could go home. However, the admiral warned Burke that his people were not to inform others of what had happened. Spouses could be told, but no one else.[177]

After catching a few hours of sleep, Burke returned to the Pentagon for a few hours of work before driving to Anacostia Naval Air Station for a flight to Moffett Field, California, where he was to meet Admiral Radford and his party and escort them back to Washington.[178]

The Navy Gets Its Chance to Testify

On Saturday morning, 1 October 1949, Secretary Matthews met in a Top Policy Group meeting with his senior advisers. Admiral Radford and the two counsels from the House committee, Gillin and Horwitz, were also present.[179] James Gillin again made his plea for the Navy to help end the hearings. He was fully supported by Secretary Matthews. Arthur Radford, who had been fully briefed by Arleigh Burke on recent events during the flight from California, argued with great conviction that the Navy was ready to present its case to the committee and must be heard. His impassioned plea carried the day with the Navy representatives. Matthews was upset that, as he saw it, Radford would dare to challenge his authority, but kept his feelings to himself, unwilling to confront the well-prepared, confident admiral directly.[180] Arrangements were made for the Navy group to meet with Carl Vinson on Monday morning.

On 3 October Matthews, Denfeld, Radford, and the others trooped over to Vinson's office where they were greeted by the congressman and General Counsel Joseph Keenan.[181] For the next two hours the group debated whether to proceed with the Navy's portion of the hearings. During the course of the meeting, the debate went back and forth. Secretary Matthews recommended delaying the hearings because he and the Navy weren't ready. Vinson, too, clearly wanted to postpone the hearings until at least the new year. Radford countered that the Navy was ready for the hearings now. As Fitzhugh Lee recalled:

> Radford stated that he had made three trips to Washington for the purpose [of testifying], that... [he] was ready to testify, that he thought the rest of the Navy witnesses were, and asked that he be permitted to do so because he was filling a post of high responsibility in the Pacific and felt that he could not properly be away from it so much.[182]

In the end Radford persuaded Carl Vinson to hold off on announcing a delay in the hearings. Although Vinson didn't give the group a final decision, Radford left the meeting believing that Vinson was still inclined to delay.[183] Nonetheless when the group left the chairman's office at noon, Radford was buoyant and Matthews silently hostile. Radford later recalled, "If Mr. Matthews had any feelings about my statements at that time he kept them to himself."[184]

Because he was not involved in the Navy's preparations for the hearings, John Crommelin was unaware of what had transpired in Vinson's office. He was determined to keep the Navy hearings on track, even if it meant martyring himself. In late September fate delivered the means into his hands. Vice Admiral Bogan had sent Crommelin a courtesy copy of his memorandum to the Secretary.[185] On 29 September Crommelin was given copies of the endorsements to Bogan's letter by the Administrative Aide to the DCNO (Air).[186] With these documents in his possession John Crommelin believed that he could force a reopening of the hearings.

In the early afternoon of 3 October, just two hours after the conclusion of the Vinson-Radford meeting, Crommelin met with an Associated Press newsman in the sixth-floor stairwell of the National Press Building. There he handed over sanitized copies of the Bogan letter and the endorsements from Radford and Denfeld.[187] The resulting story made headlines the following day. "Navy Big Brass Blasts Defense Setup" read the banner headline in the *Washington Times-Herald.* That evening Crommelin told his friend Jim Austin, UPI Bureau Chief, to release word that he had supplied the letters to the press.[188] Secretary Matthews quickly ordered the captain suspended from duty, but the suspension was of little concern to Crommelin now that he had accomplished his mission. In the aftermath Air Force supporters and even Matthews argued that Bogan's letter and the endorsements by Radford and Denfeld had been written for just such an eventuality. But this was not true.[189] Fitzhugh Lee later explained, "Actually Raddy advised Matthews to withdraw his dispatch which invited such letters—for fear that it might have this or equally bad consequences."[190]

Whatever Carl Vinson might ultimately have decided about resumption of the House Armed Services Committee hearings, Crommelin's action (and the press attention it received) forced the chairman to reconvene the hearings as soon as possible. Some weeks later Fitzhugh Lee commented to Davis Merwin, "As regards Crommelin, a great many people pleaded with him not to do anything which would upset the apple cart.... [Yet] after it was done, many in the Navy could not help but realize that the hearings would not have been re-opened without his action."[191]

In the final few days before the House Armed Services Committee hearings resumed, Radford, Burke, and the rest of the team pushed to finish their preparations. During this period Radford met with Admiral

Denfeld and convinced him that the presentations should go forward as planned.[192]

The House Armed Services Committee resumed its hearings on the B–36 investigation on 5 October 1949. In a short session Chairman Vinson thanked the committee counsels and staff for their work on the investigation, declared the B–36 hearings officially closed, and asked that the committee convene in its regular capacity the following day "to ascertain the views of the representatives of the Navy" on developments in the Defense Department.[193] It was so voted.

Conclusions

In testimony before the House Armed Services Committee in August 1949 the Air Force successfully defended itself and the B–36 program against the aspersions cast by the Anonymous Document. The last-minute revelation that this compilation of unproven (and unprovable) gossip and innuendo had been drafted by the special assistant to the Under Secretary of the Navy publicly besmirched not only Cedric Worth's reputation but also the Navy's. Most people outside the service believed that the Worth document and John Crommelin's well-timed public outbursts were part of a high-level Navy attempt to damage the Air Force.

By a mixture of chance, circumstance, and far-from-adequate planning, however, the Navy was able to ready itself in the late summer of 1949 to present its views to the House Armed Services Committee on national military strategy and the importance of strengthening naval aviation. This accomplishment was entirely due to a few dedicated individuals working under the leadership of Arthur Radford and Arleigh Burke. Without their efforts the Navy would not have been given the opportunity to redeem itself in the eyes of Congress.

Chapter 9

The "Revolt of the Admirals"

On 6 October 1949 Secretary Francis Matthews led off the Navy testimony at the opening session of the Unification and Strategy hearings. Before delivering his prepared remarks, Matthews surprised those present by declaring that Admiral Arthur Radford's testimony should be heard in executive session because of its effect on the country's national security. This accomplished, Matthews then read his statement, remarking, "On various occasions, when asked about it, I have stated that in my opinion the general morale of the Navy is good; and, furthermore, I want to say now that . . . there is every reason why it should be good."[1] He stated further that he was convinced that any impairment in morale was to be found among the minority of naval aviation personnel who refused to support unification.[2] Matthews emphasized, "No matter how sincere they may claim to be, nor how zealously they may crusade for their objectives, it cannot be conceded that they monopolize the loyalty, the honor, or the patriotic devotion of Navy men, even among naval aviators."[3]

The Secretary of the Navy's testimony was not enthusiastically received by many of those present. A number of naval officers responded to portions of the Secretary's prepared remarks with loud guffaws.[4]

That afternoon the committee heard Admiral Radford's testimony in executive session. The members then voted to allow the presentation to be given in open session. The next morning the admiral repeated his testimony for everyone in the hearing room. He began his statement by attempting to elevate the discussion from the B–36 program itself to the more important issue of the theory of warfare for which the B–36 was a symbol—the "atomic blitz," which promised a cheap and easy victory. Radford emphasized, "The type of war we plan to fight must fit the kind of peace we want. We cannot look to the military victory alone, with no thought to the solution of the staggering problems that would be generated by the death and destruction of an atom blitz."[5]

Radford questioned the usefulness of an atomic blitz on several grounds. First he did not feel that the threat of atomic annihilation would necessarily prevent war. Also he did not believe that using atomic weapons in high-altitude bombing could provide U.S. military leaders

AP/Wide World Photos

Admiral Arthur Radford, CINCPAC/CINPACFLT, *far left*, delivers his statement in open session during the House Armed Services Committee's Unification and Strategy Hearings, 7 October 1949.

with the ability to selectively destroy only military targets. Wide-scale destruction of civilian targets would be a concomitant part of any current atomic targeting effort. If atomic weapons were used under the existing circumstances, they would result in a Pyrrhic victory, at best. Finally he felt that if the American people knew that an atomic blitz meant attacking civilian targets, they would view such warfare as morally indefensible.[6] Radford emphasized to the committee that he was not opposed to the use of atomic weapons. He made it clear, however, that he wanted these weapons used principally against military targets rather than urban-industrial ones.

Because the B–36 was the symbol for this type of warfare, Radford also discussed the merits of this bomber. He argued that the decision on whether the B–36 was a satisfactory weapon had to be based on two questions: (1) Could the aircraft "be intercepted and destroyed in unacceptable numbers on unescorted missions at all speeds and altitudes at which it can operate"? and (2) If it reaches a target, "can it hit what needs to be hit from high altitude?"[7] Arthur Radford testified:

> I am aware that you have been given testimony calculated to show (1) that the B–36 can, with acceptable losses, perform unescorted missions by day or by night; (2) that inadequate radar performance makes it difficult to intercept by day or by night at altitudes over 40,000 feet; (3) that during the next five years there will be no night fighter capable of giving the B–36 serious trouble; and (4) that in time of war the B–36 from altitudes greater than 40,000 feet will be able to perform effective and precise bombing by day and by night.
> *These assertions are not valid.* The unescorted B–36 is unacceptably vulnerable. The B–36 cannot hit precision targets from very high altitudes under battle conditions.[8]

In place of "slow, expensive, very vulnerable, single-purpose heavy bombers" such as the B–36, he urged the procurement of small, fast bombers and extremely high-performance fighters.[9] Radford told the committee that the technical answers to specific questions would be provided by a team of naval officers and aeronautical engineers following his own presentation.

The Navy technical witnesses who followed Radford examined particular aspects of B–36 vulnerability and bombing capability in substantial detail. Captain Frederick M. Trapnell, commanding officer of the Naval Air Test Center at Patuxent River, Maryland, was the first technical witness. Trapnell provided a general overview of the technical issues of B–36 detection and interception:

> As for the radar [detection] problem—at the naval air test center we get good results in detecting, tracking, and controlling jet fighters—at altitudes well above 40,000 feet—with radar equipment that is 4 years old—and without any special electronic aids in the planes. Because the B–36 is a vastly more favorable target than these jet fighters, we expect even better results against it.[10]

On the question of intercepting and shooting down the heavy bomber, Trapnell was just as positive:

> Gun for gun, the interceptor is comparatively vulnerable but is a very small maneuvering target. The B–36 is a very large one and, for all practical purposes, [because of the interceptor's large speed advantage] is nonmaneuvering. Interceptor superiority [over the bomber] is favored by the factors of surprise, initiative, and deception, and it is assured by numbers.[11]

He suggested that the enemy would employ two or three interceptors against each B–36, thus assuring a high kill ratio.

The other technical witnesses dealt in some detail with radar detection, high-altitude interception, the effect of darkness and bad weather on bomber interception, the effect of speed and altitude on a bomber's combat radius, and the difficulties in hitting precise targets from high altitudes using radar. With regard to the last point Commander Eugene Tatom, head of the Aviation Ordnance Branch at the Bureau of Ordnance, remarked:

> How good is our high altitude bombing? Under perfect conditions, with a target which can be seen and which cannot be mistaken, and with all instruments and the bombing computer working perfectly, it is [only] good enough to hit a large target such as a railway yard or great oil refinery from 40,000 feet.[12]

The technical witnesses were followed by a series of the Navy's active and retired senior flag officers, who spoke about the moral and strategic issues at stake. Rear Admiral Ralph Ofstie, Naval Member of the Military Liaison Committee to the Atomic Energy Commission, delivered a particularly strong condemnation of the Air Force's conception of strategic air warfare, stressing that it was morally wrong. He decried that service's intended bombing of urban areas, noting, "The intent of wholesale extermination of enemy civilians certainly does not enter into the official definition of strategic air warfare. However, strategic bombing, as now accepted, unavoidably includes random mass slaughter of men, women, and children in the enemy country."[13] The other senior naval officers who testified (or had statements read to the committee) in favor of the Navy's overall strategic viewpoint comprised the bulk of the service's senior wartime leadership, including Fleet Admirals Ernest King, Chester Nimitz, and William Halsey; Admirals Raymond Spruance and Thomas Kinkaid; and former Marine Corps Commandant General Alexander Vandegrift.

The closing statement of the Navy presentation was scheduled to be given by Admiral Louis Denfeld. The CNO's appearance was eagerly awaited both by the proponents of naval aviation and by those on the other side of the fight. The latter were hoping (even expecting) that Denfeld would repudiate the views of the earlier Navy witnesses.

Until almost the last minute even those close to Admiral Denfeld in the Office of the Chief of Naval Operations were uncertain of which way his testimony would go. Members of his staff had been working fitfully on Denfeld's statement since at least mid-July, but in early October the CNO had not made a decision on the tack he would pursue. Up until the final days Louis Denfeld was receiving conflicting advice from his immediate staff. His Administrative Aide, Red Yeager, was always advising him to take it easy, saying, "Boss, if you don't, you're gonna be fired." Meanwhile Walter Karig, his public relations adviser, was telling him, "Boss, you've got to fire everything there is in the locker.... You've got to do everything you can do."[14]

NHC, Radford Papers

Admiral Radford in a lighter moment during the committee hearings.

During this period the CNO was asked on a number of occasions by Matthews if he had prepared his statement. Admiral Denfeld later explained the Secretary's concern: "[Matthews] was very anxious that I back him up on his statement and that I go along with him and with Secretary Johnson with regard to unification, and more or less throw over what he called the dissident aviators."[15] After Denfeld had replied noncommittally several times, Matthews finally said to him, "Admiral, I believe we should select a time at which you and I can get together and prepare your statement."[16] On 4 October Captain Karig sent the CNO a memorandum, telling him, "To put it bluntly and impolitically, I think the immediate future of the Navy depends on your actions in the next couple of weeks."[17] Nonetheless Denfeld held off making the decision until the last possible moment.

With his scheduled appearance only a few days away Louis Denfeld was finally forced to get off the fence. General Shaw commented:

I'm sure I heard Karig or [George] Russell... talking... that the day or two days before Denfeld was... scheduled to appear, he had not yet made

Admiral Louis E. Denfeld, Chief of Naval Operations from 15 December 1947 to 2 November 1949.

up his mind whether he would appear *at all*. And ... these guys were saying that Denfeld had come in that morning and told them that his wife had said to him at breakfast ... "Louie, are you going to stand up and be counted or aren't you?" And he said ... "I am."[18]

With his decision finally made, Admiral Denfeld gave the go-ahead to his staff to polish up the final version of his statement the day prior to his scheduled appearance before the committee. That night a group, including Captain Don Griffin (the original drafter), Arleigh Burke, Rear Admiral Ossie Colclough, Admiral Radford, Rear Admiral Robert Dennison, and Denfeld himself, put the final touches on the statement. It was not ready until early the next morning.[19]

On the afternoon of 13 October Louis Denfeld presented his testimony to the House Armed Services Committee. The CNO did not have time to show his prepared testimony to Secretary Matthews beforehand. He wouldn't have done so in any case, since he believed Matthews would have tried to get him to change it, something Denfeld had no intention of doing.[20] Once he began his testimony, it became immediately evident that, instead of backing the Johnson Defense Department, he was siding with Radford and the naval aviators. He announced, "As the senior military spokesman for the Navy, I want to state forthwith that I fully support the broad conclusions presented to this committee by the naval and marine officers who had preceded me."[21] Admiral Denfeld then proceeded to detail his concerns about issues such as the effect of budget cuts on the Navy's fighting strength, the role of the Joint Chiefs of Staff in providing additional money for the B-36 while advocating the cancellation of the Navy's flush-deck carrier, and the need to give predominant weight to service views in determining forces necessary for that service.[22]

In addition to these specific issues, the CNO saw the defense of the Navy's raison d'etre as equally important. He believed that he had to overturn the thinking steadily gaining ground on Capitol Hill that the Navy was somehow of secondary importance in the atomic age. He explained to the committee members:

"Why do we need a strong Navy when any potential enemy has no navy to fight?" I read this in the press, but, what is more disturbing, I hear it repeatedly in the councils of the Department of Defense. As a result, there is a steady campaign to relegate the Navy to a convoy and antisubmarine service, on the grounds that any probable enemy possesses only negligible fleet strength. This campaign results from a misunderstanding of the functions and capabilities of navies and from the erroneous principle of the self-sufficiency of air power. ... Fleets never in history met opposing fleets for any other purpose than to gain control of the sea—not as an end in itself, *but so that national power could be exerted against the enemy.*[23]

Denfeld then lauded the Navy's warfighting capabilities, from its antisubmarine forces and offensive carrier task forces to its amphibious warfare forces and the extremely important combat component provided by the Marine Corps.[24]

In conclusion Denfeld pointed to the value of allowing differing service perspectives to be publicly aired in hearings. Although he was aware that some viewed this situation as regrettable, he stated, "I believe, however, it would have been immeasurably more regrettable had these issues remained hidden and a false sense of security been permitted to prevail."[25]

Louis Denfeld's strong testimony was a bombshell. The next morning the front page headline in the *New York Times* read, "Denfeld Sees Navy Gravely Imperiled By Chiefs' Decisions."[26] A few days later *Time* magazine, which a week earlier had titled its article on the Navy's testimony "Revolt of the Admirals," intoned, "All week long the rebels nervously waited to hear what meek 'Uncle Louie' Denfeld would say. So did Secretary Johnson, who narrowed his eyes as he told a friend: 'Denfeld hasn't been disloyal—yet.' ... Denfeld's outburst startled a few people."[27] Having taken his stand, the CNO waited to see what would happen.

Administration Reactions

Admiral Denfeld's strong statement to the House Armed Services Committee was a profound shock to those in the new Defense Department who had expected the CNO to side with his Secretary. After all, up to that time, Louis Denfeld had basically "gone along to get along" with his superiors and his fellow Chiefs. Navy Secretary Francis Matthews, who first read the statement just before Denfeld gave it, was visibly flushed when he left the hearing room that afternoon.[28] *Time* magazine later reported the comment of an unnamed high-ranking general on the impact of Denfeld's testimony: "Personal relationships have gone to hell. I don't see how they can ever be repaired within the Joint Chiefs of Staff."[29] Other officials in the Johnson Defense Department were equally upset. That evening Alfred M. Gruenther, Dwight Eisenhower's long-time friend and former Director of the Joint Staff, who had recently returned to the Army Staff, sent a copy of Admiral Denfeld's testimony to General Eisenhower, together with a note that read, "We are all quite depressed over the tone. Air Force feel strongly that Gen Collins [the new Army Chief of Staff] should return from Japan to testify next week."[30]

Louis Johnson was livid at Denfeld's defection. Over the following days he mounted his forces for a strong counterattack on the Navy's presentation. On 18 October Johnson attempted to reach Eisenhower at Columbia University to urge him to testify in favor of the administration's position. Upon hearing from the general's aide, Robert Schulz, that Eisenhower was unavailable, Johnson told Schulz, "[Denfeld's statement] is an attack against the President and civilian control and economy." While the two men were on the phone, Stuart Symington walked into Johnson's office, but before the Defense Secretary rang off, Johnson reiterated his plea for Eisenhower's help, remarking, "They really have gone below the belt this time."[31]

When the hearings resumed on Monday, 17 October, the committee heard the final two witnesses for the Navy, Marine Corps Commandant, General Clifton Cates, and his predecessor, retired General Arthur Vandegrift. Both testified to what they believed was a continuing effort on the part of the Army, under the guise of greater unification, to strip the Marine Corps of vital elements of its combat strength, particularly its air assets.[32]

The following day the rebuttal witnesses began their testimony, with Air Force Secretary Stuart Symington the first to speak. In his prepared remarks Symington carefully stayed with the main points that he had made in his appearance during the B–36 hearings. He denied that the Air Force believed an atomic blitz offered a "quick, easy, and painless war," and also that the Air Force favored mass bombing of civilians. But he avoided providing new substantive material to back up his denials.[33]

Symington went to some effort, however, to deny that the recently issued Harmon Committee report on the likely results of an atomic air offensive minimized the effectiveness of such an offensive. The Harmon Committee was the ad hoc committee which had been established in January 1949 at Secretary Forrestal's request to examine the potential results of an air offensive on the Soviet Union.[34] Admiral Denfeld had mentioned the committee's report during his testimony on 13 October. Although he had not stated directly that the report lent support to the Navy's position on the likely effects of the atomic offensive (he could not discuss its findings because it was highly classified), he did leave the members with that impression.[35]

Symington refuted this impression not with material from the report itself, which he obviously could not use, but with a carefully worded memorandum from General Harmon, implying that he and his colleagues had reported favorably on the effectiveness of projected "air atomic operations."[36] Symington's use of Harmon's memo effectively countered Denfeld's testimony by arguing "from authority."[37] Because the top secret report was unavailable to the committee, Stuart Symington's ploy was successful. We know now, however, that, on balance, the Harmon Committee report supported Admiral Denfeld's reservations about the strategic air offensive.

On the positive side the Harmon Committee report did state that the atomic bomb would be a major element of Allied military strength; if delivered in an early atomic offensive, it would constitute the only means of "rapidly inflicting shock and serious damage to vital elements of the Soviet war-making capacity." However, the report also acknowledged that even if, as assumed, the air offensive was perfectly delivered, its initial atomic portion would result in only a 30 to 40 percent reduction of Soviet industrial capacity—a loss that would not be permanent. The report also stated that the atomic offensive—despite killing as many as 2.7 million Russians and injuring 4 million more in seventy target cities—would not, per se, bring about "capitulation, destroy the roots of Communism or critically weaken the power of Soviet leadership to dominate the people." The report acknowledged that the offensive would not seriously impair the ability of Soviet armed forces to advance rapidly into selected areas of Western Europe, the Middle East, and the Far East. However, fuel and logistics disruptions caused by the initial bombing would thereafter progressively diminish Soviet capabilities.[38]

Air Force Chief of Staff Hoyt Vandenberg was the next to rebut the Navy's presentations. Like Symington, Vandenberg chose to refute the Navy's charges not with new information but by arguing from authority. On the B–36's effectiveness, for example, Vandenberg commented:

> This committee and the country have heard assertions during the last 2 weeks that the B–36 cannot do its job....
>
> I think the country should know that the officers who are in charge of the strategic bombing program...have heard these assertions again and again, have examined them with professional diligence and care...and have concluded that the assertions are unfounded.[39]

He went on to recall for the committee the "historic fact" that no AAF bombing mission in World War II was ever stopped short of its target by enemy opposition.[40] Vandenberg was reminded during questioning by Congressman Dewey Short that on raids such as those on Schweinfurt, Regensburg, and Ploesti, AAF bombers had gotten through to their targets only after sustaining unacceptable losses. Vandenberg rejoined:

> What you are quoting from, sir, is tactics and techniques of a war that is past.... We have new tactics, new technique, new speeds, new altitudes, an entirely different type of explosive. Where at one time the losses might be unacceptable, in another war, in order to destroy a target, they might be very acceptable.[41]

Another issue was whether radar bombing accuracies at 40,000 feet permitted the B–36 to perform precision bombing of enemy targets. Representative Porter Hardy, Jr. (D–Va.), closely questioned General Vandenberg on this point, reading a portion of Admiral Radford's testimony that no significant developments since the war had improved bombing accuracies at 40,000 feet *under battle conditions* over what had been obtained during World War II at 20,000 feet. Hardy asked the Air Force Chief of Staff if he knew of any significant improvements. Vandenberg replied, "In the first place the implication is that bombing at 20,000 feet was not accurate and was mass bombing. I do not believe the record will sustain that.... Additionally there have been improvements, very definite improvements in bombing equipment."[42]

Hoyt Vandenberg was being extremely optimistic, to say the least. Army Air Force analyses of its wartime bombing had demonstrated that both visual and radar bombing from 20,000 feet had been anything but precise. For example, during almost all of 1944, complete mission failures for the Eighth Air Force—in which no bomber formation placed 5 percent of its bombs within 1,000 feet of the assigned aiming point—ranged from 20 percent to 40 percent.[43] Moreover, radar bombing during latter years of the war was much less accurate than visual bombing. In late 1944 the Eighth Air Force, using H2X-radar bombing and dropping through 40 to 50 percent cloud cover, was able to place only 4.4 percent of its bombs within 1,000 feet of the aiming point and only 48.5 percent within a mile of it. Under conditions of complete cloud cover these percentages worsened to .2 percent within 1,000 feet (2 out of 1,000 bombs) and 5.6 percent within a mile.[44] Moreover, neither Vandenberg nor anyone else in the Air Force at the time he testified had a good idea what the B–36's bombing accuracy at 40,000 feet was likely to be. Although the new K-1 bombing equipment was an improvement over the wartime H2X gear, the Air Force had not seriously tested its high-altitude bombing accuracy.[45] Just a week before he testified for the second time, General Vandenberg had received a memorandum written by Major General Gordon P. Saville, the Air Force's Director of Requirements, showing that up to that time at the Air Proving Ground, only *one* B–36 had made a radar-aimed bomb release from 40,000 feet.[46]

Omar Bradley's Attack on Denfeld and the Navy

Hoyt Vandenberg was followed to the witness table by General Omar Bradley, the former Army Chief of Staff and new Chairman of the Joint Chiefs of Staff. Bradley had an imposing background as an Army general officer, having served successively in the Mediterranean and European Theaters during World War II as commander of II Corps, First Army, and Twelfth Army Group.[47] Following a postwar tour as head of the Veterans Administration, Bradley had been appointed by President Harry

Truman, a fellow Missourian, to succeed his old friend and classmate Dwight Eisenhower as Army Chief of Staff.

Holding this post from 7 February 1948 to 15 August 1949, Omar Bradley had earned a reputation as a quiet, modest (though not unassuming) officer who was not strongly partisan in his judgments of service plans and programs. Although in 1948 he had sided with the Navy on the construction of the flush-deck aircraft carrier, he reversed his thinking and favored its cancellation in April 1949. In the months prior to the House Armed Services Committee hearings, he had begun to side more and more on budget issues in Joint Chiefs of Staff meetings with his Air Force colleague Hoyt Vandenberg, a friend from the days in 1944-1945 when Vandenberg's Ninth Air Force was providing air support to Bradley's Twelfth Army Group.[48]

General Bradley had taken the job as JCS Chairman in part because he hoped that his role as a firm but fair chairman would help to avert further strife between the services.[49] One of his first actions had been to request that Admiral Denfeld select a bright young naval officer to be Bradley's Navy aide.[50] Denfeld chose Lieutenant Commander Edward L. (Ned) Beach, an outstanding submarine officer who had been Denfeld's own aide when he was Chief of the Bureau of Naval Personnel in 1946 and early 1947.[51]

Commander Beach was aware that a vital, if unofficial, part of his job was to see that General Bradley had a good reading of current Navy thinking on important national defense issues. To further this effort, Beach helped arrange a meeting soon after he reported in. The participants were two members of General Bradley's staff—Beach and Lieutenant Colonel Chester V. (Ted) Clifton, Bradley's new speech writer—and four experienced naval aviators—two from the Bureau of Aeronautics (Captains William A. Schoech and Paul Foley, Jr.), one from the Fleet (VC-5's Commanding Officer, Captain J. T. Hayward), and one from OP-36, the Atomic Defense Division of OP-03 (Commander Joseph A. Jaap). On 23 September 1949 the group met in a wide-ranging, intensive, two-hour discussion.

The announced reason for the meeting was a speech that Secretary Johnson had tasked Bradley to give. The general wanted to use the occasion to stress his understanding of the problems of the Navy.[52] As Colonel Clifton told the aviators:

> [It is] the General's impression that morale in the Navy was now at a low ebb due to recent developments, particularly the SecDef's veto of the supercarrier and that the General hoped to be able to say something to help—somewhat in the manner of the similar help given [Army] Ground Forces during a corresponding low morale period about 1 1/2 years ago.[53]

Clifton then asked the group what particularly disturbed the Navy rank and file. This gave the aviators the chance to explain their feelings about the cancellation of the flush-deck carrier and the need for employing carrier aviation in antisubmarine warfare. They also expressed their concerns about Air Force sniping at naval aviation and the need for stability in budgeting for naval aviation forces. For his part Colonel Clifton attempted to justify General Bradley's vote on the flush-deck carrier and explained how the chairman viewed future service force levels.

Two issues that the naval aviators emphasized were the similarity in Navy and Army thinking on the proper employment of air power and the importance of understanding the Navy's views on offensive carrier aviation. Regarding the first issue the naval officers expressed amazement that the ground forces did not support this mutual Navy-Army viewpoint more actively in high-level discussions. Captain Foley cited talks he had had in combat with Army division commanders who greatly preferred having Marine close air support to AAF support because air control rested with the top local commander. Yet he noted that Army officers in the postwar period always seemed to support the Air Force position of independent air command.[54]

On the second issue the aviators tied Army misperceptions of Navy thinking on offensive carrier aviation to confusion about the nature of "strategic bombing." Paul Foley explained to Colonel Clifton:

> The Navy felt that it had a particular job to do—as defined at the Key West conference. Primarily it has to gain and maintain control of the sea-routes. To do this it had to contain and destroy enemy submarines in or accessible to the area and keep open the sea-routes to advance bases. These tasks necessitated having a free hand to decide how and with what they were to be accomplished.... If it meant sinking submarines by attacking them at their bases (1000 miles away) then the Navy regarded this as a "tactical" decision and "tactical bombing" and thought it should be permitted both the weapons and the freedom to perform this mission.[55]

On this point, Clifton asked the aviators if attack missions against submarine pens couldn't be performed by embarking Air Force pilots in naval vessels. He was told in no uncertain terms that in Great Britain this same "absurd experiment" during the 1920s and 1930s had led directly to serious defects in the Royal Navy's Fleet Air Arm during the first years of World War II.[56]

Ted Clifton left this meeting with a good idea of the Navy's aviation concerns. How effectively he imparted these views to General Bradley remains unknown. It certainly appears, though, that the JCS Chairman's understanding of the Navy's viewpoint continued to be extremely limited.

Whatever conciliatory role Omar Bradley may have intended to play with the Navy in the Joint Chiefs of Staff was quickly swept aside by the fierceness of the Navy's assault in the Unification and Strategy hearings on the approved policies and strategies of the Air Force, the JCS, and the Johnson Defense Department. Bradley may have anticipated the stinging attacks by Radford and the other aviators, but when his JCS colleague, Louis Denfeld, sided with them, it proved too much for the general. To Bradley's way of thinking, the admirals were "insubordinate, mutinous," and deserving of public censure.[57] A vital point apparently lost on both General Bradley and his boss, Louis Johnson, was that in testifying before Congress, Denfeld, Radford, and the others were not being mutinous but were instead complying with the lawful request of the House Armed Services Committee to provide their frank and freely given views on the issues.[58]

Now determined to strike back at the Navy's military leadership, Omar Bradley closeted himself with Ted Clifton. Captain Beach recalled the general's method of developing speeches:

> Now, one of the things that Bradley always did was he would...get the people in[to] his office, shut the door, and then they'd go to work.... Bradley would first say, "Hey, we've got to make a speech about so-and-so." And Clifton would then research [the issue], and Bradley would tell him, "I want to talk about this, about that, and about the other thing." And Clifton would write the draft. Bradley would then work it over, and extensively so. And then Clifton would work it [over] some more, and Bradley would work it [over] some more.[59]

The resulting product would be a carefully drafted speech that reflected the general's thinking. Ned Beach remarked that Bradley put more effort into his speeches than he had seen any other senior officer do.[60]

On this occasion their combined efforts produced a statement that proved to be the strongest and most controversial of Bradley's career.[61] It was so sensitive that, for Beach's own protection, Omar Bradley refused to allow his naval aide to be involved in the drafting or even to read the completed statement before it was given.[62]

General Bradley delivered his statement to the House Armed Services Committee on the afternoon of 19 October 1949.[63] The first part (less than a quarter of the text) was a fairly measured discussion of national objectives, the need for long-range military policy and the requirement for balanced military forces. The second part, however, was a highly critical examination of the Navy's principal charges and an almost vitriolic denunciation of the Navy's leadership and strategic thinking.[64]

In countering charges that strategic bombing was militarily wrong, Bradley commented, "From a military standpoint, any damage you can inflict on the war-making potential of a nation, and any great injury you can inflict upon the morale of that nation contributes to the victory."[65] He defended strategic (mass) bombing from the charge that it was morally wrong by arguing that war itself was immoral and, in any case, such bombing would be carried out "with minimum harm to the non-participating populace."[66]

Bradley's harshest criticisms came when he discussed the Navy's charge that its offensive power was being destroyed by the actions of the Secretary of Defense and the Joint Chiefs of Staff. He saw this charge as a castigation of the Chiefs' knowledge of warfare.[67] Bradley completely dismissed the Navy's concern that, by cutting its offensive air power, the Defense Secretary was harming the country's ability to fight and win a war with the Soviet Union. "Considering again the only possible enemy we have in sight," he said, "we are faced with the real fact that the Soviet Union and her satellites have tremendous land forces and tactical aviation, but their surface navy is negligible." Bradley stated that he believed in naval aviation as part of hunter-killer task forces used to fight Soviet submarines and assure control over enemy navies but that he did not believe in using carrier aviation assets to attack land targets. Such a capability might be "nice to have," but it would not make a particularly important contribution in the initial stages of a war.[68]

Bradley then launched into an assault on the competence of the Navy's leadership:

> The truth of the matter is that very few Navy men on the staff of the Chief of Naval Operations have had any experience in large-scale land operations. Uppermost in their minds are island-hopping campaigns of the Pacific, and the battles at sea. While listening to presentations by some Navy officers before the Joint Chiefs of Staff, I have heard high-ranking Navy men arrive at conclusions that showed they had no concept whatsoever of land operations.[69]

General Bradley made his judgment of the Navy leaders' military competence even clearer by contrasting the combat backgrounds of the Army and Air Force Chiefs with, by implication, that of the Chief of Naval Operations. The JCS Chairman noted that Army Chief of Staff J. Lawton Collins had commanded a division in combat on Guadalcanal and at New Georgia and later led a corps during the Northern European campaign. He similarly pointed out that Air Force Chief of Staff Hoyt Vandenberg had commanded the Ninth Air Force during the fighting in Europe. "They have had wide experience in many operations,"

Bradley stated, "including amphibious assault and with its appropriate air and naval support." In addition, Bradley himself was the former commanding general of the Twelfth Army Group— "the largest field command ever to operate under a single commander," he reminded the members. He had also participated in the assaults on Sicily and Normandy—"the two largest amphibious operations ever conducted." As for Denfeld's wartime record, Bradley simply stated, "I was not associated with Admiral Denfeld during the war, and I am not familiar with his experiences."[70] The implication of the general's comment was left hanging in the air for the committee members to grasp.

Omar Bradley concluded his lengthy statement by accusing the Navy witnesses of rebelling against civilian control of the military by disputing the Secretary of Defense's authority and of seriously harming the national defense by testifying before the House Armed Services Committee.[71] He summed up his dismissal of Navy leaders' concerns with the insulting comment, "This is no time for 'fancy dans' who won't hit the line with all they have on every play, unless they can call the signals."[72]

The naval officers present in the hearing room were stunned not only by the content of General Bradley's statement but also by his emotional delivery. Fitzhugh Lee recalled, "I will never forget his speech. He started off quietly and gradually worked himself into an hysterical delivery in which his voice kept rising in pitch[,] and he was trembling.... I never dreamed that a four-star officer in the armed forces could so completely lose control of himself."[73]

The press had a field day with Bradley's testimony. The next day the headline in the *New York Times* read, "Bradley Accuses Admirals Of 'Open Rebellion' On Unity; Asks 'All-American Team.'"[74] The *Washington Post*'s headline the same day read, "Staff Chiefs Chairman Assails Top Admirals For Hurting Defense."[75] The accompanying article by reporter John Norris described the scene:

> In a hide-searing statement before the House Armed Services Committee, he flatly rejected every one of the Navy's complaints against strategic A-bombing, the B–36 and treatment of the Navy by the Pentagon high command.... The top-ranking officer of the armed services accused the admirals, in effect, of being prima donnas and soreheads.[76]

Because of the negative press Omar Bradley began publicly backing away from his harsher remarks, telling Hanson Baldwin the following day that his "fancy dan" comment had been misconstrued and that he had not meant to cast aspersions on Admiral Denfeld's war record. He commented, "If I made a mistake I am sorry."[77] Privately, however, Bradley remained convinced that he had little to apologize for. On 26

October Dwight Eisenhower wrote him about the press attention given to his testimony and the possibility that he might have lost his usefulness in the Defense Department. Eisenhower commented, "I know that you are too level-headed to let such statements bother you." In a postscript, Ike added, "Don't defend yourself—Don't explain—Don't worry."[78] Two days later Bradley wrote back, "I hesitated a long time before making such a strong statement, but then decided that this was a way in which I could contribute most to eventual unification. We just cannot have things stirred up on the Hill every three months."[79]

The Army Sides With the Air Force

Several Navy witnesses had stressed in their testimony that the Air Force was neglecting tactical aviation in favor of strategic air power and therefore was not adequately discharging its responsibility to provide tactical air support for the Army.[80] The Army was expected to have a particular interest in this issue at the hearings.

During 1946, when the Army Air Forces had pushed for independent service status under the pending unification legislation, Army senior officers had been concerned that if the Army divested itself of tactical aviation, the new service might not continue to furnish adequate air support to its ground forces in combat.[81] To allay these concerns, General Carl Spaatz, the AAF's Commanding General, had assured Army Chief of Staff Dwight Eisenhower that if the Army supported AAF plans for a separate service that included tactical aviation, the new service would not neglect the mission of providing air support to the Army. Lieutenant General Elwood R. (Pete) Quesada, the Air Force's first commander of the Tactical Air Command (TAC), recalled, "I wasn't there but I was told about it in no uncertain terms by Spaatz. Spaatz told me that he had made this promise to Eisenhower. 'And goddammit, don't let him down,' he said."[82]

By late 1948 the Air Force, which had been in existence for more than a year, was no longer beholden to the Army for its earlier support. Spaatz had been replaced as Air Force Chief of Staff by Hoyt Vandenberg, and changes were in the offing. The Air Force's senior leadership had determined that the two primary missions of the service were strategic bombing and (to a lesser extent) continental air defense. Everything else had to assume a greatly lowered priority.

From 1946 to December 1948 the Tactical Air Command under Quesada had built up gradually from six combat groups to eleven.[83] However, by late 1948 Air Force leaders were convinced that budget stringencies reflected in the coming fiscal year 1950 budget and the service's continued 48-group force level necessitated economizing to provide greater funding for the strategic bombardment and air defense forces. Accordingly in December 1948 Hoyt Vandenberg directed that the Tactical Air Command and the Air Defense Command (ADC) be combined into a Continental Air Command (CONAC). TAC's Ninth and Twelfth Air Forces were assigned to CONAC as subordinate units. CONAC was to allocate tactical units for specific missions and special training exercises as needed. The Tactical Air Command was reduced to a 150-man planning headquarters.[84] Lieutenant General George E. Stratemeyer, Commanding General Air Defense Command, was named CONAC commander. Pete Quesada, who felt betrayed by the downgrading of TAC, left to become the adviser to the Secretary of the Air Force for reserve matters.

Under CONAC tactical air power withered. Although all CONAC pilots were supposed to be trained in both air defense techniques and close air support, air defense had the priority. Little time or attention was devoted to perfecting ground support tactics and techniques.[85]

By the spring of 1949 officers in the Army Field Forces were concerned that tactical air no longer had a major role in Air Force plans. That spring General Jacob L. (Jake) Devers, Chief of the Army Field Forces, wrote a personal letter to Vandenberg about the situation:

> Until the reorganization [of] the United States Air Force, Ninth and Twelfth Air Forces were basically charged with tactical air force missions, operating under Tactical Air Command. As near as I can determine, United States Air Force reorganization has not charged any numbered air force or lower headquarters with tactical air force functions and missions. I do not know what plans you may have to keep alive the complex machinery of close support and to allow this specialized activity to progress.... I am therefore quite concerned over the absence of Tactical Air Force organization.[86]

As the result of Devers's letter, the Air Force initiated a top-level conference with the Army. The Army attendees at this 4 May 1949 meeting included Chief of Staff Omar Bradley, General Devers, and twelve other general officers. The Air Force was represented by Chief of Staff Hoyt Vandenberg; Lieutenant General Lauris Norstad, Deputy Chief of Staff for Operations; General Quesada; Major General Robert M. Lee, Quesada's replacement at TAC; and two other general officers. Devers took the lead for the Army, making it clear that the Air Force needed to pay attention to tactical air power. Vandenberg countered by defending Air Force capabilities and promising to promote joint Army-Air Force training. He also promised that he would look into "over enthusiasm" by certain parts of the Air Force for strategic bombing at the expense of tactical air.[87]

A few days later Lieutenant General Ennis C. Whitehead, who had replaced George Stratemeyer as CONAC commander, proposed an interim solution to Vandenberg. The Fourteenth Air Force should be designated a tactical unit to support the Army and be headquartered with the Army's command at Fort Bragg, North Carolina.[88] The Air Force Chief of Staff agreed. He had already decided that further steps should be taken to allay Army fears.[89] Accordingly on 10 June 1949 Air Force Vice Chief Muir Fairchild directed Pete Quesada to head an Air Force review board at TAC headquarters, Langley Air Force Base, Virginia.[90] The five-man Quesada Board began meeting later that month to review current Air Force doctrine on tactical air operations.

Even as the Quesada Board began its first sessions, General Devers decided to hold the Air Force's "feet to the fire." He issued a press release on 8 July 1949, stating that as a result of Army prodding, the Air Force had agreed to provide greater air support to the Army. Devers expected to see four necessary improvements: more Air Force troop carrier units, additional Air Force-Army joint training in close support operations, a satisfactory fighter-bomber for close support of ground operations, and more Air Force tactical air groups in the proposed 48-group program. In the follow-up with reporters the Army Field Forces chief said, "Air Force intentions and spirit of cooperation are fine. We are working well together. What we have now are assurances, not guarantees. But I think if we keep after them—keep bouncing them—things will be all right."[91]

Barton Leach, the coordinator of the Air Force's part in the B-36 investigation, quickly brought General Devers's press release to the attention of General Vandenberg. In a memorandum to Vandenberg, Leach reminded the Air Force Chief of Staff that Item 5 on the House Armed Services Committee's agenda for the B-36 hearings addressed whether the Air Force was concentrating on strategic bombing to such an extent that it injured tactical aviation.[92] He explained that "habitual detractors of the Air Force" had raised this issue in an attempt to strike at strategic bombing and the B-36. Leach also discussed a recent article in the *Washington Star* by pro-Navy columnist David Lawrence that talked about the Air Force's "sudden indifference to tactical air forces."[93]

Linking Lawrence's piece with Devers's action, Barton Leach stressed that the Army general's press release would indicate the following to an interested audience: 1) everything that *Washington Star* columnist David Lawrence and his pro-Navy collaborators said about Air Force indifference to tactical aviation was true; 2) nothing was done about Army concerns until Lawrence raised the issue and then General Devers took action; 3) the Air Force and the Army were at "swords points" on this issue; and 4) the Air Force reluctantly agreed to Devers's ideas under heavy pressure and Devers had no faith that the Air Force would satisfactorily carry out the arrangements unless he kept "knocking them about a bit."[94]

Leach then got to the heart of the matter. "From the point of view of the job you have asked me to do—present the Air Force case in this investigation—*this is the most damning development that has taken place.*"[95] Something clearly had to be done to silence this criticism, and Leach urged Vandenberg to take action:

> I do not know what, if anything, can be done to mitigate the damage. At the very least, you might point out to General Bradley that the Air Force is under heavy attack by its avowed enemies. Anything that provides justification for their charges and gives stature to the enemies is a body blow at the Air Force. If that body blow comes from the Army, it is twice as devastating as if it came from any other source in the world.[96]

Vandenberg found Leach's suggestion intriguing. Omar Bradley was an old friend and comrade-in-arms who certainly held no special brief for the Navy. Still, approaching Bradley was a major step to take. Hoyt Vandenberg mulled over the idea for several days before deciding to see him.[97] On the afternoon of 22 July 1949 Vandenberg telephoned Bradley. The entry in Vandenberg's daily log reads, "1330 – Tel – Gen Vandenberg to Gen Bradley – wants to talk about something – Gen Bradley said he could see him at 0945, Saturday [23 July]."[98] The two men talked for half an hour the following morning.[99] Vandenberg's argument that the Army should not be criticizing its sister service at a time when the Air Force was being attacked by the Navy apparently persuaded the Army Chief of Staff.

Omar Bradley had no love for Jake Devers, whom he had long considered to be egotistical, shallow, and not very smart.[100] It was unnecessary to press for a change in the situation, however. Devers was scheduled to retire late that summer.[101] On 30 July 1949, just a week after the Vandenberg-Bradley meeting, the Army announced General Devers's retirement, effective 30 September. Less than a month later the Army released word that General Mark Clark would succeed him as Chief of the Army Field Forces.[102]

In early October 1949 the Army staff prepared its position on the issues before the House Armed Services Committee. Given the secret understanding between the Air Force and Army Chiefs not to question publicly the Air Force's support for tactical aviation, the Army took an equivocal stand. On the question of whether the Air Force was neglecting tactical air power in concentrating on strategic aviation, the Army's Plans and Operations paper noted that the limited tactical air force "constitutes a calculated risk in air support which we have been forced to accept in view of overall budget limitations."[103]

When the Army witnesses testified during the Unification and Strategy hearings, in what was later remarked upon as a "somewhat surprising" turnabout given the Army's serious concerns about Air Force tactical aviation,[104] they proved to be even more supportive of the Air Force position than their staff position papers indicated. General Collins, Bradley's replacement as Army Chief of Staff, testified on 20 October 1949. He explained to the committee that, of the Air Force's recently approved 58-group program, "36 [groups] could be utilized for direct ground support."[105] This was not just optimistic but actually misleading (though Collins probably was unaware of this), since only the twenty fighter groups in the existing 48-group Air Force program had the "potential" for engaging in "more or less effective" ground support combat operations and, as the Quesada Board had found out, only *seven* of these groups were "properly trained and equipped for effective tactical air operations."[106]

Collins told the committee that, of course, the Army would like the Air Force to provide more groups for direct ground support. "However, the question is can we, in peacetime, support that many groups under our domestic economy." The Army Chief of Staff then remarked that the Air Force was fully cooperating with the Army and that his service was equally confident that the Navy would cooperate with the Army by providing adequate amphibious equipment for future landing operations in which the Army would participate.[107] These comments were calculated to deflect the focus of the committee's inquiry away from the Army's very real concern about weaknesses in Air Force tactical air power.

Later that day General Mark Clark testified. The new Chief of the Army Field Forces chose to avoid the subject of tactical air support altogether, and the committee failed to question him regarding his predecessor's concerns.[108]

The Army witnesses left the congressmen with the clear impression that, whatever the Navy's claims, their service saw the Air Force's support for tactical aviation as adequate under the circumstances. Their reasons for providing the members with this misleading impression were twofold. The first was the Army's natural reluctance to side with the Navy against their Air Force compatriots, with whom they shared a common background. The second was a genuine trust in the Air Force's word that it would better support the Army's requirements in the future.[109] The Army was disabused of this notion a few months later, but, fortunately for the Air Force, it was too late to have any impact on the House Armed Services Committee hearings.[110]

The Hearings End

On 21 October 1949 the House Armed Services Committee heard the last of the witnesses in the Unification and Strategy hearings. Among these was Secretary of Defense Louis Johnson, who provided self-serving testimony in his usual confident and somewhat brusque manner. He argued that the Navy witnesses, although ostensibly testifying on the vulnerability of the B-36 were in reality rebelling against unification.[111] Johnson also dismissed the Navy's criticisms directed against strategic bombing, the B-36, and his cancellation of the flush-deck aircraft carrier as misleading. On the B-36's capabilities the Defense Secretary told the committee that only a comprehensive and detailed analysis such as one conducted by the department's Weapons Systems Evaluation Group would bring the bomber's capabilities "out of the area of interservice controversy and into the area of fact."[112] Johnson encountered surprisingly little hostile questioning by the pro-Navy members of the committee. It may have been because of Carl Vinson's decision to end the hearings without further controversy.[113]

Following Johnson's testimony and a short statement from former President Herbert Hoover, Chairman Vinson recessed the committee until early January. The lengthy Unification and Strategy hearings were at an end.

Conclusions

The Navy's testimony before the House Armed Services Committee was forthright in tone and deliberate in pace. It challenged much of the accepted strategic wisdom regarding the role of the strategic air offensive in warfare, the proper use of atomic weapons, the capabilities of the B-36 as an intercontinental bomber, and the usefulness of carrier aviation. Clearly, the nature of the Navy's "revolt" served to establish doubts in the minds of some members of the committee about the efficacy of the policies that Secretary of Defense Louis Johnson was pursuing in the name of economy and unification.

The thrust of the arguments was undoubtedly bolstered by the choice of the Navy's senior witnesses, who represented the highest levels of the service's wartime and postwar officer corps. Led by Admiral Radford and given crucial support at the last moment by Admiral Denfeld, the participants made the case for a strengthened naval aviation component, and beyond that, for the importance of the Navy as a whole, at a time when the service's role in national defense was under severe attack by organizations and individuals having little understanding of its value.

Chapter 10

Aftermath

Admiral Louis Denfeld's testimony before the House Armed Services Committee had sealed his fate. In providing strong support for the naval aviators at a time when it was sorely needed, the Chief of Naval Operations earned the enmity of Louis Johnson and Francis Matthews. Although Denfeld had realized that by testifying in opposition to the views of his immediate boss he was risking a great deal, particularly the amicable working relationship that the two men had developed, he didn't believe that he would lose his job. Admiral Don Griffin, who had drafted the CNO's statement, recalled years later, "I think he recognized that... [being fired] was a possibility, but he didn't believe it would happen."[1]

Denfeld's confidence came partly from his conviction that he could count on strong support from the Navy's friends in Congress. He wrote to his friend Dudley White a few days after he testified, "I hope you will contact all our friends in the Congress to ensure that they are solidly behind us.... I feel sure that I have made bitter enemies of Johnson, Symington, and Matthews, and that a purge will be in order unless I have the complete backing of the Congress and the people."[2]

Admiral Denfeld, like most former Bureau of Personnel Chiefs, was politically attuned. He was not rebellious by nature, and he certainly wanted to keep his job as Chief of Naval Operations. In fact, much earlier in the year, well before the Unification and Strategy hearings, Denfeld had been regularly reacting to rumors that he was going to be fired. Captain Frank Manson recalled:

> Admiral Denfeld had a very close friend in the White House—Admiral William Leahy. And we used to get rumors rather frequently that... Admiral Denfeld was going to be kicked out.... And Harry Cross, who was also in our office, would go over to the Press Club. And... about once a week, he would pick up a very strong rumor that Denfeld was gone. So he'd rush back over to the Pentagon and rush in to Denfeld. "Boss, I just picked up from a correspondent... [that] they're gonna get you this week."... Denfeld would call Leahy, and Leahy would then check with the

President. And they'd call back in an hour or so, "That's just a rumor; no truth in it. Go on with your job." *This would last till the next week.*[3]

In imagining that they could continue to work together after having openly challenged Matthews's conception of secretarial authority, Denfeld misjudged the strength of his hostility toward anyone considered disloyal. While interviewing Matthews about the events of October 1949, newsman Davis Merwin found him adamant on this point: "Matthews used frequently the words 'loyalty' and 'discipline,' or their equivalent, emphasizing above all that anyone in the Department who didn't hew to his line of policy would have to 'take the consequences.'"[4] Matthews also had to consider the feelings of his boss, and Louis Johnson was furious at Admiral Denfeld for his defection. In the face of such hostility there was little that even substantial congressional support for the CNO's position could have done to keep Denfeld in his job.

Louis Denfeld is Fired

On 14 October 1949, the day after Denfeld testified, Matthews presided over a meeting of the Top Policy Committee, the group composed of the senior civilian and military officials of the Navy Department that met regularly to discuss important policy matters.[5] At the conclusion of the meeting, as the attendees trooped out of the secretary's office, Matthews called Admiral Denfeld back. The CNO returned and sat down in a chair directly in front of Matthews's desk.[6] The Secretary told Denfeld that he was "stunned" by the admiral's presentation to the committee and wanted to know why he hadn't been given a chance to read the statement ahead of time.[7] The CNO told Matthews that he was sorry that he hadn't given him a copy of the statement beforehand but "that he had not done so because he had intended to give it no matter what . . . [Matthews] thought about it."[8] Louis Denfeld also told the Secretary, "If he thought I was going to throw over the boys with whom I had worked for forty years, he was wrong, and . . . I intended to back them to the full."[9] Following Denfeld's comments, Francis Matthews told the CNO that he was "very much disappointed in his failure to keep faith with . . . [him]" in his testimony before the House Armed Services Committee and that he "could not see how . . . [they] could work together on such a basis."[10]

That afternoon Matthews was in Louis Johnson's office twice, the second time for almost an hour.[11] Later that day he had private follow-up meetings with two officers who had emerged as contenders for Denfeld's job—Admiral Richard L. Conolly, Commander in Chief, U.S. Naval

Admiral Richard L. Conolly, Commander in Chief, Naval Forces Eastern Atlantic and Mediterranean, was a serious contender for the office of Chief of Naval Operations in November 1949.

Author's Collection

Forces, Eastern Atlantic and Mediterranean (CINCNELM), and Vice Admiral Forrest Sherman, Commander Sixth Fleet.[12]

Admiral Denfeld was aware that Forrest Sherman was in the Navy Department that week. Sherman had not been one of the scheduled witnesses before the House Armed Services Committee, and Denfeld hadn't called him back to Washington, so the CNO knew that something was up.[13] One night that week Captain Walter Karig and Lieutenant Commander Frank Manson were over at Admiral's House talking with the CNO and Sherman's name came up. Manson recalled:

> [Admiral Denfeld said], "I guess Forrest Sherman is down there telling them everything they want to hear." And he was really provoked.... He didn't know whether he was gonna stay on or not but... because Forrest Sherman was back in town from the Sixth Fleet and... he hadn't called him back... [Denfeld] had... a pretty good notion of what the call was all about. And... Mrs. Denfeld... said, "Well,... if we had anything but a baking-powder biscuit Secretary, things wouldn't be so *bad*.[14]

That Thursday, while in Washington on United Nations business, Nimitz had gone to the Pentagon to pay courtesy calls on Admiral Denfeld and Secretary Matthews.[15] After waiting at least an hour in the CNO's office without seeing Denfeld, Nimitz went to the Secretary's office. The two men had never met before, but Matthews thanked Nimitz for clearing with him the statement the admiral gave before the House Armed Services Committee.[16]

Secretary Matthews telephoned Nimitz on Friday. He told the admiral that he was in need of advice and requested a meeting with him at the Hotel Barclay in New York the following morning.[17] Arriving at the Barclay, the admiral found Matthews in an agitated state. Matthews said that he was not being kept properly informed by Admiral Denfeld, whom he suspected of conspiring against him with the naval aviators. He specifically referred to the leaking of the Bogan memorandum together with the signed endorsement by the CNO, telling Nimitz "that as early as 4 October [following the press accounts of the Bogan memo] he had informed Admiral Denfeld that they could no longer work together."[18] Matthews asked Nimitz if under these circumstances it would be "appropriate" for him to get a new CNO. Nimitz told the Secretary "that he was entitled to have a CNO of his own choice and that if he was not satisfied with Admiral Denfeld it was entirely in order for him to get another man in his place."[19]

There were several procedural hurdles to get over before Denfeld could be safely removed, however. One was Matthews's request to the President two months previously that Denfeld be reappointed to a second term as Chief of Naval Operations.[20] President Truman had accepted the request and nominated Admiral Denfeld for a second term. The nomination had been reported in the press and subsequently confirmed by the Senate.[21] The second hurdle was that the Chairman of the House Armed Services Committee had explicitly stated that all testimony would be frankly and freely given without reprisals by the Department of Defense against anyone testifying and that the committee would not permit or tolerate any such reprisals.[22]

Francis Matthews therefore could not give the real reason for wanting to get rid of Admiral Denfeld. As a cautious and astute lawyer, he realized that he would have to give a reason for the CNO's dismissal that predated Denfeld's testimony before the committee. Matthews thus chose the 4 October meeting that he had had with the CNO, following the leaking of the Bogan memorandum to the press.[23]

By 20 October Matthews and Johnson had decided upon Forrest Sherman as Louis Denfeld's replacement. Sherman, who had been instrumental in arranging the compromise that led to passage of the National Security Act of 1947, had an excellent reputation with people in the White House. In addition, although he was a naval aviator, he had no particular stake in the Navy's case before the House Armed Services

Committee and had not testified during the hearings.[24] He was also an ambitious officer who had no overriding qualms about taking over the CNO's job under such circumstances.[25] That afternoon Louis Johnson's friend, columnist Drew Pearson, dropped in on the Defense Secretary. He recounted the meeting in his private diary:

> Went down to see Louis Johnson. Stuart Symington was in his office when I walked in; both looking quite pleased at the way the B–36 hearings were turning out and both ribbing me for my panning of their air junketing.... Johnson is going to testify tomorrow and it looks as if his statement will be pretty good. He says categorically that Denfeld will be kicked out and replaced by Forrest Sherman. Bradford [*sic*] won't be changed immediately. They don't want to make a martyr of him.[26]

With the selection of Forrest Sherman made, the Johnson Defense Department began floating trial balloons around Washington to the effect that Admiral Denfeld would be relieved as Chief of Naval Operations.[27] The rumor was taken seriously by Democratic Representative F. Edward Hebert of Louisiana, a member of the House Armed Services Committee, and on 24 October he sent a strong letter to committee Chairman Carl Vinson in which he stated:

> Now comes the reported move to punish Admiral Denfeld, Admiral Radford and others for their testimony before the Committee. If this is allowed to happen it will be a direct affront to you and the Members of the Committee. Such action would be a deliberate defiance to your guarantee that there would be no reprisals against officers who testify.[28]

Hebert urged Vinson to carry through with the promises he and the committee had made to the witnesses. Vinson, however, knew that there was little he or his committee could do immediately to prevent the Johnson Defense Department from taking its intended actions, particularly since Congress was in recess until January.

Events moved quickly to a conclusion. In the late morning of 25 October 1949 Francis Matthews and Louis Johnson went to the White House for a meeting with President Truman.[29] Truman was perfectly willing to replace Denfeld, but one of his concerns was how his earlier nomination of the admiral for a second term would affect his power to remove him from office. The Secretary of Defense therefore had his General Counsel's office draw up a memorandum on the question and sent it to the White House the following day. The memo stated that there were no legal problems connected with the President taking such action, since he had the power to remove an executive officer appointed by him and confirmed by the Senate before the official's fixed term had expired. Moreover, the Senate's confirmation of Denfeld's nomination to a second term had no force because the President had not yet appointed him to it.[30]

Francis Matthews spent most of 26 October working at his apartment, presumably drafting the letter requesting that President Truman relieve Admiral Denfeld as CNO.[31] Louis Denfeld remained unaware of the Secretary's intentions. That day he wrote a friend, "The situation at the moment is quite delicate. I can't tell just what will happen."[32] Arleigh Burke wrote to Fitzhugh Lee of the eerie quiet then prevailing in Washington:

> The scene in Washington reminds me of being in the eye of a hurricane. Things are very quiet. . . .
>
> As you probably know, the Secretary of Defense and the Secretary of the Navy saw the President yesterday afternoon. There is no information on what happened. . . .
>
> There are rumors in the paper that Admiral Sherman is to be CNO, but as nearly as we can tell, and we have been trying to find out, these are all trial balloons emanating from some place rather high in the Democratic party but I don't think from the President. I don't know what the score is on this.[33]

On 27 October Matthews sent his letter to President Truman. It read in part, "On Tuesday the fourth of this month, events had taken such a course that, in a conference I had with Admiral Denfeld early that day, I frankly stated to him that I feared his usefulness as Chief of Naval Operations had terminated."[34] Stating that he could no longer work in a harmonious relationship with the CNO, Matthews asked that Truman authorize the transfer of Denfeld to other duties and select a successor at the earliest opportunity.[35] Harry Truman's short answer approving Matthews's recommendation was issued the same day. Late that afternoon Truman announced at a press conference that Louis Denfeld was being replaced as CNO.[36] Copies of Matthews's letter and Truman's memorandum were given to the press.[37] On hearing the news, Father Maurice Sheehy, the Secretary's long-time booster, was outraged. He wrote to Admiral Arthur Radford a few days later, "Until Monday I had hoped that Matthews might become Secretary of the Navy—but he still prefers being a political stooge."[38]

Matthews had not had the decency to inform Admiral Denfeld that he was asking for his relief. Denfeld first heard of the matter when he was telephoned by Bob Dennison, the President's Naval Aide.[39] Admiral Griffin recalled, "[I] happened to be there that . . . [evening] when Louie Denfeld got a call from Dennison saying, 'The following is on the wire right now,' and that was that he was being fired."[40] Admiral Denfeld was not officially told of his relief though until 10:15 the following morning when he met with the Secretary.[41] Despite the obvious strain of the occasion, both men endeavored to keep the short meeting cordial.[42] Matthews offered Denfeld the chance of relieving Admiral Richard Conolly in London as CINCNELM. Louis Denfeld asked for time to consider the offer.[43]

The announcement of Denfeld's dismissal as CNO was angrily received by several members of the House Armed Services Committee. On 28 October 1949 Chairman Carl Vinson issued a statement to the press from his home in Milledgeville, Georgia:

> Admiral Denfeld has been made to walk the plank for having testified before the Armed Services Committee....
>
> ...Suffice it to say that this reprisal against Admiral Denfeld for having painted the picture as he sees it in the Navy will be dealt with in the Committee's report and on the floor of the House in January.[44]

Four other committee members, Democratic Congressmen Hebert of Louisiana and Lansdale G. Sasscer of Maryland, and Republican Congressmen W. Sterling Cole of New York and Leslie C. Arends of Illinois issued a joint statement decrying the removal of Denfeld and stating that "Congress must not abdicate to the improper exercise of executive authority."[45] Republican Senator William F. Knowland of California, a member of the Senate Armed Services Committee, went even further, calling for Francis Matthews's resignation.[46]

At the time of President Truman's 27 October press conference there was already strong press speculation that Denfeld would be replaced as CNO by Vice Admiral Forrest Sherman, who was secretly en route to Washington from the Mediterranean by commercial airliner.[47] After extensive delays en route Sherman's plane finally arrived in New York on 1 November 1949.[48] Accompanied by Matthews's aide, Captain Richard P. Glass, Sherman flew to Baltimore on the Navy Secretary's plane. He was taken by car to Washington's Mayflower Hotel, where Matthews was waiting. The two men then went to the White House for an off-the-record meeting with the President, who officially told Admiral Sherman that he was to be the new Chief of Naval Operations.[49] Matthews and Sherman then journeyed to the Navy Secretary's office in the Pentagon, arriving there just after 4:30 p.m.[50] A few minutes later Matthews telephoned Admiral Denfeld concerning the CINCNELM job. Denfeld told the Secretary that he had not yet come to a decision and requested sixty days of leave following his relief.[51]

At 5:30 p.m. Secretary Matthews hosted a press conference in his office for Admiral Sherman.[52] During a barrage of questioning Forrest Sherman was asked if he would have trouble getting along with his fel-

Admiral Forrest P. Sherman, Chief of Naval Operations from 2 November 1949 to 22 July 1951.

National Archives 80-G-421847

low members of the Joint Chiefs of Staff. The admiral laughingly remarked that he hoped he would have no difficulty getting along with his colleagues, some of whom he had known for many years. When asked about the issue of whether the Navy needed the flush-deck aircraft carrier, however, Sherman declined to comment.[53]

Following a meeting the next morning with Matthews, Sherman, and Denfeld, the Navy Secretary issued a press statement stating that he had renewed his earlier offer for Admiral Denfeld to relieve Richard Conolly as CINCNELM.[54] It was the first public notice that Denfeld had been given the chance to replace Conolly in London. At 3:00 that afternoon in Secretary Matthews's office Forrest Sherman was sworn in as Chief of Naval Operations.[55] It was a short ceremony. Louis Denfeld offered the new CNO his congratulations. He then left the Pentagon to begin a sixty-day leave in his home state of Massachusetts. As he left the building, he was surprised and pleased to see a group of several hundred Navy and Marine Corps personnel assembled on the building's steps to see him off. As he walked past them, the officers and enlisted personnel saluted him. As a final gesture of their respect for the outgoing CNO, they broke into applause as he got into a waiting automobile and kept up the applause until his car had turned down the driveway.[56]

The "Rebels" Are Put To Flight

Admiral Forrest Sherman moved into his new job with dispatch. Among his first actions was a decision to abolish Arleigh Burke's OP–23 shop. OP–23 had first come under fire from the opposition in the days following the conclusion of the Navy testimony. The first major article attacking Burke's organization was a 19 October column by Drew Pearson clearly inspired by his Air Force and Defense Department contacts. Pearson wrote in his "Washington Merry-Go-Round" column:

> Today there operates backstage in the Navy a secret publicity bureau almost solely dedicated to smearing the Army and the Air Force and disrupting unification.
>
> The publicity bureau is called 'Operation 23' [sic] and it consists of 12 officers and 17 enlisted men, all on regular duty and officially assigned to this detail.[57]

Pearson went on to name Arleigh Burke as the head of the "bureau" and Commander Tom Davies as second in command.[58] Eleven days later *Washington Star* reporter John Giles broke the story that on Secretary Matthews's order OP–23 had recently been investigated by the Naval Inspector General.[59] Thereafter, additional negative stories on OP–23's role in the office of the Chief of Naval Operations began appearing in the press.

With the unfavorable press attention that OP–23 was garnering, Burke and his people were aware by the end of October that their shop had become a political liability for OPNAV. On 2 November 1949 Burke wrote his classmate Ken Ringle, "As you may have noted in the newspapers[,] Burke has got[ten] his most prominent physical aspect in the bight again. This time I think they are going to pull it closed."[60] With regard to OP–23's fate Burke commented, "I expect that my shop will likely be closed because we are under attack constantly by the Air Force and SecDef's office and nothing we can do now can be accomplished without criticism, even if it has to be manufactured."[61]

The following morning Burke was notified that OP–23 was being disestablished immediately. At 8:00 a.m. on 3 November Captain Burke assembled his officers to give them the news. According to the memorandum for record on the meeting, "Captain Burke stressed that the breaking up of OP–23 was no purge. He said there was nothing anyone in the shop could do from now on that would do any good because of the adverse publicity given to the office."[62] He told them that there should be no griping about any person in uniform, and Admiral Sherman in particular. At the end of the meeting, Arleigh Burke asked each man what he desired for his next duty assignment.

That evening the Defense Department's joint military press section issued a terse announcement that Admiral Sherman had ordered OP–23 "disbanded and dissolved" and its personnel and official duties assigned to other offices, because its principal functions had been completed.[63] At about the same time unnamed Pentagon sources told reporters that Sherman's action demonstrated how the new CNO would deal with future dissenters.[64] Although this was the lesson the Johnson Defense Department wanted the public to learn from OP–23's abolishment, it was not what Forrest Sherman intended. The following day, while on a previously scheduled visit by the Joint Chiefs of Staff to Fort Benning, Georgia, Sherman was interviewed by a local reporter. The news of OP–23's demise had been in the morning papers, and the man asked the admiral if Burke would be sent to sea duty. As he recounted, "Admiral Sherman smiled rather grimly and immediately, almost explosively, replied: 'No, Captain Burke will *not* be sent to sea. He will be given high and responsible duties consonant with his rank and ability.'" As the reporter was about to leave, Sherman called him back and said, "Here's something else you can put in your paper: I consider Captain Burke one of the finest officers in the United States naval service."[65]

Arleigh Burke had already applied for a month's leave. Before he left Washington, Admiral Sherman summoned him for a short meeting. The new CNO reassured Burke that he was going to continue to support a strong Navy. Burke related in a letter to Fitzhugh Lee just before he left:

Adm. Sherman . . . told me he was going to fight for

(a) a realization within the Army and Air Force that a strong Navy is needed

(b) explaining to the Navy what is happening and why

(c) a balance between [the] shore establishment and combat Navy to have the best possible combat Navy.[66]

On 10 November Burke left town for a month of fishing and visiting in Florida. He had not stated a preference for his next duty assignment, preferring instead to place the matter of his future career in the hands of his superiors.[67] On 14 November 1949 Admiral Radford wrote to "buck up" Burke in the aftermath of recent events. Radford remarked, "I hate to think where we *might* be had we not had your loyal service in a key role. I am grateful for it. I am sure that the Navy and the country, if they were fully informed, would be equally grateful. (Sometime—they will!)"[68]

At the time Arleigh Burke went on leave, people in OPNAV were aware that the Selection Board for rear admiral would be meeting shortly, and that Burke and his classmates Fred Trapnell and John Crommelin, who were only a few numbers "below the zone," might be in the group under consideration for promotion.[69] The Selection Board was composed of Vice Admirals Harry Hill (president) and Felix Stump and Rear Admirals Daniel E. Barbey, Allan McCann, John Cassady, Harold M. Martin, Roscoe F. Good, Charles B. Momsen, and Felix L. Johnson.[70]

When the Selection Board met on 14 November 1949, the group decided to vote on Arleigh Burke first, in order to avoid criticism that the members had passed over good people in order to select the younger officer. Selection for flag rank required a favorable vote from six of the nine-member group. Burke, who was considered throughout the Navy to be one of the outstanding officers of his generation, received nine votes.[71] The board then went on to select twenty-one additional officers; it turned in its report to Secretary Matthews on 23 November.[72]

A day or two after he received the report, Matthews sent for Admiral Hill and other members of the board. Admiral Stump recounted, "He called us in and told us, 'You gentlemen are responsible for my having had no sleep last night. Why you would select an officer who... has done the things that Captain Burke has done, I don't know.'"[73]

At some point after talking with Hill and the others, the Secretary decided to strike Burke's name from the selection list. When Matthews informed Admiral Sherman of his decision, the CNO strongly advised against it. Matthews, however, remained adamant.[74] Some days later he instructed the Selection Board to reconvene and select another officer in place of Burke. Secretary Matthews specifically suggested that the board consider Captain Richard Glass, his Special Assistant for Public Relations, ostensibly because Burke would have another chance for promotion, while Glass had already been passed over. The Selection Board selected Glass under duress on 28 November, turning in its revised selection list to the Secretary the following day.[75]

The Navy's rumor mill got the bad news quickly. On 30 November Captain A. B. (Abe) Vosseller, a Navy member of the Weapons Systems Evaluation Group, wrote to Fitzhugh Lee, "The selection board results have not been announced but the disquieting rumor is going around that the board has been reconvened to remove Arleigh Burke's name."[76]

In due course the selection list was submitted for President Truman's approval. Truman was at his summer White House in Key West, Florida, on a working holiday.[77] When the list arrived, it was handed to his Naval Aide, Bob Dennison, for delivery to the President. Dennison was horrified to see that Burke's name had been stricken.[78] He was a classmate of Arleigh Burke's and knew him to be an outstanding officer. He went over to the base library to get some texts on the legal aspects of selection boards. From these Dennison reaffirmed his understanding that only the President had the right to strike a name from a list submitted by a duly constituted selection board.

Early the following morning Dennison went into the living room where the President was writing at his desk. Before Harry Truman signed a selection list, he always asked his aide whether any injustice had been done. Dennison recalled:

> So I said, "This time, Mr. President, if you asked me if any injustice had been done I'd have to say yes. But I want to do some special pleading. And may I step out of my role as your Naval Aide for a moment?" Then he said, "Well, take the stuffing out of your shirt and sit down and tell me what the problem is."[79]

Dennison explained to the President what Matthews had done and reminded him that only he had the authority to take such an action. Truman said, "You told me that Burke was Chief of Staff for Admiral Mitscher." When Dennison agreed, Truman replied, "I was very much impressed by Admiral Mitscher. And if Burke was good enough to be his Chief of Staff he must be a real good officer."[80] The President then put the selection board papers in the desk drawer.

Normally the President returned signed selection board lists within a few days of receiving them. When weeks went by without the Navy list being sent back to Matthews, he and Secretary Johnson became concerned.[81] In the meantime news of Arleigh Burke's removal from the selection list was leaked to the press. For the next several weeks press accounts of the action variously castigated President Truman, Francis Matthews, and Louis Johnson for seeking a reprisal against one of the Navy's best officers for his part in the congressional hearings.[82]

The President finally returned from Key West on 20 December. A few days later he sent for Bob Dennison and told him that Johnson and Matthews were on their way to the White House for a meeting. Truman told his Naval Aide to wait in the Cabinet Room until after they had gone. After Johnson and Matthews left, Truman came and got Dennison. The President was smiling broadly. He said to Dennison, "Guess what happened?" When his aide remarked that the matter must have been settled, the President responded, "Yes, it is.... Burke's name has been reinstated on the list and this other officer [Captain Glass] ... also remains selected.... And the best part of it is that Johnson and Matthews think that they thought the whole thing up themselves."[83]

Rear Admiral Robert L. Dennison, Naval Aide to President Truman, helped to save Burke's career in December 1949.

National Archives 80–G–14366

On 29 December 1949 Secretary Matthews released the news of the President's approval of the line selection board list.[84] The following morning newspapers around the country reported that Arleigh Burke had been put back on the selection list for rear admiral.[85] A few days later in a letter to Admiral J. W. Reeves, Arleigh Burke remarked, "It was a big surprise to find my name on the list under the circumstances. I still haven't recovered."[86]

Burke's selection proved a bright spot in an otherwise difficult time for the Navy. Admiral Denfeld mulled over whether to accept the CINC-NELM job for some weeks before finally coming to a decision.[87] He would have preferred to remain on active duty, but he gradually became aware that, by accepting this duty assignment under the circumstances, he would be playing into the hands of Matthews and Johnson. Indeed, Arthur Radford had been writing Denfeld's close friends expressing his strong hope that the former CNO would not accept the new appointment. He wrote to Rear Admiral Richard E. Byrd, "Not only is it not befitting that he should be offered and accept a job two steps down from his last one, but his presence in Europe (instead of Washington) and his position under Sherman and Matthews would handicap him in giving further frank views to Congress in the next session."[88]

282   *Revolt of the Admirals*

On 14 December 1949 Louis Denfeld wrote a personal letter to Secretary Matthews confirming an earlier verbal comment that he was turning down the CINCNELM assignment.[89] Slightly more than a month later he submitted his request for retirement, effective 1 March 1950.[90]

Denfeld and Burke had been the two principal objects of Francis Matthews's wrath, but several other officers had also been seen (incorrectly) by some observers to have been unwitting martyrs. Jerry Bogan, the commander of the First Task Fleet, had been in that job since February 1946 and was overdue for rotation to a shore command. In early December 1949 he was offered the job as Commander Fleet Air, Jacksonville, replacing Rear Admiral J. H. Cassady, who was fleeting up to Deputy Chief of Naval Operations (Air).[91] The Jacksonville job was a rear admiral's billet, and Admiral Bogan wanted to remain at sea. When he couldn't get another three-star sea command, he chose to retire despite the advice of his friends Arthur Radford and John Dale Price.[92] Nonetheless, for the rest of his life Jerry Bogan remained convinced he had been axed by Francis Matthews because Crommelin had leaked his letter to the Secretary.[93]

Similarly Spike Blandy was none too popular with the Secretary after his testimony at the Unification and Strategy hearings. Nonetheless his retirement was not due to the Secretary's animosity. Blandy chose to retire of his own accord as of 1 February 1950 and was succeeded as Commander in Chief, Atlantic and Atlantic Fleet, by Vice Admiral William M. Fechteler, DCNO (Personnel).[94]

John Crommelin also determined his own fate. By speaking out as he did, Crommelin had seriously damaged his chances for promotion to rear admiral. Nonetheless, the new CNO gave him one last opportunity to straighten himself out. Captain Frank Manson recalled:

> After Forrest Sherman came in as CNO, . . . [he] knew that I knew John Crommelin quite well. So, he'd asked me to go talk to John and see if I couldn't get him to pipe down. . . . [Sherman] said, "And tell him not to worry, that I'll take care of him. I'll see to it that his career isn't hurt, but tell him just to pipe down."[95]

Manson did as asked telling Crommelin as well that Admiral Sherman had given Manson his personal assurances that he would get the naval aviation program back on track.

Captain Crommelin replied, "Young man, I *appreciate* this. . . . And you go tell Admiral Sherman that I *appreciate* this advice and I'll certainly take it under consideration."[96] A few weeks later, rebellious to a fault, Crommelin made another of his many speeches castigating the Johnson De-

Admiral Forrest Sherman, CNO, confers with Admiral Arthur Radford, CINC-PAC/CINCPACFLT, in San Diego, July 1950.

fense Department. This proved too much for Forrest Sherman. Crommelin, a self-made martyr, was forced into retirement a few months later.

The Results of the Unification and Strategy Hearings

With the House Armed Services Committee in recess and OPNAV in the hands of a new Chief of Naval Operations, the final months of 1949 and first months of 1950 were a time of retrenchment for the Navy after the clamorous events of the previous summer and fall. Just what had been accomplished by the Navy's participation in the Unification and Strategy hearings remained in question for most naval officers. Certainly the Johnson Defense Department, reinvigorated by its apparent victory over the recalcitrant naval aviators, moved ahead with its budget cutbacks for the fiscal year 1951 budget. In January 1950 Admiral Sherman was forced to acknowledge that the number of Navy carrier air groups would be nine for fiscal year 1951—down from fourteen the previous fis-

National Archives 80-G-682046

Forrestal (CVA 59), the first of the new class of large attack carriers, runs sea trials just prior to its commissioning in September 1955.

cal year and twenty-four the year before.[97] The Navy's active attack carriers would be six—a drop of five since fiscal year 1949.[98]

The continued slide of the Navy's aviation strength was not lost on the press. It merely reinforced the perception following the Unification and Strategy hearings that the Navy had failed to make its case. What the press could not see, however, was the gradual change of mind on the air power issue by a number of key congressmen on the House Armed Services Committee, most notably Carl Vinson. On 18 December 1949, Dewey Short, the ranking Republican on the committee, wrote Admiral Radford that "[Bryce] Harlow of our Professional Staff, has been working hard on the report, but individual Members of our Committee have pretty strong convictions and I am confident they will assert them when the final draft is adopted."[99] The first overt indication of a new congressional attitude was Vinson's announcement in committee on 10 January 1950 that the report on agenda items 3 to 7 (discussed in Navy testimony) would be handled separately from that on the first two items, because "they covered matters of national importance which should be treated in a constructive manner."[100]

In mid-February 1950 Carl Vinson sounded out Captain Ira H. Nunn, the Navy's Legislative Liaison, about the effect that the committee's report might have on Admiral Sherman's position. Vinson was worried that a report critical of Secretary of Defense Johnson and Secretary of the Navy Matthews might harm the new CNO's standing within the Defense Department. Nunn assured him that so long as Sherman was not mentioned in the report, it would not have a significant impact. Vinson then asked the officer where the Navy's shipbuilding and conversion program stood. When told that it was then under consideration by Louis Johnson, the congressman asked if Sherman wanted him to "move in on" the Defense Secretary now. When Nunn replied in the negative, Vinson said that he was prepared to do so any time Sherman wanted him to.[101]

In the last days of February the House Armed Services Committee finalized its report on the Unification and Strategy hearings. The majority of the committee, by now pro-Navy in its outlook, voted to keep a strong report. In reality the effort took some masterful planning on Vinson's part. Rear Admiral Ossie Colclough, now retired and Dean of the George Washington University Law School, was called in by Dewey Short and given the inside account, which he relayed to Arthur Radford:

> As you can imagine, there was considerable strife in the Committee over the main part of the Report, led by Paul Kilday [a strong pro-Air Force member]. I gather the first draft of the Report was purposely made even stronger, in order that our friends could recede and still end up with a strong report. The real story is that Carl and Dewey "got together."[102]

In exchange for Vinson's support for a strong main report, Short supported Vinson in opposing the Supplementary Statement, which called for the U.S. Department of Justice to investigate the removal of Admiral Denfeld as CNO in reprisal for his testimony before the committee.

The committee's report was released on 1 March. That same day Carl Vinson sent a copy of the report to General Dwight Eisenhower in New York. In an accompanying letter Vinson wrote, "This report very accurately reflects my convictions on the matters discussed therein. I hope you will have an opportunity to examine it carefully some time in the future."[103]

Although the Unification and Strategy report did not call for the reinstatement of the canceled flush-deck carrier, it expressed a solidly pro-naval aviation viewpoint in a number of major respects. Among the most important conclusions was the view that intercontinental strategic bombing was not synonymous with air power—that U.S. air power consisted of Air Force, Navy, and Marine air power, and, of these, strategic bombing

Forrestal underway at flight quarters during its initial working-up period, March 1956. Note the AJ–1 Savage heavy attack aircraft in landing position.

The new A3D all jet-powered heavy attack aircraft. This aircraft, designed to operate from large-deck aircraft carriers like those of the *Forrestal* class, was the mainstay of the Navy's long-range atomic bombing capability from the mid-1950s through the early 1960s.

constituted but one aspect.[104] The report also made it clear that difficulties between the Air Force and the Navy would continue, not so much because of service prejudices and jealousies, but because of "fundamental professional disagreements on the art of warfare."[105]

All things considered, the Unification and Strategy report vindicated the Navy's October presentation. As Dewey Short later commented to Admiral Radford, "You and your associates gave clear, frank, and honest statements, which for the most part, were irrefutable.... The results cannot be accomplished immediately, but it seems to me there is evidence that much good has come from the hearings and the report."[106]

Evidence of the change in House Armed Services thinking on the flush-deck carrier was not long in coming. In April 1950 during the committee's hearing on H.R. 7764 to authorize the construction of modern naval vessels, Admiral Sherman was repeatedly questioned by Representative L. Mendel Rivers (D–S.C.) about the Navy's need for a flush-deck carrier. The CNO finally acknowledged that such a ship would "probably be needed at sometime in the future."[107] He was seconded by the committee chairman.[108] However, because Secretary of Defense Louis Johnson still remained adamantly against the flush-deck carrier, Vinson was careful not to put the new Chief of Naval Operations in an embarrassing position by openly calling for a new carrier at this hearing.[109] Louis Johnson had made his feelings on the flush-deck carrier issue clear to Forrest Sherman only a month earlier when approving a request from Sherman for the new authorization program for Navy shipbuilding. Johnson had hand-written on the paper, "[This is] OK—No super carriers or increased carrier size."[110] Thus despite increasing support for a new carrier, the House Armed Services Committee did not press the Navy on this issue during the spring and summer of 1950.

The aviators in OPNAV reopened the idea of a new flush-deck carrier in early March 1950, but Admiral Sherman had taken the matter under his own "positive control." Navy planner Captain C. W. Lord explained to his boss, Rear Admiral Stuart H. Ingersoll, Assistant Chief of Naval Operations (Plans):

> Admiral Cassady [DCNO (Air)] opened the meeting [on the flush-deck carrier] by stating that the recent publication of information that the Navy was planning to build a 55,000 ton flush-deck carrier was a breach of faith on the part of a press correspondent. He warned that the discussion of such a ship should not go beyond naval circles until such time *as Admiral Sherman thought it propitious to press for authority to build one.*[111]

In part because of Louis Johnson's continued opposition, but also because of his own questions as to whether the new carrier should be a true flush-deck ship or have a fixed or retractable island, Sherman continued to hold off on making the carrier decision into early 1951.[112]

The outbreak of the Korean War in June 1950 and President Truman's sudden firing of Johnson in mid-September helped bring naval and congressional support for a new flush-deck carrier into the open. On 29 November 1950 Under Secretary Dan Kimball recounted a conversation with Vinson: "[He] is more than ever convinced that we not only have to have a more modern aircraft carrier, but we must have a number of them. He believes that in case of emergency the carrier would probably be our best weapon."[113]

With solid backing from Carl Vinson and his committee,[114] the new flush-deck carrier (CVB 59), soon named *Forrestal*, was authorized in March 1951.[115] The contract for the ship was let four months later.[116] With this action the modernization of naval aviation was once again placed on track.

Conclusions

It is only from the perspective afforded by a thorough examination of the documentary record of the late 1940s that we can see just how pivotal the "revolt of the admirals" was for the future of naval aviation. Until now most historians have accepted the judgment of the press at the time that the Navy's fight was a failure. It was anything but a failure.

Had Radford, Denfeld, Burke, and all the other committed proponents of naval aviation not made a stand when they did, it is highly unlikely that the fortunes of carrier aviation would have been turned around so dramatically. It can be further argued that, if the Navy had not made its case with Carl Vinson and the House Armed Services Committee in the October 1949 hearings, there would have been no advanced aircraft carriers for the Navy even after the outbreak of the Korean conflict. For if the Navy had not demonstrated that it needed such carriers to fulfill its power projection responsibilities, it is probable that the money Congress appropriated for upgrading carrier aviation strength in the wake of the Korean conflict would have been earmarked only for the modernization of the existing *Essex-* and *Midway-*class attack carriers. Instead, Navy witnesses convinced important members of the House Armed Services Committee that the Strategic Air Command was not the sum total of U.S. offensive air power and that, indeed, the Navy's carrier aviation furnished a vital portion of the country's military air assets—one that was complementary to the larger Air Force segment. In so doing, they laid the groundwork for the resurrection of the Navy's aircraft carrier program.

Chapter 11

Conclusions

It is difficult for a historian more than forty years after an event to grasp fully just how powerful the passions and prejudices were that gripped its participants. The emotions that surrounded and, indeed, infused the "revolt of the admirals" and its attendant conflicts were forged by long-standing disagreements over the nature of air power and the roles of the separate services in its projection. The tactics that Billy Mitchell used during the 1920s and early 1930s to seek a separate service status for the Air Corps outraged naval aviators, even as they provided succor to the sometimes beleaguered Army aviators. This split between two groups of military officers who were like-minded in their spirit of adventure and dedication to the skills of flying festered over time.

Part of the problem stemmed from the vastly differing conceptions that each group had about aviation's role, both within their services and as a part of the larger national defense. Since the early days at the Air Corps Tactical School at Langley Field, most Army Air Corps aviators had been imbued with a doctrine that stressed the dominant, even war-winning, potential of centrally directed strategic bombardment. These Air Corps officers believed that strong formations of self-protecting, long-range bombers, employing precision bombing to destroy significant military and industrial targets, would almost inevitably crush an enemy's will to resist even as they denied the enemy the ability to resupply or strengthen forces in the field.

Naval aviators from the outset were less enamored with doctrine than their Army counterparts, probably because of the nature of taking off from and landing on a rolling, pitching ship somewhere at sea. Just perfecting the mechanics of flying under such circumstances proved an all-absorbing task in the early years. The naval aviators too were always aware of the interdependence that existed between their aircraft and the seaborne bases from which they operated. An aircraft carrier without its air group was merely a floating hangar; an aircraft at sea without a place to land was a pending accident statistic. This interdependence made naval aviators less likely to question the value of the duties performed by their nonflying shipmates than were their army counterparts. This was true even when, in the interwar years, many Blackshoe officers lacked the vision to understand naval aviation's potential to extend the Fleet's offensive reach and multiply its punch.

During World War II the combat experienced by both air arms taught hard lessons about the mutability of doctrine. Nonetheless the Army Air Forces emerged from the war with its strategic bombardment doctrine largely intact. Senior AAF leaders were convinced that air power had come close to winning the decisive victories against Germany and Japan and that only the slowness of the air buildup and the inadequate resources allocated to its needs denied it its rightful, war-winning impact.

Navy leaders, both aviators and nonaviators, emerged from the war convinced of carrier aviation's importance to the Fleet's offensive and defensive effectiveness. They no longer looked upon carrier aircraft as an augmentation to the striking power of the battle line but as the Fleet's premier striking arm. Moreover, from the middle of the Pacific war onward, this carrier air power had been increasingly directed against enemy land targets—airfields, naval bases, ports, refineries—rather than primarily against enemy naval forces at sea. This development was in line with the strategic concept (often misunderstood by continental powers) that the purpose of powerful navies was not to oppose other navies, but instead to gain and maintain control of the seas in order to influence events on land. In the course of the bloody Pacific fighting the old belief that carrier aircraft were inherently inferior to enemy land-based aircraft was rapidly dispensed with (at least by the naval aviators) in the face of aircraft kill-ratios that increasingly favored U.S. carrier aircraft in the final years of the war.

The early postwar period was a difficult time for both Army and Navy pilots. The renewed fight for unification—and within it, Air Force separation from the Army—pushed both sides toward the extremes of their positions. Some AAF leaders talked privately of the integration of all Army and Navy air power under a single operational entity, even as diehard naval aviators foretold dire consequences for the country's national security if the Air Force obtained independence from its parent service.

Unification of the armed forces was achieved in 1947 despite the best efforts of many of the Navy's senior aviators to maintain the status quo. However much advocates of unification had hoped this legislation would rectify the problems they saw in defense organization, the passage of the National Security Act of 1947 did not settle the deeper issues that divided the services. The fight moved from unification per se to the question of service roles and missions. The Air Force was convinced that the Navy had designs on its mission of strategic air warfare. The Navy was equally convinced that Air Force attempts to circumscribe the strength and capabilities of its force of aircraft carriers was only the first step in the eventual elimination of carrier air power. Senior naval aviators took little comfort in seeing their fears apparently realized following Louis Johnson's appointment as Secretary of Defense.

During 1947 and 1948 both sides fought for their positions with a panoply of peacetime weapons. They battled for their share and more of diminishing defense budgets with all of the skill and tenacity that their planners and analysts could muster. Likewise they courted allies in Congress and the public through public relations programs of varying effectiveness. By early 1948, however, it became apparent to the Navy's uniformed leaders that their service was in danger of losing the PR fight to a better organized Air Force campaign to become the dominant military arm of the United States.

As war planning progressed and defense spending decreased, the Air Force's strategic bombers assumed a larger role in the country's security plans. Senior naval aviators and planners were convinced that the Air Force's true capabilities in strategic air warfare were much lower than its leaders were willing to admit. By this time most of the Air Force's near-term expectations for accomplishing its primary wartime offensive mission had become inextricably linked with the enormous B–36 bomber. This aircraft was thought capable of carrying out round-trip atomic bombing strikes of urban-industrial targets in the Soviet heartland from bases in the continental United States. The World War II–designed plane had great carrying capacity, but it lacked adequate combat speed in an era of jet-powered fighter-interceptors.

The Navy's near-term offensive hopes were pinned to the huge flush-deck aircraft carrier—a super carrier intended to operate long-range attack aircraft capable of carrying atomic weapons to a radius of 1,700 nautical miles. To operate such large aircraft, however, the carrier had to have no permanent projections above its flight deck—a design feature that found mixed support even within the naval aviation community. The operational viability of this design could be determined only by building and testing the ship.

The departure of James Forrestal as Secretary of Defense and the arrival of Louis Johnson in late March 1949 set the stage for a final showdown between the Navy and the Air Force over the fate of carrier aviation. The dramatically increased B–36 procurement in early 1949, coupled with Johnson's cancellation of the flush-deck carrier, provided the final impetus for the events that have since been characterized as the "revolt of the admirals."

The drafting and distribution of the Anonymous Document by two people assigned to the Navy Department resulted in the House Armed Services Committee's investigation of the B–36 program. The Air Force's senior leaders successfully defended their bomber against the Anonymous Document's baseless accusations of collusion by senior officials in awarding the aircraft's contracts for financial gain. But they were unable to prevent the committee from exploring issues that transcended this particular aircraft program—issues of national military strategy, the morality of targeting enemy cities for atomic attacks, and the role of the Navy and naval aviation in the atomic era.

A combination of circumstances allowed the Navy's senior aviators to testify before the House Armed Services Committee in a second set of hearings on unification and strategy. As a result of these hearings Congress better understood the complementary nature of land- and sea-based air power and the importance of carrier aviation to national defense. This understanding led to congressional support for a resurrection of the Navy's carrier aviation, particularly a new flush-deck aircraft carrier, even before U.S. participation in the Korean War provided the funds to expand the overall aviation program. Thus the Navy's development of the *Forrestal*-class super carriers, which provided the backbone of the service's power projection capabilities from the mid-1950s onward, was in large part a direct result of the Navy's impassioned testimony before the House Armed Services Committee in October 1949.

The 1949 congressional hearings did not significantly lessen the competition between the two services. The major doctrinal divergences and disagreements over roles and missions that sparked the "revolt" remained intact. The Korean War merely submerged these differences temporarily as the Air Force and the Navy scrambled to meet a conventional military threat for which neither was well prepared. By the mid-1950s the two services were again staking out their respective doctrinal territories in the context of the Eisenhower administration's New Look policy. This competition continues today in an era of putative military "jointness." The services' differing strategic perspectives and doctrines, which result in part from their operating environments, guarantee that the services will have competing views on roles and missions.

The early postwar period was a hectic and confusing time for the United States and its leaders. Defense decision makers attempted to maintain the country's expanded security commitments in the face of declining budgets and diminished military capabilities. Not surprisingly their efforts had a mixed result. Over the last decade and a half historians with access to newly available documentary material on U.S. diplomatic and defense policies during the Truman years have begun to unravel the complexities of this turbulent period and reweave the events into a fabric understandable to the larger public. As a part of this fabric, the events surrounding the "revolt of the admirals" deserve to be better understood on their own terms, stripped of service myopia and myths that have encumbered them over the intervening decades. It is hoped that this book has accomplished some of this necessary work.

Abbreviations

AAF	Army Air Forces
AC/AS	Assistant Chief of Air Staff
ACNO	Assistant Chief of Naval Operations
ACTS	Air Corps Tactical School
AEC	Atomic Energy Commission
AFOAT	Assistant for Atomic Energy
AFSWP	Armed Forces Special Weapons Project
AID	Air Intelligence Division
AMC	Air Materiel Command
AP	Associated Press
ASW	Antisubmarine Warfare
BB	Battleship
BUAER	Bureau of Aeronautics
BUPERS	Bureau of Personnel
BUSHIPS	Bureau of Ships
CAP	Combat Air Patrol
CB	Large Cruiser
CEP	Circular Error Probable
CG	Commanding General
CIA	Central Intelligence Agency
CINCLANT	Commander in Chief, Atlantic
CINCNELM	Commander in Chief, Eastern Atlantic and Mediterranean
CINCPAC	Commander in Chief, Pacific
CL	Light Cruiser
CNO	Chief of Naval Operations
COMAIRPAC	Commander Air Force, Pacific Fleet
COMINCH	Commander in Chief, United States Fleet
COMNAVEU	Commander Naval Forces, Europe
CONAC	Continental Air Command
CONUS	Continental United States
CV	Aircraft Carrier
CVA	Heavy Aircraft Carrier (later Attack Aircraft Carrier)
CVB	Aircraft Carrier, Large
DA	*Dal'naya aviatsiya* (Soviet long-range aviation)

DCNO	Deputy Chief of Naval Operations
DCS/O	Deputy Chief of Staff for Operations
FM	Fat Man (atomic bomb)
FY	Fiscal Year
GE	General Electric
IG	Inspector General
JATO	Jet-Assisted Take-Off
JCS	Joint Chiefs of Staff
JPS	Joint Staff Planners
JSPG	Joint Strategic Plans Group
JSPC	Joint Strategic Plans Committee
JSSC	Joint Strategic Survey Committee
JWPC	Joint War Plans Committee
kt	Kiloton (measurement of atomic/nuclear yield)
LOC	Line of Communications
LSM	Landing Ship, Medium
MD–LC	Manuscript Division, Library of Congress
MED	Manhattan Engineer District
MK	Mark (designation used for ordnance)
NA/WNRC	National Archives, Washington National Records Center
NAS	Naval Air Station
NME	National Military Establishment
NDL	Navy Department Library, Naval Historical Center
NHC	Naval Historical Center
NSC	National Security Council
NSPS	Navy Strategic Plans Study
OA	Operational Archives, Naval Historical Center
OPNAV	Office of the Chief of Naval Operations
OSD	Office of the Secretary of Defense
ONI	Office of Naval Intelligence
OSI	Office of Special Investigations
PACUSA	Pacific Air Command, U.S. Army
PIO	Office of Public Information
POL	Petroleum-Oil-Lubricants
PR	Public Relations
RAF	Royal Air Force
RG	Record Group
R&D	Research and Development
SAC	Strategic Air Command
SCB	Ship Characteristics Board
SCOROR	Secretary's Committee on Research on Reorganization

Secretary of the Air Force
Secretary of the Army
Secretary of Defense
Secretary of the Navy
Secretary of War
Antisubmarine Submarine
Tactical Air Command
Top Secret
Top Secret Air Adjutant General
United Kingdom
Secretary's Committee on Unification
United Press International
United States
United States Army
United States Air Force
United States Marine Corps
United States Navy
United States Strategic Bombing Survey
Union of Soviet Socialist Republics
Vice Chief of Naval Operations
Variable Discharge Turbine
Very Heavy Bomb (Group)
Very Long Range
Voyenno-vozdushnyye sily (Soviet Air Force)

End Notes

Introduction

1. For information on Forrestal's retirement and Johnson's assumption of power, see Steven L. Rearden, *History of the Office of the Secretary of Defense*, vol. 1, *The Formative Years, 1947–1950* (Washington: Historical Office, Office of the Secretary of Defense, 1984), 43–50. For an interesting perspective on the closing months of Johnson's sometimes-troubled tenure as Assistant Secretary of War under Secretary Harry Woodring, see Forrest C. Pogue, *George C. Marshall: Ordeal and Hope, 1939–1942* (New York: Viking Press, 1966), 19–22, 39–40. This is the second volume of Pogue's masterful four-volume biography of Marshall.

2. One important exception to this blanket statement was the reporting of the *New York Times*'s military correspondent, Hanson Baldwin, who because of his long-standing contacts with the naval aviation community and the Navy in general (he was a 1924 graduate of the U.S. Naval Academy) was able to provide some insightful commentaries on the Navy's actions and thinking during this period.

1. Air Power Doctrines

1. Quoted in Archibald D. Turnbull and Clifford L. Lord, *History of United States Naval Aviation* (New Haven, CT: Yale University Press, 1949), 161.

2. Donald B. Duncan and H. M. Dater, "Administrative History of U.S. Naval Aviation," *Air Affairs* 1 (Summer 1947): 529. The naval aviation issue is not discussed in Mary Klachko's biography of Admiral Benson. She goes so far as to argue that Benson in 1919 "lost no time in developing plans to continue the expansion of the navy's air arm." Mary Klachko, with David F. Trask, *William Shepard Benson: First Chief of Naval Operations* (Annapolis: Naval Institute Press, 1987), 166, 236n.

3. Duncan and Dater, "Administrative History of Naval Aviation," 530.

4. Quoted in Ashbrook Lincoln, "The United States Navy and Air Power, A History of Naval Aviation, 1920–1934" (Ph.D. diss., University of California, 1946), 3.

5. Duncan and Dater, "Administrative History of Naval Aviation," 530.

6. Turnbull and Lord, *History of U.S. Naval Aviation*, 187–88.

7. Ibid., 188; and Lincoln, "United States Navy and Air Power," 98.

8. Lincoln, 98; and Duncan and Dater, "Administrative History of Naval Aviation," 530.

9. Lincoln, 98–99.

10. Duncan and Dater, 530–31.

11. See David A. Rosenberg and Floyd D. Kennedy, Jr., *History of the Strategic Arms Competition 1945–1972, Supporting Study: US Aircraft Carriers in the Strategic Role*, Part I, *Naval Strategy in a Period of Change: Interservice Rivalry, Strategic Interaction, and the Development of Nuclear Attack Capability, 1945–1951* (Falls Church, VA.: Lulejian & Associates, 1975), I-5–I-6.

12. See memo, R. R. Paunack, Unit Observer, Aircraft Squadrons, Battle Force (on board U. S. S. *Langley*) to Fleet Observer, Blue, 21 Mar 1927, 4–5; and memo, Commander in Chief, U.S. Fleet to CNO, ser 11-Rd-(0), 4 May 1927, 2–3, both in M964, RG 38, *Records Relating to US Navy Fleet Problems I to XXII, 1923–1941* (Washington: National Archives, 1974), reel 8, microfilm, Navy Department Library (NDL), Naval Historical Center.

13. Quoted in Clark G. Reynolds, *The Fast Carriers: The Forging of an Air Navy* (New York: McGraw-Hill, 1968), 17.

14. CAPT F. J. Horne, "Naval Aviation: Its Employment with the Fleet," lecture delivered at the Army Air Corps Tactical School, 29 Mar 1928, 1, box 7, Strategic Plans Division Records (hereafter Strategic Plans), Operational Archives (OA), NHC.

15. Ibid., 2.

16. Ibid., 30.

17. Horne, "Cooperation Between the Army and the Navy in the Employment of Aviation," lecture delivered at the Army Air Corps Tactical School, 1 Mar 1929, 6–8, box 7, Strategic Plans, OA.

18. See *United States Fleet Problem IX, 1929: Report of the Commander in Chief United States Fleet, Admiral H. A. Wiley, U.S.N.* 18 Mar 1929, 31, box 37, WW II Action Reports File, OA.

19. Horne, "Cooperation Between the Army and the Navy in the Employment of Aviation," 8.

20. See *Annual Report of the Commander-in-Chief, United States Fleet for the Period 1 July, 1928 to 21 May, 1929*, 21 May 1929, 53; and *Annual Report of the Commander-in-Chief, United States Fleet, for the Period 1 July, 1929 to 30 June, 1930*, 1 Aug 1930, 31–32, in *1929–1931 Secret and Confidential Files, General Records of the Department of the Navy (RG 80)*, National Archives (NA) microfilm, NDL.

21. *Annual Report of the Commander-in-Chief, United States Fleet, for the Period 1 July, 1930 to 30 June, 1931*, 23 Jul 1931, 20 in *1929–1931 Secret and Confidential Files*.

22. *Annual Report of the Commander-in-Chief, United States Fleet, for the Period 1 July, 1931 to 30 June, 1932*, 21 Jul 1932, 17 in *1929–1931 Secret and Confidential Files*.

23. CDR P. N. L. Bellinger, "Naval Aviation," lecture delivered at the Army War College, 13 Feb 1934, 3, box 1, Strategic Plans, OA.

24. Ibid., 11.

25. Calculated from table 28; *Naval Aviation Combat Statistics: World War II*, OPNAV–P–23V NO. A129 (Washington: Air Branch, Office of Naval Intelligence, 17 Jun 1946), 76. A copy of this unissued study, presented to the author in February 1989 by Stuart B. Barber, is in the Operational Archives.

26. Of the 12,268 Japanese planes destroyed by U.S. carrier aircraft during the war, 93 percent were Japanese land-based planes; 72 percent of these planes were destroyed in Japan's inner defense zone (Japan, the Ryukus, Formosa, and the Philippines). Encl. to memo, CAPT R. W. Berry, Aide to SECDEF, to VADM Arthur W. Radford, VCNO, 5 Oct 1948, "A21/1-1 Navy, Apr–Dec 1948" folder, Series I, OP-23 Records, OA.

27. For background information on Trenchard and Gorrell, see H. A. Jones, *The War in the Air: Being the Story of The Part Played in the Great War by the Royal Air Force*, vol. 6 (Oxford: Clarendon Press, 1922–37), 110–117, 135–37ff.; and Maurer, comp. and ed., *The U.S. Air Service in World War I*, 4 vols. (Washington: Albert F. Simpson Historical Research Center, Maxwell AFB, AL and Office of Air Force History, Headquarters USAF, 1978–79), 1:4–14 and 2:141–57.

28. See Raymond R. Flugel, "United States Air Power Doctrine: A Study of the Influence of William Mitchell and Giulio Douhet at the Air Corps Tactical School, 1921–1935" (Ph.D. diss., University of Oklahoma, 1965), 183–234; and John F. Shiner, *Foulois and the U.S. Army Air Corps, 1931–1935* (Washington: Office of Air Force History, 1983), 44–46.

29. Alfred F. Hurley, "The Aeronautical Ideas of General William Mitchell" (Ph.D. diss., Princeton University, 1961), 110.

30. Flugel, "United States Air Power Doctrine," 62; and Hurley, "Aeronautical Ideas of Mitchell," 110–11.

31. Flugel, ibid.

32. Quoted in Hurley, "Aeronautical Ideas of Mitchell," 146–47.

33. See ibid., 162–63; and also Mitchell's testimony during the Department of Defense and Unification of Air Service hearings held by the House Committee on Military Affairs in 1926, as quoted in Robert F. Futrell, *Ideas, Concepts, Doctrine: A History of Basic Thinking in the United States Air Force*,

1907–1964, 2 vols. (Maxwell AFB, AL: Aerospace Studies Institute, Air University, 1971), 1:50. The reason for Mitchell's change in thinking on strategic bombardment remains a historical question.

34. Hurley, "Aeronautical Ideas of Mitchell," 193.

35. See Flugel, "United States Air Power Doctrine," 76–78; and Louis A. Sigaud, *Douhet and Aerial Warfare* (New York: G. P. Putnam's Sons, 1941), 3–9.

36. Giulio Douhet, *The Command of the Air*, trans. Dino Ferrari (New York: Coward-McCann, 1942), 5, 9–10. This edition contains most of the author's significant writings on air power.

37. Ibid., 10.

38. Ibid., 25.

39. Ibid., 34.

40. For a complete discussion of these points, see ibid., 14–23.

41. Ibid., 22. See also his comments regarding this issue in his monograph *The Probable Aspects of the War of the Future*, in ibid., particularly 196–97.

42. Douhet, *Command of the Air*, 58.

43. Ibid., 24.

44. Ibid., 51.

45. Ibid., 49, 51.

46. Ibid., 44.

47. The extent of Douhet's influence on U.S. air power advocates in the interwar years remains a subject of controversy with historians.

48. See Thomas A. Fabyanic, "A Critique of United States Air War Planning, 1941–1944" (Ph.D. diss., Saint Louis University, 1973), 2.

49. Ibid., 3.

50. Raymond Flugel demonstrated the significant influence of Douhet's *Command of the Air* by comparing portions of the text with Douhet's work. See ibid., 185–200.

51. Fabyanic, "Critique of Air War Planning," 13. The *Air Force Dictionary* defines a target system as "a system of targets each of which is functionally related either horizontally or vertically to every other target in the system." Woodford A. Heflin, ed., *The United States Air Force Dictionary* (Maxwell AFB, AL: Air University Press, 1956), 514.

52. Fabyanic, "Critique of Air War Planning," 33–34.

53. The Tactical School used the term "disorganize."

54. Fabyanic, "Critique of Air War Planning," 44. See also Kenneth Schaffel, "Muir S. Fairchild: Philosopher of Air Power," *Aerospace Historian* 33 (Fall/Sep 1986): 167.

55. For a discussion of British attempts at night precision bombing, see Sir Charles Webster and Noble Frankland, *The Strategic Air Offensive Against Germany, 1939–1945*, vol. 1, *Preparation* (London: HMSO, 1961), 213–32.

56. Quoted in *A Brief History of Strategic Bombardment 1911–1971* (March AFB, CA: Headquarters, 15th Air Force, 1971), 17.

57. See "Extract of Report to Chief of the Air Corp [*sic*], of Major John W. Egan, On Completion of Observer Duty With R.A.F. November 26, 1941"; and memo "Brief for General Spaatz," 10 Dec 1941, both in box 18, James H. Doolittle Papers, Manuscript Division, Library of Congress (hereafter MD–LC).

58. Ltr, Spaatz to Arnold, 24 Aug 1942; and Encl. D to JCS 97/1, 11 Sep 1942, 12, both in box 32, 1941–1946 Double Zero Files, OA.

59. Encl. D to JCS 97/1, 13.

60. Quoted in William R. Emerson, *Operation Pointblank: A Tale of Bombers and Fighters*, The Harmon Memorial Lectures in Military History, no. 4 (Colorado Springs: USAF Academy, 1962), 23. Eaker's highly sanguine view was not necessarily representative of the views of lower-level commanders. For an earlier, more cautious view, see extracts from an August 1942 report (title unknown), "1. Capabilities of Day Heavy Bombardment Without Fighter Protection (High Altitude)," n.d. [after 21 Aug 1942], box 78, Carl A. Spaatz Papers, MD–LC.

61. Untitled speech written for General Arnold, n.d. [Nov 1944] (hereafter Arnold Speech), 17, box 7, Elwood R. Quesada Papers, MD–LC.

62. During October 1943, 9.9 percent of VIII Bomber Command's aircraft were shot down and 41.7 percent sustained damage. Emerson, *Operation Pointblank*, 25.

63. Barry D. Watts, *The Foundations of US Air Doctrine: The Problem of Friction in War* (Maxwell AFB, AL: Air University Press, 1984), 63.

64. Arnold Speech, 22.

65. In this regard, the USSBS's preliminary assessment of the bombing stated:

> Whatever the target system, all of the evidence suggests not only the importance of full destruction but the importance of sustained destruction. No indispensable industry was permanently put out of commission by a single attack; attacks had to be repeated before recuperation was made possible. To destroy an important target system and keep it destroyed required extremely heavy, accurate and sustained attack. Memo, Franklin D'Olier, Chairman USSBS, to SECWAR, 11 Jun 1945 [revised 22 Jun 1945], 4; enclosed with ltr, SECWAR to President, 2 Jul 1945, box 157, Cabinet File, President's Secretary's File, Harry S. Truman Library, Independence, MO.

66. See USSBS, *Over-all Report (European War)* (Washington: USSBS, 1945), 42–45; and USSBS, *The Effects of Strategic Bombing on the German War Economy* (Washington: Overall Economic Effects Division, USSBS, 1945), 146.

67. USSBS, *Effects on the German War Economy*, 146.

68. See USSBS, *Over-all Report (European War)*, 29. For detailed information, see USSBS, *The German Anti-Friction Bearings Industry* (Washington: Equipment Division, USSBS, 1947), 1–2, 30–33, 54–61 ff.

69. Emphasis in original. USSBS, *Over-all Report (European War)*, 69–70.

70. USSBS, *German Submarine Industry Report* (Washington: Munitions Division, USSBS, 1947), 33. The de Haviland Mosquito was a fast, light bomber, originally intended for photo reconnaissance work. It later was judged one of the outstanding British aircraft of the war.

71. In its preliminary review of bombing effectiveness, the USSBS noted: "The attacks on transportation were not effective until they were made heavy and wide-spread. So long as they remained scattered and comparatively infrequent, repair was prompt." Memo, D'Olier to SECWAR, 11 Jun 1945, 2.

72. See comments in USSBS, *Over-all Report (European War)*, 64.

73. The eventual effectiveness of these attacks was due to the paralysis of German coal movements: the bombing drastically reduced train traffic in and out of the Ruhr. See D'Olier to SECWAR, 11 Jun 1945, 2; and also Alfred C. Mierzejewski, *The Collapse of the German War Economy, 1944–1945: Allied Air Power and the German National Railway* (Chapel Hill: University of North Carolina Press, 1988).

74. Hugh Odishaw, "Radar Bombing in the Eighth Air Force" (typescript), n.d. [mid-1946], 106, box 80, Spaatz Papers, MD–LC. Pin-point bombing was defined in this manner in the report:

> For all practical purposes, pin-point bombing means the bombing done by the best method during the particular period. From 1 September 1944 through 31 December 1944, pin-point bombing means 30% of bomb falls within a radius of 1,000 feet of the aiming point, 64.3% within one-half mile, 82.4% within one mile, 91.5% within 3 miles, and 92.2% within five miles. Ibid., 107.

75. The Strategic Bombing Survey noted that bombing done by H2X through cloud cover as low as 4/10 to 5/10 produced only 16.7 percent of the bomb hits within 1,000 feet of the aiming point that visual bombing did. Ibid., 14.

76. USSBS, *Over-all Report (European War)*, 72.

77. USSBS, *The Strategic Air Operation of Very Heavy Bombardment in the War Against Japan (Twentieth Air Force) Final Report* (Washington: Army and Army Air Section, Military Analysis Division, USSBS, 1946), 7–8.

78. See USSBS, *The Effects of Strategic Bombing on Japan's War Economy* (Washington: Over-all Economic Effects Division, USSBS, 1946), 41–55; and Futrell, *Ideas, Concepts, Doctrine* 1:147–48. For a contemporary Navy appraisal of the XX Bomber Command's effort, see memo, CAPT Paul D. Stroop, F-15, to F-1, 3 Nov 1944, box 76, Strategic Plans, OA.

79. Memo, LCDR Roger Kent, F-152, to Stroop, 10 Oct 1944, box 53, Strategic Plans. For the much closer targets on Japanese-occupied Formosa, B-29s could carry bomb loads of 11,000 to 13,000 pounds.

80. Compiled from Chart 4 in USSBS, *Very Heavy Bombardment in the War Against Japan*, 5.

81. See USSBS, *Effects of Strategic Bombing on Japan's War Economy*, 63.

82. Futrell, *Ideas, Concepts, Doctrine* 1:147–48.

83. Emphasis added. USSBS, *Very Heavy Bombardment in the War Against Japan*, 11.

84. Ibid.

85. James L. Cate and James C. Olson, "Urban Area Attacks," in *Army Air Forces in World War II*, vol. 5, *The Pacific: Matterhorn to Nagasaki, June 1944–August 1945*, eds. Wesley J. Craven and James L. Cate for Office of Air Force History, USAF (Chicago: University of Chicago Press, 1953), 609. An example of the cost of high-altitude bombing, particularly on missions using small numbers of bombers (fifty to seventy aircraft), is found in four missions against Tokyo flown from 3 December 1944 through 27 January 1945. On these missions, the XXI Bomber Command averaged aircraft losses of 10.1 percent and aircraft damage of 31.3 percent. Calculated from "Tokyo High Altitude Day Missions" chart in "Comparison of Loss and Damage Rates in Various Types of Missions," XXI Bomber Command *Air Intelligence Report* 1 (26 Apr 1945): 16, box 177, WW II Command File, OA.

86. USSBS, *Very Heavy Bombardment in the War Against Japan*, 12; and Cate and Olson, "Urban Area Attacks," 614–23. The figures for the damage inflicted by the incendiary attacks are from "A Partial Appraisal of the Results of B-29 Attacks on Urban Industrial Areas," n.d. [29 Aug 1945], 2, 4, box 27, Subject File 1942–50, Public Information Division, Office of Information Services (hereafter Public Information Division Records), Secretary of the Air Force Records (RG 340), National Archives, Washington National Records Center (NA/WNRC), Suitland, MD. See also the "Incendiary Strikes" chart in "Preliminary Survey of 20th A.F. Target Damage," Twentieth Air Force *Air Intelligence Report* 1 (Oct 1945): 20–21, box 177, WW II Command File, OA.

87. See USSBS, *Effects of Strategic Bombing on Japan's War Economy*, 63.

88. Quoted in Cate and Olson, "Urban Area Attacks," 626–27.

89. USSBS, *Very Heavy Bombardment in the War Against Japan*, 13.

90. "Press Conference of Major General Curtis E. LeMay, 19 June 1945," 24, box 29, Public Information Division Records, RG 340, National Archives, Washington National Records Center, Suitland, MD (hereafter NA/WNRC).

91. The Strategic Bombing Survey later found that the drop in Japanese morale attendant to the fire bombing was only one of several factors that together brought about Japan's defeat. See USSBS, *Effects of Strategic Bombing on Japanese Morale* (Washington: Morale Division, USSBS, 1947), 6, 137–46.

2. Unification, Service Rivalries, and Public Relations

1. See Lawrence J. Legere, Jr., "Unification of the Armed Forces" (Ph.D. diss., Harvard University, 1950), 99–100; and Benton V. Davis, Jr., "Admirals, Politics and Postwar Defense Policy: The Origins of the Postwar U.S. Navy, 1943–1946 and After" (Ph.D. diss., Princeton University, 1962), 84.

2. *New York Times*, 19 Feb 1932; quoted in Robert Greenhalgh Albion and Robert Howe Connery, with the collaboration of Jennie Barnes Pope, *Forrestal and the Navy* (New York: Columbia University Press, 1962), 254.

3. Append. to encl. to JCS 560, 2 Nov 1943, 5–6; encl. to memo, ADM Ernest J. King to SECNAV, 4 Nov 1943; attached to ltr, Chairman, General Board (GB) to SECNAV, GB No. 466, ser 258, 14 Dec 1943, box 599, 1943 Secret SECNAV–CNO Records, RG 80, NA.

4. GB No. 446, ser 258, 2–3.

5. Memo, Special Planning Section to CNO, via VCNO, OP-50B, 17 Dec 1943, box 10, Harry E. Yarnell Papers, OA.

6. Demetrios Caraley, *The Politics of Military Unification: A Study of Conflict and the Policy Process* (New York: Columbia University Press, 1966), 25.

7. Quoted in Curtis W. Tarr, "The General Board Joint Staff Proposal of 1941," *Military Affairs* 31 (Summer 1967): 87.

8. See Davis, "Admirals, Politics and Postwar Defense," 119; and Paul Y. Hammond, *Organizing for Defense: The American Military Establishment in the Twentieth Century* (Princeton: Princeton University Press, 1961), 191.

9. Quoted in Legere, "Unification of the Armed Forces," 273.

10. See summary of Army testimony in memo, General Board to SECNAV et al., GB No. 446, ser 267–X, 26 May 1944, 4, box 170, Strategic Plans, OA.

11. Caraley, *Politics of Military Unification*, 28.

12. Davis argues with some justification that if the Navy witnesses had been forced to testify first, they would have had little to say. Davis, "Admirals, Politics and Postwar Defense Policy," 117.

13. Legere, "Unification of the Armed Forces," 276.

14. See Davis, "Admirals, Politics and Postwar Defense Policy," 107–8; and the summary of Navy testimony in GB No. 446, ser 267–X, 26 May 1944, 7–8.

15. Typed copy of *First Report of the House Select Committee on Post-War Military Policy*, 15 Jun 1944, 4, box 170, Strategic Plans, OA.

16. Ltr, Forrestal to Palmer Hoyt, 2 Sep 1944; quoted in Walter Millis, ed., with the collaboration of E. S. Duffield, *The Forrestal Diaries* (New York: Viking Press, 1951), 60.

17. Ltr, Gates to King, 3 May 1945, 1, box 5, Ernest J. King Papers, OA.

18. Ibid., 2.

19. Transcript labeled "Minutes of Top Policy Meetings, Meeting No. 20, 7 May 1945 . . . ," 1–2, box 2, Top Policy Group Minutes, RG 80, NA.

20. Ibid., 3–4.

21. Ibid., 19–20.

22. Copy of ltr, Walsh to SECNAV, 15 May 1945, 3; attached to ltr, Forrestal to Walsh, 27 May 1945, box 37, 1941–1946 Double Zero Files, OA.

23. Ltr, Forrestal to Walsh, 27 May 1945.

24. For information on Forrestal's and Eberstadt's earlier business association, see Albion and Connery, *Forrestal and the Navy*, 77.

25. See "Memorandum of Meeting, 9 June 1945, Room 2500," Box 23, Records of the Secretary of the Navy James Forrestal, 1940–47 (hereafter Forrestal Records), RG 80, NA.

26. Ltr, Forrestal to Eberstadt, 19 Jun 1945, same box. The draft of this "mandate" had been revised and approved by Eberstadt and the others at the 9 June meeting. See "Memorandum of Meeting, 9 June 1945," 3–4.

27. In his dissertation Vincent Davis states that he finds it difficult to accept Eberstadt's initial open-mindedness on the unification issue. Davis, "Admirals, Politics and Postwar Defense," 377n. Nonetheless, contemporary records show various instances of this open-mindedness. See, for example, "MEMORANDUM OF MEETING held 15 June 1945," same date, box 23, Forrestal Records, RG 80, NA.

28. Ltr, Eberstadt to Forrestal, 11 Oct 1945, same box.

29. Memo, Eberstadt to Forrestal, 27 Sep 1945, same box.

30. Caraley, *Politics of Military Unification*, 40–41.

31. Ltr, Forrestal to Eberstadt, 6 Oct 1945, box 23, Forrestal Records, RG 80, NA.

32. Caraley, *Politics of Military Unification*, 63.

33. Statement of General of the Army George C. Marshall, Senate, Committee on Military Affairs, *Department of Armed Forces—Department of Military Security: Hearings on S. 84 and S. 1482*, 79th Cong., 1st sess., 17 Oct–17 Dec 1945, 50.

34. Caraley, *Politics of Military Unification*, 99.

35. See Statement of Hon. James Forrestal, Senate Committee on Military Affairs, *Hearings on S. 84 And S. 1482*, 103; and the comments of Deputy COMINCH Admiral R. S. Edwards to Forrestal, in entry for 25 Aug 1945, xerographic copy of typescript, section labeled "Forrestal Papers...Diary, vol. 2...Aug 1945" (hereafter Forrestal Diaries), 449, box 15, Privileged Manuscript Collection, OA. The original Forrestal Diaries are in the Forrestal Papers at Princeton University.

36. See Caraley, *Politics of Military Unification*, 62.

37. Untitled transcript of a meeting between Secretary Forrestal and senior naval officers on unification, 31 Jan 1947, 2–3; enclosed in binder labeled "'Unification Folder' Dec 1946–May 1947," "A1/2-1/4 Navy Proposals S&C" folder, Series II, OP-23 Records, OA. This group of papers on unification was compiled for Forrestal's personal use. See also entry for 9 May 1945, Forrestal Diaries, vol. 1, Mar 1944–Feb 1945, 330, box 15, Privileged Manuscript Collection, OA.

38. Caraley, *Politics of Military Unification*, 73.

39. See Perry McCoy Smith, *The Air Force Plans for Peace, 1943–1945* (Baltimore: Johns Hopkins Press, 1970), 34–35.

40. Herman S. Wolk, *Planning and Organizing the Postwar Air Force, 1943–1947* (Washington: Office of Air Force History, 1984), 90.

41. Memo, Arnold to Chief of Staff, Attn: Special Planning Division, WDSS, 5 Jun 1945, 1, File No. 70, box 16, Top Secret Air Adjutant General (TS AAG) Files, General File 1944–53, Director of Plans, Deputy Chief of Staff, Operations (hereafter DCS/O General File 1944–53), Headquarters U.S. Air Force Records (RG 341), NA.

42. See, for example, the covering memo from CAPT George L. Russell to FADM King, 11 Jul 1945, filed with *Analysis of JCS 749/12*, n.d. [circulated 14 Jul 1945], box 22, Forrestal Records, RG 80, NA. This study was the Navy Department's detailed analysis of the JCS Special Committee's Report.

43. For an official narrative of the 1946 fight over roles and missions, see James F. Schnabel, *The History of the Joint Chiefs of Staff: The Joint Chiefs of Staff and National Policy*, vol. 1, *1945–1947* (Washington: Historical Division, Joint Secretariat, Joint Chiefs of Staff, 1979), 238–47.

44. For the Marine Corps' reaction to the roles and missions fight in this period (a subject beyond the scope of this study), see Gordon W. Keiser, *The US Marine Corps and Defense Unification, 1944–47: The Politics of Survival* (Washington: National Defense University Press, 1982).

45. Encl. A to JCS 1478/8, 20 Feb 1946, 27–29; attached to memo, BGEN A. J. McFarland to FADM Leahy et al., SM-5058, 21 Feb 1946 "JCS Completed Papers 1478–1478/19" folder, Office of the Chief of Naval Operations, Navy Secretariat for JCS Matters Records (hereafter Navy Secretariat Records), OA.

46. JCS 1478/9, 6 Mar 1946, 49; attached to memo, McFarland to Leahy et al., SM-5182, 6 Mar 1946, same folder.

47. Wolk, *Planning and Organizing the Postwar Air Force*, 90.

Notes to pages 35–39

48. Emphasis added. Untitled memo marked "Dictated by Gen Spaatz during conversation with Gen Norstad," 19 Oct 1945, box 22, Spaatz Papers, MD–LC.

49. Ibid.

50. JCS 1478/10, 15 Mar 1946, 51, attached to office memo, H. C. Bruton, Admin Aide to CNO, to VADM Arthur D. Radford, 18 Mar 1946, "JCS Completed Papers 1478–1478/19" folder, Navy Secretariat Records, OA.

51. Ibid., 52.

52. Although JCS 1478/11 (Eisenhower's paper of 15 Mar 1946) is not totally declassified in official JCS records, it is completely available in printed form (from the original in Army files) in Louis Galambos, ed. *The Papers of Dwight David Eisenhower*, vol. 7, *The Chief Of Staff* (Baltimore: The Johns Hopkins University Press, 1978), 927–31. See also General Eisenhower's unofficial memo sent directly to the Joint Chiefs on 3 Apr 1946 but later formally introduced to the JCS docket as JCS 1478/13. Memo, Chief of Staff, U.S. Army, 2 Apr 1946, attached to memo, Eisenhower to Leahy et al., 3 Apr 1946, "JCS Completed Papers 1478–1478/19" folder, Navy Secretariat Records, OA.

53. Memo from Sherman to CNO, no serial, 17 Mar 1946; filed with JCS 1478/11, "JCS Completed Papers 1478–1478/19" folder, Navy Secretariat Records, OA.

54. Ibid.

55. See Encls. A and B to JCS 1478/12, 30 Mar 1946, same folder.

56. See the Record of Action filed with the 1478–1478/19 papers.

57. Copy of ltr, President Truman to Robert Patterson and James Forrestal, 15 Jun 1946, encl. to ltr, W. Stuart Symington to J. H. Doolittle, 31 Oct 1946, box 27, Papers of James H. Doolittle, MD–LC.

58. For Radford's personal comments see his draft autobiography (copy of typescript with penciled corrections), "A Brief Resume of the Life and Experiences of Arthur W. Radford, Admiral, United States Navy (Ret.)—February 4, 1966" (hereafter Radford Autobiography), [1]: 471–78, Post 1 Jan 1946 Command File, OA.

59. Emphasis in original. Entry for 19 Jun 1946, Forrestal Diaries, vol. 5, May 1946–Sep 1946, 1113, box 16, Privileged Manuscript Collection, OA.

60. Ibid.

61. See the AAF's comments on this issue in an untitled, undated memo enclosed with Symington's ltr to Doolittle, 31 Oct 1946.

62. Entry for 4 Nov 1946, "Personal Log of Vice Admiral Radford: 2 Jul 46–21 Feb 47" (hereafter Radford Personal Log), box 1, Arthur W. Radford Papers, OA.

63. Ibid.

64. During a golf game on Saturday, 2 Nov 1946, Symington had told Forrestal that "they were not doing so well and would be open to some discussion." Comment by Admiral Radford to Ferdinand Eberstadt in transcript entitled "Recording of Telephone Conversation between Admiral Radford in Washington and Mr. Eberstadt in New York," 8 Nov 1946, inserted in Radford Personal Log: 2 Jul 46–21 Feb 47. See also the entry for 7 Nov 1946.

65. Memo, VADM Sherman to SECNAV, 12 Nov 1946, 2, inserted between entries for 12 and 13 Nov 1946, Forrestal Diaries, vol. 6, Oct 1946–Mar 1947, 1331, box 16, Privileged Manuscript Collection, OA.

66. See ltr, VADM Radford to Mr. William F. Schaub, Bureau of the Budget, 20 Nov 1946, box 2, Series I, DCNO (Air) Correspondence, DCNO (Air) Records, OA.

67. Ltr, Spaatz to James E. Webb, 6 Dec 1946, 1, box 4, Special Interest File, 1948, General File by Organization and Subject 1947 – Jan 1953, Correspondence Control Division, Office of the Administrative Assistant (hereafter cited as Symington Special Interest Files), Secretary of the Air Force Records (RG 340), NA/WNRC.

68. Ibid., 4. See also Donald E. Wilson, "The History of President Truman's Air Policy Commission and Its Influence on Air Policy, 1947–1949" (Ph.D. diss., University of Denver, 1978), 38–39.

69. See transcript of Air Planning Group meeting, 7 Jan 1947, 3, box 37, Series V, Air Planning Group Files, DCNO (Air) Records, OA. Spaatz had made the point in his 6 December letter to Webb that, *as the AAF interpreted the President's letter,* "it has been decided by the Commander in Chief that the Air Force crews are to man the land based planes." Ltr, Spaatz to Webb, 6 Dec 1946.

70. Eyes Only Memo, VADM Robert B. Carney to Nimitz, via Ramsey, 25 Nov 1946, 1, box 2, 1942–1947 Double Zero Files, OA. Carney was basing his view upon discussions in the Ship Characteristics Board about the increasing size and weight of future carrier aircraft.

71. Ibid., 2–3.

72. Hanson W. Baldwin, "Air Dispute Remains: Naval Aviators Still Oppose Creation of Separate Department," *New York Times*, 26 Jan 1947—copy of article enclosed with ltr, Nimitz to Radford, 28 Jan 1947, box 1, Series I, DCNO (Air) Records, OA. The date of the Flag Selection Board briefing is based upon a reading of Radford's Log. Entries for 13–21 Nov 1946, Radford Personal Log: 2 Jul 46–21 Feb 47, box 1, Radford Papers, OA.

73. Entry for 4 Dec 1946, Forrestal Diaries, 6:1366.

74. Ltr, Forrestal to CAPT J. P. W. Vest, Commanding Officer, USS *Franklin D. Roosevelt*, 13 Jun 1947; attached to ltr, BGEN T. A. Sims, Executive Officer to the Assistant Secretary of War for Air, to Assistant Secretary Symington, 24 Jun 1947, box 4, Special Interest File, 1948, Symington Special Interest Files, RG 340, NA/WNRC.

75. The list of personnel present is drawn from the entry for 11 Jan 1947, Radford Personal Log: 2 Jul 1946–21 Feb 1947; and a 13 Jan 1946 memo on the meeting, which was drafted but not sent to Truman, on the advice of Assistant Secretary John Kenney and Admirals Forrest Sherman and Tommy Robbins. Box 30, Forrestal Records, RG 80, NA. For a partial listing, see Baldwin, "Air Dispute Remains."

76. RADM Frank D. Wagner, Chief of Naval Air Training; RADM Felix B. Stump, Chief of Naval Air Technical Training; and RADM Clifton A. F. Sprague, Chief of Naval Air Basic Training.

77. Transcript of a meeting between Secretary Forrestal and senior naval officers on unification, 31 Jan 1947, 48.

78. Draft memo, Forrestal to the President, 13 Jan 1946, 2.

79. Interestingly, neither Forrestal's diary nor Radford's log provides an account of this meeting. However, Forrestal's draft memo to the President does furnish a good summary of the major points put forward in the session by the majority of the naval aviators present.

80. Ltr, Stump to Nimitz, 13 Jan 1947, "S Correspondence 1946–1950" folder, Series II, Papers of Chester W. Nimitz, OA.

81. Ibid. Stump's remarks were a reference to the comments made by some of the naval aviators at the meeting to the effect that if the AAF was made a separate administrative entity, then "all Naval aviators should also join with the Army Air Forces in the organization of an Air Force of the United States because otherwise the future promotion and status of Naval aviators would be seriously jeopardized." Draft memo, Forrestal to the President, 13 Jan 1946, 2.

82. Ltr, Nimitz to Stump, 16 Jan 1947, "S Correspondence 1946–1950" folder, Series II, Nimitz Papers, OA.

83. Ltr, Forrestal to the President, 13 Jan 1947; attached to memo James Webb to President, 24 Jan 1947, box 29, Confidential File, White House Central Files, Truman Library.

84. Memo, Webb to the President, 24 Jan 1947; and ltr, Truman to SECNAV, 24 Jan 1947, same box.

85. For a discussion of this agreement and the President's reaction, see Caraley, *Politics of Military Unification*, 152–54.

86. Memo, CNO to the Aeronautical Board, 29 Jan 1947, box 1, Series I, DCNO (Air) Records, OA.

87. Copy of ltr from Spaatz to Radford, 31 Jan 1947; "A19/2 Key West Conference (Roles & Missions) S&C" folder, Series II, OP-23 Records.

308   *Notes to pages 43–46*

88. Ibid.

89. Ltr, Radford to Spaatz, OP–50C ser 13P50C, 4 Feb 1947; and copy of ltr, Radford to Spaatz, ser 14P05, 8 Feb 1947, both in "A19/2 Key West Conference (Roles & Missions) S&C" folder.

90. Copy of ltr, Spaatz to Radford, 10 Feb 1947, same folder. President Truman had stated that any changes in planning for aircraft procurement for fiscal year 1948 would have to be programmed within the totals included for this purpose in his 1948 budget. Ltr, Truman to SECNAV, 24 Jan 1947.

91. Ltr, Spaatz to Radford, 10 Feb 1947.

92. See, ltr, Spaatz to Nimitz, 11 Mar 1947, box 1, 1942–1947 Double Zero Files, OA; and copy of ltr, Nimitz to Spaatz, OP–03 ser 31P03, 19 Mar 1947, "A7–1/3 Air Force (SPAATZ)" folder, Series I, OP–23 Records, OA. These letters were subsequently stenciled and distributed for information to all Flag officers on 28 May 1947.

93. Radford had asked Sherman to speak about the AAF's position to Norstad, his colleague in the drafting of unification legislation. Memo, Radford to OP–09, 17 Feb 1947, box 1, Series I, DCNO (Air) Records, OA.

94. Emphasis added. Report from Col. William Westlake, Assistant to Director [of Public Relations] for Army Air Forces, to Commanding General AAF, 23 Sep 1944, 1–2, box 31, Subject File 1942–50, Public Information Division Records, RG 340, NA/WNRC.

95. Ibid., 14.

96. Eyes Only ltr, Arnold to Spaatz, 26 Sep 1944, File No. 54, box 14, TS AAG Files, DCS/O General File 1944–53, RG 341, NA.

97. Wolk, *Planning and Organizing the Postwar Air Force*, 81, 89–90, 100–103; and draft ltr, BGEN Frank F. Everest to LTGEN Nathan F. Twining, n.d.; encl. to memo, Everest to COL H. W. Bowman, Chief, Office of Information Services, 28 Sep 1945, box 27, Public Information Division Records, RG 340, NA/WNRC.

98. Wolk, *Planning and Organizing the Postwar Air Force*, 103; and ltr, LTGEN Twining, Commander Air Technical Service Command (ATSC), to BGEN J. H. Houghton, Miami ATSC, 22 Dec 1945, Exhibit A in *Progress Report ATSC Educational Program Supporting the President's Plan for the Unification of the Armed Forces, 15 January 1946* (Dayton, OH: Logistics Planning Division, ATSC, 1946), box 32, Public Information Division Records, RG 340.

99. General Carl Spaatz, "Air Power Pre-Eminent," speech given to the Business Advisory Council, Hot Springs, VA, 27 Oct 1945, 1, box 22, Spaatz Papers, MD–LC. Spaatz had begun standing in as Commanding General for the ailing Hap Arnold in September 1945. David R. Mets, *Master of Airpower: General Carl A. Spaatz* (Novato, CA: Presidio Press, 1988), 312. In February 1946 he officially succeeded Arnold as head of the Army Air Forces.

100. See Spaatz, "Airpower and the Future," speech given to the Society of Automotive Engineers, New York, 11 Oct 1945, 6, box 22, Spaatz Papers, MD–LC. See also [Dr. Bruce C. Hopper?] "Notes To Be Used By Gen Spaatz in Interview by Mr. Shalett, New York Times," 5, enclosed with memo, Sidney Shalett, War Department Correspondent, *New York Times*, to MGEN Lauris Norstad, 4 Jan 1946, box 25.

101. See H. H. Arnold, *Second Report of the Commanding General of the Army Air Forces*, 27 Feb 1945 (Washington: Headquarters, AAF, 1945), 93–94; and *Third Report of the Commanding General of the Army Air Forces to the Secretary of War* 12 Nov 1945 (Washington: Headquarters, AAF, 1945), 61–62.

102. *The United States Air Force Dictionary* (Maxwell AFB, AL: Air University Press, 1956), 34, defines air power as "that part of the military establishment of a nation made responsible as a single organization for the principal employment of this power; in the US, the United States Air Force."

103. War Department Field Manual 100–20, *Command and Employment of Air Power*, 21 Jul 1943, 2; quoted in Thomas J. Mayock, "Notes On the Development of AAF Tactical Air Doctrine," *Military Affairs* 14 (Winter 1950): 186.

104. Spaatz, "Air Power Pre-Eminent," 3–4; Spaatz, "Airpower and the Future," 6; and "Remarks of Gen. Carl Spaatz at Wings Club, 1 October 1945," 2, box 22, Spaatz Papers, MD–LC.

105. See Arnold, *Third Report of the Commanding General of the Army Air Forces*, 62; and Mets, *Master of Airpower*, 307–8.

106. Emphasis added. Ltr from Spaatz to Giles, 26 Mar 1945, File No. 51, box 13, TS AAG Files, DCS/O General File 1944–53, RG 341, NA. See also Spaatz's "*Strategic Air Power* (Fulfillment of a Concept)," draft of article for *Foreign Affairs*, Feb 1946, 12, box 25, Spaatz Papers, MD–LC. For the printed version of the article, see *Foreign Affairs* 24 (Apr 1946): 385–96.

107. Ltr, Kenney to Arnold, 10 Feb 1945; attached to ltr, Arnold to Kenney, 3 Mar 1945, File No. 46, box 13, TS AAG Files, DCS/O General File 1944–53, RG 341.

108. See, for example, the memo, H. W. Bowman, Chief, Office of Information Services, to Commanding General AAF, 5 Dec 1945, box 25, Spaatz Papers, MD–LC.

109. William Bradford Huie, *The Fight for Air Power* (New York: L. B. Fischer, 1942).

110. See General Knerr's diary entries for 26–27 Sep 1945, box 6, Hugh J. Knerr Papers, MD–LC. Murray Green argues that, during the war, Knerr had shown signs of "mellowing with age and war experience," and that at the time Huie approached him in 1945, Knerr seemed quite ready to let old wounds (i.e., his harsh published attacks on the Navy) "be bound up and healed." Murray Green, "Hugh J. Knerr: The Pen and the Sword," in *Makers of the Air Force*, ed. John L. Frisbee (Washington: Office of Air Force History, USAF, 1987), 124. Green's claim is totally misleading, as anyone who takes the time to read Knerr's postwar (1945–1949) official papers and personal correspondence can judge.

111. "*Part I* Brief of Service. Hugh J. Knerr, Major General, U.S. Air Force," box 13, Knerr Papers, MD–LC. For a useful (though selective) account of Knerr's background, see Green, "Knerr: The Pen and the Sword," 99–117. Green appears to be unaware of the collection of Knerr papers in the Manuscript Division of the Library of Congress. He cites the collection of Knerr's papers at the Air Force Academy and the Hap Arnold and Frank Andrews papers at the Library of Congress but not the Knerr papers there.

112. Green, "Knerr: The Pen and the Sword," 102.

113. Huie's book, *The Fight for Air Power*, was based in large part on a series of pro-air power, anti-Navy articles written by Huie and then-retired Air Corps Lieutenant Colonel Hugh Knerr that had appeared during 1941 and 1942 in the magazine *The American Mercury*. Huie later admitted in his book, *The Case Against the Admirals*, that *The Fight for Air Power* was also a joint effort by Knerr and Huie. Knerr's name was removed from the book following his return to active duty in mid-1942, and evidence of his collaboration was hastily erased from the text, primarily to reduce any effects its anti-Navy polemics might have on War Department–Navy Department relations. For information on this matter, see William Bradford Huie, *The Case Against the Admirals: Why We Must Have a Unified Command* (New York: E. P. Dutton, 1946), 126–27; and Green, "Knerr: The Pen and the Sword," 117–18, 120.

114. Diary entry for 27 Sep 1945, box 6, Knerr Papers, MD–LC.

115. Ltr, William Bradford Huie to Knerr, 8 Oct 1945, box 6, Knerr Papers, MD–LC. At this time Everest, in addition to his regular duty in the Office of the Assistant Chief of Air Staff for Plans, was assigned to the AAF's special organizational planning group that was working on the AAF plan for unification. See "Everest, Frank Fort, Lt. Gen. USAF (366A)," in *Generals of the Army and the Air Force* (Dec 1954), 7. This source erroneously dates the start of Everest's service on the special planning group as November 1945.

116. Emphasis in original. Ltr, Huie to Knerr, 8 Oct 1945.

117. Ibid.

118. See ltr, Huie to Knerr, 22 Oct 1945; and, particularly, ltr, Huie to Knerr, 2 Nov 1945, both in box 6, Knerr Papers, MD–LC.

119. See memo, RADM H. B. Miller, Director of Public Information, to Radford, SCOROR, OOR ser 99957, 7 Mar 1946; memo, CAPT Walter Karig, SCOROR, to Miller, 13 Mar 1946; ltr, Miller to Bennett Cerf, 26 Mar 1946; and "Book Questioned By Navy Banned," *New York Times*, 31 Mar 1946; all in "A7–1/8 (Huie) S&C" folder, Series II, OP–23 Records, OA.

120. Huie, *Case Against the Admirals*, 9.

121. Ltr, Nimitz to Eisenhower, 9 Mar 1946; quoted in Galambos, *Papers of Dwight Eisenhower* 7:909.

122. Emphasis in original. Memo, Eisenhower to Hull and Collins, 9 Mar 1946, printed in ibid., 7:909.

123. Forrestal's old friend Ferdinand Eberstadt, in a confidential letter to the Navy Secretary, noted that he had talked to the head of Dutton's (Huie's publisher) and that sales of the book "were very disappointing," running only a few thousand. Ltr, Eberstadt to Forrestal, 10 May 1946; "A7–1/8 (Huie) S&C" folder, Series II, OP–23 Records, OA.

124. Emphasis in original. Unsigned memo [probably from Brackley Shaw, Special Assistant to the Assistant Secretary for Air] to Symington, 12 Sep 1946, box 4, Special Interest File 1948, Symington Special Interest Files, RG 340, NA/WNRC. See also Shaw's draft memo, 4 Nov 1946, same box.

125. Stuart Symington's words come from his letter to J. H. "Jock" Whitney, 30 Oct 1946, 3; encl. to ltr, Symington to Doolittle, 31 Oct 1946.

126. Emphasis in original. CAPT Frank A. Manson, USN (Ret.), interview by author, 28 Jan 1989, Annapolis, MD, tape recording.

127. Stephen F. Leo, interview by George M. Watson, Jr., 18 Aug 1982, K239.0512–1558, U.S. Air Force Oral History Program, Center for Air Force History, Bolling AFB, Washington, DC, 10, 13.

128. Ibid., 12.

129. Ltr, Symington to General R. E. Wood, Sears, Roebuck and Co., 13 May 1948, encl. to ltr, Symington to GEN Dwight D. Eisenhower, President, Columbia University, 14 May 1948, box 113, Principal File, Dwight D. Eisenhower Papers, Pre-Presidential 1916–52, Dwight D. Eisenhower Library, Abilene, KS.

130. Memo for Sullivan, no ser, 9 Feb 1948, box 13, Radford Papers, OA.

131. Memo, CAPT L. A. Thackrey to SECNAV, no ser, 6 Apr 1948, box 5, Double Zero Files 1947–1950—Admiral Louis E. Denfeld Papers (hereafter Denfeld Double Zero Files), OA.

132. Ibid.

133. During FY 1948, Air Force strength stood at 55 groups.

134. Ltr, Denfeld to Dudley A. White, 6 Apr 1948, box 6, Louis E. Denfeld Papers, OA.

135. During World War II the Pacific Ocean Areas Command under Admiral Nimitz was the only theater command to operate as a true "joint command." Its J–2 (Intelligence) and J–4 (Logistics) Divisions were headed by Army general officers and one of the two plans sections of the J–3 (Plans and Operations) Division was headed by an Army brigadier general.

136. Ltr, Nimitz to Mr. E. M. (Ted) Dealey, 6 Dec 1948; "D Correspondence 1946–1950" folder, Series II, Nimitz Papers, OA.

137. Copy of ltr, David Botter to Mr. H. C. Withers, Managing Editor, 10 Dec 1948; encl. to ltr, Ted Dealey to Nimitz, 14 Dec 1948, same folder.

138. Ibid.

139. *Final Report: War Department Policies and Programs Review Board*, 11 Aug 1947, 23; encl. to memo, CNO to Dist. List, 4 Dec 1947, box 6, Denfeld Double Zero Files, OA.

140. Ibid., 24.

141. Ltr, RADM Robbins to RADM Charles R. (Cat) Brown, 15 Jan 1948, unnumbered box, Papers of Thomas H. Robbins, Jr., Naval Historical Foundation (NHF), Washington Navy Yard. For a conventional account of the Nimitz Valedictory, see Michael A. Palmer, *Origins of the Maritime Strategy:*

American Naval Strategy in the First Postwar Decade, Contributions to Naval History, No. 1 (Washington: Naval Historical Center, 1988), 36–37, 104*n.*

142. Ltr, Robbins to Brown, Robbins Papers, NHF.

143. Ibid.; and ltr, Robbins to ADM D.C. Ramsey, CINCPAC/CINCPACFLT, 9 Jan 1948, Robbins Papers.

144. Emphasis in original. *The Future Employment of Naval Forces,* P–514, copy in "A1/EM–3/4–2 CNO (Nimitz Valedictory)" folder, Series I, OP–23 Records, OA.

145. NSPS [Navy Strategic Plans Study] 3, "Study of Carrier Attack Force Offensive Capabilities," OP–30W, A16–3(17), 7 Mar 1947, box 497, Strategic Plans, OA. Contrary to Palmer's recent history on the period, the valedictory did not advocate Navy employment of "land-based nuclear-capable bombers" against enemy targets. Palmer, *Origins of the Maritime Strategy,* 37. Unfortunately, Palmer misinterpreted the thrust of the Navy argument on this point due to an out-of-context reading of a phrase on page 8 of the pamphlet.

146. See Office of Public Relations Evaluation Memorandum (M–140), "A Summary of Editorial Reaction for the Period 4–17 January, 1948," 28 Jan 1948, 3–5; and ltr, CAPT E. M. Eller, Director of Public Information, to Nimitz, DPI ser 1394, 21 Jan 1948; both in "'Future Employment of Naval Forces'—Nimitz" folder, Series III, Nimitz Papers, OA.

147. Emphasis added. Ltr, Nimitz to Sherman, 15 Jan 1948, "*S* Correspondence 1946–1950" folder, Series II, Nimitz Papers, OA. On Nimitz's enthusiasm about the valedictory, see also ltr, Nimitz to Robbins, 12 Jan 1948, "A1/EM–3/4–2 CNO (Nimitz Valedictory)" folder, Series I, OP–23 Papers, OA.

148. Ltr, Sherman to Nimitz, 7 Feb 1948, "*S* Correspondence 1946–1950" folder, Series II, Nimitz Papers, OA.

149. Emphasis added. Memo from Spaatz to Symington, 7 Jan 1948, 1, box 28, Spaatz Papers, MD–LC.

150. Ibid., 3–4.

151. Emphasis added. Ibid., 5.

152. For basic information on Louis Denfeld's term as CNO, see Paolo E. Coletta, "Louis Emil Denfeld 15 December 1947–1 November 1949," in *The Chiefs Of Naval Operations,* ed. Robert W. Love (Annapolis: Naval Institute Press, 1980), 193–206.

153. Admiral Robert B. Carney, USN (Ret.), interview by author, 30 Aug 1988, Washington, DC, tape recording.

154. For detailed information on the 1947 politicking for CNO, see the correspondence in the VADM William M. Fechteler, CAPT Harold A. Latta, USNR, FADM William D. Leahy, and RADM Thomas L. Sprague folders, in box 1, Denfeld Papers, OA. See also the Leahy folder, box 4. Admiral Carney specifically commented on Admiral Leahy's role in securing Denfeld's appointment. Carney interview.

155. On 21 August an unnamed "high government official" had said to Forrestal, "'Mr. Secretary, you are well aware that there is no man in the Navy who has the ability to obtain appropriations from Congress equal to that of Admiral Denfeld. Admiral Denfeld is tremendously liked by the Congress, and particularly the respective Committees in the House and Senate on Appropriations." Quoted in ltr, Latta to Denfeld, 22 Aug 1947, box 1, Denfeld Papers, OA.

156. Carney interview. See also Palmer, *Origins of the Maritime Strategy,* 40–41.

157. Admiral Charles D. Griffin, USN (Ret.), interview by author, 10 Dec 1985, Washington, DC, tape recording.

158. Ltr, Denfeld to Latta, 16 Aug 1947; and ltr, Latta to Denfeld, 16 Aug 1947, both in box 1, Denfeld Papers, OA. Admiral Denfeld had written Radford in August, "I have not made any plans in the event that I should be selected for the big job, but as my oldest friend in Naval Aviation I am going to lean heavily on you." Denfeld to Radford, 14 Aug 1947, box 56, Radford Papers, OA.

159. Ltr, Denfeld to RADM T. L. Sprague, 13 Oct 1947, box 1, Denfeld Papers, OA.

160. Ltr, Radford to Denfeld, 22 Aug 1947, 3, box 56, Radford Papers, OA.

312   *Notes to pages 58–61*

161. For a contrary view, see Palmer, *Origins of the Maritime Strategy*, 40.

162. In June 1948 Arctic and Antarctic explorer RADM Richard E. Byrd wrote to Denfeld complimenting him on sticking with his choice of Radford as VCNO, even under opposition. He commented: "You knew that it was right to appoint Raddy as VCNO. You had a Hell of a lot of opposition. But you stood firm and refused to compromise. *The Navy is the beneficiary.* You could not possibly have a more loyal backer and fighter for what is right than Raddy." Emphasis in original. Byrd to Denfeld, 2 Jul 1948, box 2, Denfeld Papers, OA.

163. For Steve Leo's comments on the Navy PR setup, see Leo oral history, Center for Air Force History, 22–23, 54.

164. Quoted in transcript, "Minutes of Top Policy Meetings, Meeting No. 37, 22 October 1945...," 19, box 3, Top Policy Group Minutes, RG 80, NA. Prior to his PIO assignment in the department Miller had been hand-picked by Forrestal to turn around inadequate Navy PR efforts in the Pacific war as CINCPAC/CINCPOA's public affairs officer. Rear Admiral Harold B. Miller, USN (Ret.), interview by author, 6 Oct 1990, Shawnee Mission, KS, tape recording.

165. Quoted in Top Policy Meeting transcript, 22 Oct 1945, 20.

166. Manson interview, 28 Jan 1989.

167. For information on Sullivan's time at Treasury, see his comments in John L. Sullivan, interviews by Jerry N. Hess, 27 Mar and 13 Apr 1972, interview 138, transcript, Truman Library, 4–7. His apparent aspirations for the period following his Navy Department tour are mentioned in a number of interviews that Jerry Hess conducted with various Truman administration figures for the Truman Library.

168. Vice Admiral Fitzhugh Lee, who as a captain had been John Sullivan's aide during 1947 and 1948, wrote of the Secretary's likability. Written answers to author queries, 2; attached to ltr, Lee to author [15 Mar 1986]. For a discussion of his lack of aggressiveness, see the comments of Marx Leva, one of James Forrestal's special assistants, in Marx Leva, interviews by Jerry N. Hess, 9 Dec and 12 Jun 1970, interview 76, transcript, Truman Library, 65, 90.

169. Ltr, VADM J. W. Reeves Jr. to Radford, 16 Sep 1949, box 36, Radford Papers, OA.

170. Emphasis in original. Manson interview, 28 Jan 1989.

171. Ibid.

172. Memo, Karig to CNO, 21 Jun 1948, box 4, 1948 Double Zero Files, OA.

173. See Personal and Confidential memo, Denfeld to Sullivan, 10 Jul 1948, box 3, Denfeld Double Zero Files, OA.

174. In early 1949 high-level Air Force concern over Hanson was so strong that its Office of Special Investigations (OSI) was ordered to conduct a background investigation into Hanson's letter-writing activities. See "Re: Activities of Hugh L. Hanson," 7 Feb 1949, box 39, Special Interest File 1949, Symington Special Interest Files, RG 340, NA/WNRC.

175. Ltr, Symington to Sullivan, 22 Jan 1948, box 13, Radford Papers, OA. Copies of the complete Symington-Sullivan correspondence on Hanson can be found as exhibits to the OSI report on Hanson.

176. Memo for File by CAPT Fitzhugh Lee, 14 May 1948, box 13, Radford Papers.

177. Ibid.; and Memo for File by Lee, 1 Jul 1948, same box.

178. Stuart B. Barber, interview by author, 25 Feb 1989, Arlington, VA, tape recording.

179. Copy of ltr, Barber to Forrestal, 12 Jul 1947, 1, "A21/1–1 Navy (April 47 thru March 1948)" folder, Series I, OP–23 Records, OA.

180. Ibid., 3–4.

181. *Naval Aviation Combat Statistics World War II*, OPNAV–P–23V No. A129 (Washington: Air Branch, Office of Naval Intelligence, 17 Jun 1946). Information on SCOROR's role in its suppression can be found in copy of SCOROR memo, 29 Jul 1946 and copy of memo, Robbins to CNO, 2 Aug 1946, both in "A21/1–1 Navy (1917 thru July 1948) S&C" folder, Series II, OP–23 Records, OA.

182. Assorted newspaper clippings; U.S Government Messenger Envelope labeled "Navy Letters," Stuart B. Barber Papers, loaned to author by Mr. Barber for use in this study.

183. Emphasis in original. Barber interview.

184. Emphasis in original. Ibid.

185. Various clippings and carbons of letters to the editor; U.S. Government Messenger Envelope labeled "Letters 47–9 Navy," Barber Papers. Stuart Symington was convinced by the man who handled the letters-to-the-editor column that Diogenes was a Navy admiral. Fitzhugh Lee, after talking off the record with Barber (whom he suspected of having written under this pseudonym), was able to reassure Sullivan that such was not the case. Memo for File by Lee, 14 May 1948; and Barber interview.

186. Barber interview.

187. Copy of memo, Leo to Director of Public Relations, Navy Dept., 21 Apr 1948, box 13, Radford Papers, OA.

188. Memo, Sullivan to Forrestal, 3 Jun 1948, same box.

189. Ltr, Barber to A. H. Kirchhofer, 25 Apr 1948, U.S. Government Messenger Envelope labeled "Buffalo News," Barber Papers.

190. Ltrs, Kirchhofer to Barber, 28 Apr 1948; Barber to Kirchhofer, 30 Apr 1948; and Kirchhofer to Barber, 1 May 1948, all in Barber Papers.

191. "Naval Aviation's Air Combat Record Detailed on Occasion of Its 37th Anniversary," Press Release, Navy Department, 9 May 1948, box 13, Radford Papers, OA.

192. Carbon of untitled, typed article by "Richard Essex", [early May 1948], encl. to ltr from Barber to Kirchhofer, 4 May 1948, Barber Papers.

193. Kirchhofer had written to the Navy's director of public relations that no officer on active duty or Navy official had anything to do with "the production of this material." Ltr, Kirchhofer to RADM E. C. Ewen, 10 May 1948, box 13, Radford Papers. For Navy denials of responsibility for the article, see memo, Sullivan to Forrestal, 3 Jun 1948; and ltr, Sullivan to Congressman W. Sterling Cole, same date, ibid.

194. Not once in his perusal of official material gathered on the *Buffalo Evening News* story did the author find any mention of Stuart Barber's name.

3. Atomic Weapons and War Planning

1. For a discussion of this effort, see Schnabel, *JCS and National Policy* 1:137–45.

2. JCS 1477, 18 Aug 1945; attached to memo, C. J. Moore to Leahy et al., SM–2943, 19 Aug 1945, "JCS Completed Papers 1471–1477/10" folder, Navy Secretariat Records, OA.

3. Schnabel, *JCS and National Policy* 1:277.

4. Encl. to JCS 1477/1, 30 Oct 1945, 2; attached to memo from BGEN A. J. McFarland to Leahy et al., SM–3958, 31 Oct 1945, "JCS Completed Papers 1471–1477/10" folder, Navy Secretariat Records, OA.

5. Ibid., 4–5, 13.

6. Ibid., 4.

7. JCS 1477/10, 31 Mar 1946, 57.

8. Quoted in W. A. Shurcliff, *Bombs At Bikini: The Official Report of Operation Crossroads* (New York: Wm. H. Wise, 1947), 10.

9. Msg, CNO to CINCPAC, 121430Z Oct 1945, box 7, 1941–1946 Double Zero Files, OA; Shurcliff, *Bombs at Bikini*, 10–11; and Schnabel, *JCS and National Policy* 1:283.

10. Memo, King to SECNAV, 26 Nov 1945; attached to ltr, Truman to SECNAV, 29 Nov 1945, box 2, Top Policy Correspondence, RG 80, NA.

11. Shurcliff, *Bombs at Bikini*, 11; and Schnabel, *JCS and National Policy* 1:284.

314 *Notes to pages 68–75*

12. Shurcliff, 11–13; and Schnabel, 284–87. For information on the reasons for choosing Bikini, see Shurcliff, 16–20.

13. For information on the original schedule and its postponement, see memo, Commander Joint Task Force One to CNO et al., 28 Jan 1946; memo, Blandy to Nimitz, JTF1 Serial M–6, 21 Mar 1946 (with encl); and memo, Blandy to Nimitz, JTF1 Serial M–7, 22 Mar 1946, all in box 40, 1941–1946 Double Zero Files, OA.

14. Encl. 1 to memo, COL Elmer J. Rogers, Acting Chief S & P Division, AC/AS–5, to GEN Eaker, 22 Jul 1946, [1], File No. 25, box 8, TS AAG Files, DCS/O General File 1944–53, RG 341, NA; and encl. D to JCS 1691/7, 16 Oct 1947, 68–69, "JCS Completed Papers 1691–1691/10–1691 Series" folder, Navy Secretariat Records, OA.

15. See Lloyd J. Graybar, "Bikini Revisited," *Military Affairs* 44 (Oct 1980): 121. For a possible indication of General Spaatz's disappointment, see Routing and Record Sheet (R&RS), Deputy Commander, AAF to MGEN LeMay, 23 Jul 1946; attached to memo from Deputy Commander, AAF to AC/AS–1 et al., 5 Aug 1946, File No. 25, box 8, TS AAG Files, DCS/O General File 1944–53, RG 341, NA.

16. Encl. 1 to memo, Rogers to Eaker, 22 Jul 1946, [3].

17. The AAF preliminary brief on the Able Test noted the miss distance as being 1,955 feet. Memo, Rogers to Eaker, 22 Jul 1946. It should be noted that the Mk III bomb design was not aerodynamically efficient.

18. Encl. D to JCS 1691/7, 69–70; and Shurcliff, *Bombs at Bikini*, 164–66.

19. Shurcliff, 167–68.

20. Lloyd J. Graybar, "The 1946 Atomic Bomb Tests: Atomic Diplomacy or Bureaucratic Infighting?," *The Journal of American History* 72 (Mar 1986): 904–5.

21. "The Evaluation of the Atomic Bomb as a Military Weapon: The Final Report of the Joint Chiefs of Staff Evaluation Board for Operation Crossroads," 30 Jun 1947; Encl. C to JCS 1691/10, 132–33; JCS Completed Papers 1691–1691/10–1691 Series" folder, Navy Secretariat Records, OA.

22. John T. Greenwood, "The Atomic Bomb—Early Air Force Thinking and the Strategic Air Force, August 1945–March 1946," *Aerospace Historian* 34 (Fall/Sep 1987): 159. At about the same time Major General Lauris Norstad (AC/AS–5 [Plans]) had directed his Policy and Strategy Division to prepare a study on the future uses and requirements for the atomic bomb. R&RS, AC/AS–5 to Chief of Air Staff, 23 Aug 1945; attached to R&RS, COL Willard A. Libby, Assistant Chief of Air Staff, to AC/AS–5, same date, File No. 21, box 7, TS AAG Files, DCS/O General File 1944–53, RG 341, NA

23. Greenwood, "The Atomic Bomb."

24. Typed copy of orders from LTGEN Ira C. Eaker, Deputy Commander, AAF, to GEN Carl A. Spaatz et al., 14 Sep 1945; attached to copy of Spaatz Board Report, 23 Oct 1945, box 22, Spaatz Papers, MD–LC.

25. Spaatz Board Report, 3.

26. Such targets included fuel production and refining plants, bridges, tunnels, surface vessels, and enemy air installations. Ibid., 4–5, 8.

27. Ibid., 6–9.

28. See memo from Arnold to SecWar, 24 Oct 1945, box 38, Arnold Papers, MD–LC; and Greenwood, "The Atomic Bomb," 161.

29. Typed comment by Hap Arnold at the end of the Spaatz Board Report, 7; Untitled copy of Spaatz Board Report, Tab A to unsigned memo for Assistant Secretary of War for Air W. Stuart Symington entitled "Deputy Chief of Air Staff, Research and Development," n.d. [early Feb 1946?], in binder labeled "Functions of the Assistant Chief of Air Staff–5 and the Deputy Chief of Air Staff for Research and Development," File No. 80, box 17, TS AAG Files, DCS/O General File 1944–53, RG 341, NA. This was a briefing folder prepared for Symington by General Eaker.

30. The Spaatz Board report had recommended that an officer "of the caliber of... Curtis E. LeMay" be appointed to the new position.

31. "ORGANIZATION: Deputy Chief of Air Staff for Research and Development," AAF Regulation No. 20-62, 10 Jan 1946; Tab B to memo, "Deputy Chief of Air Staff, Research and Development," box 17, TS AAG Files.

32. "Deputy Chief of Air Staff, Research and Development."

33. John T. Greenwood, "The Emergence of the Postwar Strategic Air Force, 1945–1953," in *Air Power and Warfare: The Proceedings of the 8th Military History Symposium United States Air Force Academy, 18–20 October 1978*, ed. Alfred F. Hurley and Robert C. Ehrhart (Washington: Office of Air Force History, Headquarters USAF and United States Air Force Academy, 1979), 220.

34. The other two commands were the Tactical Air Command and the Air Defense Command.

35. Extracts from SAC's mission statement; *Development of Strategic Air Command, 1946–1976* (Offutt AFB, NE: Office of the Historian, Headquarters Strategic Air Command, 1976), 2.

36. In this period a VHB group generally consisted of four eight-plane squadrons. In 1947 SAC attained a level of sixteen VHB groups, and in 1948 SAC had two Heavy (B-36) Bomb Groups and twelve Medium (B-29 and B-50) Bomb Groups. Only portions of these groups were equipped with aircraft, however.

37. See Greenwood, "Postwar Strategic Air Force," 221; and Harry S. Borowski, *A Hollow Threat: Strategic Air Power and Containment Before Korea* (Westport, CT: Greenwood Press, 1982), 38–39.

38. Forty-six B-29s were originally modified to carry atomic bombs. A few more were modified during 1946–1948. In March 1948 the entire Air Force inventory of SILVERPLATE B-29s consisted of thirty-five aircraft. See Greenwood, "Post Strategic Air Force," 221; and Table 2 in David A. Rosenberg, "U.S. nuclear stockpile, 1945 to 1950," *The Bulletin of the Atomic Scientists* 38 (May 1982): 30.

39. For a detailed history of the Manhattan Engineer District and the development of the atomic bomb, see Vincent C. Jones, *United States Army in World War II, Special Studies*, MANHATTAN: *The Army and the Atomic Bomb* (Washington: Center of Military History, United States Army, 1985). For specific information on the limited number of wartime U.S. military personnel cleared for information on the bomb project, see David A. Rosenberg, "Toward Armageddon: The Foundations of United States Nuclear Strategy, 1945–1961" (Ph.D. diss., University of Chicago, 1983), 3–4.

40. MGEN D. M. Schlatter, Assistant for Atomic Energy, DCS/Operations, *The United States Air Force and Atomic Warfare: A Report to the Chief of Staff*, 11 May 1949 [first of two volumes], 2, box 16, Assistant for Atomic Energy General Decimal Files 1949, Deputy Chief of Staff, Operations Records, RG 341, NA.

41. Memo, Powers to Chief of Air Staff, 14 Sep 1945; attached to memo, Spaatz (as Chairman of the "Spaatz Board") to Deputy Chief of Air Staff, 13 Nov 1945, File No. 21, box 7, TS AAG Files, DCS/O General File 1944–53, RG 341, NA.

42. Memo, Spaatz to Deputy Chief of Air Staff, 13 Nov 1945. In late October 1945, a Military Advisory Board, composed of five Army and five Navy officers, was established to advise General Groves on the atomic energy requirements of the armed services. LeMay and his alternate, Colonel Roscoe C. Wilson, were the AAF members. Greenwood, "The Atomic Bomb," 162.

43. On this point see George F. Lemmer, *The Air Force and the Concept of Deterrence, 1945–1950* (Washington: USAF Historical Division Liaison Office, 1963), 35–36 (sanitized version).

44. R&RS, Eaker to AC/AS-1, 14 Mar 1946, File No. 22, box 7, TS AAG Files, DCS/O General File 1944–53, RG 341, NA.

45. See R&RS, LeMay to AC/AS-3 and AC/AS-4, 7 Jan 1946; attached to memo, Eaker to Commander Joint Task Force One, 18 Jan 1946, File No. 21, same box.

46. Schlatter, *The United States Air Force and Atomic Warfare*, 2.

47. Memo, Streett (for CG, SAC) to CG, AAF, SAC 353, 29 Jul 1946; attached to 3d Ind. memo, BGEN Hood, Deputy Chief of Air Staff, to CG, SAC, 27 Aug 1946, box 629, Air Adjutant General Decimal File 1946–47, Army Air Forces Records (RG 18), NA.

48. 1st Ind. memo, BGEN Hood to CG, SAC, 12 Aug 1946; attached to 3rd Ind. memo, Hood to CG, SAC, 27 Aug 1946.

49. 3rd Ind. memo, Hood to CG, SAC, 27 Aug 1946; and 1st, Ind. memo, Hood to CG, SAC, 12 Aug 1946.

50. Schlatter, *The United States Air Force and Atomic Warfare*, 9.

51. The Mk I was some 28 inches in diameter and 126 inches long and weighed approximately 8,900 pounds. The heavier and much bulkier Mk III was 60 inches in diameter and 128 inches long and weighed approximately 10,300 pounds. Chuck Hansen, *US Nuclear Weapons: The Secret History* (Arlington, TX: Aerofax, Inc. and Orion Books, 1988), 121, 124. The largest bomb regularly carried by Navy carrier-based aircraft during the war weighed 2,000 pounds.

52. Copy of memo, CNO to All Bureaus, Boards and Offices in the Navy Department, OP-09 ser 8P09, 13 Nov 1945, encl. C to memo, CAPT Steadman Teller, OP-601, to VADM D. C. Ramsey, VCNO, via VADM Arthur Radford, no ser, n.d. [mid-Oct 1946], box 1, DCNO (Air) Records, OA.

53. Ibid.

54. For detailed information on many of the Navy Department's technical activities in connection with the Bikini tests, see "An Administrative History of the Bureau of Ships During World War II," vol. 4 (Washington, Historical Section, Bureau of Ships, n.d.), unpublished manuscript, NDL, 329–96.

55. See memo, Teller to Ramsey, n.d. [mid-Oct 1946]; memo, VADM W. H. P. Blandy, OP-06, to ASST SECNAV, no ser, 29 Apr 1946, "OP-06-Proposed Function of" folder, Joint Research & Development Board 1946–1947 Records, OA; and copy of memo, RADM H. G. Bowen, Chief, Research and Inventions, to CNO, no ser, 11 Jan 1946, "Incoming Miscellaneous CAPT de Florez 6/6/45 to 3/8/46" folder, Research and Inventions/Office of Naval Research Records, OA.

56. See App. 1 to David A. Rosenberg and Floyd D. Kennedy, Jr., *History of the Strategic Arms Competition, 1945–1972, Supporting Study: US Aircraft Carriers in the Strategic Role, Part I—Naval Strategy in a Period of Change: Interservice Rivalry, Strategic Interaction, and the Development of Nuclear Attack Capability, 1945–1951* (Falls Church, VA: Lulejian & Associates, 1975).

57. In mid-December 1946 Bernard Brodie interviewed a number of senior naval officers about their views on the atomic bomb in connection with a project he was doing for the Library of Congress. For the published version of this study see "U.S. Navy Thinking on the Atomic Bomb," in Bernard Brodie and Eilene Galloway, *The Atomic Bomb and the Armed Services*, Public Affairs Bulletin No. 55 (Washington: Library of Congress Legislative Reference Service, 1947), 24–41. OP-23 files contain a positive photocopy of Brodie's original typescript, on which has been marked the identity of the holder of each of the views discussed. Those who spoke with Brodie included CNO Fleet Admiral Nimitz; VADM Forrest Sherman, DCNO (Operations); VADM E. L. Cochrane, Chief of the Material Division, Office of the Assistant Secretary of the Navy; VADM W. H. P. Blandy, Commander Eighth Fleet; and RADM William Parsons.

58. "U.S. Navy Thinking on the Atomic Bomb," 4–5, encl. to ltr, Brodie to Ramsey, 30 Dec 1946, "A16–9 Atomic Warfare (1947–1948)" folder, Series I, OP-23 Records, OA.

59. Ibid., 6. VADM Sherman supplied this view.

60. Ibid., 8–9. RADM Parsons supplied this view.

61. Ibid., 9–11. Parsons also made these points.

62. Ibid., 12–15. Sherman and Blandy expressed these views to Brodie. For information on ship protection against atomic effects, see ibid., 16–19, giving the views of Blandy, Cochrane and Parsons.

63. For detailed information on JCS thinking on USSR foreign policy actions in 1945–1947, see Schnabel, *JCS and National Policy* 1:13–133.

64. Memo, CDR Willis Sargent, USNR, to ADM Harold R. Stark, 7 Jun 1945, 1, box A4, Harold R. Stark Papers, OA. Sargent noted that Dr. Philip Mosely, political adviser to Ambassador Winant on the European Advisory Commission, had read the paper and concurred in the views expressed.

65. Bruce R. Kuniholm, *The Origins of the Cold War in the Near East: Great Power Conflict and Diplomacy* (Princeton: Princeton University Press, 1980), 257–58. See also memo, CAPT Tully Shelley, COM-

NAVEU Staff, to Stark et al., 2 Jul 1945; attached to note from Stark to Admiral of the Fleet Sir Andrew Cunningham, 3 Jul 1945, box A4, Stark Papers, OA.

66. Schnabel, *Joint Chiefs of Staff and National Policy*, 1:58; and Walter S. Poole, "From Conciliation to Containment: The Joint Chiefs of Staff and the Coming of the Cold War, 1945–1946," *Military Affairs* 42 (Feb 1978): 13.

67. Kuniholm, *Origins of the Cold War in the Near East*, 261–65.

68. For detailed information on the Iranian situation, see ibid., 270–98, 304–50.

69. Ibid., 212.

70. JCS 1545, 9 Oct 1945; attached to memo, McFarland to Leahy et al., SM–3716, 10 Oct 1945, 4, "JCS Completed Papers 1545–1551/2" folder, Navy Secretariat Records, OA.

71. See Rosenberg, "Foundations of United States Nuclear Strategy," 28–30, 58.

72. For an interesting analysis arguing that early postwar intelligence assessments seriously overestimated Soviet ground forces capabilities and that, accordingly, the Soviet threat to Western Europe in this period was illusory, see Matthew A. Evangelista, "Stalin's Postwar Army Reappraised," *International Security* 7 (Winter 1982/1983): 110–38. Although he effectively makes the point that Soviet capabilities were probably much lower than the U.S. intelligence community estimated at the time, Evangelista fails to acknowledge the low readiness of U.S. and Western European military forces during this period that, in comparison, would have made even a significantly lower Soviet capability threatening. This lack of a net assessment casts doubt on his underlying thesis.

73. See, for example, Air Intelligence Division (AC/AS–2—ONI), Intelligence Report 100–1, "*Summary of Presentation on Russia Given by A–2 on 12 March*," 21 Mar 1946, 6–7, File No. 25, box 8, TS AAG Files, DCS/O General File 1944–53, RG 341, NA.

74. During this period, the Army Air Forces' (later the Air Force's) Air Intelligence Division (AID) was jointly staffed by AAF and Navy intelligence personnel. Therefore, approved AID studies reflected agreed Air Forces–Navy air intelligence assessments.

75. Von Hardesty, *Red Phoenix: The Rise of Soviet Air Power, 1941–1945* (Washington: Smithsonian Institution Press, 1982), 85–86, 195–96, 219; and Air Chief Marshal Sir Phillip Joubert, "Long Range Air Attack," in *The Soviet Air and Rocket Forces*, ed. Asher Lee (New York: Frederick A. Praeger, 1959), 106.

76. AID Intelligence Report 100–1, 4. This early assessment gave the ER–4's range as 3,000 miles, which proved to be about 15 percent too high.

77. Ibid., 5.

78. Memo, MGEN Lauris Norstad, AC/AS–5, to Spaatz, 9 May 1946, 1, File No. 22, box 7, TS AAG Files, DCS/O General File 1944–53, RG 341, NA.

79. Air Intelligence Division Study No. 45/1, "*Soviet Capabilities for Producing and Utilizing B–29 Type Aircraft During the Period 1 January 1946–1 January 1952*," 1 Nov 1946, 3, File No. 26, box 9, TS AAG Files, ibid. These were the only two B–29s that had fallen into Soviet hands intact according to Army Air Forces intelligence. Ibid.; and Air Policy Board Briefing (AC/AS–2), 16 Sep 1947, 1, box 28, Spaatz Papers, MD–LC. Nonetheless unclassified postwar accounts have credited the Soviets with interning three or even four B–29s. See Hardesty, *Red Phoenix*, 86, 231*n*; and Joubert, "Long Range Air Attack," 107.

80. AID Study No. 45/1, 1, 5. These estimates were scaled back significantly in later years.

81. Memo, MGEN George C. McDonald, AC/AS–2, to CG, AAF, 31 Dec 1946; attached to memo, Eaker to McDonald, 6 Jan 1947, File No. 26, box 9, TS AAG Files, DCS/O General File 1944–53, RG 341, NA; and Air Policy Board Briefing (AC/AS–2), 16 Sep 1947, 1.

82. Memo, Vandenberg to the President, [Special Study No. 3], 26 Aug 1946, [2], Box 249, Intelligence File, President's Secretary's File, Truman Library. See also Central Intelligence Group Special Study No. 4, "Soviet Military Intentions," 18 Sep 1946, box 250, same file.

83. "Presentation Given to President by Major General Lauris Norstad on 29 October 1946. 'Postwar Military Establishment'," 30 Oct 1946, 3–4, File No. 28, box 9, TS AAG Files, DCS/O General File 1944–53, RG 341, NA.

84. Ibid., 4, 10.

85. See Rosenberg, "Foundations of United States Nuclear Strategy," 31.

86. Central Intelligence Group, ORE 3/1, "Soviet Capabilities for the Development and Production of Certain Types of Weapons and Equipment," 31 Oct 1946, box 254, Intelligence File, President's Secretary's File, Truman Library.

87. Air Intelligence Division Study No. 136, *Significant Developments of Scientific Warfare in Russia,*" 29 Nov 1946, 1, File No. 26, box 9, TS AAG Files, DCS/O General File 1944–53, RG 341, NA.

88. In August 1945 General Groves authorized the release of an unclassified history of the Manhattan Project's development of the atomic bomb written at his request by Henry D. Smyth, chairman of the Physics Department at Princeton and consultant to the Manhattan District. It was republished with modifications by the Princeton University Press that same year. See Henry D. Smyth, *Atomic Energy for Military Purposes: The Official Report on the Development of the Atomic Bomb Under the Auspices of the United States Government, 1940–1945* (Princeton: Princeton University Press, 1945).

89. Air Policy Board Briefing (AC/AS–2), 16 Sep 1947, 3–4, and accompanying chart entitled "When Can They Have the Bomb?"; JIC 395/1, 8 Jul 1947, 3–4, Sec. 5, CCS 471.6 (8–15–45), Joint Chiefs of Staff Records (RG 218), NA; and Air Intelligence Division Study No. 137, "Intelligence Estimate for 1956," 24 Oct 1946, 2, File No. 26, box 9, TS AAG Files, DCS/O General File 1944–53, RG 341, NA.

90. JIC 395/1, 3–4.

91. See ORE 3/1.

92. Emphasis in original. JIC Policy Memo No. 2 (JICM–2A), 29 Mar 1948; Sec. 9, CCS 471.6 (8–15–45), RG 218, NA.

93. Air Policy Board Briefing (AC/AS–2), 16 Sep 1947, 3.

94. See "A Presentation by Lieutenant General George E. Stratemeyer, Commanding General, Air Defense Command on the Requirements for an Air Defense of the United States of America before Honorable W. Stuart Symington, the Secretary of the Air Force and General Carl Spaatz, Chief of Staff, United States Air Force, 23 October 1947," box 34, Hoyt S. Vandenberg Papers, MD–LC; and "Memorandum by the Chief of Staff, U.S. Air Force to the Joint Chiefs of Staff on Air Defense of the United States"; attached to memo, Vandenberg to Secretary, Joint Chiefs of Staff, n.d. [16 Nov 1949], box 1, Muir S. Fairchild Papers, MD–LC. The latter document, of which this copy is the second draft, became JCS 2084 of 16 Nov 1949.

95. See Schnabel, *JCS and National Policy* 1:145.

96. App. A to JCS 1518, 19 Sep 1945, 3; attached to memo, McFarland to Leahy et al., SM–3459, 20 Sep 1945, "JCS Completed Papers 1518–1519/11" folder, Navy Secretariat Records, OA.

97. Ibid., 4, 8.

98. Ibid., 7, 9, 11.

99. Memo, CNO (signed by Ramsey) to CINCPAC, OP–007 ser 0033P00, n.d. [18 Jun 1946]; attached to JCS 1518/4, "JCS Completed Papers 1518–1519/11" folder, Navy Secretariat Records, OA.

100. Schnabel, *JCS and National Policy* 1:149; and Rosenberg, "Foundations of United States Nuclear Strategy," 58.

101. Schnabel, 150–53.

102. Ibid., 158. See also Rosenberg, "Foundations of United States Nuclear Strategy," 59–61.

103. See, for example, the component study by the Service Members, Joint Intelligence Staff, JIS 267/1/ "D"—"Intelligence Estimate of Specific Areas in Southern Europe, the Middle and Near East and Northern Africa (Strengths and Dispositions of Soviet Armed Forces)," 14 Oct 1946, Sec. 3, CCS 381 USSR (3–2–46), RG 218, NA.

104. Copy of ltr, Clifford to Leahy, 18 Jul 1946; Encl. B to JCS 1696, 25 Jul 1946, "JCS Completed Papers 1695–1700" folder, Navy Secretariat Records, OA.

105. Encl. A to JCS 1969, 17.

106. Rosenberg, "Foundations of United States Nuclear Strategy," 58; and Greenwood, "Emergence of the Postwar Strategic Air Force," 226.

107. JCS 1630/3, 20 Jun 1946; attached to memo, McFarland to Leahy et al., SM–6068, 20 Jun 1946, "1627–1630/5" folder, Navy Secretariat Records, OA.

108. JCS 1630/4, 1 Jul 1946; attached to memo, McFarland to Leahy et al., SM–6162, 2 Jul 1946; and JCS 1630/5, 12 Jul 1946, same folder.

109. David A. Rosenberg, "American Postwar Air Doctrine and Organization: The Navy Experience," in *Air Power and Warfare: The Proceedings of the 8th Military History Symposium, United States Air Force Academy, 18–20 October 1978*, ed. Alfred F. Hurley and Robert C. Ehrhart (Washington: Office of Air Force History, Headquarters USAF and USAF Academy, 1979), 250; and Rosenberg, "The Origins of Overkill: Nuclear Weapons and American Strategy, 1945–1960," *International Security* 7 (Spring 1983), 11–12.

110. Greenwood, "Emergence of the Postwar Strategic Air Force," 226–27.

111. JCS 1725/1, 13 Feb 1947, 10; attached to memo, McFarland to Leahy et al., SM–7596, 13 Feb 1947, "JCS Completed Papers 1725–1725/10" folder, Navy Secretariat Records, OA. The JPS, whose members had not yet been cleared for access to atomic energy information, had no idea how small the actual number of bombs in the stockpile was in early 1947. In reality, there were no more than a dozen extant. See table 1 in Rosenberg, "U.S. nuclear stockpile," 26.

112. JCS 1725/2, 12 Mar 1947, 40; attached to memo, McFarland to Leahy et al., SM–7780, 13 Mar 1947, "JCS Completed Papers 1725–1725/10" folder, Navy Secretariat Records, OA.

113. Decision on JCS 1725/2, 1 May 1947, same folder.

114. JCS 1764/1, 14 Jul 1947, 8; attached to memo, CAPT W. G. Lalor to Leahy et al., SM–8590, 15 Jul 1947, "JCS Completed Papers 1761–1768" folder, Navy Secretariat Records.

115. Decision Amending JCS 1764/1, 13 Aug 1947, same folder.

116. "*Air Force War Planning and Supporting Studies*," Tab D to memo, GEN Hoyt Vandenberg, Vice Chief of Staff, to Secretary Symington, 6 Nov 1947, File No. 28, box 9, TS AAG Files, DCS/O General File 1944–53, RG 341, NA; and Robert D. Little, *Organizing for Strategic Planning, 1945–1950: The National System and the Air Force* (Washington: USAF Historical Division Liaison Office, [1964]), 22 (sanitized version).

117. Greenwood, "Emergence of the Postwar Strategic Air Force," 228.

118. Rosenberg, "Foundations of United States Nuclear Strategy," 82.

119. Tab D to memo, Vandenberg to Symington, 6 Nov 1947; and Rosenberg, ibid.

120. Tab D to memo, Vandenberg to Symington, 6 Nov 1947.

121. Greenwood, "Emergence of the Postwar Strategic Air Force," 229.

122. Kenneth W. Condit, *The History of the Joint Chiefs of Staff: The Joint Chiefs of Staff and National Policy*, vol. 2, *1947–1949* (Washington: Historical Division, Joint Secretariat, Joint Chiefs of Staff, 1978), 275.

123. See JCS 1745, 3 Feb 1947; attached to memo, McFarland to Leahy et al., SM–7524, 4 Feb 1947; and memo, McFarland to Joint Strategic Survey Committee and Joint Staff Planners, SM–7698, 26 Feb 1947, filed with JCS 1745, "1745/–1745/28" folder, Navy Secretariat Records, OA.

124. JCS 1745/1, 25 Feb 1947, 5; attached to memo, McFarland to FADM Leahy et al., SM–7693, 25 Feb 1947, "1745/–1745/28" folder, Navy Secretariat Records, OA.

125. Memo, Brereton to CG, AAF, 7 Jul 1947; attached to memo, Vandenberg (for Spaatz) to Brereton, 30 Jul 1947, File No. 29, box 10, TS AAG Files, DCS/O General File 1944–53, RG 341, NA.

126. Memo, Vandenberg to Brereton, 30 Jul 1947.

127. See memo (with encl), F. H. Schneider, Secretary, Joint Staff Planners, to CAPT T. B. Hill et al., PM-587, 15 Sep 1947, Sec. 6, CCS 471.6 (8-15-45), RG 218, NA.

128. Rosenberg, "Foundations of United States Nuclear Strategy," 95; and JCS 1745/15, 27 Jul 1948, attached to memo, Lalor to Leahy et al., SM-10561, 27 Jul 1948,"1745/-1745/28" folder, Navy Secretariat Records, OA.

129. JCS 1745/4, 28 Oct 1947, 14; attached to memo Lalor to Leahy et al., SM-9121, 28 Oct 1947, "1745/-1745/28" folder, Navy Secretariat Records, OA; and memo, Leahy (for the JCS) to Chairman, AEC, 29 Oct 1947, Sec. 7, CCS 471.6 (8-15-45), RG 218, NA. The actual number of atomic bombs—normally left blank in JCS documents—was handwritten in this copy of Leahy's memorandum by Captain Lalor "on advice of General Gruenther."

130. JCS 1745/5, 8 Dec 1947, 18, Sec. 8, CCS 471.6 (8-15-45), RG 218.

131. Decision on JCS 1745/7, 17 Dec 1947; enclosed with JCS 1745/7, "1745-1745/28" folder, Navy Secretariat Records, OA.

132. In October 1947, in the wake of the passage several months before of the National Security Act of 1947, the Joint Staff was reorganized. Among other actions taken, the Joint Staff Planners were redesignated the Joint Strategic Plans Committee, and the Joint War Plans Committee became the Joint Strategic Plans Group.

133. Rosenberg, "Foundations of United States Nuclear Strategy," 96-97, 98.

134. Condit, *JCS and National Policy* 2:276.

135. Ibid., 277.

136. App. to JCS 1844, 9 Mar 1948, 5; attached to memo, Lalor to Leahy et al., SM-9752, 9 Mar 1948; "1844-1844/21" folder, Navy Secretariat Records, OA.

137. Condit, *JCS and National Policy* 2:280-82.

138. Rosenberg, "Foundations of United States Nuclear Strategy," 108; and Rosenberg, "American Atomic Strategy and the Hydrogen Bomb Decision," *The Journal of American History* 66 (Jun 1979): 68.

139. Lemmer, *Air Force and the Concept of Deterrence*, 37.

140. Entries of 5 and 6 May 1948, William D. Leahy Diary, MD-LC; quoted in Robert H. Ferrell, *The American Secretaries of State and Their Diplomacy*, vol. 15, *George C. Marshall* (New York: Cooper Square Publishers, 1966), 246, 293n; and Rosenberg, "Foundations of United States Nuclear Strategy," 109. See also JCS 1844/6, 13 May 1948; attached to memo, Lalor to Denfeld et al., SM-10146, 14 May 1948, "1844-1844/21" folder, Navy Secretariat Records, OA.

141. Rosenberg, "Foundations of United States Nuclear Strategy," 109; Ferrell, *Marshall*, 246; and JCS 1844/6.

142. Rosenberg, "Foundations of United States Nuclear Strategy," 110.

143. For useful discussions of the Berlin blockade, see Rearden, *The Formative Years, 1947-1950*, 288-304; and Condit, *JCS and National Policy* 2:113-152.

144. Memo, Royall to NSC, 19 May 1948; Annex B to State Department memo, n.d., printed in Department of State, *Foreign Relations of the United States 1948* (hereafter *FRUS 1948*), vol. 1, part 2, *General: The United Nations* (Washington GPO, 1976), 573.

145. See Rearden, *The Formative Years*, 435; and commentary on background of NSC 30, *FRUS 1948*, 1, pt. 2:624-25n.

146. Memo, "Meeting—The President and Secretary Marshall—Atomic Bomb," 15 Jul 1948, filed with entry for 15 Jul 1948, Forrestal Diaries, vol. 11, 1 May 1948-31 Jul 1948, 2362, box 17, Privileged Manuscript Collection, OA.

147. Memo, "Lunch—Secretary Marshall, Secretary Royall, General Bradley—Use of the A-Bomb in War Planning," 28 Jul 1948, filed with entry for 28 Jul 1948; Forrestal Diaries, 11:2393.

148. NSC 30: "United States Policy On Atomic Warfare," 10 Sep 1948, *FRUS 1948*, 1, pt. 2:628.

149. NSC 20/4: "Report by the National Security Council on U.S. Objectives With Respect to the USSR to Counter Soviet Threats to U.S. Security," 23 Nov 1948, *FRUS 1948*, 1, pt. 2:669.

150. Condit, *JCS and National Policy* 2:285–86; and JCS 1952/1, 25 Dec 1948, 6–10, 18, Sec. 1, CCS 373 (10–23–48), RG 218, NA.

151. Condit, *JCS and National Policy* 2:289–94; JCS 1844/46, 8 Nov 1949, 366, attached to memo, Lalor to Bradley et al., SM–2275–49, 9 Nov 1949, "1844/46" folder; JCS 2056/3, 23 Nov 1949, attached to memo, Lalor to Bradley et al., SM–2410–49, 25 Nov 1949, "2056/3" folder, both in Navy Secretariat Records, OA; and JCS 1952/11, 10 Feb 1950, 163, 194, Bulky Package Part 2C, CCS 373 (10–23–48), RG 218, NA. See also Walter S. Poole, *The History of the Joint Chiefs of Staff, The Joint Chiefs of Staff and National Policy*, vol. 4, *1950–1952* (Washington: Historical Division, Joint Secretariat, Joint Chief of Staff, 1979), 161–64.

152. For a discussion of joint war planning in 1950–1952, see Poole, ibid., 165–77.

153. Borowski, *A Hollow Threat*, 4. Lack of space precludes a detailed look at SAC's strengths and weaknesses during this period. For information on this subject, see, among others, Borowski, ibid.; and Borowski, "Air Force Atomic Capability from V-J Day to the Berlin Blockade—Potential or Real?" *Military Affairs* 44 (Oct 1980): 105–110; Greenwood, "Emergence of The Postwar Strategic Air Force," 219–36; Lemmer, *Air Force and the Concept of Deterrence*, 33–39; Rosenberg, "Foundations of United States Nuclear Strategy," 83–84, 108–9, 117–19; and Rosenberg, "American Atomic Strategy and the Hydrogen Bomb Decision," 65, 70–71.

154. Memo, BGEN Thomas S. Power, Deputy AC/AS–3, to Deputy Chief of Air Staff, 10 Apr 1947, File No. 27, box 9, TS AAG File, DCS/O General File 1944–53, RG 341, NA.

155. Air Policy Board Briefing (AC/AS–2), 16 Sep 1947, 5, 6, and Chart No. 5 (showing representative Soviet urban-industrial centers).

156. Until well into the 1950s the Air Force, in drawing up its target folders, relied primarily upon captured German wartime photographic and cartographic intelligence for detailed information on Soviet cities. This intelligence did not extend to cities beyond the Urals. See Borowski, *A Hollow Threat*, 104; and "Air Force Atomic Capability from V-J Day to the Berlin Blockade," 107.

157. For the B–29: chart entitled "Capabilities of Bombers"; box 28, Spaatz Papers, MD–LC; for the B–50 (specifically the B–50A): ltr (with encl), William M. Allen, President, Boeing Airplane Company, to Secretary Symington and General Spaatz, 18 Mar 1948, box 28, Strategic Air Group Correspondence 1949–51, Director of Research and Development—Deputy Chief of Staff, Development Files, RG 341, NA. The radius provided for each aircraft was derived from the range given in the original documents, using the standard formula (radius = 2/5 range) and converting from nautical miles to statute miles where necessary. According to the B–50 performance data chart provided in a recent reference work, the B–50A's combat radius (as a mature aircraft) was 1,905 nautical miles (2,194 statute miles). Marcelle Size Knaack, *Encyclopedia of U.S. Air Force Aircraft and Missile Systems*, vol. 2, *Post–World War II Bombers, 1945–1973* (Washington: Office of Air Force History, USAF, 1988), 200–201.

158. Extract copy of "Verbatim Minutes, First Meeting, USAF Aircraft and Weapons Board, Last Day: 22 August 1947," 625; Tab FF to Inspector General, USAF, "Report of Special Inquiry Into the B–36 Procurement Program 2 June–2 July 1948", box 38, Special Interest File, 1949, Symington Special Interest Files, RG 340, NA/WNRC.

159. "Discussion Following Air Force Presentation to the Combat Aviation Subcommittee, Congressional Aviation Policy Board, Room 4E–870, The Pentagon, 21 Jan 1948," 11, File No. 40, box 12, TS AAG Files, DCS/O General File 1944–53, RG 341, NA. This verbatim, typed copy of the question-and-answer period was corrected and marked for downgrading from Top Secret to Secret. In this copy Symington's words "we would do quite a considerable" were crossed through and the words "this may involve a certain" were substituted for use in the Secret version of the text.

160. In this regard, see BGEN Thomas S. Power's negative comments in reply to GEN Partridge's remarks. Extract copy of "Verbatim Minutes, First Meeting, USAF Aircraft and Weapons Board," 625.

161. See the comments of Major General Partridge and Lieutenant General Joseph McNarney in extract copy of "Verbatim Minutes of Second Meeting, USAF Aircraft and Weapons Board, 27–30 January 1948," 189; Tab FF to "Report of Special Inquiry Into the B–36 Procurement Program."

162. See Spaatz Board Report, 3.

163. Emphasis added. Rosenberg, "Foundations of United States Nuclear Strategy," 74.

164. Emphasis in original. Memo, MGEN Partridge to Deputy Chief of Air Staff for Research and Development, 7 Jun 1946, 1-2, box 629, Air Adjutant General Decimal File 1946–47, RG 18, NA. The initial memo on this subject, which provided the exact text for Partridge's memo, was BGEN Alfred R. Maxwell, Chief, Requirements Division, AC/AS–3, to Partridge, 1 May 1946, in same folder.

165. See Rosenberg, "Foundations of United States Nuclear Strategy," 84–85.

166. Quoted in Robert F. Futrell, *Ideas, Concepts, Doctrine* 1:218.

167. Quoted in Rosenberg, "Origins of Overkill," 15; citing Robert F. Little, *The History of Air Force Participation in the Atomic Energy Program, 1943–1953*, vol. 2, *Foundations of an Atomic Air Force and Operation SANDSTONE, 1946–1948* (Washington: Air University Historical Liaison Office, 1955), 264–65. See also Rosenberg, "Foundations of United States Nuclear Strategy," 116–17.

168. See the typed transcript entitled "Secretary of Defense Budget Meeting With the Three Secretaries and the Joint Chiefs of Staff 4 October 1948—1035—Room 2C–260 Morning Session," B.P. [Bulky Package] Part I, CCS 370 (8–19–45), RG 218, NA.

169. Memo, "Budget Meeting," 15 Oct 1948, filed with entry for 15 Oct 1948, Forrestal Diaries, vol. 13, Oct 1948–Nov 1948, 2575, box 17, Privileged Manuscript Collection, OA.

170. Memos, Forrestal to JCS, 23 Oct 1948; and Forrestal to JCS, 25 Oct 1948, Sec. 1, CCS 373 (10–23–48), RG 218, NA. The first memo became an enclosure to JCS 1952 of 25 October 1948 and the second became an enclosure to JCS 1953 with the same date.

171. JCS 1952/1, 21 Dec 1948, 4, Sec. 1, CCS 373 (10–23–48), RG 218, NA.

172. See the JCS 1952/2–1952/10 and the JIC 439/2–439/9 series of papers, in Secs. 1–5, CCS 373 (10–23–48), RG 218, NA.

173. See memo, RADM C. D. Glover to Gruenther, Director, Joint Staff, 27 Apr 1949; and encl. A to memo, Lalor to Denfeld et al., SM–802–49, 3 May 1949; both in Sec. 2, CCS 373 (10–23–48).

174. JCS 1953, 25 Oct 1948; and encl. to JSPC 906/1, 2, both in Sec. 1, CCS 373 (10–23–48).

175. Summary of JSPC Meeting, 9 Dec 1948; and memo, Lalor to Harmon et al., SM–75–49, 12 Jan 1949; both in Sec. 1, CCS 373 (10–23–48).

176. See Borowski, *A Hollow Threat*, 135–49; and J. C. Hopkins, *The Development of Strategic Air Command, 1946–1981 (A Chronological History)* (Offutt AFB, NE: Office of the Historian, Headquarters Strategic Air Command, 1982), 1–14.

177. Curtis E. LeMay, with MacKinley Kantor, *Mission With LeMay* (Garden City, NY: Doubleday, 1965), 429–30.

178. Emphasis in original. Memo, Parsons to OP–03, via OP–30, 8 Nov 1948, box 243, Strategic Plans, OA.

179. Emphasis in original. Ibid.

180. Ibid.

181. Emphasis added. Untitled memo on the FY 1950 budget situation, marked "Put in my diary," 20 Dec 1948, filed with entry for 20 Dec 1948, Forrestal Diaries, vol. 14, 1 Dec 1948–28 Feb 1949, 2699–2700, box 17, Privileged Manuscript Collection, OA. Forrestal was in Europe from 11 to 15 November 1948. See itinerary labeled *"Itinerary of European Trip,* 9–16 November 1948," filed with entry for 9 Nov 1948, Forrestal Diaries, 13:2632–2636.

182. Emphasis in original. Ltr, LeMay to LTGEN Lauris Norstad, Deputy Chief of Staff, Operations, 15 Dec 1948, 3, box B 195, Curtis E. LeMay Papers, MD–LC.

183. Ibid., 1; and Rosenberg, "Foundations of United States Nuclear Strategy," 118.

184. Borowski, *Hollow Threat*, 166–67.

185. Chart 13, "SAC Evaluation Missions: Radar Bombing Accuracy," in Headquarters Strategic Air Command, "*Springfield Radar Bombing Evaluation*," 7 Jul 1952, box B 106, LeMay Papers, MD–LC.

186. LeMay, with Kantor, *Mission With LeMay*, 433.

4. Navy Thinking on Atomic Weapons and the Strategic Air Offensive

1. See, for example, "Planning Guidance for Joint Medium-Range Emergency Plan," Encl. A to memo, CNO to JCS, OP–30B ser 00014P30, 5 Apr 1948, 3, box 244, Strategic Plans, OA. This memo became JCS 1844/2 of 6 Apr 1948.

2. "Study for the Development of Naval Requirements," OP–30W, no ser, 4 Mar 1947, 5, box 194, Strategic Plans, OA.

3. The discussion by David Rosenberg of OP–06's (and the Navy's) interest in atomic weapons during 1946 downplays this interest much too severely. See Rosenberg, "American Postwar Air Doctrine and Organization," 248–50.

4. Emphasis added. Copy of memo, President to Secretary of State et al., 15 Aug 1945, box 12, Radford Papers, OA.

5. Secretary Forrestal was in the Pacific for the atomic tests at Bikini Atoll.

6. Ltr, Acting SECNAV to President, 24 Jul 1946, box 158, Cabinet File, President's Secretary's File, Truman Papers, Truman Library.

7. Ltr, President to Acting SECNAV, 27 Jul 1946, same box.

8. Memo, Chief, BUAER to SECNAV, AER–1, n.d. [early Nov 1947 – Secretary Sullivan wrote his written concurrence on the memo on 7 Nov], 1, box 1, Classified Correspondence of Secretary John L. Sullivan (hereafter Sullivan Correspondence), General Records of the Navy Department 1947– (RG 428), NA.

9. It had originally been drafted by the War and Navy Departments and sent in January 1947 to the President as part of a joint letter on unification from Secretary of War Patterson and Secretary Forrestal.

10. For example, see the paper entitled "Strategic Bombing," n.d. [early 1948?], box 11, Secretary General's Office File 1942–49, Air Board Papers, RG 340, NA/WNRC.

11. For a discussion of this point, see Condit, *JCS and National Policy* 2:277–94.

12. Memo from OP–30V to OP–30, no ser, 7 Feb 1947, 2, box 111, Strategic Plans, OA.

13. Ibid., 4.

14. In March 1951, Air Force Secretary Thomas Finletter wrote to General Vandenberg:

> I can see a substantial political advantage in having some medium bombers deployed in the U.K. . . . On the other hand there is the question: how many? Ever since General LeMay told me many months ago [spring 1950] that he felt that a sneak attack could knock out our medium bomber fleet stationed in the U.K. I have been wondering about the deployment of so many as three, now two, groups there. Eyes Only memo, Finletter to Vandenberg, 7 Mar 1951, box 84, Vandenberg Papers, MD–LC.

15. To see how the Navy's thinking had evolved by mid-1949, see the correspondence on this issue between OP–05 and OP–03: memo, VADM John Dale Price, DCNO (Air) to CNO, OP–50 ser 00058P50, 22 Apr 1949; memo, VADM Arthur Struble, DCNO (Operations) to CNO, OP–301 ser 000234P30, 27 May 1949; memo, RADM M. B. Gardner, ACNO (Operations) to OP–05, OP–03 ser 00091P03, 7 Jul 1949; and memo, VADM C. T. Durgin, DCNO (Air), to OP–03, OP–503E ser 00093P50, 27 Jun 1949; all in box 250, Strategic Plans, OA.

16. "The Tenets of Naval War Planning presented by Rear Admiral W. F. Boone, U.S.N. at The Air University, Maxwell Field, Alabama, on 18 April 1949," 9–10; "A16–11 War Plans S&C" folder, Series II, OP–23 Records, OA.

17. Ibid., 11.

18. Emphasis added. [UNICOM ?] "Some Fundamentals Regarding Sea–Air Power and the U.S. Navy," n.d. [mid-1948], 10, "A20/4 Eberstadt Comte. Briefing Data S&C" folder, ibid.

19. Of course the Air Force received the opposite impression from its analyses of the USSBS reports. For a useful discussion of the work of the USSBS and the differing responses of its AAF and Navy participants, see David MacIssac, *Strategic Bombing in World War Two: The Story of the United States Strategic Bombing Survey* (New York: Garland Publishing, 1976).

20. Ofstie, a naval aviator, had also served as the Navy member of the Joint Chiefs of Staff Evaluation Board for the atomic bomb tests at Bikini. Ofstie biographical data, box 481, Officer Bios Collection, OA.

21. "The Carrier Air Attack on Japan," 26 Sep 1947, 1, 3–4, box 3, Ralph A. Ofstie Papers, OA. This paper may have been prepared for use as a lecture.

22. Ibid., 6.

23. Copy of ltr, Group Captain T. U. Rolfe, RAF, to RADM Thomas B. Inglis, Chief of Naval Intelligence, 16 Jul 1947; and ltr, Inglis to Rolfe, 29 Jul 1947, box 3, Ofstie Papers, OA.

24. Emphasis in original. Copy of memo, Ofstie to CNO, 16 Sep 1947, "A–16 War, Preparation, Conduct & Trans. S&C" folder, Series II, OP–23 Records, OA.

25. Memo, DCNO (Operations) to CNO, OP–30L ser 000126P30, 10 Apr 1948, 2, box 244, Strategic Plans, OA.

26. Memo, RADM E. A. Cruise to CNO, OP–55 ser 0001P55, 10 Apr 1948, box 13, Radford Papers, OA.

27. Ibid. In this same regard Admiral Styer's memo had stated, "The Navy's concept of proper strategic bombing operations requires the use of modern high performance, high speed, high altitude jet propelled bombers operating from advanced bases with jet fighter escort." Memo from DCNO (Operations) to CNO, 10 Apr 1948, 2.

28. Emphasis in original. "Comment on FROLIC as a Brief for Medium-Range Planning," Encl. B to memo, CNO to JCS, 5 Apr 1948, 1–2.

29. Air Force General Joseph T. McNarney was the senior member and chairman of the Budget Advisory Committee established at Secretary Forrestal's request to advise the service chiefs on the proper allocation of funds under a $14.4 billion ceiling for FY 1950.

30. Typed transcript, "Secretary of Defense Budget Meeting With the Three Secretaries and the Joint Chiefs of Staff 4 October 1948 – 1035 – Room 2C–260 Morning Session," 49–50; B.P. [Bulky Package] Part I, CCS 370 (8–19–45), RG 218, NA.

31. Ibid., 57.

32. Ibid., 61.

33. For information on the budget wrangling in the days following the meeting of 4 October, see Murray Green, "Stuart Symington and the B–36" (Ph.D. diss., The American University, 1960), 31–47, ff.; and Condit, *JCS and National Policy* 2:233–47.

34. A November 1948 memorandum from the head of the Air Warfare section of OP–05 discussed Navy carrier air targets in the following manner:

> The [carrier] task groups will be used offensively to keep our lines of communication open. The air groups will destroy enemy aircraft on the ground and in the air, bottle up enemy submarines and shipping by mining, attack enemy submarines and other naval forces at sea, disrupt enemy lines of communication, [and] destroy enemy installations. Memorandum, RADM Cruise to Secretary of the Air Board, OP–55 ser 0007P55, 26 Nov 1948, box 4, 1948 T/S [Top Secret] Control Office Files, OA.

35. As an example of Navy concerns on this point, see the observations in the memo, Ofstie to OP–32V [Assistant Chief, Air Branch, Naval Intelligence], 2 Oct 1947, box 3, Ofstie Papers, OA.

36. See the Memo for the President drafted by VADM Forrest Sherman for FADM Nimitz, OP–30 ser 0003P03, 4 Jun 1946, "A16–5 Submarine Warfare *Top Secret*" folder, Series III, OP–23 Records, OA.

37. For a useful discussion of this concept, see Palmer, *Origins of the Maritime Strategy*, 24–27.

38. Memo, CAPT George W. Anderson, Jr. to CDR R. C. Santee, OP–34C5, OP–30V ser 0157P30, 11 Oct 1946, box 107, Strategic Plans, OA.

39. NSPS [Navy Strategic Plans Study] 3, "Study of Carrier Attack Force Offensive Capabilities," OP–30W, A16–3(17), 7 Mar 1947, 2, 6, box 497, Strategic Plans, OA.

40. App. A to NSPS 3, untitled, OP–30W2, 5 Nov 1946, 13.

41. NSPS 3, 4.

42. See copy of memo, Anderson [to CNO], no ser, 7 Jan 1948, 2, "A21/1–1 Navy (April 47 thru March 1948)" folder, Series I, OP–23 Records, OA.

43. Palmer, *Origins of the Maritime Strategy*, 42–43, argues that under Radford's influence as VCNO, OPNAV expanded its concept of targeting beyond what had been laid out in NSPS 3. But this is a misconception. A careful reading of documents such as the February 1948 Navy presentation before the House Appropriations Naval Subcommittee and the presentation to the Eberstadt Committee on National Security Organization (both cited by Palmer in support of his viewpoint) fails to reveal any such expansion.

44. Admiral Denfeld expressed it in this manner to Admiral Leahy in February 1948: "Foreseeable future development of both VLR [Very Long Range] aircraft and the super-bases which they will require does not provide sufficient substantiation of the Air Force position to warrant the exclusion of the potential capacity of carriers to contribute substantially to long-range air operations." Memo, CNO to Leahy, OP–30X ser 65P30, 28 Feb 1948, 2, "A19/2 Key West Conference (Briefing Pamphlet) S&C" folder, Series II, OP–23 Records, OA.

45. Sec. 3 of untitled briefing paper labeled "Navy Presentation beginning about 14 March (OFF-TACKLE)," n.d. [mid-Mar 1949], 2, "1844/46" folder, Navy Secretariat Records, OA.

46. Several weeks earlier he had sent two memos detailing aspects of his thinking on this issue to RADM J. J. Clark, ACNO (Air). See copy of memo, Gallery to Clark, no ser, 14 Nov 1947; and copy of memo from Gallery to Clark, no ser, 17 Nov 1947, both in "A16–11 War Plans *Top Secret*" folder, Series III, OP–23 Records, OA.

47. Emphasis added. Memo, Gallery to DCNO (Air), OP–57 ser 00124P57, 17 Dec 1947, 3, box 6, Denfeld Double Zero Files, OA. This is the signed original of Gallery's memorandum.

48. Ibid., 10.

49. Admiral Duncan sent his original copy of the memo to Admiral Sherman, DCNO (Operations), for his information and comments. Upon receiving Sherman's comments, Duncan then routed the original, together with Sherman's and his own comments, to all DCNOs, the VCNO, the CNO, and the Assistant Secretary of the Navy for Air.

50. Emphasis in original. Handwritten comment (signed with the initials FS) on Office Memorandum sent to Sherman by Duncan, n.d.; attached to Gallery memo.

51. Handwritten comment on printed note form from DCNO (Air) to all DCNOs et al., n.d., attached to Gallery memo.

52. The typed copy (and a carbon copy) of the Gallery memo in Symington's Special Interest Files is a version made from a copy of the Navy original by a non-Navy source. A comparison of Gallery's original memo in CNO's files with the Symington copy reveals not only slight changes in format but an obvious mistake in the file designation of the document that should have been readily apparent to a Navy reader. Symington copy of Gallery memo, box 4, Special Interest File, 1948, Symington Special Interest Files, RG 340, NA/WNRC.

53. Green, "Stuart Symington and the B–36," 54n. It should be recalled that the Key West meeting on armed forces' roles and missions had just concluded on 14 March.

54. Ibid.; and "Sullivan Censures Top Navy Official," *New York Times*, 10 Apr 1948, 7.

55. Memo from Denfeld to SECNAV, 8 Apr 1948, box 2, Denfeld Double Zero Files, OA. David Rosenberg (based on an interview with Admiral Gallery) commented that Gallery's "extreme position" had met with the outright disapproval of the CNO. Rosenberg, "American Postwar Air Doctrine and Organization," 254. On the contrary: In his memo to Secretary Sullivan the CNO noted, "I not only consider that Rear Admiral Gallery's initiative in preparing the paper was commendable and proper, but that the paper itself demonstrates the type of constructive thinking which the Navy tries at all times to encourage." Memo, Denfeld to SECNAV, 8 Apr 1948.

56. A number of naval officers believed that it had been leaked by the Air Force to cause the Navy unfavorable publicity. Although this must remain supposition, Drew Pearson did have good contacts in the Air Force at that time (with both Stuart Symington and Steve Leo), and his relationship with the Navy—dating back to James Forrestal's days as SECNAV—was not good.

57. Paul Y. Hammond, "Super Carriers and B–36 Bombers: Appropriations, Strategy and Politics," in *American Civil-Military Decisions: A Book of Case Studies*, ed. Harold Stein (Birmingham: University of Alabama Press, 1963), 558 (note 57); and "Sullivan Censures Top Navy Official," *New York Times*, 10 Apr 1948, 7.

58. Memo, Spaatz to Symington, 7 Jan 1948, 2, box 28, Spaatz Papers, MD–LC. This was a reference to the Executive Order issued by Truman following the signing of the National Security Act of 1947.

59. In October 1946 the AAF Assistant Chief of Staff for Intelligence had commented in a memo to General Spaatz, "The [Navy-Air Power] line is beautiful—first kill off the Army—then let the Navy and Air stand as the requirements—then argue that carrier air power can dominate the Mediterranean and you have the Navy and Air merged into one service claiming the budget—NAVY." Memo, MGEN George C. McDonald, AC/AS–2, to Spaatz, 17 Oct 1946, box 262, Spaatz Papers, MD–LC.

60. These criticisms of carrier capabilities are taken from a variety of official Air Force documents.

61. Emphasis in original. Memo, McDonald to Spaatz, 18 Oct 1946, box 262, Spaatz Papers, MD–LC.

62. Draft memo, LTGEN Lauris Norstad to Spaatz, 10 Mar 1948, 2, box 28, Spaatz Papers, MD–LC. For an extensive critique of the capabilities of the large, flush-deck aircraft carrier for atomic bombing, see the fifty-nine-page study "Department of the Air Force Memorandum—The Super Carrier (CVA-58) Project," 7 Apr 1949, box 97, Vandenberg Papers, MD–LC.

63. Entry for 23 Jan 1948, Radford Personal Log: Jan 1948 to—, box 1, Radford Papers, OA.

64. "Conference with Mr. Forrestal, Admiral Radford, Leva and General Spaatz, 28 January 1948," 3, box 28, Spaatz Papers, MD–LC.

65. Ltr, Sherman to Forrestal, 28 Feb 1948, 1, box 4, Forrest P. Sherman Papers, OA. Forrestal's letter is not present in the folder.

66. For a brief discussion of the Key West meeting, see Rearden, *Formative Years, 1947–1950*, 395–97.

67. "Functions of the Armed Forces and the Joint Chiefs of Staff," 12, att. to memo, SECDEF to the Secretaries of the Army, Navy, and Air Force and JCS, 21 Apr 1948, encl. to memo, CNO to All Ships and Stations, OP–21D ser 1631P21, 26 Apr 1948, "A19/2 Key West Conference" folder, Series I, OP–23 Papers, OA. The Key West agreement specifically defined strategic air warfare as "air combat and supporting operations designed to effect, through the systematic application of force to a selected series of vital targets, the progressive destruction and disintegration of the enemy's war-making capacity to a point where he no longer retains the ability or the will to wage war." The definition listed a number of vital targets; all but one were industrial, or resource related. Ibid., 15.

68. Ibid., 11.

69. See "Notes for Friday—Opening of Meeting," 11 Mar 1948, inserted in Forrestal Diaries, vol. 10, Feb 1948–Apr 1948, 2131, box 17, Privileged Manuscript Collection, OA.

70. Entry of 11 Mar 1948 [dictated 16 Mar], ibid., 2129.

71. Entry of 15 Mar 1948 [dictated 16 Mar], ibid., 2135.

72. "In considering the statement 'To be prepared to participate in the over-all air effort as directed by the Joint Chiefs of Staff,' ... it was stressed that the capabilities of naval aviation should be utilized to the maximum, including a specific provision that the Navy would not be prohibited from attacking targets, inland or otherwise, to accomplish its mission." JCS 1478/24, 7 Jul 1948, 207, "A19/2 Key West Conference" folder, Series I, OP–23 Records, OA.

73. Copy of memo, Lee to SECNAV, 8 Jul 1948, "A19/2 Key West Conference S&C" folder, Series II, OP–23 Records, OA.

74. Memo, Lee to SECNAV, 14 Jul 1948, box 14, Radford Papers, OA.

75. At this 7 July press conference, in response to a question on whether the Navy could use the atomic bomb, James Forrestal had stated: "The whole purpose and spirit of that statement [regarding strategic air] was to bar the Navy from the concept of preparing the use of its air power for strategic purposes *in the sense of the destruction of industrial areas of large critical territories in enemy countries.*" Emphasis added. Quoted in ibid.

76. This reconstruction of the incident was provided by Secretary Sullivan's former aide some eighteen months after the original events. Ltr, Lee to CAPT Richard W. Ruble, Aide to SECNAV, 3 Aug 1949, box 16, Radford Papers. OA.

77. Memo, "Dinner—the Three Secretaries—Air Force and Naval Air," 19 Jul 1948 (but dated at bottom 7–22–48), filed with entry for 19 Jul 1948, Forrestal Diaries, vol. 11, May 1948–31 Jul 1948, 2370, box 17, Privileged Manuscript Collection, OA. Following this dinner James Forrestal concluded that the problem might be settled by assigning the atomic bomb to the Air Force on the basis of "dominant interest" and limiting naval aviation's use of it to "sorties upon strategic targets at the direction of the Air Force" and "sorties upon purely naval targets," but giving the Navy the right of appeal first to the JCS and then to the Secretary of Defense. Ibid.

78. Ltr, Lee to Ruble, 3 Aug 1949.

79. Emphasis added. Encl. to memo from Symington to Sullivan, 21 Jul 1948, box 2, Sullivan Correspondence, RG 428, NA. Another copy can be found in box 52, Vandenberg Papers, MD–LC.

80. A gun-type weapon relied upon a propellant charge to drive a smaller projectile of fissionable material down a tube—essentially a gun barrel (hence the term, gun-type)—running the length of the bomb casing and into a larger fissionable target to form the supercritical mass needed for the atomic explosion. See Hansen, *US Nuclear Weapons*, 20–21. On 27 April 1948, the Navy had demonstrated a potential carrier atomic capability by launching two large, P2V–2 patrol planes (using jet-assisted take-off [JATO] deck runs) from the *Midway*-class aircraft carrier *Coral Sea*.

81. See Schlatter, *The United States Air Force and Atomic Warfare*, 7. See also Hansen, *U.S. Nuclear Weapons*, 21.

82. Memo, Sullivan to Symington, 9 Aug 1948, with encl.; attached to memo from Symington to Sullivan, 21 Jul 1948, box 2, Sullivan Correspondence, RG 428, NA.

83. Rosenberg, "U.S. nuclear stockpile," 27.

84. App. to encl. to JCS 1823/7, 21 Oct 1948, sec. 12, CCS 471.6 (8–15–45), RG 218, NA.

85. Hansen, *US Nuclear Weapons*, 34.

86. Rosenberg, "American Atomic Strategy and the Hydrogen Bomb Decision," 71; and Rosenberg, "U.S. nuclear stockpile," 28.

87. The Air Force had opened the fight on 23 March 1948. At the time General Spaatz staked a claim to exclusive control by the Air Force by asking the Joint Chiefs to recommend to the Secretary of Defense that the Air Force Chief of Staff be designated the executive agent of the JCS for directing and supervising the operational functions of the AFSWP. See Condit, *JCS and National Policy* 2:177ff.

88. For more on the Air Force viewpoint, see Schlatter, *The United States Air Force and Atomic Warfare*, 10–14.

89. Emphasis added. Memo, "Conversation With General Vandenberg—Atom Bomb, Use of—Weapons Programs," 28 Jul 1948, filed with entry for 28 July 1948, Forrestal Diaries, 11:2389. Forrestal told Vandenberg that, although he was solidly behind the Air Force's claim for predominance in the field of strategic air warfare, he "would not extend that to denial to another service of the development of a weapon [i.e., the flush-deck aircraft carrier] which it thought it needed in its own particular field." Ibid., 2388.

90. Memo, Forrestal to Spaatz and Towers, 9 Aug 1948, box 1, 1948 Double Zero Files, OA.

91. Memo, Spaatz and Towers to Forrestal, 18 Aug 1948, attached to Forrestal memo, 9 Aug 1948.

92. "Secretary Forrestal and Joint Chiefs Plan Weekend Conference," National Military Establishment Press Release No. 135–48, 20 Aug 1948, "A19/3 Newport Conference" folder, Series I, OP–23 Records, OA.

93. In the second meeting at Newport, Admiral Radford stated, "From this discussion I understand General V [Vandenberg] to agree that the Air Force cannot now state that the A bomb is to be used exclusively for the purpose of strategic bombing." Both Vandenberg and Forrestal agreed that this was correct. Then Vandenberg commented, "As I see it, by pinning it down [making the Air Force executive agent for AFSWP] as we have, we can now go out and protect you. Our first reaction was 'keep everybody out'. Now we have the responsibility for inviting you in." "Agreed Final Version of Minutes of Newport Meeting 20–22 August 1948," 27, box 1, 1948 Double Zero Files, OA. See also pages 21–23.

94. See "Newport Conference Discussed Before Senior Military Officers," OSD Press Release No. 140–48, 24 Aug 1948, 2, 4–6, same box.

5. Super Carriers and B–36 Bombers

1. Discussion of the 6A carrier's development process is based principally upon the hearings of the General Board from 1945 through 1950, the General Board's aircraft carrier files, and Norman Friedman, *U.S. Aircraft Carriers: An Illustrated Design History* (Annapolis: Naval Institute Press, 1983), 225–53.

2. Memo, CNO to CAPT V. Schaeffer et al., OP–31 ser 099131, 27 Apr 1945, box 160, Strategic Plans, OA. See also memo, CAPT A. A. Burke to Judge Advocate General, OP–23 ser 067P23, 11 May 1949, 1 (hereafter "History of the 6A Carrier Project"), CNO Chronological File, Post 1 Jan 46 Command File, OA.

3. Memo, SECNAV to Chairman General Board, 29 Jun 1945, box 194, Strategic Plans, OA.

4. Memo, SECNAV to Chairman General Board and Chiefs of Bureaus of Ships, Ordnance, and Aeronautics, no ser, 10 May 1945, same box.; and Friedman, *U.S. Aircraft Carriers*, 225.

5. Memo, RADM C. L. Brand, BUSHIPS, to Chairman General Board, BUSHIPS ltr C–CV/S1–1(400), 12 Oct 1945, 3, box 83, General Board Records, RG 80, NA. The CVB–41-class carrier had a standard displacement of 46,050 tons. Ibid., encl. A.

6. See memos, CAPT W. T. Rassieur, OP–03–5, to CAPT V. Schaeffer et al., OP–03–5 ser 009903, 2 Jul 1945; and Rassieur to Schaeffer et al., OP–03–513 ser 0012403, 13 Jul 1945, both in box 160, Strategic Plans, OA.

7. The study was modified in April 1946 to the final C–2 design. The quoted portion of this sentence is taken from a photocopy of memo, Chief BUAER to CNO (OP–04), BUAER ser Aer–SI–2, 7 Jun 1946, box 199, Strategic Plans.

8. See Encl. A to memo, Cochrane to Chairman General Board, 26 Nov 1945; and memo, with encl., from OP–05 to OP–04, OP–517 ser 018P517, 15 Mar 1946, box 83, General Board Records, RG 80, NA.

9. Rear Admiral Emerson E. Fawkes, USN (Ret.), interview by CAPT John F. Barlow, USN (Ret.), and author, 14 Jul 1984, Arlington, VA, tape recording. Fawkes was then head of the Dive Bomber Design Desk at BUAER. This interview was conducted by the author and his father for a forthcoming history of the Navy's Heavy Attack program.

10. Memo, RADM H. B. Sallada to CNO, BUAER ser C30035, 11 Dec 1945; Encl. A to memo, DCNO (Air) to CNO, OP–517 ser 04P517, 8 Jan 1946, "A19/2 Key West Conference (Briefing Pamphlet) S & C" folder, Series II, OP–23 Records, OA.

11. Such aircraft would be incapable of being struck below, i.e., taken down to the hanger deck for maintenance and storage.

12. Memo, Sallada to CNO, 11 Dec 1945.

13. Ibid.

14. Fawkes interview. Fawkes had drafted the letter sent to CNO by Sallada. The July 1946 official description of the aircraft—designated the XAJ–1—noted, "Its performance is designed to permit carrier (CVB) take-off with an 8000# bomb load...." Aviation Circular Letter No. 126–46, Memo, CNO to All Ships, Stations and Units Concerned with Naval Aircraft, OP–517B19 ser 089P517, 25 Jul 1946, "A–2 (AJ) (N.A.) Documentation" folder, Naval Aviation History Branch, NHC.

15. Vice Admiral Frederick L. Ashworth, USN (Ret.), Recollections recorded in response to written questions submitted by Captain Barlow and the author, Feb 1984, Santa Fe, NM, tape recording. Captain Ashworth was responsible for the air applications of atomic weapons in OP–36. For an interesting, but not wholly accurate written account of this action, see Vincent Davis, *The Politics of Innovation: Patterns in Navy Cases.* Monograph No. 3, 1966–67, Monograph Series in World Affairs (Denver: University of Denver, 1967), 11–13.

16. For information on the Mk III special weapon, see Hansen, *US Nuclear Weapons*, 122–24. The Mk III was superseded by the improved but similarly sized Mk IV during 1949–1950. Ibid., 124–25.

17. Fawkes interview.

18. The fourth part of the program—the coordinated design and development of escort fighters for long-range bombers—was to parallel the bomber development. Memo, Sallada to CNO, 11 Dec 1945.

19. Memo, CNO to Chief BUAER, OP–517 ser 042P517, 28 Dec 1945; Encl. B to memo, VADM M.A. Mitscher, DCNO (Air), to CNO, OP–517B1 ser 04P517, 8 Jan 1946, "A19/2 Key West Conference (Briefing Pamphlet) S&C" folder, Series II, OP–23 Records, OA.

20. Rough draft paper, "Reasons for 6A Carrier," 30 Jun 1949, 4, "A21/1–1/1 Carrier" folder, Series I, OP–23 Records; and "Naval Warfare and Carriers"—Presentation by CAPT Arleigh Burke to the Joint Chiefs of Staff on 6A carrier [according to typed notation on document], Apr 1949, 4–5; "File No. 98–A," unnumbered box, Arleigh A. Burke Papers, OA.

21. Testimony of VADM J. H. Cassady, DCNO (Air), Hearing on "Attack Carrier (New Construction) (10–50)," 25 Oct 1950; *Hearings before the General Board of the Navy 1950*, vol. 4 (Wilmington, DE: Scholarly Resources Inc., 1983), 15:996, microfilm, NDL. Admiral Cassady told the General Board that the ability of a flush-deck carrier to operate in all weather had been more important to Mitscher than its ability to handle larger aircraft. Ibid. The U.S. Navy's first aircraft carrier, the converted collier *Langley* (CV 1), and the escort carrier *Long Island* (AVG 1, later CVE 1) were the service's earlier flush-deck aircraft carriers.

22. Radford's view was apparently related to his concern that the Navy might be prohibited from operating land-based ASW and reconnaissance aircraft under a unification agreement with the War Department. See Radford Autobiography, [2]:48.

23. Memo, Mitscher to CNO, 8 Jan 1946.

24. Memo, CAPT W. V. Saunders to Assistant SECNAV for Air Sullivan, 14 Jan 1946, "A19/2 Key West Conference (Briefing Pamphlet) S&C" folder, Series II, OP–23 Records, OA.

25. See handwritten notation by Sullivan, and staff comments, on Office Memo, 22 Jan 1946; and Sullivan's handwritten notation at the bottom of memo, Mitscher to CNO, 8 Jan 1946, same folder.

26. Memo, CNO to OP–04 and OP–05, OP–09 ser 09P09, 7 Feb 1946, same folder.

27. Friedman, *U.S. Aircraft Carriers*, 241; and "Digest of Information Constituting the Background of Action Concerning a New Carrier," 1; att. to untitled statement on the 6A carrier drafted by OP–502D, Fall 1948, "A21/1–1/1 Navy—Carrier (S&C)" folder, Series II, OP–23 Records, OA.

330   *Notes to pages 137–141*

28. See "CVB–X Design Study '1'," PD No. 1352, 20 May 1946, box 83, General Board Records, RG 80, NA.

29. Friedman disparagingly referred to the CVB–X at this point as "a rather grotesque single-purpose carrier design, much more a complement to the fleet carrier than an alternative." Friedman, *U.S. Aircraft Carriers*, 242. This design, however, was precisely what the Operations Division in 1946 was looking for in this special-purpose carrier. Admiral Sherman commented in June of that year, "As further advances in Naval Warfare come along it will be increasingly necessary to use single purpose ships, relying on other bottoms for support." Photocopy of memo, OP–03 to OP–04, OP–34D ser 0383P34, 12 Jun 1946, 3, box 199, Strategic Plans, OA.

30. Memo, OP–03 to OP–04, 12 Jun 1946, 2–3.

31. Friedman, *U.S. Aircraft Carriers*, 242–44.

32. See, for example, the testimony of RADM L. C. Stevens, Hearing on "Panama Canal—Navy Requirements in Canal Modernization," 20 Nov 1946, *Hearings before the General Board of the Navy 1945–47*: vol. 1, 13:82, microfilm.

33. Testimony of VADM R. B. Carney, Hearing on "Shipbuilding and Conversion Program Fiscal 1949," 23 Jul 1947, *Hearings before the General Board of the Navy 1947*: vol. 2, 13:398.

34. By this time, Ship Characteristics Board Project 4—the postwar fleet carrier (CV)—had been merged with Project 6—the CVB–X—to become the new Project 6A Carrier.

35. "Digest of Information Concerning a New Carrier," 2. This delay also accorded with the wishes of the Bureau of Ships.

36. These figures differ from those given in Friedman, *U.S. Aircraft Carriers*, 241. He may have been using figures supplied at a much earlier stage of the design study process.

37. The 90,000-pound heavy attack aircraft for the 6A carrier went through several design studies from 1946 through early 1949. The first design, the ADR–42 (for Bureau of Aeronautics Design Research Division Study 42), was used for planning purposes until early 1948. It was replaced first by the ADR–62 and then by the ADR–64. Each design differed slightly in certain characteristics. The characteristics given here for the ADR–42 are largely taken from memo, CAPT H. D. Riley to RADM C. D. Glover et al., OP–30X, no ser, 22 Nov 1947, box 86, Strategic Plans, OA.

38. Friedman, *U.S. Aircraft Carriers*, 248. The weight of the ADR–45A used here, which differs from that given in Friedman, is taken from BUAER source material. The prototype XF2D–1 was later redesignated the F2H–1 Banshee.

39. Testimony of VADM Robert Carney, Hearing on "Shipbuilding and Conversion Program Fiscal 1949," 23 Jul 1947, *Hearings before the General Board of the Navy 1947*: vol. 2, 13:397–98.

40. "Digest of Information Concerning a New Carrier," 2.

41. "Ship Characteristics Board Proposed Characteristics Project 6A (CV-Flush Deck)," 20 Aug 1947, 2, Encl. A to memo, Senior Member, Ship Characteristics Board, to CNO, OP–04B ser 0164P04B, 22 Aug 1947, box 83, General Board Records, RG 80, NA.

42. "Proposed Characteristics Project 6A," 20 Aug 1947, 1. Follow-on planning in the office of the DCNO (Air) eventually called for the CVX (6A) air group to consist of twenty-four ADR–62 heavy attack aircraft. See memo, Price to VCNO, OP–501 ser 0001P50C, 3 Feb 1948, 1 and attachment, "Air Group Complements," box 4, T/S Control Office Files, OA.

43. "Digest of Information Concerning a New Carrier," 2.

44. "History of the 6A Carrier Project," 1.

45. Public Law 291—the Second Supplemental Surplus Appropriations Rescission Act of 1946—directed the completion of all combatant vessels under construction on 1 Mar 1946 that were more than 20 percent complete on that date. The vessels covered by this law included one battleship, one heavy cruiser of a class larger than those previously built, seven destroyers, two destroyer escorts, and two submarines. Testimony of Secretary Sullivan, 19 May 1948, in Congress, House, Committee

on Appropriations, Subcommittee on Navy Department Appropriations, *Department of the Navy Appropriation Bill for 1949: Supplemental Hearings*, 80th Cong., 2d sess., 1948, 4–6.

46. The Navy originally asked for money in FY 1949 to build fourteen ships and convert eight more. Webb agreed to a reduced Navy program to build six ships (including the 6A carrier) and convert three others. Memo with enclosures, RADM H. G. Hopwood, Director of Budget and Reports, to SECNAV, 5 Feb 1948, box 1, Sullivan correspondence, RG 428, NA.

47. Copy of ltr, Webb to SECNAV, 19 Dec 1947, box 1, Denfeld Double Zero Files, OA. The battleship *Kentucky* was 73 percent complete and the large cruiser *Hawaii* was "something like 84 percent" complete at the time of the work stoppage. Testimony of Secretary Sullivan, 19 May 1948, in House, *Navy Appropriation Bill for 1949: Supplemental Hearings*, 4.

48. Draft Memo for the Record, 25 Mar 1948, 6, att. to DM–16, memo, MGEN Alfred Gruenther, Director Joint Staff, to Admiral Leahy et al., 26 Mar 1948, "A19/2 Key West Conference (Roles & Missions) S&C" folder, Series II, OP–23 Records, OA.

49. Memo titled "Meeting with the President – Key West Conference Report," 15 Mar 1948, enclosed with entry for 15 Mar 1948, Forrestal Diaries, 10:2135. In the printed version of the Forrestal Diaries, editor Walter Millis assumed that "HA" meant "high altitude," and this interpretation of Forrestal's cryptic abbreviation has been followed by subsequent historians. Millis, *Forrestal Diaries*, 393. It is much more likely, however, that HA stood for "heavy attack," and is how the abbreviation is interpreted here.

50. See, for example, testimony of Secretary Sullivan, 19 May 1948, House, *Navy Appropriation Bill For 1949: Supplemental Hearings*, 11; and Jim G. Lucas, "Joint Chiefs Ready to Rip Veil Off Air Power Battle," *Washington Daily News*, 21 May 1948, 26. For support of their view that the JCS had approved the 6A carrier, Sullivan and Denfeld were relying on their interpretations of JCS actions in connection with JCS 1796/6 and the agreements reached at Key West.

51. See undelivered "Statement of General Spaatz Before a Subcommittee of the Senate Armed Services Committee," 21 May 1948; and answers prepared for Spaatz by LTGEN Lauris Norstad in response to questions asked by Congressman Evrett P. Scrivener, 19 May 1948, marked "not sent," both in box 29, Spaatz Papers, MD–LC. On 25 May 1948 Spaatz made public his view that the Air Force had not approved the 6A carrier plan in the JCS paper sent to the Finletter Commission, in a prepared statement and in his answers to questions from reporters at a National Press Club luncheon following his retirement as Air Force Chief of Staff. See typed copy (excerpts?) of newspaper article (from the *Baltimore Sun*?), encl. to note from unnamed member of the Joint Staff to Gruenther, 26 May 1948, CCS 561 (5–26–48), RG 218, NA.

52. Ltr, Denfeld to Congressman Charles A. Plumley, Chairman, Naval Subcommittee on Appropriations, 28 May 1948, box 2, Denfeld Double Zero Files, OA.

53. Emphasis added. Memo, Lalor to Gruenther, 27 May 1948, CCS 561 (5–26–48), RG 218, NA.

54. The Bureau of Ships believed that the last of the four flush-deck carriers could be delivered by 1 July 1955. However, it thought that the expectation of having the first 6A carrier operational during FY 1952 was overly optimistic. See memo, VADM J. D. Price, DCNO (Air), to VCNO, OP–501 ser 0002P50C, 10 Feb 1948, 1, box 4, 1948 T/S Control Office Files, OA.

55. See Ship Characteristics Board Memo 17–48, 27 Apr 1948, Ship Characteristics Board Files, Post 1 Jan 1946 Command File, OA.

56. Testimony of Secretary Sullivan, 11 Jun 1948; in Congress, Senate, Committee on Appropriations, Subcommittee on Navy Department Appropriations, *Navy Department Appropriation Bill for 1949: Hearings*, 80th Cong., 2d sess., 1948, 11.

57. Secretary Forrestal had expressed his views on this point to General Hoyt Vandenberg in July 1948: "I said I was against the development of a new fleet of super-carriers by the Navy but I felt it was most important that one such ship, capable of carrying the weight of a long range bombing plane, go forward." Memo titled "Conversation with General Vandenberg—Atom Bomb, Use of—Weapons Programs," 28 Jul 1948, filed with entry for 28 July 1948, Forrestal Diaries 11: 2388. See also Radford Autobiography [2]:663–64.

58. 1st Ind. memo, CNO to SECNAV, OP–34D ser 0613P34, 3 Aug 1948, box 2, 1948 Double Zero Files, OA.

59. Public Law 753, 80th Cong., 2d sess., 24 Jun 1948, 10.

60. Memo, CNO to SECNAV, OP–33V1 ser 1032P33, 22 Jul 1948, with First Endorsement, same date, box 2, 1948 Double Zero Files, OA.

61. On 29 July 1948 the President authorized construction of the aircraft carrier in a private shipyard. Memo, CNO to Chief, Bureau of Ships, OP–414 ser 1416P414, 12 Aug 1948, box 3, same file; and "History of the 6A Carrier Project," 3.

62. Discussion of the B–36's development process is based principally upon the Air Force's Strategic Air Group Research and Development correspondence files; and [MGEN Frederick H. Smith, Jr., Mr. Frederick M. Sallagar and others], "History of B–36 Procurement," n.d. [submitted to the Secretary of the Air Force on 26 July 1949], box 42, Vandenberg Papers, MD–LC. The text of Smith's B–36 procurement history is available most readily in Congress, House, Committee on Armed Services, *Investigation of the B–36 Bomber Program: Hearings*, 81st Cong., 1st sess., 1949, 44–90.

63. "History of B–36 Procurement," 1-1.

64. Ibid., 1-2; and Marcelle Size Knaack, *Encyclopedia of U.S. Air Force Aircraft and Missile Systems*, vol. 2, *Post–World War II Bombers 1945–1973* (Washington: Office of Air Force History, United States Air Force, 1988), 6.

65. See "Telephone Conversation Between: Mr. Girdler, Consolidated Aircraft, San Diego, Calif. and Mr. H. E. Talbott," 21 Jul 1942, box 28, Strategic Air Group Correspondence 1949–51 (hereafter Strategic Air Group), Director of Research and Development—Deputy Chief of Staff, Development Files, RG 341, NA.

66. In March 1943 Consolidated Aircraft Corporation merged with Vultee Aircraft Corporation. The new company became Consolidated Vultee Aircraft Corporation (Convair).

67. Memo, MGEN E. M. Powers, AC/AS–4 to CG Air Materiel Command (AMC), 25 Mar 1946, 1, box 28, Strategic Air Group, RG 341, NA.

68. Meyers K. Jacobsen and Ray Wagner, *B–36 in action* (Carrollton, TX: Squadron/Signal Publications, 1980), 5.

69. "History of B–36 Procurement," 4-2. In August 1944, a formal procurement contract for the 100 B–36s replaced the earlier AAF letter of intent.

70. Ibid., 5-1.

71. Ibid., 5-2.

72. General Arnold approved retention of the B–36 contract on 6 Aug 1945.

73. "History of B–36 Procurement," 6-1.

74. Memo, Powers to CG AMC, 25 Mar 1946, 4.

75. Emphasis added. Memo, Powers to CG, AMC, 3 Apr 1946, box 28, Strategic Air Group, RG 341, NA.

76. Murray Green, "Stuart Symington and the B–36" (Ph.D. diss., The American University, 1960), 74; quoting from an article by J. H. Higgs, *St. Louis Globe–Democrat*, 27 Aug 1946.

77. "Inhabited Regions of World Now in Range of B–36's Atomic Bombs," Press Release, War Department Public Relations Division, Press Section, AAF, 7 Nov 1946, "M–1 *B–36* News Released thru April **1949**" folder, Series I, OP–23 Records, OA.

78. Copy of ltr, GEN George C. Kenney to Spaatz, 12 Dec 1946, enclosed with ltr, Spaatz to Kenney, 16 Jan 1947, box 28, Strategic Air Group, RG 341, NA.

79. Ibid.

80. Memo, LTGEN Nathan Twining to AC/AS–4, 27 Dec 1946, 1, 4–5, same box.

81. Msg TSBPA3B-12-3, Bombardment Branch, AMC to CG, AAF, Attn. AC/AS-4, 3 Dec 1946, 1-2, 4; and memo, BGEN Alden R. Crawford, Chief Research & Engineering Division, AC/AS-4, 12 Dec 1946, both in same box.

82. Memo, BGEN F. H. Smith, Jr., Secretary USAF Aircraft & Weapons Board, to members, USAF Aircraft & Weapons Board, 8 Oct 1947, same box; and History of B-36 Procurement," 9-1.

83. "History of B-36 Procurement," 9-2.

84. Chronological chart, encl. to memo, COL J. W. Sessums to W. Barton Leach, 5 Jul 1949, box 27, Strategic Air Group, RG 341, NA.; and Jacobsen and Wagner, *B-36 in action*, 7.

85. Convair also proposed to examine the costs for refitting the A and B model B-36 aircraft with the VDT engines. Proposal wired from Convair to HQ USAF, encl. to memo, COL Leslie O. Petersen, Acting Chief Requirements Div, AC/AS-3, to Research & Engineering Div, AC/AS-4, 8 Sep 1947, box 28, Strategic Air Group, RG 341, NA.

86. One factor influencing this renewed interest was the Air Force's concern about the future use of Convair's leased Government plant at Fort Worth once the original contract was completed. "History of B-36 Procurement," 11-1.

87. Memo, LTGEN H. A. Craig, Deputy Chief of Staff for Materiel, to CG AMC, 5 Dec 1947, box 28, Strategic Air Group, RG 341, NA.

88. Emphasis added. Negative photocopy of memo, Kenney to Spaatz, SAC 452.1 1st Ind, 3 Nov 1947; Tab NN to Inspector General, USAF, "Report of Special Inquiry into the B-36 Procurement Program 2 June-2 July 48," box 38, Special Interest File 1949, Symington Special Interest Files, RG 340, NA/WNRC.

89. Memo, Kenney to Spaatz, 26 Jan 1948, box 28, Spaatz Papers, MD-LC.

90. "History of B-36 Procurement," 16-2.

91. Ibid., 16-3.

92. Copy of memo, Norstad to Craig, 24 Apr 1948, encl. to copy of Craig's 1st Ind. to undated ltr, HQ AMC, 25 Jun 1948, box 28, Strategic Air Group, RG 341, NA.

93. Green, "Stuart Symington and the B-36," 90; and "History of B-36 Procurement," 16-7–16-8.

94. Undated, unsigned memo on Symington's role in the B-36 program, dictated by the Air Force Secretary about 16 Jun 1949 [date supplied in Murray Green, "Stuart Symington and the B-36," 91n], 4; and copy of memo from LTCOL Beverly H. Warren, Chief Fort Worth Air Force Procurement Field Office, AMC, to MGEN K. B. Wolfe, MCPPXF, 27 May 1948, with enclosures; encl. to memo, Warren to COL George L. Wertenbaker, MCPPXF-1, 6 Jun 1949, both in box 51, Special Interest File 1950, Symington Special Interest Files, RG 340, NA/WNRC.

95. Green, "Stuart Symington and the B-36," 91-92.

96. Emphasis added. Memo, Symington to Forrestal, 5 Jun 1948, box 28, Strategic Air Group, RG 341, NA.

97. Symington memo, [16 Jun 1949], 3; and memo, Symington to Vandenberg, 7 Jun 1948, box 59, Vandenberg Papers, MD-LC.

98. Symington memo, [16 Jun 1949], 2.

99. The aircraft was originally designated the B-50C. For information on the B-50C/B-54, see unsigned memo for COL J. W. Sessums, n.d. [Jun or Jul 1949], box 28, Strategic Air Group, RG 341, NA.

100. "History of B-36 Procurement," 17-5.

101. Ibid., 17-6; and Green, "Stuart Symington and the B-36," 95, citing General Fairchild's Memo for the Record, 25 Jun 1948. The five aircraft removed from the original contract in order to pay for the VDT engine installations could not be reinstated because the additional costs that the program had incurred by this time.

102. Knaack, *Post–World War II Bombers*, 21.

103. By the end of 1948, the Air Force had accepted twenty-one B–36As from Convair. Ibid., 22.

104. Emphasis added. Memo, Powers to SECAF, 23 Jul 1948, box 28, Strategic Air Group, RG 341, NA.

105. "History of B–36 Procurement," 19-5.

106. The U.S. intelligence community was not aware in 1948 that the swept-wing MiG–15 was operational, nor did it become aware of the full extent of the aircraft's capabilities until after the start of the Korean War. See Central Intelligence Agency (CIA) Intelligence Memorandum No. 200, "Soviet Aviation Day," 19 Jul 1949, 2; and CIA Report IM–203, "The Soviet Air Forces: Summary," 25 Jul 1949, 5 and 10 (table); both in box 2, CIA File (Special Eval.—ORE), Records of the National Security Council, Truman Papers, Truman Library. Air Force–Navy air intelligence reports in the 1951–1952 period were estimating the MiG–15's maximum speed at about 580 knots (668 mph) at sea level and its service ceiling at 50,000 feet.

107. Quoted in Robert Hotz, "New B–36 to Give USAF Greater Range: Data released for first time on B model of giant bomber, soon to go into service," *Aviation Week*, 18 Oct 1948, 12. Interestingly, it was outgoing SAC commander, George Kenney, who provided the information that he expected the B–36 "eventually to have a maximum range of 12,000 miles with an effective bomb load." See memo, G. B. Woods to Barrows, Under SECAF, 15 Oct 1948, enclosed with office memo, Woods to BGEN D. L. Putt, Director of Research & Development, AC/AS–4, 18 Oct 1948, box 28, Strategic Air Group, RG 314, NA.

108. The Air Staff requested AMC's evaluation of the proposal on 3 November. Msg, Putt to CG AMC, 3 Nov 1948, box 28, Strategic Air Group, RG 341, NA.

109. They also were to be equipped with jet pods.

110. "History of B–36 Procurement," 19-6; and Knaack, *Post–World War II Bombers*, 29.

111. Memo, Powers to CG AMC, 17 Jan 1949, box 28, Strategic Air Group, RG 341, NA.

112. The Air Force accepted the first B–36Ds in August 1950. Knaack, *Post–World War II Bombers*, 32.

6. A Time of Crisis and Change

1. For information on the events in China in 1948 and 1949 from the perspective of Defense decision makers, see Rearden, *The Formative Years* 1: 221–32; and Condit, *JCS and National Policy* 2:440–83.

2. Memo (with enclosures), RADM E. G. Allen, Director of Budget and Reports, to SECNAV, 20 Feb 1946, filed in "JCS Completed Papers 1478–1478/19" folder, Navy Secretariat Records, OA.

3. Ibid.; and "Synopsis of Statement by Vice Admiral Forrest P. Sherman, USN, Deputy Chief of Naval Operations (Operations), Before the Committee on Naval Affairs, United States Senate, on H.R. 4421, February 14, 1946," 3–4, and chart [12], box 197, Strategic Plans, OA. The figure for aircraft includes both operating aircraft and nonoperating aircraft (those in overhaul, transit, support, or reserve status).

4. Memo on highlights of estimates for naval appropriations for FY 1947, encl. to memo, Harold D. Smith, Director, Bureau of the Budget, to the President, 20 Mar 1946, box 158, Cabinet File, President's Secretary's File, Truman Library.

5. "Statement by Fleet Admiral Chester W. Nimitz, U. S. Navy, Chief of Naval Operations, Before the House Appropriations Committee, March 13, 1946," 5–6, box 40, 1941–1946 Double Zero Files, OA; and App. B to "Basic Post War Plan No. 2," 2; encl. to memo, CNO to Distribution List, 21 Mar 1946, "*COMINCH-CNO* Planning Material *1946*" folder, Post 1 Jan 46 Plans File, OA.

6. This amount did not include an additional $500 million that the Navy was authorized to transfer from its stock fund to its general accounts. Edward A. Kolodziej, *The Uncommon Defense and Congress, 1945–1963* (Columbus: Ohio State University Press, 1966), 50–56. Kolodziej's book provides an excellent discussion of congressional actions on defense budgets during this period.

7. "Information with reference to Fiscal Year 1948 Navy Budget Estimates," n.d. [early Feb 1947], 1–2, table A and table B; encl. to ltr from SECNAV Forrestal to Senator Chan Gurney, OP–001B ser 012P001, 7 Feb 1947, box 7, Top Policy Correspondence, RG 80, NA.

8. Kolodziej, *Uncommon Defense and Congress*, 67–70.

9. Office of Budget and Reports, Navy Department," 1949 Budget Review," 22 Aug 1947; and "Maximum Budget Ceiling, Fiscal Year 1949," 28 Jul 1947, both in box 7, Top Policy Correspondence, RG 80, NA.

10. Remarks by Congressman Charles A. Plumley, in Congress, House, Committee on Appropriations, Subcommittee on Navy Department Appropriations, *Department of the Navy Appropriation Bill for 1949: Hearings*, 80th Cong., 2d sess., 1948, 1.

11. For information on the Prague coup and Clay's war warning message, see Rearden, *The Formative Years*, 279–84.

12. See memo, Truman to SECDEF, 13 May 1948; encl. to memo, Truman to CNO, same date, box 2, 1948 Double Zero Files, OA.

13. Statement of Secretary of the Navy John L. Sullivan, in House Committee on Appropriations, Subcommittee on Navy Department Appropriations, *Department of the Navy Appropriation Bill for 1949: Supplemental Hearings*, 80th Cong., 2d sess., 1948, 3.

14. Kolodziej, *Uncommon Defense and Congress*, 88.

15. For a detailed examination of the National Military Establishment's FY 1949 budget process, see Rearden, *The Formative Years*, 309–33.

16. For good discussions on the battle over the FY 1950 defense budget, see Rearden, *The Formative Years*, 335–60; Condit, *JCS and National Policy*, 205–47; and Warner R. Schilling, "The Politics of National Defense: Fiscal 1950," in *Strategy, Politics, and Defense Budgets*, ed. Warner R. Schilling, Paul Y. Hammond, and Glenn H. Snyder (New York: Columbia University Press, 1962), 1–266.

17. See Rearden, 344, 346.

18. Entry for 8 Jan 1949, Dwight D. Eisenhower Diaries, printed in Robert H. Ferrell, *The Eisenhower Diaries* (New York: W.W. Norton, 1981), 152.

19. These memos can be found most readily in box 4 of the W. Stuart Symington Papers, Truman Library. Because of their Eyes Only designation (used by Symington to keep them out of the hands of Forrestal's "pro-Navy" assistants) they were removed from the Symington Special Interest Files now available at the National Archives' facility at the Washington National Records Center. Representative examples include Symington's eyes-only memos to Forrestal of 1 May 1948, 10 September 1948, and 28 January 1949.

20. Entry for 4 Feb 1949, Eisenhower Diaries, in Ferrell, *The Eisenhower Diaries*, 156.

21. Copy of memo, SECNAV to All Bureaus, Boards and Offices, Navy Department and Headquarters, U.S. Marine Corps, UNICOM–179, 15 Dec 1948, box 20, Burke Papers, OA. The most comprehensive account of the letter-leaking incident is found in CAPT Robert A. Rowe, USN (Ret.), "Some History of the Secretary's Committee on Unification—(UNICOM)," n.d., 8–11, same box.

22. Copy of memo, SECNAV to All Bureaus et al., 14 Jul 1948, same box.

23. BGEN Samuel R. Shaw, USMC (Ret.), interview by author, 29 Jul 1987, Alexandria, VA, tape recording.

24. Ibid.; and comments by General Shaw in ADM Arleigh A. Burke, USN (Ret.), Interview by Benis M. Frank, BGEN Samuel R. Shaw, USMC (Ret.), and COL Donald J. Decker, USMC (Ret.), 26 Jul 1983, transcript, History and Museums Division, Headquarters, U.S. Marine Corps, Washington, 18–19.

25. When asked about it years later, these reasons were among those that Admiral Burke gave for being chosen to head OP–23. Burke oral history, History and Museums Division, USMC, 12–13.

26. ADM Arleigh A. Burke, USN (Ret.), copy of corrected typed manuscript "Notes in regard to OP–23," 2, box 23, Burke Papers, OA.

27. Thackrey headed UNICOM until its disestablishment and then served as the acting head of the newly created OP–23, pending Burke's arrival.

28. Burke, *A study of OP-23 and its role in the Unification debates of 1949, Special Series: Volume IV* (Annapolis: U.S. Naval Institute, 1983), 75. This volume is a combined written account and oral history transcript dealing with the early months of OP-23. For OP-23's official mission, objectives, and functions, see encl. to memo from CNO to All Bureaus et al., OP-23 ser 1P23, 23 Dec 1948, box 3, 1948 Double Zero Files, OA.

29. Burke oral history, History and Museums Division, USMC, 17.

30. Hammond, "Super Carriers and B-36 Bombers," 505.

31. ADM Arleigh A. Burke, interview by author, 25 Sep 1986, Fairfax, VA, tape recording. See also Jeffrey G. Barlow, "The 'Revolt of the Admirals' Reconsidered," in *New Interpretations in Naval History: Selected Papers from the Eighth Naval History Symposium*, ed. William B. Cogar (Annapolis: Naval Institute Press, 1989), 232–33.

32. Emphasis in original. Manson interview, 28 Jan 1989.

33. Ibid.

34. Ltr, Burke to Mendenhall, 6 Jan 1949, "File No. 21," unnumbered box, Burke Papers, OA.

35. ADM Arleigh A. Burke, USN (Ret.), interview by author, 27 Apr 1987, Fairfax, VA, tape recording.

36. Admiral Arleigh A. Burke, USN (Ret.), copy of corrected typed manuscript, "OP-23 in 1949," A60–A61, box 22, Burke Papers, OA. These rules, which apparently were not put into written form, were provided from memory by Admiral Burke and RADM Joseph L. Howard (SC), USN (Ret.), a former OP-23 staffer.

37. For examples of some of these early assignments, see the draft article prepared by OP-23 for Secretary Sullivan's submission to *Reader's Digest*, "What It Takes to Win a War," n.d. [mid-Feb 1949]; the rough draft of a speech to be given at the Naval Academy by Admiral Radford, n.d. [mid-Feb 1949]; and the rewritten draft of a letter for Admiral Denfeld to send to Congressman Robert L. Coffey, Jr., on the 6A carrier, 14 Feb 1949 (signed and sent on 18 Feb); all in "File No. 21," unnumbered box, Burke Papers, OA.

38. Burke, "OP-23 in 1949," A49.

39. Ltr, Eberstadt to Forrestal, 31 May 1948, encl. to memo, Forrestal to SECARMY et al., 2 Jun 1948, box 5, Special Interest File 1948, Symington Special Interest Files, RG 340, NA/WNRC. The Commission on Organization of the Executive Branch of the Government (the Hoover Commission) was established by Congress in mid-1947 to investigate and make recommendations by January 1949 "on how to promote economy, efficiency and improved service in federal agencies...." *Congress and the Nation, 1945–1964: A Review of Government and Politics in the Postwar Years* (Washington: Congressional Quarterly Service, 1965), 1458. Eberstadt had accepted the offer of former President Herbert Hoover, the chairman of the commission, to head its Committee on the National Security Organization in early May 1948. See "Memorandum: Re Job for Hoover Commission," 10 May 1948, box 72, Ferdinand Eberstadt Papers, Seeley Mudd Library, Princeton University.

40. Some 245 people were interviewed in person and scores of others by telephone. See Jeffrey M. Dorwart, *Eberstadt and Forrestal: A National Security Partnership, 1909–1949* (College Station: Texas A&M University Press, 1991), 164.

41. Richard F. Haynes, *The Awesome Power: Harry S. Truman as Commander in Chief* (Baton Rouge: Louisiana State University Press, 1973), 111; and draft memo, SECNAV to SECDEF, OP-100L ser 133OP100, 14 Sep 1948, box 2, 1948 Double Zero Files, OA.

42. Memo, Symington to Forrestal, 14 Sep 1948, box 5, Special Interest File, 1948, Symington Special Interest Files, RG 340, NA/WNRC.

43. See Memo for the Record, 17 Aug 1948, 3; encl. to memo, John H. Ohly, Special Assistant to SECDEF, to SECNAV and SECAF, 19 Aug 1948, enclosed with memo, H. G. Beauregard to SECNAV et al., 23 Aug 1948, box 2, 1948 Double Zero Files, OA.

44. Regarding opposition to a strong JCS Chairman and to the emergence of a general staff, see, for example, Statement of Ferdinand Eberstadt in Congress, Senate, Committee on Armed Services,

National Security Act Amendments of 1949: Hearing on S. 1269 and S. 1843, 81st Cong., 1st sess., 24, 29 Mar; 6, 7, 11, 12 Apr; 5 and 6 May 1949, 54–56; Testimony of ADM Louis E. Denfeld (for the Joint Chiefs of Staff), ibid., 110–11; Testimony of GEN Omar N. Bradley, ibid., 116; and Statement of Herbert Hoover, ibid., 128. See also Statement of Herbert Hoover (and comments by Carl Vinson) in Congress, House, Committee on Armed Services, *Full Committee Hearings on S. 1843, To Convert the National Military Establishment Into an Executive Department of the Government, To Be Known as the Department of Defense, To Provide the Secretary of Defense With Appropriate Responsibility and Authority, and With Civilian and Military Assistants Adequate To Fulfill His Enlarged Responsibility*, 81st Cong., 1st sess., 28 Jun 1949, 2716–2718; and Statement of General Bradley, ibid., 2879–2883.

45. Ltr, Burke to Thackrey, 4 Feb 1949, "File No. 21" folder, unnumbered box, Burke Papers, OA.

46. Marx Leva interview by Jerry N. Hess, 9 Dec 1969 and 12 Jun 1970, interview 16 transcript, 40; and Wilfred J. McNeil, interview by Jerry N. Hess, 19 Sep 1972, interview 294, transcript, 102, both in Truman Library. See also the comments by Millis, *Forrestal Diaries*, 547.

47. Former Navy Secretary John Sullivan recalled: "In the previous June [1948] he was not in good shape, but he made a comeback, and in September was more like his old self. Very early in October he began issuing me contradictory orders, and from then on he went downhill, and very fast." John L. Sullivan, interviews by Jerry N. Hess, 27 Mar and 13 Apr 1972, interview 138, transcript, Truman Library, 55.

48. Emphasis in original. ADM Robert L. Dennison, interviews by Jerry N. Hess, 10 Sep 1971, 6 Oct 1971, and 2 Nov 1971, interview 105, transcript, Truman Library, 22–23. Admiral Dennison also recounted this story, with slightly more detail, in an interview with the author. ADM Robert L. Dennison, USN (Ret.), interview by author, 23 Feb 1977, Washington, DC, tape recording.

49. For information on the latter point, see the discussions in Samuel P. Huntington, *The Soldier and the State: The Theory and Politics of Civil-Military Relations* (Cambridge: The Belknap Press of Harvard University Press, 1957), 445; Morton H. Halperin, "The President and the Military," *Foreign Affairs* 50 (Jan 1972): 316; and Arnold A. Rogow, *James Forrestal: A Study of Personality, Politics, and Power* (New York: Macmillan Company, 1963), 272–73.

50. Millis, *Forrestal Diaries*, 548–49. Louis Johnson apparently was in the White House that morning and met with Forrestal following the Secretary's initial meeting with the President. Ibid.

51. Copy of letter of resignation, 2 Mar 1949, filed with entry for 2 Mar 1949, Forrestal Diaries, vol. 15, 1 Mar 1949–, 2790, box 17, Privileged Manuscript Collection, OA.

52. Pogue, *Marshall: Ordeal and Hope*, 20.

53. Quoted by Admiral Dennison; Dennison oral history, Truman Library, 31.

54. Information on Louis Johnson's background comes from the biographical entry on Johnson in Anna Rothe, ed., *Current Biography Who's News and Why 1949* (New York: H. W. Wilson, 1950), 299.

55. Johnson had been led to believe that Woodring would retire within four months of his appointment as Assistant Secretary. Glenn D. Paige, *The Korean Decision, June 24–30, 1950* (New York: Free Press, 1968), 31.

56. Pogue, *Marshall: Ordeal and Hope*, 20.

57. Consolidated's major contract in the early postwar period was for production of the B–36. Johnson spoke about his appointment to Consolidated's board of directors in his testimony at the B–36 hearings:

> During visits with President Roosevelt in late 1941, the President discussed with me the production problems of the Consolidated Aircraft Corp.... The President asked me to be his 'eyes and ears' and to keep him advised regarding Consolidated's production of aircraft. Some time later, I receive a call from the chairman of the board of Consolidated, after new management had taken over, asking me to serve on the board of directs.... I put the question to the White House.
>
> Steve Early, then Secretary to President Roosevelt, telephoned and asked me to serve on the board of directors of Consolidated. He said that was what the President wanted. I accepted and became a director as of August 13, 1942. Statement of Louis Johnson, House Armed Services Committee, *B–36 Bomber Program: Hearings*, 476–77.

338 *Notes to pages 176–180*

58. See biographical entry on Louis Johnson in Rothe, *Current Biography 1949*, 300; and Paige, *Korean Decision*, 30–31.

59. Indeed, Admiral Denfeld was aware in mid-November 1948 that Johnson was insisting that the position of Secretary of Defense was the only job he wanted. See ltr, Denfeld to RADM O. S. Colclough, Commander Submarine Force, Pacific Fleet, 20 Nov 1948, 1, box 2, Denfeld Papers, OA.

60. Emphasis added. Entry of 13 Jan 1949, Tyler Abell, ed., *Drew Pearson: Diaries, 1949–1959* (New York: Holt, Rinehart & Winston, 1974), 9.

61. He had first met Johnson in the summer of 1948 at the Bohemian Grove encampment. Ltr, Denfeld to Dudley A. White, President, Sandusky Newspapers, Inc., 28 Feb 1949, box 6, Denfeld Papers, OA.

62. Emphasis added. Ltr, Denfeld to Dennison, 9 Mar 1949, box 3, Denfeld Papers. This assurance marked a change in Admiral Denfeld's thinking. In November 1948, before he had personally talked with Louis Johnson, he had written to Ossie Colclough, "I believe that they will have to give him something, but I hope it is not the Defense job for as you know, he is very Army-minded and was a very stormy petrel when he and Woodring were in the War Department." Ltr, Denfeld to Colclough, 20 Nov 1948, 2.

63. Ltr, Holden to Denfeld, 22 Mar 1949, 3, box 3, Denfeld Papers, OA. Holden went on to assure Denfeld that because of Johnson's "political viewpoint," Holden was organizing in "a big way" for the Navy. Ibid.

64. Ltr, Eisenhower to Hazlett, 12 Aug 1949, 3, box 56, Principal File, Eisenhower Pre-Presidential Papers, Eisenhower Library.

65. The Air Force issued a press release on 11 Jan 1949 stating that it was going to buy 39 B–36 aircraft in addition to the 95 already on order. B–36 Chronology note card for date of 12 Feb 1949, box 17, Radford Papers, OA; and memo entitled "Chronology," no author [CAPT Charles D. Griffin], n.d. [Aug or Sep 1949], 2, box 21, Radford Papers.

66. Memo, Powers to CG, AMC, 17 Jan 1949, box 28, Strategic Air Group Records, RG 341, NA.

67. Memo, Symington to Forrestal, 28 Jan 1949, box 41, Vandenberg Papers, MD–LC.

68. Quoted in memo, Symington to Forrestal, 25 Feb 1949, 1, box 42, Principal File, Eisenhower Pre-Presidential Papers, Eisenhower Library. See also the extract from the Summary Minutes of the Fairchild Board; quoted in Green, "Stuart Symington and the B–36," 103–4.

69. Memo, Symington to Forrestal, 28 Jan 1949.

70. Memo, Forrestal to JCS, 3 Feb 1949, encl. to JCS 1979 of 3 Feb 1949, "1978, 1979, 1980, 1981, 1982, 1983" folder, Navy Secretariat Records, OA.

71. Memo, CAPT C. W. Wilkins, Admin. Aide to CNO, to Denfeld, OP–007 ser 174–49, 9 Feb 1949, same folder.

72. Memo, Symington to Forrestal, 4 Feb 1949, appended to memo, W. J. McNeil to JCS, 7 Feb 1949, encl. to JCS 1979/1 of 7 Jan 1949, same folder.

73. Annex B to memo, Symington to Forrestal, 4 Feb 1949.

74. Memo, Forrestal to JCS, 12 Feb 1949, encl. to JCS 1979/2 of 14 Feb 1949, same folder.

75. Memo, Denfeld (for JCS) to Forrestal, 21 Feb 1949, encl. to JCS 1979/3 of 21 Feb 1949, same folder.

76. Testimony of Marx Leva, House Armed Services Committee, *B–36 Bomber Program: Hearings*, 465. For the Committee on Aeronautics' views, see its memo to the Executive Secretary, Research and Development Board, AR 55/1.1, 11 Feb 1949; Att. D to Item 2(b), 21st Agenda, AR 55/1, Committee on Aeronautics, Research and Development Board, 28 Feb 1949, "F-8 *B–36* Research & Develop. Board Comte. On Aero. (Procurement) Top Secret" folder, Series III, OP–23 Records, OA.

77. Testimony of Marx Leva, House Armed Services Committee, *B–36 Bomber Program: Hearings*, 466.

78. According to Marx Leva, the Air Force had forecast its request in a memorandum sent to Forrestal on 23 March. Ibid., 467.

79. The Fairchild Board appointed to review the Air Force's 48 group program had found that "the B–54 offered substantial increases in speed, range, and bomb capacity" over the Air Force's existing B–29 and B–50 medium bombers. Memo, Symington to Forrestal, 25 Feb 1949, 3, box 42, Eisenhower Pre-Presidential Papers, Eisenhower Library.

80. Testimony of Marx Leva, House Armed Services Committee, *B–36 Bomber Program: Hearings*, 467.

81. Johnson's pro-Convair sympathies couldn't have hurt the Air Force's case for the program changes, but there is no evidence that it had a significant impact on his decision, one which, after all, merely followed the path set by his predecessor.

82. Millis, *Forrestal Diaries*, 551.

83. Memo, Pace to Eisenhower, 1 Apr 1949, quoted in Green, "Stuart Symington and the B–36," 128.

84. Memo, Vandenberg to Symington, 2 Apr 1949, box 32, Vandenberg Papers, MD–LC.

85. Ibid.

86. Memo, Johnson to Pace, 2 Apr 1949, quoted in Green, "Stuart Symington and the B–36," 128.

87. Memo on JCS actions in connection with flush-deck carrier and B–36 bomber programs, Burke to Radford, n.d. [Aug or Sep 1949], box 19, Radford Papers, OA; and B–36 Chronology note card for date of 5 Apr 1949, box 17, Radford Papers.

88. This kind of spur-of-the-moment decision making by a Chief, without the benefit of having been briefed on the issue by his staff, often leads to decisions which are contrary to a service's interests.

89. Memo, Burke to Radford, n.d. [Aug or Sep 1949]; and memo from CAPT Fitzhugh Lee to Radford, 12 Aug 1949, attached to memo entitled "Chronology," n.d. [Aug 1949], box 21, Radford Papers.

90. Memorandum for the Press from Department of the Air Force, No. 161, 5 Apr 1949, "M–1 B–36 News Released thru April 1949" folder, Series I, OP–23 Records, OA. An advance copy of the press release had been given to General Vandenberg the previous day. Memo, Lee to Radford, 12 Aug 1949, box 21, Radford Papers.

91. Decision on JCS 1979/4, 9 Apr 1949; "1978, 1979, 1980, 1981, 1982, 1983" folder, Navy Secretariat Records, OA.

92. Emphasis in original. Memo, Eisenhower to Forrestal, n.d. [21 Dec 1948], box 42, Principal File, Eisenhower Pre-Presidential Papers, Eisenhower Library.

93. Diary entry, 27 Jan 1949, Louis Galambos, ed., *The Papers of Dwight David Eisenhower*, vol. 10, *Columbia University* (Baltimore: Johns Hopkins University Press, 1984), 336. General Eisenhower told President Truman in early February 1949 that the Air Force-Navy conflict was "professional and almost political" in nature. Briefing outline marked "Notes I used in conversation with Pres. on Feb. 9, 1949," box 116, Principal File, Eisenhower Pre-Presidential Papers, Eisenhower Library.

94. For Eisenhower's request and the Navy's response, see ltrs, Eisenhower to Denfeld, 3 Jan 1949; Denfeld to Eisenhower, 10 Jan 1949, and Denfeld to Eisenhower, 28 Jan 1949, all in box 34, same file.

95. Diary entry, 2 Feb 1949, in Galambos, *Eisenhower Papers* 10:461.

96. Undoubtedly a major source of Eisenhower's view was the extensive briefing on the need for aircraft carriers that he received on 1 February. See Memorandum for File, LT Robert A. Rowe, OP–23, 3 Feb 1949, "File No. 21," unnumbered box, Burke Papers, OA; and Captain Robert A. Rowe, telephone interview by author, 22 Apr 1989, Rancho Palos Verdes, CA, tape recording.

97. Air Force opposition to the maintenance of a significant number of fleet carriers first became apparent during the preparation of service positions on the FY 1950 budget. The Air Force proposed that the Navy be allowed to retain only four of the current (FY 1949) eleven fleet carriers on active status, under the $14.4 billion budget required by President Truman. For a discussion of the fight in the JCS over the FY 1950 budget, see Condit, *JCS and National Policy* 2:205–47.

98. Draft memo (by Leach), Vandenberg to SECDEF, 8 Feb 1949, attached to memo from Leach to Vandenberg, 9 Feb 1949, box 7, Symington Papers, Truman Library. Other copies of this memo are in box 52, Vandenberg Papers, MD–LC.

99. Memo, Leach to Vandenberg, 31 Mar 1949, same box.

100. Draft memo, Vandenberg to Forrestal, 8 Feb 1949.

101. Emphasis added. Memo, Leach to Vandenberg, 31 Mar 1949.

102. Ltr, Leach to Symington, 11 Apr 1949, box 7, Symington Papers, Truman Library.

103. Ltr, Johnson to Eisenhower, 15 Apr 1949, 1, box 62, Principal File, Eisenhower Pre-Presidential Papers, Eisenhower Library. President Truman had approved assigning the name USS *United States* to the 6A carrier on 2 Feb 1949.

104. Ibid.

105. Ibid., 3.

106. Knowing that the individual Chiefs had received copies of the letter, Eisenhower did not write to the JCS on the matter until 20 Apr 1949. By that time the JCS had already met to discuss the issue. For Eisenhower's message to the JCS, see memo, Eisenhower to Bradley et al., 20 Apr 1949, box 62, Principal File, Eisenhower Pre-Presidential Papers, Eisenhower Library. See also his letter to Secretary Johnson of the same date, contained in same box.

107. The Joint Chiefs of Staff had journeyed down to meet with Eisenhower at Key West in early April. During a series of meetings on the FY 1950 and FY 1951 budgets, which took place from 8–12 April, the subject of the carrier was discussed, "though," according to Louis Johnson, "not in any great detail." Testimony of Louis Johnson; House Committee on Armed Services, *The National Defense Program—Unification and Strategy: Hearings*, 81st Cong., 1st sess., GPO, 1949, 619. See also Galambos, *Eisenhower Papers* 10:551–52n.

108. Admiral Radford recalled that he was relieved by John Dale Price on 16 April and "left Washington that same day." Radford Autobiography [2]:613.

109. Note from Wilkins to Price, 16 Apr 1949, attached to Denfeld's copy of SM–673–49, with encl., box 36, JCS Office Files, Navy Secretariat Records, OA. The note went on to say, "[Admiral Denfeld] said if you wish to talk to him about it he would be glad to see you Monday a.m." Ibid.

110. Sullivan oral history, Truman Library, 58–59. In this interview Sullivan mistakenly recalled that the meeting had taken place on Wednesday, which would have made the date it occurred the 20th, not the 18th of April.

111. Multilith copy of ltr, Sullivan to Johnson, 26 Apr 1949, box 6, Denfeld Papers, OA. Sullivan's letter is also printed in House Armed Services Committee, *Unification and Strategy: Hearings*, 622–23.

112. Sullivan oral history, Truman Library, 59.

113. See the press accounts of the keel-laying summarized from stories in the *New York Herald Tribune*, the *Washington Post* (AP), and the *Washington Times-Herald* (UPI), 19 Apr 1949, in "Pertinent Press Items for Attention of Secretary Johnson"—4/20, box 237, Analysis Branch, Office of Public Information, Assistant Secretary of Defense (Legislative & Public Affairs) Records (hereafter PIO–OSD Records), Secretary of Defense Records (RG 330), NA; and att. to memo, CAPT Lewis S. Parks, Aide to Under SECNAV, to Secretary Sullivan, 20 Apr 1949, box 6, 1949 Double Zero Files, OA.

114. Memo, Gruenther to Denfeld et al., DM–131, 18 Apr 1949, sec. 1 (only section), CCS 561 (5–26–48), RG 218, NA; and Condit, *JCS and National Policy* 2:317.

115. Ltr, Leach to Symington, 20 Apr 1949, 1–3, box 7, Symington Papers, Truman Library.

116. Memo, CAPT W. R. Hollingsworth, Admin. Aide to VCNO, to Radford, 22 Apr 1949, 2, box 25, Radford Papers, OA.

117. Draft memo for SECDEF, n.d. [21 Apr 1949], 1, box 36, JCS Office Files, Navy Secretariat Records, OA. Written on the draft in pencil is the following note: "Prepared by 05 [DCNO (Air)] Rejected by 00 [CNO] and rewritten as ser 002P00 of 4/22/49."

118. Ibid., 4.

119. Memo, Hollingsworth to Radford, 22 Apr 1949.

120. Penciled comment on memo from Hollingsworth to Radford, ibid. The hurried nature of this request is shown by the fact that as late as 19 April, Captain Burke was informing his boss, Rear Admiral Wellborn, DCNO (Administration), that OP-23 had the job of preparing the Navy's presentation to the JCS on the 6A carrier and hoped to have it ready by Monday, 25 April. Memo, Burke to Wellborn, 19 Apr 1949, "File No. 23" folder, unnumbered box, Burke Papers, OA.

121. Typed copy [on JCS letterhead] of memo, Lalor to Gruenther, 14 Oct 1949, box 36, JCS Office Files, Navy Secretariat Records, OA.

122. Memo, Denfeld to SECDEF, OP-00 ser 0002P00, 22 Apr 1949, encl. to memo from COL John H. Ives, Deputy Secretary JCS, to Denfeld et al., SM-714-49, 23 Apr 1949, CCS 561 (5-26-48), RG 218, NA.

123. Memo, Lalor to Gruenther, 14 Oct 1949.

124. See draft memo for SECDEF; encl. to memo, Lalor to Leahy et al., SM-10221, 27 May 1948, CCS 561 (5-26-48), RG 218, NA.

125. Memo from Bradley to SECDEF, 22 Apr 1949; encl. to SM-714-49, 23 Apr 1949. Bradley had also noted that the planes of a carrier task force possessed the capability "of penetrating 700 miles inland." He agreed with this capability but argued that this was sufficient, given the limited usefulness of carrier aircraft against land targets. Ibid.

126. Memo, Lalor to Gruenther, 14 Oct 1949.

127. Memo, Vandenberg to SECDEF, 23 Apr 1949; encl. to SM-714-49, 23 Apr 1949, CCS 561 (5-26-48), RG 218, NA.

128. Ibid. A penciled note at the bottom of SM-714-49 states, "Capt. Stephens says their records indicate the SECDEF's office signed [for the documents] at exactly 1030."

129. Memo, Burke to Radford, n.d. [Aug or Sep 1949], 6-7. The press release obviously had been prepared some hours earlier. See Vice Admiral Herbert D. Riley's recollection from his Naval Institute oral history, as quoted in Paolo E. Coletta, *The United States Navy and Defense Unification, 1947-1953* (Newark: University of Delaware Press, 1981), 138. On this point, see also Stacy V. Jones, "The inside story of the big carrier that wasn't built...," *Liberty*, Aug 1949, 40.

130. Emphasis added. Memo, Johnson to SECNAV, 23 Apr 1949; encl. to memo, Lalor to Denfeld et al., SM-715-49, 25 Apr 1949, CCS 561 (5-26-48), RG 218, NA. For the press release, see "Memorandum to the Press No. M-17-49, 23 Apr 1949", "A7-1/10-1 SECDEF M Series" folder, Series I, OP-23 Records, OA.

131. Johnson admitted in testimony before the House Armed Services Committee that he made his decision on the fate of the carrier on the evening of 22 April—which, of course, is before he had received the official copies of the Chiefs' memoranda. See House Armed Services Committee, *Unification and Strategy: Hearings*, 620. However, his actual decision clearly appears to have antedated 22 April by some days.

132. See the testimony of Louis Johnson, ibid., 619-20. Although he may have seen earlier versions of material incorporated into the final Air Force memorandum, given his closeness to Stuart Symington at the time, he is unlikely to have seen preliminary drafts of the final memo because the Air Force was rushed in getting it finished on Friday. A final comment that should be made about the Defense Secretary's veracity on this issue is that Johnson could not have read the individual service views in a *finished* form, whether in draft or otherwise, before they were delivered to his office on the morning of 23 April. This fact is documented by an internal JCS memorandum that the Secretary of the Joint Chiefs of Staff sent to the Director of the Joint Staff later in 1949. In this memo Captain Lalor stated that prior to the time that the official memoranda were sent to the Secretary of Defense's office at 10:30 on the morning of 23 April, "no copies of the individual Chiefs' views were shown by Ives or myself to anyone outside of your office or our offices." Memo, Lalor to Gruenter, 14 Oct 1949.

133. Sullivan oral history, Truman Library, 59. See also Admiral Denfeld's testimony, House Armed Services Committee, *Unification and Strategy: Hearings*, 360.

134. In his OSD history, Steven Rearden stated that Eisenhower had recommended canceling the project. *The Formative Years*, 412 and 607n. An examination of Eisenhower's folders of correspon-

dence with Johnson, however, demonstrates this was not the case. Eisenhower's short note to Johnson telling him that he had referred the matter to the Chiefs is the only communication Eisenhower had with Johnson between the receipt of Johnson's letter asking Eisenhower to have the Chiefs reexamine the question of the 6A carrier and the receipt of a second Johnson letter informing Eisenhower of the Secretary's decision to cancel the carrier. Further, Johnson's letter to Eisenhower of 25 April, detailing his decision on the carrier, makes it clear that there had been no telephone conversation with Eisenhower during the intervening period. Johnson's letter noted:

> Many thanks for your letter of April 20. As you have seen from the newspapers, the Joint Chiefs did not delay their decision on the super aircraft carrier. They submitted their views to me on Friday, the 22nd [*sic*], and after consideration and consultation with the President, I directed the Navy on Saturday to take action to discontinue work on the ship. Ltr, Johnson to Eisenhower, 25 Apr 1949, box 62, Principal File, Eisenhower Pre-Presidential Papers, Eisenhower Library.

135. See ltr, Eisenhower to his friend Swede Hazlett, 27 Apr 1949, box 56, same file.

136. In his testimony before the House Armed Services Committee in October 1949, Johnson prefaced his specific comments on the cancellation decision with a discussion of the savings he was hoping to achieve in defense spending. This statement, coupled with the general climate of budget cutbacks in 1949 and early 1950, led people to speculate that the flush-deck carrier had been canceled by Johnson largely for budgetary reasons.

137. See Rearden, *The Formative Years*, 411–12; and David A. Rosenberg, "American Postwar Air Doctrine and Organization, Navy Experience," 258.

138. Davis Merwin, former publisher of the *Minneapolis Star*, was at the time the owner and publisher of the *Daily Pantagraph* (Bloomington, IL). Merwin, a Marine veteran, was a strong supporter of naval aviation. Part of his access in Washington may have existed because Adlai Stevenson was his first cousin and close friend.

139. Emphasis added. Copy of ltr, Merwin to COL John H. Hinrichs, USA, 8 Nov 1949, 2, box 17, Radford Papers, OA. Merwin provided the earliest and most complete account of his one-and-a-quarter-hour meeting with Secretary Johnson in a letter five days after the meeting to his close friend John Cowles, the owner of the Des Moines and Minneapolis newspapers and *Look* magazine:

> The other impolitic statement by Johnson that left me flabbergasted, was that naval strikes from carriers would be limited definitely and permanently to a 750 mile radius. Johnson said that the current radius was of the order of 530 miles, and that he was thus being generous in allowing an extension of the distance.... As Johnson put it, the question was not one of spending more money to get the additional radius, it was rather a slightly heated announcement of his determination to keep the Navy from encroaching.... I asked Johnson his reasons and he said the Navy wasn't going to be allowed to get into strategic bombing. Copy of ltr, Merwin to Cowles, 27 Jun 1949, enclosed with ltr, Merwin to Radford, 4 Dec 1949, 2–3, box 50, Radford Papers.

Following his interview with the Defense Secretary, David Merwin was handed over to the Air Force by Louis Johnson for a three-hour briefing (Merwin termed it an "indoctrination") on the B–36.

140. Transcript entitled "Telephone Conservation Between Mr. Sullivan and Mr. W. John Kenney 1441 April 26, 1949", Secretary Sullivan's Daily Log, box 9, John L. Sullivan Papers, Truman Library. This document was supplied to the author by archivist Dennis Bilger of the Truman Library following the opening of the Sullivan Papers in November 1990.

141. Memo, Sullivan to the President, 24 Apr 1949, box 158, Cabinet File, President's Secretary's File, Truman Library.

142. Dennison oral history, Truman Library, 107. See also Sullivan oral history, Truman Library 62.

143. ADM Robert L. Dennison, USN (Ret.), interviews by John T. Mason, Jr., 8 Nov 1972, 9 Jan 1973, 17 Jan 1973, 30 Jan 1973, 27 Mar 1973, 11 Apr 1973, 9 May 1973, 12 Jun 1973, 10 Jul 1973, 17 Jul 1973, and 25 Jul 1973, transcript, U.S. Naval Institute, Annapolis, MD, 188. In his oral history done the pre-

vious year for the Truman Library, Dennison had said that he couldn't remember if Ross had come to the office or had talked with Sullivan on the phone. Dennison oral history, Truman Library, 108.

144. Ibid.

145. Fitzhugh Lee, interviews by Etta-Belle Kitchen, 11 Jul 1970 and 9 Aug 1970, Coronado, CA, transcript, U.S. Naval Institute, Annapolis, MD, 199–200.

146. The President met with Sullivan and the others at 11:45 a.m. The meeting lasted for less than fifteen minutes. See entry for 25 Apr 1949, 1949 Daily Sheets, President's Appointment Schedule, box 91, President's Secretary's File, Truman Library.

147. Sullivan oral history, Truman Library, 62, 74.

148. Ibid., 62–63. See also Dennison oral history, Truman Library, 107–8; and Dennison oral history, USNI, 187–88. In his oral history, Sullivan mistakenly said that Ross's visit had occurred on a Wednesday. The 26th, however, was a Tuesday.

149. Ltr, Sullivan to Johnson, 26 Apr 1949.

150. Ibid.

151. The time of the White House announcement of Sullivan's resignation is taken from Sullivan's comment to Kenney in "Telephone Conversation Between Sullivan and Kenney, 26 Apr 1949, 1441."

152. See "Pertinent Radio Items for Attention of Secretary Johnson"—4/27; and "Pertinent Press Items for Attention of Secretary Johnson"—4/28, box 237, PIO–OSD Records, RG 330, NA.

153. Ltr, Merwin to Cowles, 27 Jun 1949, 2.

154. Ibid. Johnson told the House Armed Services Committee:

> Mr. Sullivan was not for unification, would not support unification and I believe on March 26 [sic], two days before I was sworn in . . . he tendered to the President of the United States his resignation as Secretary of the Navy and knew it was accepted, because he was not in accord with unification and because I had told him there was no room on my team on the civilian side for anybody who wouldn't loyally and enthusiastically support unification. Testimony by Louis Johnson, House Armed Services Committee, *Unification and Strategy: Hearings*, 622.

This half-truth was repeated by Steven Rearden in his *The Formative Years*, 412n. While it is true that Sullivan had submitted a letter of resignation to the President on 24 March, it was a *pro forma* letter sent to coincide with James Forrestal's departure as Secretary of Defense. In mid-April 1949 Sullivan had no intention of resigning as Secretary of the Navy. Furthermore, his resignation had not been accepted by President Truman. The earlier resignation letter is printed in the House hearings, ibid., 623. During late 1948 and early 1949, John Sullivan apparently had thought of leaving his Navy post, possibly for another job in the administration, but by April 1949 he had decided to stay on as SECNAV. See ltr, Denfeld to Colclough, 20 Nov 1948, 1 and ltr, Denfeld to RADM R. E. Byrd, 12 Jan 1949, both in box 2; and ltr, Denfeld to Dennison, 9 Mar 1949, box 3, Denfeld Papers, OA.

155. See typed carbon "Remarks by Secretary John L. Sullivan at departure ceremony today: 24 May 1949," box 25, Radford Papers, OA; and the "period in office" entry for Kenney in the untitled, typed list of Secretaries, Under Secretaries, and Assistant Secretaries of the Navy, n.d. [late 1951], [3], box 3, Dan A. Kimball Papers, Truman Library. Sullivan had also asked Admiral Denfeld to resign, since he thought that this would strengthen further the impact of his resignation in protest. Denfeld declined, because he felt that he "would help the Navy better by staying." Sullivan oral history, Truman Library, 64–65.

156. Louis H. Renfrow, interviews by Jerry N. Hess, 12 and 15 Mar 1971, interview 99, transcript, Truman Library, 112–13. Renfrow, an American Legion crony of Johnson's, was then serving the Secretary as Special Assistant.

157. Emphasis added. "Remarks by Secretary John L. Sullivan at departure ceremony."

158. Memorandum of Information, CAPT W. R. Hollingsworth [given to CDR M. U. Beebe for Radford], 31 May 1949, [3], box 25, Radford Papers, OA.

7. The Navy's Troubles Increase

1. The view that Johnson may have been behind Radford's departure has been suggested most recently, although implicitly rather than explicitly, by Michael Palmer in his short history, *Origins of the Maritime Strategy*, 48, 105 n.

2. On 18 March 1949 Ramsey wrote the letter to Denfeld detailing his retirement plans. In a message to the department a week later, he changed the proposed date for his retirement from 1 July to 1 May 1949. Msg, CINCPACFLT to BUPERS and CNO, 242031Z Mar 1949, box 4, Denfeld Double Zero Papers, OA.

3. See Radford Autobiography, [2]: 608. It should be noted that Denfeld's decision was made some days before Louis Johnson became Secretary of Defense.

4. Ltr, Radford to Doyle, 20 May 1949, box 56, Radford Papers, OA. Many of these same points were made in other letters to his friends. See, for example, ltr, Radford to MGEN Merritt A. Edson, USMC (Ret.), 15 Apr 1949; and ltr, Radford to John W. Avirett, 2d, 14 May 1949, both in box 29, Radford Papers. On the question of Symington's role, see the harshly anti-Radford Eyes Only memo, Symington to Forrestal, 22 Nov 1948, box 4, Symington Papers, Truman Library.

5. See Radford Autobiography [2]: 607–8.

6. Emphasis in original. Manson interview, 28 Jan 1989.

7. Ibid. Captain Manson went on to note, however: "As the years rolled on after that, and then the Korean War [started], Admiral Struble changed. He was out there using those carriers [as COM-SEVENTHFLT].... And he became ... [a] much stronger ... supporter of the carrier arm of the Navy." Ibid.

8. The list of officers in attendance is taken from Memorandum for File from LT Robert A. Rowe, OP–23, 3 Feb 1949, 1, "File No. 21," unnumbered box, Burke Papers, OA.

9. Ltr, Denfeld to Eisenhower, 28 Jan 1949, box 34, Principal File, Eisenhower Pre-Presidential Papers, Eisenhower Library.

10. The length of the briefing session and the knowledge that Eisenhower was briefed on undersea warfare at the same session come from a memo written by RADM Charles Wellborn, Jr., DCNO (Administration), who was with Eisenhower during the entire four-day Navy briefing program. Memo, Wellborn to ADM John Towers, 5 Feb 1949, 1, attached to original, signed copy of Rowe's memo of 3 Feb 1949, "A1/EM–3/4 Navy S&C" folder, Series II, OP–23 Records, OA.

11. Rowe interview.

12. Struble stayed on as DCNO (Operations) into 1950 for a variety of reasons. They probably included Radford's sudden departure from OPNAV for new duty and Denfeld's likely unwillingness to bring in a new DCNO (Operations) at a time when he was already working under the handicap of having a new Navy Secretary and a new Vice Chief of Naval Operations.

13. Ltr, Reeves to Radford, 8 Aug 1949, box 36, Radford Papers, OA.

14. Ibid.

15. Ltr, Reeves to Radford, 22 Aug 1949, same box.

16. Ltr, Radford to Reeves, 30 Aug 1949, same box.

17. Emphasis added. Memo, Vandenberg to McKee, n.d. [early Mar 1949], box 97, Vandenberg Papers, MD–LC.

18. Ibid.

19. Ibid. Vandenberg concluded his memorandum by noting,

> I realize only too well that this is strong stuff, loaded with explosives. On the other hand, so long as we believe that the national security is not being assured ... we cannot be peaceful. *We should continue the fight and carry it to the public in the same aggressive manner so ably demonstrated by Mr. Symington in the past.*" Emphasis added. Ibid.

20. Handwritten notes in General Knerr's hand (prepared for a talk?), entitled "Gremlins in the Defense Department," n.d. [Spring 1949?], [4–5], box 11, Knerr Papers, MD–LC.

21. Knerr notes, [6–7].

22. Ibid., [7].

23. At the time, it had about 15 million subscribers and 60 million readers.

24. Ltr, Palmer to Spaatz, 23 Nov 1948, box 29, Spaatz Papers, MD–LC. See also ltr, Spaatz to Palmer, 9 Dec 1948, same box.

25. William Bradford Huie, "Which Is the Bulwark in This Atomic Age?—A Navy—Or An Air Force?" *Reader's Digest*, Dec 1948, reprinted in House Armed Services Committee, *B–36 Bomber Program: Hearings*, 580.

26. Ltr, Karig to Dashiell, 26 Nov 1948, box 2, Kimball Papers, Truman Library.

27. Memo, Karig to Under SECNAV, n.d. [21 Dec 1948], ibid.

28. For the other three articles by Huie, see "'Let Americans Take Heart'—The Facts Which Must Prevent War," *Reader's Digest*, Jan 1949; "Our Best Hope for Peace: Why We Must Have the World's Best Air Force," *Reader's Digest*, Mar 1949; and "Here Is Proof That For 40 Years the People Have Been Right, and the Army and Navy Bureaucrats Have Been Wrong, in the Struggle for American Air Power," *Reader's Digest*, Apr 1949; all reprinted in House Armed Services Committee, *B–36 Bomber Program: Hearings*, 583–97.

29. Ltr, Alsop to Sommers, 12 Jan 1949, [3], box 26, Joseph and Stewart Alsop Papers, MD–LC. It should be noted that the Alsop brothers were strong supporters of the 70-Group Air Force.

30. Planned expenditure on *United States* during FY 1950 was to be $27.5 million—22 percent of the $124,855,000 total estimated cost. Unmarked chart on costs of the new ships in the FY 1949 shipbuilding and conversion program, n.d. [Dec 1948], box 3, Denfeld Double Zero Files, OA.

31. The Navy originally had requested $225 million for its FY 1950 shipbuilding and conversion program. This amount covered the cost of 33 new vessels (28 of them LVTs [Landing Vehicles Tracked]) and 29 conversions, including two *Essex*-class carriers to be modernized to the 27A configuration. A revised Navy request for $52 million for the FY 1950 shipbuilding and conversion program (a reduction of $173 million over its original request), together with $279 million to cover the increased costs of the FY 1949 and prior year programs, was eventually approved by the Bureau of the Budget. See memo, CNO to SECNAV, OP–414 ser 0504P414, 4 Dec 1948, box 2, 1948 Double Zero Files, OA; and memo, RADM H. G. Hopwood, Director of Budget and Reports, to SECNAV, no ser, 15 Feb 1949, with attached copy of memo, Frank Pace, Jr., Director, Bureau of the Budget, to SECDEF, 10 Feb 1949, box 5, Denfeld Double Zero Files, OA.

32. The 27A configuration was designed to enable the *Essex*-class carriers to operate heavy aircraft (up to take-off weight of 52,500 lbs. fully loaded [for the AJ–1]), jet aircraft, and pilotless aircraft.

33. Memo, Denfeld to SECNAV, OP–414 ser 0203P414, 3 May 1949, box 25, Radford Papers, OA.

34. Ibid.

35. Copy of ltr, Kimball to Johnson, 4 May 1949; encl. to memo, W. J. McNeil to JCS, 16 May 1949, CCS 561 (5–26–48), RG 218, NA.

36. Memo, McNeil to JCS, 16 May 1949.

37. Memo, Lalor to Denfeld et al., SM–900–49, 17 May 1949, CCS 561 (5–26–48), RG 218, NA..

38. Emphasis added. Memo, Vandenberg to SECDEF, 26 Apr 1949, box 52, Vandenberg Papers, MD–LC.

39. Unsigned memo, OP–05 to OP–09, 23 May 1949, box 4, Denfeld Double Zero Files, OA.

40. Memorandum of Information from Hollingsworth [for Radford], 31 May 1949, [4], box 25, Radford Papers, OA.

41. Ibid.

42. Ibid.

43. Memo, Struble to Wedemeyer et al., 1 Jun 1949, box 52, Vandenberg Papers, MD–LC. Struble's proposed compromise paper consisted of three sections, labeled a, b, and c. Section a was a statement that the JCS recommended approval of supplemental priorities 2, 3, and 4. Section b was a one-paragraph Navy view supporting approval of priority 1 (the CV conversions). Section c was left blank by Struble for the inclusion of the Army and Air Force views on priority 1.

44. Memo, BGEN Joseph Smith, Acting Director, Plans and Operations, to Vandenberg, 2 Jun 1949, same box.

45. Francis Matthews had reported on board on 25 May.

46. Typed note by Hollingsworth, stapled to typed copy of memo from JCS to SECDEF, 2 Jun 1949, box 25, Radford Papers, OA; and entry of 6 Jun 1949, 1949 Daily Log of Secretary of the Navy Francis P. Matthews (hereafter Matthews Daily Log), box 43, Francis P. Matthews Papers, Truman Library.

47. Emphasis in original. Memo, SECNAV to SECDEF, OP–05B ser 0005P05, 6 Jun 1949, 1–2, box 41, DCNO (Air) Records, OA. This memo, dictated after the meeting by Rear Admiral J. H. Cassady, ACNO (Air), was a summary of the points that had been orally presented to the Defense Secretary.

48. Hollingsworth note stapled to memo of 2 Jun 1949.

49. Ibid.

50. Memo, Denfeld (for JCS) to SECDEF, 10 Jun 1949, CCS 561 (5–26–48), RG 218, NA.

51. Memo, Johnson to SECARMY, et al., 13 Jun 1949, same section.

52. Typewritten note stapled to typed copy of SECDEF's untitled draft speech, n.d., box 25, Radford Papers, OA.

53. For the gist of the arguments likely presented by Admiral Carney, see memo, CNO to SECNAV, OP–04 ser 00048P04, 16 Jun 1949, "A21/1–1/1 Carrier *Top Secret*" folder, Series III, OP–23 Records, OA. Admiral Carney drafted this memorandum for Admiral Denfeld's signature.

54. Carney interview.

55. Ibid.

56. National Military Establishment, Office of Public Information Release No. 35–49S, "Address by Louis Johnson, Secretary of Defense, Before the National War College," 21 Jun 1949, 4, encl. to memo, CAPT H. E. Sears, Acting Chief of Public Relations, to CNO, 23 Jun 1949, box 5, 1949 Double Zero Files, OA; and Rearden, *The Formative Years*, 412. To assure surprise for the announcement, the news of the approval of the carrier modernization had intentionally been left out of the printed version of Johnson's speech distributed ahead of time to the press.

57. Kimball had been appointed to a position in the Navy Department in March 1949. He had fleeted up from Assistant Secretary of the Navy for Air to Under Secretary only two and a half months later, when Secretary Sullivan and Under Secretary Kenney resigned in protest of the flush-deck carrier's cancellation.

58. For information on Kimball's background and thinking at the time he took over as Assistant SECNAV (Air), see Robert Hotz, "Navy Air Boss Once Army Pilot," *Aviation Week*, 21 Mar 1949, 14–15.

59. Ltr, Kimball to Hecht, 21 Jun 1949, box 3, Kimball Papers, Truman Library.

60. Emphasis added. Note, Kimball to Early, 21 Jun 1949, same box.

61. Assistant Secretary of the Air Force Eugene M. Zuckert remarked, "I think Johnson became inordinately concerned with how he would look in the press and on the Hill. I think he thought that the job really depended—this maybe is a cruel overstatement—but depended more upon his public relations than on what he did." Eugene M. Zuckert, interview by Jerry N. Hess, 27 Sep 1971, interview 107, transcript, Truman Library, 25. See also ltr, Eisenhower to Swede Hazlett, 24 Feb 1950, 4, box 56, Principal File, Eisenhower Pre-Presidential Papers, Eisenhower Library. Comments on Johnson's political posturing on defense matters in the hopes of succeeding Truman as President can also be found in a number of Air Force memoranda in Hoyt Vandenberg's papers.

62. This action would avoid any political fallout over the issue of replacing a prominent Catholic. Truman's Naval Aide remarked, "Well, this was Johnson's reasoning, you see. There might be a kickback. Sullivan resigns and he was a Catholic, so the thing to do is put in another Catholic. That was the primary requirement, a political requirement, of course." Dennison oral history, USNI, 195.

63. Sullivan oral history, Truman Library, 73.

64. Matthews had been a member of the executive committee of the National Conference of Catholic Charities from 1931 to 1934 and had been the Supreme Knight of the Knights of Columbus from 1939 to 1945. Biographical entry on Francis Matthews in Rothe, ed., *Current Biography Who's News and Why 1949*, 413–14.

65. Ltr, Right Reverend Maurice Sheehy to Radford, 17 May 1949, box 53, Radford Papers, OA. See also ltr, Sheehy to Radford, 7 May 1949.

66. Ltr, Sheehy to Radford, 17 May 1949, same box.

67. Griffin interview, 10 Dec 1985.

68. At his first news conference in Omaha, Nebraska, after being named Secretary, Matthews was asked by a reporter what experience he had had with the Navy. He replied, "Well, nothing, except—and this is off-the-record—I own a rowboat up at my summer home [in Minnesota]." Quoted in John A. Giles, "The Navy's Secretary Walks Alone," *Washington Evening Star*, 23 Oct 1949, C-2.

69. Certain observers to the events of the "revolt of the admirals" have long believed that the Anonymous Document was the product of the efforts of a sizeable number of people in the Navy Department, perhaps including high Navy officials. This viewpoint has been put forth consistently in writings by Air Force proponents. This view notwithstanding, a detailed investigation of all of the relevant Navy records relating to its role in the events of 1949 and interviews with many of the key participants fail to reveal that anyone other than Worth and Davies knowingly participated in drafting the Anonymous Document.

70. Typed biographical statement (on Under SECNAV letterhead), "Cedric Worth Special Assistant to the Under Secretary of the Navy," n.d. [late Jun–early Jul 1949] (hereafter Worth biographical data), box 1, Kimball Papers, Truman Library; and testimony of Cedric Worth, House Armed Services Committee, *B-36 Bomber Program: Hearings*, 546–52.

71. Typed list of Secretaries, Under Secretaries, and Assistant Secretaries of the Navy, n.d. [late 1951], [5]; and Worth biographical data.

72. Worth biographical data; and testimony of Captain David L. McDonald, Third Day, 7 Sep 1949, transcript of Court of Inquiry "to inquire into circumstances surrounding preparation of anonymous document furnished members of Congress concerning contracts for B-36 aircraft and other matters" (hereafter Naval Court of Inquiry), 66 (numbering is sequential throughout document), copy 32 of multilith document, "H-1 *B-36* Naval Court of Inquiry *Top Secret*" folder, Series III, OP-23 Records, OA. This was OP-23's file copy of the transcript.

73. In a paper on the "revolt of the admirals" delivered to the U.S. Naval Academy's Eighth Naval History Symposium in 1987, the author (basing his remarks on an interview with Admiral Davies) argued that Davies had not taken an active part in drafting the Anonymous Document. Indeed, Admiral Davies had told the author:

> I had no idea what Cedric was going to do with the information [I had given him about the technical aspects of the B-36], and, as a matter of fact, I was completely taken aback when he showed me the document that he had written, which had all kinds of stuff in it which I hadn't told him.... [H]e showed it to me just a few hours before he handed it to [Congressman] Van Zandt." Rear Admiral Thomas D. Davies, USN (Ret.), interview by author, 11 Aug 1987, Washington, DC, tape recording.

Nonetheless, subsequent interviews by the author with Captain Frank Manson, Stuart Barber, and Admiral Arleigh Burke, together with a careful rereading of the transcript of the Navy Court of Inquiry on the preparation of the Anonymous Document, now lead the author to believe that Admiral Davies' role in drafting the document was more pivotal than he was willing to acknowledge, even thirty-eight years later. For the author's original comments on this issue, see Barlow, "'The Revolt of the Admirals' Reconsidered," 234.

74. Davies' testimony, Second Day, 6 Sep 1949, Naval Court of Inquiry, 24.

75. Davies interview; and Burke interview, 27 Apr 1987. Davies had been assigned to UNICOM in an additional-duty capacity in early December 1948 and was kept on when UNICOM's people were transferred to OP–23.

76. Paul Hammond asserted that Davies was the assistant head of OP–23. Paul Y. Hammond, "Super Carriers and B–36 Bombers, 506. But this was not true. In fact, Captain Calvin E. Wakeman served as OP–23's assistant head or executive officer but more by reason of position as the next senior officer in the division than because OP–23 required a highly formalized chain of command.

77. Manson interview, 28 Jan 1989.

78. The effort began at least as early as the first week in April 1949. Several of the rumors contained in the Anonymous Document were told to Tom Davies by James Maher of Lockheed Aircraft during Davies' visit to California from 3 to 10 April 1949. Commander Davies attempted to obtain additional information confirming these rumors as soon as he returned to Washington. Davies' testimony, Second Day, 6 Sep 1949, Naval Court of Inquiry, 29–33.

79. Testimony of Harold Mosier, Fourth Day, 8 Sep 1949, Naval Court of Inquiry, 108.

80. There is no exact date for the completion of the Anonymous Document. In his testimony before the House Armed Services Committee Cedric Worth could remember only that it was available some time in April 1949. Testimony of Cedric Worth, House Armed Services Committee, *B–36 Bomber Program: Hearings*, 535.

81. The numbered sections were preceded by three unnumbered introductory paragraphs. The "Anonymous Document"—mimeograph copy of untitled paper, n.d. [Apr 1949]; att. to memo (on SECAF letterhead notepaper) from COL Glenn W. Martin, executive to Secretary of the Air Force, to Clark Clifford, White House, 22 JUL 1949, box 11, Clark M. Clifford Papers, Truman Library. This paper appears to be one of the original copies of the Anonymous Document given to one of the members of Congress by Cedric Worth. In coming to this conclusion, the author has compared this paper with a variety of other copies, including another mimeographed version (clearly marked "copy") found in box 1, Kimball Papers, Truman Library, and a typed version found in JCS files, sec. 5, CCS 373 (10–23–48), RG 218, NA.

82. Hammond, "Super Carriers and B–36 Bombers," 492.

83. See note 73, above.

84. Testimony of Glenn Martin, Fourth Day, 8 Sep 1949, Naval Court of Inquiry, 125.

85. Ibid.

86. General Vandenberg first touted the ability of the B–36 to successfully evade air defense interception in February 1949. Discussing operations of B–36 bombers in tests against air defenses at Eglin Air Force Base, he noted:

> Defensively the conditions were supposedly ideal. The attack was made in broad daylight. A radar network, manned by the most experienced technicians in the AF was alerted and ready. Jet interceptor fighters were standing by. But the B–36 successfully bombed Eglin from an altitude of 40,000 feet and returned to its base without having been effectively intercepted. GEN Hoyt S. Vandenberg, "The Air Force is not a One-Weapon Force," *Air Force Policy Letter*, 25 Feb 1949, 1, quoted in Robert L. Smith, "The Influence of USAF Chief of Staff General Hoyt S. Vandenberg on United States National Security Policy" (Ph.D. diss., The American University, 1964), 116.

87. Robert Hotz, "Improved B–36 is Planned by Strategists," *Aviation Week*, 14 Mar 1949, 13. See also Hanson W. Baldwin, "War Plane Orders Face Examination by Congressmen . . . B–36 Claims Scrutinized . . . ," *New York Times*, 24 May 1949.

88. Hotz, "Improved B–36," 13. In an editorial a week later *Aviation Week* reported a comment from Air Force Chief of Staff Hoyt Vandenberg that "his main concern now is not how to protect the

B–36 against enemy fighters but how to develop USAF fighters capable of stopping a B–36 type assault on the United States." "B–36 vs. Fighters—Analysis," *Aviation Week* 21 Mar 1949, 7.

89. Typed copy of article—Jim G. Lucas, "Is Air Force or Navy Right About the B–36?" *Washington Daily News*, 15 Mar 1949; "A21/1–2 Air Force" folder, Series I, OP–23 Records, OA.

90. Green, "Stuart Symington and the B–36," 144.

91. Testimony of W. Stuart Symington, House Armed Services Committee, *B–36 Bomber Program: Hearings*, 238.

92. Testimony of Dan A. Kimball, ibid., 612–13.

93. Copy of ltr, Kimball to Van Zandt, 2 May 1949; attached to note, Kimball to Symington, 17 May 1949, box 39, Special Interest File 1949, Symington Special Interest Files, RG 340, NA/WNRC.

94. Quoted in David Lawrence, "Altitude Jet Fighter Tests by Navy Show B–36 Is Vulnerable," *Washington Evening Star*, 10 May 1949.

95. See the story by Lucas in the *Washington Daily News*, 17 May 1949. The content of Kimball's letter was probably leaked to Lucas by Cedric Worth. See testimony of Dan Kimball, House Armed Services Committee, *B–36 Bomber Program: Hearings*, 612–13.

96. Copy of House Armed Services Committee resolution, together with copy of ltr, Vinson to Louis Johnson, 18 May 1949, attached to original, signed memo from Johnson to JCS, 19 May 1949, sec. 2, CCS 373 (10–23–48), RG 218, NA.

97. Memo, Johnson to JCS, 19 May 1949.

98. See the wording of his memo to the Chiefs.

99. Memo, VADM J. D. Price, VCNO, to all DCNOs, OP–09 ser 21P09, 20 May 1949, box 6, 1949 Double Zero Files, OA.

100. See the OP–05B draft comment, no ser, enclosed with memo RADM J. H. Cassady to OP–03, no ser, 21 May 1949, box 8, 1949 Double Zero Files. For the results of Air Force high-altitude intercept testing, see, for example, Air Force reports contained in "A21/4 Jet Aircraft S&C" folder, Series II, OP–23 Records, OA.

101. Ltr, Radford to Hugh Hanson, 23 May 1949, box 29, Radford Papers, OA.

102. Copy of memo, JCS (signed by Denfeld) to SECDEF, 27 May 1949, attached to copy of memo, COL John H. Ives, Deputy Secretary, JCS, to Denfeld, Hull and others, 1 Jun 1949, box 25, Radford Papers.

103. Memo, Ives to Denfeld et al., 1 Jun 1949.

104. Jim G. Lucas, "Ban on B–36 Duel Jolts Air Admirals," *Washington Daily News*, 2 Jun 1949, 39. Lucas himself was convinced that Johnson was trying to sabotage Admiral Denfeld's position with the uniformed Navy. Following a conversation he had in confidence with Lucas, one Navy Department staffer wrote:

> [Lucas] believes that Mr. Johnson is out to sabotage Admiral Denfeld's position within the Navy, i.e., destroy the confidence and respect that the Navy has for Admiral Denfeld and thereby weaken the Navy generally. He says that Mr. Johnson told him that although Admiral Denfeld voted against cancellation of the CVA [the *United States*] in the JCS, he went to the White House with Mr. Johnson and told the President that he really didn't mean to vote against the cancellation of the carrier. Lucas says that he knows of six other correspondents that Johnson has said the same thing to. Mr. Johnson also told him that he was going to recommend that President reappoint Admiral Denfeld for another two years (divide and conquer). Typed note from [Mr. Elton F.?] Drake labeled "Rumors from grape vine! Note the source!!" 13 Jun 1949, box 25, Radford Papers, OA.

105. Ltr, Price to Radford, 1 Jun 1949, box 60, Radford Papers.

8. The Navy and the B–36 Hearings

1. See Lowell Mellett, "House Committee Opens Up Large Subject of Military Propaganda," *Washington Evening Star*, 22 Mar 1949.

2. The Joint Chiefs of Staff had approved the short-range Joint Emergency War Plan TROJAN on 28 January 1949. The target list for the proposed atomic offensive in TROJAN consisted of a broad range of industrial facilities in 70 cities in the Soviet Union. See Condit, *JCS and National Policy* 2:285–86.

3. The article went on to note, "By coincidence or not, investigation showed yesterday that there are 70 Russian cities, according to the Rand-McNally world atlas, which have a population of 100,000 or more." Charles Corddry, "Forrestal Asks Expansion of B–36 Force," *New York Herald Tribune*, 15 Mar 1949. The *Washington Daily News* version of the story had appeared the previous day.

4. "Air Power 'Lobby' Warned By Vinson: House Committee Threatens to Investigate Those in Defense Who Deprecate Branches," *New York Times*, 6 Apr 1949, 5.

5. Ibid.; and Hammond, "Super Carriers and B–36 Bombers, 491. For Symington's denial of Air Force responsibility for the leak, see Eyes Only memo from Symington to Forrestal, 14 Mar 1949, box 42, Principal File, Eisenhower Pre-Presidential Papers, Eisenhower Library.

6. Quoted in "Air Power 'Lobby' Warned," *New York Times*.

7. See "Let's Keep the Record Straight on the B–36 Investigation and Related Matters"—Extension of Remarks of Hon. James E. Van Zandt of Pennsylvania, 20 Jul 1949, *Congressional Record*, vol. 95, Daily ed. (21 Jul 1949), A4892.

8. Manson interview, 28 Jan 1989.

9. Ibid.

10. Hammond, "Super Carriers and B–36 Bombers," 497.

11. Negative photocopy of "Statement of James E. Van Zandt, M. C. in the House of Representatives[,] May 26, 1949", 1, attached to memo (on SECAF letterhead notepaper), COL Glen W. Martin, Executive to SECAF, to Clark Clifford, White House, 22 Jul 1949, box 11, Clifford Papers, Truman Library.

12. See ibid., 2–5.

13. Slip copy of H.Res. 234, 81st Cong., 1st sess., "A18/1-3 Investigations" folder, Series I, OP–23 Records, OA. A transcript of the committee's hearing on the matter is printed in Armed Services Committee, *B–36 Bomber Program: Hearings*, 2–7.

14. Copy of "Agenda of B–36 Investigation," 9 Jun 1949, attached to copy of ltr, Vinson to SECNAV Matthews, 9 Jun 1949, box 21, Radford Papers, OA.

15. Ltr, Vinson to Matthews, 9 Jun 1949.

16. Green, "Stuart Symington and the B–36," 164–65.

17. "Dr. W. B. Leach Of Harvard Receives Air Force Award," National Military Establishment Press Release No. M–60–49, 10 May 1949, "A7–1/10–1 SecDef M Series" folder, Series I, OP–23 Records, OA.

18. Green, "Stuart Symington and the B–36," 165.

19. Leach's 2 Jun 1949 outline for developing the Air Force's case, listed in Hammond, "Super Carriers and B–36 Bombers," 498.

20. Green, "Stuart Symington and the B–36," 165–66. Detailed materials on the B–36 program and the Air Force's preparation for the hearings are in boxes 38–40, Special Interest File, 1949; and box 51, Special Interest File, 1950, Symington Special Interest Files, RG 340, NA/WNRC.

21. Draft memo, Cassady to Price; encl. to memo, Cassady to Ofstie et al., 9 Jun 1949, "A-3 *B–36* Unofficial & Personal Letters & Memos, *Top Secret*" folder, Series III, OP–23 Records, OA. This memo was drafted before the Navy's receipt of Congressman Vinson's 9 June letter.

22. Memo, Ofstie to OP–05B, 13 Jun 1949, box 4, Ofstie Papers, OA.

Notes to pages 219–223   351

23. Typed, unsigned, undated [15 Jun 1949] note, probably by CAPT W. R. Hollingsworth, Admin. Aide to VCNO, attached to copy of memo, COL John Ives, Deputy Secretary, JCS, to JCS, SM–1108–49, 15 Jun 1949, "B–1 B–36 Task Force Chronology *Top Secret*" folder, Series III, OP–23 Records, OA.

24. Copy of ltr, Vinson to Matthews, 14 Jun 1949, same folder; and copy of ltr, Vinson to Denfeld, 14 Jun 1949, box 78, 1965 Double Zero Files, OA.

25. See the comments in Burke, copy of corrected typed manuscript "Notes in regard to OP–23," 286–87, box 23, Burke Papers, OA.

26. Ibid., 283–84.

27. Memo, Burke to Struble, 17 Jun 1949, box 4, Ofstie Papers, OA.

28. For the reactions of RADM W. F. Boone, ACNO (Strategic Plans), and RADM R. E. Libby, Chief, General Planning Group, see OP–23 Memo for Files, 17 Jun 1949; and memo, Libby to OP–03, 18 Jun 1949, encl. to memo, LCDR R. T. Swenson to Committee on B–36 Capabilities, 22 Jun 1949, both in "B–1 B–36 Task Force Chronology *Top Secret*" folder, Series III, OP–23 Records.

29. Memo for Record, 22 Jun 1949, 1–2, box 4, Ofstie Papers, OA. In addition to the committee items assigned, Rear Admirals Brown and Libby and Captain Griffin were tasked with drafting a paper on "The Nature of a Future War."

30. Memo, Boone to OP–03, no ser, 6 Jul 1949, attached to memo, Struble to Brown, no ser, 7 Jul 1949, box 4, Denfeld Double Zero Files, OA.

31. Memo, Gardner to Brown, no ser, n.d. [7 Jul 1949 ?], attached to memo, Struble to Brown, 7 Jul 1949.

32. Memo, Struble to Brown, 7 Jul 1949.

33. Memo (with encl.), Brown to Under Secretary's Task Force, 7 Jul 1949, box 19, Radford Papers, OA.

34. This sentence was capitalized for emphasis in the original. Copy of memo, Carney to Brown, OP–04 ser 00054P04, 8 Jul 1949, box 4, Denfeld Double Zero Files, OA.

35. Copy of memo, Price to Brown OP–09 ser 0003P09, n.d. [8 Jul 1949 ?], "B–1 B–36 Task Force Chronology *Top Secret*" folder, Series III, OP–23 Records, OA.

36. Ltr, Burke to Radford, 8 Jul 1949, box 16, Radford Papers, OA.

37. Ibid.

38. See memo for Mr. Kimball, OP–03 ser 0059P03, n.d.; encl. to memo, Brown to the Under Secretary's Task Force, 14 Jul 1949, box 4, Ofstie Papers, OA.

39. Admiral Denfeld had signed and sent over a more detailed but not significantly stronger letter on 18 July. See ltr, Denfeld to Vinson, 18 Jul 1949, "B–1 B–36 Task Force Chronology *Top Secret*" folder, Series III, OP–23 Records, OA.

40. Complete copies of the various drafts can be found in separate folders in box 19 of the Radford Papers.

41. [OP–23], typed report prepared for the record entitled "A History of the Investigation of the B–36," n.d. [completed on or shortly after 2 Nov 1949], 11, box 9, Denfeld Papers, OA; and Burke, "Notes in regard to OP–23," 290.

42. Ltr, Burke to Radford, 22 Jul 1949, 1, box 16, Radford Papers, OA.

43. Ibid., 2.

44. Emphasis in original. Ltr, Brown to Burke, 11 Aug 1949, "File No. 98–A," unnumbered box, Burke Papers, OA.

45. Handwritten note by CAPT Hollingsworth, n.d. [20 Jun 1949], attached to copy of Memo of Understanding by the Budget Advisory Committee, 18 Jun 1949, box 25, Radford Papers, OA.

46. Copy of memo, Durgin to Carney, OP–05B ser 0006P05, 27 Jun 1949, same box.

47. See Rearden, *The Formative Years, 1947–1950*, 371–72.

48. Memo, Johnson to SECARMY et al., 5 Jul 1949, box 25, Radford Papers, OA.

49. See Condit, *JCS and National Policy* 2:266.

50. Briefing booklet entitled "Analysis of NME Budget by Vice Adm. R. B. Carney USN, Navy Member JCS (BAC)," n.d. [Jul 1949], [8], box 4, Denfeld Double Zero Files, OA.

51. Ltr, Burke to Radford, 8 Jul 1949, 2.

52. Memo of Information by Hollingsworth, n.d. [11 Jul 1949], [3], box 25, Radford Papers, OA.

53. Ltr, Burke to Radford, 18 Jul 1949, box 16, Radford Papers.

54. Copy of memo, Chief BUAER to CNO, via DCNO (Air), BUAER ser 06988, 25 Jul 1949,"F–8 B–36 Procurement *Top Secret*" folder, Series III, OP–23 Records, OA.

55. Unsigned OP–05 memo, marked "Background info—*not submitted*," no ser, n.d. [early Jul 1949], box 25, Radford Papers, OA.

56. [Op–23], "A History of the Investigation of the B–36," 21.

57. Ltr, Metsger to Radford, 19 Jul 1949, box 34, Radford Papers, OA; and RADM A. B. Metsger, USN (Ret.), interview by author, 10 Aug 1987, Arlington, VA, tape recording.

58. Metsger interview.

59. Xerographic copy of typewritten original, CDR A. B. Metsger, "Crisis in Naval Aviation 26 July, 1949," 21 [numbering of document below]; contained in RADM A. B. Metsger, USN (Ret.), "Crisis in Defense: Congressional Hearings 1949," n.d. [circa 1980], box 19, Burke Papers, OA. This was the paper Metsger used in briefing Admiral Radford. Metsger interview.

60. Metsger, "Crisis in Naval Aviation," 21 and 24.

61. Ltr, Burke to Radford, 18 Jul 1949; ltr, CAPT Fitzhugh Lee to Burke, 30 Jul 1949, "File No. 26," unnumbered box, Burke Papers, OA; and written answer to author queries, Lee to author, [15 Mar 1986], 6 and 8.

62. Ltr, Radford to Burke, 30 Jul 1949; "File No. 98–A," unnumbered box, Burke Papers, OA.

63. Ltr, Burke to Lee, 2 Aug 1949, 2–3, box 16, Radford Papers, OA.

64. "Vinson Pledges No Delay in Bomber Probe," *Washington Post*, 5 Aug 1949.

65. Ltr, Burke to Radford, 5 Aug 1949, box 16, Radford Papers, OA.

66. Original signed ltr, Vinson to Matthews, 6 Aug 1949, attached to OPNAV routing slip dated 8 Aug 1949, box 78, 1965 Double Zero Files, OA.

67. Ltr, Matthews to Vinson, 8 Aug 1949, attached to ltr, Vinson to Matthews, 6 Aug 1949.

68. See testimony of Robert A. Lovett, House Armed Services Committee, *B–36 Bomber Program: Hearings*, 26–29, 33–34, 41.

69. See Statement of MGEN Frederick H. Smith, Jr., ibid., 44–90.

70. Testimony of GEN George C. Kenney, ibid., 120.

71. Ltr, Kenney to Symington, 18 Jun 1949, 3, box 39, Special Interest File, 1949, Symington Special Interest Files, RG 340, NA/WNRC. This letter is also printed in the hearings volume (122–23).

72. Testimony of General Kenney, House Armed Services Committee, *B–36 Bomber Program: Hearings*, 120.

73. Testimony of LTGEN Curtis E. LeMay, ibid., 150.

74. This was a misleading statement. In March 1949 Brigadier General D. L. Putt, Director of Research and Development, Office of Deputy Chief of Staff, Materiel, had informed his boss:

> Certainly our jet fighters can attain the same altitude as the B–36. They can maintain a speed superiority at that altitude, and, consequently can successfully attack the B–36 at that altitude.

The same facts apply to Navy fighters. However, the important premise is not whether the fighters can shoot down the airplane at that altitude but rather whether or not the fighters can find a target at that altitude. Our prognosis is, that the fighters will be unsuccessful in intercepting bombers above 40,000 feet eighty percent of the time, until the ground electronic equipment has been improved considerably. Memo, Putt to Deputy Chief of Staff, Materiel, 28 Mar 1949, box 28, Strategic Air Group, RG 341, NA.

75. Testimony of General LeMay, House Armed Services Committee, *B–36 Bomber Program: Hearings*, 152–53.

76. Testimony of GEN Hoyt S. Vandenberg, ibid., 190.

77. Ibid., 202. Vandenberg's answer to the question was confusing. He may have meant to indicate that *interception* of the B–36 at 40,000 was almost impossible, but that is not what he said.

78. Testimony of W. Stuart Symington, ibid., 206–7.

79. Ibid., 207.

80. "Bi-Weekly Report of B–36 Difficulties: Report No. 10," 7 Jul 1949, 4, box 38, Special Interest File, 1949, Symington Special Interest Files, RG 340, NA/WNRC. Each copy of the report in this file was personally seen by Symington, stamped "Noted by the Secretary of the Air Force" and initialed. The section in the 7 July report on the 20mm gun problems was specifically denoted by several pencil markings.

81. "Bi-Weekly Report of B–36 Difficulties: Report No. 12," 4 Aug 1949, 2, same box.

82. "Experts & Explanations," *Time*, 22 Aug 1949, 13. Following receipt of a copy of the Anonymous Document in June 1949, Stuart Symington had initiated an investigation of its paternity by the Air Force Office of Special Investigations (OSI). OSI's resulting report stated that Cedric Worth, Glenn Martin, and Harold Mosier "are reliably reported to have collaborated in the preparation of the 'Anonymous Document,'" and that Commander Thomas Davies "is known to have actively participated in developing information" contained in the document. The only other naval officer mentioned by name in the report as being linked with the Anonymous Document was Lieutenant (jg) Samuel P. Ingram, USNR. Office of Special Investigations Report, *Relevant Information Concerning Current Attacks Upon U.S. Air Force and Its Personnel With Particular Reference to the B–36 Program*, n.d. [late July 1949], 2, 6, 17, box 39, Special Interest File, 1949, Symington Special Interest Files, RG 340, NA. A copy of the report was furnished to Congressman Carl Vinson and the House committee in early August. For information on the OSI report, see various pages of Green, "Stuart Symington and the B–36." Because Worth's (and, by implication, the Navy's) authorship of the Anonymous Document was not disclosed in committee testimony until 24 August, the *Time* article's comments were obviously the result of a leak.

83. The recess was to allow a special subcommittee to travel out to California to take testimony from individuals who, for one reason or another, could not get to Washington to testify.

84. Burke, "Notes in regard to OP–23," 328.

85. "Analysis of Testimony to Date (12 August 1949)," 1, "A/1 Chron. (1949) S&C" folder, Series II, OP–23 Records, OA. See also "Abstract of undeveloped points in testimony to date (12 August)", box 4, Ofstie Papers, OA.

86. Burke, "Notes in regard to OP–23," 297.

87. Memo, Burke to Briscoe, no ser, 15 Aug 1949, 1, box 4, Ofstie Papers, OA.

88. Ibid., 2–3, 6.

89. Burke, "Notes in regard to OP–23," 329.

90. See entries for 22–25 Aug 1949 in Radford Personal Log: 30 Apr 1949–3 Apr 1951, box 2, Radford Papers, OA.

91. Memo, Radford to Keenan, 24 Aug 1949, "1–2 *B–36* Witness Lists *Top Secret*" folder, Series III, OP–23 Records, OA; and ltr, Burke to Radford, 12 Aug 1949, box 16, Radford Papers, OA.

92. "Suggested Order of Presentation," n.d. [mid-Aug 1949], "I-2 *B–36* Witness Lists *Top Secret*" folder, Series III, OP–23 Records, OA.

93. See testimony of Cedric R. Worth, House Armed Services Committee, *B–36 Bomber Program: Hearings*, 524–57ff.

94. "The B–36 Bombs the Black Paper," *Newsweek*, 5 Sep 1949, 13.

95. Ltr, Symington to Leach, 20 Apr 1950, box 7, Symington Papers, Truman Library.

96. United Press, "Navy Fathered Memo on B–36, Vinson Says," *Washington Daily News*, 25 Aug 1949. The *Washington Times Herald*'s headline to the same UPI story was "Vinson Links Navy Bloc to Smear."

97. "Meet the Author," *Time*, 5 Sep 1949, 14.

98. Ltr, Burke to Mrs. Guy Ray, 26 Aug 1949, "File No. 26," unnumbered box, Burke Papers, OA.

99. Comments of Carl Vinson, House Armed Services Committee, *B–36 Bomber Program: Hearings*, 654–55.

100. Emphasis in original. Department of Defense Office of Public Information, Analysis Branch, "B–36 Investigation," 30 Aug 1949, box 42, Vandenberg Papers, MD–LC.

101. Condit, *JCS and National Policy* 2:515.

102. Ibid., 517–18.

103. Emphasis in original. Ltr, Lee to Burke, 30 Aug 1949, box 16, Radford Papers, OA.

104. See copy of directive SECNAV to ADM Thomas C. Kinkaid, no ser, 25 Aug 1949, "H–1 B–36 Naval Court of Inquiry *Top Secret*" folder, Series III, OP–23 Records, OA.

105. Although Murray Green characterized the Court proceedings as a charade, the inquiry was a serious effort that was impeded in its work by a lack of solid evidence linking anyone other than Worth to the intentional act of composing and distributing the document. See Green, "Stuart Symington and the B–36," 211–36.

106. Memo, Symington to Naval Court of Inquiry, 22 Sep 1949, box 6, Symington Papers, Truman Library.

107. Ibid.

108. Tom Davies recalled his relief at the outcome, "Actually, Cedric Worth took the blame himself. And that saved me in the sense that they didn't go any further, once he said that." Davies interview, 11 Aug 1987.

109. See the entries for 2–7 Sep 1949, Radford Personal Log: 30 Apr 1949–3 Apr 1951, box 2, Radford Papers, OA.

110. Ltr, Radford to Davis Merwin, 8 Mar 1950, 4, box 34, Radford Papers, OA.

111. Ibid., 2–3.

112. Ltr, Matthews to Radford, 14 Sep 1949, same box.

113. "Telephone conversation between Mr. Matthews and Mr. Joseph Keenan 1645 14 September 1949," inserted between entries for 29 Aug 1949 and 14 Sep 1949, Matthews Daily Log.

114. Ltr, Denfeld to Radford, 24 Sep 1949, box 5, Denfeld Papers, OA.

115. See ltr, Radford to VADM J. W. Reeves, Jr., 30 Aug 1949, box 36, Radford Papers, OA.

116. Burke, copies of group of typewritten pages written as part of an earlier version of "Notes in regard to OP–23" (hereafter "Notes [Earlier Version])," 291, box 24, Burke Papers, OA.

117. RADM J. L. Howard, USN (Ret.), "Comments on Admiral Burke's OP–23 Draft (Beginning p. A188) by J. L. Howard," n.d., 4/5–5/5, box 19, Burke Papers.

118. Ibid.; and Burke, "Notes (Earlier Version)", 291.

119. Edward P. Stafford, "Saving Carrier Aviation—1949 Style," U.S. Naval Institute *Proceedings* 116 (Jan 1990): 49.

120. CAPT John G. Crommelin, USN, "Statement of Captain John G. Crommelin, U.S. Navy on the B-36 Investigation," 10 Sep 1949, 4-5; and Crommelin, "The General-Staff Concept," n.d. [10 Sep 1949], 6; both stamped 12 Sep 1949 and encl. with copy of memo, Burke to Radford, 12 Sep 1949, box 4, Ofstie Papers, OA.

121. See, for example, "Pentagon Crippling Power of Navy, Captain Says, Risking His Career," *New York Times*, 11 Sep 1949, 1, 47.

122. Memo, Burke to Crommelin, 14 Sep 1949, "File No. 27," unnumbered box, Burke Papers, OA. See also ltr, VADM Felix B. Stump, Commander Air Force, Atlantic Fleet, to Crommelin, 16 Sep 1949, encl. with ltr, Stump to Burke, 16 Sep 1949, same file.

123. Msg, SECNAV to CINCPAC et al., 142127 Sep 1949, box 4, Ofstie Papers, OA.

124. Copy of memo, Bogan to SECNAV, ser 0183, 20 Sep 1949, box 4, Denfeld Double Zero Files, OA. This copy from CNO's personal files lacks both the serial number and date.

125. Copy of first endorsement on Bogan's memo, Radford to SECNAV, no ser, 22 Sep 1949, bound into VADM Gerald F. Bogan, USN (Ret.), interviews by CDR Etta-Belle Kitchen, USN (Ret.), 25 Oct and 26 Oct 1969, transcript, U.S. Naval Institute, Annapolis, MD. This copy lacks the date of submission.

126. Second endorsement on Bogan's memo, CNO to SECNAV, ser 03P00, 28 Sep 1949, box 9, 1950 Double Zero Files, OA.

127. [OP-23], "A History of the Investigation of the B-36," 25.

128. Entry for 27 Sep 1949, Matthews Daily Log.

129. Memo for File, no ser, 28 Sep 1949, 1, box 55, Radford Papers, OA. This is a transcript of a 28 September telephone conversation between Arleigh Burke and Fitzhugh Lee. Burke was relating information to Lee (for Admiral Radford) that had been passed along to him at Admiral John Dale Price's request by Captain E. E. Woods.

130. Emphasis in original. Ibid.

131. Ibid.

132. Ibid., 1-2.

133. Ibid., 2.

134. Ibid.

135. Horowitz even suggested that the presentation should be a joint Air Force-Navy one. Ibid., 3.

136. Ibid. When Burke commented to Admiral Price that attempting to combine several issues of such complexity into a single agenda item was impossible to accomplish in a satisfactory manner, Price responded that he "knew that" but "to do it anyway." Ibid.

137. Entry for 28 Sep 1949, Matthews Daily Log.

138. Shaw interview. Sam Shaw was recounting the story of the meeting as he heard it later from General Cates.

139. Ibid. In recounting this story to Colonel Shaw, General Cates remarked, "Christ Almighty! Now's the time to charge." Ibid.

140. Memo for File, 28 Sep 1949, 3.

141. Emphasis added. Ibid., 4. Admiral Denfeld had told this to Admiral Briscoe later that morning, and Briscoe had relayed this information to Captain Burke. Ibid.

142. Ibid., 3.

143. Ibid., 4.

144. Shaw interview. OP-23 had just moved its offices from Main Navy to the fourth deck of the Pentagon. Because of space limitations, Burke was forced to share an office with several of his senior people, including Sam Shaw, Snowden Arthur, and Joe Howard.

145. Memo for File, 28 Sep 1949, 5.

146. Shaw interview.

147. John G. Norris, "Navy Cramps Admirals in B–36 Inquiry," *Washington Post*, 29 Sep 1949, 1.

148. Ibid.

149. Entry for 29 Sep 1949, Matthews Daily Log.

150. Davis Merwin, "Memorandum of Conversation, Wednesday, January 11, 1950 with Secretary of the Navy Matthews," 2; encl. to ltr, Merwin to Radford, 27 Jan 1950, box 34, Radford Papers, OA.

151. As Davis Merwin later recorded, "Matthews labeled this 'rank insubordination' pointing out the, to him, absurdity of such a gesture, when Price's CNO was present and he, Matthews, the head of the Department, was being likewise defied by deference to an officer not in the chain of command." Ibid. When Admiral Radford later read this account, he commented, "It is amazing to me that Mr. Matthews labeled such a suggestion 'rank insubordination'. He was perfectly at liberty to over-ride it. As far as I know, the only reason that he did not over-ride it was that he was not sure himself what was the right thing to do." Ltr from Radford to Merwin, 8 Mar 1950, 4.

152. "Telephone conversation between Mr. C. B. Allen and Mr. Matthews 0830 30 October [September] 1949," misdated and filed between the entries for 29 and 30 Oct 1949, Matthews Daily Log.

153. As Matthews told his friend the Right Reverend Maurice Sheehy, "Now the . . . [newspaper story by Jack Norris], Thursday, that's the leak somewhere. We're going to find out who did it and *they'll take the consequences.*" Emphasis added. "Telephone Conversation Between Reverend Sheehy and Mr. Matthews 0850 1 October 1949," filed with entry for 1 Oct 1949, Matthews Daily Log.

154. Entry for 29 Sep 1949, Matthews Daily Log. McCann, a highly respected submariner who had recently served on the General Board, had taken over as Naval Inspector General on 14 June 1949. VADM McCann's official biography, dated 25 May 1950, Box 408, Officer Bios Collection, OA.

155. Entry for 29 Sep 1949, Matthews Daily Log.

156. Merwin, "Memorandum of Conversation with Secretary Matthews," 2.

157. Ibid.

158. Entry for 29 Sep 1949, Matthews Daily Log. Just a few minutes before this, Matthews had met with Captain Woods for a second time.

159. Matthews Daily Log for that day shows that McCann had another quick meeting with the Secretary less than fifteen minutes after the 3:52 p.m. session.

160. Captain Charles Snowden Arthur, USN (Ret.), interview by author, 1 Oct 1993, Washington, DC, tape recording. From Arthur's description, the Reserve lieutenant was probably the "infamous" Sam Ingram.

161. Shaw interview; and Rear Admiral Joseph L. Howard (SC), USN (Ret.), telephone interview by author, 28 Sep 1993, San Diego, CA, tape recording.

162. Shaw interview.

163. Arthur interview.

164. Ibid.

165. Howard interview. Sam Shaw sensed what was happening because he knew who Admiral McCann was. As a junior officer in *Tuscaloosa* (CA 37), Shaw had served with the admiral's son. He could also tell that McCann was not there on a social call. As he remarked about seeing the admiral enter the office, "That man—something he's got a hold of . . . he doesn't like it, for sure." Shaw interview.

166. Howard interview.

167. Ibid.

168. Emphasis in original. Shaw interview.

169. Howard interview.

170. Shaw interview; and Howard interview.

171. Howard interview.

172. Shaw interview.

173. Howard interview.

174. Ibid.

175. Shaw interview.

176. Ibid.; and Howard interview.

177. Howard interview; Shaw interview.

178. Radford had departed NAS Barbers Point for Washington at 1700 (local time) on 29 September. Entry for 29 Sep 1949, Radford Personal Log: 30 Apr 1949–3 Apr 51, box 2, Radford Papers, OA.

179. Entry for 1 Oct 1949, Matthews Daily Log.

180. Merwin, "Memorandum of Conversation with Secretary Matthews," 2; and ltr, Radford to Merwin, 8 Mar 1950, 4.

181. Entry for 3 Oct 1949, Matthews Daily Log.

182. Ltr, Lee to CAPT Walter Karig, 21 Nov 1949, box 21, Radford Papers, OA.

183. Ibid.

184. Ltr, Radford to Merwin, 8 Mar 1950, 4.

185. Bogan oral history, USNI, #1–123.

186. Memo, Naval Inspector General to SECNAV, OP–08 ser 045P08, 7 Oct 1949, 5, box 9, 1950 Double Zero Files, OA.

187. Stafford, "Saving Carrier Aviation—1949 Style," 44, 50.

188. Ibid., 50.

189. High-level Air Force thinking on this point is most evident in Murray Green's account of the events. Green asserted that top Navy uniformed officials had held a conference in Coronado, CA, beginning on 20 Sep 1949, at which the Bogan letter and the endorsements were written. He further stated that the "obvious" objective of these leaders was to release the correspondence to the Congress and the public in order "to reopen the investigation on more favorable terms." Green, "Stuart Symington and the B–36," 237–38. For Matthews's own feelings, see typewritten copy of North American Newspaper Alliance (NANA) interview of Matthews by Martin S. Hayden—"Matthews Believes 'Admirals' Revolt' Is Over, Feels He Has Won 'One Fight in a Long Battle'—Against Navy Cuts When Proposed and Still Opposes Them," for release 8 Nov 1949, 2, encl. with ltr, Fitzhugh Lee to Hanson Baldwin, 21 Nov 1949, box 21, Radford Papers, OA.

190. Ltr, Lee to Karig, 18 Nov 1949, box 21, Radford Papers, OA. See also ltr, Lee to Baldwin, 21 Nov 1949.

191. Ltr, Lee to Merwin, 17 Nov 1949, box 17, Radford Papers.

192. Burke, "Notes in regard to OP–23," 89.

193. House Armed Services Committee, *B–36 Bomber Program: Hearings*, 660–61.

9. The "Revolt of the Admirals"

1. Testimony of Francis P. Matthews, House Armed Services Committee, *Unification and Strategy: Hearings*, 7.

2. Ibid., 8–9.

3. Ibid., 9.

4. See Paolo Coletta, "An Interview with John T. Mason, Jr., Director of Oral History," Comment and Discussion section, U.S. Naval Institute *Proceedings* 100 (Feb 1974): 94.

5. Testimony of ADM Arthur W. Radford House Armed Services Committee, *Unification and Strategy: Hearings*, 41.

6. See ibid., 50–51.

7. Ibid., 42.

8. Emphasis added. Ibid., 43.

9. Ibid., 46. Under questioning, Radford suggested the Air Force's B–47 all-jet medium bomber as the kind of aircraft he was advocating in place of the B–36. See ibid., 83.

10. Statement of CAPT Frederick M. Trapnell, ibid., 133.

11. Ibid., 134–35. For technical information supporting Trapnell's testimony on interception of the B–36, see "Problems Involved in Attacking the B–36 With the F2H (Pilot's Viewpoint)," encl. to ltr, CDR W. J. Widhelm, Director, Tactical Test, Naval Air Test Center, to Ofstie, 1 Jul 1949; and memo, Trapnell to Ofstie, no ser, 2 Jul 1949, both in box 4, Ofstie Papers, OA.

12. Statement of CDR Eugene Tatom, House Armed Services Committee, *B–36 Bomber Program: Hearings*, 170. As a measure of how poor the Strategic Air Command's bombing accuracies were at this time SAC CEPs (circular error probables) for routine radar bombing averaged 6,075 feet (only half the bombs dropped falling within a circle *2.3* miles in diameter drawn around the intended aiming point, the other half falling outside of it,) during October–December 1948, and during all of 1949 they still averaged above 4,300 feet. Chart, "Radar Bombing Accuracy CEP–RBS Record (First) Runs All SAC Bomb Wings," in *Strategic Air Command Progress Analysis, 1 November 1948 to 31 October 1953*, 26, box B 98, LeMay Papers, MD–LC.

13. Statement of RADM Ralph A. Ofstie, House Armed Services Committee, *B–36 Bomber Program: Hearings*, 186.

14. Manson interview, 28 Jan 1989.

15. Copy of ltr, Denfeld to Davis Merwin, 13 Feb 1950, box 17, Radford Papers, OA.

16. Merwin, "Memorandum of Conversation with Secretary Matthews," 3.

17. Memo, CAPT Walter Karig to CNO, no ser, 4 Oct 1949, 3, box 78, 1965 Double Zero Files, OA.

18. Emphasis in original. Shaw interview, 29 Jul 1987.

19. Griffin interview, 10 Dec 1985.

20. Ltr, Denfeld to Davis Merwin, 13 Feb 1950.

21. Statement of ADM Louis E. Denfeld, House Armed Services Committee, *Unification and Strategy: Hearings*, 350.

22. Ibid., 350–61.

23. Emphasis added. Ibid., 352–53.

24. Ibid., 353–55.

25. Ibid., 361.

26. William S. White, "Denfeld Sees Navy Gravely Imperiled By Chiefs' Decisions," *New York Times*, 14 Oct 1949, 1.

27. "Facts & Fears," *Time*, 24 Oct 1949, 27.

28. Merwin, "Memorandum of Conversation with Secretary Matthews," 3; and Griffin interview.

29. "Facts & Fears," *Time*, 24 Oct 1949, 27.

30. Note from Gruenther to Eisenhower, Thursday 6 P.M. [13 Oct 1949], box 48, Principal File, Eisenhower Pre-Presidential Papers, Eisenhower Library.

31. Memo, MAJ Robert L. Schulz, Eisenhower's aide, to Eisenhower, 18 Oct 1949, box 118, same file.

32. See Statement of GEN Clifton B. Cates, House Armed Services Committee, *Unification and Strategy: Hearings*, 394–96.

33. See Symington statement, ibid., 402–3.

34. See the discussion of its establishment in chapter 3. For information on the Harmon Committee's deliberations, see David A. Rosenberg, "American Atomic Strategy and the Hydrogen Bomb Decision," *The Journal of American History* 66 (Jun 1979): 72–73; and Condit, *JCS and National Policy* 2:304–7.

35. Denfeld statement, House Armed Services Committee, *Unification and Strategy: Hearings*, 352; and the subsequent testimony of Denfeld and former Harmon Committee member Rear Admiral Tom B. Hill, ibid., 363–64.

36. See memo, Harmon to Symington, n.d. [15 Oct 1949], printed in ibid., 404. In reality the Air Force was so upset by the critical sections of the Harmon Committee report that in the JCS, Air Force Chief of Staff Hoyt Vandenberg had pressed for omission of parts relating to the negative side effects of the air offensive and for major revisions in the report's conclusions. These changes were defeated only by the strong pleas of Admiral Denfeld. See Rosenberg, "American Atomic Strategy and the Hydrogen Bomb Decision," 73.

37. Murray Green, writing years before the Harmon Committee's report was declassified, accepted Harmon's comments as proof that Denfeld and Tom Hill had cited the report falsely. Green, "Stuart Symington and the B–36," 262–67.

38. Typewritten Navy brief on the 11 May 1949 Harmon Committee report, 2–5, "AI/EM–3/7 Joint Chiefs of Staff *Top Secret*" folder, Series III, OP–23 Records, OA. A declassified, lightly sanitized copy of the complete report is available as JCS 1953/1, 12 May 1949, in the CCS 373 (10–23–48) files, RG 218, NA.

39. Statement of GEN Hoyt S. Vandenberg, House Armed Services Committee, *Unification and Strategy: Hearings*, 456.

40. Ibid., 457.

41. Vandenberg testimony, ibid., 465.

42. Ibid., 480.

43. AAF Bombing Accuracy Report #1, 11 Apr 1945, cited in memo, A. A. Brown, Deputy Director, Operations Evaluation Group, to RADM R. P. Briscoe, OP–34, OEG ser (LO) 1256–49, 23 Aug 1949, 3, box 19, Radford Papers, OA. The period under analysis was from 1 January to 1 November 1944.

44. Table XII, "Estimated Per Cent of Bombs within Standard Distances According to Type of Bombing, 1 September 1944–31 December 1944," in Odishaw, "Radar Bombing in the Eighth Air Force," 93.

45. In fact the decision to accelerate the B–36 high-altitude bombing accuracy tests appears to have come only in the wake of the Navy's testimony at the hearings. See handwritten office memo, MGEN Frank F. Everest, Assistant Deputy Chief of Staff (Operations), to Vandenberg, 12 Oct 1949, box 34, Vandenberg Papers, MD–LC. The Air Force Air Proving Ground estimated that it would require 30 days to accomplish this accelerated testing. Ibid. As it turned out, the tests were not completed until the end of January 1950. Memo, MGEN Carl A. Brandt, Director of Requirements, to Vice Chief of Staff, 2 Feb 1950, box 1, Fairchild Papers, MD–LC.

46. Memo, MGEN Gordon P. Saville to Norstad, n.d. [12 Oct 1949], attached to office memo, Everest to Vandenberg, 12 Oct 1949. At the time this memo was written, Headquarters USAF was awaiting data from SAC on its own limited B–36 high-altitude bombing tests.

47. For information on Bradley's combat career, see Omar N. Bradley, *A Soldier's Story* (New York: Henry Holt, 1951). In 1969–1970, during a military tour at the U.S. Army Military History Research Collection (now the U.S. Army Military History Institute), Carlisle Barracks, Pennsylvania, the author worked on General Bradley's personal and official papers.

48. As an example of the wartime informality of the Bradley-Vandenberg relationship, see ibid., 549–50.

49. Omar N. Bradley and Clay Blair, *A General's Life* (New York: Simon and Schuster, 1983), 505.

50. Ltr, Denfeld to Bradley, 26 Aug 1949, box 2, Denfeld Papers, OA.

51. CAPT Edward L. Beach, USN (Ret.), interview by author, 23 Aug 1990, Washington, DC, tape recording.

52. For an account of the speech as delivered, see Walter W. Ruch, "Bradley Says Navy Has Adequate Role," *New York Times*, 13 Oct 1949, 5. Ironically, it was given just a day before Louis Denfeld's impassioned testimony before the House Armed Services Committee.

53. Copy of typewritten document by CAPT Paul Foley, Jr., "Summary of conference held in the Pentagon, Friday, 23 Sep 1949, Room 2E864, 0830–1030," 28 Sep 1949, 1, "File No. 98–A," unnumbered box, Burke Papers, OA.

54. Ibid., 4.

55. Ibid., 6–7.

56. Ibid., 7.

57. Bradley and Blair, *A General's Life*, 510.

58. See the comments of committee chairman Carl Vinson on this point, House Armed Services Committee, *Unification and Strategy: Hearings*, 1–2.

59. Beach interview.

60. Ibid.

61. Bradley and Blair, *A General's Life*, 510.

62. Beach interview. He recalled that the other members of the staff finally allowed him to read the speech after Bradley had left to deliver it on the Hill.

63. "19 Oct 1949 Statement of General Omar N. Bradley, Chairman, Joint Chiefs of Staff, Before the Armed Services Committee of the House of Representatives Unification," in *The Collected Writings of General Omar N. Bradley*, vol. 4, *Testimony, 1946–1949* (Privately printed, copy no. 41, n.d.), 222–72, author's collection. The material in this six-volume collection consists of photo offset reproductions of the original multilith documents. The published version of Bradley's statement is to be found in House Armed Services Committee, *Unification and Strategy: Hearings*, 515–37. For the reader's benefit, all citations from General Bradley's statement will be to the published version of the text.

64. In his interview Captain Beach expressed the view that there was no intent on Bradley's part to "dig" the Navy. Although this idea may have been expressed to Beach by the rest of the staff in the days following Bradley's delivery of his statement, even a casual reading of the text reveals that Bradley's words were meant to attack the Navy in a deliberate manner.

65. Statement of GEN Omar N. Bradley, House Armed Services Committee, *Unification and Strategy: Hearings*, 522.

66. Ibid. In making this comment, the general was either demonstrating a complete naivety about the effects that U.S. atomic bombing would have on the Russian civilian populations in the seventy targeted urban-industrial areas, or he was being deliberately untruthful.

67. See ibid., 530. In Bradley's original text, the words referring to the insinuation that the JCS were ignorant "as to how a war should be carried on" were underlined. See the copy of this page reproduced in *Collected Writings of General Bradley* 4:257.

68. Bradley statement, 528.

69. Ibid.

70. Ibid., 530–31.

71. Ibid., 533, 536–37.

72. Ibid., 536. Captain Beach remarked that Bradley and Clifton were unaware of how this comment would be taken. When he read the general's statement just after Bradley had left for the Hill, Beach zeroed in on the "fancy dan" comment. When Beach told the other staffers that the general shouldn't say this, they responded, "It's too late now,... [Bradley's] gone. [But] why not? There's

Notes to pages 262–265   361

nothing meant by it." The subsequent press reaction to this comment convinced Bradley and the staff that Beach had been right. In fact Bradley later told Ned Beach that he wished he had gotten Beach's "input on that item." Beach interview.

73. Written answer to author query, Lee to author, [15 Mar 1986], 9, author's collection.

74. William S. White, "Bradley Accuses Admirals Of 'Open Rebellion' On Unity; Asks 'All-American Team,'" *New York Times*, 20 Oct 1949, 1. See also Hanson W. Baldwin, "Bradley Bombs Navy, General's Bitter Words to Committee Stun Admirals, Widen Service Chasm," ibid., 3.

75. John G. Norris, "Staff Chiefs Chairman Assails Top Admirals For Hurting Defense," *Washington Post*, 20 Oct 1949, 1.

76. Ibid.

77. Baldwin, "Bradley's Charges Upset Washington," *New York Times*, 21 Oct 1949, 1.

78. Ltr, Eisenhower to Bradley, 26 Oct 1949, attached to ltr, Bradley to Eisenhower, 28 Oct 1949, box 13, Principal File, Eisenhower Pre-Presidential Papers, Eisenhower Library.

79. Ltr, Bradley to Eisenhower, 26 Oct 1949. Captain Beach remarked on this point, "In fact, Bradley had to take the position that he'd carefully... written his... statement and that he... didn't believe in revising it after the fact." Beach interview.

80. See particularly the statement of BGEN Vernon E. Megee, USMC, House Armed Services Committee, *Unification and Strategy: Hearings*, 193–200.

81. See the comments of LTGEN Elwood R. Quesada, USAF (Ret.), quoted in Joseph W. Caddell, "Orphan of Unification: The Development of United States Air Force Tactical Air Power Doctrine" (Ph.D. diss., Duke University, 1984), 79. These were taken from an official Air Force oral history with General Quesada.

82. Comment by General Quesada in Richard H. Kohn and Joseph P. Harahan, ed., *Air Superiority in World War II and Korea: An Interview with Gen. James Ferguson, Gen. Robert M. Lee, Gen. William Momyer, and Lt. Gen. Elwood R. Quesada* (Washington: Office of Air Force History, USAF, 1983), 65.

83. Alfred Goldberg, ed., *A History of the United States Air Force, 1907–1957* (Princeton: D. Van Nostrand, 1957), 140.

84. The information on the TAC/ADC consolidation and Vandenberg's reasons for adopting it come from Alfred Goldberg and Robert D. Little, *History of Headquarters USAF, 1 July 1949 to 30 June 1950* (Washington: Air University Historical Liaison Office, Department of the Air Force, 1954), 5; Goldberg, *History of the United States Air Force*, 139–40; Phillip S. Meilinger, "Hoyt S. Vandenberg: The Life of a General" (Ph.D. diss., University of Michigan, 1985), 280–81; and Caddell, "Orphan of Unification," 127–28.

85. Shortly after Lieutenant General Ennis Whitehead reported in as the new CONAC commander in May 1949, he toured the command's facilities. After visiting the various gunnery ranges, he was convinced that air-to-ground gunnery had been receiving too much emphasis. He accordingly ordered the emphasis switched to air-to-air gunnery in order to improve air defense training. Donald M. Goldstein, "Ennis C. Whitehead, Aerospace Commander and Pioneer" (Ph.D. diss., University of Denver, 1970), 383.

86. Ltr, Devers to Vandenberg, n.d. [marked Spring 1949], 2, quoted in Caddell, "Orphan of Unification," 210–11.

87. Caddell, 212, citing Memo for Record by LTCOL Stanley R. Larsen, Assistant Secretary, Army General Staff, 5 May 1949, 1–3.

88. Ltr, Whitehead to Vandenberg, 11 May 1949, 1–2, attached to office memo for Vandenberg, n.d. [mid-May 1949], box 43, Vandenberg Papers, MD–LC. Eventually established at nearby Pope Air Force Base, Tactical Air Force (Provisional) was solely a planning and staff organization with no assigned tactical air units. Caddell, "Orphan of Unification," 275.

89. Vandenberg's decision was in response to a 26 Apr 1949 request by General Lee, the commander of TAC, that a board be set up to review tactical air doctrine and equipment. See Caddell, "Orphan of Unification," 286.

90. See memo, Fairchild to Quesada, 10 Jun 1949, and attached directive, AFCAG–13A 334 of 13 Jun 1949, box 6, Elwood R. Quesada Papers, MD–LC.

91. Quoted in "Who Cashes In?" News and Comment section, *Infantry Journal*, Aug 1949, 30–31. As an indication of early press interest in this matter, see John A. Giles, "Gray Denies Dispute Between Army, AF on Tactical Support," *Washington Evening Star*, 10 Jul 1949.

92. Memo, Leach to Vandenberg, 8 Jul 1949, 1, box 42, Vandenberg Papers, MD–LC.

93. See David Lawrence, "Army Ground Forces Held Almost Without Direct Support, Tactical Air Arm Called Neglected As Millions Go Into Strategic Bombers," *Washington Evening Star*, 8 Jun 1949.

94. Memo, Leach to Vandenberg, 8 Jul 1949, 1–2.

95. Emphasis added. Ibid., 2.

96. Ibid., 3.

97. The Leach memo was written on Friday, 8 July. The following week Vandenberg was busy meeting with the Chiefs on the fiscal year 1951 budget at White Sulphur Springs. When he returned to the office on Monday, 18 July, he had General Norstad summon Barton Leach for a meeting. He had several meetings with Leach that week—the last including Secretary Symington and three others. Entries for 11 Jul, 12–16 Jul, 18 Jul, 19 Jul, and 22 Jul 1949, Manila envelope marked "Diaries [Daily Log], 1 July 1949 to 31 August 1950," box 2, Vandenberg Papers, MD–LC.

98. Entry for 22 Jul 1949, ibid.

99. Entry for 23 Jul 1949, ibid.

100. This was Omar Bradley's wartime assessment of Devers, according to Clay Blair. Bradley and Blair, *A General's Life*, 210. See also 443, 464.

101. Ltr, Whitehead to Vandenberg, 11 May 1949, 1.

102. *Facts On File Yearbook 1949* (New York: Facts On File, 1950), 246, 277; and "New Field Forces Chief," "News and Comment" section, *Army and Navy Journal*, 27 Aug 1949, 1974.

103. MGEN R. E. Duff, Acting Director of Plans and Operations, Summary Sheet with attachments, 10 Oct 1949, cited in Caddell, "Orphan of Unification," 219.

104. Caddell, 218. Caddell was unaware of the Barton Leach memo and the subsequent Vandenberg-Bradley meeting, however.

105. Statement of GEN J. Lawton Collins, House Armed Services Committee, *Unification and Strategy: Hearings*, 545. On 18 October 1949 Congress passed the fiscal year 1950 defense appropriation bill, which provided an additional $851 million for an Air Force strength of *fifty-eight* groups. This was well above what the administration had requested, and when President Truman signed the bill on 29 October, he announced that he was impounding the extra funds. As a result the Air Force's strength remained at the administration's level of forty-eight groups. Rearden, *The Formative Years, 1947–1950*, 356; and "Summary Comparison of Forces for Military Departments, Fiscal 1949 Actual, Fiscal 1950 Budget Program, and Fiscal 1951 Estimates," revised 19 Sep 1949, Appendix A to JCS 1800/56, 22 Sep 1949, "JCS 1800/43 thru 1800/64" folder, Navy Secretariat Records, OA.

106. "Notes on Fifth Meeting of USAF Board of Review," 2, box 6, Quesada Papers, MD–LC. The one Light Bomber Group in the program was limited to the accuracy provided for LORAN (long-range navigation based on pulsed radio signals from two or more pairs of ground stations of known location to provide aircraft position), since its B–45 bombers lacked proper electronic bomb sights. Ibid., 3.

107. Collins statement, 545.

108. See Statement of GEN Mark Clark, House Armed Services Committee, *Unification and Strategy: Hearings*, 569–70ff.

109. See Caddell, "Orphans of Unification," 222.

110. For an extended analysis of the Air Force's subsequent failure to live up to its promises regarding tactical air support for ground forces, see ibid., 242-327. In this regard, the first draft of the Quesada Board's "Formal Report" on tactical air operations had stated:

This Board is of the opinion that if the Air Force should continue its present *relatively negative tactical air policies* for a period of four to six more years the Army will have compiled a dossier of facts which will completely justify its requisitioning a budget for its own air force on the grounds that [the] USAF *has neither been able to meet nor has it physically discharged its responsibilities for providing support to the ground forces.* The board considers that the Air Force has been derelict in meeting its responsibilities toward the surface forces for providing them a full and complete air-ground cooperation training program. Emphasis added. "First Draft, Report of USAF Board of Review for Tactical Air Operations," 8, attached to memo, COL William B. Reed, Quesada Board Recorder, to Quesada, 27 Sep 1949, box 6, Quesada Papers, MD–LC.

This strong statement was replaced in the final draft with a heavily watered-down version asserting that there was a "recurring suspicion" that the Air Force was placing inadequate emphasis on tactical air operations and that the service's failure to satisfactorily provide for tactical air operations in concert with "continental U.S. surface forces" was being "misconstrued" as proof that the Air Force was neither capable of meeting nor was conscientiously discharging its tactical air responsibilities. "Formal Report of the Board of Review," 7, same box.

111. Statement of Louis Johnson, House Armed Services Committee, *Unification and Strategy: Hearings*, 612.

112. Ibid., 614. In late April 1949, WSEG had been tasked with the evaluation of the likely effectiveness of the strategic air offensive against vital elements of the Soviet war-making industry.

113. On the lack of questioning, see Rearden, *The Formative Years*, 419–20. In a Memo for File written on 27 October 1949, Rear Admiral Ralph Ofstie noted:

1. On Thursday, 20 October, a meeting was held in the office of Chairman Vinson of the House Armed Services Committee. It was attended by SecDef Johnson, SecNav Matthews, SecAir Symington, Admiral Denfeld, General Vandenberg (?), and Committee members. General Bradley was not present.

2. The subjects of discussion at this meeting have been held very close by the participants. It is significant, however, that when SecDef Johnson testified the following day, he was not "put on the pan" as Vinson had threatened nor was he questioned by the minority members. Likewise Cong. Cole, who had anticipated playing a major part when Johnson came on the stand, did not even attend the hearing.

3. It is very evident that a "deal" was made to close up the Hearings with dispatch and with a minimum of further controversy. Memorandum for File, 27 Oct 1949, box 4, Ofstie Papers, OA.

10. Aftermath

1. Griffin interview, 10 Dec 1985.

2. Ltr, Denfeld to Dudley A. White, 18 Oct 1949, box 6, Denfeld Papers, OA.

3. Emphasis added. Manson interview, 28 Jan 1989.

4. Merwin, "Memorandum of Conversation with Secretary Matthews," 1.

5. The meeting began at 9:35 a.m. Entry for 14 Oct 1949, Matthews Daily Log.

6. Memo by Matthews on the 14 Oct 1949 meeting, n.d. [14 Oct 1949 ?], 1, box 158, Cabinet File, President's Secretary's File, Truman Library.

7. Louis E. Denfeld, "Reprisal: Why I Was Fired," *Collier's*, 18 Mar 1950, 62. In his memo, Matthews asserted that Denfeld had started talking without waiting for him to say anything, but this seems highly unlikely. Matthews memo, 1.

8. Matthews memo.

9. Copy of ltr, Denfeld to Davis Merwin, 13 Feb 1950.

10. Matthews memo, 2.

11. Entry for 14 Oct 1949, Matthews Daily Log.

12. Ibid. Matthews had first met individually with Conolly and Sherman on 10 October. The next day he again had short meetings with the two men. On 12 October Matthews and his two aides had lunch with Vice Admiral Sherman. They had a similar lunch with Admiral Conolly on 13 October. See entries for 10–13 Oct 1949, Matthews Daily Log.

13. In a newspaper interview several weeks later, Secretary Matthews acknowledged that he had ordered Sherman back to Washington.

14. Emphasis in original. Manson interview, 28 Jan 1989.

15. E. B. Potter, *Nimitz* (Annapolis: Naval Institute Press, 1976), 446.

16. Ltr, Nimitz to Monsignor Maurice S. Sheehy, 13 Feb 1950; "S Correspondence 1946–1950" folder [second of two], Series II, Nimitz Papers, OA.

17. Potter, *Nimitz*, 446. To ensure absolute secrecy, Matthews apparently telephoned Nimitz from his home. He left the office for the day earlier than usual, and there is no record of the telephone call in his daily log. See the list of telephone calls in the entry for 14 Oct 1949, Matthews Daily Log.

18. Ltr, Nimitz to Sheehy, 13 Feb 1950.

19. Ibid.

20. Memo, Matthews to the President, n.d. [early Aug 1949], box 4, Denfeld Double Zero Files, OA.

21. See "Adm. Denfeld Retained As CNO," *Army and Navy Journal*, 13 Aug 1949, 1430; and memo, Nathaniel H. Goodrich, Assistant General Counsel, Department of Defense, to Marx Leva, 26 Oct 1949, 1, 4, box 158, Cabinet File, President's Secretary's File, Truman Library.

22. See the opening statement of Carl Vinson, House Armed Services Committee, *Unification and Strategy: Hearings*, 2.

23. In his biography of Nimitz, Potter states that Nimitz advised Matthews not to list the CNO's testimony before the committee among his reasons for asking for Denfeld's removal, because "all officers had been guaranteed against reprisals for their testimony." Potter, *Nimitz*, 447. This scenario is highly unlikely. First, as a lawyer, Matthews hardly needed to be told that such an action could have dangerous consequences. Second, Nimitz himself denied that in their meeting Matthews had brought up the CNO's testimony as a reason for wanting him replaced. Nimitz wrote to Father Sheehy just a few months later:

> I read Secretary Matthews' [27 October] letter to the President in which he asked for Denfeld's replacement, and I noted that he said in that letter that as early as 4 October he had decided he wanted a new Chief of Naval Operations. Inasmuch as Mr. Matthews had made the same statement to me considerably before Denfeld's removal [during the 15 October meeting] *I cannot accept the statement that Denfeld was removed by Secretary Matthews as an act of reprisal for the testimony which he gave before the House Armed Services Committee on 13 October.* Emphasis added. Ltr, Nimitz to Sheehy, 13 Feb 1950.

24. Sherman told the press on 1 November that he had "preferred not to testify" and that if he had been called upon to give testimony, he would have had "little to say except answer some questions." Quoted in Austin Stevens, "Sherman Chosen Navy Chief, Says He Backs Unity 100%," *New York Times*, 2 Nov 1949, 19. Fitzhugh Lee (and Admiral Radford) believed that Matthews had not wanted Sherman to testify. See ltr, Lee to Merwin, 1 Dec 1949, box 17, Radford Papers, OA.

25. Manson interview, 28 Jan 1989.

26. Entry of 20 Oct 1949, Abell, ed., *Drew Pearson: Diaries*, 86–87.

27. See [OP-23], "A History of the Investigation of the B-36," 39, box 9, Denfeld Papers, OA.

28. Copy of ltr, Hebert to Vinson, 24 Oct 1949, box 19, Radford Papers, OA.

29. Entry for 25 Oct 1949, Matthews Daily Log.

30. See memo, Nathaniel Goodrich to Marx Leva, 26 Oct 1949, 1–2, 4.

31. Entry for 26 Oct 1949, Matthews Daily Log.

32. Ltr, Denfeld to Captain Edward C. Holden, USNR, 26 Oct 1949, box 3, Denfeld Papers, OA.

33. Ltr, Burke to Lee, 26 Oct 1949, box 16, Radford Papers, OA.

34. This excuse was all too obvious. Indeed, in his memo for the record that he sent to Truman, Matthews stated that, in his *14 October* meeting with the CNO, he had told Denfeld that because of the admiral's failure to keep faith with the Secretary in the matter of his testimony before the committee, he could not see how they could work together. Matthews memo, n.d. [14 Oct 1949], 2. Admiral Denfeld later commented to Davis Merwin: "He is cleverly trying to lay stress on the Crommelin matter and the Bogan letter to put up a smoke screen so that it will look as though he fired me for those two incidents, before my testimony before the Committee, but you and I know that our relations were most cordial up to the time I made my statement and that is the reason I was replaced." Ltr, Denfeld to Merwin, 13 Feb 1950, box 17, Radford Papers, OA.

35. Original signed ltr, Matthews to Truman, 27 Oct 1949, 2–3, box 11, National Intelligence Authority File, Clifford Papers, Truman Library.

36. See "Adm. Denfeld Loses Post in Service Row," *Army and Navy Journal*, 29 Oct 1949, 1.

37. See White House press release copy of ltr, Matthews to Truman, 27 Oct 1949, attached to press release copy of memo, Truman to SECNAV, same date, box 83, George M. Elsey Papers, Truman Library.

38. Ltr, Sheehy to Radford, 28 Oct 1949, box 53, Radford Papers.

39. The Secretary's pitiful excuse for not talking to Denfeld on 27 October was that he was going to the President for authority to make the transfer and if the President didn't approve, "then there was nothing to talk to him about." "Telephone conversation between Mr. Matthews and Mr. Cedric Foster 1111 28 October 1949", inserted between entries for 27 and 28 Oct 1949, Matthews Daily Log.

40. Griffin interview

41. L. S. Sabin, "An Interview with John T. Mason, Jr., Director of Oral History," Comment and Discussion section, U.S. Naval Institute *Proceedings* 99 (Nov 1973): 87; and entry for 28 Oct 1949, Matthews Daily Log.

42. "Telephone conversation between Mr. Matthews and Mr. Bradbury 1125 31 October 1949," 3, inserted between entries for 29 Oct and 31 Oct 1949, Matthews Daily Log.

43. "Telephone conversation between Mr. Matthews and Cedric Foster 1111 28 October 1949".

44. Copy of typed press statement by Carl Vinson, 28 Oct 1949; encl. to ltr, Vinson to Admiral W. H. Standley, USN (Ret.), 31 Oct 1949, attached to ltr, Standley to Denfeld, 18 Nov 1949, box 9, Denfeld Papers, OA.

45. Quoted in "House Committee Members Angered at Denfeld Relief," *Army and Navy Journal*, 5 Nov 1949, 250.

46. Ibid.

47. See "Adm. Denfeld Loses Post," 221. In order to maintain secrecy, Matthews and Johnson used State Department communications to order Sherman to return to the United States in civilian clothes and on board a civilian airliner. Palmer, *Origins of the Maritime Strategy*, 53.

48. See ltr, ADM J. H. Towers, USN (Ret.), Vice President of Pan American World Airways System, to Sherman, 2 Nov 1949; and ltr, Sherman to Towers, 11 Nov 1949, both in box 4, Sherman Papers, OA. Sherman came back on a Pan American aircraft.

49. The details on Sherman's itinerary on 1 November are from Stevens, "Sherman Chosen Navy Chief," 1, 19. Secretary Matthews' official log for that day reveals only that he first arrived at the office at 4:30 p.m. Entry for 1 Nov 1949, Matthews Daily Log.

50. Entry for 1 Nov 1949, Matthews Daily Log.

51. Ibid.

52. Stevens, "Sherman Chosen Navy Chief," 19. The time of the press conference is provided by the Matthews Daily Log.

53. Stevens, "Sherman Chosen Navy Chief," 19.

54. See "Statement Released by Secretary of the Navy Francis P. Matthews November 2, 1949," filed with entry for 2 Nov 1949, Matthews Daily Log.

55. Entry for 2 Nov 1949, ibid.

56. Austin Stevens, "Sherman Inducted As New Navy Chief," *New York Times*, 3 Nov 1949, 1, 18; and John G. Norris, "Sherman Takes Post at Helm of Navy," *Washington Post*, 3 Nov 1949.

57. Drew Pearson, "Admirals Running Handout Mill," *Washington Post*, 19 Oct 1949. The designation of OP–23 as "Operation 23" clearly denotes a non-Navy Department source.

58. This inaccurate description of Davies as "second in command" of OP–23 (probably designed to link OP–23 directly with the drafting of Cedric Worth's Anonymous Document) was accepted at face value by subsequent writers, including Paul Hammond. For Davies' true status, see memo, CNO to SECNAV, OP–23 ser 148P23, 2 Nov 1949, 3, "File No. 28," unnumbered box, Burke Papers, OA.

59. John A. Giles, "Navy Unit's Role In Services Fight Under Scrutiny: Documents Are Seized; 3,300 Middies Cheer Denfeld at Game," *Washington Evening Star*, 30 Oct 1949. See also memo, Burke to CAPT Richard P. Glass, Aide to SECNAV, 31 Oct 1949, ibid. Giles and other reporters who later contacted Burke for confirmation of Giles's story were familiar with the details of the investigation itself. However they apparently were unaware of when it had occurred and why it was ordered. This would appear to point to an Air Force or OSD source for the story.

60. Ltr, Burke to CAPT K. D. Ringle, 2 Nov 1949, "File No. 28," unnumbered box, Burke Papers, OA..

61. Ibid. See also "History of the Investigation of the B–36," 41.

62. Untitled memo dictated by Burke, 3 Nov 1949, "File No. 28," unnumbered box, Burke Papers, OA..

63. C. B. Allen, "Sherman Ends Naval Division That Led Feud," *New York Herald Tribune*, 4 Nov 1949; John G. Norris, "Sherman Dissolves 'OP 23' Unit, Called Key to Fight by Navy," *Washington Post*, 4 Nov 1949; and Lloyd Norman, "OP–23 Board Dissolved by Chief's Order," *Washington Times Herald*, 4 Nov 1949. OP–23 was officially disestablished on 4 November 1949. Copy of memo, CNO to All Bureaus and Offices, Navy Department, and Headquarters USMC, OP–23 ser 149P23, n.d. [5 Nov 1949], box 19, Burke Papers, OA.

64. "Death Blow Struck Navy Policy Unit," *Los Angeles Times*, 4 Nov 1949; and "Sherman Scatters Navy Rebels," *Washington Daily News*, 4 Nov 1949.

65. Emphasis in original. Ltr, Charles G. Ewing to Burke, 5 Sep 1951, "File No. 28," unnumbered box, Burke Papers, OA.

66. Ltr, Burke to Lee, 9 Nov 1949, box 16, Radford Papers, OA.

67. Burke told his friend Alvin Herzig, "We will be back in a month—at which time I will get a new assignment. Where I don't know—but it[']s the top peoples['] problem—not mine." Ltr, Burke to Herzig, 9 Nov 1949, "File No. 28," unnumbered box, Burke Papers, OA.

68. Emphasis in original. Ltr, Radford to Burke, 14 Nov 1949, box 55, Radford Papers, OA.

69. See David McConnell, "Admiral's Rank For Crommelin Is a Possibility," *New York Herald Tribune*, 7 Nov 1949. Although not among the thirty-nine people formally scheduled to be considered by the Selection Board, Burke and the two others from the Class of 1923 were only a few "numbers" below them. Ibid.; and "Crommelin Promotion Could Be Considered by New Navy Board," *Washington Evening Star*, 7 Nov 1949.

70. John G. Norris, "Dissident Admirals Left Off Navy's New Promotion Board," *Washington Post*, 10 Nov 1949.

71. ADM Felix B. Stump, USN (Ret.), interviews by John T. Mason, Jr., 7 Jan 1963, 18 Apr 1963, 7 Aug 1963, 25 Jun 1964, and 22 Jul 1964, transcript, Oral History Research Office, Columbia University, New York City, NY, 247.

72. Jack Steele, "Truman Denies Change in Navy Promotion List," *New York Herald Tribune*, 16 Dec 1949. This submission date appears to be supported by the Secretary's appointment calendar, which shows a short meeting with Vice Admiral Harry Hill at 3:19 p.m. on the 23rd. Entry for 23 Nov 1949, Matthews Daily Log.

73. Stump oral history, Columbia University, 245. Secretary Matthews' daily schedule shows a meeting with Vice Admiral Hill at 10:55 a.m. on 25 November. Entry for 25 Nov 1949, Matthews Daily Log.

74. Ltr, RADM J. W. Reeves, Jr. to Burke, 4 Jan 1950, attached to ltr, Burke to Reeves, 5 Jan 1949, "File No. 29," unnumbered box, Burke Papers, OA.

75. Steele, "Truman Denies Change." Matthews's calendar for those days shows two short morning meetings with an Admiral Hill (no other identification) on the 28th and an afternoon meeting on the 29th. Entries for 28 and 29 Nov 1949, Matthews Daily Log.

76. Ltr, Vosseller to Lee, 30 Nov 1949, box 16, Radford Papers, OA.

77. President Truman was at Key West from 28 November to 20 December 1949. Information from the President's schedule provided to author by Dennis Bilger of the Truman Library.

78. Dennison interview, 23 Feb 1977.

79. Ibid. See also Dennison oral history, Truman Library, 137–38.

80. Dennison interview, 23 Feb 1977.

81. Ibid.

82. See, for example, Bert Andrews, "Capt. Burke, Unification Critic, Taken Off Navy Promotion List," *New York Herald Tribune*, 13 Dec 1949; Robert W. Ruth, "Cole Charges Reprisal Against Navy Officer," *Baltimore Sun*, 14 Dec 1949; "Truman Denies Report That Burke Was Taken From Admiral List," *Washington Evening Star*, 15 Dec 1949; Hanson Baldwin, "Navy Vents Wrath At Slight To Burke In Unification Row," *New York Times*, 16 Dec 1949, 1; and L. Edgar Prina, "31-Knot Burke a Hero to Seadogs, Man Taken Off Promotion List Deemed Just About Navy's Finest Officer," *New York Sun*, 20 Dec 1949.

83. Dennison interview, 23 Feb 1977. See also Dennison oral history, Truman Library, 139–40.

84. ALNAV 118, 29 Dec 1949, "File No. 28," unnumbered box, Burke Papers, OA.

85. See, for example, "Truman Promotes Pentagon 'Rebel' ", *New York Times*, 30 Dec 1949, 1; John G. Norris, "Burke on Admiral List, Crommelin Off, 23 Captains Promoted, Senate Must Act on Slate," *Washington Post*, 30 Dec 1949, 1, Robert W. Ruth, "Capt. Burke Promoted, Admiral Blandy Retires," *Baltimore Sun*, 30 Dec 1949, 1, and "An Admiral Now Despite Key Role in Defense Row, Capt. Arleigh A. Burke Moves Up," *Kansas City Times*, 30 Dec 1949, 1.

86. Ltr, Burke to Reeves, 5 Jan 1950, "File No. 29," unnumbered box, Burke Papers, OA.

87. See, for example, ltr, Denfeld to ADM Harold R. Stark, USN (Ret.), 17 Nov 1949; att. to ltr, Stark to Denfeld, 2 Nov 1949, box 9, Denfeld Papers, OA.

88. Ltr, Radford to Byrd, 1 Dec 1949, box 20, Radford Papers, OA. In a letter to Ossie Colclough, Radford further noted, "In a way, by accepting Conolly's job under the circumstances, Louis would be assisting Sherman in sticking the knife in Conolly. I personally feel that Conolly backed Louis to the limit, and was a genuine and loyal friend." Ltr, Radford to Colclough, 21 Nov 1949, box 31, Radford Papers.

89. Original signed ltr, Denfeld to Matthews, 14 Dec 1949, box 27, Matthews Papers, Truman Library.

90. Memo, Denfeld to SECNAV, via Commandant, First Naval District and CNO, 19 Jan 1950; att. to memo from CNO to SECNAV, 24 Jan 1950, box 8, 1950 Double Zero Files, OA.

91. See memo, Sherman to SECNAV, 16 Dec 1949, box 145, Agencies File, President's Secretary's File, Truman Library. This memo was the new CNO's list of recommendations for assignments to key billets for the remainder of fiscal year 1950.

92. See ltr, John Dale Price to Radford, 22 Dec 1949; and ltr, Radford to Price, 31 Dec 1949, box 60, Radford Papers. For additional information on Bogan's decision and on the unfortunate final outcome, see memo, Sherman to SECNAV, 14 Jan 1950, 2nd encl. to ltr from Bogan, ser 1159, 30 Dec

1949; and ltr, Sherman to Senator William F. Knowland, 11 Jan 1950, both in box 8, 1950 Double Zero Files, OA; and ltr from Sherman to Radford, 9 Jan 1950, box 36, Radford Papers, OA.

93. For Bogan's views, see various pages of his USNI oral history.

94. Memo, Sherman to SECNAV, 16 Dec 1949; and memo, Sherman to JCS, OP–03 ser 17P03, 19 Jan 1950, box 42, JCS Office Files, Navy Secretariat Records, OA. See also ltr, Price to Radford, 12 Nov 1949; and ltr, Radford to Price, 21 Nov 1949, both in box 60, Radford Papers, OA.

95. Manson interview, 28 Jan 1989.

96. Emphasis in original. Ibid.

97. "Minutes of Press Conference Held by Secretary of Defense Louis Johnson 10 Jan 1950, 2:30 p.m., Room 3E–869," 12–13, box 62, Principal File, Eisenhower Pre-Presidential Papers, Eisenhower Library.

98. Memo, CNO to JCS, ser 00086P33, 27 Dec 1949, box 28, T/S Control Office Files, OA; and Memo for Files by OP–003, no ser, 13 Jul 1951, 3–5, box 7, Sherman Papers, OA.

99. Ltr, Short to Radford, 18 Dec 1949, box 37, Radford Papers, OA.

100. Memo, F. M. Sallagar to Stuart Symington, 10 Jan 1949, attached to cover note, MAJ Robert Hogg, Exec. Asst. to CS/USAF, to Hoyt Vandenberg, same date, box 42, Vandenberg Papers, MD–LC.

101. Memo, CAPT Ira H. Nunn to Sherman, 17 Feb 1950, box 4, 1953 Double Zero Files, OA.

102. Ltr, Colclough to Radford, 10 Mar 1950, box 31, Radford Papers, OA.

103. Ltr, Vinson to Eisenhower, 1 Mar 1950, attached to ltr, Eisenhower to Vinson, 4 Mar 1950, box 118, Principal File, Eisenhower Pre-Presidential Papers, Eisenhower Library.

104. Congress, House, Committee on Armed Services, *Unification and Strategy: A Report*, 81st Cong., 2d sess., 1 Mar 1950, H. Doc. No. 600, 54.

105. Ibid.

106. Ltr, Short to Radford, 5 Apr 1950, box 37, Radford Papers, OA.

107. Congress, House, Committee on Armed Services, *Full Committee Hearings on H. R. 7764, To Authorize the Construction of Modern Naval Vessels, and for Other Purposes*, 81st Cong., 2d sess., 25 Apr 1950, 5958.

108. Ibid., 5961.

109. See ibid., 5962.

110. Office memo, Lyle S. Garlock, ASST to ASST SECDEF McNeil, recording Secretary Johnson's comments attached to the original copy of the request, n.d. [17 Mar 1950]; att. to office memo, Garlock to Sherman, 17 Mar 1950, box 9, 1950 Double Zero Files, OA.

111. Emphasis added. Memo, OP–301F1 to OP–30, no ser, 9 Mar 1950, 1, box 257, Strategic Plans, OA. See also its att., memo, DCNO (Air) to Distribution List, OP–502D ser 0048P50, 3 Mar 1950.

112. See notes "New CVB," n.d. [mid-May 1951], box 7, Sherman Papers, OA; and testimony of CDR J. L. Counihan, Hearing on "Attack Carrier (New Construction)," 24 Oct 1950, *Hearings Before the General Board of the Navy 1950: Vol 4* (Wilmington, DE: Scholarly Resources, 1983), 15:961, microfilm, 967–68.

113. Memo for Record by Kimball, 29 Nov 1950, box 2, Kimball Papers, Truman Library. A month earlier, in an interview in *U.S. News & World Report*, Vinson had expressed the same sentiment. See "Why Bigger Draft Is Coming, An Interview With Carl Vinson," *U.S. News & World Report*, 27 Oct 1950, 45.

114. See, for example, ltr, Dewey Short to Radford, 24 Jun 1950, box 37, Radford Papers, OA.

115. Although initially designed as a flush-deck carrier, *Forrestal* was redesigned in 1953 and eventually built with a fixed island, following the Navy's successful 1952 tests of the British-inspired angled flight deck.

116. See encl. (on shipbuilding programs) to memo, VADM James Fife, DCNO (Operations), to ADM Duncan, 11 Aug 1951, "1800/138—1800/165" folder, Navy Secretariat Records, OA; Scot MacDonald, "Evolution of Aircraft Carriers: CVA's Built To Meet Modern Needs," *Naval Aviation News*, November 1963, 24; and Norman Friedman, *U.S. Aircraft Carriers*, 256.

Bibliography

This book is based largely upon research conducted in the archival collections of a variety of repositories in the Washington, D.C., area and at the Truman and Eisenhower presidential libraries. Valuable material was also found in doctoral dissertations by individuals who had special access to the papers of one or another of the services. The most important Washington-area repositories for this study were the Operational Archives of the Naval Historical Center, the National Archives, the Manuscript Division of the Library of Congress, and the Washington National Records Center in Suitland, Maryland.

Primary Sources

The Naval Historical Center's Operational Archives, located at the Washington Navy Yard, maintains extensive holdings of classified and unclassified U.S. Navy records dating from the pre-World War II period to the present. Both declassified and unclassified official and personal papers were used for this study. The official papers included the records of the Immediate Office of the Chief of Naval Operations (designated the Double Zero Files); the Strategic Plans Division Records (material on strategic planning and policy generated or held by OP–30 and its successors); the Top Secret Control Office Records (Top Secret documents generated within or received by the Office of the Chief of Naval Operations, which were maintained by a central office for security purposes); the Deputy Chief of Naval Operations for Air Records (selected official and personal-official correspondence files of successive Deputy Chiefs of Naval Operations for Air, together with certain additional materials from OP–05 files); and the OP–23 Records (materials largely relating to unification and matters concerning service roles and missions that were generated or received by the Organizational Research and Policy Division of the office of the Deputy Chief of Naval Operations for Administration and its predecessors, SCOROR [Secretary's Committee on Research on Reorganization] and UNICOM [Secretary's Committee on Unification]) from 1945 through 1949.

The materials from some of the Operational Archives' extensive collection of personal papers proved equally valuable for this study. Those of greatest importance included the papers of Admiral Arthur W. Radford, Admiral Arleigh A. Burke, and Vice Admiral Ralph A. Ofstie. Radford's unification files, assembled and originally maintained for him during his tour as Commander in Chief, Pacific and Commander in Chief, Pacific Fleet by then Captain Fitzhugh Lee, are invaluable in furnishing copies of otherwise hard-to-find documents on the roles and missions debates. The papers kept by Arleigh Burke which relate to his role as head of OP–23 are vital to an understanding of the events of 1949. Ralph Ofstie's papers provide additional valuable insights into Navy thinking at the time.

A number of records collections were consulted at the National Archives. In addition to various Navy records found in Record Groups (RG) 38, 72, 80, and 428, selected records from the National Archives' extensive holdings of Headquarters, United States Air Force (RG 341) files were used, particularly the Strategic Air Group Records (research and development correspondence on Army Air Forces and U.S. Air Force bomber programs from the wartime period through the early 1950s) and the Top Secret Air Adjutant General Records (the first twenty-three boxes of which were declassified in 1991). Other collections examined at the National Archives included RG 218 (Records of the Joint Chiefs of Staff) and RG 330 (Records of the Office of the Secretary of Defense).

At the Manuscript Division of the Library of Congress, the voluminous collections of personal papers of former Army Air Forces Commanding Generals and Air Force Chiefs of Staff were examined, including those of Generals Arnold, Spaatz, Vandenberg, Twining, White, and LeMay. The papers of Carl Spaatz and Hoyt Vandenberg proved the most valuable for this study.

At the Washington National Records Center, Suitland, Maryland, a number of collections under National Archives control were used. The most fruitful was the Symington Special Interest Files in RG 340 (Records of the Secretary of the Air Force). The Special Interest Files consist of some fifty-seven boxes of material on roles and missions and other issues of potential controversy that were assembled for the use of Air Force Secretary Stuart Symington. Although they must be used together with materials now available in the Symington Papers at the Truman Library, these files constitute an invaluable source on high-level Air Force thinking in the early postwar period.

The Truman Presidential Library in Independence, Missouri, holds a vast collection of materials relating to Harry S. Truman's terms as President of the United States. For this study the Navy- and Air Force-related materials in the President's Secretary's File and the Papers of Clark M. Clifford, Dan A. Kimball, Francis P. Matthews, John L. Sullivan, and W. Stuart Symington proved the most important. The most useful material available at the Eisenhower Presidential Library in Abilene, Kansas, turned up in the Principal File of the Eisenhower Pre-Presidential Papers. Here can be found General Dwight D. Eisenhower's correspondence with Defense Secretaries James V. Forrestal and Louis A. Johnson relating to his service during 1949 as a part-time advisor to the Secretary of Defense and temporary presiding officer of the Joint Chiefs of Staff.

Secondary Sources

The most useful dissertations on issues relevant to the "revolt of the admirals" are Lawrence J. Legere, Jr.'s "Unification of the Armed Forces," Murray Green's "Stuart Symington and the B–36," and B. Vincent Davis's "Admirals, Politics and Postwar Defense Policy." Only the last work has been published in book form.

Lawrence Legere was a major in the U.S. Army when he completed his dissertation in 1950—the year of the denouement of the "revolt." He briefly traces the development of Army-Navy relations from the American Revolution forward but concentrates on the issue of armed services unification in the twentieth century. The author did much of his dissertation research in the Army's Office of the Chief of Military History, where he reviewed and cited War Department copies of Joint Chiefs of Staff unification documents from World War II and the early postwar period. Legere was able to cite only secondary sources for his account of the 1947–1950 period. But his adroit handling of information from the large number of articles in professional military journals from these years allowed him to make useful comments about doctrinal thinking in the armed forces, particularly in the Air Force.

Murray Green drafted "Stuart Symington and the B–36" on his own time while a civilian employee of the Air Force. Because of his official standing and his previous service in Air Force Secretary Stuart Symington's office, Green was given access to an extensive number of then security-classified Air Force files on Navy-Air Force roles and missions disputes, including the B–36 bomber controversy—the previously mentioned Symington Special Interest Files. He was allowed to cite and quote from many of the documents contained in these files. The result is a study that faithfully reflects a contemporary, high-level Air Force perspective on the events of 1948–1949. Because of the overwhelming amount of Air Force material used in its preparation, however, the dissertation provides only a single service perspective on the subject.

Vincent Davis finished his dissertation on "Admirals, Politics and Postwar Defense Policy" in 1961. When published five years later by the University of North Carolina Press, it was entitled *Postwar Defense Policy and the U.S. Navy, 1943–1946*. Although his study did not furnish details on the events of 1949, it did provide an insightful overview of the Navy's World War II planning for its role in the postwar period. Like Green, Davis based his analysis upon documents in classified files; in this case, it was the Navy's records on postwar planning. In addition Davis conducted interviews and corresponded with a large number of senior naval officers and civilian officials. His study therefore contains much informed commentary on the Navy's thinking during the war with regard to postwar force structure and on its roles-and-missions debate with the Army and its increasingly vocal component, the Army Air Forces.

Given the importance of the "revolt of the admirals" as an example of the postwar debate on military strategy, it is surprising how few published works have attempted to examine it seriously. Walter Millis's 1958 book, *Arms and the State*, touched on the "revolt" but did not explore its depths. Similarly, a thoughtful paper presented at the Harvard Law School by James Freund of the Defense Policy Seminar and eventually published in *The Air Power Historian* used the events of 1949 to theorize about the nature of bureaucratic conflict in the defense establishment.

Until political scientist Paul Y. Hammond published his monograph-length study in 1963, no sustained analyses of the Navy-Air Force fight had appeared. Hammond's study, "Super Carriers and B–36 Bombers," soon became the standard account because of its detailed examination of the events surrounding the "revolt," its thorough analytical style, and its measured prose. Historians of postwar U.S. defense policy continue to rely upon it as the most comprehensive and accurate account of the events.

Although there is much to praise in the Hammond monograph, it suffers from two weaknesses. The first is a lack of balance resulting from too much reliance on contemporary news stories for its facts. The second is a perspective on the Navy's role in the events that appears overly colored by the author's privileged access to selected Air Force materials. Hammond was not privy to official Navy documents.

Most accounts of the "revolt of the admirals" written since publication of Paul Hammond's study have used his narrative version of the events uncritically. Accordingly these works have failed to challenge his conclusions regarding the Navy's role in the "revolt" and the long-term results of the hearings.

NOTE: Bibliographical listings for some newspaper accounts omit page numbers; these articles were found as clippings in various manuscript collections.

Primary Sources

Manuscript Collections

Dwight D. Eisenhower Library, Abilene, KS.
    Eisenhower Pre-Presidential Papers
    Alfred M. Gruenther Papers

National Archives and Records Administration, Washington, DC.
- RG 18: Air Adjutant General Records
- RG 38: COMINCH Records
- RG 72: Bureau of Aeronautics Records
- RG 80: General Board Records
  Records of Secretary of the Navy James Forrestal, 1940–1947
  SecNav–CNO Records
  Top Policy Group Correspondence
  Top Policy Group Minutes
- RG 218: Joint Chiefs of Staff Records
- RG 330: Office of Public Information, Assistant Secretary of Defense (Legislative & Public Affairs) Records
  Office of the Secretary of Defense Records
- RG 341: Assistant for Atomic Energy General Decimal Files, 1949
  Strategic Air Group Records
  Top Secret Air Adjutant General Files
- RG 428: Classified Correspondence of Secretary Francis P. Matthews (1949–1950)

  Classified Correspondence of Secretary John L. Sullivan

National Archives and Records Administration, Washington National Records Center, Suitland, MD.
- RG 340: Air Board Papers
  Public Information Division Records
  Symington Special Interest Files
- RG 428: Secretary of the Navy Records

Manuscript Division, Library of Congress, Washington, DC.
  Joseph and Stewart Alsop Papers
  Henry H. Arnold Papers
  James H. Doolittle Papers
  Ira C. Eaker Papers
  Muir S. Fairchild Papers
  Ernest J. King Papers

Hugh J. Knerr Papers
Curtis E. LeMay Papers
Elwood R. Quesada Papers
Carl A. Spaatz Papers
Nathan F. Twining Papers
Hoyt S. Vandenberg Papers
Thomas D. White Papers

Naval Historical Center, Washington, DC.
  Naval Aviation History Branch
    Aircraft Carrier Files
    Aircraft Files
  Operational Archives
    Official Files:
      DCNO (Air) Records
      Miscellaneous Records of the Office of Information (CHINFO)
      Navy Secretariat for JCS Matters Records
      Officer Bios Collection
      OP–23 Records
      Post 1 January 1946 Command File
      Post 1 January 1946 Plans File
      Post 1 January 1946 Reports File
      Records of the Immediate Office of the Chief of Naval Operations (Double Zero Files)
      Research and Inventions/Office of Naval Research Records
      Strategic Plans Division Records
      Top Secret Control Office Records
      World War II Command File
    Personal Papers (including Privileged Manuscript Collection):
      Arleigh A. Burke Papers
      Louis E. Denfeld Papers
      James V. Forrestal Diaries (xerographic copy)
      James V. Forrestal Papers
      Ernest J. King Papers
      William D. Leahy Papers
      Samuel Eliot Morison Office Files
      Chester W. Nimitz Papers
      Ralph A. Ofstie Papers
      Arthur W. Radford Autobiography (xerographic copy)
      Arthur W. Radford Papers

Forrest P. Sherman Papers
Harold R. Stark Papers
Harry E. Yarnell Papers

Seely Mudd Library, Princeton University, Princeton, NJ.
Ferdinand Eberstadt Papers
James V. Forrestal Papers

Harry S. Truman Library, Independence, MO.
Clark M. Clifford Papers
Confidential File, White House Central Files
George M. Elsey Papers
Dan A. Kimball Papers
Francis P. Matthews Papers
National Security Council Records, Truman Papers
President's Secretary's File, Truman Papers
John L. Sullivan Papers
W. Stuart Symington Papers

Naval Historical Foundation, Washington, DC.
Thomas H. Robbins, Jr., Papers

Center for Air Force History, Bolling Air Force Base, Washington, DC.
Various limited circulation official histories

Other Manuscript Material
Author's correspondence with Vice Admiral Fitzhugh Lee, USN (Ret.)
Papers of Stuart B. Barber, Arlington, VA (loaned to the author for this study)

Congressional and Executive Documents

Arnold, H. H. *Second Report of the Commanding General of the Army Air Forces to the Secretary of War.* February 27, 1945. Washington: Headquarters AAF, 1945.

———. *Third Report of the Commanding General of the Army Air Forces to the Secretary of War.* November 12, 1945. Washington: Headquarters AAF, 1945.

Headquarters Army Air Forces. *Mission Accomplished: Interrogations of Japanese Industrial, Military, and Civil Leaders of World War II.* Washington: Assistant Chief of Air Staff, Headquarters AAF, 1946.

The United States Strategic Bombing Survey. *Over-All Report (European War).* Washington: USSBS, 1945.

———. *The Effects of Strategic Bombing on the German War Economy.* Washington: Over-All Economic Effects Division, USSBS, 1945.

———. *The Strategic Air Operation of Very Heavy Bombardment in the War Against Japan (Twentieth Air Force) Final Report.* Washington: Army and Army Air Section, Military Analysis Division, USSBS, 1946.

———. *Summary Report (Pacific War).* Washington: USSBS, 1946.

———. *Bombing Accuracy, USAAF Heavy and Medium Bombers in the ETO.* 2d ed. Washington: Military Analysis Division, USSBS, 1947.

———. *The Defeat of the German Air Force.* Washington: Military Analysis Division, USSBS, 1947.

———. *The Effects of Strategic Bombing on Japanese Morale.* Washington: Morale Division, USSBS, 1947.

———. *The German Anti-Friction Bearings Industry.* Washington: Equipment Division, USSBS, 1947.

———. *German Submarine Industry Report.* Washington: Munitions Division, USSBS, 1947.

———. *Statistical Appendix to Over-All Report (European War).* Washington: USSBS, 1947.

———. *The War Against Japanese Transportation 1941–1945.* Washington, Transportation Division, USSBS, 1947.

U.S. Congress. House. Committee on Appropriations. Subcommittee on Navy Department Appropriations. *Department of the Navy Appropriation Bill for 1949: Hearings.* 80th Cong., 2d sess., 1948.

———. *Department of the Navy Appropriation Bill for 1949: Supplemental Hearings.* 80th Cong., 2d sess., 1948.

———. Committee on Armed Services. *Full Committee Hearings on S. 1843, To Convert the National Military Establishment Into an Executive Department of the Government, To Be Known as the Department of Defense, To Provide the Secretary of Defense With Appropriate Responsibility and Authority, and With Civilian and Military Assistants Adequate to Fulfill His Enlarged Responsibility.* 81st Cong., 1st sess., 28 June, 1949.

———. *Investigation of the B–36 Bomber Program: Hearings.* 81st Cong., 1st sess., 9–12, 17–19, 22–25 August and 5 October, 1949.

———. *The National Defense Program—Unification and Strategy: Hearings.* 81st Cong., 1st sess., 6–8, 10–13, 17–21 October 1949.

———. *Unification and Strategy: A Report.* 81st Cong., 2d sess., 1 March 1950. House Document No. 600.

———. *Full Committee Hearings on H.R. 7764, To Authorize the Construction of Modern Naval Vessels, and for Other Purposes.* 81st Cong., 2d sess., 25 April 1950.

U.S. Congress. Senate. Committee on Appropriations. Subcommittee. *Navy Department Appropriation Bill for 1949: Hearings on H.R. 6772, a Bill making Appropriations for the Department of the Navy and the Naval Service for the Fiscal Year Ending June 30, 1949, and for Other Purposes.* 80th Cong., 2d sess., 1948.

———. Committee on Military Affairs. *Department of Armed Forces—Department of Military Security: Hearings on S. 84 and S. 1482.* 79th Cong. 1st sess., 17 October–17 December 1945.

———. Committee on Armed Services. *National Security Act Amendments of 1949: Hearing on S. 1269 and S. 1843.* 81st Cong., 1st sess., 24 and 29 March, 6, 7, 11, and 12 April, 5 and 6 May, 1949.

U.S. Department of the Navy. *Naval Aviation Combat Statistics: World War II.* OPNAV-P-23V No. A129. Washington: Air Branch, Office of Naval Intelligence, 17 June 1946 [withdrawn from circulation before general issuance].

———. *United States Naval Aviation, 1910–1980.* NAVAIR 00-80P-1. Washington: Prepared at the direction of the Deputy Chief of Naval Operations (Air Warfare) and the Commander Naval Air Systems Command, 1981.

———. *U.S. Naval Aviation in the Pacific.* Washington: Office of the Chief of Naval Operations, 1947.

U.S. Department of State. *Foreign Relations of the United States, 1948.* Vol. 1, Part 2, *General; The United Nations.* Washington: GPO, 1976.

U.S. Department of War. *Final Report: War Department Policies and Programs Review Board.* 11 August 1947. Washington: War Department, 1947.

Microfilm Publications (in Navy Department Library)

Hearings before the General Board of the Navy. Wilmington, DE: Scholarly Resources Inc., 1983.

1929–1931 Secret and Confidential Files, General Records of the Department of the Navy (RG 80). Washington: National Archives, n.d.

Records Relating to US Navy Fleet Problems I to XXII, 1923–1941. Washington: National Archives, 1974.

Published Diaries, Memoirs and Papers

Abell, Tyler, ed. *Drew Pearson: Diaries 1949–1959.* New York: Holt, Rinehart & Winston, 1974.

Bradley, Omar N. *A Soldier's Story.* New York: Henry Holt & Co., 1951.

———. *The Collected Writings of General Omar N. Bradley.* Vol. 4, *Testimony 1946–1949.* Privately printed, copy no. 41, n.d. Author's collection.

Bradley, Omar N., and Clay Blair, Jr. *A General's Life.* New York: Simon and Schuster, 1983 [Despite its appearance, this book in reality is a biography, not an autobiography].

Clark, J. J., and Clark G. Reynolds. *Carrier Admiral.* New York: David McKay Co., 1967.

Ferrell, Robert H., ed. *The Eisenhower Diaries.* New York: W. W. Norton & Co., 1981.

Galambos, Louis, ed. *The Papers of Dwight David Eisenhower,* Vol. 7, *The Chief of Staff.* Baltimore: Johns Hopkins University Press, 1978.

———. Vol. 10, *Columbia University.* Baltimore: Johns Hopkins University Press, 1984.

Jurika, Stephen, ed. *From Pearl Harbor to Vietnam: The Memoirs of Admiral Arthur W. Radford.* Stanford, CA: Hoover Institution Press, 1980.

Millis, Walter, ed., with the collaboration of E. S. Duffield. *The Forrestal Diaries.* New York: Viking Press, 1951.

Richardson, James O., with George C. Dyer, *On the Treadmill to Pearl Harbor: The Memoirs of Admiral James O. Richardson, USN (Retired), as told to Vice Admiral George C. Dyer, USN (Retired).* Washington: Naval History Division, 1973.

Interviews and Oral History Collections

Interviews by author. Author's personal collection.

Arthur, Charles S., Captain, USN (Ret.). 1 October 1993. Washington. Tape recording.

Ashworth, Frederick L., Vice Admiral, USN (Ret.). Recollections recorded in response to written questions submitted by Captain John F. Barlow, USN (Ret.), and author, February 1984. Santa Fe, NM. Tape recording.

Barber, Stuart B. 25 February 1989. Arlington, VA. Tape recording.

Beach, Edward L., Captain, USN (Ret.). 22 August 1990. Washington. Tape recording.

Burke, Arleigh A., Admiral, USN (Ret.). 25 September 1986. Fairfax, VA. Tape recording.

———. 27 April 1987. Fairfax, VA. Tape recording.

Carney, Robert B., Admiral, USN (Ret.). 30 August 1988. Washington. Tape recording.

Davies, Thomas D., Rear Admiral, USN (Ret.). 11 August 1987. Washington. Tape recording.

Dennison, Robert L., Admiral, USN (Ret.). 23 February 1977. Washington. Tape recording.

Fawkes, Emerson E., Rear Admiral, USN (Ret.). Interview by Captain John F. Barlow, USN (Ret.), and author, 14 July 1984. Arlington, VA. Tape recording.

Griffin, Charles D., Admiral, USN (Ret.). 10 December 1985. Washington. Tape recording.

Howard, Joseph L., Rear Admiral (SC), USN (Ret.). Telephone interview, 28 September 1993. San Diego, CA. Tape recording.

Manson, Frank A., Captain, USN (Ret.). 28 January 1989. Annapolis, MD. Tape recording.

———. Telephone interview, 12 February 1989. Falls Church, VA. Notes.

———. Telephone interview, 8 April 1989. Falls Church, VA. Tape recording.

Metsger, Alfred B., Rear Admiral, USN (Ret.). 10 August 1987. Arlington, VA. Tape recording.

Miller, Harold B., Rear Admiral, USN (Ret.). 6 October 1990. Shawnee Mission, KS. Tape recording.

Rowe, Robert A., Captain, USN (Ret.). Telephone interview, 22 April 1989. Rancho Palos Verdes, CA. Tape recording.

Shaw, Samuel R., Brigadier General, USMC (Ret.). 29 July 1987. Alexandria, VA. Tape recording.

Oral History Research Office, Columbia University, NY (*Copies in Operational Archives, Naval Historical Center*).

Conolly, Richard L., Admiral, USN (Ret.). Interviews by Donald F. Shaughnessy, 1958 and 1959. Transcript.

Fechteler, William M., Admiral, USN (Ret.). Interviews by John T. Mason, Jr., 7 March 1961, 10 April 1961, 9 October 1961, 23 January 1962, 5 February 1962, 19 March 1962, and 22 May 1962. Transcript.

Stump, Felix B., Admiral, USN (Ret.). Interviews by John T. Mason, Jr., 7 January 1963, 18 April 1963, 7 August 1963, 25 June 1964, and 22 July 1964. Transcript.

Center for Air Force History, Bolling Air Force Base, Washington, DC.

Leo, Stephen F. Interview by George M. Watson, Jr., 18 and 19 August 1982. K239.0512–1558, transcript.

Harry S. Truman Library, Independence, MO.

Dennison, Robert L., Admiral, USN (Ret.). Interviews by Jerry N. Hess, 10 September 1971, 6 October 1971, and 2 November 1971. Interview 105, transcript.

Leva, Marx. Interviews by Jerry N. Hess, 9 December 1969 and 12 June 1970. Interview 76, transcript.

McNeil, Wilfred J. Interview by Jerry N. Hess, 19 September 1972. Interview 294, transcript.

Renfrow, Louis H. Interviews by Jerry N. Hess, 12 and 15 March 1971. Interview 99, transcript.

Sullivan, John L. Interviews by Jerry N. Hess, 27 March 1972 and 13 April 1972. Interview 138, transcript.

380   Bibliography

Zuckert, Eugene M. Interview by Jerry N. Hess, 27 September 1971, interview 107, transcript.

U.S. Marine Corps Historical Center, Washington, DC *(Copy in Arleigh A. Burke Papers, Operational Archives, Naval Historical Center).*

Burke, Arleigh A., Admiral, USN (Ret.). Interview by Benis M. Frank, Brigadier General Samuel R. Shaw, USMC (Ret.), and Colonel Donald J. Decker, USMC (Ret.), 26 July 1983. Transcript.

U.S. Naval Institute, Annapolis, MD (*Copies in Operational Archives, Naval Historical Center*).

Baldwin, Hanson W. Interviews by John T. Mason, Jr., 24 February–8 December 1975. Volume 2, transcript.

Bogan, Gerald F., Vice Admiral, USN (Ret.). Interviews by Commander Etta-Belle Kitchen, USN (Ret.), 25 and 26 October 1969. Transcript.

Burke, Arleigh A., Admiral, USN (Ret.). Interviews by John T. Mason, Jr., 7 November 1980, 28 January 1981, 26 February 1981, 26 March 1981, 30 April 1981 and 28 May 1981. "A Study of OP–23 and its Role in the Unification Debates of 1949," Special Series: Volume IV, transcript.

Dennison, Robert L., Admiral, USN (Ret.). Interviews by John T. Mason, Jr., 8 November 1972, 9, 17, and 30 January 1973, 27 March 1973, 11 April 1973, 9 May 1973, 12 June 1973, and 10, 17, and 25 July 1973. Transcript.

Griffin, Charles D., Admiral, USN (Ret.). Interviews by John T. Mason, Jr., 15 and 28 January 1970, 4 February 1970, 2 and 14 April 1970, 26 May 1970, 4 and 11 June 1970, and 7 July 1970. Volume 1, transcript.

Lee, Fitzhugh, Vice Admiral, USN (Ret.). Interviews by Commander Etta-Belle Kitchen, USN (Ret.), 11 July 1970 and 9 August 1970. Transcript.

Wellborn, Charles, Jr., Vice Admiral, USN (Ret.). Interviews by John T. Mason, Jr., 9 and 30 November 1971, 15 December 1971, 4 January 1972, 8 and 24 February 1972, and 7, 14 and 26 April 1972, and 10 May 1972. Transcript.

Secondary Sources

Books, Monographs, and Studies

Air Force Association. *Who's Who in the Air Force: Biographies of Key Personnel of the United States Air Force Around the World.* A supplement to *Air Force Magazine.* 1954 Edition. Washington: Air Force Association, 1954.

Albion, Robert Greenhalgh, and Robert Howe Connery, with the collaboration of Jennie Barnes Pope. *Forrestal and the Navy.* New York: Columbia University Press, 1962.

Borowski, Harry. *A Hollow Threat: Strategic Air Power and Containment Before Korea.* Westport, CT: Greenwood Press, 1982.

Boyle, Andrew. *Trenchard*. New York: W. W. Norton & Co., 1962.

Brodie, Bernard. *The Heritage of Douhet*. Project RAND Research Memorandum RM-1013. Santa Monica, CA: RAND Corporation, 1952.

———. *Strategy in the Missile Age*. Princeton: Princeton University Press, 1959.

———. *War and Politics*. New York: Macmillan Co., 1973.

Brodie, Bernard, and Eilene Galloway. *The Atomic Bomb and the Armed Services*. Public Affairs Bulletin No. 55. Washington: Library of Congress Legislative Reference Service, 1947.

Byrd, Martha. *Chennault: Giving Wings to the Tiger*. Tuscaloosa: University of Alabama Press, 1987.

Caraley, Demetrios. *The Politics of Military Unification: A Study of Conflict and the Policy Process*. New York: Columbia University Press, 1966.

Carter, Kit C., and Robert Mueller, comps. *The Army Air Forces in World War II. Combat Chronology 1941–1945*. Washington: Albert F. Simpson Historical Research Center, Air University, and Office of Air Force History, USAF, 1973.

Clark, Keith C., and Laurence J. Legere, eds. *The President and the Management of National Security: A Report by the Institute for Defense Analysis*. New York: Frederick A. Praeger, 1969.

Coffey Thomas M. *Hap: The Story of the U.S. Air Force and the Man who Built It: General Henry H. "Hap" Arnold*. New York: Viking Press, 1982.

Cogar, William B., ed. *New Interpretations in Naval History: Selected Papers from The Eigth Naval History Symposium*. Annapolis: Naval Institute Press, 1989.

Coleman, Ted, with Robert Wenkam. *Jack Northrop and the Flying Wing: The Story Behind the Stealth Bomber*. New York: Paragon House, 1988.

Coletta, Paolo E., ed. *American Secretaries of the Navy*, Vol. 2, *1913–1972*. Annapolis: Naval Institute Press, 1980.

———. *The United States Navy and Defense Unification 1947–1953*. Newark: University of Delaware Press, 1981.

Condit, Doris M. *History of the Office of the Secretary of Defense*. Vol. 2, *The Test of War 1950–1953*. Washington: Historical Office, Office of the Secretary of Defense, 1988.

Condit, Kenneth W. *History of the Joint Chiefs of Staff: The Joint Chiefs of Staff and National Policy*. Vol. 2, *1947–1949*. Washington: Historical Division, Joint Secretariat, Joint Chiefs of Staff, 1978.

Congress and the Nation, 1945–1964: A Review of Government and Politics in the Postwar Years. Washington: Congressional Quarterly Service, 1965.

Copp, Dewitt S., for the Air Force Historical Foundation. *A Few Great Captains: The Men and Events That Shaped the Development of U.S. Air Power*. Garden City, NY: Doubleday & Co., 1980.

———. *Forged in Fire: Strategy and Decisions in the Air War over Europe 1940–45*. Garden City, NY: Doubleday & Co., 1982.

Craven, Wesley F., and James L. Cate, ed., for Office of Air Force History, USAF. *The Army Air Forces in World War II*. 7 Vols. Chicago: University of Chicago Press, 1948–1958.

Davis, Vincent. *Postwar Defense Policy and the U.S. Navy, 1943–1946*. Chapel Hill: The University of North Carolina Press, 1966.

———. *The Admirals Lobby*. Chapel Hill: University of North Carolina Press, 1967.

———. *The Politics of Innovation: Patterns in Navy Cases*. Monograph Series in World Affairs No. 3: 1966–67. Denver, CO: University of Denver, 1967.

De Seversky, Alexander P. *Victory Through Air Power*. New York: Simon and Schuster, 1942.

Dickens, Admiral Sir Gerald. *Bombing and Strategy: The Fallacy of Total War*. London: Sampson Low, Marston & Co., 1947.

Donovan, Robert J. *Tumultuous Years: The Presidency of Harry S Truman 1949–1953*. New York: W. W. Norton & Co., 1982.

Dorwart, Jeffrey M. *Eberstadt and Forrestal: A National Security Partnership, 1909–1949*. College Station: Texas A&M University Press, 1991.

Douhet, Giulio. *The Command of the Air*. Translated by Dino Ferrari. New York: Coward-McCann, 1942.

Earle, Edward Meade, ed., with the collaboration of Gordon A. Craig and Felix Gilbert. *Makers of Modern Strategy: Military Thought from Machiavelli to Hitler*. Princeton: Princeton University Press, 1943.

Emerson, William R. *Operation Pointblank: A Tale of Bombers and Fighters*. Harmon Memorial Lectures in Military History. Colorado Springs: United States Air Force Academy, 1962.

Ferrell, Robert H. *The American Secretaries of State and Their Diplomacy*. Vol. 15, *George C. Marshall*. New York: Cooper Square Publishers, 1966.

Fifteenth Air Force, Headquarters. *A Brief History of Strategic Bombardment 1911–1971*. March AFB, CA: Headquarters Fifteenth Air Force, 1971.

Frankland, Noble. *The Bombing Offensive Against Germany: Outlines and Perspectives*. London: Faber & Faber, 1965.

Friedman, Norman. *U.S. Aircraft Carriers: An Illustrated Design History.* Annapolis: Naval Institute Press, 1983.

Frisbee, John L., ed. *Makers of the United States Air Force.* Washington: Office of Air Force History, USAF, 1987.

Futrell, Robert F. *Ideas, Concepts, Doctrine: A History of Basic Thinking in the United States Air Force, 1907–1964.* 2 Vols. Maxwell AFB, AL: Aerospace Studies Institute, Air University, 1971.

Glines, Carroll V., Jr. *The Compact History of the United States Air Force.* New York: Hawthorn Books, 1963.

Goldberg, Alfred. *A History of the United States Air Force 1907–1957.* Princeton: D. Van Nostrand Co., 1957.

Goldberg, Alfred, and Robert D. Little. *History of Headquarters USAF, 1 July 1949 to 30 June 1950.* Washington: Air University Historical Liaison Office, Department of the Air Force, 1954.

Hammond, Paul Y. *Organizing for Defense: The American Military Establishment in the Twentieth Century.* Princeton: Princeton University Press, 1961.

Hansell, Haywood, Jr. *The Air Plan That Defeated Hitler.* Atlanta, GA: Printed by author, 1972.

Hansen, Chuck. *US Nuclear Weapons: The Secret History.* Arlington, TX: Aerofax and Orion Books, 1988.

Hardesty, Von. *Red Phoenix: The Rise of Soviet Air Power, 1941–1945.* Washington: Smithsonian Institution Press, 1982.

Haynes, Richard F. *The Awesome Power: Harry S. Truman as Commander in Chief.* Baton Rouge: Louisiana State University Press, 1973.

Heflin, Woodford A., ed. *The United States Air Force Dictionary.* Maxwell AFB, AL: Air University Press, 1956.

Holley, I. B., Jr. *An Enduring Challenge: The Problem of Air Force Doctrine.* Harmon Memorial Lectures in Military History. Colorado Springs: United States Air Force Academy, 1974.

Hopkins, J. C. *The Development of Strategic Air Command 1946–1981 (A Chronological History).* Offutt AFB, NE: Office of the Historian, Headquarters Strategic Air Command, 1982.

Hewlett, Richard G., and Francis Duncan. *A History of the United States Atomic Energy Commission.* Vol. 2, *Atomic Shield, 1947/1952.* University Park: Pennsylvania State University Press, 1969.

Huie, William Bradford. *The Fight for Air Power.* New York: L. B. Fischer, 1942.

———. *The Case Against the Admirals: Why We Must Have a Unified Command.* New York: E. P. Dutton & Co., 1946.

Huntington, Samuel P. *The Soldier and the State: The Theory and Politics of Civil-Military Relations.* Cambridge: Belknap Press of Harvard University Press, 1957.

Hurley, Alfred F. *Billy Mitchell: Crusader for Air Power.* New York: Franklin Watts, 1964.

Hurley, Alfred F., and Robert C. Ehrhart. *Air Power and Warfare: The Proceedings of the 8th Military History Symposium United States Air Force Academy, 18–20 October 1978.* Washington: Office of Air Force History, Headquarters USAF, and United States Air Force Academy, 1979.

Jacobsen, Meyers K., and Ray Wagner. *B–36 in Action.* Carrollton, TX: Squadron/Signal Publications, 1980.

Jones, H. A. *The War in the Air: Being the Story of the Part Played in the Great War by the Royal Air Force.* Vol. 6. Oxford: Clarendon Press, 1937.

Jones, Vincent C. *United States Army in World War II. Special Studies. Manhattan: The Army and the Atomic Bomb.* Washington: Center of Military History, United States Army, 1985.

Kaplan, Fred. *The Wizards of Armageddon.* New York: Simon and Schuster, 1983.

Keiser, Gordon W. *The US Marine Corps and Defense Unification 1944–47: The Politics of Survival.* Washington: National Defense University Press, 1982.

Kennett, Lee. *A History of Strategic Bombing.* New York: Charles Scribner's Sons, 1982.

Knaack, Marcelle S. *Encyclopedia of U.S. Air Force Aircraft and Missile Systems.* Vol. 2, *Post-World War II Bombers 1945–1973.* Washington: Office of Air Force History, USAF, 1988.

Kohn, Richard H., and Joseph P. Harahan, eds. *Air Superiority in World War II and Korea: An Interview with Gen. James Ferguson, Gen. Robert M. Lee, Gen. William Momyer, and Lt. Gen. Elwood R. Quesada.* Washington: Office of Air Force History, USAF, 1983.

Kolodziej, Edward A. *The Uncommon Defense and Congress, 1945–1963.* Columbus: Ohio State University Press, 1966.

Kuniholm, Bruce R. *The Origins of the Cold War in the Near East: Great Power Conflict and Diplomacy.* Princeton: Princeton University Press, 1980.

Lapica, R. L., ed. *Facts on File Yearbook 1949.* New York: Facts on File, 1950.

Lee, Asher, ed. *The Soviet Air and Rocket Forces.* New York: Frederick A. Praeger, 1959.

LeMay, Curtis E., with MacKinley Kantor. *Mission with LeMay.* Garden City, NY: Doubleday & Co., 1965.

LeMay, Curtis E., with Bill Yenne. *Superfortress: The Story of the B–29 and American Air Power.* New York: McGraw-Hill Book Co., 1988.

Lemmer, George F. *The Air Force and the Concept of Deterrence, 1945–1950.* Washington: USAF Historical Division Liaison Office, 1963.

Little, Robert D. *Organizing for Strategic Planning, 1945–1950: The National System and the Air Force.* Washington: USAF Historical Division Liaison Office, [1964].

Love, Robert W., ed. *The Chiefs of Naval Operations.* Annapolis: Naval Institute Press, 1980.

MacIssac, David. *Strategic Bombing in World War Two: The Story of the United States Strategic Bombing Survey.* New York: Garland Publishing, 1976.

Macmillan, Norman. *The Royal Air Force in the World War.* Vol. 4, *1940–1945 (II).* London: George G. Harrap & Co., 1950.

Maurer, Maurer, comp. and ed. *The U.S. Air Service in World War I.* 4 vols. Washington: The Albert F. Simpson Historical Research Center, Maxwell AFB, AL, and Office of Air Force History, USAF, 1978–1979.

———. *Aviation in the U.S. Army, 1919–1939.* Washington: Office of Air Force History, USAF, 1987.

Matthews, Lloyd J., and Dale E. Brown, eds. *The Parameters of War: Military History From the Journal of the U.S. Army War College.* Washington: Pergamon-Brassey's, 1987.

McClendon, R. Earl. *The Question of Autonomy for the United States Air Arm, 1907–1945.* Maxwell AFB, AL: Documentary Research Division, Air University, 1950.

Messinger, Charles. *"Bomber" Harris and the Strategic Bombing Offensive, 1939–1945.* New York: St. Martin's Press, 1984.

Mets, David R. *Master of Airpower: General Carl A. Spaatz.* Novato, CA: Presidio Press, 1988.

Mierzejewski, Alfred C. *The Collapse of the German War Economy, 1944–1945: Allied Air Power and the German National Railway.* Chapel Hill: University of North Carolina Press, 1988.

Millis, Walter, with Harvey C. Mansfield and Harold Stein. *Arms and the State: Civil-Military Elements in National Policy.* New York: The Twentieth Century Fund, 1958.

Mortensen, Daniel R. *A Pattern for Joint Operations: World War II Close Air Support North Africa.* Historical Analysis Series. Washington: Office of Air Force History and U.S. Army Center of Military History, 1987.

Murray, Williamson. *Strategy for Defeat: The Luftwaffe, 1933–1945.* Maxwell AFB, AL: Air University Press, 1983.

Paige, Glenn D. *The Korean Decision, June 24–30, 1950.* New York: Free Press, 1968.

Palmer, Michael A. *Origins of the Maritime Strategy: American Naval Strategy in the First Postwar Decade.* Contributions to Naval History No. 1. Washington: Naval Historical Center, 1988.

Paret, Peter, ed., with the collaboration of Gordon A. Craig and Felix Gilbert. *Makers of Modern Strategy from Machiavelli to the Nuclear Age.* Princeton: Princeton University Press, 1986.

Perry, Mark. *Four Stars.* Boston: Houghton Mifflin Co., 1989.

Pogue, Forrest C. *George C. Marshall: Ordeal and Hope, 1939–1942.* New York: Viking Press, 1966.

Poole, Walter S. *The History of the Joint Chiefs of Staff: The Joint Chiefs of Staff and National Policy.* Vol. 4, *1950–1952.* Washington: Historical Division, Joint Secretariat, Joint Chiefs of Staff, 1979.

Possony, Stefan T. *Strategic Air Power: The Pattern of Dynamic Security.* Washington: Infantry Journal Press, 1949.

Potter, E. B. *Nimitz.* Annapolis: Naval Institute Press, 1976.

———. *Admiral Arleigh Burke.* New York: Random House, 1990.

Raven, Alan. *Essex-Class Carriers.* Warship Design Histories. Annapolis: Naval Institute Press, 1988.

Rearden, Steven L. *History of the Office of the Secretary of Defense.* Vol. 1, *The Formative Years, 1947–1950.* Washington: Historical Office, Office of the Secretary of Defense, 1984.

Reynolds, Clark G. *The Fast Carriers: The Forging of an Air Navy.* New York: McGraw-Hill, 1968.

Rogow, Arnold A. *James Forrestal: A Study of Personality, Politics, and Power.* New York: Macmillan Co., 1963.

Rosenberg, David A., and Floyd D. Kennedy, Jr. *History of the Strategic Arms Competition, 1945–1972. Supporting Study: US Aircraft Carriers in the Strategic Role, Part I—Naval Strategy in a Period of Change: Interservice Rivalry, Strategic Interaction, and the Development of Nuclear Attack Capability, 1945–1951.* Falls Church, VA: Lulejian & Associates, 1975.

Rothe, Anna, ed. *Current Biography Who's News and Why 1949.* New York: H. W. Wilson Co., 1950.

Sampson, Jack. *Chennault.* New York: Doubleday & Co., 1987.

Saundby, Air Marshal Sir Robert. *Air Bombardment: The Story of its Development.* London: Chatto & Windus, 1961.

Saunders, Hilary St. George. *Royal Air Force, 1939–1945.* Vol. 3, *The Fight Is Won.* London: HMSO, 1954.

Saward, Dudley. *Bomber Harris: The Story of Marshal of the Royal Air Force Sir Arthur Harris, Bt, GCB, OBE, AFC, LLD, Air Officer Commanding-in-Chief, Bomber Command, 1942–1945.* Garden City, NY: Doubleday & Co., 1985.

Schaffer, Ronald. *Wings of Judgment: American Bombing in World War II.* New York: Oxford University Press, 1985.

Schilling, Warner R., Paul Y. Hammond, and Glenn H. Snyder. *Strategy, Politics, and Defense Budgets.* New York: Columbia University Press, 1962.

Schnabel, James F. *The History of the Joint Chiefs of Staff: The Joint Chiefs of Staff and National Policy.* Vol. 1, *1945–1947.* Washington: Historical Division, Joint Secretariat, Joint Chiefs of Staff, 1979.

Sherrod, Robert. *History of Marine Corps Aviation in World War II.* Washington: Combat Forces Press, 1952.

Sherry, Michael S. *Preparing for the Next War: American Plans for Postwar Defense, 1941–45.* New Haven, CT: Yale University Press, 1977.

———. *The Rise of American Air Power: The Creation of Armageddon.* New Haven, CT, and London: Yale University Press, 1987.

Shiner, John F. *Foulois and the U.S. Army Air Corps, 1931–1935.* Washington: Office of Air Force History, 1983.

Shurcliff, W. A. *Bombs at Bikini: The Official Report of Operation Crossroads.* New York: Wm. H. Wise & Co., 1947.

Sigaud, Louis A. *Douhet and Aerial Warfare.* New York: G. P. Putnam's Sons, 1941.

———. *Air Power and Unification: Douhet's Principles of Warfare and Their Application to the United States.* Harrisburg, PA: The Military Service Publishing Co., 1949.

Smith, Perry M. *The Air Force Plans for Peace, 1943–1945.* Baltimore: Johns Hopkins University Press, 1970.

Smyth, Henry D. *Atomic Energy for Military Purposes: The Official Report on the Development of the Atomic Bomb Under the Auspices of the United States Government, 1940–1945.* Princeton: Princeton University Press, 1945.

Spaight, J. M. *The Beginnings of Organized Air Power: A Historical Study.* London: Longmans, Green & Co., 1927.

Stafford, Edward F. *"All Enemies Foreign or Domestic": Captain John G. Crommelin, U.S. Navy and "The Revolt of the Admirals."* Chester, MD: Privately printed, n.d.

Stein, Harold, ed. *American Civil-Military Decisions: A Book of Case Studies.* Birmingham: University of Alabama Press, 1963.

Strategic Air Command, Headquarters. *The Development of Strategic Air Command 1946–1976.* Offutt AFB, NE: Office of the Historian, Headquarters Strategic Air Command, 1976.

Suchenwirth, Richard. *Historical Turning Points in the German Air Force War Effort.* USAF Historical Study No. 189. Maxwell AFB, AL: USAF Historical Division, Research Studies Institute, Air University, 1959.

Taylor, Theodore. *The Magnificent Mitscher.* New York: W. W. Norton & Co., 1954.

Turnbull, Archibald D., and Clifford L. Lord. *History of United States Naval Aviation.* New Haven, CT: Yale University Press, 1949.

Watts, Barry D. *The Foundations of US Air Doctrine: The Problem of Friction in War.* Maxwell AFB, AL: Air University Press, 1984.

Webster, Sir Charles, and Noble Frankland. *The Strategic Air Offensive Against Germany, 1939–1945.* Vol. 1, *Preparation.* London: HMSO, 1961.

———. *The Strategic Air Offensive Against Germany, 1939–1945.* Vol. 4, *Annexes and Appendices.* London: HMSO, 1961.

Wolk, Herman S. *Planning and Organizing the Postwar Air Force 1943–1947.* Washington: Office of Air Force History, USAF, 1984.

Zuckerman, Solly. *From Apes to Warlords: The Autobiography (1904–1946) of Solly Zuckerman.* London: Hamish Hamilton, 1978.

Articles

"Address by Louis Johnson, Secretary of Defense, Before the National War College," National Military Establishment, Office of Public Information Release No. 35–49S, 21 June 1949.

"Adm. Denfeld Loses Post in Service Row." *Army and Navy Journal,* 29 October 1949, 221, 237, 241.

"Adm. Denfeld Retained as CNO." *Army and Navy Journal,* 13 August 1949, 1430.

"Adm. Sherman Made CNO; Supports Unity." *Army and Navy Journal,* 5 November 1949, 251.

"Air Power 'Lobby' Warned by Vinson: House Committee Threatens to Investigate Those in Defense who Deprecate Branches." *New York Times,* 6 April 1949, 5.

Allard, Dean C. "Interservice Differences in the United States, 1945–1950." *Airpower Journal* 3 (Winter 1989): 71–85.

Allen, C. B. "Sherman Ends Naval Division That Led Feud." *New York Herald Tribune*, 4 November 1949.

"An Admiral Now Despite Key Role in Defense Row, Capt. Arleigh A. Burke Moves Up." *Kansas City Times*, 30 December 1949, 1.

Anders, Roger M. "The Atomic Bomb and the Korean War: Gordon Dean and the Issue of Civilian Control." *Military Affairs* 52 (January 1988): 1–6.

Andrews, Bert. "Capt. Burke, Unification Critic, Taken Off Navy Promotion List." *New York Herald Tribune*, 13 December 1949.

"An Interview With John T. Mason, Jr., Director of Oral History at the U.S. Naval Institute." U.S. Naval Institute *Proceedings* 99 (July 1973): 42–47.

"B–36 Investigation." Department of Defense Office of Public Information, Analysis Branch, 30 August 1949.

"B–36 vs. Fighters—Analysis." *Aviation Week*, 21 March 1949, 7.

Baldwin, Hanson W. "Air Dispute Remains: Naval Aviators Still Oppose Creation of Separate Department." *New York Times*, 26 January 1947.

———. "War Plane Orders Face Examination by Congressmen . . . B–36 Claims Scrutinized. . . ." *New York Times*, 24 May 1949.

———. "Bradley Bombs Navy, General's Bitter Words to Committee Stun Admirals, Widen Service Chasm." *New York Times*, 20 October 1949, 3.

———. "Bradley's Charges Upset Washington." *New York Times*, 21 October 1949, 1.

———. "Navy Vents Wrath at Slight to Burke in Unification Row," *New York Times*, 16 December 1949, 1, 26.

Barlow, Jeffrey G. "'The Revolt of the Admirals' Reconsidered." In *New Interpretations in Naval History: Selected Papers from the Eighth Naval History Symposium*, edited by William B. Cogar, 224–43. Annapolis: Naval Institute Press, 1989.

Bauer, K. Jack. "Dan Able Kimball 31 July 1951–20 January 1953." In *American Secretaries of the Navy*, Vol. 2, *1913–1972*, edited by Paolo E. Coletta, 829–41. Annapolis: Naval Institute Press, 1980.

Bogan, G. F. "Naval Warfare." *Air Affairs* 3 (Spring 1950): 320–31.

"Book Questioned By Navy Banned." *New York Times*, 31 March 1946.

Borowski, Harry R. "Air Force Capability from V–J Day to the Berlin Blockade—Potential or Real?" *Military Affairs* 44 (October 1980): 105–10.

Boylan, Bernard L. "The Search for a Long Range Escort Plane 1919–1945." *Military Affairs* 30 (Summer 1966): 57–67.

Boyle, James M. "The XXI Bomber Command: A Primary Factor in the Defeat of Japan." *The Airpower Historian* 11 (April 1964): 49–53.

Brodie, Bernard. "New Tactics in Naval Warfare." *Foreign Affairs* 24 (January 1946): 210–23.

———. "U.S. Navy Thinking on the Atomic Bomb." In *The Atomic Bomb and the Armed Services*, Bernard Brodie and Eilene Galloway, 24–41. Public Affairs Bulletin No. 55. Washington: Library of Congress Legislative Reference Service, 1947.

"Buying Probe Gets Support But No Action: Congressional Democrats Seem Ready to Block Proposed Procurement Investigation." *Aviation Week*, 30 May 1949, 12.

Cate, James L., and James C. Olsen. "Urban Area Attacks." In *The Army Air Forces in World War II*, Vol. 5, *The Pacific: Matterhorn to Nagasaki, June 1944 to August 1945*, edited by Wesley F. Craven and James L. Cate for Office of Air Force History, USAF, 608–44. Chicago: University of Chicago Press, 1953.

———. "Iwo Jima." In *The Army Air Forces in World War II*, Vol. 5, *The Pacific: Matterhorn to Nagasaki, June 1944 to August 1945*, edited by Wesley F. Craven and James L. Cate for Office of Air Force History, USAF, 577–607. Chicago: University of Chicago Press, 1953.

———. "Precision Bombardment Campaign." In *The Army Air Forces in World War II*, Vol. 5, *The Pacific: Matterhorn to Nagasaki, June 1944 to August 1945*, edited by Wesley F. Craven and James L. Cate for Office of Air Force History, USAF, 546–76. Chicago: University of Chicago Press, 1953.

Cate, James L., and E. Kathleen Williams. "The Air Corps Prepares for War, 1939–41." In *The Army Air Forces in World War II*, Vol. 1, *Plans and Early Operations, January 1939 to August 1942*, edited by Wesley F. Craven and James L. Cate for Office of Air Force History, USAF, 101–50. Chicago: University of Chicago Press, 1948.

Cline, Ray S., and Maurice Matloff. "Development of War Department Views on Unification." *Military Affairs* 13 (Summer 1949): 65–74.

Coletta, Paolo E. "An Interview With John T. Mason, Jr., Director of Oral History." Comment and Discussion section. U.S. Naval Institute *Proceedings* 100 (February 1974): 94–95.

———. "The Defense Unification Battle, 1947–50: The Navy." *Prologue* 7 (Spring 1975): 6–17.

———. "Francis P. Matthews 25 May 1949–31 July 1951." In *American Secretaries of the Navy*, Vol. 2, *1913–1972*, edited by Paolo E. Coletta, 783–827. Annapolis: Naval Institute Press, 1980.

———. "John Lawrence Sullivan 18 September 1947–24 May 1949." In *American Secretaries of the Navy*, Vol. 2, *1913–1972*, edited by Paolo E. Coletta, 747–80. Annapolis: Naval Institute Press, 1980.

———. "Louis Emil Denfeld 15 December 1947–1 November 1949." In *The Chiefs of Naval Operations*, edited by Robert W. Love, 193–206. Annapolis: Naval Institute Press, 1980.

"Comparison of Loss and Damage Rates in Various Types of Missions." *Air Intelligence Report* (XXI Bomber Command) 1 (26 April 1945): 15–18.

Corddry, Charles. "Forrestal Asks Expansion of B–36 Force." *New York Herald Tribune*, 15 March 1949.

"Crommelin Promotion Could Be Considered by New Navy Board." *Washington Evening Star*, 7 November 1949.

Dater, Henry M. "Tactical Use of Air Power in World War II: The Navy Experience." *Military Affairs* 14 (Winter 1950): 192–200.

Davis, Richard G. "Bombing Strategy Shifts, 1944–45." *Air Power History* 36 (Winter 1989): 33–45.

"Death Blow Struck Navy Policy Unit." *Los Angeles Times*, 4 November 1949.

Denfeld, Louis E. "Reprisal: Why I Was Fired." *Collier's*, 18 March 1950, 13–15, 62, 64.

Duncan, Donald B., and H. M. Dater. "Administrative History of U.S. Naval Aviation." *Air Affairs* 1 (Summer 1947): 526–39.

Eaker, Ira. "Part II, Memories of Six Air Chiefs: Westover, Arnold, Spaatz." *Aerospace Historian* 20 (Winter, December 1973): 188–96.

Eastman, James N., Jr. "The Development of Big Bombers." *Aerospace Historian* 25 (Winter/December 1978): 211–19.

"Effects of Incendiary Attacks." *Air Intelligence Report* (XXI Bomber Command) 1 (29 March 1945): 9–12.

"8th AF Sub Patrol Training." *Army and Navy Journal*, 23 August 1947.

Evangilista, Matthew A. "Stalin's Postwar Army Reappraised." *International Security* 7 (Winter 1982/1983): 110–38.

"Everest, Frank Fort, Lt. Gen. USAF (366A)." *Generals of the Army and the Air Force* 2 (December 1954): 7–8.

"Experts & Explanations." *Time*, 22 August 1949, 13.

"Facts & Fears." *Time*, 24 October 1949, 26–27.

Fagg, John E. "The Strategic Bomber Strikes Ahead." In *The Army Air Forces in World War II*, Vol. 3, *Europe: Argument to V–E Day, January 1944 to May 1945*, edited by Wesley F. Craven and James L. Cate for Office of Air Force History, USAF, 278–322. Chicago: University of Chicago Press, 1949.

———. "The Climax of Strategic Operations." In *The Army Air Forces in World War II*, Vol. 3, *Europe: Argument to V–E Day, January 1944 to May 1945*, edited by Wesley F. Craven and James L. Cate for Office of Air Force History, USAF, 715–55. Chicago: University of Chicago Press, 1949.

———. "Mission Accomplished." In *The Army Air Forces in World War II*, Vol. 3, *Europe: Argument to V–E Day, January 1944 to May 1945*, edited by Wesley F. Craven and James L. Cate for Office of Air Force History, USAF, 783–808. Chicago: University of Chicago Press, 1949.

Falk, Stanley L. "General Kenney, the Indirect Approach, and the B–29s." *Aerospace Historian* 28 (Fall/September 1981): 146–55.

Ferguson, Arthur B. "Pointblank." In *The Army Air Forces in World War II*, Vol. 2, *Europe: Torch to Pointblank, August 1942 to December 1943*, edited by Wesley F. Craven and James L. Cate for Office of Air Force History, USAF, 665–706. Chicago: University of Chicago Press, 1949.

Finney, Robert T. "Early Air Corps Training and Tactics." *Military Affairs* 20 (Fall 1956): 154–61.

Freund, James C. "Part I, The 'Revolt of the Admirals': A Study of the 1949 Congressional Hearings on Unification and Strategy." *The Airpower Historian* 10 (January 1963): 1–10.

———. "Part II, The 'Revolt of the Admirals': A Study of the 1949 Congressional Hearings on Unification and Strategy." *The Airpower Historian* 10 (April 1963): 37–42.

Futrell, Robert F. "Tactical Employment of Strategic Airpower in Korea." *Airpower Journal* 2 (Winter 1988): 29–41.

"General Devers Reports." *Infantry Journal*, November 1949, 31–32.

Giles, John A. "Gray Denies Dispute Between Army, AF on Tactical Support." *Washington Evening Star*, 10 July 1949.

———. "The Navy's Secretary Walks Alone." *Washington Evening Star*, 23 October 1949, C-1–C-2.

———. "Navy Unit's Role In Service Flight Under Scrutiny: Documents Are Seized; 3,000 Middies Cheer Denfeld at Game." *Washington Evening Star*, 30 October 1949.

Goldberg, Alfred. "AAF Aircraft of World War II." In *The Army Air Forces in World War II*. Vol. 6, *Men and Planes*, edited by Wesley F. Craven and James L. Cate for Office of Air Force History, USAF, 193–227. Chicago: University of Chicago Press, 1955.

―――. "Roles and Missions." In *a History of the United States Air Force, 1907–1957*, edited by Alfred Goldberg, 115–19. Princeton, NJ: D. Van Nostrand Co., 1957.

―――. "Strategic Air Command—The Deterrent Force." In *A History of the United States Air Force, 1907–1957*, edited by Alfred Goldberg, 121–27. Princeton, NJ: D. Van Nostrand Co., 1957.

Goldman, Ben. "The Aluminum Bough: Evolution of Tactical Air Command." *The Airpower Historian* 11 (April 1964): 54–59.

Graybar, Lloyd, J. "Bikini Revisited." *Military Affairs* 44 (October 1980): 118–23.

―――. "The 1946 Atomic Bomb Tests: Atomic Diplomacy or Bureaucratic Infighting?" *The Journal of American History* 72 (March 1986): 888–907.

Green, Murray. "Hugh J. Knerr: The Pen and the Sword." In *Makers of the United States Air Force*, edited by John L. Frisbee, 99–126. Washington: Office of Air Force History, USAF, 1987.

Greenwood, John T. "The Emergence of the Postwar Strategic Air Force, 1945–1953." In *Air Power and Warfare: The Proceedings of the 8th Military History Symposium United States Air Force Academy, 18–20 October 1978*, edited by Alfred F. Hurley and Robert C. Ehrhart, 215–44. Washington: Office of Air Force History, Headquarters USAF and United States Air Force Academy, 1979.

―――. "The Atomic Bomb—Early Air Force Thinking and the Strategic Air Force, August 1945–March 1946." *Aerospace Historian* 34 (Fall/September 1987): 158–166.

Greer, Thomas H. "Air Arm Doctrinal Roots, 1917–1918." *Military Affairs* 20 (Winter 1956): 202–16.

Halperin, Morton H. "The President and the Military." *Foreign Affairs* 50 (January 1972): 310–24.

Hammond, Paul Y. "Super Carriers and B–36 Bombers: Appropriations, Strategy and Politics." In *American Civil-Military Decisions: A Book of Case Studies*, edited by Harold Stein, 465–564. Birmingham: University of Alabama Press, 1963.

Hansell, Haywood S., Jr. "Gen. Muir S. Fairchild: Strategist, Statesman, Educator." *Air Force Magazine*, January 1979, 72–74.

―――. "Brig. Gen. Kenneth N. Walker, Prophet of Strategic Airpower." *Air Force Magazine*, November 1979, 92–94.

―――. "General Laurence S. Kuter 1905–1979." *Aerospace Historian* 27 (Summer/June 1980): 91–94.

―――. "Harold L. George: Apostle of Air Power." In *Makers of the United States Air Force*, edited by John L. Frisbee, 73–97. Washington: Office of Air Force History, USAF, 1987.

Haynes, Richard F. "The Defense Unification Battle, 1947–50: The Army." *Prologue* 7 (Spring 1975): 27–31.

Hensel, H. Struve. "The Military Budget: A Navy View." *Newsweek*, 14 February 1949, 25.

Holley, I. B., Jr. "An Air Force General: Laurence Sherman Kuter." *Aerospace Historian* 27 (Summer/June 1980): 88–90.

Hotz, Robert. "New B–36 to Give USAF Greater Range: Data Released for First Time on B Model of Giant Bomber, Soon to Go Into Service." *Aviation Week*, 18 October 1948, 12.

———. "Improved B–36 is Planned by Strategists." *Aviation Week*, 14 March 1949, 13.

———. "Navy Air Boss Once Army Pilot: But He Still Sees Future for Aircraft Carriers, and Thinks Interservice Competition Produces Progress." *Aviation Week*, 21 March 1949, 14–15.

"House Committee Members Angered at Denfeld Relief." *Army and Navy Journal*, 5 November 1949, 249–50.

Huston, James A. "Tactical Use of Air Power in World War II: The Army Experience." *Military Affairs* 14 (Winter 1950): 166–85.

"Inhabited Regions of World Now in Range of B–36's Atomic Bombs." Press Release, War Department Public Relations Division Press Section, AAF, 7 November 1948.

Johnson, Robert E. "Why the Boeing B–29 Bomber, And Why the Wright R–3350 Engine?" *American Aviation Historical Society Journal* 33 (Fall 1988): 174–88.

Jones, Stacy V. "The inside story of the big carrier that wasn't built. . . ." *Liberty*, August 1949, 13, 40–42.

Joubert, Air Chief Marshal Sir Phillip. "Long Range Air Attack." In *The Soviet Air and Rocket Forces*, edited by Asher Lee, 101–16. New York: Frederick A. Praeger, 1959.

Knox, Dudley W. "Unification and Integration." *Infantry Journal* 66 (February 1950): 8–11.

Krauskopf, Robert H. "Part I, The Army and the Strategic Bomber 1930–1939." *Military Affairs* 22 (Summer 1958): 83–94.

———. "Part II, The Army and the Strategic Bomber 1930–1939." *Military Affairs* 22 (Winter 1958–1959): 208–15.

Lawrence, David. "Altitude Jet Fighter Tests by Navy Show B–36 Is Vulnerable." *Washington Evening Star*, 10 May 1949.

———. "Army Ground Forces Held Almost Without Direct Support; Tactical Air Arm Called Neglected As Millions Go Into Strategic Bombers." *Washington Evening Star*, 8 June 1949.

LeMay, Curtis E. "Strategic Air Power: Destroying the Enemy's War Resources, 2. The Command Realities." *Aerospace Historian* 27 (Spring/March 1980): 9–15.

"Let's Keep the Record Straight on the B–36 Investigation and Related Matters." Extension of remarks of Hon. James E. Van Zandt of Pennsylvania, 20 July 1949. *Congressional Record*. Vol. 95. Daily ed. (21 July 1949), A4892.

Lincoln, Ashbrook. "The United States Navy and the Rise of the Doctrine of Air Power." *Military Affairs* 15 (Fall 1951): 145–56.

Lucas, Jim G. "Joint Chiefs Ready to Rip Veil Off Air Power Battle." *Washington Daily News*, 21 May 1948, 26.

———. "Is Air Force or Navy Right About the B–36?" *Washington Daily News*, 15 March 1949.

———. "Ban on B–36 Duel Jolts Air Admirals." *Washington Daily News*, 2 June 1949.

MacDonald, Scott. "Evolution of Aircraft Carriers: CVAs Built to Meet Modern Needs." *Naval Aviation News*, November 1963, 24.

MacIssac, David. "The Strategic Bombing Offensive: New Perspectives." *Air University Review* 18 (July–August 1967): 81–85.

———. "The Air Force and Strategic Thought, 1945–1951." Working Paper No. 8. International Security Studies Program. Washington: The Wilson Center, 1979.

———. "Voices from the Central Blue: The Air Power Theorists." In *Makers of Modern Strategy from Machiavelli to the Nuclear Age*, edited by Peter Paret, with Gordon A. Craig and Felix Gilbert, 624–47. Princeton: Princeton University Press, 1986.

Mark, Eduard. "A New Look at Operation STRANGLE." *Military Affairs* 52 (October 1988): 176–84.

Maycock, Thomas J. "Notes on the Development of AAF Tactical Air Doctrine." *Military Affairs* 14 (Winter 1950): 186–91.

McBane, Robert B. "The B–36—Air Force Global Bomber." *Army Information Digest* 4 (August 1949): 25–33.

McConnell, David. "Admiral's Rank for Crommelin is a Possibility." *New York Herald Tribune*, 7 November 1949.

McFarland, Keith D. "The 1949 Revolt of the Admirals." *Parameters* 11 (June 1981): 53–63.

McFarland, Stephen L. "The Evolution of the American Strategic Fighter in Europe, 1942–44." *The Journal of Strategic Studies* 10 (June 1987): 189–208.

"Meet the Author." *Time*, 5 September 1949, 14.

Meilinger, Phillip S. "The Admirals' Revolt of 1949: Lessons for Today." *Parameters* 19 (September 1989): 81–96.

———. "Hoyt S. Vandenberg and the Independent Air Force." *Air Power History* 37 (Fall 1990): 27–36.

Mellett, Lowell. "House Committee Opens Up Large Subject of Military Propaganda." *Washington Evening Star*, 22 March 1949.

Moody, Walton S. "United States Air Forces in Europe and the Beginning of the Cold War." *Aerospace Historian* 23 (Summer/June 1976): 75–85.

Mrozek, Donald J. "Nathan F. Twining: New Dimensions, a New Look." In *Makers of the United States Air Force*, edited by John L. Frisbee, 257–80. Washington: Office of Air Force History, USAF, 1987.

"New Field Forces Chief." News and Comment section, *Army and Navy Journal*, 27 August 1949, 1474.

Norman, Lloyd. "OP-23 Board Dissolved By Chief's Order," *Washington Times Herald*, 4 November 1949.

Norris, John G. "Navy Cramps Admirals in B–36 Inquiry." *Washington Post*, 29 September 1949, 1.

———. "Staff Chiefs Chairman Assails Top Admirals for Hurting Defense." *Washington Post*, 20 October 1949, 1.

———. "Sherman Takes Post at Helm of Navy," *Washington Post*, 3 November 1949.

———. "Sherman Dissolves 'Op 23' Unit, Called Key to Fight by Navy." *Washington Post*, 4 November 1949.

———. "Dissident Admirals Left Off Navy's New Promotion Board." *Washington Post*, 10 November 1949.

———. "Burke on Admiral List, Crommelin Off, 23 Captains Promoted; Senate Must Act on Slate." *Washington Post*, 30 December 1949, 1.

"Op–23 Disbanded." *Army and Navy Journal*, 5 November 1949, 251.

Parrish, Noel F. "Hoyt S. Vandenberg: Building the New Air Force." In *Makers of the United States Air Force*, edited by John L. Frisbee, 205–82. Washington: Office of Air Force History, USAF, 1987.

Parton, James. "The Thirty-One Year Gestation of the Independent USAF." *Aerospace Historian* 34 (Fall/September 1987): 150–57.

Pearson, Drew. "Admirals Running Handout Mill." *Washington Post*, 19 October 1949.

Peck, Earl G. "B–47 Stratojet." *Aerospace Historian* 22 (Summer/June 1975): 61–64.

"Pentagon Crippling Power of Navy, Captain Says, Risking His Career." *New York Times*, 11 September 1949, 1, 47.

Poole, Walter S. "From Conciliation to Containment: The Joint Chiefs of Staff and the Coming of the Cold War, 1945–1946." *Military Affairs* 42 (February 1978): 12–16.

"Preliminary Survey of 20th A.F. Target Damage." *Air Intelligence Report* (Twentieth Air Force) 1 (October 1945): 20–21.

Prina, L. Edgar. "31-Knot Burke a Hero to Seadogs: Man Taken Off Promotion List Deemed Just About Navy's Finest Officer," *New York Sun*, 20 December 1949.

"Revolt of the Admirals." *Time*, 17 October 1949, 21–23.

Reynolds, Clark G. "Forrest Percival Sherman 2 November 1949–22 July 1951." In *The Chiefs of Naval Operations*, edited by Robert W. Love, 209–32. Annapolis: Naval Institute Press, 1980.

Rosenberg, David A. "American Postwar Air Doctrine and Organization: The Navy Experience." In *Air Power and Warfare: The Proceedings of the 8th Military History Symposium United States Air Force Academy, 18–20 October 1978*, edited by Alfred F. Hurley and Robert C. Ehrhart, 245–78. Washington: Office of Air Force History, Headquarters USAF and United States Air Force Academy, 1979.

———. "American Atomic Strategy and the Hydrogen Bomb Decision." *The Journal of American History* 66 (June 1979): 62–87.

———. "U.S. Nuclear Stockpile, 1945 to 1950." *The Bulletin of the Atomic Scientists* 38 (May 1982): 25–30.

———. "The Origins of Overkill: Nuclear Weapons and American Strategy, 1945–1960." *International Security* 7 (Spring 1983): 3–71.

Ruch, Walter W. "Bradley Says Navy Has Adequate Role." *New York Times*, 13 October 1949, 5.

Ruth, Robert W. "Cole Charges Reprisal Against Navy Officer." *Baltimore Sun*, 14 December 1949.

———. "Capt. Burke Promoted; Admiral Blandy Retires," *Baltimore Sun*, 30 December 1949, 1.

Sabin, L. S. "An Interview with John T. Mason, Jr., Director of Oral History." Comment and Discussion section. U.S. Naval Institute *Proceedings* 99 (November 1973): 86–87.

Schilling, Warner R. "The Politics of National Defense: Fiscal 1950." In *Strategy, Politics, and Defense Budgets*, Warner R. Schilling, Paul Y. Hammond, and Glenn H. Snyder, 1–266. New York: Columbia University Press, 1962.

Schlight, John. "Elwood R. Quesada: Tac Air Comes of Age." In *Makers of the United States Air Force*, edited by John L. Frisbee, 177–204. Washington: Office of Air Force History, USAF, 1987.

Schratz, Paul R. "The Admirals' Revolt." U.S. Naval Institute *Proceedings* 112 (February 1986): 64–71.

Shaffel, Kenneth. "Muir S. Fairchild: Philosopher of Air Power." *Aerospace Historian* 33 (Fall/September 1986): 165–71.

"Sherman Scatters Navy Rebels." *Washington Daily News*, 4 November 1949.

Smith, Perry M. "Douhet and Mitchell: Some Reappraisals." *Air University Review* 18 (September–October 1967): 97–101.

Spaatz, Carl A. "Strategic Air Power: Fulfillment of a Concept." *Foreign Affairs* 24 (April 1946): 385–96.

———. "Budgeting for Land-Sea-Air Power." *Newsweek*, 10 January 1949, 24.

Stafford, Edward P. "Saving Carrier Aviation—1949 Style." U.S. Naval Institute *Proceedings* 116 (January 1990): 44–51.

Steele, Jack. "Truman Denies Change in Navy Promotion List." *New York Herald Tribune*, 16 December 1949.

Stevens, Austin. "Sherman Chosen Navy Chief; Says He Backs Unity 100%." *New York Times*, 2 November 1949, 1, 19.

———. "Sherman Inducted As New Navy Chief," *New York Times*, 3 November 1949, 1, 18.

"Summary of Damage to Urban Areas and Industrial Targets in Japan." *Air Intelligence Report* (XXI Bomber Command) 1 (16 June 1945): 9–12.

Tarr, Curtis W. "The General Board Joint Staff Proposal of 1941." *Military Affairs* 31 (Summer 1967): 85–90.

"The B–36 Bombs the Black Paper." *Newsweek*, 5 September 1949, 13–15.

"Truman Denies Report that Burke Was Taken From Admiral List." *Washington Evening Star*, 15 December 1949.

"Truman Promotes Pentagon 'Rebel.'" *New York Times*, 30 December 1949, 1, 12.

"XXI BomCom Operations." *Air Intelligence Report* (XXI Bomber Command) 1 (29 March 1945): 3–5.

United Press. "Navy Fathered Memo on B–36, Vinson Says." *Washington Daily News*, 25 August 1949.

———. "Death Blow Struck Navy Policy Unit." *Los Angeles Times*, 4 November 1949.

"Vinson Pledges No Delay in Bomber Probe." *Washington Post*, 5 August 1949.

Warner, Edward. "Douhet, Mitchell, Seversky: Theories of Air Warfare." In *Makers of Modern Strategy: Military Thought from Machiavelli to Hitler*, edited by Edward Mead Earle, with Gordon A. Craig and Felix Gilbert, 485–503. Princeton: Princeton University Press, 1943.

White, William S. "Denfeld Sees Navy Gravely Imperiled by Chiefs' Decisions." *New York Times*, 14 October 1949, 1.

———. "Bradley Accuses Admirals of 'Open Rebellion' on Unity; Asks 'All-American Team'." *New York Times*, 20 October 1949, 1.

"Who Cashes In?" News and Comment section. *Infantry Journal* (August 1949): 30–31.

"Why Bigger Draft Is Coming: An Interview With Carl Vinson." *U.S. News & World Report*, 27 October 1950, 40–46.

Wolk, Herman S. "A Review Article of THE AGE OF DETERRENCE." *The Airpower Historian* 11 (October 1964): 121–23.

———. "The Defense Unification Battle, 1947–50: The Air Force." *Prologue* 7 (Spring 1975): 18–26.

———. "George C. Kenney: The Great Innovator." In *Makers of the United States Air Force*, edited by John L. Frisbee, 127–50. Washington: Office of Air Force History, USAF, 1987.

———. "George C. Kenney: MacArthur's Premier Airman." In *We Shall Return: MacArthur's Commanders and the Defeat of Japan, 1942–1945*, edited by William M. Leary, 88–114. Lexington: University Press of Kentucky, 1988.

Zaloga, Steven J. "Soviet Air Defense Radar in the Second World War." *The Journal of Soviet Military Studies* 2 (March 1989): 104–16.

Newspapers, Magazines, and Journals

Air University Quarterly Review, 1947–1950

Army and Navy Journal, 1949–1950

New York Times, 1948–1949

Aviation Week, 1948–1949

Newsweek, 1948–1949

Time, 1948–1949

Doctoral Dissertations and Masters Theses

Caddell, Joseph W. "Orphan of Unification: The Development of United States Air Force Tactical Air Power Doctrine." Ph.D. diss., Duke University, 1984.

Davis, Benton Vincent, Jr. "Admirals, Politics and Postwar Defense Policy: The Origins of the Postwar U.S. Navy, 1943–1946 and After." Ph.D. diss., Princeton University, 1961.

Fabyanic, Thomas A. "A Critique of United States Air War Planning, 1941–1944." Ph.D. diss., Saint Louis University, 1973.

Flugel, Raymond R. "United States Air Power Doctrine: A Study of the Influence of William Mitchell and Giulio Douhet at the Air Corps Tactical School, 1921–1935." Ph.D. diss., University of Oklahoma, 1965.

Goldstein, Donald M. "Ennis C. Whitehead, Aerospace Commander and Pioneer." Ph.D. diss., University of Denver, 1970.

Green, Murray. "Stuart Symington and the B–36." Ph.D. diss., The American University, 1960.

Hurley, Alfred F. "The Aeronautical Ideas of General William Mitchell." Ph.D. diss., Princeton University, 1961.

Legere, Lawrence J. "Unification of the Armed Forces." Ph.D. diss., Harvard University, 1950.

Lincoln, Ashbrook. "The United States Navy and Air Power: A History of Naval Aviation, 1920–1934." Ph.D. diss., University of California, 1946.

Meilinger, Phillip S. "Hoyt S. Vandenberg: The Life of a General." Ph.D. diss., University of Michigan, 1985.

Moll, Kenneth L. "Nuclear Strategy, 1945–1949: America's First Four Years." M.A. thesis, University of Omaha, 1965.

Parrish, Noel F. "Behind the Sheltering Bomb: Military Indecision from Alamogordo to Korea." Ph.D. diss., Rice University, 1968.

Rosenberg, David A. "Toward Armageddon: The Foundations of United States Nuclear Strategy, 1945–1961." Ph.D. diss., University of Chicago, 1983.

Smith, Robert L. "The Influence of U.S.A.F. Chief of Staff General Hoyt S. Vandenberg on United States National Security Policy." Ph.D. diss., The American University, 1964.

Wilson, Donald E. "The History of President Truman's Air Policy Commission and its Influence on Air Policy 1947–1949." Ph.D. diss., University of Denver, 1978.

Index

A3D Skywarrior heavy attack aircraft [Douglas], 143, 287 (photo)
Acheson, Dean, 176
ADR–42 heavy attack aircraft, 137, 139, 141, 330
ADR–45A heavy attack aircraft, 139, 141
ADR–62 heavy attack aircraft, 330
ADR–64 heavy attack aircraft, 330
Aeronautical Board, 43
Air Corps Tactical School (ACTS), 11–13, 108, 291
Air Defense Command, 264
Air Force. *See also* Army Air Forces
   48-group program, 268, 339
   58-group program, 267, 362
   70-group program, 52
   Aircraft and Weapons Board, 96
   aircraft performance questions, 60
   Air Intelligence Division, 317
   anti-Navy complaints and accusations, 163
   Armor Institute, 230
   and B–36 bomber hearings, 218–19, 226–30, 233, 353
   budget/appropriations, 178–79, 263–64, 339, 341, 362
   and flush-deck carrier, 122, 183–84, 185, 187
   forces, 263–64
   and Harmon Committee Report, 359
   intelligence, 321
   legislation, 4
   Office of Special Investigations (OSI), 234, 312, 353
   opposition to naval aviation, 107, 121–30, 197–200, 201, 326, 331, 339
   Ordnance Department, 230
   public relations campaigns, 197–99, 206–7
   records of, 370
   relationship with Army, 263–67, 362–63
   reorganization, 177–78, 264
   and roles and missions, 178, 263, 327, 371
   support for, 4, 51–52
   strategic bombardment doctrine, 8–11, 19, 109
   war planning concerns, 95–99
Air Intelligence, 95
Air Materiel Command (AMC), 149, 150, 151, 154, 156, 177, 230
Air Policy Board, 95
Air power, defined, 308
Air power doctrines. *See also* Strategic air offensive
   Air Corps Tactical School doctrine, 11–13
   carrier air doctrine, 3–8, 291–92
   pursuit doctrine, 12
   tactical, 361
   strategic bombardment doctrine, 8–11, 14, 17, 83, 291
   World War II European theater and, 13–17
   World War II Pacific theater and, 17–21
Air Service Field Officers School, 11
Air Service Tactical School, 11
Air University, 102
Air War College, 110, 122
Aircraft. *See* Navy fighter aircraft; specific aircraft
Aircraft carriers
   Air Force position on, 201
   air support, 115–16
   angled flight deck for, 368
   Army position on, 186
   atomic weapons delivery, 106–8, 128–29, 316
   bomber development for, 133–34
   budget/appropriations issues, 139, 140, 142–43, 162, 222–24, 253, 330
   capabilities, 80, 133–34, 316
   Coral Sea (CVB 43), 107, 327
   CVA (Heavy Aircraft Carrier), 144
   CVB–X, 137, 139, 330. *See also United States*
   CVB 41 class, 132. *See also Midway*-class
   Essex (CV 9), 138 (photo)

402   Index

Essex-class, 9 (photo), 21, 132 (photo), 140, 201, 202, 203–4, 213, 289
Fast Carrier Task Force, 8, 21, 165
first, 6
and fleet exercises, 6
flush-deck, 1, 107, 128, 131–45, 157, 182–88, 190, 191, 195, 201, 202, 207, 253, 258–59, 276, 285, 287–88, 293, 294, 329, 331, 342, 368
Forrestal (CVA 59), 284 (photo), 286 (photo), 287, 288, 368
improvements to, 21
Independence-class light carriers (CVLs), 21
and Mediterranean, 121–22
Midway (CVB 41), 125, 126, 133 (photo), 135 (photo), 138 (photo)
Midway-class (CVBs 41, 42, 43), 107, 131, 289
missions and responsibilities, 106, 115–16, 128–29
modernization/replacement program, 107, 140, 201–4, 213, 289, 331, 346
targets, 115–20, 324, 325
27A configuration, 201, 345
size comparison, 138 (photo)
task forces, 107, 116, 135, 324, 341
United States (CVA 58), 1, 138 (photo), 140 (photo), 142 (photo), 143 (photo), 145 (photo), 182–88, 185 (photo), 190, 197, 200, 201, 208, 210, 217, 221, 236, 326, 345
vulnerabilities, 121, 122, 184
Aircraft engines and propulsion
GE J-47, 154–56, 229
Pratt & Whitney R-4360-41, 149–50, 153
reciprocating-engine/turbojet, 134
turbine engine, 134, 150
variable discharge turbine (VDT), 150, 152, 153–54, 156, 333
Aircraft Industries Association, 193
AJ-1 Savage heavy attack aircraft [North American], 108 (photo), 134, 140, 286 (photo), 345
Allen, C. B., 240
Alsop, Stewart, 200, 345
American Legion, 174, 176
Anderson, F. L., 76–77
Anderson, George W., Jr., 115, 186, 219

Anonymous Document, 206–9, 215–16, 217, 228, 230, 232, 234, 245, 293–94, 347, 348, 353
Antisubmarine warfare, 33, 37, 38, 39, 38, 39, 43, 44, 80, 115, 259, 329
Arends, Leslie C., 275
Arkansas (ex-BB 33), 68, 71, 72 (photo)
Armed Forces Special Weapons Project (AFSWP), 101, 128, 130, 327
Army
aircraft capabilities, 352–53
unification stance, 255, 263–67
Army Air Corps, 1
Johnson and, 175
strategic bombing doctrine, 8–11, 291
Tactical School, 6
Army Air Forces (AAF). *See also* Air Force
Air Intelligence Division, 85, 317
air power doctrine, 3, 14–17, 19–20, 21, 292
Air War Plans Division, 13, 98
appropriations campaign, 38, 43
and atomic weapons, 74–77, 97
AWPD–1 plan, 13
capabilities, 39
creation, 13
Office of Public Relations, 50, 60
Plans Directorate, 97
postwar reorganization, 72, 75, 95
public relations campaign, 44–52
and research and development, 75
roles and responsibilities, 25, 33, 39, 42, 43, 45, 46, 307
and strategic air offensive, 88, 89–90, 97–98, 256–57
targeting, 97
and unification, 25, 30–32, 38, 46, 48–50, 306, 309
war plans, 89–90, 92
Army Air Service, 4, 11–12
Army and Navy Munitions Board, 28
Army Field Forces, 264
Army-Navy agreement, 33
Arnold, Henry H. (Hap), 13, 21, 31 (photo), 32, 33, 35, 45–46, 48, 49, 68, 74, 75, 146, 308, 370
Arthur, Charles Snowden, 241, 356
Ashworth, Frederick L., 134, 329

Index 403

Assistant Chief of Naval Operations for Organizational Research and Policy. *See* OP-23
Atomic Bomb Striking Force, 75
Atomic energy
  international control of, 88, 89
  Military Advisory Board, 315
  ships powered by, 106
  Smyth report, 85
  Soviet program, 85
  Truman policy, 106-7
Atomic Energy Commission (AEC), 90, 91, 111, 250
Atomic weapons. See also War Plans
  AAF position on, 46, 74-77, 314
  bombing of Japan, 20, 21, 65, 74
  carrier delivery of, 106-8, 125-27
  core design, 127
  delivery methods, 80
  and deterrence, 85, 102, 103, 200
  early Service thinking on, 72-74
  Harmon Committee report, 255
  history of development of, 318
  JPS study, 91
  Mk I "Little Boy", 78, 127, 316, 327
  Mk III "Fat Man", 66, 73, 78, 91, 107, 127, 134, 316, 329
  Mk IV, 127, 329
  moral issues, 110, 247-48, 261, 360
  Navy position on, 78-80, 106, 115-21
  and Navy roles and missions, 123, 327
  operational control of, 129
  plutonium production, 127
  policymaking on, 93, 178, 327
  psychological effects, 100
  security of information about, 76, 85, 106, 215, 318, 319, 320
  Soviet test of, 233
  Soviet threat and, 81-86, 233
  stockpiles, 85-86, 90, 101, 127, 128, 233, 320
  and strategic air offensive, 108-14
  strategic vs. tactical value, 65-66
  targeting, 91-92, 94-96, 97, 98-99, 115-21, 123, 215, 314, 328, 360
  testing, 66, 68-73, 77, 79, 127
  training, 101
  uranium-235 (Oralloy) production, 127
Austin, Jim, 244
Aviation Week, 209

Azerbaijan, 81-82

B-17 Flying Fortress bomber [Boeing], 13, 14, 149, 228
B-24 Liberator bomber [Consolidated], 14
B-29 Superfortress bomber [Boeing], 98, 149
  atomic bomb delivery, 68, 70, 80, 94, 95, 96-97, 315
  bomb groups, 178
  capabilities, 18, 96, 112-13, 303, 321, 339
  forward bases for, 94
  photos, 18, 96
  SILVERPLATE aircraft, 75, 95, 315
  Soviet internment and copies of, 83-84, 317
  suggested use by Navy, 43, 44
  and VHB operations, 17, 18, 19
  weaponeers, 77-78
B-32 Dominator bomber [Consolidated Vultee], 147
B-36 bomber hearings, 217-22, 224-33, 237-39, 243-45, 353
B-36 Peacemaker bomber [Consolidated Vultee]
  Air Corps planning for, 145-46
  Air Force testimony on, 227-31
  Anonymous Document on, 206-9, 215-16, 217, 228, 230, 232, 234, 245, 293-94, 347, 348, 353
  atomic targets, 94
  B-36A model, 150, 152, 153 (photo), 154, 155, 179, 333, 334
  B-36B model, 149, 151, 152, 153, 154, 155, 177, 179, 210, 228, 333
  B-36C model, 150, 151
  B-36D model, 156 (photo), 179, 209-10, 228, 229 (photo), 334
  cancellation discussions, 152
  capabilities, 97, 146-47, 149, 150-51, 154, 155, 227, 230, 248-50, 256-57, 268, 293, 334, 348, 359
  comparative performance, 153-54, 155, 228, 352-53
  congressional investigation of, 1, 105, 209, 217-18, 224-25, 265
  conversion to tankers, 152
  defensive armament, 227-30

404 *Index*

delays, 147–48, 229
demonstration, 155
design competition, 146
economic concerns, 154
engines, 149–50, 151, 152, 153, 154–56, 333
funding for, 179, 182, 253, 333
interception tests, 209–12
jet pods for, 156, 177, 178, 209–10, 228, 229, 334
K–1 bombing system, 156, 177, 179, 180, 257, 359
modifications in, 177–82, 333
Navy testimony on, 219–20, 231–33, 235, 238, 243–45, 294
procurement, 146, 151–52, 178–80, 206–9, 332, 333, 338
problems, 146–48, 208
public relations, 148–49, 215
and Soviet atomic weapons test, 233
and strategic bombing issues, 239, 255–57
Van Zandt and, 216–22, 228
Very Heavy Bomb groups, 147
vulnerabilities, 210, 228, 230, 248–50, 352–53
XB–36, 146, 148
YB–36, 146
B–45 Tornado bomber [North American], 362
B–47 Stratojet bomber [Boeing], 155, 358
B–50 Superfortress bomber [Boeing], 94, 96, 97, 112–13, 149, 150, 153, 154, 178, 179, 321, 339
B–50A, 98 (photo)
B–54 [B–50C] bomber [Boeing], 153–54, 179, 182, 333, 339
Bachman, L. A., 166
Baldwin, Hanson, 262, 299
Barber, Stuart B., 60, 61–62, 63, 148, 153, 207, 300, 313, 347
Barbey, Daniel E., 279
Barrows, Arthur S., 152, 170, 218–19
Baruch Plan, 89
Beach, Edward L. (Ned), 258, 260, 360–61
Bellinger, P.N.L., 8
Benson, William S., 4, 299
Berlin crisis, 92–93, 154, 159
Berry, Robert W., 170

Bikini atomic tests, 66, 67 (photo), 68, 69–73 (photos), 77, 79, 314, 324
Blandy, William H. P. (Spike), 37 (photo), 47, 56, 57, 68, 78 (photo), 79, 164, 211, 239, 282, 316
Boeing Aircraft Company, 146
Bogan, Gerald F. (Jerry), 236–37, 244, 272, 282, 357, 365
Bomb groups
43rd, 95
509th, 74, 76, 95, 96 (photo)
Light, 362
Heavy Strategic, 177–78
VHB, 95, 147, 315
Bombers. *See also specific models*
accuracy under enemy fire, 14
aerial refueling, 97
capabilities, 110, 303
carrier-based, 133–34
Douhet's concept, 11
forward bases for, 87, 89, 147, 324
long-range, 75, 83
Soviet, 83
supersonic, 113, 324
unescorted formations, 13, 14–15, 303
Very Long Range, 325
Bombing
area attack, 108, 111, 112
costs, 303
Dayton bombing mission, 102–3
effectiveness, 302, 303
Eight Air Force bombing accuracies, 17, 257, 302
H2X, 17, 257, 303
high-altitude precision, 17, 19, 108, 256–57, 303, 359
incendiary, 19
K–1 system, 156, 177, 179, 180, 257, 359
night area, 13
night precision, 13, 227
Norden bomb sight, 17
one-way (suicide) missions, 96–97
radar-assisted, 17, 19, 108, 256–57, 302, 303, 358
pinpoint, 302
precision attack, 108
SAC bombing accuracies, 358
system attack, 112
and target selection, 12–13, 16–17, 111, 301

THUNDERBOLT exercise, 112
units, 11
Very Long Range Bombardment, 45
Boone, W. F., 110, 166, 195, 219, 220
Borowski, Harry, 95
Botter, David, 52–53
Boyd, J. M., 167
Bradley, Omar N.
  Army Chief of Staff, 164, 203, 264, 267
  Chairman, Joint Chiefs of Staff, 257, 258, 263, 359
  and Devers, 266
  and flush-deck carrier, 142, 185, 186, 258, 341
  and JCS, 180
  and Navy, 258, 261
  papers of, xvii, 359
  personality, 258
  photos, 124, 129, 130, 175, 178
  and Unification and Strategy hearings, 260–63, 360–61, 363
  and Vandenberg, 258, 266
  and war planning, 93, 99
  wartime service, 257
Braisted, F. A., 167
Brereton, Lewis H., 90
Brett, George H., 146
Bridges, Styles, 52, 56
Briscoe, Robert P., 166–67, 219, 220, 224–25, 231, 238, 355
Brodie, Bernard, 316
Brown, Charles R. (Cat), 219, 220, 221–22, 224, 351
Brown, John Nicholas, 62, 170, 207
Budget Advisory Committee, 324
Buchanan, Charles A., 170
Buffalo Evening News, 62–63, 313
Bureau of Aeronautics (BUAER), 5, 38, 41, 60–61, 132–33, 134, 135, 137, 139, 140, 207, 210, 328
Bureau of Construction and Repair, 4, 5
Bureau of Engineering, 5
Bureau of Navigation, 5
Bureau of Ordnance, 5, 250
Bureau of Personnel (BUPERS), 56
Bureau of Ships (BUSHIPS), 131–32, 137, 139, 140, 331
Bureau of the Budget, 38–39, 43, 141, 159–60, 180, 182, 201
Bureau of Yards and Docks, 5

Burke, Arleigh A.
  and B–36 hearings, 219, 220, 223, 224–27, 230, 231, 232, 233–34, 236, 238, 239, 243, 245, 347
  background, 165
  and Inspector General investigation, 242, 366
  on naval aviation budget, 223
  and OP–23, 165, 166, 168, 169, 171, 173, 207, 236, 238, 239, 241, 242, 277–78, 335, 341
  papers of, xviii, 370
  personality and management style, 173
  photo, 168
  selection to rear admiral, 279, 280–81, 366
  reprisals for congressional testimony, 2, 274, 277–79, 366
  and Unification and Strategy hearings, 244–45, 253, 289, 355
Burrough, Edmund W., 37 (photo)
Byrd, Richard E., 281, 312

Cairo-Suez, U.S. forward bases in, 92
Caraley, Demetrios, 29
Carney, Robert B., 40, 56–57, 107, 114, 140, 202, 203, 204, 221, 223, 307
Carrier aviation. *See also* Naval aviation
  Air Force concern over, 121–22, 259
  appropriations decline, 224, 283–84
  capabilities, 8, 341
  Japanese planes destroyed by, 300
  offensive, 259
  targets, 115–20, 324, 325
  training for, 33, 35
  World War II operations, 121
Carter, William J., 47
Case Against the Admirals, 49–50, 309, 310
Cassady, J. H., 219, 220, 279, 282, 288, 329, 346
Cates, Clifton B., 165, 238, 255, 355
Central Intelligence Agency, 85
Central Intelligence Group, 84, 85
Chase, J. V., 8
Chiang Kai-shek, 159
Chief of Naval Air Technical Training, 42
Chief of Naval Intelligence, 85
Chief of Naval Operations (CNO), 4, 33, 34, 53, 56–58, 74, 107, 135, 137, 144,

See also Denfeld; King; Nimitz; and Sherman
China, Communist victory in, 159
Churchill, Winston S., 81
Clark, G. W., 167
Clark, Mark W., 266, 267
Clay, Lucius D., 160
Clifford, Clark M., 87, 370
Clifton, Chester V. (Ted), 258, 259, 260, 360
Cochrane, E. L., 47, 316
Colclough, O. S. (Ossie), 47, 253, 285, 338, 367
Cold War. *See* Soviet Union
Cole, W. Sterling, 275
Collins, J. Lawton, 49, 164, 254, 261, 268
Command of the Air, 10
Commander Air Force Pacific Fleet (COMAIRPAC), 61
Commander in Chief, Atlantic Fleet, 41
Commander in Chief, U.S. Fleet (COMINCH), 7 (photo), 27, 74
Commander Task Force 58, 135
Commander Joint Task Force One, 68
Commander U.S. Naval Forces, Europe (COMNAVEU), 81
Commission on Organization of the Executive Branch of the Government (Hoover Commission), Committee on the National Security Organization, 171
Congress. *See also* House of Representatives; Senate
    Armed Services Committees, 183
    Appropriations Committees, 183
    Congressional Aviation Policy Board, 97, 122
    and support for unification, 51–52
Conolly, Richard L., 37 (photo), 47, 163 (photo), 164, 239, 270, 271 (photo), 275, 276, 364, 367
Consolidated Vultee Aircraft Corporation. *See* Convair
Continental Air Command (CONAC), 264, 361
Convair, 146, 147, 150, 151, 152, 153, 154, 175, 177, 209, 217, 226, 332, 333, 334, 337, 339
Cooke, Charles M., Jr., 7 (photo)
Coontz, Robert E., 4, 5

Coral Sea (CVB 43), 107, 327
Corddry, Charles, 215
Corn, W. A., 166
Corsair. *See* F4U
Cowles, John, 342
Craig, H. A., 152
Craven, Thomas T., 4, 5
Crawford, J. G., 166
Crommelin, John G., 235–36, 237, 244, 245, 279, 282–83, 365
Cross, Harold E. (Harry), 269
Cruise, E. A., 112–13, 167
Czechoslovakia, Soviet invasion of, 160

Daniels, Josephus, 4
Dashiell, Alfred, 199
David Taylor Model Basin, 142, 143, 145
Davies, Thomas D., 207, 208, 209, 226, 227, 230, 234, 277, 347, 348, 353, 354, 366
Davis, B. Vincent, Jr., 371–72
Dealey, Ted, 52
Deane, Charles B., 209
Defense Department. *See* Department of Defense
Denbo, R. W., 167
Denby, Edwin, 5
Denfeld, Louis E. 164, 200, 203
    and Air Force 70 Group plan, 52
    background, 58
    and B–36 bomber, 179, 180, 182, 212, 219–20, 221, 225, 231, 235, 238, 239, 240
    Bradley's attack on, 257–63
    and CINCNELM offer, 276, 281, 367
    Chief of Naval Operations, 56–59, 60, 129, 142, 163, 166, 168, 175, 178, 252, 311, 343, 344, 355
    Chief of Personnel and DCNO (Personnel), 37, 47
    and congressional appropriations, 311
    and decision to support aviators, 251, 253
    dismissal of, 2, 270–77, 285, 365
    and flush-deck carrier, 142, 184, 186, 187, 189, 325, 340
    and Gallery memorandum, 120
    and Johnson, 176, 213, 254–55, 269, 270, 338, 349

and Matthews, 2, 235, 240, 243, 251, 253, 254, 269, 270, 272, 273, 274, 275, 276, 282, 363, 364, 365
and Navy public relations, 58–59, 60
and Navy roles and missions, 124, 129, 236, 253–54, 324
and OP-23, 168
personality and management style, 193, 311, 339
photos, 37, 124, 129, 163, 175, 178, 252
and Radford, 57–58, 163, 193, 244–45, 281–82, 311, 312, 367
retirement, 282
selection as CNO, 56–57, 311
and Shipbuilding and Conversion Program, 201
and unification, 165, 237
and Unification and Strategy hearings, 239, 244–45, 250–54, 255, 260, 268, 269, 289, 363
and strategic air offensive, 99, 100, 113, 114, 120, 359
and Struble, 197, 344
Dennison, Robert L., 173–74, 189, 253, 274, 279–80, 281 (photo), 343
Department of Defense, 171, 172, 173, 233, 268
Department of National Defense, 23, 30
Deputy Chief of Air Staff for Research and Development, 66, 90
Deputy Chief of Naval Operations (DCNO)
for Administration (OP–02), 166, 202
for Air (OP–05), 27, 35, 56, 57–58, 78, 80, 135, 136, 137, 139, 219, 223, 224, 369
Guided Missiles Division of, 80
for Logistics (OP–04), 137, 137, 166–67, 202
for Operations (OP–03), 80, 120, 166–67, 196–97, 201, 219, 221
Atomic Defense Division of, 80
for Special Weapons (OP–06), 77, 79–80
Deputy Commander in Chief, U.S. Fleet, 27
Devers, Jacob L. (Jake), 264, 265, 266
Dewey, Thomas E., 175
Dillon, John H., 170
Directorate of Intelligence, 98–99

Doolittle, James H. (Jimmy), 15 (photo), 49, 204
Douhet, Giulio, 9, 10–11, 12, 46, 301
Doyle, A. K. (Artie), 193
Draper, W. H., 170
DUALISM Exercise, 102
Dudley, Paul L., 166
Duncan, Donald B. (Wu), 61–62, 117, 120, 196–97
Durgin, C. T. (Cal), 202, 223, 224–25, 231

Eaker, Ira C., 14, 45, 74, 75, 76–77, 148
Early, Stephen T., 204, 205, 235
Eberstadt, Ferdinand, 28–29, 171, 173, 310, 336
Eberstadt Committee, 171
Eighth Air Force, 13–14, 15, 16–17, 75, 96, 108, 257
Eisenhower, Dwight D.
on Air Force–Navy conflict, 182, 339
Army Chief of Staff, 35, 170, 258
and atomic weapons use, 88–89, 90
and B–36 bomber, 179, 180, 181
and flush-deck carrier, 182, 184, 185, 187, 188, 340, 342
on Forrestal, 162, 163–64
on Johnson, 177, 342
and Marine Corps, 35
and Navy budget, 222, 223
New Look policy, 294
papers of, 370–71
presiding officer of the Joint Chiefs of Staff, 179, 180, 182, 184, 185, 187, 188, 340, 344
and unification, 49, 195–96, 263
and Unification and Strategy hearings, 254–55, 263, 285
Engel, Albert J., 120
Engines. *See* Aircraft engines and propulsion
ER–4 bomber, 83, 317
Essex (CV 9), 138 (photo)
Essex, Richard. *See* Barber, Stuart
Esterbrook, Bob, 62
Everest, Frank F., 48, 49, 187, 309
Executive Order 9877, 107, 123

F2H–1 Banshee fighter [McDonnell], 210, 211, 330
F4U Corsair fighter [Chance-Vought], 8, 21
F4U–5 Corsair, 210

Index

F6F Hellcat fighter [Grumman], 8, 21
F7U Cutlass fighter [Vought], 143
F8F-2 Bearcat fighter [Grumman], 210
F9F-2 Panther fighter [Grumman], 210
F-80C Shooting Star fighter [Lockheed], 210
F-84 Thunderjet fighter [Republic], 210
F-86A Sabre fighter [North American], 210, 227
Fairchild, Muir S., 99–100, 152, 265
Fairchild Board, 178, 339
Farber, William S., 37 (photo), 47
Fast Carrier Task Force, 8, 21, 165
Fawkes, Emerson E., 328, 329
Fechteler, William M., 166, 202, 282
FH-1 Phantom fighter [McDonnell], 140
Figallo, Bruno, 140
Fifteenth Air Force, 75, 108
Fifth Fleet, 7
Fight for Air Power, 48, 309
Finletter, Thomas K., 323
Fitch, Aubrey W., 7 (photo)
Fleet Problem VII, 6
Fleet Problem IX, 7
Foley, Kate, 189, 258, 259
Forrestal (CVA 59), 284 (photo), 286 (photo), 287, 288, 368
Forrestal, James V.
  and atomic weapons, 78, 92, 93, 107, 125–26, 255, 327
  attitude toward Navy as SECDEF, 162, 163
  and B-36 bomber, 152, 177, 179
  and defense budget, 160, 161–62
  and flush-deck carrier, 122–23, 131, 142, 144, 182, 328, 331
  Hanson and, 60–61
  personality and management style, 130, 337
  photos, 7, 26, 34, 37, 124, 129, 175
  and Navy roles and missions dispute, 123, 124, 125–26, 129–30, 141, 162, 199
  resignation of, 173–74, 175, 337
  Secretary of Defense, 59, 60–61, 92, 93, 99, 113, 122–23, 124, 129, 142, 144, 152, 170, 176, 177, 183, 199, 293, 337, 371
  Secretary of the Navy, 1, 26, 27, 78
  and strategic air offensive, 99–103, 113, 122, 328
  and unification issue, 26, 27, 28–29, 30, 32, 37–38, 40–41, 42–43, 47, 49, 51, 52, 53, 58, 63, 128, 170, 193, 307
  War Council meeting, 175 (photo)
Fort Bragg, 265
Foster, J. G., Jr., 166
Fourteenth Air Force, 265
Franklin D. Roosevelt (CVB 42), 107, 131, 211
Freund, James C., 372
Future Employment of Naval Forces, 54

Gallery, Daniel V., 117, 120–21, 167
Gallery memorandum, 53, 117, 120–21, 325, 326
Gardner, M. B. (Matt), 202, 220, 221
Gates, Artemis L. (Di), 27–28
General Board, 3, 140, 165
George, Harold L., 13
Giles, Barney M., 46, 277
Giles, John A., 366
Gillin, James M., 237, 238, 240, 243
Glass, Richard P., 275, 279
Glenn Martin Aircraft Company, 208
Godney, W. K., 167
Good, Roscoe F., 279
Goodyear Tire and Rubber Company, 84
Gorrell, Edgar S., 9
Grant, E., 167
Gray, Gordon, 170
Green, Murray, 354, 357, 371, 372
Greenslade, J. F., 166
Griffin, Charles D. (Don), 57, 220, 253, 269, 274, 351
Groves, Leslie R., 71, 76, 77, 97, 315, 318
Gruenther, Alfred M., 124 (photo), 129 (photo), 130 (photo), 164, 254, 341

Hale, P. G., 166
Halsey, William F., 236, 250
Hammond, Paul Y., 169, 208, 348, 366, 372
Hanford, Washington, plutonium production facility, 127
Hansen, Chester B., 203
Hansen, Chuck, 127
Hanson, Hugh L., 60–61, 63, 148, 153, 207, 312
Harding, Warren G., 5
Hardison, O. B., 167

Hardy, Porter, Jr., 256–57
Harlow, Bryce, 284
Harmon Committee, 101, 255
Harmon Committee Report, 255–56, 359
Harmon, Hubert R., 101, 255
Hawaii (CB 3), 141, 331
Hayward, J. T., 258
Hazlett, Edward E. (Swede), 177
Hebert, E. Edward, 273, 275
Hecht, Frank, 204–5
Heffernan, J. B., 167
Hellcat. *See* F6F
Hensel, H. Struve, 28
Herzig, Alvin, 366
Hicks, Frederick C., 5
Hicks, R. L., 166
Hill, Harry W., 240, 279, 367
Hill, Tom B., 240, 359
Hiroshima, 20, 21, 65, 74, 78, 79, 101
Hobbs, A., 167
Holden, Edward C., Jr., 176–77, 338
Hollingsworth, William H., 202–3
Hood, Reuben C., Jr., 76, 77
Hoover, Herbert, 173
Horne, Frederick J., 6, 7
Hornet (CV 8), 21
Horowitz, Solis, 237, 238, 240, 243, 355
House of Representatives. *See also* B–36 bomber hearings; and Unification and Strategy hearings
  Appropriations Committee, 4, 120
  Armed Services Committee, 1, 105, 142, 185, 200, 209, 211, 216, 217, 224, 225–33, 235, 237, 240, 244, 245, 248, 253, 260, 265, 266, 267, 268, 271, 272, 273, 275, 285, 288, 353
  Naval Affairs Committee, 5, 200
  Naval Appropriations Subcommittee, 160
  Select Committee on Post-War Military Policy. *See* Woodrum Committee
Howard, Joseph L. (Joe), 236, 241, 242
Huie, William Bradford, 48–49, 198, 200, 209, 309, 310
Hull, John E., 49, 183–84
Huntington (CL 107), 165
Hurley, Alfred, 10
Hussey, George F., Jr., 47

Independence (ex-CV 22), 70

Independence-class light carriers (CVLs), 21
Intelligence
  Air Intelligence Division (AID), 317
  Assistant Chief of Staff for Intelligence, 85, 122, 326
  Chief of Intelligence, War Department General Staff, 85
  Chief of Naval Intelligence, 85
  economic intelligence, need for better, 112
  Office of Naval Intelligence, 116
  on projected Soviet atomic weapons stockpile, 85–86, 233
  on Soviet atomic development, 86, 233
  on Soviet defensive capabilities, 155, 334
  on Soviet military threat, 80, 81–86, 93–94, 317
  on Soviet offensive air capabilities, 83–84, 317
  on Soviet vulnerabilities, 95–96
  on targets in Soviet Union, 95–96, 321

Ingersoll, Stuart H., 288
Inglis, Thomas B., 166
Ingram, Samuel P., 353, 356
Iran, Soviet Union and, 81–82

J–47 engine. *See* Aircraft engines and propulsion
Jaap, Joseph A., 258
Jacobs, Randall, 7 (photo)
Japan, 48
  aircraft losses, 300
  atomic bombing of, 20, 21, 65, 74, 78, 79
  fire bombing of, 19, 45, 48, 111–12, 303
  U.S. air bases in, 83, 91
Johnson, Felix L., 279
Johnson, Louis A.
  and American Legion, 174
  Assistant Secretary of War, 174, 337
  and B–36 bomber, 180–81, 211, 212, 217, 230, 233, 234, 337, 339, 363
  and B–54 cancellation, 180–81
  background, 1, 174–76, 337
  and Burke's selection to rear admiral, 280–81
  and defense budgets, 223, 224, 283–84
  and Denfeld, 176, 213, 254–55, 269, 270, 273, 338, 349

410 *Index*

and *Essex* conversions, 201, 203–4
firing of, 288
and flush-deck carrier, 1, 2, 138, 183, 184, 187, 188, 189, 190, 191, 207, 208, 210, 288, 341, 342
and Matthews, 205, 206, 270, 273, 280, 365
and naval aviation, 176–77, 194, 197, 203, 338, 342
personality and management style, 174, 190, 205, 268
photo, 181
political ambitions, 346
pro-Air Force position, 188, 191, 194, 197
and Radford, 193, 344
reprisals for Navy testimony, 269, 270, 273, 278, 280
Secretary of Defense, 1, 2, 138, 176–77, 180, 181, 183, 337, 338, 371
and Shipbuilding and Conversion Program, 201, 203, 204, 213, 285, 346
and Sullivan, 1, 181, 184, 187, 189, 190, 191, 340, 343
and unification, 251, 268, 273, 343, 363
and Unification and Strategy hearings, 254–55, 268, 363
Joint Chiefs of Staff
and atomic weapons, 65, 68, 89, 93
and B–36 bomber, 179, 180, 211–12
chairman, 173, 258
and defense budgets, 162, 223–24, 340, 362
and flush-deck carrier, 141, 142, 184–85, 186, 331, 340, 342
and Key West Agreement, 124, 326
and Newport Agreement, 129–30
photos, 124, 129, 130, 175, 178
and postwar military policy, 65
and roles and missions dispute, 129–30, 141
and Shipbuilding and Conversion Program, 201
and Strategic Air Offensive, 100, 359
and unification issue, 24, 25, 27, 32, 371
and war planning, 86, 87, 89, 91, 93, 94
Joint Intelligence Committee, 85–86, 100
Joint Staff Planners (JPS), 66, 82, 86, 87, 88, 91, 92, 319, 320

Joint Strategic Plans Committee (JSPC), 92, 100, 320
Joint Strategic Plans Group (JSPG), 91, 92, 320
Joint Strategic Survey Committee (JSSC), 32–33, 65, 72, 82–83, 90, 91
Joint War Plans Committee (JWPC), 87, 90, 91, 320

Karig, Walter, 59–60, 169, 194, 199–200, 250, 251, 271
Kearsarge (CV 33), 126
Keenan, Joseph B., 232, 235, 243
Kenney, George C., 45, 47, 48, 101, 148–49, 150, 154, 227, 230, 334
Kenney, W. John, 141, 170, 175 (photo), 188, 190
Kentucky (BB 66), 141, 331
Kepner, William E., 15 (photo)
Key West Conference, 123, 325
Kiland, I. N., 166, 202
Kilday, Paul J., 285
Kimball, Dan A., 1, 201, 203, 204, 207, 210, 211, 220, 221–22, 231, 232, 288, 346, 349, 370
King, Ernest J., 7 (photo), 27, 68, 78, 250
Kinkaid, Thomas C., 250
Kirchhofer, A. H., 62–63, 313
Korean War, 83, 288, 289, 294, 334
Knerr, Hugh J., 48–49, 199, 309
Knowland, William F., 275
Knox, Frank, 25, 26, 27
Kuniholm, Bruce R., 82

Lalor, William G., 143, 341
Langley (CV 1), 6, 138 (photo), 329
Langley Field, Virginia, 11, 265, 291
Lawrence, David, 265
Leach, W. Barton, 183–84, 185, 218, 232, 265, 266, 362
Leahy, William D., 56, 66, 87, 92, 93, 124, 142, 143, 269–70, 324
Lederer, William J., 199
Lee, Fitzhugh, 124–25, 225, 233, 238, 239, 243, 244, 262, 274, 278, 279, 312, 313, 355, 370
Lee, Robert M., 264, 361
Legere, Lawrence J., 371
LeMay, Curtis E.
and B–36 capabilities, 227, 230

and bonus damage, 99
Chief of Staff, U.S. Army Strategic Air Forces, Pacific, 74
Commander XXI Bomber Command, 19, 20
Commanding General, Strategic Air Command, 101, 102, 103, 323
Deputy Chief of Air Staff for Research and Development, 66, 68, 75, 76–77, 90, 315
and incendiary bombing of Japanese cities, 19–20
papers of, 370
photos, 20, 66
and SAC capabilities 101-3, 323
Leo, Stephen F., 50, 51 (photo), 61, 62, 164 (photo)
Leva, Marx, 170, 338
Lexington (CV 2), 7–8
Libby, R. E., 166, 219, 220
Lockheed Aircraft Corporation, 348
Lockwood, Charles A., Jr., 47
Long Island (AVG 1, CVE 1), 329
LORAN, 362
Lord, C. W., 288
Los Alamos National Laboratory, 71
Lovett, Robert A., 25, 146, 226
Lucas, Jim, 211, 212, 349

Maas, Melvin J., 122
MacArthur, Douglas, 23
Mahabad, Kurdish Republic of, 82
Maher, J. E., 167, 348
Manhattan Engineer District, 71, 75, 76, 77, 79
Manhattan Project, 76, 78, 315, 318
Manning, John J., 47
Manson, Frank A., 50, 58–59, 169, 194–95, 208, 216, 269, 271, 282, 344, 347
Mao Tse-tung, 159
Mariana Islands, 18–19
Marine Corps, 25, 33, 35, 223, 254, 259, 305
Marshall, George C., 23–24, 29–30, 32, 35, 65, 93
Martin, Glenn L., 208, 209, 215, 353
Martin, Harold M., 279
Martin, Joseph W. (Joe), 52
Martyn, John W., 170

Matthews, Francis P.
and Anonymous Document, 234
and B–36 bomber hearings, 219, 221, 225, 226, 231, 239–40
background and experience, 1, 205–6, 347
and Burke's selection to rear admiral, 279, 280–81, 367
and Conolly, 270, 364
and Denfeld, 2, 235, 240, 243, 251, 253, 254, 269, 270, 273, 274, 275, 276, 282, 363, 364, 365
and *Essex* conversions, 203, 272
and Johnson, 205–6, 270, 273, 280, 365
and naval aviation, position on, 236, 241
and Nimitz, 271–72, 364
and OP–23, 241
papers of, 370
personality and management style, 206, 244, 356
photo, 205
Secretary of Navy, 1, 205–6, 347
and Sherman, 270, 272, 273, 275, 276, 279, 364, 365
reprisals for Navy testimony, 2, 269, 270, 273, 275, 277, 279, 365
and unification, 235
and Unification and Strategy hearings, 238–40, 243, 244, 247, 251, 285, 356, 363
Maxwell Field, Alabama, 12, 110
McCandless, B., 167
McCann, Allan R., 240, 241, 242–43, 279, 356
McCormick, John, 56
McDill, Alexander S., 220, 226
McDonald, George C., 122, 326
McIntire, Ross T., 47
McKee, William F., 66 (photo), 197–98
McMahon, Brian, 68
McMahon, F. W., 167
McMullen, Clements, 101
McMullen, D. R., 167
McNarney, Joseph T., 113, 151, 152, 324
McNaughton, Frank, 216
McNeil, Wilfred J., 124 (photo), 170
Mendenhall, W. E. (Goat), 169
Merwin, Davis, 188, 190, 240, 244, 270, 342, 356, 365

Metsger, A. B., 225, 352
Midway (CVB 41), 125, 126, 133 (photo), 135 (photo), 138 (photo)
Midway-class (CVBs 41, 42, 43), 107, 131, 209
MiG–15 Fagot fighter [Mikoyan-Gurevich], 155, 334
Military Liaison Committee (to AEC), 111
Miller, Harold B. (Min), 58, 312
Millis, Walter, 372
Mitchell, William (Billy), 4, 9–10, 12, 23, 291
Mitscher, Marc A., 21, 41, 135, 136, 165, 280, 329
Moebus, L. A. (Fish), 166, 195
Moffett, William A., 5
Molotov, Vyacheslav, 81
Momsen, C. B., 166, 195, 279
Montreux Convention, 81
Mose, J. B., 167
Mosely, Philip E., 316
Mosier, Harold G., 208, 353
Mosquito bomber, 16, 302
Murphy, Joseph N., 134
Mustang. *See* P–51

Nagasaki, 20, 21, 65, 74, 78
Nagato, 71
National Military Establishment. *See also* Department of Defense
  anti-Navy sentiments, 212
  atomic weapons policy of, 94
  Barber articles and, 62
  and B–36 bomber, 211
  budget/appropriations, 56, 99, 159, 160, 162, 163, 188, 222–24, 334, 362
  and carrier aviation support, 121
  creation of, 52
  and flush-deck carrier, 128, 207
  organization, 170
  photo of top officials, 124
  roles and missions controversy, 124, 128, 191
National Security Act Amendments of 1949, 173
National Security Act of 1947, 52, 53, 55, 57–58, 59, 107, 171, 173, 200, 235, 272, 292
National Security Council, 28, 29, 93, 94, 110

National Security Resources Board, 29
National War College, 204
Naval Air Test Center, Patuxent River, Maryland, 108, 249
Naval aviation. *See also* Carrier aviation
  Air Force opposition to, 121–30
  civilian supporters, 61
  funding issues, 24, 222, 259
  importance of, 2
  integrated approach, 5–6, 291–92
  Louis Johnson and, 194
  long-range atomic bombing, 120, 287
  policy development, 3–4
  roles and missions, 6, 121–30, 292
  strengthening of, 27
  thirty-seventh birthday of, 62
Naval Aviation Combat Statistics: World War II, 61
Naval aviators
  as atomic weaponeers, 76
  effect of unification on, 307
  Radford and, 57–58
  training, 35, 59
  unification position of, 40–42
Naval Appropriations Act for 1922, 5
Naval Court of Inquiry, 234, 354
Naval War College, 129
Navy
  atomic weapons position, 78–80, 120, 314, 327
  Basic Naval Establishment Plan, 224
  Bradley denunciation of, 260–63
  and B–36 bomber hearings, 219–22, 224–26, 227, 230–32, 234–36, 237–40, 243–45, 351, 355, 356
  budget/appropriations, 159–64, 223, 283–84, 308, 330, 334, 339, 345
  carrier air doctrine, 3–8, 21
  forces, 80, 159–60, 161, 334
  leadership team (1946), 37 (photo)
  morale, 258–59
  organization (1946), 47, 72, 74
  Office of Public Information, 58, 59
  public relations campaign, 58–63
  roles and missions, 33, 43, 53–54, 123–26, 129–30, 141, 164, 182–83, 221, 253–54, 327, 371
  Shipbuilding and Conversion Program, 139–40, 141, 144, 201, 285, 330, 331, 345

and strategic air offensive, 108–14, 182–83, 324, 327
Strategic Plans Division, 54, 109, 115–16, 369
targeting plans, 115–21, 311,325
Navy ASW aircraft, 39–40, 43, 44, 327
Navy attack aircraft, 107, 108 (photo), 119, 125 (photo), 126 (photo), 132–34, 141, 286 (photo), 287 (photo), 327, 330, 331
Navy fighter aircraft, 6, 8, 329, 353 *See also specific types*
Navy League, 204–5
Nevada (ex-BB 36), 68, 70, 71 (photo)
New York Times, 254, 262
Newport Conference, 129–30
Newport News Shipbuilding and Dry Dock Company, 185
Newsweek magazine, 232
Newton, W. H., 167
Nimitz, Chester W., 170
  and atomic weapons, 80, 88, 316
  and carrier aircraft development, 136–37
  Chief of Naval Operations, 33, 34, 37, 47, 53, 58
  CINCPAC/CINCPOA, 7, 310
  and Matthews, 271–72, 364
  photos, 7, 34, 37, 55
  and Sherman, 35
  and Unification and Strategy hearings, 250
  and unification issue, 27, 41, 42, 49, 52–56, 58
  and Valedictory, 52, 53–56, 121, 122
Ninth Air Force, 31, 258, 264
Norden bombsight, 17
Norris, Jack, 239, 240, 242, 262
Norstad, Lauris
  Assistant Chief of Air Staff for Plans, 33, 44, 84–85
  Chief of Staff, Twentieth Air Force, 19
  Deputy Chief of Staff, Operations, 152, 154, 218, 264, 362
  as member of the Spaatz Board, 74
  photos, 44, 124, 129, 130
  and Spaatz, 33, 35, 44
  and unification, 38, 44
NSC 20/4, 93
NSC 30, 93

Nunn, Ira H., 285

Oak Ridge, Tennessee, uranium-235 production, 127
Odlum, Floyd B., 208
Office of the Chief of Naval Operations (OPNAV), 78–79, 143–44
  and aircraft carrier conversion program, 201
  Atomic Energy Division (OP–36) of, 240, 258, 329
  briefings on Navy roles and missions, 182–83
  budget/appropriations concerns, 222–24
  and Denfeld, 56
  Metsger briefing on status of, 225
  and naval aviation, 3–4, 40, 196
  organization, 166–67
  papers of, 369
  Special Weapons Division (OP–06) of, 106
  and *United States*, cancellation of, 186, 187
Office of Naval Intelligence, 61
Office of Special Investigations (OSI), 234, 312, 353
Ofstie, Ralph A., 111–12, 219, 220, 250, 324, 363, 370
Ohly, John H., 170
Okinawa, 92
Our Air Force—Keystone of National Defense, 10
OP–23 (Organizational Research and Policy Division)
  abolition of, 277–78
  establishment of, 164–73
  information leak, suspected of 241, 356
  Inspector General investigation of, 241–43, 277, 366
  offices of, 355
  operating rules, 169, 171, 336
  personnel, 207, 366
  press characterization of, 169
  records of, 369
  responsibilities, 168–69, 336, 341
  review of Air Force B–36 testimony, 230
  and statement of fundamental principles for Navy, 171

and Unification and Strategy testimony, 237–43
Operations
BIG TOWN, 96 (photo)
CROSSROADS, 68, 71–72
SANDSTONE, 127
Operations Deputies (Little Chiefs), 196, 202–3
Organizational Research and Policy Division. *See* OP–23

P2V Neptune ASW aircraft [Lockheed], 43, 127, 137, 207
P2V–3C heavy attack aircraft, 125 (photo), 126 (photo)
P4M Mercator ASW aircraft [Martin], 43
P–38 Lightning fighter [Lockheed], 15
P–47 Thunderbolt fighter [Republic], 15, 149
P–51 Mustang fighter [North American], 15
Pacific Air Command, U.S. Army (PACUSA), 83
Pace, Frank, Jr., 180, 181
Palmer, Paul, 199
Panama Canal, 8
Paris Peace Conference, 87
Parsons, William S., 79 (photo), 80, 101–2, 167, 316
Partridge, Earle E., 66 (photo), 96–97
Patterson, Robert P., 32, 38, 42–43, 49
Pearson, Drew, 53, 120, 176, 273, 277
Pensacola (ex-CA 24), 71 (photo)
Pershing, John J., 30
Peurifoy, John E., 176
Philadelphia Bulletin, 120
Philadelphia Inquirer, 120
Pihl, Paul E., 167, 220
Plumley, Charles A., 160
Pogue, Forrest C., 174, 299
Pope Air Force Base, 361
Potsdam Conference, 81
Powers, Edward M., 76, 148, 154, 177
Price, John Dale, 142, 166, 184, 189, 194–97, 203, 212, 219, 220, 221, 237–38, 239, 240, 282, 340, 355, 356
Propulsion. *See* Aircraft engines and propulsion
Public relations campaigns

Air Force, 44–52, 148–49, 197–200, 215, 293
B–36, 148–49, 215
and defense appropriations, 215
Navy, 58–63, 293
Putt, D. L., 352–53

Quackenbush, R. S., Jr., 167
Quesada, Elwood R. (Pete), 263, 264
Quesada Board, 265, 267, 362–63

R–4360–41 engine. *See* Aircraft engines and propulsion
Radar, 17, 19, 21, 108, 148, 210
Radford, Arthur W.
and aircraft funding issues, 43, 44, 223
and atomic weapons policy, 247–48, 328
and B–36 bomber, 211, 222, 224–27, 230, 231–32, 236, 238, 239, 240, 248–49, 358
Commander in Chief, Pacific, and Pacific Fleet 193, 194, 195, 212, 222, 283
and Denfeld, 57–58, 163, 193, 244–45, 281–82, 311, 312, 367
Deputy Chief of Naval Operations for Air, 35, 37–38, 41, 47, 136, 329
and flush-deck carrier, 136, 329
and Matthews, 206, 234–35, 356
and Navy roles and missions, 124, 129, 245, 328, 329
papers of, xviii, 370
photos, 37, 41, 124, 129, 136, 163, 194, 248, 251, 283
and reprisals for testimony, 273, 274, 278–79
and strategic air offensive, 1–2, 122, 247–48
and Struble, 197
and unification, 35, 37–38, 40, 41, 58, 59, 193, 236–37, 307, 329
and Unification and Strategy hearings, 1, 243–45, 247–48, 251, 253, 257, 268, 273, 284, 285, 287, 289, 356, 357
Vice Chief of Naval Operations, 57–58, 124, 136, 163, 166, 184, 194, 312, 340
Ramsey, Dewitt C. (Duke), 37 (photo), 41, 42, 47, 56, 88, 163 (photo), 193, 194 (photo), 344
Ranger (CV 4), 138 (photo)
Rayburn, Samuel T. (Sam), 209

RB–36B reconnaissance aircraft, 177
Reader's Digest, 198–200, 209, 345
Rear Admiral Selection Board (1949), 279
Reeves, J. W., Jr., 59, 196, 197, 281
Reconnaissance, 33, 37, 38, 39, 43, 177
  aircraft, 156, 177, 329
Renfrow, Louis H., 190–91
Research and Development Board, Committee on Aeronautics, 179
Riggs, Ralph S., 166
Riley, Herbert D., 109
Ringle, Kenneth D. (Ken), 277
Rivers, L. Mendel, 287
Robbins, Thomas H., 53–54
Rockets, 14, 80
Roosevelt administration, 59, 174, 175
Rosenberg, David Alan, 326
Ross, Charles, 189–90, 343
Rowe, Robert A., 195–96
Royal Air Force (RAF), 13, 16, 112
Royal Navy Fleet Air Arm, 259
Royall, Kenneth C., 93, 114 (photo), 126, 170, 171, 175 (photo), 181 (photo)
Rumble, C. A., 166
Russell, George L., 238, 240, 251

Sakawa, 68, 70 (photo)
Sallada, Harold B., 41 (photo), 47, 133, 135, 225, 329
SANDSTONE atomic tests, 127
Saratoga (ex-CV 3), 7–8, 71
Sargent, Willis H., 316
Sarper, Selim, 81
Sasscer, Lansdale G., 275
Saunders, William V., 137
Saville, Gordon P., 257
SB2C Helldiver bomber [Curtiss], 135 (photo)
Schaede, F. B., 167
Schlatter, David M., 77
Schoech, William A., 258
Schofield, Frank H., 8
Schulz, Robert, 255
Second Supplemental Surplus Appropriations Rescission Act of 1946, 330–31
Secretary of the Air Force. See Finletter; Symington
Secretary of the Navy. See Forrestal; Matthews; Sullivan
Secretary of War, 42–43, 86. See also Stimson

Secretary of Defense. See also Forrestal; Johnson
  and single chief of staff idea, 171, 173
Secretary's Committee on Research of Reorganization (SCOROR), 51–52, 53–54, 61, 165, 369
Secretary's Committee on Unification (UNICOM), 164–65, 335, 369
Senate
  Appropriations Committee, 144, 201
  Armed Services Committee, 215, 275
  Military Affairs Committee, 32
  Naval Affairs Committee, 28
Service rivalries. *See also* Unification of services
  and budget maneuvers, 114, 162
  escalation of, 162
  carrier atomic weapons delivery and, 107
  JSSC report and, 33
  Gallery memorandum and, 53
  Nimitz Valedictory and, 53–54, 121
  OP–23 and, 169
  Price and, 195
  strategic air offensive and, 113, 114, 182
  unification and, 105
Shangri-la (CV 38), 132 (photo)
Shanklin, E. W., 166
Shaw, Brackley, 218, 219
Shaw, Samuel R., 165, 241, 242, 251, 356
Sheehy, Maurice S., 206, 274, 356
Sheppard, Harry R., 160
Sherman, Forrest P.
  and atomic weapons, 80, 120, 316
  and Burke, 278, 279
  Chief of Naval Operations, 276, 279, 283, 285, 367
  Commander Sixth Fleet, 54
  and Crommelin, 282–83
  DCNO (Operations), 35, 38, 80
  and flush-deck carrier, 137, 139, 276, 287, 288, 330
  and Forrestal, 123, 164
  and Nimitz, 35
  photos, 37, 276, 283
  and politicking for CNO, 56, 271, 272, 274, 364
  and roles and missions, 35, 55, 120, 123, 276
  selection as CNO, 273, 365
  and unification, 38, 41

and Unification and Strategy hearings, 271, 364
Shipbuilding and Conversion Program, 139–40, 141, 144, 201, 285, 330, 331, 345
Ship Characteristics Board (SCB), 137, 139–40, 141, 144
Short, Dewey, 235, 256, 284, 285, 287
SILVERPLATE aircraft, 75, 95, 315
Simpler, Leroy C., 62
Smith, Frederick H., Jr., 219, 226
Smyth, Henry D., 318
Snyder, Charles P., 37 (photo)
Solomons, E. A., 166
Sommers, Martin, 200
Souers, Sidney, 56
Soviet Union
  air force, 83
  atomic energy program of, 85
  atomic weapons test, 233
  B-29 internment and copies, 83–84, 317
  and Berlin crisis, 92–93, 154, 159
  Bykovo Military Airfield in, 83–84
  capabilities for intercepting B-36, 227
  and Czechoslovakia, 160
  and Iran, 81–82, 87, 116
  MiG-15, 155, 334
  projected atomic weapons stockpile of, 85–86, 233
  Red Army, 82–83
  submarines, 115
  threat to Far East, 83
  threat to U.S., 80, 81–86, 93–94
  threat to Western Europe, 317
  and Turkey, 81, 87, 115–16
  targets in, 95–96, 115–21, 321
  war planning against, 86–96
Spaatz, Carl A.
  Air Force Chief of Staff 170
  and Air Force public relations campaign, 199
  and Air Force role in ASW, 39
  on air power dominance, 46, 48, 55–56
  and aircraft carrier role, 128–29, 142, 331
  and Armed Forces Special Weapons Project, 327
  and atomic weapons, 74, 76, 77, 90
  and B-36 bomber, 148, 149, 150–51

  on carrier aviation training, 33, 35
  Commanding General, Army Air Forces, 33, 36, 308
  and Continental Air Forces, 75
  Eighth Air Force, 13–14, 15
  and naval procurement requests, 39, 43–44, 331
  and Nimitz Valedictory, reaction to 55–56
  papers of, 370
  photos, 15, 31, 36, 124
  retirement, 142
  on strategic bombing, 21
  on roles and missions, 33, 35, 55–56, 121, 122, 124, 307
  and unification, 33, 39, 45, 46, 48, 49, 263
Spaatz Board, 74, 97, 315
Sprague, T. L., 57
Spruance, Raymond A., 7 (photo), 250
St. Louis Globe-Democrat, 148
Stalin, Joseph, 81, 159
Stark, Harold R., 81
Stevens, Leslie C., 41 (photo)
Stimson, Henry L., 25, 174
Stone, E. E., 166
Stonesifer, J. N., 167
Strategic Air Command (SAC)
  and atomic weapons, 77, 95
  and B-36 aircraft, 154, 182
  and bombing accuracies, 102–3, 358, 359
  and bonus damage, 99
  combat readiness of, 101–3, 321
  Commanding General of, 100, 101, 102, 103
  creation of, 75
  and Dayton bombing exercise, 102–3
  effectiveness of, 182
  EWP 1–49, 99
  forward bases, 92, 109, 323
  mission and responsibilities, 75, 95, 105
  OPLAN 14–47, 90
  value of, 200
  Very Heavy Bomb Groups, 95, 315
Strategic air offensive
  Air Force opposition to Navy role in, 88, 121–30, 182
  budget issues and, 113
  defense against, 80

defined, 326
effectiveness of, 255–56
Forrestal's concerns, 99–103
flush-deck carrier and, 183
land-sea tandem force, 110–11
moral issues, 110, 250
Navy doubts about, 108–14, 182, 324
Navy role in, 106, 110–11, 115–21, 141, 182–83, 324, 325, 327
public relations campaign, 206–7
Soviet threat and, 105–6
and tactical air operations, 264, 265
targeting, 89–90, 97–98, 115–21, 326
Unification and Strategy hearing report and, 285, 287
Strategic air warfare, defined, 326
Stratemeyer, George E., 264, 264
Streett, St. Clair, 77
Struble, Arthur D. (Rip), 195, 196, 197, 202, 203, 212, 219, 220, 221, 222, 344, 346
Stump, Felix B., 42, 196, 279, 307
Styer, C. W., 112
Submarines, Soviet, 115
Sullivan, John L., 164
  Assistant Secretary of Navy for Air, 37, 47, 136–37
  and B–36 bomber, 210
  and carrier aircraft development, 136–37
  and flush-deck carrier, 141, 142, 144, 184, 187, 188, 189, 340
  on Forrestal, 337
  and Johnson, 1, 181, 184, 187, 189, 190, 191, 340, 343
  and Matthews, 205
  and Navy's atomic role, 106–7, 124–27
  papers of, 370
  personality and management style, 59, 312
  photos, 37, 57, 60, 114, 181
  and public relations, 59
  resignation and replacement, 188–91, 205, 343, 346
  Secretary of the Navy, 51, 57, 59, 60, 114, 141, 142, 144, 170, 181, 188, 210
  and strategic air offensive, 101, 120
  and Symington, 125–27
  and unification, 41, 51, 52, 165
Symington, W. Stuart

and Anonymous Document, 215–16, 230, 353
and Air Force reorganization, 178
Air Force Secretary, 1, 55, 97, 114, 120, 122, 151, 152, 170, 175, 177, 178, 181, 183, 210, 335
Assistant Secretary of War for Air, 38, 39, 50–51, 148
and B–36 bomber, support for, 1, 148, 151, 152, 153, 154, 177, 178, 179, 180–81, 210, 215–16, 217, 218, 227, 230, 232, 233, 234, 255, 273
and B–54 cancellation, 180
and Barber letter-writing campaign, 313
and Denfeld, 269
and flush-deck carrier, 183, 185
and Gallery memorandum, 120
and Hanson letter-writing campaign, 60
papers of, 370
personality and management style, 59
photos, 39, 114, 164, 175, 181
and Navy roles and missions, 39, 114, 120, 122, 125, 126, 127, 163
and Nimitz Valedictory, 55
on one-way (suicide) missions, 99
and public relations, 50–51, 164
and Strategic Air Command, 101
Sullivan and, 125–27
and unification, 38, 50–51, 122, 171, 193
and Unification and Strategy hearings, 255, 273, 363

Tactical Air Command (TAC), 263, 264, 265, 361
Taft, Robert A. (Bob), 52
Target selection, 12–13, 16–17, 111
  and atomic weapons, 89–90, 91–92, 93–94, 97, 98–99, 115–21, 314, 350
  "bonus damage" concept, 99
  intelligence for, 321
  lines of communication, 111, 115–16
  Navy, 115–21, 137
  in Soviet Union, 118–19, 137, 321, 350
  transportation, 111, 116
  World War II, 111–12
Tatom, Eugene, 250
Taylor, David W., 4
Thackrey, Lyman A. (Red), 51–52, 54, 168, 173
Thebaud, Hewlett, 166, 254

THUNDERBOLT exercise, 112
Time magazine, 232, 353
Todd, C. R., 166
Towers, John H., 128–29
Trapnell, Frederick M., 249, 279
Trenchard, Hugh M., 9
Truculent Turtle, 207
Truman, Harry S.
  atomic energy policy, 88, 106–7
  atomic weapons policy, 68, 92, 107
  and B–36 bomber, 179
  and Berlin crisis, 93–94, 159
  and Burke's selection to rear admiral, 279–80
  and defense appropriations, 43, 159, 160–61, 162, 223, 308, 339, 362
  and flush-deck carrier, 141, 143, 144, 183, 343
  and Forrestal's resignation, 173–74
  Johnson and, 175–76, 288
  Matthews and, 206, 273, 274, 365
  and Navy roles and missions, 37–38, 123
  papers of, 370
  and Paris Peace Conference, 87
  and presidential campaign of 1948, 175–76
  and reprisals for Navy testimony, 272, 273–74, 275
  and strategic air offensive, 103
  and Soviet threat, 81, 84, 87, 93–94, 233
  and Sullivan's resignation, 189
  and unification, 32, 339
TU–2 Bat bomber [Tupolev], 83
TU–4 Bull bomber [Tupolev], 83, 86
Tupolev, A. N., 83
Turkey, Soviet pressures on, 81, 115–16
Tuscaloosa (CA 37), 356
Twelfth Air Force, 264
Twelfth Army Group, 258, 262
Twentieth Air Force, 20, 45, 111
Twining, Nathan F., 148, 149, 370
Tydings Bill, 171, 173
Tydings, Millard E., 209, 215

Unification and Strategy hearings
  administrative reactions, 254–57
  Army testimony, 263–67
  end of, 268
  Navy testimony, 247–54, 272, 282, 363
  preparation for, 238–39, 243–45
  reprisals for testimony, 2, 269, 270, 272, 273, 275, 277, 279, 285
  results, 283–89, 294
Unification of services
  Army Air Forces position, 30–32, 33, 35, 37, 38, 44–52, 292
  Army proposals and rationales, 29, 30
  Denfeld and, 56–58
  budget/funding issues, 29, 30, 31–32, 38–39, 43, 253
  Forrestal and, 26, 27, 28–29, 30, 32, 37–38, 40–41, 42–43, 47, 49, 51, 52, 53, 58, 63
  House hearings on, 1, 24, 26–27, 190, 243–45
  Johnson slander of Sullivan, 190
  JSSC report, 32–33
  land-based aircraft issue, 43
  legislation, 32
  and Marine Corps role, 25, 33, 35, 305
  Navy coordination of efforts on, 165
  Navy opposition to, 23, 24, 26, 30, 35, 40, 59–63, 292, 304, 305
  Nimitz Valedictory, 52–56
  opponents, 26, 28–29, 193
  Patterson-Forrestal agreement on, 42–43
  proponents, 23–24, 25, 32, 48–50, 56
  public relations campaigns, 44–52, 58–63
  roles and missions disputes, 25, 32–44, 253–54, 294
  Struble and, 195–96
  training issue, 35
  War Department's initial opposition to, 23
  waste and duplication issues, 24, 25, 26–27, 128, 199

United Kingdom, U.S. SAC bases in, 92, 109, 323
United States (CVA 58), 1, 138 (photo), 140 (photo), 142 (photo), 143 (photo), 145 (photo), 185 (photo), 182–88, 190, 197, 200, 201, 208, 210, 217, 221, 236, 326, 345
United States Strategic Bombing Survey (USSBS), 16, 111, 132, 302, 303, 324
U.S. Strategic Air Forces, 15, 31

Index

Van Zandt, James E., 209, 210, 211, 216–22, 228, 230
Vandegrift, Alexander A., 35, 47, 250, 255
Vandenberg, Hoyt S.
  anti-Navy policy line, 197–98, 201
  and Armed Forces Special Weapons Project, 128, 328
  and atomic weapons, 74, 91, 128, 328
  Air Force Chief of Staff, 128, 175, 178, 344, 362
  Assistant Chief of Air Staff for Operations, Commitments, and Requirements, 74
  and Bradley, 258, 266
  and carrier conversion program, 204
  and B–36 bomber, 147, 150, 151, 152, 181, 219, 227–28, 230, 256, 348, 353
  and B–54 cancellation, 180
  Commanding General Ninth Air Force, 31, 258, 261
  and flush-deck carriers, 122, 142–43, 183, 331
  and Navy Shipbuilding and Conversion Program, 204
  papers of, 370
  photos, 31, 129, 130, 151, 175, 178
  on Soviet threat, 84
  and strategic air offensive, 100, 129, 265, 266, 323, 362
  and Tactical Air Command, 264, 361
  and unification, 264, 265, 344
  and Unification and Strategy hearings, 256–57, 363
Vaughn, Harry H., 174
Veterans Administration, 257
Veterans of Foreign Wars, 230
Very Heavy Bomb Groups, 95
Vice Chief of Naval Operations, 41, 57–58, 88, 139. *See also* Price; Radford; Ramsey
Variable discharge turbine engine. *See* Aircraft engine and propulsion
Vinson, Carl
  and Anonymous Document, 209, 215–16, 217, 234
  B–36 bomber hearings, 226, 230, 231, 232
  B–36 bomber investigation, 210, 211, 212, 218, 219–20, 221
  and carrier aviation, revitalization of, 2, 368
  and Defense Department structure, 173
  and flush-deck carrier program, 185, 288
  House Naval Affairs Committee, 200
  pro-Air Force position, 200
  pro-Navy position, 284, 285
  and reprisals for Navy testimony, 275
  and Van Zandt resolution and speech, 217
  and Unification and Strategy hearings, 238–39, 243, 244, 245, 268, 273, 275, 284–85, 289, 363
Vinson, Fred M., 114 (photo)
Vosseller, A. B. (Abe), 279

Wadsworth, James W., 24–25
Wakeman, Calvin E., 348
Wallace, W. J., 166
Walsh, David I., 28
War Council, 175, 181, 203, 204
War Department, 53, 174
  Final Report: War Department Policies and Program Review Board, 53, 117
  Intelligence, 85
  postwar military establishment, 84–85
  Public Relations Division, 148
  Special Planning Division, 32
  unification, position on, 23, 53
War planning. *See also* Atomic weapons; Target selection
  Air Force concerns, 95–99
  and atomic weapons policy, 88–89, 90, 92–94, 102–3, 113
  war plans
    BROILER, 90, 91–92
    CHARIOTEER, 92
    EARSHOT, 90
    EARSHOT JUNIOR, 90
    ERASER, 92
    FLEETWOOD, 94
    FROLIC, 92, 109, 113
    HALFMOON, 92, 94, 109
    HARROW, 92
    MAKEFAST, 89–90, 98
    medium-range, 113
    NSPS 3 study, 115–16, 325
    OFFTACKLE, 94–95, 109, 117

PINCHER, 87, 89, 90
REAPER, 95
SHAKEDOWN, 95
strategic concepts for, 86
TROJAN, 94, 215, 220, 350
War Production Board, 28
Washington Daily News, 210, 215, 349
Washington Post, 239, 262
Washington Star, 265, 277
Washington Times-Herald, 244
Weapons Systems Evaluation Group (WSEG), 100, 183, 184, 268, 279, 363
Webb, James E., 39, 141
Wedemeyer, Albert C., 124 (photo), 129 (photo), 130 (photo), 164
Wellborn, Charles, Jr., 16, 202, 341, 344
Wellings, A. J., 167
White, Dudley A., 52, 269
White, Thomas D., 370
White Sulfur Springs, 223–24, 362
Whitehead, Ennis C., 264–65, 361
Whitney, C. V., 170
Wilkins, C. W., 184
Willett, E. F., 28
Wilson, Roscoe C., 315
Wolfe, Kenneth B., 152, 219
Woodring, Harry H., 174
Woodrum, Clifton A., 25
Woodrum Committee, 25, 26, 27, 28
Woods, Edwin E., 237, 238, 240–41, 355, 356
Wooldridge, E. T., 167
Worth, Cedric R., 1, 207, 208, 209, 215, 232, 233, 234, 245, 347, 349, 353, 354, 366
World War I
OPNAV in, 4
World War II, 8, 9
carrier operations, 121
Black Thursday [Schweinfurt raid], 14–15, 256
China-Burma-India Theater, 17
Combined Bomber Offensive, 112
European Theater, 13–17, 89
German invasion of Russia, 146
Pacific Theater, 17–20, 45, 111, 135
strategic bombing effectiveness, 109, 292, 302
Wright Field, Dayton, Ohio, 84, 148, 150

XAJ–1 heavy attack aircraft [North American], 107, 329
XB–52 bomber [Boeing], 157
XF2D–1 [F2H–1 Banshee] fighter, 139, 141, 330
XR 60–1 Constitution, 41
XX Bomber Command, 17, 18
XXI Bomber Command, 19, 20

Yarnell, Harry E., 24
Yeager, Howard A. (Red), 163 (photo), 250
Yorktown (CV 10), 9, 138 (photo)

Zeke [Zero] aircraft, 8
Zuckert, Eugene M., 170, 346